Japan's Total Empire

Twentieth-Century Japan: The Emergence of a World Power
Irwin Scheiner, Editor

Japan's Total Empire

Manchuria and the Culture of Wartime Imperialism

LOUISE YOUNG

University of California Press

BERKELEY   LOS ANGELES   LONDON

Publication of this work was generously supported by a grant from the Japan Foundation.

University of California Press
Berkeley and Los Angeles, California

University of California Press, Ltd.
London, England

Library of Congress Cataloging-in-Publication Data

Young, Louise, 1960–
    Japan's total empire : Manchuria and the culture of wartime
imperialism / Louise Young.
        p.   cm.—(Twentieth-century Japan ; 8)
    Includes bibliographical references and index.
    ISBN 0-520-21071-9 (cloth : alk. paper)
        1. Manchuria (China)—History—1933–1945.   2. Mukden Incident,
1931.   3. Japan—History—1926–1945.   4. World politics—1933–
1945.   I. Title. II. Series.
DS783.7.Y67   1998
325'.352' 09518—dc21   97-1715
                                                            CIP

Manufactured in the United States of America
9 8 7 6 5 4 3 2 1

In memory of
Louise Merwin Young
1903–1992

A Study of the East Asian Institute, Columbia University

The East Asian Institute is Columbia University's center for research, publication, and teaching on modern East Asia. The Studies of the East Asian Institute were inaugurated in 1962 to bring to a wider public the results of significant new research on modern and contemporary East Asia.

Contents

Map and Tables

Acknowledgments

Without the support of numerous individuals and institutions, this study could never have been completed; their help is gratefully acknowledged. Carol Gluck gave timely and inspirational support at every stage of the project, from her help in shaping its conceptual categories when it was still a dissertation proposal, to her suggestions for some last-minute improvements to the conclusion when it had become a book. Meticulous readings by Elizabeth Blackmar, Henry Smith, Arthur Tiedemann, Jack Snyder, and especially John Dower helped me rethink and reframe my ideas. Geoffrey Chambers, Kēvin Shea, Elizabeth Tsunoda, Barbara Satō, Kim Brandt, and Crawford Young were always available to read and discuss drafts. Laura Hein, Yanni Kotsonis, Kären Wigen, Roger Chickering, Satō Kazuki, Julie Rousseau, Hyung Gu Lynn, Emily Young, and Imura Tetsuo made helpful suggestions on sections of the book. Carol Gluck's graduate seminars at Columbia University provided both insight and enthusiasm in generous measure, as did Carter Eckert's students at Harvard. For sharing with me in Japan their advice, contacts, and considerable private libraries I am indebted to Igarashi Takeshi, Eguchi Keiichi, Okabe Makio, Asada Kyōji, Awaya Kentarō, Kimijima Kazuhiko, Kobayashi Hideo, Okamoto Kōichi, and Yanagisawa Asobu. The staffs of the Tokyo University Libraries, the National Diet Library, the Tokyo Chamber of Commerce Library, Waseda Library, and the Kindai Bungakukan provided service which frequently transcended the call of duty. I am particularly grateful to Ikuta Atsuko at the Ie no hikari kyōkai Reference Department, Shiraishi Hiroshi at the National Institute for Defense Studies, and Imura Tetsuo at the Institute of Developing Economies. Financial assistance was provided by Columbia University during the fall of 1988, by the Japan Foundation for fourteen months of research in Tokyo from January 1989 through the spring of 1990, and by the Giles Whiting Foundation for dissertation write-up during 1990–1991. Special thanks are due to the Reischauer Institute for offering a congenial environment and the financial support that enabled me to begin to turn a dissertation into a book.

Note on Sources

Most primary materials cited in the notes can be located in the following Tokyo archives: Tokyo University Libraries, Waseda University Library, National Diet Library, Kindai bungakukan, Ie no hikari kyōkai, Tokyo Chamber of Commerce, and the Institute of Developing Economies. Unless otherwise indicated, the place of publication for all Japanese-language publications is Tokyo.

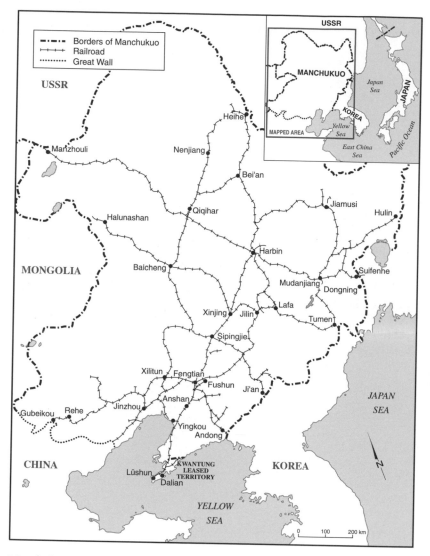

Manchukuo circa 1944

PART I

THE MAKING OF
A TOTAL EMPIRE

1   Manchukuo and Japan

Today the words *"Empire of Japan"* evoke multiple meanings: one set of images for former colonial subjects, another for former enemies in the Pacific War, and yet another for the Japanese themselves. No epoch did more to inscribe these words with meaning than the period between 1931 and 1945, when Japan moved aggressively to expand its overseas territory, occupying first China and then Southeast Asia, and initiating a series of military conflicts against Nationalist and Communist forces in China, against the Soviet Union, against the United States, and against the British Empire. At the heart of the new empire Japan won and then lost in the military engagements of these years lay the puppet state of Manchukuo in Northeast China.

Although Manchukuo was created in 1932, its roots went back to 1905, when Japan acquired a sphere of influence in the southern half of Manchuria as a result of victory in the Russo-Japanese War. A mix of formal and informal elements, the South Manchurian sphere of influence was anchored by long-term leases on the Liaodong Peninsula and on lands held by Japan's colonial railway company, the South Manchurian Railway, which the Japanese knew as Mantetsu. Over these leased territories, which represented but a small fraction of South Manchuria, Japan ruled directly through a formal colonial apparatus. Over the rest of South Manchuria Japan exerted influence indirectly, through the relationship with local Chinese rulers, through economic dominance of the market, and through the constant threat of force by its garrison army.

The first phase of Japanese involvement situated the sphere of influence in Manchuria within a rapidly expanding empire. By the end of World War I, the empire included Taiwan, Korea, the Pacific island chains the Japanese called Nan'yō, the southern half of Sakhalin, as well as participation in the unequal treaty system in China. Initially, Manchuria occupied a peripheral position within this wider empire: it was neither the strategic focus of foreign policy nor the site where key innovations in imperial management took place. But all this changed after 1931, as Japanese focused their energies on the construction of a new kind of empire in the Northeast.

The new face of empire showed itself in three areas of activity—military conquest, economic development, and mass migration. First, under the guidance of the garrison force known as the Kwantung Army, thousands spilled their blood in a series of military campaigns from 1931 to 1933 collectively designated the Manchurian Incident. In the course of these campaigns, Japan brought all of Manchuria under military occupation, extending formal control to the Amur River and the border of Soviet Siberia in the north, and to the Great Wall of China in the south. Second, under a new regime of colonial management known as the controlled economy, the Japanese-run Manchukuo government conducted a bold experiment in planned economic development and state capitalism. The project involved the integration of the two economies, tying Manchurian development to domestic production goals through the creation of the Japan-Manchuria bloc economy. Third, an ambitious plan to send five million Japanese farmers to settle in the Manchurian hinterland was designed to create a new generation of "continental Japanese" who would secure a more thorough domination of colonial society. Linking social policy in the metropolis and the empire, the Japanese government sought to make the Manchurian population 10 percent Japanese through the export of impoverished tenant farmers, who were the most visible manifestation of Japan's rural crisis.

In the service of these three endeavors, over a million Japanese soldiers, entrepreneurs, and agricultural emigrants crossed the waters that separated Japan from the continent. While they invested their futures and sometimes their lives in the building of Manchukuo, at home many times their number labored over the empire in indirect, though no less essential, ways. During the military campaigns of the Manchurian Incident, a wave of war hysteria swept Japanese society. War fever generated the domestic political and social support that gave the Kwantung Army freedom of action to engage in aggressive military imperialism, as Japanese fought to defend "the Manchurian lifeline" (*Manshū seimeisen*). Businessmen and intellectuals, inspired by utopian visions of economic opportunity, used their social standing to sell the idea of staking Japan's future on "Manchurian development" (*Manshū kaihatsu*). Local elites led rural communities to endorse plans to send as many as half their villagers to colonize Manchuria and build "a new heaven on earth" (*shintenchi*). Although they never set foot in Manchuria, these different groups of people were empire builders nonetheless.

Together they constructed the metropolitan infrastructure of empire. Japan's empire building in Manchuria thus produced two imperial systems—one in the colony and one in the metropolis. In Manchuria, Japanese established a state apparatus, structures of economic domination, and mechanisms of social control; at home they built a parallel set of political and social structures to mobilize the resources essential to the success of the imperial project. These efforts, and the transformations they wrought, are the subject of this book.

STUDYING EMPIRE

Historians have usually examined Japanese expansion in Manchuria from the top down, studying the formation of empire almost entirely as an activity of state. Consisting of policy studies, analyses of bureaucratic politics, and monographs on key military figures, the historical record presents a portrait of the official mind of empire. Accounts of the military occupation of Manchuria in the early 1930s have focused on the question of who made the decision for war. Was it an act of subimperialism and insubordination on the part of Kwantung Army officers in Manchuria? Or was it directed by responsible government authorities in Tokyo?[1]

1. Dated, but still useful historiographical essays dealing with the debate over Japanese military expansionism are Waldo H. Heinrichs, Jr., "1931–1937," and Louis Morton, "1937–1941," both in Ernest R. May and James C. Thomson, Jr., eds., *American-East Asian Relations: A Survey* (Cambridge: Harvard University Press, 1972), pp. 243–290. The key works on the military history of the Manchurian Incident in English include: Robert J. C. Butow, *Tojo and the Coming of the War* (Stanford: Stanford University Press, 1961), pp. 28–47; Alvin D. Coox, "The Kwantung Army Dimension," in Peter Duus, Ramon H. Myers, and Mark R. Peattie, eds., *The Japanese Informal Empire in China, 1895–1937* (Princeton: Princeton University Press, 1989), pp. 395–428; James B. Crowley, *Japan's Quest for Autonomy: National Security and Foreign Policy, 1930–1938* (Princeton: Princeton University Press, 1966), pp. 82–186; Sadako N. Ogata, *Defiance in Manchuria: The Making of Japanese Foreign Policy, 1931–1932* (1964; reprint, Westport, Conn.: Greenwood Press, 1984); Mark R. Peattie, *Ishiwara Kanji and Japan's Confrontation with the West* (Princeton: Princeton University Press, 1975), pp. 87–181; and Takehiko Yoshihashi, *Conspiracy at Mukden: The Rise of the Japanese Military* (New Haven: Yale University Press, 1963). For analysis of the Japanese debate

Studies of Japan's economic development of Manchuria have also concentrated on state actors. Taking up different components of economic policy, the debate in this case has revolved around the question of assessing the success or failure of the Manchurian experiment. Was the controlled economy in Manchuria a bold innovation in industrial policy that provided the foundation for the postwar "economic miracle"? Or was it a risky experiment with heavy industrialization through economic autarky, doomed to failure because of the dependence of Japan's capital- and resource-poor national economy on Western markets?[2]

---

that divides scholarly interpretations into Marxist and non-Marxist camps, see Hatano Sumio, "Japanese Foreign Policy, 1931–1945: Historiography," in Sadao Asada, ed., *Japan and the World, 1853–1952: A Bibliographic Guide to Japanese Scholarship in Foreign Relations* (New York: Columbia University Press, 1989), pp. 217–240. The Japanese literature on the subject is voluminous, but successive revisions of the Marxist interpretation of the Manchurian Incident can be traced in Rekishigaku kenkyūkai, ed., *Manshū jihen*, vol. 1 of *Taiheiyō sensōshi* (Aoki shoten, 1971); Fujiwara Akira and Imai Seiichi, eds., *Manshū jihen*, vol. 1 of *Jūgonen sensōshi* (Aoki shoten, 1988); and Eguchi Keiichi, *Jūgonen sensō no kaimaku*, vol. 4 of *Shōwa no rekishi* (Shōgakkan, 1988). The non-Marxist interpretation is represented by the first of the seven-volume series, *Taiheiyō sensō e no michi: kaisen gaikôshi*, translated into English under James William Morley, ed., *Japan Erupts: The London Naval Conference and the Manchurian Incident, 1928–1932* (New York: Columbia University Press, 1984); and Inoue Mitsusada et al., eds., *Kindai 2*, vol. 5 of *Nihon rekishi taikei* (Yamakawa shuppansha, 1989).

2. For the "doomed experiment" interpretation, see Michael A. Barnhart, *Japan Prepares for Total War: The Search for Economic Security, 1919–1941* (Ithaca: Cornell University Press, 1987), pp. 22–49, 64–114. For the "bold innovation" thesis, see Chalmers Johnson, *MITI and the Japanese Miracle: The Growth of Industrial Policy, 1925–1975* (Stanford: Stanford University Press, 1982), pp. 116–156, esp. pp. 124–136. Discussions of the Manchurian economy in English include W. G. Beasley, *Japanese Imperialism 1894–1945* (Oxford: Clarendon Press, 1987), pp. 175–197; Kang Chao, *The Economic Development of Manchuria: The Rise of a Frontier Economy*, Michigan Papers in Chinese Studies, no. 43 (Ann Arbor: Center for Chinese Studies, 1982); F. C. Jones, *Manchuria since 1931* (New York: Oxford University Press, 1949), pp. 100–220; Ramon H. Myers, *The Japanese Economic Development of Manchuria, 1932 to 1945* (New York: Garland, 1982); Nakagane Katsuji, "Manchukuo and Economic Development," in Peter Duus, Ramon H. Myers, and Mark R. Peattie, eds., *The Japanese Informal Empire in China, 1895–1937* (Princeton: Princeton University Press, 1989), pp. 133–158; Ann Rasmussen Kinney, *Japanese Investment in Manchurian Manufacturing, Mining, Transportation, and Communications, 1931–1945* (New York: Garland, 1982); and Kungtu C. Sun, *The Economic Development of Manchuria in the First Half of the Twentieth Century* (Cambridge: Council on East Asian Studies, Harvard University, 1973), pp. 75–102. In Japanese see Asada Kyōji and Kobayashi Hideo, eds., *Nihon teikokushugi no Manshū shihai: jūgonen sensōki o chūshin ni* (Jichōsha, 1986), pp. 547–926; Kobayashi Hideo, *"DaiTōa kyōeiken" no keisei to hōkai* (Ochanomizu shobō, 1975), pp. 47–91, 167–176; Manshūshi kenkyūkai, ed., *Nihon*

While the subject is not much discussed in English, the considerable body of Japanese-language work on the colonization of Manchuria falls into two camps, between which lies an interpretive gap. One camp consists of academic studies of the formation and implementation of settlement policy within the framework of Japanese aggression. These works stress the exploitation of the Chinese and Korean peasants who worked the lands in Northeast China. The other camp is made up of popular accounts by former colonists, which tell the story of their own victimization. These focus on the tragic denouement of Manchurian colonization for the many Japanese colonists who died at the hands of Chinese and Russian soldiers at the end of the war. Whether, as agents of the imperial state, the colonists were victimizers of the people of Northeast China or were themselves victims remains the point of contention between the two camps. Yet despite their differences, both interpretations of colonists-as-victims and colonists-as-victimizers share the assumption that colonists were controlled by the state.[3]

At the root of this historiographical preoccupation with the state is the issue of responsibility: responsibility for empire and responsibility for war. Public memory in Japan avoids the question and adheres to the view, enshrined by the Tokyo War Crimes Trial, that a military cabal seized hold of government and forced the people into a reckless war. Even after fifty years, the pervasiveness of this narrative of victimization—what Carol Gluck has called "history in the passive voice"[4]—is striking. Despite the popular conviction that ordinary people were not the agents but the victims of their imperial past, there is an increasingly vocal call among the community of progressive scholars in Japan to investigate the "people's war responsibility" and "fascism at the grass roots."[5] This challenge suggests

---

teikokushugika no Manshū (Ochanomizu shobō, 1972), pp. 1–211; and Okabe Makio, *Manshūkoku* (Sanseidō, 1978), pp. 75–146.

3. Representative of the policy studies critical of Manchurian colonization are the essays in Manshū iminshi kenkyūkai, ed., *Nihon teikokushugika no Manshū imin* (Ryūkei shosha, 1976). Representative of the colonists' view is Mantakukai, ed., *Dokyumento Manshū kaitaku monogatari* (Azusa shoten, 1986).

4. Carol Gluck, "The Idea of Showa," *Daedalus* 119, no. 3 (Summer 1990), pp. 12–13.

5. These are the titles of two recent books on World War II that focus on popular support for Japanese expansion in Asia: Takahashi Hikohiro, *Minshū no gawa no sensō sekinin* [The People's War Responsibility] (Aoki shoten, 1989), and Yoshimi Yoshiaki, *Kusa no ne no fashizumu: Nihon minshū no sensō taiken* [Fascism at the Grass Roots: The War Experience of the Japanese People], vol. 7 of *Atarashii sekaishi* (Tōkyō daigaku shuppankai, 1987). Two very suggestive applications of this approach to the Manchurian Incident are Eguchi Keiichi, *Nihon*

the need to revise the historical record on Manchukuo, for missing from the picture are the millions of people who were involved in its construction—through war support associations, business unions, colonization committees, and countless other organizations. It clearly took more than ministers and generals to make an empire, and this book examines how society—both the institutions and the individuals that comprised it—was engaged in the empire-building process. The state is not eclipsed as an object of analysis, but rather the focus is on the roles of both state and society and the ways in which they mobilized each other for the imperial project.

Since the concepts of "state" and "society" are here used to formulate the problem of agency, a brief word is in order about what is meant by these terms. I understand them, first, to signify an expression of power in relationship to one another and to the empire. The state wields power in its ordering of society, while society exercises power in its shaping of the state. As each projects its power overseas, both state and society become agents of empire. Second, such power is deployed through institutions. State power operates through bureaucratic organizations: government ministries, agencies, and committees. Social power is similarly effected through organizations such as chambers of commerce, political parties, and women's groups. In both state and society such institutions provide the vehicles through which individuals effect power by collective action. In other words, institutions mediated the relationship between the individual and the empire, whether that individual was a government official or a private citizen. To ask the question, then, Who were the agents of empire? involves looking at the roles of both private and public institutions in mobilizing support for Manchukuo. It means seeing how Manchukuo looked from the bottom up as well as from the top down, and depicting the popular, as well as the official, mind of empire.

Although the concepts of state and society are here paired as dichoto-

---

teikokushugi shiron: Manshū jihen zengo (Aoki shoten, 1975), pp. 149–196, and Awaya Kentarō, "Fasshoka to minshū ishiki," in Eguchi Keiichi, ed., *Nihon fashizumu no keisei,* vol. 1 of *Taikei Nihon gendaishi* (Nihon hyōronsha, 1978), pp. 251–302. Iwanami shoten's recent eight-volume series on Japanese colonialism has expanded on this theme, devoting two entire volumes to "popular" imperialism— vol. 5 on Japanese expatriates in the colonies and vol. 7 on colonialism and popular culture: Ōe Shinobu et al., eds., *Bōchō suru teikoku no jinryū,* vol. 5 of *Iwanami kōza kindai Nihon to shokuminchi* (Iwanami shoten, 1993); and Ōe Shinobu et al., eds., *Bunka no naka no shokuminchi,* vol. 7 of *Iwanami kōza kindai Nihon to shokuminchi* (Iwanami shoten, 1993).

but
she
didn't

mous categories to make a point about the involvement of non-government actors in the imperial project, a final caveat must be added about the problem with defining them in oppositional terms. In any specific instance the boundary line between state and society is extremely fuzzy, making it difficult to say where state ends and society begins. Are public school teachers, for instance, state actors or social agents? If army officers are part of the state, where do conscript soldiers belong? The arbitrariness of the answers to such questions suggests that rather than posing state and society as a dichotomy, we should conceive them as reflections of one another, or alternate formulations of the same entity. Mobilized for empire all individuals become extensions of the state even as they remain members of society.

Though fundamentally empires are social products, they are not much studied as popular enterprises. Preoccupied with identifying a theoretical model that would explain the causes of imperialism—and particularly the sudden burst of European expansionism in the late nineteenth century—literature on European and American imperialism has tended to focus on the rival merits of economic and political theories of causality. In the former instance, this meant showing how the structures of an expanding industrial capitalism sought to open and control new overseas markets. In the latter, scholars focused on the decision making of both metropolitan leaders and their on-site agents. They identified the motives for the so-called new imperialism in both the rivalrous dynamics of the international system as well as growing political instability on the borders of the European empires in Asia and Africa. For a long time divisions within the Anglo-American academy between Marxist and anti-Marxist scholars fossilized this debate into a series of revisions of the capitalist theory of imperialism on one side and debunking attacks on the other.[6]

In recent years this has changed, as historians of imperialism have taken up the question of culture. Beginning in the early 1980s, books on empire and technology, science, ideology, propaganda, popular culture, and other topics have appeared, shifting the focus away from political and economic structures of empire.[7] Although this conversion to culture reinvigorated

6. See Roger Owen and Bob Sutcliffe, eds., *Studies in the Theory of Imperialism* (London: Longman, 1972), pp. 1–70, 117–142, for samples of this debate. For a summary of the various positions, see Wolfgang J. Mommsen, *Theories of Imperialism*, trans. P. S. Falla (Chicago: University of Chicago Press, 1980), pp. 70–141.

7. There has been a recent explosion of work on culture and imperialism, largely inspired by Edward W. Said's pioneering study *Orientalism* (New York:

the study of imperialism, cultural theories of imperialism have only begun
to challenge the monocausal terms of the older debate. In much of this
literature culture simply supplanted economy or politics as the sole independent variable. And yet, in the empires of the nineteenth and twentieth
centuries, it is impossible to reduce the roots of expansionism to a single
cause. No more than Marxist theories of imperialism, power-politics models, or arguments about subimperialists and turbulent frontiers, can studies
of the cultural construction of empire account for the multidimensional
nature of experience. In an age of unified markets, globalized mass communications, and the exposure of the individual to multiple systems of
meaning, it is impossible to look at the economic without considering the
political, to study the cultural without thinking about the social, to discuss
the national without reference to the international. Therefore we need to
look at ways in which economics, politics, culture, and society work together as a unit and the ways in which national systems are integrated
into international systems. We need, in short, a total theory of imperialism.

TOTAL IMPERIALISM

Like many abstract concepts, imperialism is a term that resists concrete
definition. Most historians deploy the term to describe the annexation of
territory and imposition of alien rule over the peoples that live there:
domination formalized in the creation of institutions of direct colonial
administration. More problematic are instances of informal domination—
where a country retains nominal independence, but falls within another
nation's "sphere of influence." Historians agree that the colonization of
Senegal by France or Ceylon by Great Britain were expressions of impe-

---

Vintage, 1978), which was recently reformulated as *Culture and Imperialism* (New
York: Knopf, 1993). Said theorizes the relationship between culture and empire in
a sophisticated way, situating cultural production within the institutions of imperial domination. Said is chiefly interested in explaining the structures and conventions of high culture rather than elucidating a theory of imperialism. Thus, his
work has introduced a new methodology for studying the impact of imperialism
on culture, but is not as helpful for thinking about the relationship the other way
around. Several new volumes of essays on the subject are moving in this direction,
studying the cultural technologies of colonialism as well as the cultural effects of
the colonial encounter. See Nicholas B. Dirks, ed., *Colonialism and Culture* (Ann
Arbor: University of Michigan Press, 1992), and Amy Kaplan and Donald E. Pease,
eds., *Cultures of United States Imperialism* (Durham, N.C.: Duke University Press,
1993).

rialism. But whether Soviet influence in Eastern Europe or American interventions in Indochina are properly characterized as "imperialism" is a
subject of debate. My own definition of imperialism, designed to charac-
terize Japan's relationship to China during the late nineteenth and early
twentieth centuries, accommodates both formal or direct, and informal or
indirect, mechanisms of domination. Imperial domination implies that the
dominated society not only is altered by the interventions of the dominating society, but loses its ability to reject those interventions. The Chinese, for example, were not in a position to tell the Japanese to go home
in 1907 or 1932. By contrast the Japanese could and did send their European advisors away in the 1890s. The former was a relationship defined by
imperialism, while the latter illustrated Japan's measure of independence
from European control. A further characteristic that distinguishes imperialism from other forms of influence is the scale of the disparity of power
between the two societies and the one-sided pattern of intervention that
emerges. In this way, imperialism is different from interdependence. Japanese influenced basic decisions which structured the economic and political conditions of Northeast China, but Chinese had no such power in
Japanese government circles. Such interventions, moreover, may be effected through both formal and informal channels. Hence, the term *imperialism* is not synonymous with colonialism, but rather subsumes it.
Japanese conditioned social life in Northeast China both through formal
colonial institutions—the Kwantung governor general and the Manchukuo government—as well as through such informal methods of control
as military threat, market dominance, and the cultivation of a collaborative
elite.

how about US r Japan?

A final distinction may be added here between imperialism as process
and empire as structure. Imperialism is empire building; it represents the
process of constructing a relationship of domination. Empire signifies what
is built—the structures that produce and reproduce dominance. For Japan
and Manchukuo this distinction captures both the mercurial dynamism of
the process as well as the ossified weightiness of the structures that together, incongruously, characterized the imperial project.

The phenomenon of imperialism can be traced back to the beginnings
of recorded history; its early modern period began with the European voy-
ages of exploration at the turn of the sixteenth century. Here I address
imperialism in the nineteenth and twentieth centuries when the features
identified with modernity inscribed themselves on the processes of imperialism and created what I call total empires. Conditioned by the advent of

the nation-state, industrial capitalism, and other revolutions of the modern age, imperialism became increasingly multidimensional, mass-mobilizing, and all-encompassing. The relationship between modernity and empire, moreover, was dialectical: just as modernization conditioned the growth of empire, the process of imperialism shaped the conditions of modern life. An attempt to puzzle out the evolving relationship between modernity and empire occupies the theoretical heart of this book.

The political revolution of the nation-state represented a key element in this relationship, transforming the meaning of imperialism in the nineteenth century. The rise of nations and nationalism meant that imperialism was increasingly an enterprise of both nation and state, in contrast to the crown colonies of the Americas and the trading factories of Asia that were established under the charter of the absolutist monarchies of early modern Europe. Indeed, imperialism became fundamental to modern projects of state making and nation building, both in Japan—as the government's designating itself "the Great Empire of Japan" (*DaiNihon teikoku*) and the patriotic popular response to the Sino-Japanese War suggest—and elsewhere around the globe. Moreover, the articulation of constitutional contracts that bound states to represent the interests of society meant that imperialism henceforth would be a joint endeavor. If a faction within the government—such as the Japanese Army—sought to expand the nation's power overseas, it needed to mobilize social support for the task. Similarly, private groups with imperial ambitions—such as Japanese business organizations—pressured their governments to lend state support to their plans. Such developments led to the emergence of an imperialized nationalism, while making imperial policy the crucible of a growing intimacy between state and society.

All of this was occurring, of course, in the midst of the global expansion of industrial capitalism. The advent of the industrial revolution in Europe stimulated integration of colonial markets into the world economy in a manner that facilitated the export of colonial wealth and resources to the industrial metropole and tended to hinder the development of industrial capitalism in the colonial periphery. Although Japanese colonial policies stimulated economic development in Manchuria and Korea, Japan, too, sought access to colonial export markets and colonial sources of cheap raw materials in order to maintain its own industrial production. Moreover, industrial capitalism not only produced a new form of economic integration between metropolitan and colonial societies, it also stimulated the emergence of what is known as social imperialism—that is, the projection overseas of the social discontents and dislocations engendered by industrialization at home.[8] In Japan's case, social imperialism operated both to diffuse radical demands of factory workers and to deflect class tensions in a rural economy battered by the effects of industrialization. Finally, industrial capitalism was responsible for the mass production and commodification of culture, and, hence, the invention of what we know as mass culture. The mass production of culture transformed the nature of the imperial project because it created new vehicles for the mobilization of popular support. In Japan and elsewhere, war fevers, yellow journalism, and what J. A. Hobson called in 1901 the "psychology of jingoism" became familiar features of modern empires.

In these ways the revolutions associated with modernity revolutionized imperialism. I have named the new imperialism "total" both to describe the phenomenon itself and to suggest a methodology for its study. The term does not signify absolute or totalitarian, but is used, rather, as an analogue of "total war." Like total war, total empire was made on the home front. It entailed the mass and multidimensional mobilization of domestic society: cultural, military, political, and economic. The multidimensionality of total empire relates to the question of causality as well. Manchukuo emerged from multiple, overlapping, and mutually reinforcing causes; it was an empire propelled by economic forces as well as strategic imperatives, by political processes and cultural determinants, by domestic social forces as well as international pressures. In themselves, none of these variables explains or determines imperialism; rather, their synergy or concatenation is what gave total imperialism its peculiar force. Empire in this sense is overdetermined. Finally, in using the term *total* I want to convey the widespread, even comprehensive, character of Manchukuo's impact on Japanese society. The process of empire building in Manchuria touched the lives of most Japanese in the 1930s in one way or another.

This is not to suggest that all modern empires were total in this way. All overseas interests, whether formal colonies or informal spheres of influence, held the potential of becoming total empires—but not all did. By my definition French Algeria and British India were almost certainly total empires, and perhaps others were as well. But without careful comparative research it would be reckless to venture a taxonomy of total empires or to

---

8. The classic work on social imperialism is Hans-Ulrich Wehler, *Bismarck und der Imperialismus* (Cologne: Kiepenheuer and Witsch, 1969), a study of Germany's sudden conversion to empire in the late nineteenth century. The argument is summarized in English in Hans-Ulrich Wehler, "Bismarck's Imperialism 1862–1890," *Past and Present*, no. 48 (August 1970), pp. 119–155.

hypothesize more precisely about the common historical conjunctures that bring them about. In Japan's case it is clear that some imperial projects were more important than others, and that imperial interests in the Nan'yō (Pacific Islands), Taiwan, and Korea all meant different things at different times. Japan's experience suggests, as well, that nations build one total empire at a time. Before the emergence of Manchukuo in the 1930s, only Korea in the 1890s and early 1900s ever involved domestic society to a degree that approached my sense of total.[9]

Understood in these terms, Manchukuo was a total empire. This book tells the story of its construction: a process of empire building that was multicausal and multidimensional, all-encompassing and, by the end, all-consuming.

MANCHUKUO IN JAPAN

This is a story, first of all, about an imperial relationship. Imperialism wove an increasingly intricate web of connections between empire and metropolis. Military occupation set in place one network of ties; economic development engendered another. Both of these were intertwined with the associations generated by Japanese settlement. Each soldier who fought to defend the Manchurian lifeline, each shipment of cement used for the development of Manchukuo, and each tenant farmer who settled in the new heaven on earth added to the whole. This expanding web of connections locked Japan and Manchukuo into an intimate embrace, and meant, increasingly, that when Manchukuo caught a cold, Japan sneezed. Whether it was the infectious inflation of the late 1930s and 1940s or the spreading arrests of alleged Japanese Communists that began with Mantetsu (the South Manchurian Railway) in 1942–1943, such sneezes revealed the often unforeseen transformations that imperialism wrought on metropolitan society. For total empire building was a dialectical process in this sense as well, and with the passage of time this process deposited more of Japan in Manchukuo and more of Manchukuo in Japan.

This book concentrates on the latter dimension of this dialectic—the story of Manchukuo in Japan. It is an account of empire building at home, focusing on the proliferating intersections between Manchukuo and the course of daily life—Japanese encounters with Manchukuo in local politics,

9. Peter Duus's recent work on the social and economic dimensions of empire building in Korea provides strong evidence for including Korea in the category of total empire: Peter Duus, *The Abacus and the Sword: The Japanese Penetration of Korea, 1895–1910* (Berkeley: University of California Press, 1995).

in schools, or in the morning news. The increasing frequency of such encounters naturalized the new empire. Over the course of the 1930s Manchukuo became ordinary and unexceptional—just another feature of the everyday landscape. The empire that began as a war devolved into a way of life.

My account of this process looks at imperialism through Japanese eyes. Like the ideas of other empire builders, Japanese views of Manchukuo were essentially solipsistic. Chinese and Korean residents of Northeast China had their own perceptions of the Japanese occupation, but these rarely penetrated the Japanese consciousness. Instead, Japanese interpreted Chinese actions to fit their own ideology of imperialism, painting military resistance as banditry or the mass immigration by southern Chinese as signaling a desire for Japanese-style order and justice. But even more striking than such intrusions of Asian others into Japanese imperial narratives was their frequent absence from these accounts. In Japanese dramatizations of the Manchurian Incident, the Chinese enemy was usually a faceless threat that hovered just off stage. Depictions of the hygienic new cities of Manchukuo kept the Chinese urban masses out of sight. Rural Manchuria, for its part, was imagined as empty, flat space—a vast frontier awaiting Japanese settlement. This depopulation of the imaginary landscapes of Manchukuo was an expression of the imbalance of power between Japanese and their others. Neither Chinese nor Koreans in Manchuria had a channel through which they could project their power back to metropolitan Japan, no means by which they could write themselves fully into the narratives of Japanese imperialism. This did not mean that Asian subjects of the Japanese empire had no agency in their own history. In their choices to collaborate or resist, Chinese and Koreans helped determine the shape of Japan's total empire. Their stories are every bit as complicated and contradictory as those of the Japanese. But for the most part colonial subjects were not agents of the history with which this book is primarily concerned, for they did not participate in the building of Manchukuo within Japan.

AGENTS OF EMPIRE

The builders of Manchukuo were a motley crew. Visions of empire fired the imaginations of a mixed collection of right-wing officers, reform bureaucrats, and revolutionaries of left and right, making bedfellows of erstwhile opponents. One could hardly imagine a more unlikely set of coimperialists than the right-wing pan-Asianist Ōkawa Shūmei, the author of Japan's most famous anti-war poem "Yosano Akiko," the left-wing revolutionary Comintern spy Ozaki Hotsumi, and the sadistic military police officer Amakasu Masahiko. Yet all these people, and many others, shared the dreams of Manchukuo and worked with one another to bring those dreams to reality.

This did not mean that they held the same vision of Manchukuo's future. Far from it: their ideas were frequently at odds with one another. Where intellectuals saw in Manchukuo's new colonial cities an urban utopia, rural reformers dreamt of agrarian paradise; where businessmen looked upon Manchukuo as the remedy to a faltering capitalist economy, radical army officers saw it as the means to overturn capitalism itself. These contending visions and the political and social conflict that they represented are very much a part of the story of empire in Manchukuo. Although opposition to the imperial project was sometimes forcibly silenced or drowned out, more often it was coopted. Persuaded that the new empire had something to offer them, groups that had been indifferent or even hostile to expanding Japan's position in Northeast China in the 1920s joined together to build Manchukuo in the 1930s. Mobilized for empire, their particular and often contradictory agendas became incorporated into the increasingly complex and unwieldy plans for Manchukuo.

Empire was thus a collaborative project. As Manchukuo grew more elaborate, the mobilization of domestic resources intensified and drew in an increasingly inclusive sweep of Japanese society. During the military occupation, Manchurian policy commanded the attention of both national cabinet officials and local party politicians. Chambers of commerce and labor unions lobbied with equal fervor for their share of Manchurian development. The colonization movement mobilized the energies of tenants and landlords, men, women, and children. From the top down and from the bottom up, agents of empire sought to involve all segments of Japanese society in the Manchukuo project.

To mobilize popular support for Manchukuo, imperial activists used existing institutions and also created new ones. Thus much of my account will focus on schools, army regiments, political parties, mass media, and other social, cultural, economic, and political institutions, showing the ways in which they were shaped and reshaped into vehicles for empire building. Whether one looks at the mass media spreading the war fever of the early thirties, academic institutions recruiting engineers to build heavy industry in the new empire, or government agencies organizing the resettlement of hundreds of thousands of Japanese farmers in the Manchurian plain, a variety of organizations played a part in the ongoing process of mobilization for empire.

The paper trail of these various agents of empire has led me beyond the collections of government documents and papers of leading statesmen through which historians have customarily read the imperial record on Manchukuo. Unlike the documents of government policy, however, there is no established body of sources that constitute the archives of civil society. A letter from one bureaucrat to another elucidates the ideas behind a policy decision, but how do we trace the thoughts of the popular mind of empire? To gain as broad a picture as possible, this study adopts an eclectic approach to sources, exploring the idea of Manchukuo as it was represented in popular magazines, pulp fiction, chamber of commerce records, propaganda pamphlets from the Army and Colonial Ministries, and military police reports. I also read city and prefectural histories from all parts of Japan for information about the local political impact of the Manchurian Incident and war-support campaigns. Recognizing the importance of continental travel as a vehicle for disseminating images of Manchurian development, I look at travel diaries, company histories of the tourist industry, travel guides, and such miscellany as maps, postcards, and souvenirs. And I analyze the numerous village studies produced by the Imperial Agricultural Association, the Ministry of Agriculture and Forestry, and the Manchurian Emigration Council, which document with great detail the history of the Manchurian colonists and the impact of their exodus on home villages. From such an array of sources, this book tells the story of Manchukuo from the point of view of the Japanese who built the new empire.

CULTURE AND IMPERIALISM

To a large extent, Manchurian empire building took place in the realm of the imagination." The imperial project generated three distinct imaginings of Manchukuo, cultural constructions that changed as the trajectory of imperial expansion moved from military occupation to economic development to colonial settlement. Japanese first knew Manchukuo as a battlefield; later it became associated with various schemes for economic renovation. Finally, they envisioned it in terms of hardy pioneers in an expansive frontier. For those at home, this succession of imagined empires was as real as their physical embodiments across the sea. In other words, for the vast majority of Japanese, the ideas and symbols of popular culture provided the primary medium through which they would experience Manchukuo.

My attempt here to map the imaginative terrain of empire rests on a three-fold conceptualization of culture. First, since my analysis separates

government from non-government initiatives concerning Manchukuo, I
distinguish between official and mass cultures of imperialism, the former
disseminated through government propaganda apparatuses and the latter
through the mass media. Second, because I am trying to locate the idea of
Manchukuo within a particular confluence of circumstances in the 1930s,
I understand culture as a historical construction. That is to say, ideas, practices, and even traditions are not timeless and immutable inheritances from
the past, but represent, rather, the inventions of specific historical moments. Finally, in order to place Manchukuo within the larger historical
context of Japanese imperialism and understand how initiatives in Manchukuo both broke with and recapitulated the past, I look at culture as a
process. The idea of Manchukuo did not suddenly appear full-blown, but
evolved through a process of cultural invention and reinvention. In other
words, Japanese imagined and reimagined "Manchukuo" in ways that innovated new imperial practices while drawing on the cultural accumulations of fifty years of empire building.

   In all three senses, imperial culture intersected with economic, social,
military, and political spheres. The Americanist Richard Slotkin put this
well when he wrote: "The cultural historian tries to construct a historical
account of the development of meaning and to show how the activities of
symbol-making, interpretation, and imaginative projection continuously
interlock with the political and material processes of social existence."[10]
This means pointing out not only that social existence shapes the imagination, but also the reverse. Ideas about the economy shape its structures;
political opinions are institutionalized in new programs and new bureaucracies; militarism helps direct the course of the military. In the context of
Manchukuo, this dialectical relationship between ideas and institutions interwove the dreams and deeds of empire.

   The pages that follow tell the story of total empire in Manchukuo from
shifting vantage points. I begin in Chapter Two with an international history of Japan's advance into Northeast China, situating Manchukuo within
the larger context of Japan's colonial empire. Tracing the developmental
logic of Japan's expansion in East Asia, this chapter looks to the international context for the answers to the question, Why did Manchukuo be-

---

10. Richard Slotkin, *Gunfighter Nation: The Myth of the Frontier in Twentieth-
Century America* (New York: Harper Perennial, 1992), p. 5.

come the centerpiece of the Japanese empire in the 1930s? Chapters Three through Nine comprise the heart of the study and focus on the processes of domestic mobilization for each of the three facets of the imperial project in Manchukuo: military, economic, and migratory.

Starting with the watershed events of 1931, Part Two (Chapters Three and Four) attempts to explain, in social and political terms, the domestic forces behind the new military imperialism of the 1930s. Why did the Manchurian Incident become a turning point for Japanese imperialism, and what did it signify for those at home? The answers I find relate the popularization of the new imperialism to the growth of institutions of mass culture and mass politics.

Following the turn to economic methods of imperial expansion in the mid 1930s, Part Three (Chapters Five and Six) takes up the radical experiment in colonial development. These chapters focus on the mobilization of two key segments of the middle class: business elites and intellectuals. In spite of their mistrust of army policy in the puppet state of Manchukuo, both groups were instrumental in supplying the enormous resources necessary for Manchurian development. Looking at the hopes and fears different groups of Japanese projected onto the new empire, I argue that what brought these unlikely allies together was a shared vision of the utopian potential of Manchukuo.

Part Four (Chapters Seven through Nine) formulates an explanation for why Manchurian colonization grew into a nationwide social movement and a major government initiative in the 1930s. In my answer I trace the emergence of agrarian social imperialism—the broad support for the resettlement of impoverished Japanese farmers to the Manchurian countryside in order to resolve the social crisis that industrial capitalism had produced in Japanese farm villages. The Manchurian solution to the problem of the villages was promoted with equal fervor by reformists in and out of government. Together, their participation in the colonization movement brought about a new relationship between state, society, and empire. For bureaucrats in a central government experimenting with techniques of social management, and for rural activists who were demanding greater government responsibility for the social health of farm villages, Manchurian colonization represented a new level of state involvement with rural society on one hand, and a new level of rural involvement in the empire on the other.

Collectively, these chapters describe the efforts of rich and poor, of officials and private citizens, of urban and rural residents to build an empire in Manchukuo. Although this is overwhelmingly a domestic story, it begins in the empire itself. It was international pressures that drove Kwantung Army conspirators to undertake the Manchurian Incident in 1931, and it was in the arena of foreign policy that the event demarcated the sharpest break with the past.

2 The Jewel in the Crown
The International Context of Manchukuo

Japanese expansion in Northeast China in the 1930s was part of a complex geometry of imperialism, comprised of the Japanese, their rivals for empire in the Asia-Pacific region, and the peoples over whom they sought dominion. Both governments and communities took part in the imperial enterprise, and in each case the course of empire was directed by the institutions that shaped the possibilities for individual action, as well as the individuals themselves. To take one example, the Kwantung Army officers who played such a prominent role in the creation of Manchukuo operated within a multiplicity of frameworks. Institutionally, they occupied positions within a colonial garrison army, which itself was part of a larger military bureaucracy, and, beyond that, one branch of the Japanese government. Living in the Northeast, the officers were part of an expatriate community of Manchurian Japanese, who were themselves members of a greater colonial elite. The configuration of international power at a given moment in time prescribed the interactions of these officers with different groups of Chinese, as it did their relations with Westerners in China. In this sense, the outcome of an imperial intervention initiated by Kwantung Army officers could not be reckoned in a single equation: it required a more complicated computation, taking into account bureaucratic politics, the politics of collaboration, and the diplomacy of imperialism. These were the power grids overlaying the Manchurian situation; the calculations they engendered defined the geometry of empire.

They were not static configurations of power. The spatial dimensions of empire changed over time, and there were good reasons for—even a logic to—the transitions. The creation of Manchukuo was part of this logic and thus represented a particular phase in the chronology of Japanese imperialism. In 1931 the initiation of a new military imperialism in Northeast

21

China marked a turning point for the Japanese empire. Thereafter Japanese made Manchukuo the centerpiece of their empire; they crafted it into the jewel in Japan's imperial crown. Why 1931 became the moment of departure for a new kind of imperialism is a complicated question to which I will come back over and again in the course of this book. The answers suggested in this chapter focus on the external pressures on Japanese policy, in particular the ways in which Japan and its imperial rivals responded to the challenge of the Chinese Nationalist movement. I rephrase the question of imperial chronology slightly: What defined the character of the new imperialism in Manchukuo? How was it set apart from earlier phases? The answers in this case look to the significance of Japanese characterizations of Manchukuo as "autonomous" of Western influence—going it alone against Western opposition—and "revolutionary" in the approach to colonial subjects—embracing the challenge of Chinese nationalism through the creation of a new kind of colonial state.

Defining the new imperialism at once in terms of Japan's relationship to the West and its relationship to Asia was a resonant dualism in the history of Japanese imperialism. Since the beginnings of Japanese expansionism in the 1870s and 1880s, the course of empire building had moved through several distinct phases, each defined by changing constructions of this same dualism. Thus the phases of empire building represented on one hand major transitions in Japan's relationship with Europe and the United States as it moved from being the object of imperial ambitions to becoming an imperial rival and enemy. On the other hand, each phase also marked an accumulation of experience with colonial subjects, the acquisition of new cultural forms of colonial capital, which were then deployed in the next phase. Knowledge garnered from this wealth of experience—both in the diplomacy of imperialism and the arts of colonial management—provided the foundation on which Manchukuo was built. For this reason, the story of the jewel in the crown demands a return to Manchukuo's imperial beginnings in order to separate out the old from the new.

IMPERIAL BEGINNINGS

The first push for influence in Northeast China gathered force at a turning point in the history of the Japanese empire. Victories in wars with China (1894–1895) and Russia (1904–1905) gained Japan entry into the ranks of the world's great military powers. During the same period, the new commercial treaties of 1894 and the Anglo-Japanese Alliance of 1902 signaled Japan's admittance into the Western community of nations on terms of equality. These were momentous steps for a nation that, in 1853, had been forced by American gunboats to accept unequal treaties—the same treaties that turned China into a quasi-colony of Europe before Japanese eyes. The specter of China's humiliation provided a powerful incentive for Japan to expand in self-defense.

Yet Japan's turn to imperialism was more than a simple reaction to Western pressure. The expansionist impulse sprang as well from the social and political upheavals of the mid nineteenth century and drew on a sophisticated discourse on Asia.[1] Together, internal and external forces propelled Japan into the precocious imperial activism of the 1870s and 1880s. As American and European commerce wreaked havoc on native industry, Japanese statesmen used European international law to enlarge their national territory, asserting claims to Ezo (present-day Hokkaidō), and the Kurile, Ryūkyū (Okinawa), and Bonin Islands. The Japanese government launched a military expedition to Taiwan in 1874, and sent soldiers and gunboats to Inchon in 1876 to force Korea to sign a commercial treaty, even while lobbying European diplomats unsuccessfully for the revision of their own unequal treaties. Thus it was that Japan began its career as a modern imperial power under the imperialist gun, escaping its aggressors by becoming an aggressor itself.

Japanese empire builders first trained their guns on Korea. In the official discourse of Meiji Japan, intervention in Korean court politics and an increasingly belligerent Sino-Japanese struggle for influence represented a new approach to Asia, one fusing older Confucian ideas with newer Western conceptions of international relations. Replacing China as the head of a Confucian family of nations, Japan had the prerogative to guide younger Asian brothers down the path it had itself so recently trod— toward Western-style modernization, civilization, and enlightenment. Articulated in the language of military geopolitics, it was strategically imperative to secure the Korean peninsula, transformed metaphorically into a "dagger pointed at the heart of Japan." In an international order where the "strong devour the weak," Japanese concluded they could either join the West as a "guest at the table" or be served up with China and Korea as part of the feast.[2] Such were the narratives of imperial mission in the

[handwritten margin note: 1900s, not 1890s]

---

1. For Japanese relations with Asia during the Tokugawa period, see Ronald Toby, *State and Diplomacy in Early Modern Japan: Asia in the Development of the Tokugawa Bakufu* (Stanford: Stanford University Press, 1984), and Marius Jansen, *China in the Tokugawa World* (Cambridge: Harvard University Press, 1992).

2. For a useful essay summarizing the Meiji discourse on Asia, see Marlene J. Mayo, "Attitudes toward Asia and the Beginnings of Japanese Empire," in Grant

formative years of empire, shaped by ambitions to dominate Korea. And it was that mission that led Japan, pursuing empire in Korea, on into Northeast China.

The desire for a foothold in Manchuria, known to the Chinese as the Three Eastern Provinces, or simply the Northeast, emerged within Japanese Army circles as early as the 1880s.[3] If control over Korea was essential to defend the home islands, then Manchuria's strategically placed Liaodong Peninsula was critical to secure Korea. When the Sino-Japanese rivalry over Korea erupted into war in 1894 and Japan proved victorious, the army added a Liaodong leasehold to the terms for peace. But a new rival for domination of the region deprived Japan of the Liaodong concession and soon threatened even the influence won in Korea itself. Supported by France and Germany in the Triple Intervention of 1895, Russia forced Japan to retrocede the Liaodong Peninsula to China. Quickly concluding its own agreement for a leasehold in 1898, Russia then invested heavily in its new sphere of influence in Manchuria and began to push into Korea as well. Tensions escalated and war soon broke out, Japan's second imperial contest over Korea. Victorious once again, Japan declared a protectorate over Korea and appropriated Russian interests in South Manchuria. Although it would later be claimed that the Russo-Japanese War was fought over Manchuria, Korea was the paramount objective and the real prize of the war. Indeed, army concerns notwithstanding, the lack of general interest in Manchuria led to a serious debate in 1905 over whether to sell the Russian rights to an American railway magnate. The government decided, of course, to keep Manchuria. But the point to remember is that at the outset, Japanese interests in Northeast China were overshadowed by the then favorite son of the Japanese empire—Korea.[4]

K. Goodman, comp., *Imperial Japan and Asia: A Reassessment* (New York: East Asian Institute, Columbia University, 1967), pp. 6–30. For a compilation of different accounts of the origins of Meiji imperialism see Marlene J. Mayo, comp., *The Emergence of Imperial Japan: Self-defense or Calculated Aggression?* (Lexington, Mass.: D. C. Heath, 1970).

3. The strategic concerns of late Meiji imperialism are discussed in James B. Crowley, "From Closed Door to Empire: The Formation of the Meiji Military Establishment," in Bernard S. Silberman and H. D. Harootunian, eds., *Modern Japanese Leadership* (Tucson: University of Arizona Press, 1966), pp. 261–285.

4. On Meiji imperialism in Korea, see Hilary Conroy, *The Japanese Seizure of Korea, 1868–1910: A Study of Realism and Idealism in International Relations* (Philadelphia: University of Pennsylvania Press, 1960), and Duus, *Abacus and Sword*.

With a new diplomatic status, a new military reputation, and a new collection of colonial possessions, Japan turned a fresh page in its imperial history. During this second, developmental, phase of empire, Japan's sphere of influence in Northeast China took shape. An admixture of formal and informal elements, Manchuria represented the two faces of Japan's nascent empire.[5] The Portsmouth Peace Treaty of 1905 transferred to Japan all Russian rights and interests in South Manchuria, originally signed over by China in 1898. These comprised 1) the balance of the twenty-five-year leasehold over the Liaodong Peninsula, which under Japanese rule became the Kwantung Leased Territory and included the port of Dalian and the naval base of Lüshun; 2) the southern spur of the Russian-built Chinese Eastern Railway, which ran from Changchun to Lüshun and which the Japanese renamed Mantetsu (the South Manchurian Railway); and 3) the so-called railway zone, which included a land corridor on either side of the railway track and the railway towns adjacent to important stations. As the result of the Portsmouth Peace Treaty, the Kwantung Leased Territory and the Japanese sections of the railway towns became effective colonial possessions, administered as part of Japan's growing formal empire. The rest of Manchuria, however, remained under Chinese government jurisdiction; Japanese influence was informal and their control indirect. Under these circumstances, the expansion of Japanese interests relied on using a combination of threat and bribery to extract ever more concessions from the local Chinese leadership. Equally important, such negotiations were never simply between Japan and China, but were embroiled in the multilateral intricacies of China diplomacy.

The diplomacy of imperialism turned, in China, on a complex interplay between Chinese domestic politics and European rivalries, punctuated in the early twentieth century by American and Japanese entries onto the imperialist playing field, the Russian and Chinese revolutions, and World War I. From the establishment of the unequal treaty system in the mid nineteenth century to the "carve up of China" into spheres of interest in the late 1890s, European powers had joined together to wrest from China concessions of collective benefit.[6] But behind the front of unity, commercial

5. On Japanese imperialism in Manchuria before 1931, see Ken'ichiro Hirano, "The Japanese in Manchuria, 1906–1931: A Study of the Historical Background of Manchukuo," Ph.D. dissertation, Harvard University, 1983; Herbert P. Bix, "Japanese Imperialism and Manchuria, 1890–1931," Ph.D. dissertation, Harvard University, 1972; and Herbert P. Bix, "Japanese Imperialism and the Manchurian Economy, 1900–1931," *China Quarterly* 51 (July–September 1972), pp. 425–443.

6. For a definitive treatment of the treaty port system, see John K. Fairbank,

competition was cutthroat: Europeans suspiciously scrutinized every move their rivals made.

Imperialist pressures heightened the domestic political crisis, leading in 1911 to the overthrow of the Qing dynasty and the establishment of the Chinese Republic. Yet the end of imperial rule brought neither a halt to foreign aggression nor an abatement of political unrest. Far from it: both internal and external pressures intensified in the wake of the revolution. As Chinese leaders came and went and the seat of government jumped from city to city, the country descended into military and political chaos. Between 1915 and 1922, rivalries between local warlord armies erupted into ten separate civil wars and turned China's political map into a constantly shifting power grid. Onto this kaleidoscopic political landscape Japanese cast increasingly calculating eyes. To an officialdom newly attuned to the importance of export expansion, logic decreed China—with the commercial opportunities offered by an already mythically prodigious market—to be the next frontier.[7] Their position in Korea was secured by annexation in 1910; maneuvering against Western rivals for a piece of China now occupied the attention of foreign policy makers.

Having learned from the experience of the Triple Intervention that diplomatic isolation spelled disaster, policy makers developed tactics for exploiting European rivalries to gain cover for Japanese expansion. The Anglo-Japanese Alliance of 1902 was the first successful application of this strategy. The British were interested in halting Russian expansion in China; by guaranteeing French neutrality, the alliance encouraged Japan to do the job for them. The policy of playing pawn to British interests in Asia served Japan well. Not only was the alliance essential to victory against Russia, but it allowed Japan to occupy German holdings in Asia during World War I. While this conflict withdrew European power from China, Japan moved in to press the Twenty-one Demands on the Chinese government, gaining an extension of Japanese rights in the Northeast, the transfer of German interests in Shandong, and other concessions to what

Trade and Diplomacy on the China Coast: The Opening of the Treaty Ports, 1842–1954, 2 vols. (Cambridge: Harvard University Press, 1953).

7. For economic concerns see Peter Duus, "Economic Dimensions of Meiji Imperialism: The Case of Korea, 1895–1910," in Ramon H. Myers and Mark R. Peattie, eds., *The Japanese Colonial Empire, 1895–1945* (Princeton: Princeton University Press, 1984), pp. 128–171; and William D. Wray, "Japan's Big-Three Service Enterprises in China, 1896–1936," in Peter Duus, Ramon H. Myers, and Mark R. Peattie, eds., *The Japanese Informal Empire in China, 1895–1937* (Princeton: Princeton University Press, 1989), pp. 31–64.

Japanese were now calling their "special relationship" with China. When the war ended, opportunities for unilateral action closed up, of course, but in the new arrangements set forth at the Washington Conference of 1922, Japan joined its rivals to present a recast united imperialist front to China. Looking back, the empire had progressed far since the days of the Triple Intervention. The inexperienced protégé of Great Britain had learned to ride the winds of Europe's political storms, and its special relationship with China was now secured in the legal embrace of the diplomacy of imperialism.[8]

As China diplomacy preoccupied Japanese foreign policy makers, the development of a growing array of colonial possessions was absorbing the attention of a new group of colonial administrators. Building up the apparatus of colonial rule in Taiwan (1895), Karafuto (1905), the Kwantung Leased Territory (1905), Korea (protectorate 1905, annexed 1910), and the equatorial Pacific Islands known as Nan'yō (occupied 1914, League of Nations mandate 1919), an empire which the Meiji discourse on Asia had only vaguely imagined grew a material dimension and sunk experiential roots.[9] In the diverse Asian communities over which they ruled, Japanese created a network of new institutions to concentrate political power in their own hands, extract financial profits, and suppress any resistance to the Japanese-imposed political and economic order. To meet the first objective, the new rulers established the powerful office of the governor general, granting to this single authority combined executive, judicial, and legislative powers. Buttressing the power of the governors general were military garrisons which collectively constituted a sizable overseas force: two divisions in Korea, one in the Kwantung Leased Territory, and several

8. On Great Power rivalries in China in the first two decades of the twentieth century, see Ian H. Nish, *The Anglo-Japanese Alliance: The Diplomacy of Two Island Empires 1894–1907* (London: Athlone Press, 1966); Ian H. Nish, *Alliance in Decline: A Study in Anglo-Japanese Relations 1908–23* (London: Athlone Press, 1972); Peter Lowe, *Great Britain and Japan, 1911–1915: A Study of British Far Eastern Policy* (London: Macmillan, 1969); and Madeleine Chi, *China Diplomacy, 1914–1918* (Cambridge: East Asian Research Center, Harvard University, 1970).

9. The best summary treatment of Japanese colonialism is found in three essays by Mark R. Peattie: "The Japanese Colonial Empire, 1895–1945," in Peter Duus, ed., *The Twentieth Century,* vol. 6 of *The Cambridge History of Japan* (New York: Cambridge University Press, 1988), pp. 217–270; "Introduction," in Ramon H. Myers and Mark R. Peattie, eds., *The Japanese Colonial Empire, 1895–1945* (Princeton: Princeton University Press, 1984), pp. 3–52; and "Japanese Attitudes toward Colonialism, 1895–1945," in Ramon H. Myers and Mark R. Peattie, eds., *The Japanese Colonial Empire, 1895–1945* (Princeton: Princeton University Press, 1984), pp. 80–127.

regiments in Taiwan. These units, particularly the Korea and Kwantung Armies, evolved into seasoned imperial troops with their own distinctive esprit de corps.

" In order to make colonialism pay," Japanese authorities organized financial institutions such as the Banks of Taiwan and Korea, charging them to take control of the monetary system and to finance colonial trade and investment. To facilitate the exploitation of what were, at the time of annexation, overwhelmingly agricultural economies, Japan set up semipublic companies such as Mantetsu (the South Manchurian Railway) and the Oriental Development Company. These restructured the landholding arrangements and oversaw the transfer of large blocks of land into Japanese hands. They promoted the commercialization of agriculture and steered production toward such profitable export crops as sugarcane in Taiwan, rice in Korea, and soybeans in the Kwantung Leased Territory.

Standing between the political and economic apparatus of the colonial state on one hand, and native society on the other, were the agents of enforcement—the colonial policemen. These factotums of Japanese administration performed a wide variety of tasks. In addition to their ordinary policing duties, they collected taxes, mobilized labor for road construction, oversaw land purchases, enforced tenant agreements, and taught school. To carry out all these functions, Japan built up enormous colonial police forces. In Korea and Taiwan, for example, the police operated through four levels of administration. At the base of this structure the colonial state maintained 2,599 police substations in Korea in 1926 and 1,510 in Taiwan in 1931. The total forces numbered 18,463 (40 percent native) and 11,166 (20 percent native), respectively.[10]

Such were the institutions Japanese developed to rule their formal empire in the early twentieth century, and which shaped and schooled the first generation of colonial elite. Adjusting this experience colonizing Asia to fit with the imagined Asia of the past, Japanese discourse on colonialism sharpened the definition of the imperial project and its local colorations. When Japanese spoke now of "Japan and Asia," distinct images of Taiwan, Korea, China, and Manchuria leapt to mind. To the abstract notion of "empire" were now attached concrete details: a police station in Seoul, a colonial currency in Taiwan, the pyramids of soybean cake stacked on the

10. Ching-chih Chen, "Police and Community Control Systems in the Empire," in Ramon H. Myers and Mark R. Peattie, eds., *The Japanese Colonial Empire, 1895–1945* (Princeton: Princeton University Press, 1984), pp. 213–239.

Dalian wharves. Empire had smells and sounds; it could be touched and tasted.

In their first articulations of an imperial mission, Japanese had used various metaphors to describe their new relationship with Asia: as head of an East Asian family of nations, as victor in an international struggle for survival, as vigilant defender against the threat of a peninsular dagger that pointed at Japan. Whether expressed in Confucian, Social Darwinist, or geopolitical terms, early Meiji calls for the expansion of Japanese interests in Asia represented prescriptions for future behavior, not descriptions of existing relationships. However, colonial experience gradually transformed moralistic imperatives of Confucian tutelage into the crisp bureaucratic professionalism of the science of colonial management; older goals of enlightenment (*kaika*) made way for the new teleology of progress (*hattatsu*).

In the international jungle of the new era it was no longer Asia but the West with which Japan battled for survival. The lines of advantage that military leaders called on their countrymen to secure in the 1890s became the lines of sovereignty in subsequent decades. Soldiers first fought and won these territories; then they patrolled them against enemies within and without. In the process, experience infused geopolitical imperatives with memories of sacrifice, death, and the hates of war.

In Northeast China, as elsewhere, a distinct variation of colonial mission emerged, merging the historical specificity of this dominated territory with the broader goals of the empire as a whole. Inscribed in the slogan "managing Manchuria" (*Manshū keiei*), the quest for empire in the Northeast combined strategic and economic imperatives in equal measure. It is to the development of these interests in the early years of *Manshū keiei* that I now turn.

"MANAGING MANCHURIA"

In 1905 and 1906 the Japanese government established a Kwantung governor general to administer the Kwantung Leased Territory and created a network of consulates throughout the Northeast to act for the Foreign Ministry. Their influence, however, was quickly overshadowed by the growing prominence of the institutions created to spearhead the military and economic penetration of the new continental foothold. Indeed, the Kwantung Army and Mantetsu together defined the nature of empire in the Northeast.

In keeping with the strategic importance accorded the new acquisition, a sizable military presence was established in the Northeast. The Kwantung garrison (reorganized in 1919 under its better-known appellation, the Kwantung Army) was composed of a regular army division and a heavy siege artillery battalion, both stationed within the Kwantung Leased Territory.[11] Supplementing this force were six independent garrison battalions of railway guards deployed along the railway zone, making a total troop strength of some 10,000 men. Except for a temporary loss of two railway guard battalions during military retrenchment in the late twenties, the Kwantung Army remained at this strength until the outbreak of the Manchurian Incident in 1931.

Fearing a revenge attack after the Russo-Japanese War, Japanese Army planning concentrated on countering the Russian threat by turning Manchuria into a strategic buffer zone. Staff officers believed that in order to defend Japanese interests it was imperative to expand Mantetsu's lines into a network connecting Japan, Korea, and Manchuria which could move men and materiel quickly into position in north Manchuria. Thus the Kwantung Army was assigned a two-fold strategic mission: first, to help secure concessions from the Chinese to build new rail lines deemed strategically necessary; and second, to ensure that Manchuria remained free of the political and military disturbances beginning to spread throughout China.

Over the course of the following two decades, the Kwantung Army pursued this mission with zealous determination. Acting sometimes at the behest of the army high command or with the unofficial support of civilian officials, and sometimes on independent initiative, Kwantung Army officers made the army into an agent of subimperialism. To the plotters, the revolutionary overthrow of China's imperial dynasty in 1911 and its subsequent descent into civil war provided a stream of opportunities to reshape the Chinese political situation to Japanese advantage. In the Northeast, Kwantung Army intrigues turned on nurturing the power base of the collaborationist warlord Zhang Zuolin and scheming to wrest Manchuria and Mongolia from Chinese control.[12]

11. On the early history of the Kwantung Army see Shimada Toshihiko, *Kantōgun: zaiMan rikugun no dokusō* (Chūō kōronsha, 1965), pp. 2–74; Coox, "The Kwantung Army Dimension," pp. 395–409; and Alvin D. Coox, *Nomonhan: Japan against Russia, 1939*, vol. 1 (Stanford: Stanford University Press, 1985), pp. 1–19.
12. The most thorough treatment of the relationship between Zhang Zuolin (Chang Tso-lin) and the Japanese is found in Gavan McCormack, *Chang Tso-lin in Northeast China, 1911–1928: China, Japan, and the Manchurian Idea* (Stanford: Stanford University Press, 1977).

(US-style)

The practice of seconding military advisers to Chinese leaders (an estimated fifty Japanese officers advised Zhang's army in 1928) provided ample opportunity for various forms of Japanese intervention.[13] During the late teens and twenties these military advisers supplied influence, information, funds, weapons, and even Japanese soldiers to ensure Zhang's victory over rival warlords. None of this came free, of course, and in exchange Japanese advisers secured promises of mining, railway, lumbering, and other concessions.

At a low point in what had always been an uneasy partnership between Zhang and the Japanese, Kwantung Army plotters decided they were best rid of him. Leading the conspiracy, Colonel Kōmoto Daisaku ordered the destruction of Zhang's railway car while he was traveling north to Fengtian. Russian-made bombs, the suitably attired corpses of three murdered Chinese, and secret papers were left on the scene to deflect suspicion onto one of Zhang's rival warlords. The conspirators anticipated that Zhang's death would lead to major disturbances, giving the Kwantung Army a pretext to occupy Manchuria and install a puppet leader. But although the war minister proposed dispatching additional troops to Manchuria for just this purpose, the rest of the Japanese cabinet refused, and the Kwantung Army plot to precipitate war with China and occupy the Northeast failed. Nevertheless, nothing was done to dislodge the conspirators or to quell the destabilizing predilection of Kwantung Army officers for military intrigue and imperial agitation.

While the Kwantung Army labored to strengthen Japan's strategic position on the continent, the mighty South Manchurian Railway (Mantetsu) undertook to open Manchuria to economic exploitation. A semipublic concern created in 1906 to manage the former Russian railway network with a capitalization of 200 million yen (increased to 440 million in 1920), Mantetsu was easily Japan's largest corporation. Mantetsu quickly expanded the Russian-built railway into an enterprise of staggering proportions. In addition to running freight and passenger services, the company operated coal mines at Fushun and Yantai as well as harbor and port facilities at Andong, Yingkou, and in the hub of Japanese activities in the Northeast, Dalian. Mantetsu maintained warehouses for goods and hotels for travelers; it administered the railway zone, which involved running schools and hospitals, as well as collecting taxes and managing public utilities. The research wing of Mantetsu became the center of Japanese colonial research, generating studies on all aspects of imperial policy

13. McCormack, pp. 119–124.

throughout the formal and informal empire. Within a decade of operation, Mantetsu began to launch a string of subsidiary corporations. These included Dalian Ceramics, Dalian Oil and Fat, South Manchurian Glass Company, Anshan Iron and Steel Works, electric light companies and gas plants in the major cities, a shale oil factory, a machine workshop, and plants to mill flour and refine sugar.[14]

For the first twenty-five years of its existence Mantetsu was an extremely profitable enterprise. Company assets rose from 163 million yen in 1908 to over a billion in 1930. A rate of return of 20 to 30 percent for all but a few of these years meant that not only was it the largest of Japan's companies, but frequently the most profitable as well.[15] During the 1920s yearly revenue for this single company averaged 218 million yen, a sum equal to about a quarter of total Japanese tax revenue.[16] The great majority of company revenue (75 percent) was generated by freight services.[17] While the railway transported significant quantities of millet, sorghum, and coal, the key to Mantetsu profits was soybeans—exported to Europe for manufacture into vegetable fats and oils, and to Japan for fertilizer and feed. Mantetsu's development of the soybean trade reshaped Manchuria's agricultural economy into a heavily commercialized export economy reliant on the production of a single crop. It was the classic pattern of an extractive, colonial economy. Soybean production increased four times between 1907 and 1927, by which time half the world's supply came from Northeast China. By monopolizing transportation and storage facilities, Mantetsu was able to charge premium rates on export-designated agricultural produce and maintain the company's extraordinary profitability.[18]

14. On the early history of Mantetsu, see Ramon H. Myers, "Japanese Imperialism in Manchuria: The South Manchurian Railway Company, 1906–1933," in Peter Duus, Ramon H. Myers, and Mark R. Peattie, eds., *The Japanese Informal Empire in China, 1895–1937* (Princeton: Princeton University Press, 1989), pp. 101–132; Manshikai, *Manshū kaihatsu yonjūnenshi*, vol. 1 (Manshū kaihatsu yonjūnenshi kankōkai, 1964), pp. 152–236; Andō Hikotarō, ed., *Mantetsu: Nihon teikokushugi to Chūgoku* (Ochanomizu shobō, 1965), pp. 11–152; and Bix, "Japanese Imperialism and the Manchurian Economy," pp. 425–443.

15. Nakamura Seishi, "Hyakusha rankingu no hensen," *Chūō kōron keiei mondai* (special issue, Fall 1977); *Kigyō tōkei sōran* (Tōyō keizai shinpōsha, 1943); Myers, "Japanese Imperialism," pp. 110, 115.

16. Japanese tax revenue was 175 million yen in 1920, 895 in 1925, and 835 in 1930: Andō Yoshio, ed., *Kindai Nihon keizaishi yōran*, 2d ed. (Tōkyō daigaku shuppankai, 1979), p. 18. For Mantetsu revenues see Manshikai, vol. 1, p. 299.

17. Myers, "Japanese Imperialism," p. 111.

18. Bix, "Japanese Imperialism and the Manchurian Economy," pp. 425–443; McCormack, p. 7.

By 1931, large numbers of Japanese had acquired an immediate taste of empire in service to one of these two institutions. Since the Kwantung Army was not composed of a permanent garrison unit, but rather was made up of regional divisions rotated for two-year postings, officers and conscripts from all over Japan saw service in Manchuria. By 1930, divisions based in Utsunomiya, Kyoto, Himeiji, Zentsūji, Hiroshima, Sendai, Asakawa, and Kumamoto had taken their turns in the Kwantung Army.[19] Moreover, Japan had fought one major military engagement on Manchurian soil and launched a second from the Manchurian garrison. The Russo-Japanese War mobilized over a million soldiers, a figure that exhausted the military reserve system and meant that one in eight households sent a family member to Manchuria. The casualty rate was very high—close to half a million dead and wounded, leaving a popular association of the Manchurian battleground with sacrifice and grief.[20] The Siberian Intervention, launched against the newly constituted Soviet Union from 1918–1922, involved 240,000 men. Here the fighting was much less bitter and casualties were a fraction of the Russo-Japanese War figure, but the four-year conflict deposited yet another layer of military experiences into public memories of Manchuria.[21]

Brought over to carry out the rapidly expanding activities of Mantetsu, the Japanese civilian population of Manchuria grew rapidly from 16,612 in 1906 to 233,749 in 1930.[22] Together with their dependents, Mantetsu employees accounted for about a third of this population; a large fraction of the rest were involved in commercial operations indirectly dependent on Mantetsu. Indeed, everyone's livelihood was reliant on the continuation of Mantetsu activities, just as company services—transportation, housing, sewage, electricity, entertainment, and much more—were an omnipresent feature of expatriate life in Manchuria.[23]

Mantetsu gave to the Japanese civilian population a predominantly elite, overwhelmingly urban cast. After briefly experimenting with importing unskilled labor from Japan, the company abandoned higher-priced Japa-

19. Coox, *Nomonhan*, vol. 1, p. 6.

20. Mobilization and casualty figures from Inoue Kiyoshi, *Nihon teikokushugi no keisei* (Iwanami shoten, 1968), pp. 227–239, and Iguchi Kazuki, "Nisshin, Nichiro sensōron," in Rekishigaku kenkyūkai and Nihonshi kenkyūkai, eds., *Kindai 2*, vol. 8 of *Kōza Nihon rekishi* (Tōkyō daigaku shuppankai, 1985), pp. 86–87. For a photographic record of the Russo-Japanese War, see Mainichi shinbunsha, *Nisshin Nichiro sensō*, vol. 1 of *Ichiokunin no Shōwashi: Nihon no senshi* (Mainichi shinbunsha, 1979), pp. 78–205.

21. Alvin Coox lists casualties at 12,000: Coox, *Nomonhan*, vol. 1, p. 9.

22. Manshikai, vol. 1, p. 84.

23. Hirano, p. 148.

nese workers in favor of the economies of Chinese labor. This meant that Mantetsu's Japanese work force—grown from 10,754 in 1910 to 21,824 in 1930—was of an exclusively elite character: it was an aristocracy of skilled laborers, white-collar workers, professionals, managers, and administrators.[24] The private commercial and manufacturing sector that sprouted from Mantetsu's foundations did not alter the sociological balance in the Japanese community. The private sector divided into two groups, one of giant firms like the Mitsui Trading Company, the Yokohama Specie Bank, and the Ōkura Trading Company, which bought from, sold to, and financed Mantetsu, and the other of small owner-operated shops, restaurants, and consumer-manufacturing establishments which catered to the expatriate community. The Japanese work force supported by the large firms was managerial and professional, and that supported by the small concerns, petit-bourgeois. The port city of Dalian, where almost half (100,000) of the 230,000 Japanese residents in Manchuria lived in 1930, well illustrated this trend. Less than 1 percent (1,000) of Japanese were involved in the manual occupations of farming or fishing, and only .3 percent (282) were found in mining. In contrast, 25 percent (24,507) were occupied in manufacturing, 23 percent (22,575) in commerce, 22 percent (21,823) in transportation, and 20 percent (19,532) in public service (schoolteachers, bureaucrats, and policemen).[25]

Like the memories of sacrifice on the battlefield and evocations of pride in service to the Kwantung Army, participation in the economic project in Manchuria created fertile ground for the imperial imagination, generating visions of colonial privilege and cosmopolitanism. In the strategic imperatives of the Kwantung Army, "managing Manchuria" meant quelling civil unrest and manipulating the warlords. In the economic mission of Mantetsu, it signified managing the soybean trade, tending to company investments, servicing the Japanese community, and controlling Chinese society. Such was the apprehension of *Manshū keiei* on the eve of the Manchurian Incident—the product of an empire built to the strategic and economic specifications of the Kwantung Army and Mantetsu.

After eighty years of experience with the diplomacy of imperialism, two imperial wars, and a thirty-five-year-old colonial empire, Japan had at its disposal a sophisticated understanding of international law, an army practiced in colonial warfare, and a seasoned colonial bureaucracy. This represented the overall accumulation of Japanese imperial capital in 1931.

24. Manshikai, vol. 1, p. 297.
25. *Manshū keizai zuhyō* (Dalian: Dalian shōkō kaigisho, 1934), p. 7.

In Manchuria itself, twenty-five years of investment had produced the well-entrenched sphere of influence that spread out from the colonial core in the Kwantung Leased Territory, anchored by the multifarious investments of Mantetsu and guarded by the Kwantung Army. A quarter of a million Japanese lived in this partially informal empire; many more had come once and returned home. Yet compared with the efforts that followed, all this would seem inconsequential—a short preamble to the extraordinary history of Manchukuo. Something changed in 1931, and with this change empire building took on a new urgency, a new audacity, and a new vision.

THE CHALLENGE OF CHINESE NATIONALISM

The immediate forces behind Japan's shift in gears emerged out of the breakdown, in the late 1920s, of the system of imperialist diplomacy in China. On the Chinese political front, the character of the civil war changed as the corrosive warlord conflicts gave way to a struggle between nascent Nationalist and Communist organizations to mobilize popular support and lead the unification of the country, with critical implications for foreign powers. Republican China's first modern political party, the Nationalist party, or Guomindang, was originally organized in 1912 by anti-Manchu revolutionaries associated with Sun Zhongshan (Sun Yat-sen). After moving through a series of reorganizations, the Guomindang fell under the leadership of Jiang Jieshi (Chiang Kai-shek) in the 1920s and expanded rapidly. By 1926 it boasted a powerful national organization and an army of 85,000 troops. The Chinese Communist party also grew to power in the turbulent years of the twenties. Formed in 1921 with advisers, money, and arms from the Soviet Union (and, initially, a political alliance with the Nationalists), the Communist party began to organize workers and students in large numbers. By late 1925, Chinese Communist party membership reached 20,000.[26]

Both the Nationalists and the Communists represented a new form of mass mobilization whose popular strength was directed first at unloosing the political grip of the warlords. Their challenge to the regional military rulers culminated in the Northern Expedition of 1926–1928. Setting off from Guangzhou in the south, Jiang Jieshi led his army north to Beijing, driving some warlords into retreat and absorbing others into his swelling

26. The best general histories of Sino-Japanese relations during the Republican period are by Marius B. Jansen: *The Japanese and Sun Yat-sen* (Cambridge: Harvard University Press, 1967), and *Japan and China: From War to Peace, 1894–1972* (Chicago: Rand McNally, 1975), pp. 224–314.

notice how she curries favor
Fairbank, Jansen, etc.

forces along the way. Uniting the country under the single, centralized political authority of the Guomindang, Jiang's Northern Expedition briefly ended the era of political fragmentation and chaos. Yet soon after unification, the Nationalist-Communist alliance unraveled, leading to the outbreak of a new sort of civil war. The Nationalists emerged as the clear victors in the first phase of conflict. Jiang's bloody surprise attack on Communist organizations in Shanghai in April 1927 and the suppression of Communist-organized "Autumn harvest" insurrections the following fall decimated the Communist movement. Their scattered forces retreated into the hills of the southeast where, under the leadership of Mao Zedong, the peasant-based organization of the People's Liberation Army took shape and developed its strategies of guerrilla warfare. The Communists used these strategies with growing effect, challenging the Nationalist hold over a politically unified China.

Both the Nationalists and the Communists rode to power on the rising tide of anti-imperialist nationalism. The inception of the Chinese Nationalist movement is usually dated from the May Fourth Movement of 1919. After witnessing their own officials at the Paris Peace Conference sell out the former German holdings in Shandong to the interests of Japanese imperialism, enraged students organized a nationwide series of demonstrations. From that point on anti-imperialist protests became an increasingly common occurrence in Shanghai, Hankou, and other foreign centers of manufacture and trade. Merchants and workers joined with students to boycott and strike against foreign enterprises. The protesters frequently singled out British and Japanese firms, since these two nations dominated foreign economic influence in China. Both countries were divided over how to best respond to the Nationalist challenge, flip-flopping from military suppression to appeasement and back again. Coordinated imperialist action was the casualty to such confusion. Thus when the British used force to suppress protest in May and June of 1925, Japanese officials adopted a conciliatory attitude, urging cotton manufacturers to compromise with strikers. Later, when British policy makers decided to back Jiang's moderation against Communist radicalism, their loans and diplomatic support contrasted sharply with Japan's military expeditions to Shandong in 1927 and 1928. What was true for Britain and Japan was equally certain for the other foreign interests in China. Individual national interests overrode advantages of collective action, as bilateral negotiations swept aside the cooperative diplomacy prescribed by the Washington Conference.

In 1929, the collapse of the American stock market and ensuing shock wave of global depression dealt the interimperialist alliance another profound blow. All parties responded to the economic crisis with economic nationalism. As they sought to barricade their own interests against any competitors, the imperatives of economic survival seemed to leave less and less room for compromise. To Japanese policy makers this meant sealing off their extensive investments in Manchuria from the rest of China, for special steps seemed necessary to secure a sphere of interest from the forces of Chinese nationalism.

In the Northeast, the rise of the Nationalist movement changed the relationship between Japan and its local collaborators. The increasingly forceful demands for the recovery of economic and political concessions from Japan—expressed in newspapers and through boycotts, strikes, and demonstrations—put pressure on the local warlord Zhang Zuolin to appease some of these demands lest he, like his rivals to the south, find himself the target of nationalist anger. The pressures he was under from nationalist protesters strengthened Zhang's hand in bargaining with the Japanese, who kept up their own demands throughout the 1920s. Zhang maneuvered shrewdly between these two opposing forces, using each as a shield to stave off the other. Although Zhang's repression never permitted boycott and strike activity to reach the intensity it did in the south, whether by accident or design protesters sometimes slipped through his control, as happened in the 1923 Jilin and Qiqihar demonstrations demanding the return of the Kwantung leasehold and railway rights. Japanese officials never entirely believed his protestations of helplessness; they grew increasingly irritated with both Zhang's pleas for patience and his promises to respond to demands later, when nationalist tempers had cooled.[27]

Even worse, Zhang and his allies were beginning to make investments that would compete with Japanese enterprises and threaten its economic dominance. These included railways and a port facility aimed at creating a parallel Chinese transportation and marketing network in order to break Mantetsu's monopoly. Zhang also established a cotton mill in Fengtian, and his associates created companies for sugar, timber, and coal production. With Zhang's encouragement, Chinese-owned public utilities sprang up, and Chinese merchants opened new businesses throughout the growing cities of the Northeast. While Japanese colonial officials looked on in outrage, the man whose wars they had bankrolled and whose armies they had protected seemed to betray their trust.

27. McCormack refers to this as "two-faced diplomacy": McCormack, pp. 124–126.

who?

Complaints about Zhang's insincerity mounted; but when Kwantung Army officers conspired to resolve the situation by assassinating Zhang, they gravely miscalculated. Zhang Zuolin was succeeded by his son, Zhang Xueliang, who proved to be even less tractable than Zuolin. Well aware of Japan's role in his father's death, Xueliang took his revenge by pushing harder than ever for rights recovery, stepping up investments, and—the crowning blow—signing an agreement with Jiang Jieshi that brought Manchuria under the control of the Guomindang. While this did not mean full political and military integration, Zhang Xueliang now referred all diplomatic matters to the Guomindang, greatly complicating Japanese negotiations concerning Manchuria. Their worst fears appeared to have been realized when Jiang Jieshi announced in the spring of 1931 that the new principles of Guomindang foreign policy included the return of the Kwantung Leased Territory and the recovery of rights to operate Mantetsu.

The sense of crisis among the Japanese in the Northeast intensified, as a fall in profits in the late 1920s seemed to confirm that the nationalist strategy of economic encirclement was working. Though the contraction in colonial revenues was in fact caused by other factors—Mantetsu profits fell due to a drop in world demand for soybeans rather than the Chinese railroad network, and Japanese shopkeepers were imperiled by competition from a Mantetsu consumer co-op and not Chinese merchants—the Japanese blamed it squarely on what they called the "anti-Japanese movement." Within the various sectors of the colonial state and at every level of colonial society, people compiled catalogs of grievances: obstructions to land purchases, illegal seizures of goods, triple taxing, refusal to permit construction of previously agreed upon railways, unpaid debts, scurrilous newspaper reports, hostility in textbooks, assaults, vandalism, and murder. Settler society organized itself and began to lobby the metropolitan government. Through petitions and speeches they insisted on firm measures to settle the "over 500 pending cases" in what became the catchphrase of an appeal for military intervention.[28]

Responding in part to these lobbying activities, in part out of their own perception of the gathering crisis, government officials began to discuss options for an independent Manchuria. This was not entirely a new idea, for since the 1911 Revolution Japanese policy makers had flirted with the possibility of severing Manchuria from China. The issue was seriously taken up at the Eastern Conference of 1927, and in 1929 the Kwantung

28. Ogata, p. 18.

Army began developing operational plans for occupation. Matters came to a head in the summer of 1931, when the Wanbaoshan and Nakamura Incidents became the focal point of agitation for military intervention.

The Wanbaoshan Incident involved a dispute over irrigation rights between 200 immigrant Koreans, whose settlement in eastern Manchuria had been facilitated by the Japanese authorities, and a handful of Chinese landowners. In a climate of hostility where the Chinese regarded the Koreans as tools of Japanese aggression in Manchuria and the Japanese responded angrily to harassment of Japanese nationals (as the Koreans in Manchuria were considered), the dispute quickly escalated. Chinese police told the Koreans to leave, but Japanese consular police insisted they could stay. A group of 400 Chinese farmers then attacked the Koreans and were in turn fired at and driven off by the Japanese police.[29]

In the meantime, the arrest and execution of a Japanese intelligence officer by Chinese soldiers created a second cause célèbre. When discovered near the border of Inner Mongolia, far into the Russian sphere of interest in north Manchuria, army captain Nakamura Shintarō claimed he was an agricultural expert. However, because his belongings included a military map, narcotic drugs, weapons, and surveying instruments, the Chinese soldiers assumed he was a military spy and shot him.[30]

In and of themselves, there was nothing extraordinary about these two incidents; similar things had occurred numerous times in the past. But in the contentious atmosphere of 1931 they became lightning rods for resentments on both sides. While Chinese nationalists rioted against the Japanese, the Japanese settler organizations Yūhokai and the Manchurian Youth League dispatched representatives to Japan to make speeches and lobby government officials. They were joined by right-wing organizations, political party hawks, and army spokesmen who supported their demands for government action to end the "outrages."[31]

By 1931 there was widespread consensus among the Japanese in Northeast China about the need for a new approach. Although this imperial establishment was a big fish in its own pond, it figured very little in the sea of international and domestic concerns which beset Japan at that time.

29. Yoshihashi, pp. 143–144; Edward Earl Pratt, "Wanpaoshan, 1931: Japanese Imperialism, Chinese Nationalism and the Korean Problem in Northeast China on the Eve of the Manchurian Incident," Master's thesis, University of Virginia, May 1983.

30. Yoshihashi, pp. 143–145.

31. Ogata, p. 18.

This would change, however, as a series of increasingly ambitious imperial projects carried out over the 1930s made Manchuria the centerpiece of the empire and led to the birth of Manchukuo.

THE PUPPET STATE OF MANCHUKUO

The Kwantung Army set the construction of Manchukuo in motion with the military conquest of the Northeast known as the Manchurian Incident. Between September 18, 1931, and the Tanggu Truce of May 31, 1933, a series of campaigns brought the four provinces of Jilin, Liaoning, Heilongjiang, and Rehe under Japanese military control. The occupation began with a conspiracy engineered by Kwantung Army officers. What had failed in 1928 worked to spectacular effect in 1931. Staging an explosion of Mantetsu track near the Chinese military base in the city of Fengtian (now known as Shenyang), the conspirators used the alleged attack as a pretext to open fire on the Chinese garrison. Over the ensuing days and months the army quickly escalated the situation, first moving to occupy the railway zone and then embarking on the operations to expel from Manchuria the estimated 330,000 troops in Zhang Xueliang's army. Unlike in 1928, the metropolitan government ultimately sanctioned army action; the army high command in Tokyo refused to rein in their forces in Manchuria, and the cabinet was unwilling to relinquish territory gained in a fait accompli. Thus the Kwantung Army was permitted to overrun the Northeast, and Japan found itself in full possession of Manchuria.[32]

Early in the campaign, it became clear to the plotters that their home government would not approve the formal annexation of the Northeast and the creation of a Japanese colony in Manchuria. Instead, they enlisted the collaboration of powerful Chinese, organized a "Manchuria for the Manchurians" movement, and declared Manchukuo an independent state. Manchukuo was created in March 1932 with Chinese serving as the titular ministry and department heads; actual power, however, resided with the Japanese vice-ministers and the Japanese-dominated General Affairs Board. Japan quickly recognized Manchukuo and signed a mutual defense treaty making the Kwantung Army responsible for its national security. Behind the fiction of the puppet state, Japan had effectively turned Manchuria into a colony of rule. As transparent as this fiction may have seemed to many, Japanese labored mightily to convince themselves and others of

32. For basic sources on the military history of the Manchurian Incident, see Chapter 1, note 1.

the truth of Manchurian independence. In the puppet regime they sought a form of colonial state that represented a new kind of collaboration between imperialist and subject, a formula for colonial rule neither formal nor informal that would accommodate nationalist demands for sovereignty and self-determination.

What Manchurian independence in fact accommodated were Kwantung Army demands for greater authority. Assuming position of all the key posts in the new state, the Kwantung Army created for itself an imperium in imperio. Before the establishment of Manchukuo, the army shared power with Mantetsu and, to a lesser extent, with the Kwantung governor general and the Japanese consulate. In the administrative reorganization, however, the latter two were effectively excluded from the decision-making loop while Mantetsu was forced into a subordinate relationship with the Kwantung Army. Moreover, in a parallel reorganization in Japan, the Army Ministry outmaneuvered the Colonial and Foreign Ministries, dominating the newly created Manchurian Bureau. This gave the military control over official communications between Japan and Manchukuo. Thus, not only did the Manchukuo government give the Kwantung Army a vehicle for expanding its power within the Northeast, but it also provided a channel for extending its influence over metropolitan government.

The size, reputation, and hubris of the Kwantung Army increased in tandem with the expansion of its power base in the new colonial state. Troop strength grew rapidly, reaching its peak at twelve divisions in 1941. The rapid and efficient occupation of Manchuria greatly enhanced the prestige of the army and brought the Kwantung garrison a wave of adulatory publicity. As the army redefined its strategic mission to focus on the threat from the Soviet Union along the Manchukuo-Siberian border, Kwantung Army units were built up into the crack troops of the Imperial Army. Preparing for a decisive strike north, the Kwantung Army forayed into Soviet territory, provoking border skirmishes that flared into war in the Nomonhan Incident of 1939. At the same time, the expulsion of Zhang's forces south of the Great Wall created a new turbulent frontier over which the army was anxious to establish control, spawning yet another series of plots and connivances to push down into north China and beyond. Interpreting liberally its mandate for the defense of Manchukuo, the army drove relentlessly forward to expand the territory under its control.[33]

33. For a brief account of the Kwantung Army, see Coox, "The Kwantung Army Dimension," pp. 409–428. For exhaustive treatment, see Coox, *Nomonhan*, vols. 1–2.

The second phase in the construction of Manchukuo was economic. The puppet state became more than just a military project when the metropolitan government stepped up its involvement, gambling heavily on a bold experiment in the restructuring of the colonial economy. Against the backdrop of unprecedented economic crisis, the Japanese government began to view industrial development of Manchukuo as the means to rejuvenate the economy and create a self-sufficient trade zone protected from the uncertainties of the global marketplace. The military luster imparted by the early triumphs of the Kwantung Army was now enhanced by the investments that made Manchukuo a jewel of unrivaled value. The levels of money that poured in provided some of the most dramatic testimony of the Japanese commitment to Manchukuo. In Manchukuo's first five years, Japanese invested 1.2 billion yen, a figure almost equal to the 1.75 billion yen supplied to the region over the previous twenty-five years. Between 1932 and 1941, 5.86 billion yen were injected into Manchukuo, more than the 5.4 billion yen accumulated in the entire overseas empire—China, Korea, Taiwan, Manchuria, Karafuto, and Nan'yō—by 1930.[34]

It was more than just capital that Japanese invested. Starting in 1933, the metropolitan government sent a parade of bureaucrats including Kishi Nobusuke, Shiina Etsusaburō, Minobe Yōji, Kōda Noboru, and Shiseki Ihei to take up important posts in the Manchukuo administration.[35] Mostly from the Ministry of Commerce and Industry, these men were among the brightest of a new breed of planners—the "new bureaucrats"—interested in developing industrial policies to extend government management over the economy.[36] Unlike the pool of colonial bureaucrats who had spent their careers in the empire and identified themselves with the colonies they

34. Hayashi Takehisa, Yamazaki Hiroaki, and Shibagaki Kazuo, *Nihon shihonshugi*, vol. 6 of *Kōza teikokushugi no kenkyū: ryōtaisenkan ni okeru sono saihensei* (Aoki shoten, 1973), p. 250; Kaneko Fumio, "Shihon yushutsu to shokuminchi," in Ōishi Kaichirō, ed., *Sekai daikyōkōki*, vol. 2 of *Nihon teikokushugishi* (Tōkyō daigaku shuppankai, 1987), p. 337; Hikita Yasuyuki, "Zaisei kin'yū kōzō," in Asada Kyōji and Kobayashi Hideo, eds., *Nihon teikokushugi no Manshū shihai: jūgonen sensō o chūshin ni* (Jichōsha, 1986), pp. 866, 889.

35. Johnson, *MITI and the Japanese Miracle*, pp. 130–132.

36. Sometimes called the reform bureaucrats, the term *new bureaucrats* is loosely applied to officials who supported a variety of state-strengthening economic and social reforms which often had a fascist tinge. For more detail, see Johnson, *MITI and the Japanese Miracle*, pp. 116–156; Barnhart, pp. 71–76, 171–175; and William Miles Fletcher, *The Search for a New Order: Intellectuals and Fascism in Prewar Japan* (Chapel Hill: University of North Carolina Press, 1982), pp. 88–105.

managed, these policy makers had little or no overseas experience; their concerns were with the domestic economy. For them, Manchukuo represented a laboratory in which to test economic theories which they would later apply to Japan.

At the heart of the Manchurian experiment were two novel ideas of economic governance beginning to circulate in the industrialized world, though never before applied to a colony. The first, state-managed economic development, borrowed the Soviet model for the command economy. The second, the self-sufficient production sphere, or bloc economy, drew on economic analyses of military production in World War I. Replacing the old mandate for "managing Manchuria," the new economic mission of development (*kaihatsu*) called for coordinated industrialization of Japan and Manchukuo and aimed at military self-sufficiency.[37]

Under the banner of "Manchurian development," the Manchukuo government created twenty-six new companies by the end of 1936, one company per industry in such fields as aviation, gasoline, shipping, and automobiles.[38] Five-year plans were instituted beginning in 1937, setting ambitious production targets. While Manchurian development was skewed toward heavy industrialization, the agricultural sector was also brought within the sphere of government planning. Although policies like the introduction of new crops and the establishment of agricultural extension services and marketing cooperatives were geared primarily toward enhancing Japan's agricultural self-sufficiency, the developmentalist agenda of the Manchukuo government also sought to legitimate the colonial project in the eyes of the subject population. Recognizing that poverty created a breeding ground for anti-imperialist sentiment and communist agitation, administrators tried to eliminate some of the economic causes of discontent. Of course, developmental policies aimed at improving the welfare of the Chinese peasantry were easily compromised when they conflicted with imperatives for resource extraction or the interests of the collaborating Chinese elite. Nevertheless, the rhetoric of colonial development showcased new ideals of social reform that borrowed from the movement to mitigate rural poverty within Japan.

The new program transformed Mantetsu's role in the colonial economy. Previously, the economy was its private domain, and Mantetsu executives

37. For basic references, see Chapter 1, note 2.
38. Hara Akira, "1930 nendai no Manshū keizai tōsei seisaku," in *Manshūshi kenkyūkai*, ed., *Nihon teikokushugika no Manshū* (Ochanomizu shobō, 1972), p. 46.

presided over an imperium in imperio. In the face of the Kwantung Army's advance into economic management, however, Mantetsu retreated from its mining and manufacturing activities, concentrating on management of its transportation network. Final control over its empire of subsidiaries was relinquished in 1937 to Manchurian Heavy Industries, the large public-private firm created to coordinate the industrial production targets of the Five-Year Plan. This represented a defeat for Mantetsu in its struggle with the army for control over the government institutions left vacant by the withdrawal of Zhang Xueliang from Manchuria. Victorious, the army used its domination of the puppet state of Manchukuo to initiate the heavy industrialization of the colonial economy and to reconfigure the institutions for managing Manchuria. Forced by these initiatives into a series of unprofitable investments in the new state-run industries and a network of strategic railways, Mantetsu's capital strength and profitability were gradually whittled away.

There were compensations. The new program put a premium on planning and generated an enormous demand for research. Mantetsu became the brain trust for Manchukuo development, later expanding into a center of planning for the empire as a whole. Mantetsu's prestige as a research institute reached its peak in the early 1940s, when the Research Department commanded a staff of 2,200 to 2,300 researchers.[39] In addition to its new role in planning, Mantetsu was given a free hand in the economic development of north China—rapidly becoming the next frontier for Japanese imperial expansion—to offset its loss of jurisdiction in the Manchurian economy.

Following close on the heels of the new military and economic programs, the announcement in 1936 of the Japanese government's intent to carry out mass Japanese emigration to Manchuria signaled a third radical departure for the imperialist project. Grand in scope, the plan aimed to send five million farmers, a figure equivalent to one-fifth of the 1936 farm population, to a "new paradise" in Manchuria in the space of twenty years. By placing in Northeast China a large settler community that would reproduce itself, Japanese hoped to mount their imperial jewel in a permanent setting.[40]

The settler community created by the government's colonization pro-

---

39. Ishidō Kiyotomo, "Mantetsu chōsabu wa nan de atta ka (II)," no. 17 of "Mantetsu chōsabu kankeisha ni kiku," *Ajia keizai* 28, no. 6 (June 1987), p. 55.
40. On the Manchurian settlement program, see Manshū iminshi kenkyū-kai, ed.

gram bore little resemblance to the Japanese society that had grown up in Manchuria in the years before Manchukuo. The older community was exclusively urban; the new settlements were in the countryside. A privileged elite of administrators, entrepreneurs, and professionals made up the urban community; the rural immigrants were drawn from the ranks of impoverished tenant farmers and the lumpen proletariat. Unlike the colonial elite, who eagerly flocked to the continent in the 1930s, swelling the urban population to close to a million in 1940,[41] the farm immigrants needed to be bribed with offers of free passage, free land, and a long list of other enticements before they would be persuaded to take advantage of the opportunities in Manchukuo.

Among other reasons, urban life was more attractive because fellow Japanese citizens comprised a large proportion of the population. In the two centers of urban settlement, Dalian and Fengtian, Japanese made up 29 percent and 59 percent of the 1932 population, respectively. The 300,000 rural settlers, in contrast, entered a world where they constituted a fraction of a percent of the estimated 34 million natives.[42] The settlers were divided among just over a thousand villages scattered throughout the rural hinterland. Often the sole Japanese outpost for many miles, these immigrant villages were swallowed up in the Chinese multitudes that surrounded them. In addition, few of the urban Japanese intended to take up permanent residence in Manchuria, a fact much lamented by the ideologues of colonization. Since urban settlers had financial mobility, they often chose to return to Japan after finishing their tour of duty in the colonial service or their company's Manchurian branch. The agricultural settlers, however, came for good. The price of government aid was a lifetime commitment to their new home. Even if they changed their minds, returning to Japan was far from easy. They had severed ties with their home villages, selling off land and property, and in most cases they were financially dependent on the government and would be hard pressed to find funds to pay the fare home. Unlike their urban counterparts, the rural settlers were stuck in Manchuria—permanent residents, if not out of choice, out of necessity.

Government involvement in the welfare of the farm settlements extended far beyond what was provided urban colonists. Rather like the economy itself, the immigrant villages were state-planned and state-managed. A swelling bureaucracy and ever-larger budget appropriations were given

41. Manshikai, vol. 2, p. 84.
42. Mantetsu, ed., *Manshū nenkan: Shōwa 8 nen* (Dalian: Manshū bunka kyō-kai, 1933), pp. 38–39.

over to the micro-management of the immigrant villages. Everything from the number of livestock to the crop mix was prescribed by plan. State-run cooperatives bought colonists' produce and sold them seed, fertilizer, and sundries for everyday use. State agricultural agents advised them and reported on their progress. Such attention aimed to secure their long-term survival and, at the same time, to ensure that colonists stayed put on the land.

Like everything about Manchurian government policy, there was a heavy military coloration to the agricultural settlement program. Behind the big budgets and the state preoccupation with the welfare of the colonists lay a two-fold strategic agenda. First, in constructing Japanese villages in north Manchuria along the border with Siberia, administrators aimed to create a human buffer zone against the Soviet Union. Second, by settling Japanese in the rural centers of the Chinese resistance movement, officials hoped to deter further guerrilla warfare against the colonial state. To prepare them for their paramilitary role, the state included military maneuvers in the course of training provided to all agricultural settlers, and issued them arms along with tools and seeds when they arrived in their new homes. In effect, the settlers were turned into a strategically deployed reserve of the Kwantung Army.

Through the agricultural settlement program, Manchukuo administrators created a new colonial society, one comprised of a weak and subordinated farming class that could be controlled in ways not possible with the urban colonists. Like the gamble for power by the Kwantung Army in 1931 and the risks taken to test out the planned economy, settlement was an experiment; it was an attempt to create a new instrument of the colonial state.

These three projects involved more money, more resources, and more people with each passing month. Each step grew bolder and each decision more brash, as Manchukuo increasingly defined the cutting edge of imperial policy. By the late 1930s Manchukuo had become synonymous with the Kwantung garrison, pride of the Imperial Army, with the command economy and the yen bloc, and with the noble labors of the settlers who tilled the rich earth of Manchuria. What had been developed in the Northeast to meet the challenge of nationalism in China created a model for the construction of a new kind of empire. Japanese applied this model to an Asia where the rise of anti-imperialist nationalisms threatened the old formulas for imperialist cooperation and colonial management. In this way, the creation of Manchukuo ushered in an era of autonomous imperialism for Japan in Asia.

AUTONOMOUS IMPERIALISM

This third phase of imperialism lasted until the end of World War II. What Japanese officials called "autonomous diplomacy" signified two departures from past practice. First, it meant liberating imperial interests in Asia from a consideration of relations with the West. In the past, fearing diplomatic isolation, Japanese policy makers took careful stock of how a potential move in Asia was likely to be received in the West. Interventions were preceded by judicious multilateral negotiations. After 1931, however, the "Manchurian problem," the "China question," and the "advance south" all were decided unilaterally and in the face of Western opposition. The stand-off between Japan and the great powers in the League of Nations in 1932–1933 signaled this change in direction. In the spring of 1933, failing to gain Western endorsement for its actions in Northeast China, Japan left the League and isolated itself diplomatically. Of their own volition, Japanese statesmen withdrew from the great power club into which they had labored so long to gain entry.

Second, autonomy betokened a new independence for the colonial armies. In this sense the origin of the new phase of imperialism in a Kwantung Army conspiracy was of more than passing importance. Indeed, military faits accomplis followed one upon the other, as aggressive field officers took their lead from the success of the Manchurian Incident. Since Meiji times, imperial expansion began with military conquest. But by the 1930s, the imperial garrisons had multiplied and the institutional complexity of the armed services opened new possibilities for subimperialists. The trigger-happy proclivity of the garrison armies turned the boundaries of the empire into a rolling frontier. And as the army gained influence over political institutions both at home and in the empire, the tendency to resort to force when negotiations stalled only grew stronger.

This "shoot first, ask questions later" approach to empire building drew Japan into a series of military conflicts. At first, China and the Soviet Union responded to Japan's go-fast imperialism with concessions.[43] In the early 1930s, the Nationalists were too busy fighting the Communists to resist the takeover of Manchuria. Stalin, preoccupied with agricultural collectivization, the five-year plans, and purging the party, decided to sell off the Chinese Eastern Railway in 1935 and retreat before Japan's advance into north Manchuria. But after the formation of a united Chinese Communist-

---

43. The phrase comes from John W. Dower, *Empire and Aftermath: Yoshida Shigeru and the Japanese Experience, 1878–1954* (Cambridge: Council on East Asian Studies, Harvard University, 1979), p. 85.

Nationalist front in 1936 and the Soviet fortifications of the Manchurian-Soviet border, both China and the Soviet Union began to stand their ground. War broke out with China in 1937, and with the Soviet Union in 1938 and 1939.

Similarly, American and European interests in Asia were initially consumed with domestic economic problems and the dissolution of the international financial system. The day before the Manchurian Incident, Great Britain went off the gold standard; there was little attention to spare for the Far East. Although after 1937 the United States opposed Japan indirectly by supplying Jiang Jieshi with war materiel, only in 1940, after the outbreak of war in Europe and the Japanese advance into Indochina, did the United States begin embargoes on strategic materials to Japan. The tightening of the economic screws led to the decision, once again, to attack; from December 1941, Japan was fighting a war against Britain and the United States, and the boundaries of the empire became an endless war front. In the process, the empire and the war grew indistinguishable. The hallmark of the new imperialism was a perpetual state of war. From the creation of Manchukuo to the occupation of Southeast Asia, policy makers and foot soldiers alike were propelled by a sense of crisis and the extraordinary needs of a nation at war.

Following the model pioneered in Manchukuo, the autonomous phase of empire also denoted a new kind of colonial rule. This was signaled first in official rhetoric, which sought to depict the Japanese colonial state as the ally of anti-colonial nationalism. First, Manchuria was "liberated" from China by a movement for independence; later, Japanese set up an administration in Southeast Asia under the slogan "Asia for the Asiatics." As vacuous and self-serving as these declarations seem in retrospect, at the time they were initially effective in mobilizing support both among Japanese at home and among the Asians who helped Japan create the new colonial institutions.

The organizational structure of the puppet state which was developed in the Northeast subsequently became the prototype for the creation of a string of collaborationist regimes in occupied China.[44] In Southeast Asia, the picture was more complex. With the support of local nationalist movements, Japan drove out Western colonial rulers, establishing two types of

---

44. On the occupation of China, see Lincoln Li, *The Japanese Army in North China, 1937–1941: Problems of Political and Economic Control* (New York: Oxford University Press, 1976), and John Hunter Boyle, *China and Japan at War, 1937–1945: The Politics of Collaboration* (Stanford: Stanford University Press, 1972).

administration. In Thailand (the sole independent country at the time of Japanese occupation), and after January 1943 in Burma and the Philippines, alliances gave Japan the power of indirect rule. In Indonesia and Malaya, the occupying forces governed through a military administration. With the exception of French Indochina, where Japan ruled in collaboration with the French authorities and was opposed by Ho Chi Minh's newly organized Vietminh, Southeast Asian nationalists cooperated with Japanese colonial rule, especially in its initial phase.[45]

Strategies of mobilization were part of the Manchuria formula. Military, political, economic, and cultural institutions were created or reshaped to organize new communities of support for Japanese rule. Ambitious young Chinese found the Manchukuo Army and military academy a route of advancement, as did their counterparts throughout the empire. Military institutions formed in the late colonial period in Burma, Korea, and elsewhere became the training ground for postcolonial elites. Similarly, Japanese established mass parties such as the Putera in Indonesia and the Kalibapi in the Philippines, patterned on Manchukuo's Kyōwakai. Throughout the empire, Japanese created joint ventures with local capital. Sometimes this was a mask for Japanese control, sometimes a cover for appropriation of native capital, and sometimes, as in Korea, a means of cultivating a collaborative elite and splitting the nationalist movement.[46] Assimilationist cultural policies were widely applied over the course of the thirties and forties, in an attempt to create an elite cadre of youth loyal to Japanese rule. These went furthest in Taiwan and Korea, where the *kōminka* (imperialization) movement sought to erase native cultural traditions,

---

45. On the Co-prosperity Sphere, see E. Bruce Reynolds, "Anomaly or Model? Independent Thailand's Role in Japan's Asian Strategy, 1941–1943," and Ken'ichi Gotō, "Cooperation, Submission, and Resistance of Indigenous Elites of Southeast Asia in the Wartime Empire," in Peter Duus, Ramon H. Myers, and Mark R. Peattie, eds., *The Japanese Wartime Empire, 1931–1945* (Princeton: Princeton University Press, 1996), pp. 243–273 and 274–301, respectively; Joyce C. Lebra, *Japanese-Trained Armies in Southeast Asia: Independence and Volunteer Forces in World War II* (New York: Columbia University Press, 1977); Willard H. Elsbree, *Japan's Role in Southeast Asian Nationalist Movements, 1940 to 1945* (Cambridge: Harvard University Press, 1953); Josef Silverstein, ed., *Southeast Asia in World War II: Four Essays* (New Haven: Yale University Southeast Asia Studies, 1966); and Alfred W. McCoy, ed., *Southeast Asia under Japanese Occupation* (New Haven: Yale University Southeast Asia Studies, 1980).

46. Carter J. Eckert, "Total War, Industrialization, and Social Change in Late Colonial Korea," in Peter Duus, Ramon H. Myers, and Mark R. Peattie, eds., *The Japanese Wartime Empire, 1931–1945* (Princeton: Princeton University Press, 1996), pp. 3–39.

replacing them with the Japanese religious practices of shrine Shinto, the use of the Japanese language, and the Japanization of given names.[47]

It was not just colonial state institutions, but also the experiment with economic autarky in Manchukuo that became the guiding spirit of the wartime Japanese empire. The integrated industrial and trading unit formed with the Japan-Manchuria bloc economy was extended first to include north China, then the rest of China, and finally Southeast Asia in a self-sufficient yen bloc. In Korea, Taiwan, and north China this involved industrialization and heavy investment, as it did in Manchukuo. The lessons of economic management learned in Manchukuo, including currency unification, production targets, semipublic development companies, and other tools of state control, were also applied in these new economies.

In all these ways the experiment in Manchukuo marked the beginning of a new imperialism, made necessary by the upsurge of revolutionary nationalist movements throughout the empires of Asia. European powers responded to the rise of Asian nationalism with a policy of appeasement, attempting to shore up the crumbling colonial edifice through political concessions in the Middle East and India. Japanese dealt with the same challenge by claiming a unity with Asian nationalism. They tried to coopt the anti-colonial movement by declaring the Japanese colonial state to be the agent of nationalist liberation.

In its international context, the story of Manchukuo focuses on the interactions of states and societies across space and time. On the global stage, Japanese empire builders acted and reacted within a specific configuration of power, the logic of which both expanded and delimited the available choices. The crumbling of the great power alliance in China in the face of the Chinese Nationalist challenge and the shockwave of global depression cleared a path for Japanese unilateral action in the late 1920s, even while it closed off possibilities for cooperative diplomacy. The considerable growth of Japan's military and industrial power relative to other regional powers—particularly China—opened up possibilities for aggression on the continent. At the same time, the gathering strength of the Guomindang closed off the option of conciliation toward China, and created a time limit in which the Japanese would have to act to expand before the Chinese Nationalists grew too strong. Similarly, the escalation of the arms race

47. Wan-yao Chou, "The Kōminka Movement in Taiwan and Korea: Comparisons and Interpretations," in Peter Duus, Ramon H. Myers, and Mark R. Peattie, eds., *The Japanese Wartime Empire, 1931–1945* (Princeton: Princeton University Press, 1996), pp. 40–68.

between Japan, the Soviet Union, the United States, and Great Britain weighted the scales toward precipitous and preemptive action on Japan's part, in order to capture territory before a military deterrent emerged to block such a move. The assembling and disassembling of alliances, the continually changing balances of power, and the dynamics of cooperation and competition that these produced all figured into the geometry of Japanese imperialism.

This same geometry of empire placed Manchuria among a number of interrelated imperial projects. What happened in central China affected Manchuria, just as events in Manchuria influenced Taiwan. Practices developed in Korea were applied in Manchuria, while Manchuria, in other aspects, became a model for Korea. While Manchuria became the dynamic centerpiece of the empire in the 1930s, the bulwark of autonomous diplomacy and the vanguard of revolutionary imperialism, the imperial strategies innovated in Northeast China were applied elsewhere in the empire as well, often more boldly and with greater consequence. The chapters that follow concentrate almost exclusively on the metropolitan response to Manchukuo. This focus on Manchukuo necessarily eclipses the domestic connections to Taiwan and Korea as well as the mobilization of popular support for the new imperial frontier in Southeast Asia. Yet, even though my narrative places it out of sight, the empire in its entirety was very much a part of the social and cultural context of the 1930s.

Manchukuo did occupy the central space of the Japanese empire of the 1930s, though this special position only developed over time. The stages of this development were intrinsic to the chronology of the Japanese empire. In the first phase, interest in continental expansion and the formation of an imperial mission in Northeast China took shape during the emergence of an imperial Japan in the late 1800s. At that point, Korea rested atop the pinnacle of imperial ambition; Manchuria represented merely a strategic buffer to keep Japan's rivals out of Korea. Acquisition of a foothold in the Northeast, however, coincided with the beginnings of a second phase of empire building, when Japan began to construct and develop institutions of domination in its burgeoning colonial empire. In the process of institution building in the Manchurian leasehold in the teens and twenties, Japanese turned the strategic buffer into an empire famed for the modernizing activities of Mantetsu and the martial spirit of the Kwantung Army. And yet, until Japanese felt their claim to the "rights and interests" in the Northeast challenged by an increasingly importunate Chinese Nationalist movement, these Manchurian holdings were merely in the second string of their colonial possessions. But when boycotts, strikes, demands for rights recovery, and the steady progress toward political unification seemed to imperil all that Japanese empire builders had worked to produce, the Manchurian empire suddenly took on new importance and new commitment. Primed for action, when the old rules for collaboration with local warlord interests broke down, Japan quickly elected a course of military confrontation. In the process, Manchuria became the testing ground for a host of experimental colonial institutions, including the puppet state, the command economy, and state-managed colonization. As the Manchurian experiment took hold and was deemed a success, it became the model for a new imperialism. In the third phase of empire, Japanese unleashed their colonial armies on Asia. The armies proceeded to engage in risky (and ultimately catastrophic) games of brinksmanship with other regional powers, even while they created institutions that were highly successful in mobilizing indigenous support for Japanese rule. Thus, inscribed in the course of expansion in the Northeast—from its beginnings at the turn of the century through the era of autonomous imperialism in the 1930s— was the developmental logic of Japanese imperialism.

These reflections on the large spatial and temporal structures of empire provide the international context for the chapters that follow. Such a context is important because the metropolitan aspect of Manchukuo with which this book is primarily concerned represents only one dimension in the wide spaces of total empire. It is important, moreover, because this book concentrates on the period between 1931 and 1945, a small, though critical, slice of time in the larger history of Japan in Manchuria. Narrowing the field of study, we now move into this different world, focusing on Japan in 1931—a nation swept up in war fever.

PART II

THE MANCHURIAN INCIDENT
AND THE NEW
MILITARY IMPERIALISM,
1931–1933

3   War Fever
Imperial Jingoism and the Mass Media

After the story broke of the military clash at Fengtian on September 18, 1931, the news of the latest action on the China continent commanded the headlines for months. War songs set fashion in popular music and battle-field dramas filled the stage and screen. None of this was completely new, of course, for war booms had accompanied earlier imperial wars against China (1894–1895) and Russia (1904–1905). Moreover, just as those war booms had profoundly influenced cultural developments, the Manchurian Incident war fever marked a turning point from the era christened "Taishō demokurashii" to what Japanese called the "national emergency" (*hijōji*) of early Shōwa.

Many currents flowed together to produce the sea change of the early thirties. Policy makers turned to military methods to contain the rise of Chinese nationalism in the Northeast. Withdrawing from the League of Nations in 1933, statesmen led the nation into an era of international isolation and on a collision course with rival imperialists. Politically, this period marked the end of party-run cabinets and the dying gasp of the organized left. The war set off a rapid military buildup and the foundation of what was called the quasi-wartime economy. War fever promoted the militarization of popular culture and encouraged the proliferation of social organizations for total war. These changes collectively constituted the for-mation of a new military imperialism.

Popular Japanese stereotypes of the "dark valley" of the 1930s conjure up images of a militaristic police state which exercised unlimited powers of political repression to coerce an unwilling but helpless populace into cooperating with the army's expansionist designs. One of the key subplots in the dark-valley version of the 1930s concerns the deliberate deception of the Japanese people through expurgated and even mendacious news reports of the military events on the continent. The role of the press and publishing industry in the governmental disinformation campaign is usually explained by reference to the notorious Peace Preservation Law of 1925, which gave the Home Ministry widespread powers of arrest and censorship. A closer look at the reaction of the mass media to the outbreak of the Manchurian Incident, however, reveals some inaccuracies in this picture of a press muzzled by government censors and publicizing with great reluctance the official story of Japan's military actions in Manchuria. In fact, without any urging from the government, the news media took the lead in promoting the war. Publishing and entertainment industries volunteered in cooperating with army propagandists, helping to mobilize the nation behind the military occupation of Northeast China. They did so, in large part, for a very simple reason: imperial warfare offered producers of mass culture irresistible opportunities for commercial expansion and profit.

Such a phenomenon was certainly not unique to Japan. As John MacKenzie has documented for the case of Britain, and others for the United States and France, the mass media throughout the industrial world played key roles in stimulating military imperialism in the nineteenth and twentieth centuries.[1] This literature raises many important and knotty theoretical issues concerning the relationship between imperialism and popular culture, three of which have particular bearing on Japan's war fever. First, what did it mean for the politics of empire that the mass media began, in increasingly sophisticated ways, to mediate the relationship between government and public? The mass media provided a key channel for the dissemination of government propaganda to the public. At the same time, it became a means for the government to gauge public reaction to events and policies, and hence, a conduit for the expression of what was being defined as "public opinion." Inserting itself between government and people, the media's treatment of current events often changed the political significance of those events for both sides.

A second issue that arises in these media studies is how we understand the cultural construction of empire when our analysis of newspapers, mov-

---

1. John M. MacKenzie, *Propaganda and Empire: The Manipulation of British Public Opinion, 1880–1960* (Manchester: Manchester University Press, 1984). On American imperialism and popular culture, see Richard Slotkin, *The Fatal Environment: The Myth of the Frontier in the Age of Industrialization, 1800–1890* (New York: Atheneum, 1985), and Slotkin, *Gunfighter Nation;* and on France, see William H. Schneider, *An Empire for the Masses: The French Popular Image of Africa, 1870–1900* (Westport, Conn.: Greenwood Press, 1982).

ies, and other organs of the mass media limits us to the production rather than the consumption of mass culture. Historians of imperial popular culture speak of "the popular image of empire" and "national myths," phrases that imply a unity in the public perception. Their studies persuasively demonstrate that the myths of the American frontier or British Christian militarism were imperial constructions produced for and consumed by a mass audience. And yet, what does "popular" mean when we cannot know how stories were read or movies interpreted by the consumers of imperial culture? Moreover, given that newspapers and film companies tailored their products to a consumer market, how much of the popular vision of empire was determined by the media itself and how much was shaped by consumer demand?

Third, this literature on mass media is concerned with how to fit media representations of a particular instance of military imperialism into a broader interpretation of imperial ideology. Whether in the heroic narrative, the stirring speech, or some other form, representations of empire building appealed to audiences in terms of morality and of necessity, for such are the conceptual categories through which societies justify military aggression. And since imperial ideologies are constantly evolving, the question becomes: What was new and what was not-so-new in the imperatives articulated in the moment? In other words, how much did the call to action in Japan's war fever of the early 1930s owe to the accumulations of a venerable imperial tradition, and how much was the product of the historical moment itself?

This chapter makes no claims to resolve these questions in all their complexity. They do, nevertheless, inform an attempt to draw out the broader significance of the imperial jingoism that animated Japanese popular culture during the Manchurian Incident. Like imperial war fevers in Europe and the United States, Japan's war fever of the 1930s revealed the relationship between an expanding marketplace for cultural manufactures and the rise of jingoism as a key force behind military imperialism.

THE NEWS WAR

In 1931 the news of war in Northeast China first spread through the press. On the morning of September 19, just hours after the Kwantung Army secretly detonated the railway track and led the assault on the Chinese military base in Fengtian, early editions throughout the country reported that Zhang Xueliang's soldiers had attacked the Japanese Army. On the front page of the nation's leading daily, the Osaka *Asahi*, Japanese read that "in an act of outrageous violence [bōgyaku], Chinese soldiers blew up a section of Mantetsu track located to the northwest of Beitaying [Military Base] and attacked our railway guards. Our guards immediately returned fire and mobilized artillery to shell Beitaying. Our forces now occupy a section of the base."

In the following days and months the reports continued, with different news organs striving to be the first to greet their audiences with the army movements of the previous day. Newspapers vied to scoop the daily progress of the Kwantung Army as they tracked its course in September step by step, recording the occupation of Fengtian, Jilin, and other cities along the South Manchurian Railway as well as the removal of Zhang Xueliang's forces to the city of Jinzhou in southwestern Manchuria. Papers battled to break the news of the aerial bombing of Jinzhou in October, the occupation of the northern city of Qiqihar in November, and the ground assault on Jinzhou in December. Headlines competed to announce most dramatically the occupation of Harbin in January, which gave Japan command of all the key Manchurian cities. In February audiences read rival accounts of the marines landing in Shanghai to quell anti-Japanese demonstrations in the Japanese concession; and in March they learned from contending sources that an independence movement had culminated in the founding of the new state of Manchukuo. For six months, the news war over Manchuria consumed the media and their reports gripped the nation.

Why did war fever break out in 1931? Why did it start with a news war? Part of the answer lies in the state of Japan's highly developed and very competitive commercial news media. Because of its level of development, the rise in demand for news from the Manchurian front spurred competition for the expanding news market. This in turn stimulated technological innovation in newspaper production as well as the diffusion of a new medium of communications, radio. Competition, technological innovation, and market expansion became key forces behind the imperial jingoism that suddenly engulfed Japan.

The press provided an excellent conduit for disseminating news of war to what was, by 1931, a highly literate and overwhelmingly newspaper-reading public.[2] The middle and upper classes had long provided the core readership for an expanding newspaper industry, but by the 1920s, the

2. For newspaper readership and the expansion of the publishing market geographically and sociologically, see Carol Gluck, *Japan's Modern Myths: Ideology in the Late Meiji Period* (Princeton: Princeton University Press, 1985), pp. 169–174, 232–233.

habit had spread to the laboring classes in urban and rural Japan. Thanks to a universal compulsory educational system in place since the 1870s, literacy rates were high among even the most economically marginal groups. For example, of the predominantly male population of day laborers in a Tokyo slum in 1922, 92 percent of the single residents and 89 percent of the heads of household could read and write.[3] For people that could not afford to subscribe, newspapers were available in bars, restaurants, barbershops, and at the meeting houses of local youth groups and reservist associations. Readership was, of course, higher than subscriber rates, and it is clear from the limited survey data available that subscriber rates themselves were high and rising. For example, 80 percent of 659 worker households surveyed in the Tokyo working-class neighborhood of Tsukishima in 1919 subscribed to newspapers; 18 percent took two or more papers.[4] Similar surveys of Tokyo working women (nurses, teachers, clerks, typists, shop attendants, and tram workers) revealed that 88 percent subscribed to a paper. In a Kyūshū mine, about half the workers surveyed subscribed, and in farm villages near Tokyo the subscriber rate was 87 percent.[5]

From its beginnings as a political press in the 1860s, the modern newspaper industry had expanded rapidly into a collection of mass-circulation news organs in the 1890s and 1900s. By 1911 there were 236 newspapers nationwide and the 7 largest dailies had circulations of over 100,000.[6] This process accelerated in the 1910s and 1920s, as the number of journals and newspapers registered under the newspaper law rose from 3,123 in 1918 to 11,118 in 1932. By 1927 the circulation of the nation's 2 leading dailies, the Osaka *Asahi shinbun* and the Osaka *Mainichi shinbun*, were over a

3. The same survey shows much lower literacy rates for women: 63 percent of single women and 55 percent of women supporting households could not read. The data was originally reported in Tōkyō-shi, *Tōkyō-shinai no kichin yado ni kansuru chōsa* (1923). Cited in Yamamoto Taketoshi, *Kindai Nihon no shinbun dokushasō* (Hōsei daigaku shuppankyoku, 1981), pp. 220–221.

4. The original survey was conducted by Naimushō eiseikyoku, *Tōkyō-shi Kyōbashi-ku Tsukishima ni okeru jitchi chōsa hōkoku* (1921). Cited in Yamamoto Taketoshi, p. 225.

5. The survey of Tokyo working women was carried out by the Tokyo metropolitan government in 1924; nine hundred women were interviewed. The survey of miners was conducted at the Ashio copper mine in 1919; 1,200 households were interviewed. The farm village survey included forty-eight households and was carried out in 1934 by the Imperial Agricultural Association (Teikoku nōkai). Since the village was located on the outskirts of Tokyo, subscriber rates were probably higher than the national average. The three surveys are discussed in Yamamoto Taketoshi, pp. 229–240.

6. Gluck, *Japan's Modern Myths*, p. 171.

million, and 9 other dailies boasted circulations of between 100,000 and 500,000.[7]

Increasingly, the newspaper industry was an instrument of national integration. The expansion of the railway and the stimulus of two wars had spurred the expansion of the large dailies outside their metropolitan markets of Osaka and Tokyo. In 1909 only 31.5 percent of the Osaka *Asahi*'s circulation fell within the Osaka city limits; of the remaining 68.5 percent, 14 percent went to Kyoto, 12 percent to the neighboring Hyōgo prefecture, 10 percent to Shiga, Wakayama, Mie, and Nara prefectures in the Kinki region, 7 percent to Ishikawa, Fukui, Toyama, Aichi, and Gifu prefectures in the Chūbu region, and 6 percent to the southern island of Kyūshū.[8] By 1923, 70 percent of Tokyo's newspaper production was sold outside the city.[9]

Yet even though the metropolitan press had penetrated provincial cities and villages by the end of the Taishō period, in many areas a resiliant provincial press proved able to resist the incursions of metropolitan cultural institutions. Indeed, the rapid development of the Osaka and Tokyo papers was matched in the provinces with a flourishing local press. Most provincial cities supported several newspapers; prefectural and regional papers complemented their numbers. For example, Toyama prefecture on the Japan Sea coast produced, in addition to 26 regional periodicals, 3 daily and 2 evening papers.[10] When the metropolitan papers tried to take over the provincial markets, in all but a few districts, such as Saitama and Kanagawa which bordered the big cities, the local press was able to withstand the challenge.[11] This was accomplished in large part by imitation of metropolitan technologies of marketing and production, something which often required mergers and other institutional restructuring. Another key factor aiding the survival of the local press was the growing tendency to subscribe to more than one paper. A 1930 nationwide survey of 13,688 youth groups found that each group took an average of 3.3 newspapers; almost 50 percent were local papers.[12]

7. Yamamoto Taketoshi, p. 412.

8. Ibid., p. 273.

9. Minami Hiroshi and Shakai shinri kenkyūjo, *Taishō bunka, 1905–1927* (Keisō shobō, 1987), p. 121.

10. Michael Lewis, *Rioters and Citizens: Mass Protest in Imperial Japan* (Berkeley: University of California Press, 1990), p. 35.

11. Yamamoto Taketoshi, p. 271.

12. The original survey is: DaiNippon renmei seinendan, *Zenkoku seinendan kihon chōsa* (1934). Cited in Yamamoto Taketoshi, p. 242.

Through the diffusion of mass marketing technology as well as the development of national markets for the metropolitan dailies, the growth of the newspaper industry fostered the formation of a nationally integrated mass culture. This meant that news coverage of events of national significance like the Manchurian Incident was disseminated quickly throughout the country. It also guaranteed a degree of uniformity of coverage, as competing papers picked up each other's stories and imitated new marketing techniques. Most of all, it meant that by 1931 Japan was a nation of news hounds. In upper-, middle-, and working-class households, in urban and rural Japan, men, women, and even children informed themselves of the events of the day through the commercial news media. Thus it was natural that the press became the medium through which the influence of the Manchurian Incident first penetrated the home front, infecting Japanese society with war fever.

For the press, the war fever offered great opportunities for market expansion. With urban markets largely saturated, the goal at this stage was a more thorough penetration of the rural market. Historian Toyama Shigeki described the inroads made in his own village at the time: "My father's family were farmers. Before the Manchurian Incident we had not taken a paper, but after articles about the local unit began to appear and articles about the war-dead in our village came out almost everybody began to take the newspaper, even tenant farmers."[13] The drive to expand circulation was pursued, as in earlier imperial wars, through innovations in format, production, and marketing techniques. During the Sino-Japanese and Russo-Japanese wars, the enormous expansion of the newspaper market had been accomplished by the increased use of, first, illustrations and, later, photographs to accompany news stories from the front, the merging of "hard" (political) and "soft" (entertainment) journalism, the switch to advertising as a primary source of revenue, and other changes.[14] Now, the Manchurian Incident news war ushered in an era of high-speed news production.

Leading the way were the *Mainichi shinbun* and *Asahi shinbun* news-

---

13. Toyama's remark was made in a roundtable discussion on the Manchurian Incident originally published as "Manshū jihen gojūnen no zadankai," *Keizai* (September 1981). Quoted in Eguchi, *Jūgonen sensō no kaimaku*, pp. 107–108.

14. D. Eleanor Westney, *Imitation and Innovation: The Transfer of Western Organizational Patterns to Meiji Japan* (Cambridge: Harvard University Press, 1987), pp. 180–206, and Donald Keene, "The Sino-Japanese War of 1894–95 and Japanese Culture," in Donald Keene, *Landscapes and Portraits: Appreciations of Japanese Culture* (Tokyo: Kōdansha International, 1971), pp. 259–299.

paper chains.[15] Both Osaka-based with various fairly independent regional editions, their respective flagship papers—the Tokyo *Asahi*, Osaka *Asahi*, Osaka *Mainichi*, and Tokyo *Nichinichi*—dominated the national news market.[16] The four large dailies deployed recently purchased fleets of airplanes and cars, and mobilized the latest printing and phototelegraphic machinery in their drive to win the news war. The Osaka *Asahi* had demonstrated dramatically the potential of airplanes to accelerate the delivery of news when it flew a photograph of the bombed-out train in which Zhang Zuolin was killed in 1928 from Seoul to Osaka, reaching the streets within twenty-four hours of the explosion.[17]

In 1931 and 1932, both companies used their airplanes to shuttle teams of correspondents and equipment back and forth between Japan and Manchuria. On September 20, the Osaka *Asahi* boasted it had already "put several planes into operation and dispatched 8 special correspondents" to the scene.[18] By November 15, the *Asahi* had sent at least 33 special correspondents to Manchuria, and by January 1, the *Mainichi* chain had sent 50.[19] Of course, long before airplanes, newspapers sent special correspondents to cover important stories. During the Sino-Japanese War in 1894–1895, for example, sixty-six newspapers sent a total of 114 reporters, 11 artists, and 4 photographers to China.[20] But the advent of the airplane changed the news-gathering process, extending the possible scale and speed of coverage.

The wedding of new technology with older practices was apparent on

15. I am indebted to Eguchi Keiichi for pointing out to me the central role of the big dailies in whipping up the war fever. See his "Manshū jihen to daishinbun," *Shisō*, no. 583 (January 1973), pp. 100–103.

16. The Osaka *Asahi* and Osaka *Mainichi* had long held the national lead in circulation figures, but not until the 1920s did their Tokyo editions overtake the decisive lead of the *Hōchi shinbun*. The campaign to take over the Tokyo market followed both companies' transformation from limited partnerships into joint stock companies after World War I, and was empowered by huge increases in capitalization. For example, *Mainichi*'s capital rose from 500 thousand yen in 1919 to 5 million yen in 1924. For circulation figures of the major Osaka and Tokyo dailies, see Yamamoto Taketoshi, p. 412. For an account of the *Mainichi* and *Asahi* campaign against the *Hōchi shinbun*, see Minami et al., *Taishō bunka*, p. 127.

17. Ikei Masaru, "1930 nendai no masu media: Manshū jihen e no taiō o chūshin toshite," in Miwa Kimitada, ed., *Saikō Taiheiyō sensō zen'ya: Nihon no 1930 nendairon toshite* (Sōseiki, 1981), p. 144.

18. Minami Hiroshi and Shakai shinri kenkyūjo, *Shōwa bunka, 1925–1945* (Keisō shobō, 1987), p. 262.

19. Abe Shingo, "Manshū jihen o meguru shinbungai," *Kaizō* (November 1931), pp. 36–39; Eguchi, "Manshū jihen to daishinbun," p. 100.

20. Westney, p. 192.

the production end as well, reflected in the Manchurian Incident "extra" (*gōgai*) war. Just as they sent correspondents to cover the earlier imperial wars, newspaper companies had used extras to break stories from the front. Now, victory in the race to break the news was decided by two new machines, the high-speed cylinder press and the wire photograph transmitter. With their capital advantages, the *Asahi* and *Mainichi* dominated the field in this new technology. Together with the news service Dentsū, they imported the nation's first telephotograph machines in 1928.[21] Between their four Osaka and Tokyo papers, the two newspaper companies owned 74 of the nation's 108 high-speed cylinder presses in 1930.[22] Hence, the *Asahi* and *Mainichi* were able to overwhelm smaller papers through sheer numbers of costly extras—sometimes putting out two separate multipage extras between the morning and evening editions—and by featuring the latest photos from the front. Writing in late October 1931, one observer commented that "after the opening of the extra war . . . all the papers put out extras. However, after the initial extras, the subsequent editions were not news so much as photographs. Therefore, the extra war was dominated by the two large papers, the *Asahi* and the *Mainichi,* and the rest were left to look on from the sidelines."[23]

Unfortunately for the large dailies, their weaker competitors were not the only contenders in the news war of 1931–1932. No sooner had the fighting broken out on the continent, than the newspapers found themselves face to face with an upstart rival in the battle for the "scoop": radio. The fierce competition between radio and newspapers was a new development. Since its founding in 1926, Japan's national broadcasting monopoly, Nihon hōsō kyōkai (NHK), had taken a back seat in news production and concentrated its efforts on pursuing an educational mission. NHK relied on the newspaper companies and wire services for their news; in return for a free supply of this information, it surrendered editorial rights and left the press to break all the stories. In 1930, however, in a move to get out from under the shadow of the press, radio began to contract directly with the wire services for news, retaining the right to edit their own stories.[24] During the Manchurian Incident, NHK moved aggressively to carve out a new position for itself in the news industry.

---

21. Minami et al., *Shōwa bunka,* p. 258.
22. Ikei, "1930 nendai," pp. 143–144.
23. Abe Shingo, "Manshū jihen o meguru shinbungai," *Kaizō* (November 1931), pp. 36–37.
24. Ikei, "1930 nendai," pp. 146–147. For founding of NHK see Gregory J.

Radio competed with the press by increasing their regular news programming from four to six times a day, as well as through *rinji nyūsu*—special unscheduled news broadcasts, or news flashes. This device was first employed, appropriately, to scoop the big dailies on the events of September 18. In a special report that interrupted the early morning calisthenics program, a six-minute news broadcast broke the story of the "clash between our railway guards . . . and the (Chinese) First Brigade. . . ."[25] On speed alone, *rinji nyūsu* gave radio a strong advantage in the news war. NHK pressed the advantage home, broadcasting *rinji nyūsu* seventeen times between September 19 and 30 alone.[26]

The number of new radio contracts rose rapidly during the national crisis. After the initial investment in the receiver (10–30 yen for a crystal radio set, 50–100 yen for a vacuum tube set), monthly rates were lower (at 75 sen) than the 1 yen per month it cost to take a newspaper. Nevertheless, the receiver represented a significant financial outlay for all but the very wealthy.[27] This made the growth in radio contracts all the more striking. At the end of 1930, 778,948 households, or 6.1 percent of the population contracted to receive radio broadcasts. By the end of 1933, this number had risen to 1,714,223 households, or 13.4 percent of the population, an increase of almost a million ratepayers in three years.[28]

At this stage, radio listening tended to be an urban practice. NHK estimated in 1934 that 36 percent of urban households had radios while only 6 percent of rural households did. But urban was not restricted to metropolitan: a substantial share of radio-listening households lived outside of

---

Kasza, *The State and Mass Media in Japan, 1918–1945* (Berkeley: University of California Press, 1988), pp. 72–101.

25. Ikei, "1930 nendai," p. 146.

26. Ibid., p. 148.

27. The price of a receiver was prohibitive for most working-class people, who often earned less than 1 yen a day. The monthly salary of a maid, for example, was 15 yen. It was within reach for some white-collar employees, such as an assistant clerk at the Communications Ministry who earned 56 yen per month. Prices and wages from Kōdansha, ed., *Shōwa e no kitai: Shōwa gannen–3 nen*, vol. 1 of *Shōwa nimannichi no zenkiroku* (Kōdansha, 1989), pp. 143, 149, 151, 153.

28. Nihon hōsō kyōkai, *Nihon hōsōshi*, vol. 1 (Nihon hōsō kyōkai, 1961), p. 281. Once interest in radio was boosted by battlefield coverage during the Manchurian Incident, numbers of new radio contracts continued to rise. Total contracts in 1934 were 1,979,000; in 1935, 2,422,000; in 1936, 2,905,000; in 1937, 3,584,000; in 1938, 4,166,000; and in 1939, 4,862,000: Kōdansha, ed., *Nitchū sensō e no michi: Shōwa 10 nen–12 nen*, vol. 4 of *Shōwa nimannichi no zenkiroku* (Kōdansha, 1989), p. 169.

Osaka and Tokyo. Of course, the higher the concentration of population, the higher the percentages of radio listeners. By 1935, 49.8 percent of Tokyo and 36.3 percent of Osaka households owned a radio, as did 26.8 percent of Kyoto-city households. Heavily urban prefectures such as Aichi (with the city of Nagoya), Hyōgo (with the city of Kobe), and Kanagawa (with the city of Yokohama) also boasted rates of 23.9 percent, 22.9 percent, and 23.7 percent, respectively. Moreover, even in the distant prefectures of Miyagi in the northeast and Fukuoka in the southern island of Kyūshū, high numbers of listeners in the prefectural capitals pushed the prefectural averages up to 12.3 percent and 12.4 percent, respectively.[29]

The news war between radio and the press quickly escalated from the supply of speedy and sensational "emergency news" to reporting in the form of a public spectacle. Newspapers, of course, had long been in the *ibento* (event) business. Like the "new journalism" of late nineteenth-century Europe and the United States, the Japanese press had begun in the 1890s to sponsor a variety of events in order to increase reader involvement and expand their market. By the end of the Meiji period, newspaper readers throughout the country were accustomed to seeing newspapers sponsor fundraising drives for victims of disaster or distress, contests and lotteries, and concerts, exhibits, lectures, and sporting events.[30] All these techniques had been used to great effect during the Sino-Japanese and Russo-Japanese wars. During the Manchurian Incident, newspapers inundated the much larger market with all the traditional *ibento*, plus a new one: newsreel screenings.

Asahi and *Mainichi* newsreels that tracked the occupation of Manchuria, stage by victorious stage, filled public halls and packed city parks. Although both newspaper and film companies had made sporadic attempts at producing regular film news during the 1920s, newspaper company footage of the Manchurian Incident brought newsreels into widespread use for the first time. As fast as new film canisters could be flown in from Manchuria, the *Asahi* and *Mainichi* screened the newsreels in city parks in Osaka, Kobe, Kyoto, and Tokyo, and circulated the films for additional showings in department stores, elementary schools, and elsewhere throughout the country. In Osaka, for example, the first installment, "The Military Clash between the Japanese and Chinese Armies" opened Sep-

29. Other prefectures with more than 10 percent of radio-listening households included Nara, Hiroshima, Okayama, Gifu, Ishikawa, Saitama, and Chiba: Kōdansha, *Nitchū sensō e no michi*, pp. 32–33.
30. Westney, pp. 187–190; Yamamoto Taketoshi, pp. 313–319.

tember 21—just three days after the clash began—and required several showings a night to accommodate the crowds. An account of the onset of the campaign for northern Manchuria, "The Nen River Battle-Front," proved to be the city's favorite for November, playing for 20,000 spectators on a single night. Five thousand stood outdoors on a chill January evening to watch marching columns of Japanese soldiers "Entering Jinzhou."[31] Since the free newsreels were a marketing tool, they were shown widely outside the urban areas, particularly in rural districts where the large dailies hoped to expand circulation. In Aichi prefecture, for example, between September 1931 and September 1932, the Osaka *Asahi* screened newsreels at 102 different locations. At least 46 of these were shown in county districts.[32]

An equally enthusiastic reception for traveling lecture series and exhibits of military paraphernalia rewarded the big dailies with popular acclaim. On November 25, the Osaka *Asahi* touched off a lecture boom with a three-day lecture series on "Reports from the Battlefield," with special correspondents lecturing to full houses in Osaka, Kobe, Kyoto, and Nagoya on their impressions of conditions on the front. A December 3 session drew a crowd of 6,000 in Osaka, and a report in Tokyo on the invasion of Jinzhou in January inspired standing ovations and three banzais for the *Asahi* from the enthusiastic crowd. Encouraged by the response to the Jinzhou lecture, the *Asahi* expanded the number of stops on its itinerary, sending the speakers to engagements in the cities of Yokohama, Yokosuka, Chiba, Sendai, Fukushima, Wakamatsu, Niigata, Nagaoka, Takada, Morioka, Hirosaki, Aomori, Akita, Yamagata, and Kanazawa.[33]

The large department stores offered space to both the *Mainichi* and *Asahi* newspaper companies for exhibits held in November and December of military paraphernalia commemorating the Manchurian Incident. After opening in Tokyo, an exhibit of "Souvenirs of the fierce campaign to take the Fengtian Beitaying" sponsored by the Tokyo *Asahi* went on to tour seventy locations to the north and west. In Tokyo, a city of 5 million, exhibit goers numbered 11,000 daily, while the national grand total topped 600,000. Beginning September 21, the Osaka *Asahi* sent an exhibit of

31. Eguchi, "Manshū jihen to daishinbun," pp. 100–103; Ikei, "1930 nendai," p. 171.
32. Eguchi Keiichi, "Manshū jihen to minshū dōin: Nagoya-shi o chūshin toshite," in Furuya Tetsuo, ed., *Nitchū sensōshi kenkyū* (Yoshikawa kōbunkan, 1984), pp. 141–143.
33. Eguchi, "Manshū jihen to daishinbun," pp. 100–103.

"Manchurian Incident Photographs" throughout western Japan, and in November they treated audiences to "Anti-Japanese Posters from China."[34]

Not to be outdone, NHK busied itself making radio an indispensable partner to the imperial pageantry of the Manchurian Incident. In the process, NHK pioneered new techniques which became a hallmark of broadcasting in the 1930s and 1940s. The most spectacular of these was the live broadcast—simultaneous radio coverage from the scene of an event. In 1931 and 1932, NHK began participating in public ceremonials throughout the country with great frequency, involving themselves in troop send-offs and welcome parades, funerals, military reviews, collection drives, and armament christenings. Like the photograph, the live broadcast closed the distance gap and made the event immediate for the listening audience. Just as the first widespread use of battlefield photography during the Russo-Japanese War had illustrated the potential of photojournalism, the first radio war demonstrated the power of broadcast communications.

Radio's live broadcasting of military ceremonies changed the local character of these events, greatly enhancing their appeal and news value. The first of the live broadcasts was a three-city air-defense drill conducted by Kobe, Kyoto, and Osaka on November 11, 1931. By the end of the year NHK had participated in three mass military funerals broadcast from Niigata and Sendai, and five send-off ceremonies from Hiroshima's Ujina Wharf. During the following year, radio audiences could tune in to live broadcasts on the average of once a week. The fifty-three live broadcasts included three prayer ceremonies held at Yasukuni, the national shrine where dead soldiers were enshrined as military gods; one air-defense drill; the "Fourth Memorial Service for the War Dead of the Sendai Unit of the Second Division" from Sendai City as well as thirteen other funerals; seven welcome parades, including the "Victorious Return of the Second Division" from in front of Sendai Station; two send-offs; twenty airplane christenings; three weapons-donation ceremonies; and an "Evening of Battle Stories Commemorating the Glorious Victory" from Tokyo's Hibiya Public Hall on June 29.[35]

NHK also developed live broadcast programs for troop entertainment. In a spectacular advertisement for their newly established radio link-up with Manchuria, NHK mobilized storytellers, singers, minstrels, comedi-

---

34. Ibid., p. 102.
35. Nihon hōsō kyōkai, *Rajio nenkan: Shōwa 8 nen* (Nihon hōsō shuppan kyōkai, 1933), p. 69. Program schedules in Ikei, "1930 nendai," pp. 149–152.

ans, and other popular entertainers to participate in an "Evening of Entertainment for Our Brothers in Manchuria." Broadcast live from Tokyo Playhouse on October 30, the "Evening of Entertainment" proved such a success that ten new programs were produced by January 24, 1932.[36] In this way, NHK used the war to market their newly developed news services, competing with the press by innovating and expanding news production.

The war-mongering behavior of radio and press in 1931–1932 was a predictable reaction to the pressures of a well-developed commercial market for news; the media sensationalized the war because consumers bought more papers and radio contracts that way. But as in the earlier imperial war booms, their actions resulted in a transformation of the news market as well. In the wake of the Manchurian Incident, the *Asahi*, the *Mainichi*, and NHK emerged as the clear leaders in a more national news market, helping to define a nationally unified response to the military crisis in the empire. As the actions of the news media revealed, the commercial relationship between the mass media and the public created a positive feedback loop in the production and consumption of media products on the theme of war, and served to inflate the Manchurian Incident war boom.

This dynamic formed an integral part of the phenomenon of jingoism. War, by this time, was known to stimulate technological leaps in fields of medicine, weaponry, and heavy industry. As Japan's experience in the war fever of 1931–1933 suggests, this also applied to developments in the mass media. The rise in demand during the Manchurian Incident provided an opportunity for the press and radio to test market innovations in format, invest in technological improvements, and put into practice new sales techniques. Such advances built upon the foundation of a well-developed national news market. The technological and commercial developments of the 1920s primed the news industry for a growth spurt once the right market conditions presented themselves. Responding energetically to these opportunities, the mass media infected the country with war fever. Essential to imperial jingoism, then, was the process of innovation and expansion in the mass production of an industrialized mass culture.

UNOFFICIAL PROPAGANDISTS

Led by the news media giants, an increasingly one-dimensional interpretation of the events in Manchuria expanded into other areas of mass cul-

36. Ikei, "1930 nendai," pp. 167–168.

ture. Books, magazines, movies, records, and other forms of popular entertainment took the sense of national crisis primed by the press and radio, and infused it with the boisterousness of a carnival, as Manchuria became the theme for vaudeville acts, Kabuki tragedies, and even restaurant menus. This cultural deluge constituted a second dimension of the imperial jingoism of the Manchurian Incident. Mass-culture industries flooded their marketplace with Manchurian-theme products, and in the process disseminated a specific package of information and a set interpretation of events on the continent. Manchurian-theme products glorified military action, heroized the colonial army, and extolled the founding of Manchukuo. Telling and retelling the epochal moments of the Sino-Japanese conflict in every conceivable cultural form, the mass media helped shape public memory of the Manchurian Incident. When representations of Manchuria moved from the factual, if selective, reportage in the news to fictionalized dramatizations on stage and screen, the complex realities of the military occupation were reduced to the simple and sanctifying patterns of myth.[37] The saturation coverage, the winnowing out of key stories that rendered symbolically the justice of Japan's war aims, and the multimedia representations of these stories all were defining characteristics of imperial jingoism.

As was true for the press, jingoism was nothing new for the publishing and entertainment industries. From the emergence of mass magazines to the birth of modern drama, the development of the mass-culture industries was profoundly influenced by the cultural production of the Sino-Japanese and Russo-Japanese wars.[38] In the decades between the earlier imperial wars and the Manchurian Incident, mass production of the *enbon* (yen book) brought the price of books down, and the publication of the entertainment magazine *Kingu* broke records for magazine circulation.[39] At the same time, popular entertainment was revolutionized by the emergence of the film and recording industry. Like the technological advance of the press in the twenties, these developments profoundly influenced the scale of imperial jingoism, magnifying its impact on Japanese society.

Another factor behind the greater contagiousness of the Manchurian

37. For a stimulating discussion of myth making and imperialism, see Slotkin, *The Fatal Environment*, pp. 1–48.
38. See Keene, pp. 259–299; Minami et al., *Taishō bunka*, p. 128; and Gluck, *Japan's Modern Myths*, pp. 135–136, 150, 171–173.
39. Before *Kingu*, best-selling magazines had circulations in the 250,000- to 260,000-issue range. *Kingu* doubled this. Yen books: Minami et al., *Shōwa bunka*, pp. 287–301; *Kingu*: Minami et al., *Shōwa bunka*, pp. 303–305.

Incident war fever was the new reach of the mass culture industries. Distribution networks in place by the end of the Meiji ensured that mass culture produced in the metropolis reached urban and rural audiences throughout the country. The history of the penetration of the rural market by metropolitan book and magazine publishers paralleled that of the press. The provincial trade of the Tokyo-based publishing industry was handled by seven major distributors, all established between 1890 and 1912.[40] Unlike publishing, where separate companies handled distribution, the early movie theaters were underwritten by such film-importing and production companies as Nikkatsu and Tenkatsu. From the establishment of Japan's first movie theater in the Asakusa neighborhood of Tokyo in 1903, the number of movie theaters grew rapidly. In 1912 the 164 first-run moviehalls nationwide were concentrated in Tokyo, Osaka, Kyoto, Kobe, Yokohama, and Nagoya, while over half of Japan's prefectures still had no theater. Less than ten years later all prefectures had at least one theater, and the numbers of first-run theaters had risen to 694. Of these, 86 were in Tokyo, 54 in Fukuoka prefecture, 47 in Hokkaidō, 39 in Osaka, and 34 in Shizuoka; the remaining prefectures had an average of 10 each.[41] Both the investments in the machinery for mass production and the growth of nationwide distribution systems in the 1920s meant that once the publishing and entertainment industries caught the war fever, they spread it farther, faster, and more dramatically than during the earlier campaigns against China or Russia.

Hard hit by the depression that had devastated the economy since 1929, the entertainment and publishing world looked upon the outbreak of the Manchurian Incident as manna from heaven. Charting trends in the book industry, a publisher's yearbook reported that "brisk sales of books on Manchuria have breathed new life into an utterly stagnated publishing industry."[42] Although before the occupation only specialty publishers like the South Manchurian Railway (Mantetsu), the China-Japan Culture Association (Chū-Nichi bunka kyōkai), or Osaka yago shoten had handled books on the subject, with the new demand for books on Manchuria, mainstream publishers took to the topic with élan. Together, Nihon hyōronsha,

40. The seven were Tōkyōdō, Hokuryūdō, Tōkaidō, Ryomeidō, Uedaya, Tōseidō, and Bunrindō.

41. In 1926 there were 1,056 theaters nationwide, or one theater per 60,000 people: Minami et al., *Taishō bunka*, pp. 122–123, 128–129.

42. *Sōgō shuppan nenkan* (Tosho kenkyūkai, 1932), p. 963.

Jitsugyō no Nihonsha, Heibonsha, Shinkōsha, and other publishers brought out more than 500 titles on Manchuria in 1932 alone. Tokyo's largest bookstores Sanseidō and Tōkyōdō described a "deluge of publications on the Manchurian problem" and a "flurry" of "orders from outside Tokyo for Manchurian books."[43]

The Tokyo Metropolitan Library Readership Survey, used by all the publishers' yearbooks as the benchmark for popular tastes, gives an idea of what sort of merchandise was moving off the shelves. Among the most read books of 1932, for example, were *Understanding New Weapons, The Army Reader,* and *The Navy Reader;* the celebrated account of a female journalist at the front, *Along with the Army in Male Attire;* and the immensely popular story of the three soldiers who exploded themselves in the line of duty, *The Unswervingly Loyal Three Human Bombs (plus The Heroic Five Human Bullets).* In the field of juvenile literature, children's favorites of 1932 and 1933 included *Our Army, Our Navy, Our Airforce,* and *Our Army and Navy—National Defense Reader for Young People;* a biography of the Russo-Japanese War hero *Admiral Nogi; Battleship Stories for Children* and *War Stories for Children; A Young Person's Guide to the Airforce and Air Battles;* a book on *Inspirational Tales of Patriotism for Little Boys and Girls;* and the children's version of *The Three Human Bombs.*[44]

Just as booksellers promoted militarism for profit, popular magazines opened their pages to army spokesmen in order to capitalize on the Manchurian fever. Special issues brought out in 1932 and 1933 featured a spate of articles on "the Manchurian problem" from a pro-military perspective. *Rekishi kōron* (History Forum) published a "Manchuria-Mongolia" issue in April 1933, with articles tracing the "special relationship" between Japan and Manchuria back to premodern times. In addition to a grisly column of hearsay from the front, "Tiny Tales of the Manchurian War," *Bungei shunjū* (Literary Chronicle) ran a special Manchurian section from March through May of 1932.[45] Even such unlikely sources as the pulp magazine *Hanzai kagaku* (Criminal Science) found a way to bring army experts on board. In an issue devoted to "The Manchurian-Mongolian Lifeline," ed-

43. *Shuppan nenkan* (Tōkyōdō, 1933), pp. 2, 465–484; *Sōgō shuppan nenkan* (1932), p. 963.
44. *Shuppan nenkan* (1933), pp. 85–89; *Shuppan nenkan* (1934), pp. 87–91.
45. Sakurai Tadayoshi, "Manshū issun shita hanashi," *Bungei shunjū* (March 1932), pp. 44–46.

itors commissioned an army general to write a feature on "The Judicial System and Punishment in Manchuria."[46]

The publishing giant Kōdansha turned its empire of high-circulation magazines into a cheering gallery for the Kwantung Army. Although they had little to say on the subject before October 1931, after that date Kōdansha magazines like *Kingu* (King), *Yūben* (Eloquence), *Kōdan kurabu* (Story Club), and *Shōnen kurabu* (Boy's Club) were filled with such articles by corporals and majors as "The Loyal and Brave Japanese Spirit— How Our Soldiers Meet Their End" and the posthumously published "Bandit Pacification Diary."[47] In 1932, *Shōnen kurabu* brought out a "Manchurian Incident" issue in February, a "ready-to-mail Manchurian Incident commemorative postcard supplement" in March, a "Patriotism" issue in April (featuring the Manchurian Incident fundraising campaign and a paper model of an airplane "now flying the Manchurian skies"), a "Navy" issue in May, and an "Airforce" issue in June. Military celebrities became regular contributors with articles like "The Last of Him" by Major General Sakurai Tadayoshi, author of the Russo-Japanese War classic *Nikudan* (Human Bullets) and subsequently the head of the army's propaganda division, the *shinbun han*.[48] Army Minister Araki Sadao frequently appeared in popular magazines, including a piece in *Fujin kurabu* (Women's Club) on "The National Emergency! The Mission of Japanese Women!"[49]

Suddenly, the languorous jazz rhythms which had been the rage only weeks before were replaced by a boom in *gunka* (war songs). Sino-Japanese and Russo-Japanese war period classics came back into vogue; as the *Asahi Yearbook* explained, "the current hostilities have given the population a new appreciation of old favorites."[50] Record companies brought out a string of war songs including "Arise Countrymen" (Okiteyo kokumin), "Ah, Our Manchuria!" (Aa waga Manshū), "The Imperial Army Marches Off" (Kōgun shinpatsu no uta), "Attack Plane" (Bakugekiki), and "Manchurian Maiden, My Manchurian Lover" (Manshū no rabaa Manshū musume).[51]

46. Lieutenant General Satō Kiyomasa, "Manshū ni okeru shihō seidō to keibatsu," *Hanzai kagaku* (March 1932), pp. 72–81.

47. Tanihagina Haruo, "Chūyū Nihon no tamashii: waga shōhei no saigo o kataru," *Kōdan kurabu* (April 1933), pp. 112–124; Mizuno Gon'ichi, "Tōhikō shuki," *Kingu* (July 1933), pp. 303–313.

48. Sakurai Tadayoshi, "Kare no saigo," *Ie no hikari* (August 1932), pp. 211–215.

49. Araki Sadao, "Hijōji! Nihon fujin no shimei," *Fujin kurabu* (April 1933), pp. 110–113.

50. *Asahi nenkan* (Asahi shinbunsha, 1933), p. 675.

51. Other popular songs included "Manshū jinei kyoku" (Manchurian Camp

The furor on screen and stage was, if possible, even more intense. For the first six months of 1932 theaters and moviehouses filled their bills with such productions as *The Glittering National Flag, The First Step into Fengtian—South Manchuria Glitters under the Rising Sun, The Four Heroic Human Pillars,* and *The Gallant Bugler.*[52] Movie companies encouraged conscripts to take a positive view of their call-up in the films *The Mobilization Order, Sentarō Goes to the Front,* and *Go to the Front, Boys!* As *Screen and Stage* wrote of *Go to the Front, Boys:* "Our home villages are facing an unprecedented crop failure. But this is nothing to the crisis facing the Japanese empire. . . . In this spirit, this movie follows the story of infantry private Aoki Sentarō, who goes to the front with a brave heart, happy to die for his country."[53]

The crisis in the empire, the heroism of battle, and the glory of sacrifice were the messages of the Manchurian Incident theme products that poured forth from Japan's culture industries, dominating the mass media in 1931 and 1932. These messages dovetailed beautifully, of course, with what the army wanted its public to hear about the Manchurian Incident. But the

---

Song), "Ajia kōshin kyoku" (Asia March), "Mamore Manmō seimeisen" (Defend Our Manchurian-Mongolian Lifeline), "Manshū jihen kouta" (Manchurian Incident Ditty), "Daixx shidan no Manshūyuki o okuru uta"(Manchurian Send-off Song), "Aa Manshū no uta" (Oh! Manchuria), "Rikusentai no uta" (Marines Song), "Sōkō ressha" (Armored Train), and "Gunji tantei no uta" (Military Spy Song): see *Asahi nenkan* (1933), p. 675; *Rekōdo* (February 1932), pp. 78, 112, unpaginated advertisement; *Rekōdo* (May 1932), unpaginated advertisement. For lyrics to several of these songs see Hamano Kenzaburō, *Aa Manshū* (Akimoto shobō, 1970), pp. 116–120.

52. The productions discussed here are drawn from the movie and play listings in *Eiga to engei,* 1932–1933. Citation of entertainment reviews and advertisements in this magazine is complicated by the fact that many of the listings are unpaginated and/or lack a title or heading. References to *Eiga to engei* will therefore be cited as follows: Name of movie or play (with English translation in square brackets): title of review article (where available), title of magazine, date of publication, and page numbers (where available). *Kagayaku kokki* [The Glittering National Flag]: *Eiga to engei* (January 1932), p. 31; *Kyokujitsu kagayaku Minami Manshū: Hōten ichibanjō* [The First Step into Fengtian: South Manchuria Glitters under the Rising Sun]: "Sensō eiga," *Eiga to engei* (April 1932); *Hitobashira yonjūshi* [The Four Heroic Human Pillars]: *Eiga to engei* (May 1932); *Yūkannaru rappa* [The Gallant Bugler]: "Gendaigeki," *Eiga to engei* (June 1932). Other titles included in the film listings were *Shanhai sensen yonjūri* [One Hundred Miles on the Shanghai Front]: *Eiga to engei* (May 1932), p. 16; *Manshū kaishingun* [The Great Manchurian Campaign]: *Eiga to engei* (April 1932); *Seikū daishūgeki* [The Great Air Assault]: "Gunji eiga," *Eiga to engei* (June 1932).

53. *Sentarō Manshū shussei* [Sentarō Goes to the Front] and *Shōshūrei* [The Mobilization Order]: "Sensō eiga,"*Eiga to engei* (April 1932). *Ikeyo wagako* [Go to the Front, Boys!]: "Gunji eiga," *Eiga to engei* (June 1932).

culture industries needed no arm twisting to advertise the army's cause: they became unofficial propagandists because crude militarism was all the crack. Audiences flocked to watch the dramas of death in battle; consumers bought up the magazines commemorating the glories of the empire. "Empire" was a fad, and such cultural fads were the rice bowl of the mass media.

Critical to the effectiveness of this informal propaganda was the popular conviction that what audiences were viewing was live history. Songwriters and dramatists lifted their material straight from the pages of the newspaper, moving from fact to fiction without skipping a beat. In dramatizing history as it unfolded, they shaded the line between news and entertainment and presented audiences with a pseudohistorical version of the events on the continent. The production of what today might be labeled "infotainment" was, at the time, another conspicuous feature of imperial jingoism. Rendering the brutality of war in the comforting conventions of melodrama and popular song, the entertainment industry obscured the realities of military aggression even as it purported to be informing audiences about the national crisis.

Newsreel screenings sponsored by the big dailies had already begun the process of transforming history into an entertaining public spectacle. Widespread shooting on location by movie companies further blurred the line between fact and fiction. All the film studios sent actors and technicians to do double duty in Manchuria, entertaining the troops one day and shooting film the next. Companies used on-location shots as a selling point in films like *Ah! The Thirty-eight Heroes of Nanling,* shot in Fengtian and Changchun. Tōkatsu Studios filmed much of their heroic accounts of the Nen River and Qiqihar campaigns on location, films they called *Japanese Cherries—The Fallen Blossoms of North Manchuria* and *Love in the Frozen Plain.*[54] Productions such as *The Great Army Parade* and *Manchuria March* dealt with the Manchurian Incident in the manner of an entertainment review. Each scene depicted an emblematic moment—the Chinese execution of the Japanese captain Nakamura bringing tensions to a head in June 1931, the occupation of Fengtian in September, and Japanese diplomats defending military action in the League of Nations in October. Shōchiku, Tōkatsu, and Shinkō film studios each brought out their own

---

54. *Aa Nanrei no sanjūhachi yūshi* [Ah! The Thirty-eight Heroes of Nanling]: *Eiga to engei* (January 1932), p. 32; *Hokuman no rakka: yamatozakura!* [Japanese Cherries! The Fallen Blossoms of North Manchuria] and *Tōgen ni fuku ai* [Love in the Frozen Plain]: "Tōkatsu eiga," *Eiga to engei* (March 1932).

version of *Manchuria March*, taking the theme music from the prize-winning hit song of the same name.[55] Such productions turned the epochal moments of the Manchurian Incident into nationalist metaphors, symbolically rendering the takeover of Northeast China in the familiar language of imperial mythology. How new events were assimilated into established myths of a heroic Japan standing tall against Western bullies and easily routing the cowardly Chinese is a question that awaits more considered treatment later. The point to take here is that by raising public awareness of the Manchurian empire through the dissemination of a fictionalized history, the entertainment industry became an agent of imperial myth making.

In its myth-making capacity, the entertainment industry created a gallery of Manchurian Incident heroes out of army reports on the outcomes of successive military operations. Kawai Pictures sensationalized the battlefield death of Captain Kuramoto (posthumously promoted to major) in *The Big-hearted Commander Captain Kuramoto*, while Tōkatsu Films memorialized his bravery in *Ah! Major Kuramoto and the Blood-stained Flag*.[56] The story of Private Yamada, captured by the Chinese during a reconnaissance mission and later rescued by a Korean interpreter, was made into the movie *Scout of North Manchuria*, the play *The Occupation of Qiqihar*, and recorded on the Victor label as the minstrel chant "Private Yamada and Mr. Tei."[57] All seven Japanese movie companies produced versions of the sensational suicide of Major Kuga Noboru, who was apotheosized by Shinkō as *The Perfect Soldier*, by Kawai as *The Yamato Spirit*, and by Tōkatsu as an *Embodiment of the Way of the Warrior*.[58] Injured and left behind when the Japanese force withdrew after the first failed assault on Shanghai, Kuga was taken prisoner by the Chinese. After he

55. *Rikugun daikōshin* [The Great Army Parade]: *Eiga to engei* (June 1932); *Manshū kōshinkyoku* [Manchuria March], play version:"Tōkyō gekijo," *Eiga to engei* (January 1932); *Manshū kōshinkyoku* [Manchuria March], movie version: "Kabata eiga," *Eiga to engei* (March 1932), p. 26.

56. *Ninjō chūtaichō Kuramoto taii* [Captain Kuramoto, the Big-hearted Commander] and *Aa Kuramoto shōsa chizome no gunki* [Aa! Major Kuramoto and the Blood-stained Flag]: "Sensō eiga," *Eiga to engei* (April 1932).

57. The movie *Hokuman no teisatsu* [Scout of North Manchuria]: *Eiga to engei* (January 1932), p. 22; the play *Chichiharu nyūjō* [The Occupation of Qiqihar]: *Eiga to engei* (February 1932), p. 44; the song "Yamada ittōhei to Teisan" [Private Yamada and Mr. Tei]: *Rekōdo* (February 1932), p. 74.

58. *Bujin no seika: Kuga shōsa* [Major Kuga: The Perfect Soldier] and *Yamato damashii: Kuga shōsa* [Major Kuga: The Yamato Spirit]: *Eiga to engei* (May 1932), p. 16. *Bushidō no seika: Aa Kuga shōsa* [Major Kuga: Embodiment of the Way of the Warrior]: "Gunji eiga," *Eiga to engei* (June 1932).

was released, he returned to the battlefield where he had fallen. He then shot himself to expiate the shame of capture. Announcing Kuga's suicide on April 1, 1932, Army Minister Araki Sadao praised Kuga's martial spirit: "Soldiers of the Imperial Army go to the battlefield to win or to die. Choosing the course of death, Major Kuga displayed the highest military spirit. We will treat him as a battlefield casualty, honoring him as if he died in battle."[59] Even the death of an Osaka *Mainichi* newspaper reporter in the course of covering the front became the stuff of heroic drama. Nikkatsu Pictures' *The Blood-stained Pen* glorified the daring and zeal of the reporter when he rushed off behind enemy lines to pursue a scoop. Describing his martyrdom, *Screen and Stage* wrote that he was struck down by an "enemy of unparalleled violence."[60]

The mass media had helped create the heroes of Japan's earlier imperial campaigns, though the numbers that crowded the Manchurian Incident heroes gallery overwhelmed the human icons of the Sino- and Russo-Japanese wars. The scale of military mobilization was, of course, much larger in the earlier campaigns. Yet the reduced number of real participants in 1931–1933 seemed to call for a multiplication of those singled out for cultural distinction. This was due in part to the fact that it was easier to glorify death when there was not much of it. Audience appetites for battlefield heroics would dull after war spread and casualty lists mounted, but in 1931 the loss of a son or husband to a new war on the continent was still an abstraction for most Japanese. A second reason for the multiplication of heroes in the Manchurian campaigns was the growth of the mass media since the earlier wars. In the cultural marketplace of 1931 there were more producers and more consumers, and hence, more competition and more chaos. In the effort to sell their products, cultural manufacturers created as many heroes as the market would bear, competing with one another to depict acts of zealous bravery and sensational death. Ultimately, the commercial initiatives of the mass media did more than army propaganda to define and popularize military heroism in the Manchurian Incident. The army provided the source of information from the battlefield, but the media told and retold these stories, imprinting heroic deeds onto public memory through repetition in song, print, and on stage. In this way media publicity gave cultural authority to the sacrifice and martyrdom of

59. On media sensationalism of Kuga's suicide, see Eguchi, *Jūgonen sensō no kaimaku*, p. 150. For Araki's statement, see ibid., pp. 157–158.

60. *Chizome no teppitsu* [The Blood-stained Pen]: "Sensō eiga," *Eiga to engei* (April 1932).

the celebrated. Had they been unsung, men like Kuga and Kuramoto would have remained anonymous.

Though entertainers spread their eulogies around during the Manchurian Incident, not all deaths were celebrated equally. Another conspicuous feature of the imperial jingoism of the early thirties was the emergence of heroes and superheroes. The sensationalizing of the "three human bombs" (or bullets), the soldiers who were blown up in the line of duty during the assault on Shanghai, cast all other new heroes into shadow. The army publicized the three deaths as a conscious act of suicide, claiming the young men had sacrificed themselves to explode a section of wire fence impeding the army's advance. Various rumors circulated at the time contradicting the army's account. Some said the three had died because their commanding officer cut the fuse too short or because he had given them the wrong type of fuse; others suggested that the men attempted to abandon the mission but their commander ordered them to follow through. And it was quietly pointed out that something was amiss with the official report because three other soldiers accompanied the mission and were able to return unharmed.[61] Soon this all became immaterial because the "three human bullets" boom in the mass media gave popular authority to the army's version of the event.

Throughout March, "three human bullets" productions swept the entertainment world. The *Screen and Stage* reported that "Tokyo's theaters, including all the major houses . . . are filled with 'three human bullets' plays. The story has been dramatized in every form, from *shinpa* (new school) to *kyūgeki* (classical drama)." No fewer than six movie versions were produced in March alone, and at vaudeville reviews at places like the Horie Dance Hall, the chorus line kicked their heels to the "Three Human Bullets Song."[62] Record companies brought out a string of "human bombs" songs, which were multiplying due to song contests in the *Asahi, Mainichi, Shōnen kurabu, Rekōdo,* and other newspapers and magazines. Yamada

61. According to Eguchi Keiichi, questions about the official version were raised in *The True Story of the "Three Human Bullets,"* written by a soldier of the same unit. This book was banned by Home Ministry authorities, but, as discussed later, a large fraction of censored publications slipped through the police net. In 1965 former Major General Tanaka Ryūkichi admitted in a television interview that the deaths were due to the officer's miscalculation of the length of the fuse: "If the officer giving the order would have made the fuse cord one meter long, those boys could have blown up the wire mesh and returned to safety." Eguchi, *Jūgonen sensō no kaimaku,* pp. 144–145, 154–157.

62. *Eiga to engei* (April 1932), frontispiece; "Sensō eiga," *Eiga to engei* (April 1932), p. 18.

Kosaku, founder of the Tokyo Philharmonic, collaborated with Koga Masao, king of popular song, to produce one prize-winning version.[63] This, though, was overshadowed by the poet Yosano Hiroshi's version, which proved by far the most popular of the "human bombs" songs.[64] Before long, even "human bullets" products appeared on the market. Entrepreneurs from the dead men's home towns began selling "three human bullets sake" and "three human bullets bean paste candy," and an Osaka department store dining room showed questionable taste in offering a "three human bombs" special: radish strips cut to simulate the explosives tube and butterburs representing the "human bombs."[65]

Like previous media fads, the "three human bullets" craze did not last long. By the summer of 1932, the entertainment world had turned its attention to the opening of the Japanese Derby, a rash of love suicides, and the Japanese victories at the Los Angeles Olympics. Interest in Manchuria picked up again the following winter, however, with the release of the League of Nations' Lytton Commission Report on the Sino-Japanese conflict and the League debate over the legitimacy of Manchukuo. Responding to the Lytton Commission's criticism of Japanese actions and the increasing certainty that Japan was losing the war of words to China, a flood of articles denounced European and American interference in Japanese affairs. Although this second media boom was as transitory as the first, the impact of war fever in the culture industries long outlasted the headlines. Media sensationalism flooded popular consciousness with images of war and empire. Such jingoism was important because it became unofficial propaganda for empire. Marketing militarism, the mass media helped mobilize popular support for the army's policy of military aggression against China, and in the process influenced foreign policy and the politics of empire.

MASS MEDIA MILITARISM AND THE CENSORSHIP QUESTION

In the context of the early thirties, this militarism in the media represented a dramatic shift from the previous decade, during which the mass media had achieved a reputation for championing pacifism and international cooperation. This raises the provocative and controversial question: How can we account for the media's conversion to militarism in the wake of the Manchurian Incident? In the argument thus far, media activism has been

63. *Asahi nenkan* (1933), p. 677.
64. Eguchi, *Jūgonen sensō no kaimaku*, pp. 156–157.
65. Ibid., p. 157.

ascribed to the mercurial nature of the cultural marketplace, situating jingoism in the string of media fads that punctuated the cultural history of the 1920s and 1930s. Taking a different position on this question, the explanation of the volte-face one hears most frequently in Japan is that this was a forced conversion: government censorship silenced media criticism of the army and prevented the expression of liberal sentiment. But both of these arguments provide only partial explanations. Newspapers and magazines were necessarily responsive to consumer demand, but editorial decisions were also driven by political and ideological beliefs. Government certainly began to tighten censorship during the Manchurian Incident, a process which intensified over the course of the decade. But in the early thirties, it was still possible for editors and directors to evade government censorship had they wanted to. Thus, the explanation for the media's conversion to militarism must also be sought in the political convictions of editors and journalists: they wrote articles in support of the Manchurian Incident because they believed army policy was justified.

Before jumping on the Manchuria bandwagon, producers of mass culture rode the Taishō fashions in urban culture. As magazine publishing entered a new era of circulation growth after World War I, leading journals such as *Chūō kōron* and *Kaizō* became champions of the movement for universal suffrage. In the early twenties, left-wing books made good business sense. A printing of 10,000 copies which sold out in two days of the second volume of Shimada Seijirō's *Chijō* (Earth) and reputed sales of over 1 million copies of Kagawa Toyohiko's *Shisen o koete* (Overcoming the Struggle) taught publishers the meaning of the term *besuto seraa* (bestseller). Both books depicted the injustice of urban poverty and championed the struggle against the degradation and exploitation of the working class. When Kagawa was arrested for his involvement in a Kobe strike in 1920, demand for his book rose, boosted by full-page newspaper ads which dramatically announced the author's arrest.[66] The triple media hit of 1929, "Tokyo March" (Kikuchi Kan's serial novel first published in the magazine *Kingu*, then made into the movie whose title song sold 250,000 records), glorified the consumer culture of Tokyo's Ginza, with its department stores, jazz halls, cafes, and crowds of *modan gaaru* (modern girls) strolling the tree-lined streets.[67] Thus, mass-culture producers were equally capable of responding to popular interest in democracy, social justice, or consumerism, as they were to an enthusiasm for military imperialism.

66. Minami et al., *Taishō bunka*, pp. 233–235.
67. Minami et al., *Shōwa bunka*, p. 472.

In the press, a long-standing policy of championing disarmament and a "soft line" toward China had earned the *Asahi* and *Mainichi* newspapers the enmity of the army and made its editors the target of physical assaults by right-wing organizations.[68] Prior to World War I, the large dailies had supported government expenditures for armaments and applauded the performance of the armed services in the Sino-Japanese and Russo-Japanese wars. But beginning with the navy's involvement in the Siemens bribery scandal of 1914, a succession of blunders brought the military under increasingly stinging editorial attacks. Both papers sharply criticized the Siberian Intervention of 1918–1922. The army's insistence that the reporters assigned to accompany the troops onboard ship quarter themselves in the stables with the horses probably did nothing to improve the newspapers' view of the expedition.[69] When the first proposals for reductions in the military budget were voted down in 1921, the newspapers took up the disarmament cause, denouncing the "tyranny of military influence" in politics. They applauded Japan's signature to the Washington Naval Limitation Treaty in 1922; they cheered the subsequent elimination of four army divisions and abandonment of plans for warship construction.[70] More damage was done to the army's reputation when news of the murder, in 1923, of fourteen socialist and labor activists by army officers and military police leaked out. The victims had been arrested during the chaos after the Tokyo earthquake. Though the army banned all coverage of the murders, the Osaka *Asahi* defied army censorship to release an extra reporting the news.[71] The army's China policy invited yet more criticism from the press. When General Tanaka Giichi's cabinet dispatched troops to Shandong in 1927 and 1928 in a show of force against the Northern Expedition of Jiang Jieshi's Nationalist Army, the papers called for diplomacy instead of strong-arm tactics. The Tokyo *Nichinichi* refused to accept the army's version of events during the second Shandong Expedition in 1928, when fighting broke out between Chinese and Japanese troops at Jinan. An editorial called on the government to "tell the truth," and protested the subsequent troop reinforcements.[72]

68. For the enmity of the army, see Eguchi, *Jūgonen sensō no kaimaku*, p. 105; for the right-wing attack on the president of the *Asahi*, see Chamoto Shigemasa, *Sensō to jaanarizumu* (San'ichi shobō, 1984), pp. 168–169.

69. After indignant protests by their editors to the Army Ministry, the reporters were furnished with cabins. Chamoto, p. 198.

70. Jansen, *Japan and China*, p. 360, and Fujiwara Akira, *Nihon gunjishi*, vol. 1 (Nihon hyōronsha, 1987), p. 164.

71. Chamoto, p. 222.

72. Eguchi, *Jūgonen sensō no kaimaku*, pp. 99–105; William Fitch Morton,

After more than a decade of criticizing army excesses and advocating diplomatic solutions to the "China problem," the *Asahi* and *Mainichi* papers made a dramatic volte-face in 1931. Close on the heels of September 18, *Asahi* managers resolved that "though the newspaper remains in favor of disarmament," in the interests of "unifying public opinion behind the army," the paper would not "criticize or oppose in any way military action or the military itself." In a more mean-spirited vein, *Mainichi* editors decided their paper would treat China "as an enemy country" and therefore refrain from using "titles and honorifics for Chinese nationals."[73] In practice, reports wired in by special correspondents in the field came straight "from the lips" of Kwantung Army spokesmen. As one contemporary described the situation, "not only did virtually all the coverage from the front take a hard-line slant," but reports from Tokyo journalists "gave preferential treatment to army information." Moreover, journalists in the rest of the country were "following suit."[74]

There were a number of factors operating to shape these decisions. Undoubtedly the government maintained a vigilant attitude toward press coverage of the Manchurian Incident and applied pressure to run progovernment articles. Editors were similarly influenced by the commercial opportunities of the war fever to give pro-military coverage of the Manchurian Incident. But neither government repression nor market pressures can entirely account for the alacrity and enthusiasm with which *Mainichi* and *Asahi* editors embraced the army's policy in Manchuria. In the twenties, they had genuinely opposed the Shandong Expeditions, but they just as sincerely regarded the occupation of Manchuria in a different light.

Tanaka Giichi and Japan's China Policy (Folkestone, Kent: Dawson, 1980), pp. 70–74, 86–95, 100–101, 118–120, 138–139; Chamoto, pp. 168–182, 192–193, 198, 222–224, 247–248.

73. These remarks were reported to the *kenpeitai* (military police) by informants and included in a *kenpeitai* report on the attitude toward the Manchurian Incident adopted by the *Asahi* and *Mainichi*: Kenpei shireikan Toyama Bunzō, "Ōsaka *Asahi* Ōsaka *Mainichi* no jikyoku ni taisuru taidō kettei ni kansuru ken hōkoku" (19 October 1931), in Fujiwara Akira and Kunugi Toshihiro, eds., *Manshū jihen to kokumin dōin*, vol. 8 of *Shiryō Nihon gendaishi* (Ōtsuki shoten, 1983), p. 96. The *kenpeitai* monitored popular reactions to the Manchurian Incident by tracking the mass media and through their network of informants in political organizations. *Kenpeitai* reports on the Manchurian Incident have been published in the document collection edited by Fujiwara Akira and Kunugi Toshihiro that was just cited. Henceforth this collection is cited as Fujiwara and Kunugi, *Manshū jihen to kokumin dōin*.

74. Abe Shingo, "Manshū jihen o meguru shinbungai," *Kaizō* (November 1931), p. 36.

While it may seem politically inconsistent to criticize the army one day and then endorse military expansionism the next, both positions were consistent with a commitment to the empire. In other words, it was possible to favor economic and diplomatic methods of protecting Japanese interests in the 1920s and yet perceive, in 1931, the need for a show of force in Manchuria. In short, editors committed themselves to unifying public opinion behind the occupation because they were convinced that the army was right.

Changes in radio programming and the initiation of a public-education campaign by NHK mirrored the support given by the national dailies to the army's position. During the year following the Manchurian Incident, NHK broadcast 279 lectures and educational programs on Manchuria, including special programming aimed at women and children. NHK began this public-opinion crusade very quickly, squeezing in 4 lectures in the last days of September. Peaking in December with 40 scheduled programs, NHK hosted military men as the most frequent speakers on their public-education programs. Moreover, the civilian contributors featured, such as political firebrand Mori Kaku and right-wing scholar Yano Jin'ichi, were hardly neutral observers in the foreign-policy debate over Manchuria.[75] Mori, for example, represented the extremist wing of the hawkish Seiyūkai party, and had acquired a reputation for his unrestrained attacks on the "pusilanimous" tactics advocated by Minseitō party doves. A close associate of General Tanaka Giichi, the symbol of a "positive" China policy, Mori himself was a firm advocate both of military expansionism on the continent and of a greater role for the army in domestic politics. Like Mori, Kyoto University professor Yano Jin'ichi was a long-time proponent of a stronger Japanese presence in Manchuria and went to work for the Kwantung Army as a propagandist for Manchukuo in 1932.

In contrast to the press, radio support for the army did not represent a shift in position, for NHK was too new to have acquired a track record on military policy. Since the founding of the NHK network in 1926, NHK was technically privately owned and managed. Government regulations, however, subjected radio to strong state controls and made it virtually an instrument of the Communications Ministry. Even so, before the Manchurian Incident NHK had not taken an active role in news reporting, nor was it used as a vehicle for political propaganda. The political and ideological role of radio was not yet fixed, and many sought to reverse the course

75. Nihon hōsō kyōkai, *Rajio nenkan: Shōwa 8 nen* (1933), pp. 10–20; radio schedules in Ikei, "1930 nendai," pp. 153–167.

NHK seemed to have embarked upon in 1931. The Minseitō-led cabinet objected to the broadcast of Mori Kaku's speech in November 1931 and was outraged when Mori deviated from the preapproved script to make an attack on cabinet policy. Leftist intellectuals were dismayed by radio's new direction, complaining, as in a petition by novelist Nogami Yaeko, of "radio serving as an organ of state since the start of the war . . . arranging events in a montage of mistaken ideology."

To criticisms of Nogami and others, a manager of the Osaka branch of NHK replied, "those on the left often say that Japanese broadcasting is trying to fulfill its foremost function as an organ for the diffusion of re-actionary thought. If one looks at the relationship with supervisory state officials, the scope of the limits on broadcast contents, etc., one cannot disagree with this observation, but it is only the organization and the system which foist [upon radio] varied functions favorable to a reactionary course—it is certainly not inevitable that we must advance along this road."[76] These words underscored the limitations of state controls. It was clear that NHK was feeling pressure from certain factions in government, but as the Osaka manager pointed out, the ultimate decisions were in hands like his. In institutions that were run by individuals and split into factions, the structure itself could not guarantee a particular outcome. Following their own inclinations, NHK managers charted a pro-army course for radio to applause from some and jeers from others. Though they may have wanted to keep the pro-army faction in the government happy, it was undoubtedly the standing ovations from the public that really made the difference.

The conversion of popular entertainment from the frivolity of the *moga* flapper to the drama of the campaigns in Manchuria was a different case once again. Dominated increasingly by fashion, mass culture had become a world of *buumu* (booms) which changed from season to season. Hence, it was not surprising that "like a see-saw," the rise of *kiwamono* (sensa-tional) and *gunjimono* (militaristic) products was accompanied by a fall in *keikō*, or proletarian, culture.[77] But unlike such Taishō fads as yo-yos or pulp fiction which eventually regained popularity, the proletarian culture movement never revived. In large degree this was the result of a campaign

76. The defense of NHK was originally published in the January 1932 and February 1932 issues of *Chōsa jihō*. Quoted in Kasza, pp. 96–97. See also Kasza's discussion of state control over NHK: ibid., pp. 72–101.

77. One publisher's yearbook described this as a "see-saw" effect: *Shuppan nenkan* (1933), p. 2.

of repression against left-wing publications waged by the Home Ministry. In addition to press and publication laws giving wide postpublication censorship powers, the Home Ministry was empowered by the Peace Preservation Law of 1925 to arrest anyone criticizing private property or advocating changes in the national polity (*kokutai*). In principle this gave the government a virtual carte blanche to repress all anti-government expression. In practice, however, the instruments of suppression were wielded selectively against such organizations as the Proletarian Arts League (Nihon puroretaria geijutsu dōmei) and the Proletarian Cinema League (Purokino). Though these laws tended not to be applied against mainstream publishers and companies, the negative examples of the left-wing organizations doubtless had a chilling effect.[78]

In any case, the left-wing artistic community required little muzzling on the Manchurian question, for few spoke out against the occupation. Far from it, many artists reacted like Yosano Akiko, the nation's most famous pacifist. Akiko and her husband, Hiroshi, produced numerous poems and songs celebrating the military occupation. Early in her career, Akiko had caused a sensation with the anti–Russo-Japanese War poem "Brother Do Not Give Your Life." Addressed to her youngest brother, her poem demands: "Did our parents make you grasp the sword and teach you to kill? For you what does it matter whether the fortress of Lüshun falls or not?" But in 1932, while her husband penned "three human bullets" lyrics, Akiko published "Citizens of Japan, A Morning Song." In it, she urged Japanese troops on "through sufferings a hundredfold" to "smash sissified dreams of compromise." Unlike the Russo-Japanese War poem, which had condemned the waste of human life in battle, Akiko's new poem glorified the heroic death of a soldier who "scatters" his body, "purer than a flower, giving life to a samurai's honor." Akiko's change of heart was apparently inspired by a trip to Manchuria in 1928, courtesy of Mantetsu. After a forty-day journey throughout the country, she returned to Japan impressed with Manchuria's progress under Japanese stewardship and convinced of the justice of Japan's colonial mission.[79]

78. Kōdansha, ed., *Tairiku ni agaru senka: Shōwa 4 nen–6 nen*, vol. 2 of *Shōwa nimannichi no zenkiroku* (Kōdansha, 1989), pp. 70–71; Kasza, pp. 38–44; Richard H. Mitchell, *Censorship in Imperial Japan* (Princeton: Princeton University Press, 1983), pp. 199–204.

79. On Akiko's conversion, see Steve Rabson, "Yosano Akiko on War: To Give One's Life or Not—A Question of Which War," *Journal of the Association of Teachers of Japanese* 25, no. 1 (April 1991), pp. 45–74. Poems on pp. 45–46, 56–60.

Had they wished, it would have been possible in 1931 and 1932 for journalists and editors to express anti-war sentiments. The press and publication laws made Japan sound like a police state, but in reality they were notoriously difficult to enforce. The postpublication censorship system's key weapon, the ban on circulation, was usually thwarted by the efforts of publishers to sell the offending merchandise before police arrived to confiscate it. In 1932 the confiscation rate of banned newspapers was estimated at 25 percent, and for books and magazines, 13.7 percent.[80] Newspapers defied Home Ministry prepublication warnings 262 times in 1931 and 1,080 times in 1932. The major papers were among the offenders.[81] During the Russo-Japanese War, though Yosano Akiko's poem and other anti-war publications such as the *Heimin shinbun* came under a storm of protest from other journalists and publishers, government censorship laws failed to prevent publication and sale.[82] What happened in 1905 was true for 1931 as well.

Looking back, the *Asahi* newspaper tried to explain its own volte-face as a case of official repression. The company history reported that "freedom of expression was not permitted after the outbreak of the Incident. . . . With the explosion at Fengtian, in a single stroke the nation entered a quasi-wartime situation and the press was completely silenced."[83] In fact, critical comments managed to get through the censor's net. In the most striking example, throughout the fall and winter of 1931–1932, forums for liberal and left-wing intellectuals such as the journals *Chūō kōron* and *Kaizō* were filled with skepticism toward the war fever. *Chūō kōron*'s October 1931 editorial opposed sending troops to Manchuria, stating that Japan's ultimate goals could not be gained by force, and accusing elements in Japan of exploiting minor conflicts in Manchuria to impose an aggressive policy. Though Home Ministry censors warned *Chūō kōron*'s editors not to repeat such sentiments,[84] the November edition featured an article by

---

80. Kasza, pp. 35–36.

81. As Kasza points out, the legal devices of banning circulation were supplemented by a number of extralegal methods to regulate journalism. Censors often issued informal postpublication warnings (*keikoku*) not to publish a similar article again, or allowed publishers to delete objectionable passages. In addition, the Home Ministry used a prepublication warning system of "instructions" (*shisatsu*), "admonitions" (*keikoku*), and "consultations" (*kondan*) for newspapers requesting self-censorship on politically sensitive matters in order to avoid the postpublication ban: Kasza, p. 31.

82. Rabson, pp. 45–74; Chamoto, pp. 94–108; Mitchell, pp. 135–136.

83. The original quotation comes from *Asahi shinbun nanajūnenshi* (1959). Quoted in Eguchi, *Jūgonen sensō no kaimaku*, p. 102.

84. Kasza, p. 48.

Marxist Inomata Tsunao on "Monopoly Capitalism and the Crisis in Manchuria and Mongolia." When this was banned outright,[85] editors blunted
subsequent criticism of the Manchurian Incident in later editions. But
though they softened the language, the criticism of government policy still
came through in a December article on the inevitable damage the occupation would do to Japanese-Western relations. Moreover, a January article
disputed the army's claim that the occupation of Manchuria was necessary
for the self-defense of treaty rights.[86]

Articles in *Kaizō* took an equally critical position, denouncing the self-
serving news war and criticizing the *Asahi* and *Mainichi* for their obse-
quious attitude toward the military.[87] In the same November issue, journalist Gotō Shinobu called the military action in Manchuria a "two-fold
coup d'etat," in the first instance against the Chinese government and in
the second against the Japanese Minseitō cabinet and the pacifist policies
of Foreign Minister Shidehara.[88] As late as April 1932, *Kaizō* printed an
article by Tokyo University professor and renowned liberal intellectual
Yanaihara Tadao, criticizing the short-sightedness of trying to overcome
Chinese nationalism with military measures.[89] Clearly the army had its
critics, and liberal journals were printing their opinions.

Especially in September and October of 1931, local papers affiliated with
the Minseitō political party also published harsh criticisms of army policy.
For example, the *Fukui nippō* reported on September 24:

> In view of the recent friction in Sino-Japanese relations it is easy to imag-
> ine the state of tension of both our troops and the Chinese Army. That
> two skittish armies stationed, as it were, cheek to jowl should clash is not
> particularly surprising or even momentous. Indeed it is nothing more than
> a local incident, but it has created such an enormous impact because of the
> general foreboding of war among the populace. . . .
>
> The army has been hammering incessantly on the theme of protecting
> rights and interests in Manchuria and is constantly recounting the details
> of [the murder by Chinese of a Japanese army captain in] the Nakamura

85. Ibid.
86. Tanaka Kuichi, "Manshū jihen to rekkoku no taiShi seisaku," *Chūō kōron*
(December 1931), pp. 2–24; Yoshino Sakuzō, "Minzoku to kaikyū to sensō," *Chūō
kōron* (January 1932), pp. 27–38.
87. Abe Shingo, "Manshū o meguru shinbungai," *Kaizō* (November 1931),
p. 36.
88. Gotō Shinobu, "Manshū mondai to sono zentō," *Kaizō* (November 1931),
p. 99.
89. Yanaihara Tadao, "Manmō shin kokkaron," *Kaizō* (April 1932), pp. 18–29.

Incident. As they are stirring up a sense of enmity toward China in dark corners and in the open sunlight we suddenly hear the unfortunate news of the clash between Chinese and Japanese troops. And we may expect, momentarily, the startling announcement of war between the two, like a sudden thunderclap in a clear blue sky. The question is—has the Incident gone that far?[90]

Although the editor of the *Fukui nippō* was remonstrated by the military police for the paper's imputation of a military conspiracy, the article went to press and people read it just the same.

Ishibashi Tanzan, editor of the influential economic journal *Tōyō keizai shinpō* and long-time advocate of a "little Japan" foreign policy, also used his journal to argue that Japan should "abandon special rights and interests in Manchuria" (*Manmō hōkiron*) throughout the early months of the Manchurian Incident. Just as he had criticized military action in China in the past, in the fall of 1931 he spoke out against "the completely mistaken" idea that the "country will die without Manchuria," arguing that there was no "profit in turning China and the Western powers into Japan's enemies." Observing that the "military action was contrary to the intent or the liking of the cabinet," Ishibashi suggested that the situation in Manchuria posed no real "national threat" and denounced the army for flaunting "the authority of the cabinet."[91]

Although opposition to the occupation was strongly voiced in the *Tōyō keizai shinpō* and elsewhere, such sentiments stood little chance of penetrating the storm of pro-military reports unleashed by radio and the national press. In the end, the voice of opposition was not silenced by government repression; it was drowned out by the mainstream news media. This, then, was the third dimension of imperial jingoism. Propaganda and censorship are usually regarded as instruments of the state, used to shape and control public opinion. Imperial jingoism, however, is the product of unofficial propaganda and private self-censorship. In Japan's case, imperial jingoism was responsive to government direction, but never perfectly controlled by it. Driven more directly by the opportunities for technological and commercial advance at a time when the national crisis stimulated de-

90. A copy of this article was included in a *kenpeitai* report on Minseitō-affiliated press coverage of the Manchurian Incident. Kenpei shireibu keimubu Fujii Shinji, "Manshū jihen ni taisuru ichi Minseikei shinbun no ronchō ni kansuru ken tsūchō" (24 September 1931), in Fujiwara and Kunugi, *Manshū jihen to kokumin dōin*, p. 36. For a description of this document collection, see note 73 in this chapter.

91. "Manmō mondai kaiketsu no konpon hōshi ikan," *Tōyō keizai shinpō* (26 September 1931, 10 October 1931). See also Eguchi Keiichi's discussion in Eguchi, *Nihon teikokushugi shiron*, pp. 220–222.

mand for Manchurian-theme products, the mass media promoted the war on its own volition and in its own interests.

DEFEND THE MANCHURIAN LIFELINE!

The war boom of 1931–1933 constituted a critical period in the ideological construction of empire. On the first anniversary of the Manchurian Incident, the chief of staff of the 3d Division, Colonel Inuzuka Hiroshi, observed how much things had changed since the beginning of the war. "At first there were quite a few Japanese who judged the army as if it were on trial. Consciousness of Manchuria was nil."[92] Yet within six months it had become all-consuming. Manchuria became a "lifeline" for which no sacrifice was too great.

The path from indifference and ignorance to nationalistic obsession was trod, for many ordinary Japanese, by skimming the daily news, listening to popular songs, or reading favorite magazines. The self-appointed educators in the mass media took to their task with enthusiasm, setting forth a popular catechism on "why we fight." This catechism explained the concurrent events in Manchuria within a framework of imperial ideology that was, by 1931, well developed. And yet the action in Manchuria was undeniably a departure from policies pursued in the 1920s. New conditions demanded new explanations. Thus the imperial myth making of the early 1930s assimilated fresh elements into old stories, reconstructing imperial ideology to make room for Manchukuo.

The first response to the popular catechism on "why we fight" became the battle cry of the Manchurian Incident: *Mamore Manshū seimeisen!* (Defend the Manchurian lifeline!). The term *lifeline* was coined by diplomat and Seiyūkai politician Matsuoka Yōsuke in an impromptu Diet speech in January 1931.[93] Picked up by the daily press in the early days of the fighting and spread throughout the mass media, the catchphrase quickly took hold of public imagination. The term *lifeline* expressed the visceral and organic sense of connection between Japan and its Manchurian empire. Japan's fate was bound to the Northeast because Manchuria was vital to Japan's survival.

This sense of dependence on Manchuria had grown on Japanese in the course of a twenty-five-year proprietorship. By 1931, Mantetsu and the

92. Inuzuka's remark was published in the September 18, 1932, issue of the *Nagoya shinbun*. Cited in Eguchi, "Manshū jihen to minshū dōin," p. 127.

93. Eguchi, *Jūgonen sensō no kaimaku*, pp. 22–23, 105.

Kwantung Leased Territory, like Taiwan and Korea, were regarded as part of Japan. Such proprietary feelings carried with them a whole complex of Japanese attitudes toward their empire. From the beginnings of empire in the Meiji period, Japanese had come to look upon the empire as part of their national identity. Japan was, after all, imperial Japan. From the same period, moreover, Japanese had been taught that their national survival depended on the possession of an empire, that Japan had expanded in self-defense. As the rise of organized Chinese nationalism seemed to imperil Japan's hold over Manchuria, the threat was understood in this broader context. Yet *lifeline* was a new term applied to Manchuria. As such, it spoke to a recently developed sense of embattlement in the Northeast. The term's popular appeal also reflected the newfound importance Japanese accorded something they had previously taken for granted. Thus, images of the Manchurian lifeline in the mass media drew on a new sense of connectedness between the ordinary citizen and this faraway place on the map. The connection was drawn in personal terms both historic and immediate, resurrecting memories of the Russo-Japanese War—also fought on Manchurian soil—and tapping the anxieties of a people in severe economic distress.

Memories of the Russo-Japanese War confused the war's aims with its subsequent peace settlement. Coming back into currency, the old slogan about the "payment of 100,000 lives and a billion yen in blood and treasure for Manchuria" implied that Japan had fought Russia in 1904 over Manchuria. As a writer for the popular magazine *Ie no hikari* (The Light of the Home) expressed it, "Japan fought both the Sino-Japanese and the Russo-Japanese wars, buried 100,000 souls in the Manchurian plain, and risked the fate of the nation to gain the rights and interests we now hold in Manchuria. These are the victory prizes [*kesshō*] won with the priceless blood and sweat of the Japanese race."[94] Forgetting that it was in fact the struggle for control over Korea that had precipitated the war and that Japan had gained its Korean colony as a result of the victory, Japanese in the 1930s somehow felt that Manchuria comprised the sole compensation for this past sacrifice, immeasurable in both personal and national terms.

By any reckoning, the Russo-Japanese War was a costly and painful experience, and it cut much deeper than the nation's first imperial war with China. The soldiers that were mobilized numbered 1,088,996, almost five times the number that fought in the Sino-Japanese War; another 945,395 went to the front in noncombat roles. The war left 81,455 dead (six times

94. "Ie no hikari shinbun," *Ie no hikari* (January 1932), p. 166.

the Sino-Japanese War) and 381,313 wounded. At 1.8 billion yen, it was nine times as expensive, and costs were offset with heavy borrowing in foreign and domestic financial markets and a host of new taxes.[95] These sacrifices were repaid with a stunning victory over one of the world's great powers. To Japanese at the time, this victory turned their country into a great nation (*taikoku*) and signaled Japan's "advance into the ranks of the world powers." But as Carol Gluck notes, the war was also viewed in terms of the "humiliating peace" that followed.[96] When the government accepted terms that fell far short of what people were led to expect, their sense of disappointment and betrayal was expressed in urban rioting against the peace treaty in 1905. The bitterness that accompanied the aftermath of war, the postwar depression, the war debt, the return of war-mutilated men, and the emptiness left by those who did not come back all bequeathed to public memory a sense of ill usage and uncompensated sacrifice. In the war fever of 1931, both the triumph of the victory and the bitterness of the peace were projected onto the Manchurian lifeline.

A popular revival in Russo-Japanese War songs and the dramatization of the epochal moments of the war on stage and screen recalled the giddy sense of pride felt when Japanese saw their nation catapulted into the forefront of international prestige and power. Tokyo theaters brought out stirring dramas like *For the Fatherland* (*Sokoku no tame ni*) and Kabuki tragedies such as *The Gold-buttoned Soldier* (*Kinboton no heitai*).[97] General Nogi, the Russo-Japanese War hero who had conducted the bloody assault on Lüshun and later stunned the nation with his suicide after the death of "his Emperor," was exalted in children's biographies and minstrel songs.[98] Tokyo's Meijiza Theater produced a "General Nogi" play in January 1932, and Kawai Pictures opened *Remember General Nogi!* (*Omoidaseyo Nogi shōgun*) the following month.[99] Other war heroes like the martyred "military god" Commander Hirose were eulogized in children's songs and stories. The boys' magazine *Shōnen kurabu* accompanied an illustrated account of Hirose's final glorious hours with a paper construction set

95. Iguchi, pp. 86–87.

96. Gluck, *Japan's Modern Myths*, p. 90.

97. See play listings in *Eiga to engei* (January 1932), p. 53, and play listings for "Shinkabukiza," *Eiga to engei* (February 1932).

98. *Rekōdo* (February 1932), p. 74; *Rekōdo* (May 1932), p. 82; *Shuppan nenkan* (1933), p. 89.

99. See play listings for "Meijiza," *Eiga to engei* (February 1932); see movie listings for "Kawai eiga," *Eiga to engei* (March 1932).

representing the Tokyo statue of Hirose. As the magazine described this "stirring" memorial to the great man, "the longer you look at it the more humbled you feel by his nobility."[100] The boom of Russo-Japanese War theme products reconnected Manchuria to the victory that had startled the world and gilded the "lifeline" with the reflected glory of the earlier campaign.

At the same time, the resurrection of elegiac Russo-Japanese War songs like "Sen'yū" (Comrade) called to mind the human cost of the war, shading images of the Manchurian lifeline with bitter memories of death and sacrifice:

> Here, many hundreds of leagues from home,
> The red setting sun of distant Manchuria
> Shines down on a stone at the edge of a field,
> Beneath which my friend lies.

> It grieves me to think of the brave hero
> Who only yesterday headed the charge —
> Ruthlessly setting upon the enemy.
> I wonder, will he sleep well here?

> At the height of the battle,
> I raced blindly to the friend
> Who had been at my side
> As he fell suddenly,
> The flag with him.[101]

Even before its resurgence in popularity during the Manchurian Incident, "Sen'yū" had made phrases such as "red setting sun" (*akai yūhi*) and "hundreds of leagues from home" (*koko wa mikuni o nanbyaku ri*) common epithets for Manchuria. Revived in 1931, "Sen'yū" reminded Japanese of the importance of defending their foothold in Northeast China. Representing Manchuria as the site of loss, the place where fathers, brothers, and comrades in arms died in heroic sacrifice, the "Sen'yū" revival strengthened the sense of connection that the lifeline was coming to represent. Manchuria must be defended, for it was all that the Japanese had left of the loved ones they mourned.

Such personalized narratives of loss were linked, invariably, with sacrifice for the nation. In "Sen'yū" this was conveyed by the reference to

---

100. Ikeda Nobumasa, "Gunshin Hirose chūsa," and "Daifuroku-Hirose chūsa no dōzō setto ni tsuite," both in *Shōnen kurabu* (May 1932), pp. 216–230.

101. Lyrics to "Sen'yū" in Hamanō, p. 119.

the flag. In "Manchuria March," the hit song of 1932, it was suggested with a verse that made Manchuria into a national monument to the Russo-Japanese War dead:

> Look over at the war memorial!
> There the bones of our heroes,
> Dead in the war between Japan and Russia,
> Are long buried.
> Stained with a red river of blood,
> The evening sun shines upon it,
> Soaring high over the endless plain.[102]

Here the personal loss of a comrade in arms was generalized to the national loss of "our heroes." Their interment transformed Manchuria into a national (family) graveyard, while the "river of blood" marked Japan's claim to Manchurian soil. Identifying Manchuria with the Russo-Japanese War, songs like "Manchuria March" made the lifeline into a metaphor for shared sacrifice and provided a blood claim to Manchurian territory.

Such blood imperatives to defend the Manchurian lifeline were also phrased in terms of a blood debt to the Russo-Japanese War generation. Employing a familiar Confucian vocabulary of familial obligation, appeals to the blood debt circulated in the mass media in 1931–1933 suggested that the young owed it to their parents to protect the Manchurian empire. A reader's poem (senryū) published in the popular magazine *Kingu* depicted service on the Manchurian battlefront forging a special bond between father and son: "Remembering Manchuria with a full heart/he leaves the warmth of the fire/to see his first born off to Manchuria."[103] Such words implied that the Manchurian Incident was, in effect, a replay of the Russo-Japanese War. This, of course, was an absurd suggestion, for engagement with an ill-equipped and poorly financed warlord force (most of which was not resisting Japanese occupation militarily) was in no way comparable to facing the full strength of the tsar's army and navy. Poetic license aside, the point of such appeals was to elicit a reenactment of the outpouring of patriotic sacrifice for which the Russo-Japanese War was also remembered.

Public memories linking the Russo-Japanese War to the Manchurian Incident fashioned Manchuria into a generational lifeline, connecting past and present and passing the burden of guardianship from father to son,

---

102. Lyrics to "Manshū kōshin kyoku" in ibid., p. 120. All translations of songs and poems from Japanese sources are the author's.
103. Asō Jirō, "Senryū," *Kingu* (April 1932), p. 245.

from one generation to the next. A tribute to the first war dead published in *Kingu* singled out Captain Kuramoto for special mention because of such a family connection: "First the father in the Russo-Japanese War and now the son in the present incident, their heroic bones abandoned to the elements on the Manchurian plain."[104] The notion of a generational lifeline also resonated with the doctrine of the family-state, the idea that all Japanese were part of one national family under the paternity of the emperor. Legally sanctioned in the Meiji constitution and promoted through the educational system, its moral prescriptions of "loyalty and patriotism" called for obedience to emperor and nation as an expression of familial piety. The idea of blood debt evoked in the Manchurian Incident war fever wedded patriotic duty toward this metaphoric national family with the personal feelings of obligation toward friends and family.

In addition to these popular images of a line of blood and spirit that indebted the living to the dead and bound them to defend Manchuria, the lifeline came to symbolize an economic umbilical chord as well. Unlike the Russo-Japanese War images, the language of economic security was a new addition to the imperial lexicon. Since before the turn of the century, apostles of empire advocated the promotion of Japanese shipping to and trade with Korea and China, pointing to the links between commercial competitiveness and international prestige.[105] But at that stage the economic importance of empire was conceived in terms of export markets. When the experience of World War I taught military planners the value of colonies as import markets, Japanese began to evaluate the empire as a resource base for industrial production.[106] This new appreciation of colonies as a source of strategic imports was reinforced by the initiation of large-scale rice imports from Korea and Taiwan after the rice riots of 1918. For the first time, Japan was dependent on the colonies for domestic food consumption.

The mass media discourse on Manchuria in 1931–1933 defined the lifeline in this new economic language of empire. Articles in best-selling magazines like *Kingu* and *Ie no hikari* called Manchuria a "bottomless

---

104. Hirose Teiichi, "Aa soretsu! Aa chūretsu! Kanjōshi Nanrei daigeki senki," *Kingu* (December 1931), p. 31.

105. Duus, "Economic Dimensions of Meiji Imperialism," pp. 131–148.

106. Barnhart, esp. pp. 17–49. See also Mark R. Peattie, "Forecasting a Pacific War 1912–1933: The Idea of a Conditional Japanese Victory," in James W. White, Michio Umegaki, and Thomas R. H. Havens, eds., *The Ambivalence of Nationalism: Modern Japan between East and West* (Lanham, Md.: University Press of America, 1990), pp. 115–132.

treasurehouse," referring to its "unlimited land" and "inexhaustible resources." In short, it was the "key to the national economy."[107] In the newly popularized vision of Northeast China, the empire was represented in terms of a resource base necessary for Japan's economic security, or even its economic survival. For a people mired in depression, the image of an economic lifeline was a powerful symbol, speaking to their hopes of an elixir as well as their fears of a fall.

An illustrated map in *Kingu* showed Manchuria as a cornucopia of resources. From the ground emerged heaps of iron ore, glinting mountains of gold, and smoky piles of coal. The endless plain teemed with livestock: galloping horses, lowing cows, roaming camels, and grazing sheep. The rich earth yielded soybeans, cotton, wheat, sorghum, barley, and countless other grains. When Japan unlocked the treasurehouse, these articles optimistically predicted, abundance would wash over Japan's shores.[108]

An essay entitled "The Resources of the Manchurian-Mongolian Warehouse" explained to readers that Manchuria represented a "new paradise [*shintenchi*] for Japanese industrial expansion" and held endless tracts of "land waiting to be cultivated." Quantifying Manchuria's bounty, the article described a natural wonderland that was "the world's leading producer of soybeans," and generated every year "10 million koku of wheat," "36 million koku of sorghum," "2.7 million head of cattle," "3.5 million horses," "4.6 million sheep," and other vast amounts of produce and livestock. Manchuria was a great underground reservoir of "the builders of civilization—iron and coal"; a wealth of timber awaited the razing of Manchuria's "expansive virgin forests." Summing it up, the author declared, "Manchuria-Mongolia is a truly boundless natural field [*kōbakutaru tennen no yokuya*] now waiting to be exploited."[109]

The maps, the cartoons, and the statistics brought home to readers that Manchurian resources were the key to their livelihood and their prosperity. At the same time, they popularized an embryonic notion of imperial autarky. Stressing Japan's poverty of resources and dependency on imports from Europe and the United States, the media introduced fears of economic

107. "Manshū wa Nihon no seimeisen," *Ie no hikari* (January 1932), p. 166.
108. "Dare ni mo wakaru Manshū jijō omoshiroi ebanashi," *Kingu* (April 1932), pp. 33–56.
109. Usami Katsuo, "Manmō no zōsuru shigen," *Hanzai kagaku* (March 1932), pp. 42–45, 49. This article was part of the special issue on Manchuria entitled *Seimeisen Manmō: shigen to fūzoku* [The Manchurian-Mongolian Lifeline: Natural Resources and Popular Customs].

blackmail into the language of imperialism.[110] In such a world, control over Manchurian resources represented a safeguard of Japanese independence.

The "lifeline" was a metaphor with many resonances. It was appealing as a rallying cry in 1931 because it effectively tapped public memories of the imperial past and at the same time spoke to the economic insecurities of the present. Joining past to present, the construction of Manchuria as a lifeline wove new themes into the existing fabric of imperial ideology. Older notions of a blood debt and the sense that Japanese had paid dearly for their empire in the Northeast were joined to newer conceptions of the economic imperatives of empire for the survival of an industrial nation. The images of the lifeline thus bound Manchuria to Japan within an organic definition of empire: Japan could sooner lose Manchuria than a person could survive the evisceration of a vital organ. Manchuria was being culturally reshaped into the heart of the empire.

COWARDLY CHINESE AND WESTERN BULLIES

The redefinition of the ties that bound Japan to Manchuria was only one of the themes that emerged out of the imperial jingoism of the early thirties. The call to arms also invoked in Japan the idea of racial "others," the categories of people against which Japanese constructed their own national identity. From the Meiji period, Japanese had conceived of international relations within a hierarchy of race, culture, and power. Acutely sensitive to Japan's place in the system, they looked upon their burgeoning empire as a manifestation of superiority over other Asian countries and a project of "catch-up" with the West. As Japanese imperialism entered a new phase in the 1930s, the imperial discourse on self and other became more overtly chauvinistic, expressing race hates and race fears vociferously. While their troops were overrunning Manchuria, the Japanese told themselves: we fight because we are better than the Chinese and because we are not afraid of the West. In these fictionalized battlefield encounters, Japanese projected inferior qualities onto racial others to accommodate a more aggressive and confrontational style of empire building.

Resentment that Chinese dared to snatch from Japanese hands the precious Manchurian lifeline was quickly transformed into victory euphoria

---

110. "Dare ni mo wakaru Manshū jijō omoshiroi ebanashi," *Kingu* (April 1932), pp. 33–56; Manshū wa Nihon no seimeisen," *Ie no hikari* (January 1932), p. 166.

as news of the fall of city after city came in over the wires. These seemingly effortless victories unleashed a wave of self-congratulatory articles about the drubbing Japan was giving China and about the ineptitude of the Chinese soldiery. The point of reference for this outpouring of abuse was the first Sino-Japanese War. As Donald Keene has shown, the war of 1894–1895 marked a turning point in Japanese views of China. Throughout most of Japanese history, China was held as an object of emulation; Chinese civilization was revered as the wellspring of Japanese culture. And although cultural reverence for China was shaken by the specter of China's humiliation during the Opium War and new competing cultural models from the West, as late as 1890 the visit of the Chinese fleet to Japan inspired fear and respect. All this changed, however, in the course of a war that engendered for China a passionate contempt and hatred.[111]

The ferocity of the war hates did not completely erase the centuries-old tradition of venerating China, embedded in a variety of Sinified artistic, philosophical, scholarly, and other cultural practices. Japanese attitudes toward their erstwhile model of civilization remained filled with ambivalences and contradictions. The scorn showered on the Chinese national character in 1931–1933 represented a new stage in the project of reconciling these ambivalences: producers of Japanese culture seemed determined to wipe out lingering feelings of cultural debt with a concentrated burst of vituperation.

Popular representations of the occupation labored to cast the Chinese in the worst possible light. Incessant boasting about the "200,000 Chinese against 10,000 Japanese" took no notice of Jiang Jieshi's widely advertised nonresistance policy. Transforming this statistic into an index of China's martial deficiency, popular magazines gave rise to a sense that each Japanese soldier was worth twenty of the enemy's.[112] As major military targets such as Fengtian and Jilin were occupied virtually without bloodshed, magazines like *Shōnen kurabu* transformed voluntary withdrawal, voluntary disarmament and other forms of nonresistance into cowardly and disorganized retreats. Resurrecting Sino-Japanese War images of Chinese cowardice, stories about the Incident invariably showed Chinese soldiers in the act of "bolting," "escaping," "running off," "hiding," or, as the favorite phrase had it, "fleeing pell-mell like scattering spider babies" (*kumo no ko*

---

111. Keene, pp. 259–299.
112. Imamura Kakichi, "Manshū no Shinahei," *Shōnen kurabu* (February 1932), p. 75.

o chirasu yō ni nigemadotte imasu).[113] Hearsay from an unidentified "eye-witness" reported the witness's surprise to see "officers creep out from under the floors" when the Japanese Army "set fire to the Chinese barracks to smoke-out hiding enemy soldiers." Such stories provided the evidence that nurtured the legend of the Chinese coward.[114]

The notion that the enemy did not fight fair added another dimension to the picture. One article on "The Chinese Soldier in Manchuria" explained that "bandit soldiers" were "just like flies, no sooner do you drive them off but they come right back out again." This construction of the enemy as outlaw did not date to the Sino-Japanese War, but drew rather on vocabularies of repression in Korea. Just as military authorities in Korea blamed "thieves and criminals" for stirring up anti-Japanese riots in 1907–1909 and "lawless elements" for the March 1 uprising of 1919, in Manchuria in 1931, the Chinese enemy was likened to "a gang of thugs." Worse still, continued the article, were "soldiers out of uniform," "nuisances" who disguised themselves as ordinary Chinese and sneaked about causing trouble. "Because the Chinese Army loses if it fights in an open and sportsmanlike manner," concluded the author, "it uses this cowardly method to harass the Japanese Army."[115]

Ultimate proof for this judgment was provided, according to popular wisdom, by China's appeal for League of Nations mediation in the Sino-Japanese dispute. A cartoon entitled "The Contest between the Monkey and the Crab over Manchuria" rearranged events to show that China attempted diplomacy only after it lost the war. The cartoon used a popular Japanese folktale about a farsighted crab and a greedy monkey to tell the story of the Sino-Japanese dispute. The original tale begins with a trade; the monkey talks the crab into surrendering a rice cake in exchange for the monkey's persimmon seed. The monkey eats the cake; the crab plants the seed; and the real trouble begins when the crab's carefully tended garden bears a fine, fruit-laden persimmon tree. It is at this point that the cartoon picks up the story, picturing the monkey (China) attempting to steal the fruit of the persimmon tree (South Manchuria) belonging to the crab (Japan). After knocking down several business-suited crabs, the mon-

113. Suzuki Gyōsui, "Teki no shōkō ressha o kōgeki suru waga hikōki," *Shōnen kurabu* (February 1932), unpaginated.

114. Takinaka Takeo, "Shōnenkan no mite kita Manshū senchi no hanashi: tetchō kara," *Shōnen kurabu* (February 1932), p. 109.

115. Imamura Kakichi, "Manshū no Shinahei," *Shōnen kurabu* (February 1932), pp. 76–77.

key starts chopping at the tree with an ax. At this point the long-suffering crab "finally exploded" and "shoved the monkey's red behind." The next frame showed a tearful monkey complaining of his mistreatment to the "animal conference."[116] This was the sequence of events that structured the popular narrative of the Manchurian Incident. In the words of a schoolboy, the moral of the story was: "Japan is good at war. China didn't win so they brought the issue to the League of Nations."[117]

This unflattering portrait of the Chinese character was rounded off with an account of easy corruptability. Again, this image was not a Sino-Japanese War construction, but had emerged in the course of the teens and twenties and reflected as much on the Japanese inclination toward corruption as it did on the putative dishonesty of the Chinese. Bribing their way through a string of warlord allies, Japanese agents in China sold their patronage for the biggest concession and sold out their erstwhile clients when a better offer came along. Perceived, ironically, as an indication of Chinese venality, the actions of Japan's China hands became the basis for a reevaluation of the Chinese national character. The mercenary theme was given wide play in 1931–1933. An article on "ordinary crimes of bribery and betrayal" illustrated the character of the Chinese soldiers with a drawing of two Chinese warlords, one with a giant "money" magnet pulling the army off the other warlord's weaker magnet. The accompanying text read, "Civil wars occur often in China but it is rare for these conflicts to be resolved by a decisive military victory. Rather, victory is decided through one side purchasing the betrayal of the enemy with money. . . . According to Japan's code of war it is shameful to allow yourself to be bought off by the enemy," but Chinese change sides "the minute they are handed some money."[118]

Moreover, just as Sino-Japanese War writers had contrasted Japanese progress with Chinese backwardness, during the Manchurian Incident Japanese took pride in their own patriotism and derided the self-absorbed indifference of the Chinese masses to the fate of the nation. The popular travel writer Gotō Asatarō frequently commented on the absence of national feeling among the Chinese. "Chinese coolies," wrote Gotō in 1932, "are happy to build sandbags for the Japanese Army because they can get money for it. The next day they sit atop the sandbags, drinking sorghum

116. "Manshū no saru kani gassen," *Shōnen kurabu* (February 1932), p. 79.
117. Hirata Minoru, "Hayaku nakayoshi ni," in "Bokura wa me no mae ni Manshū jihen o mita," *Shōnen kurabu* (February 1932), p. 68.
118. Shimonaga Kenji, "Shinahei mandan," *Kōdan kurabu* (May 1933), p. 84.

wine and watching their own soldiers being destroyed by the Japanese, saying 'Wow! Look at that!' "[119]

Drawing on paternalistic vocabularies from the colonial experience in Korea and Taiwan, magazines and newspapers drew a careful distinction between the cowardly and corrupt Chinese soldiers and those they called the "good people" (*ryōmin*). As a schoolboy expressed it, "Japan isn't fighting all of China. Just these evil soldiers."[120] During the pacification of Korea in 1907, a general in charge observed that the upper classes were the real enemy because "the lower class has been oppressed by officials and the upper class and will come to see Japanese officials as protectors of the people."[121] Similar constructions of oppressive officials and underclasses in need of Japanese rescue emerged in descriptions of the Manchurian Incident. Some accounts showed *ryōmin* welcoming the Japanese Army as liberators, grateful to be rescued from the clutches of "marauding bandits" and "venal warlords."[122] In "Battlefield Story," one Japanese soldier declared that although he spared no mercy toward the "vile Chinese soldiers," the "pathetic sight of innocent *ryōmin* or a starving child" moved him to give up his own rations.[123]

In spite of such distinctions, as stories circulated by returning soldiers conveyed to the home population, actually telling enemy from friend in the war zone was a difficult problem. One magazine discussion among Manchurian Incident veterans devoted considerable time to this issue. "Even though we are told not to kill *ryōmin*, you just can't tell them apart," confessed one soldier. Another added, "You wouldn't believe the number of Chinese who are really soldiers. You can basically consider anyone on the street in Manchuria a plainclothes soldier. They say in Jinzhou alone there were more than 300,000 of them." Under these circumstances, the soldiers explained, they had developed a simple technique for telling friend from foe: "When you see someone coming you put your gun on them. If they cry or run away, they're *ryōmin*. If they put their hands up, you know they're soldiers in urban dress." But as one personal anecdote demonstrated, you could never be too careful.

119. Gotō Asatarō, "Shina no heitai," *Kingu* (April 1932), p. 53.
120. Hirata Minoru, "Hayaku nakayoshi ni," in "Bokura wa me no mae ni Manshū jihen o mita," *Shōnen kurabu* (February 1932), p. 68.
121. Conroy, p. 366.
122. Imamura Kakichi, "Manshū no Shina no heitai," *Shōnen kurabu* (February 1932), p. 76; Hirata Minoru, "Hayaku nakayoshi ni," in "Bokura wa me no mae ni Manshū jihen o mita," *Shōnen kurabu* (February 1932), p. 67.
123. Nohara Tatsuo, "Senjō no hanashi," *Kōdan kurabu* (May 1933), p. 77.

Everybody thinks that only men are plainclothes soldiers. But there are women, kids . . . all kinds. . . . Once a young woman of twenty-two or twenty-three came up to me looking very friendly. There in front of her house stood a crippled old grandmother, again smiling in a friendly way; naturally I thought they were *ryōmin*. But then I had a bad feeling about one of them and I shouted out a warning. The old woman ran hobbling off. I strip searched the girl . . . she couldn't understand me so I gestured with my hands. . . . Underneath her clothes she was wearing two pairs of panties. Hidden inside, sure enough, there was a pistol. I did not want to kill her but she tried to hit me with the gun and that was why she died. She said something abusive before she died. Afterwards I felt sorry for her but at the time if I did not handle it right I would have been done for. I was provoked.[124]

Such words revealed the intensity of the fear and mistrust that Japanese directed at Chinese in occupied Manchuria. The anecdote recounted the story of an atrocity: the murder of a Chinese woman. It communicated to the home front the bullying and terrorization of the civilian population that was standard operating procedure during the occupation; Chinese life was held cheap. The matter-of-fact retelling of this story in a popular magazine showed that to the soldiers, the editors, and probably the audience, the murder was unexceptional. In this way, the brutality of imperialism made its practitioners brutal, both the soldiers who actually wielded the bayonettes and the cultural consumers who took part vicariously in the violence.

In the context of the war fever, the assault on the Chinese national character helped reconstitute the idea of "China" in the Japanese popular imagination. As they had over and again in the past, Japanese reworked the symbolic meaning of their relationship with China, a country that had in elemental ways given shape to Japan's own culture. In the latest phase of this process, the new imperialism of the 1930s refigured the Chinese "other" in several ways. The new racial contempt for China produced by the war fever helped to cover over any lingering sense of cultural debt that stood in the way of empire building on the continent. Moreover, by fostering race hates, the new views of China portrayed in the mass media inured people to the brutality of imperial warfare and accustomed them to hearing about increasingly violent encounters with Chinese. Since the Meiji period, pejorative racial depictions of China had provided a foil against which Japan constructed its own national identity. To this end, the disparaging racial portrayals of the Chinese soldiers that circulated in the

124. "Jissen ni sanka shita gunjin no zadankai," *Ie no hikari* (July 1932), pp. 50–51.

early 1930s represented indirect encomiums to the Japanese character, helping reforge a national identity appropriate to a more aggressive military imperialism. Go-fast imperialism, in short, required high-growth racism.

This process also affected images of Japan's other salient "other": the West. Thus, while tall tales of Chinese cowardice circulated and Japanese congratulated themselves on their own legendary military prowess, strong criticism from the West invoked shrill denunciations of outside pressure and assertions of *seigi*, or the righteousness of Japan's actions. Like the outpouring of hostility toward China, the force of this reaction emerged out of a long history of ambivalence toward the West. From the time of Perry's gunboats, as the nation fought and maneuvered to gain entry to the Western club of great powers, Japanese had both feared and admired the West. The eighty-year-old relationship was productive of a host of insults and accolades, and Japanese were acutely sensitive to each. Popular representations of the League controversy of 1931–1933 drew on this catalog of grievances, even as the outrage masked long-standing desires for Western approval and fears of diplomatic isolation. But as Japan moved to occupy Manchuria in the teeth of Western opposition and isolate itself diplomatically by withdrawing from the League, this paradigmatic shift in a foreign policy posture led to a fundamental reconstruction of the idea of the West.

Scores of articles in such unlikely sources as the farm-household magazine *Ie no hikari* gave a blow-by-blow account of the Sino-Japanese controversy in the League. While glossaries of new terms explained the meaning of "extraterritoriality," the "nine-power treaty," and the "Kellogg-Briand Pact," and told readers that the popular nickname for the Lytton Commission Report was "lack of understanding" (*ninshiki busoku*), reports on the diplomacy of the Manchurian Incident exaggerated the extent of international hostility.[125] Long experience with racial discrimination by Europeans, Americans, and British colonists in Canada, Australia, and New Zealand led Japanese to interpret Western diplomatic opposition in racial terms. "From first to last the League did not flinch from its anti-Japanese stance," reported *Ie no hikari*. "This is the predictable outcome of the current control of the League by the white race."[126] Although the sense of

125. For glossaries see "Ie no hikari shinbun," *Ie no hikari* (August 1932–December 1932).
126. Itō Kameo, "Renmei o dattai shita Nihon wa dō naru ka?" *Ie no hikari* (April 1933), p. 174.

racial isolation was nothing new, its inflation into a seemingly insurmountable obstacle was. During the Paris Peace Conference that followed World War I, Japanese diplomats had pushed hard for the inclusion of a racial equality clause in the covenant of the League of Nations. Their defeat evoked much anger in the Japanese press, but bitter feelings were tempered by victory on the two key conference demands: recognition of Japanese acquisition of former German rights in China's Shandong province and the Pacific Islands.[127] In the past, the racial gulf between Japan and the Western powers was regarded as an aggravation to be countered by skilled diplomacy. In 1931, it became the explanation for the failure of Japanese diplomacy.

The specter of a solid phalanx of white powers united against Japan led to gloomy scenarios of economic blackmail and worse. An article analyzing the diplomacy of anti-Japanism explained that the League resolutions of the fall of 1931 "treated Japan just like a burglar . . . and isolated poor Japan from the world." Although sanctions had never been seriously discussed at the League, the mass media imagined a worst-case scenario and reported that council resolutions censuring Japan's actions threatened the country with an "international economic blockade if she did not withdraw her troops."[128] In such day-by-day micro-reporting of the events at the League, a new picture emerged of Japan's relationship with Western powers. Since its founding, Japanese had felt proud of their membership on the League Council: Japan was a player in the great power club. In the context of the early thirties, this image changed. Now the League became an institution controlled by white powers who bullied and isolated Japan.

The reformulation of Japan's relationship with the Western powers in a framework of confrontation and hostility was reinforced by a flood of images of an impending conflict between the United States and Japan. A boom in war-scare literature with titles like "If Japan Should Fight" were filled with portentous references to "war clouds in the far east" and warned that it was only a matter of time before the "unavoidable clash between America and Japan."[129] In 1932 alone, seventeen books and thirty-six articles in leading journals appeared on the subject of a coming war with the

127. Louise Young, "Power and Color: Japanese Imperialism in a White World Order," Master's thesis, Columbia University, May 1987, pp. 75–114.

128. "Seppaku shite kita Manshūkoku no shōnin," *Ie no hikari* (August 1932), p. 182.

129. Hirata Shinsaku, "Nihon moshi tatakawaba," *Shōnen kurabu* (May 1932), pp. 81–92; "Manshūkoku shōnin ni taisuru kakkoku no ikō," *Ie no hikari* (November 1932), p. 56.

United States. War scares had been a reoccurring feature of the Japanese-American relationship since before the turn of the century, and the twenties had witnessed two of them. Both the 1919–1921 and the 1924–1925 scares were set off by a combination of naval rivalries and tension over American legislation against Japanese immigration. Though the announcement in May 1932 that the U.S. Atlantic Scouting Fleet would be stationed in the Pacific helped trigger a new war scare,[130] the real source of Japanese-American antagonism in 1932 and 1933 was Japan's invasion of China. In the past, predictors of war had imagined such a conflict might arise from the struggle for naval supremacy in the Pacific or racial antagonisms. Now a battle for control over China was included in the hypothetical landscape of war.

While war-scare literature exaggerated the Western threat, at the same time popular magazines seemed to spare no effort to deflate public fears of reprisals. In this way the thinly veiled anxiety behind the anti-Western bluster manifested itself in a contradictory tendency first to inflate the extent of the threat and then to minimize its significance. Participants in an illustrated roundtable discussion on Japan's withdrawal from the League in the April 1933 issue of *Kingu* dismissed the war bogey. "I cannot imagine sanctions leading to war," an army officer was quoted as saying. Another participant pointed out that since the United States was dependent on Japanese imports it would never apply sanctions. A cartoon illustration of a worried Uncle Sam trying to work out the costs of sanctions on an abacus was accompanied by the explanation, "to lose Japan's silk imports would mean a tremendous shock to the American textile industry." Another drawing, noting that a loss of the Japanese cotton market would "cause a drastic fall in cotton prices and hurt farmers which make up half the American population," symbolically rendered American suffering in the image of a mother, breasts bursting, watching in agony as her infant suckled contentedly at his own bottle. The caption read: "The country that imposes economic sanctions is the one who suffers."[131] These cartoon images conveyed the message that Japan's trading relationship with the United States implied interdependency. If Japan, like the infant, was vulnerable, then so was the more powerful American economy.

Such discussions incorporated new ideas of autarky and economic warfare into imperial rhetoric. In the past, fears of diplomatic isolation had

130. Peattie, "Forecasting a Pacific War," pp. 116–117.
131. "Kokusai renmei dattai! Nihon wa dō naru zadankai," *Kingu* (April 1933), pp. 123–124, 127.

rested on the specter of military coercion. Now they included economic pressures as well. Turning rhetorical somersaults to quell fears of outside pressures, the same *Kingu* journalist argued that even if the United States applied sanctions, with a few substitutions and "national will," overcoming trade dependence on food, oil, cotton, and so forth "would not be difficult." This point was driven home with the cartoon of a farmer seated at a traditional Japanese meal of fish, soup, and rice, and turning his back on an elegant Western-style repast. "Self-sufficiency is plenty" announced the smiling farmer.[132]

A special feature asking "What will happen to Japan after it withdraws from the League?" answered comfortingly that "Japan will not suffer in the least. The one that will suffer is the League itself. . . . Japan's withdrawal will cause the League to lose power and influence." Moreover, Japan's isolation would not last, for "before long one of the great powers will adopt a policy of allying with Japan. The white powers in the League united against Japan, but they have divergent interests. Even the U.S. and England, which now seem to be fast friends, are in fact at great odds with one another. It is extremely disadvantageous for great powers with interests in the Far East to look on Japan as a permanent enemy. Therefore they will use every opportunity to draw closer to Japan in the future."[133] In fact, concluded one observer, the only effect of withdrawal would be to liberate Japan. In a cartoon illustrating this point, a Japanese samurai used his sword of "righteousness" (*seigi*) to sever the chain tying him to an iron ball representing the League of Nations.[134] Such language telegraphed a message of defiant isolationism, conveying to the Japanese public the virtues of Japan's withdrawal from the Western club of imperialists.

In mass-media coverage of the diplomacy of the Manchurian Incident, the alternating inflation and deflation of the Western threat was mirrored by a depiction of Japan's foreign policy posture as powerless and reactive, then defiant and strong. Illustrating the reactive face, one cartoon showed Japan and China on the League of Nations boat. As China labored to steer the boat toward the shoals of "withdrawal," Japan frantically tried to keep the boat away from the shoals.[135] At the same time, the recurrent image

132. Ibid., pp. 126–127.
133. Itō Kameo, "Renmei o dattai shita Nihon wa dō naru ka?" *Ie no hikari* (April 1933), pp. 174–175.
134. Haniguchi Ken, "Hitokawa muita renmei kaigi," *Kōdan kurabu* (April 1933), p. 106.
135. Matsunami Mōji, "Hijōji Nippon no shōtai o egaku," *Ie no hikari* (December 1931), p. 33.

of a solitary Japanese soldier standing guard, his bayonet held aloft, expressed a mood of grim bravado. Accompanying one such illustration, the *Kingu* poem "Attack Us Head On" captured the sense of defiant isolationism with which popular writers greeted the news that the League had voted against Japan in February 1933:

> We stood against forty-two
> And were defeated.
> What is defeat, we are just!
> That is right, that is right,
> We are just.
> Enemy, if you come, attack us head on.
> Attack us head on![136]

In illustrations and songs like these, the mass media conveyed a powerful set of messages to their audience concerning the current foreign crisis. Sanctioning Japan's new diplomatic isolation, the mass media depicted the nation driven by forces beyond its control: Japan was compelled to take a stand—and would stand alone. At a stage in which diplomatic repercussions of the invasion of China remained at the level of moral censure, the mass media told a story of Japan single-handedly taking on a mighty host of Western armies. The choice of military metaphors to represent a diplomatic conflict was a highly significant element in the reimagining of the West. As their government was shifting gears into go-fast imperialism, Japanese began to prepare themselves for the possibility of war.

Neither anti-Western bombast nor derision of the Chinese was new to Japanese imperial rhetoric, but they came together with an explosive force and all-inclusiveness in the new xenophobia of the early thirties. It is important to add, however, that the continued popularity of such Western cultural imports as movies, music, and literature placed certain limits on the usefulness of anti-foreignism as a strategy for mobilization. Moreover, Japanese imported not just finished products, but the cultural forms that produced them. Adapting Western forms, they incorporated them into native practices. Like the cultural borrowing from China that had occurred over the centuries, Western influence could not be expunged by a burst of hostility. For a heavily Sinified and Westernized Japan, criticism of the Chinese and Western other quickly ran into criticism of the self. In the Western case particularly, contradictions between the new images of racial confrontation and the continued embrace of Western culture led to a series of private and government initiatives to eliminate Western cultural influ-

---

136. Matsumura Matahito, "Donto koi," *Kingu* (September 1933), pp. 58–59.

ence, culminating in the prohibitions on certain styles of dress and loan words during the Pacific War.[137] And, like the outbreak of war itself, these campaigns against Western decadence were anticipated in the reimagining of the West that took place during the Manchurian Incident war fever.

THE HEROIC SELF

While refiguring racial others to accommodate the new realities of empire, mass-media images of the Japanese self redefined the meaning of patriotism to fit the new era. This was accomplished through the outpouring of Manchurian Incident *bidan,* or "tales of heroism," in the press, popular magazines, and on stage and screen. A traditional form of moral story-telling that celebrated doing good deeds, *bidan* rendered the Incident in the light of personal experiences. These fictionalized experiences of imperial warfare were shaped, like the real ones, by gender. Hence one genre of *bidan* celebrated male heroism on the battlefield, while another eulogized female sacrifice on the home front. Together, these war-fever *bidan* reformulated the idea of patriotism in two striking ways.

The first of these concerned the extraordinary preoccupation of battlefield *bidan* with death. Death provided the dramatic center of the stories, and patriotic heroism was defined by martyrdom through death. In pursuit of the martyred hero, *bidan* exaggerated incidents of battlefield death in the Manchurian Incident. Although casualties during some engagements were high, there seemed to be many more bodies littering the fictionalized field of battle. The 2,530 total Japanese military deaths in the Manchurian Incident (compiled between September 1931 and July 1933) constituted a tiny fraction of those killed in the earlier wars. It certainly did not prepare people for the slaughter that was to come: 185,647 were killed in the China War between 1937 and 1941.[138] The comparatively low death tolls of the Manchurian Incident permitted the storytellers in the mass media to glibly kill off their heroes in large numbers. Much like hyperbolic accounts of the Western pressures on Japan, these depictions of untold carnage in battlefield *bidan* unwittingly prepared the nation for the days to come.

The second element in the reformulation of patriotism related to the

---

137. Ben-Ami Shillony, *Politics and Culture in Wartime Japan* (Oxford: Clarendon Press, 1981), pp. 141–151; Thomas R. H. Havens, *Valley of Darkness: The Japanese People and World War Two* (New York: Norton, 1978).

138. Iwanami shoten henshūbu, *Kindai Nihon sōgō nenpyō* (Iwanami shoten, 1968), p. 296; John W. Dower, *War without Mercy: Race and Power in the Pacific War* (New York: Pantheon Books, 1986), p. 297.

idea of sacrifice for the nation. In 1931, vocabularies of sacrifice could draw on any number of venerable traditions. The virtues of self-sacrifice for family and village were stock in trade for rural agrarian improvers; effacement of individual desires for the collective good constituted a pillar of Confucian morality. *Bushidō* (the way of the warrior) exhorted sacrifice on the battlefield for men, and the official prescription of female virtue, *ryōsai kenbō* (good wife, wise mother), urged sacrifice to the family for women. But this impressive tradition was matched by the equally venerable idea of individualistic competition, emerging from Meiji dreams of rising in the world and Darwinian metaphors of a struggle for survival.[139] In the 1920s, both the growth of consumer culture and the increasingly fierce competition for middle-class educational and employment opportunities favored the latter doctrine of self-improvement and personal success. As factory workers were demanding better pay and tenant farmers lower rents, the calls to obey social superiors and sacrifice for the collective good fell increasingly on deaf ears.

The Manchurian Incident *bidan* rescued this embattled tradition of sacrifice. Relating experiences of both soldier and housewife, *bidan* told Japanese that uncommon valor on the battlefield and extraordinary sacrifice on the home front were the highest expression of national virtue. Ironically, such appeals to sacrifice were framed, not in homilies about Japanese groupism, but in the language of personal glory and individualistic competition. Since it is frequently argued that group psychology and ideologies of collectivism played a key role in the mobilization of support for war and fascism in the 1930s,[140] it is worth underscoring the individualistic and competitive dimensions of imperial mythology in the early 1930s.

Among the crowd of martyred manly heroes that jostled for attention was Regimental Commander Koga Dentarō. As part of the "mopping-up" operations following the occupation of Jinzhou in early January 1932, Koga's cavalry regiment had occupied the walled city of Jinxi, southwest of Jinzhou. After a large "bandit" force attempted to retake Jinxi, Koga determined, against orders, that he would mount his own attack. Impatient for action, he was unwilling to stand guard over the city and wait passively for reinforcements. Leaving a platoon of some 21 men at Jinxi to guard

139. On ideologies of striving and success, see Gluck, *Japan's Modern Myths,* pp. 204–212.

140. The collectivist argument is adumbrated in R. P. Dore and Tsutomu Ōuchi, "Rural Origins of Japanese Fascism," in James William Morley, ed., *Dilemmas of Growth in Prewar Japan* (Princeton: Princeton University Press, 1971), pp. 181–209.

the flag, Koga took the remaining 130 men with him to attack a force of over 1,000. Although Koga's forces soon found themselves in desperate difficulties, upon hearing that the flag-guarding platoon was in danger, Koga split his forces again, taking half to rescue the flag and leaving the rest to "hold off the enemy." In the end this reckless course of action accomplished nothing and cost the regiment virtually all its officers, leaving Koga and 11 others dead and 19 wounded.[141] Yet Koga became one of the most celebrated heroes of the Manchurian Incident. His story was the subject of a *naniwabushi* chant on the Polidor label, of Tōkatsu and Shinkō movies, and was staged by the famous Tokyo Kokuza Theater.[142] Told and retold countless times in every popular entertainment medium, the Koga *bidan* glorified his actions as those of the archetype of military heroism.

In an illustrated version published in the boy's magazine *Shōnen kurabu*, "Ah! The Imperial Flag Is in Danger," the suicidal attack on the "bandit army" (which had multiplied into a force of 5,000) was depicted as an act of courage and daring. Without mentioning Koga's insubordination, *Shōnen kurabu* narrated the *bidan* as a series of glorious last stands at Jinxi. At each stage another band of Japanese soldiers—cut off from their comrades and hopelessly outnumbered—fought to the death to protect the flag. While the story exalted sacrifice for the nation (in the symbol of the flag), it did so by celebrating individual acts of heroism. In sequence, each of these last stands grew more dramatic and heroic. They were, in effect, a kind of competition: the reader moved up the tournament ranks, finally witnessing Koga's triumph—the most glorious act of heroism.[143]

This spirit of competitive sacrifice set Manchurian Incident *bidan* apart from their predecessors. The principal heroes to emerge from the Sino-Japanese War were Harada Jūkichi, who scaled the Gembu gate and let the Japanese forces into Pyongyang; Kiguchi Kōhei, the bugler who blew the forward charge with his dying breath; and the unknown sailor who extinguished a shipboard fire and died asking whether the enemy ship was yet sunk. These stories celebrated the gallantry of the conscript soldiers who composed the new Japanese army and who became the heroes of the Japanese masses.[144] Unlike the Koga story, which eulogized a series of futile

---

141. Eguchi, *Jūgonen sensō no kaimaku*, p. 135.
142. Songs: *Rekōdo* (May 1932), p. 82; plays: *Eiga to engei* (March 1932), p. 26; movies: "Sensō eiga," *Eiga to engei* (April 1932) and *Eiga to engei* (May 1932), p. 16.
143. Kume Gen'ichi, "Sōretsu senwa: Aa gunki ayaushi," *Shōnen kurabu* (March 1933), pp. 144–155.
144. Keene, pp. 274–281.

acts of bravado, the Sino-Japanese War stories depicted sacrifice that positively affected the outcome of the war. Thus, Harada Jūkichi became a hero when he helped the army occupy Pyongyang, while Koga sacrificed himself and his men trying to retake a flag (and a city) that his own reckless impatience had placed in danger.

Although the heroes of the Russo-Japanese War—Nogi Maresuke, Tōgō Heihachirō, Tachibana Shūta, Hirose Takeo, and the emperor himself—were, like Koga, all officers, their stories celebrated different qualities of great leadership. Hirose Takeo, for example, was heroized for his paternal benevolence when he was killed searching for a missing sailor under his command. Similarly, the Meiji Emperor was honored for expressing his concern for his troops and his subjects in an alleged 7,526 poems written during the war. In the stories that circulated about Hirose and the emperor, Russo-Japanese War heroes were portrayed as paragons of solicitude.[145] In contrast, Koga's cavalier attitude toward his soldiers' lives suggested that good leadership had nothing to do with compassion but required, conversely, ruthlessness and a steely indifference to battlefield losses. In the daring, even foolhardy Koga great leadership was defined as the willingness to take risks; concern for his troops would have interfered with this quality of leadership. Heroes of the Russo-Japanese War were also risk-takers, but combined daring with tactical expertise. Thus, Tōgō Heihachirō and Nogi Maresuke were famed for being brilliant officers who commanded key campaigns of the war—Tōgō defeating the Russian Baltic fleet and Nogi leading the siege of Lüshun. In contrast, Koga managed to bungle an assignment of guard duty in a minor operation. But this did not matter, because Manchurian Incident *bidan* redefined the meaning of heroic leadership, celebrating daring instead of skill, and bravery rather than wisdom.

Both the Sino-Japanese War stories, which focused on the heroism of the fighting man, and those of the Russo-Japanese War, which highlighted the heroism of leadership, depicted heroic sacrifice as part of a collective effort. Whether the story concentrated on the officer and his men or the soldier and his unit, the context of action was the army group that drove purposively and inexorably toward victory. In the Sino- and Russo-Japanese war *bidan* the image of the Japanese group was harmonious, a fighting organism united in mind, spirit, and purpose. In contrast, the

145. Nakauchi Toshio, *Gunkoku bidan to kyōkasho* (Iwanami shoten, 1988), pp. 3–6, 42–50, 100–105. On the emperor, see Gluck, *Japan's Modern Myths,* pp. 88–90.

narrative in the Koga *bidan* split the group into pieces, atomizing acts of heroism into a series of independent, uncoordinated operations. Each man fought to be the one who saved the flag; each strove for a more sensational act of sacrifice than the last; each sought a more heroic death. In the process the meaning of patriotism shifted from sacrifice for the group to the competitive strength of the individual.

Like other battlefield *bidan,* Koga's story conveyed the message that sacrifice through death was the only path to virtue. Unlike the earlier war heroes, many of whom survived their campaigns, no hero of the Manchurian Incident outlived his moment of glory. Rendered with images like "crimson-stained snow" and the "glittering face of death," or by the traditional metaphor of a "fallen cherry blossom," death was transformed in these *bidan* into a symbol of poignant beauty.[146] The *Shōnen kurabu* version of the Koga *bidan* departed from this convention and described Koga's last moments under the caption "The Command That Was Vomited with Blood." This decidedly unbeauteous yet arresting image of Koga's dying visage left the reader with a brutally powerful visual impression. In Koga's story, man was transformed to hero at the moment of death. It was in death that Koga earned his posthumous title, *idaina hitobashira* (a great human sacrifice). Sacrifice in the line of duty provided both the dramatic climax to and the aesthetic heart of Koga's story. Koga's last moments saw him hit and fallen, only to raise himself on his sword point to issue the forward order.

> The Commander looked so bad that the others stood blankly for a moment. Then suddenly, he was lurching up from between the bodies and they could hear his voice crying out mightily:
> "Save the flag! Forward, forward!"
> As he cried out blood spurted from his mouth and he slid to the ground. But again he pulled himself up on his sword point and forced out a raspy cry,
> "Forward, forward . . ."
> He continued thus three or four times more, falling and rising, rising and falling, till finally, face down on the grass, he moved no more.[147]

In *bidan,* the moment of death was also the moment of victory. In Koga's story, this occurred when the flag was saved by one of his lieuten-

---

146. For other examples of *bidan,* see "Manshūgun nikudan jikki," *Kingu* (March 1932), pp. 113–135; and Takeda Toshihiko, "Nishi jihen no giseisha: Nishio shōi no shi," *Kōdan kurabu* (April 1933), pp. 262–287.

147. Kume Gen'ichi, "Sōretsu senwa: Aa gunki ayaushi," *Shōnen kurabu* (March 1933), pp. 152–154.

ants. "Face dripping with enemy blood like some hideous red devil," Lieutenant Oyadomari demanded, "the flag, how is the flag?" Upon learning it was safe with the platoon, Oyadomari gasped out his final words: "Safe? It's safe? . . . I . . . I . . . if the flag is safe then I can die." While the others looked on, tears "cascading down their cheeks," Oyadomari toppled over, secure in Japan's victory.[148] In this equation of victory with death, battlefield *bidan* yet again interwove the themes of personal glory, death, and patriotism. Thus, in saving the flag for his country, Oyadomari died even as he achieved his moment of personal glory. Strikingly absent from depictions of the heroism of men like Oyadomari were acts of bravery to save the lives of comrades, protect the platoon, or otherwise sacrifice the individual for the good of the group. Rather than promoting ideologies of groupism, these stories did precisely the opposite; the paeans to individual valor and the competition for heroic martyrdom called for patriotic sacrifice through appeals to personal glory and in ideological language of individualistic success.

While battlefield *bidan* showed manly young soldiers demonstrating their virtue by dying at the front, a separate genre of home-front *bidan* glorified the heroism of their female counterparts. National and local newspapers stirred up a *bidan* boom with a flurry of articles on acts of great personal sacrifice to support fundraising campaigns and other aspects of the war effort. In a typical example, an Osaka paper published the heartrending story of the donation made by a female textile worker. Although supporting two children and an aging parent on her paltry earnings, she managed to scrape together three yen (nearly a week's wage) to send to the front.[149] The point was not that the money helped anyone. The end result of such gestures was usually left vague, for the moral of the story was to convey the nobility of the sacrificial gesture itself.

Like the battlefield *bidan,* inspirational tales of home-front virtue made the degree of loss into a measure of national virtue. The greater the sacrifice, the greater the virtue. The story of an impoverished tenant farmer's wife published in *Fujin kurabu* illustrated one of the myriad female acts of virtue.[150] And like the Koga *bidan,* her story conveyed the nobility of sacrifice through the language of individualistic competition. The account began as an old woman arrived at a local police station with what was at

---

148. Ibid., p. 155.
149. Eguchi, *Jūgonen sensō no kaimaku,* p. 113.
150. Hara Takaki, "Manshū jihen no ura ni hisomu namida no junjō jitsuwa," *Fujin kurabu* (March 1932), pp. 173–175.

the time the large sum of twenty yen. Donating the money to the war effort, she refused to give her name or have her generosity acknowledged in any way; but one of the policemen discovered who she was and learned of her tragic circumstances. Like the Osaka textile worker and thousands of other home-front heroines whose deeds were celebrated in newspapers and magazines, the story of the sacrificial act was framed in discovery. Though she had modestly sought anonymity, the reward for the farm wife's action was its revelation and that moment of fame granted by the spotlight of the mass media. In this way patriotic sacrifice was represented as a path to fame and glory, the route to patriotic stardom.

One of the main points of the story of our heroine was that throughout her long and sad life, she had staunchly refused to be a burden to others. When her second son was drafted and her husband and eldest son debilitated by illness, she was left with a fifteen-year-old daughter and a seventy-four-year-old mother to tend the farm. Still, she declined to accept any charity from the village authorities, saying, "Thank you for your kindness but it is an honor for my son to discharge his patriotic duty. No matter how difficult things are for us I cannot accept any money." This refusal to accept community support flew in the face of the homilies of mutual aid delivered by agrarian-minded bureaucrats and ideologues for community voluntary organizations. No helpful neighbors leap in to help with planting or harvesting. Instead of surrendering to the harmonious group spirit of the village community, our heroine labors valiantly alone, solitary martyr to the national cause. Such narratives were entirely self-referential, constructing patriotic sacrifice as an expression of individual will rather than group spirit.

Moreover, in a reversal of the logic of the family-state, the nation was not represented as a metaphorical family, but rather the family as a metaphorical nation. Service to the nation was carried out within the family unit. In the farm wife's story, acts of patriotic sacrifice are inspired by the example of other family members. When her second son returned from a tour of duty in Manchuria on the eve of the Manchurian Incident, he too fell ill. Learning from his sickbed of the outbreak of war between Japan and China, he fretted that he could not be there "fighting the bandits and giving his life for his country." Hearing this noble sentiment, his mother was moved to tears and could not rest until she made a gesture for the soldiers in Manchuria. Thereupon she took the entire family savings of twenty yen and donated it to the war cause. Significantly, such gestures did not aim to help one another but rather to make a grander display of patriotism—a game of suicidal one-upmanship in which each family member strove to outdo the other, competing for the greatest gesture of sacrifice.

By exaggerating personal demonstrations of patriotic sacrifice, such *bidan* promoted a peculiar vision of home-front support. Instead of exhorting people to work harder in order to increase domestic production in a time of crisis, the farm wife's story depicts the gradual evisceration of the household, leaving it a crippled, unproductive shell. After she disposed of the family savings, the farm wife's second son's condition worsened. On his death bed he took his sister's hand and apologized for being a worry to his family. "If only I could have died in Manchuria like my friend Okamoto," he lamented. Conveying his dying wish that his sister "do something for the nation" in his place, the boy's final words were: "Goodbye Manchurian Garrison Army banzai!" In keeping with her brother's deathbed wish, the sister volunteered her services as a nurse at the front. This left the farm wife and her aged mother alone to support two invalids. The story concluded with the farm wife making her daily pilgrimage to the local shrine to pray for the safety of the imperial army. If every Japanese farm family followed this prescription for patriotic action, the nation would starve. Rather than promoting some vision of the nobility of tilling the soil and keeping the home hearths burning, this story is about a farm wife who allows her family farm to run to ruin while she and her family, one by one, succumb to the allure of Manchuria. All the glory is vested in Manchuria, patriotism projected onto the empire. At the end of the story, the farm wife ritually renews her gesture of patriotic sacrifice through prayer, still lost in a Manchurian dream.

Spinning tall tales of self-sacrifice, such home-front *bidan* created the domestic female version of battlefield heroes like Major Koga. In the contest to see who was the biggest martyr, pathos outshone pathos, tragedy overshadowed tragedy, and sacrifice outdid sacrifice. In this way the Manchurian Incident *bidan* boom promoted a new competitive-style patriotism that revived the virtue of sacrifice by making it a route to personal glory and success.

The *bidan* boom was but one symptom of the imperial jingoism that helped transform both the form and content of Japanese popular culture in the early 1930s. Beginning with the news media, a commercialized mass-culture industry took the opportunity—as it had in the past—to capitalize on the war in the interests of increasing circulation. In the process of using the war fever to expand the market for cultural manufactures, the mass media grew more technologically sophisticated and achieved a more thorough penetration of the national market. Such developments in the technologies and institutions of the culture industry helped contribute to the difference in scale between the war fever of 1931–1933 and the Sino-Japanese and Russo-Japanese war fevers of an earlier age. In the intervening years between Japan's initial wars of empire and the Manchurian campaigns, the media had become progressively more mass. With mechanization and the shift toward mass production in newspaper, book, and magazine publishing, as well as the emergence of new media like radio, cinema, and records, the vehicles of imperial propaganda became infinitely more sophisticated. In this sense, massification gave to the media the power to constitute, to unify, and to mold a national opinion on imperialism.

The military imperialism initiated on September 18, 1931, spawned a new set of images of the Manchurian empire, and in the process helped transform the content of Japanese popular culture. Part reinvention and part new construction, the popular catchphrases on why Japan must fight became part of the active vocabulary of empire building. Although the ceasefire of May 1933 was followed by anti-insurgency military operations in Manchuria, mass media production of imperial propaganda never again achieved the intensity of those early years. This high-growth phase of cultural production created the first building blocks of the cultural edifice of Manchukuo, in which people at home learned to live and breathe their new empire. Appealing to people through narratives of familial obligation, xenophobia, consumerism, and competition, the first imagining of Manchukuo helped reshape the cultural practices of Taishō democracy into Shōwa militarism.

As this chapter has shown, the mass media played a central role in stimulating the outbreak of the Manchurian Incident war fever and mobilizing support for the new military imperialism. But powerful as it was, the media did not single-handedly bring about the shift away from a foreign policy supporting cooperation with Europe and the United States, disarmament, and economic imperialism in China. Reinforcing the transforming impact of the mass media were the activities of a host of other agents of empire, for military expansion in Manchuria also suited the interests of aspirants to political power and social status. It was their activities, which are the subject of the next chapter, that made Manchukuo into the policy of the government and the empire of the masses.

4 Go-Fast Imperialism
Elite Politics and Mass Mobilization

The Manchurian Incident represented an aggressive army bid for political power at home as well as in the empire. In the initial phases of the military action, the Kwantung Army deliberately subverted the authority of the central government in Tokyo and expanded the theater of war on its own initiative. After militarily occupying Manchuria, the Kwantung Army set itself up as the new political authority in the region, ruling through the puppet government of Manchukuo. Kwantung Army actions on the continent inaugurated a phase of rapid military expansionism that John Dower aptly named "go-fast imperialism."[1] At the same time, the Manchurian Incident set in motion a political chain reaction at home, culminating in the rise of army influence over the institutions of government and the formation of a popular consensus behind a paradigmatic shift in Japanese foreign policy. Together these institutional and policy changes defined the political dimension of go-fast imperialism.

The question remains why the Manchurian Incident conspiracy of 1931 succeeded, when similar plans for a Manchurian takeover had failed in 1928. Why did 1931 become a turning point for empire? Examining the see p. 43, 180 thinking of government leaders, historians of Japanese foreign policy have identified a quest for autonomy and economic security in the key policy decisions of this period.[2] Although this is an accurate representation of one aspect of bureaucratic thinking, it captures only part of the picture. To understand fully the reasons for the sea change of the early thirties, we need to consider, first, why this course of action was chosen over other

1. Dower, *Empire and Aftermath*, p. 85.
2. This is the central argument of Crowley, *Japan's Quest for Autonomy*, as well as Barnhart.

what's the point of "go-fast"? and g-far?

115

alternatives. In part, the answer to this question has to do with a growing consensus among government officials that continental expansion was the only means to secure Japan's future. But it also relates to the army's quest for political autonomy at home and how officers achieved victory in the power struggle over the factionalized bureaucracy of Japan's central government. Second, we must look beyond the realm of bureaucratic politics to see how the decision to embark on the new military imperialism played out on social and political battlefields far from the centers of government power. In doing so we find that it was the surge of popular support for the Kwantung Army's takeover of Manchuria—more than any other single factor—that guaranteed the success of the army's bid for power.

This popular endorsement did not appear spontaneously. Far from it: many Japanese labored long and hard to mobilize their countrymen and women behind the new empire. Aiding them in this endeavor was the existence, by 1931, of a variety of social and political institutions that organized people into collectivities: political parties, labor unions, voluntary associations. As in Europe, the democratization of politics and the growth of mass organizations in the late nineteenth and early twentieth centuries changed the process of imperial policy making.[3] Using these new vehicles of mass mobilization, government officials tried to enlist popular political forces in support of their course of action. At the same time, political organizations used the imperialist cause to appeal to a mass following. When imperialism became a tool of domestic politics for both government officials and private citizens, it spelled the end of a government monopoly over imperial policy; henceforth policy decisions would be made collectively. For Japan, this dynamic shaped the course of empire building in Manchukuo.

Mobilization for empire linked the high politics of state to an emerging mass public. Since the establishment of the institutions of constitutional government in 1889, relations between state and society had evolved within the framework of this political system. From the beginning, the constitutional framework placed important limits on the state-society relationship: only certain segments of society had access to and were represented by the state. These groups comprised the "public opinion" to which government policy was responsive. By 1931, however, four decades

---

3. Although it does not examine explicitly the relationship to the policy-making process, an overview of the democratization of political institutions and the emergence of mass social organizations in Europe is found in Eric Hobsbawm, *The Age of Empire: 1875–1914* (New York: Vintage Books, 1989), esp. pp. 56–141.

of political development had expanded the definition of public opinion to include not only the electorate (grown from a limited 1 percent of the population in the 1890s to universal male suffrage in 1925), but also the organs of the mass media and elite interest groups of businessmen, landlords, intellectuals, and military officers. It began in addition to include groups outside the elite, such as tenants and workers, as well as the unenfranchised—women and youth—who joined what was called the national unity on the Manchurian question. In the course of a shift to the new military imperialism in Northeast China, initiatives from inside and outside the government redefined the meaning of public opinion. While the government tried using new propaganda techniques to mobilize and unify public opinion on the Manchurian Incident, private organizations representing the interests of workers and women labored to ensure their inclusion in the "public" that was being unified. These efforts of the government and the people to reach out to one another marked a new stage in the evolution of the political relationship between state and society. Empire was an integral part of this transformation.

THE POLITICAL BATTLEFIELD

In the days and weeks following the outbreak of fighting on September 18, the cabinet became the center of a political struggle over Manchurian policy. Responding to the succession of faits accomplis by the Kwantung Army, the central government split into two opposing factions, one pushing for and the other trying to hold back military expansion. This policy dispute represented more than a difference of opinion over tactics and diplomatic priorities. Over the course of the 1920s, debates over how to best handle the "China problem" and the "Manchuria problem" had become a field on which to wage battle against political foes, whether in a rival ministry or party. At stake was not just control over policy (how Japan was to protect and expand its investments in Manchuria, Shandong, and Shanghai, its share of the China market, and its military position in the Northeast), but control over the pinnacle of institutional power in the Japanese government, the cabinet.

The army's victory on the high political battlefield made the Manchurian Incident a turning point for domestic politics. The rise of army power in the 1930s in some ways represented a return to the position of political influence which the service institutions had enjoyed in the Meiji but lost over the course of the Taishō. The army managed to reestablish its political fortunes by playing the politics of compromise, the same game that the parties had used to achieve their own rise to power in the early decades of the century. Army spokesmen forged alliances with other key players in the political arena, players who then supported the army's direction of policy and rise to power. While historians have made the point before, it bears reiteration here: the militarization of the state in the 1930s was not achieved through a rupture in the institutions of government.[4] In this sense the new military imperialism represented the outcome of Japan's constitutional decision-making process and the majority opinion of Japan's political elite.

The public nature and politicization of foreign policy were established political traditions by 1931. Since the arrival of American gunboats in 1853, government mismanagement of foreign affairs served as a rallying point for opposition movements. A strategy that proved effective in the overthrow of the shogunate in 1868 was used over the following decades against the new government. Factions within the Meiji oligarchy and groups excluded from the new government jockeyed for power by attacking the government for inaction on the "Korean problem" or failing to secure revision of the unequal treaties. Of course, public debate over foreign policy was not driven solely by political ambition. Both opportunists and true believers joined in the clamor to invade Korea in 1873 and the angry denunciations of treaty negotiations in the late 1880s.[5] Indeed, the presence of both politicians with other ends in view and extremists willing to kill and die for their cause made public foreign-policy debates potent and enduring forces in Japanese politics.

From the buildup and aftermath of the Sino- and Russo-Japanese wars in the 1890s and 1900s, to the debates over continental policy in the teens and twenties, the politics of imperialism evolved to accommodate new practices of mass politics. In the process, rallies, riots, and other political actions of the crowd added weight to one side or the other in the now familiar tug of war between "go-fast" and "go-slow" imperialism.[6] In the early days of

---

4. This argument is made by Gordon M. Berger, "Politics and Mobilization in Japan, 1931–45," in Peter Duus, ed., *The Twentieth Century*, vol. 6 of *The Cambridge History of Japan* (Cambridge: Cambridge University Press, 1988), pp. 99–153. For another articulation, see Shillony, pp. 1–43.

5. On Korea see Conroy, pp. 17–77, and the more recent treatment by Duus, *Abacus and Sword*, pp. 29–43. On treaty revision see Gluck, *Japan's Modern Myths*, pp. 114–115, and Kenneth B. Pyle, *The New Generation in Meiji Japan: Problems of Cultural Identity, 1885–1895* (Stanford: Stanford University Press, 1969), pp. 108–117.

6. On the politics of the crowd, see Lewis, pp. xvii–xxiv, 1–33, and Andrew

the Meiji, the lines were drawn between those advocating immediate conquest of Korea and those insisting that action be postponed until the country had developed greater economic and military strength. By the late 1920s, the preeminent political issue was China. Those in favor of sending military garrisons to protect Japan's continental interests against the Chinese Nationalists occupied the "go-fast" position, while those counseling reliance on diplomacy and acting in concert with Western allies occupied the "go-slow" position.

In the political struggle that followed from Kwantung Army actions in the fall of 1931, the pattern quickly reestablished itself. Out of the 1920s' legacy, two axes of conflict emerged. The most visible confrontation was between the two major political parties, the Minseitō and the Seiyūkai. During the previous decade, these two parties fought for control over the cabinet, waging political battle by attacking each other's foreign policy. In the process, both parties acquired signature foreign policies. These were dubbed "Shidehara diplomacy" and "Tanaka diplomacy," after the foreign ministers Shidehara Kijūrō, who ran the Foreign Ministry in the Minseitō (and its predecessor, the Kenseikai) cabinet, and Tanaka Giichi, who was foreign minister in the Seiyūkai cabinet. When the Minseitō/Kenseikai was in power, the Seiyūkai opposition attacked Shidehara's "weak-kneed" diplomacy, blaming Chinese boycotts of Japanese goods on the government's conciliatory attitude toward Chinese authorities, who Japanese leaders believed were behind the boycott movement. What the situation called for, in the Seiyūkai's opinion, was a show of force to demonstrate Japan's determination and convince these leaders to cooperate. The Seiyūkai opposition also denounced Shidehara's spineless attitude toward the West, accused Minseitō cabinets of compromising national defense through excessive cuts in military spending, and charged the Minseitō with being in the pocket of big business. When the Seiyūkai cabinet was in power, the tables were turned. The Minseitō opposition blamed Tanaka's heavy-handed use of force for causing the Chinese boycotts; what the situation demanded, Minseitō politicians felt, was a show of understanding plus economic incentives to bring the Chinese leaders in line. The Minseitō upbraided Tanaka for compromising national security by antagonizing the Western powers, blamed the nation's financial ills on high military budgets, and accused the party of excessive military influence.[7]

Gordon, *Labor and Imperial Democracy in Prewar Japan* (Berkeley: University of California Press, 1991), pp. 26–62.

   7. On political parties in the 1920s, see Awaya Kentarō, *Shōwa no seitō: hōkai*

In the fall of 1931, the Minseitō held the cabinet under the premiership of Wakatsuki Reijirō, and with Shidehara, of course, as foreign minister. The Kwantung Army's military action was in direct conflict with Minseitō policy. The required military expenditures undermined plans for financial retrenchment, and the use of force upset Shidehara's economic diplomacy in China. Moreover, the occupation of Manchuria violated the Washington Conference agreement to "respect the territorial integrity of China," evoking hostile reactions from the United States and Britain. In the events at Fengtian, the Kwantung Army took the government by surprise. Shidehara later claimed that he first learned of these events from the morning papers on September 19.[8] While this is scarcely credible, the cabinet certainly did hear about it after the fact. It took almost a week of frantic discussions before the cabinet could produce a course of action that satisfied all the interested parties. The resulting nonexpansion policy (*fukakudai hōshin*), embodied in the September 24 "First Official Statement," clearly set forth government opposition to a full-scale occupation of Manchuria and to any further military action.[9] Over the following weeks and months, the Minseitō cabinet struggled both to maintain this policy and to fend off a Seiyūkai campaign to bring down the cabinet. The opposition took the opportunity to step up attacks on Shidehara diplomacy, applauding the determination of the Kwantung Army and castigating the "First Official Statement" as an expression of "servility from beginning to end."[10]

This struggle was played out in local, as well as national, political arenas. When news of the Manchurian Incident broke, local Minseitō politicians regarded the information with considerable suspicion. With prefectural elections scheduled for September and October, the sudden eruption of Sino-Japanese hostilities seemed more than mere coincidence. Indeed,

---

to sengo no saishuppatsu, vol. 6 of *Shōwa no rekishi* (Shōgakkan, 1988), pp. 22–247, and Peter Duus, *Party Rivalry and Political Change in Taisho Japan* (Cambridge: Harvard University Press, 1968). On Tanaka and Shidehara diplomacy see William Fitch Morton; Akira Iriye, "The Failure of Economic Expansionism: 1918–1931," in Bernard S. Silberman and H. D. Harootunian, eds., *Japan in Crisis: Essays in Taisho Democracy* (Princeton: Princeton University Press, 1974), pp. 237–269; and Inoue Kiyoshi, " 'Manshū' shinryaku," in *Kindai 7*, vol. 20 of *Iwanami kōza Nihon rekishi* (Iwanami shoten, 1976), pp. 18–29.

8. Shidehara made this claim in his memoirs, *Gaikō gojūnen* (1951). Quoted in Eguchi, *Jūgonen sensō no kaimaku*, p. 69.

9. For text of "First Official Statement" see Gaimushō, ed., *Nihon gaikō nenpyō narabini shūyō bunsho* (Hara shobō, 1976), p. 185.

10. Awaya, *Shōwa no seitō*, p. 268.

many Minseitō politicians imagined the Manchurian Incident to be part of a Seiyūkai-army conspiracy to secure the electoral defeat of the Minseitō and pave the way for rearmament and a return to hard-line diplomacy.[11] Minseitō politicians attacked the army for "interfering in our business" and accused it of "attempting to deceive the populace" with the "secret support of the Seiyūkai." By "taking a treacherous attitude toward the current government" and using the Manchurian Incident to "shorten the life" of the Minseitō cabinet, Minseitō officials charged, the army clearly violated the injunction against military involvement in politics.[12] Throughout September and October, Minseitō papers printed editorials criticizing the army, and Minseitō-affiliated officeholders used their positions to defend the Shidehara foreign-policy line.[13]

In the meantime, within the cabinet and on the ground in Manchuria, escalating tension between Foreign Ministry representatives and army officers defined a second axis of conflict over how to settle the Manchurian Incident. Disagreements between the army minister and the foreign minister accounted for much of the week's delay between September 18 and the "First Official Statement" concerning the initiation of hostilities. The Kwantung Army report to the cabinet through the Army Ministry withheld any information concerning its own role in setting the charge on the railway track and commencing the assault on Chinese forces. Instead, it gave what would become the official line: Chinese soldiers exploded the track and attacked first. Thus, neither the cabinet nor the central army authorities were cognizant that Kwantung Army staff officers had in fact instigated and staged the Manchurian Incident.[14] Nevertheless, there was good reason to doubt the official reports from Manchuria. Since August, rumors of an impending Manchurian expedition had circulated, and re-

11. For conspiracy speculations, see *kenpeitai* report of Kenpei shireikan Toyama Bunzō, "Kokubō shisō fukyū kōenkai no jōkyō narabi sono hankyō ni kansuru ken hōkoku" (30 September 1931). This report is found on p. 39 of a document collection on the social impact of the Manchurian Incident edited by Fujiwara Akira and Kunugi Toshihiro: *Manshū jihen to kokumin dōin*. For a discussion of local Minseitō reactions to the Manchurian Incident, see Awaya, "Fasshōka to minshū ishiki," p. 267.

12. Kenpei shireikan Toyama Bunzō, "Kokubō shisō fukyū kōenkai no jōkyō narabi sono hankyō ni kansuru ken hōkoku" (30 September 1931), in Fujiwara and Kunugi, *Manshū jihen to kokumin dōin*, pp. 42–43.

13. Ibid., pp. 39–40; Kenpei shireikan Toyama Bunzō, "Gen'eki gunjin no kōen ni taisuru Okayama-ken chiji no yōkyu ni kansuru ken hōkoku" (24 September 1931), in Fujiwara and Kunugi, *Manshū jihen to kokumin dōin*, p. 35.

14. Ogata, pp. 59–61.

porters frequently questioned Wakatsuki and Shidehara about "when the war was to begin."[15] The events at Fengtian unleashed a new round of rumors of an army conspiracy, leading Shidehara to oppose the army minister's requests for reinforcements and to challenge the legality of army initiatives without cabinet approval.[16] A series of vituperative exchanges in Manchuria between Kwantung Army staff officers and Foreign Ministry representatives did not improve matters. Shortly after the fighting began on September 18, consular official Morishima Morito attempted to stop the army from occupying Fengtian, but was ordered out of the room at swordpoint.[17] When the Fengtian consul general Hayashi Kyūjirō confronted the Kwantung Army commander in chief Honjō Shigeru the following day with evidence of a Kwantung Army conspiracy, the interview precipitated a string of hostile meetings in which accusations and requests for apologies flew back and forth.[18]

Like the Seiyūkai-Minseitō confrontation, the Army Ministry–Foreign Ministry split emerged out of a long history of conflict over China policy. This was particularly pronounced in Manchuria. Since the creation of colonial institutions in 1906, the Army Ministry and Foreign Ministry had been engaged in a turf battle in the region. From the start, the two ministries were unable to agree on who should have ultimate authority, and the resulting compromise arrangement created a tangle of overlapping jurisdictions between four separate colonial institutions: Mantetsu (the South Manchurian Railway), the Kwantung garrison, the consulates, and the administration of the Leased Territory. The initial arrangements (the governor general of the Kwantung Leased Territory was appointed by the army but was under Foreign Ministry direction for all but military affairs) satisfied neither side and led to endless bickering and maneuvering. Frequent attempts were made to restructure and "unify" the administration at one or another side's expense.

The major reorganization that took place in 1919 represented a victory for the Foreign Ministry. A diplomat immediately assumed the post of governor in the new civil administration of the Kwantung Leased Territory. Moreover, the Foreign Ministry was given the key jurisdictional right over negotiations with Chinese leaders. Since changes of any kind—investments, roads, etc.—required agreements with the local authorities, the

15. Ibid., p. 57.
16. Crowley, *Japan's Quest for Autonomy*, pp. 123–127.
17. Ibid., p. 121.
18. Ogata, pp. 63–64.

right to negotiate was critical for freedom of action. Virtually excluded from the Kwantung government, the army was left with its Kwantung garrison, now reorganized into the Kwantung Army. This institutional segregation of the army strengthened tendencies, already present in the army's China hands, to advance their own agenda through independent initiative and conspiracy.[19]

This jurisdictional battle between the army and the Foreign Ministry nurtured popular perceptions of "dual diplomacy" (a phrase coined by the Foreign Ministry in the 1910s)[20] and reinforced the distinctions between career officer Tanaka's "positive" policy and career diplomat Shidehara's "cooperative" diplomacy. While the turf war was real, and differences between the two China policies significant, it is important not to overstate the unity of the Foreign Ministry faction against the army faction, or the Seiyūkai against the Minseitō. In the political scuffle that ensued over the Manchurian Incident, one finds examples of hard-line diplomats and moderate officers. Both factional rivalries within the parties and ministries, as well as alliances between them, meant that the situation was much more complex and fluid than caricatures of Shidehara and Tanaka diplomacy might suggest. Complicating things further, the Manchurian crisis competed with equally critical financial and social crises at home, and these crises spawned their own political theaters of war, complete with policy battlelines, political-party enemies, and bureaucratic allies. It was both the sense of urgency generated by the multiple dimensions of the political crisis and the fluidity of institutional rivalries that made compromise the method of conflict resolution in the Manchurian crisis.

THE NEW POLICY AND THE NEW POLITICS

In the fall of 1931, as in the years and decades that preceded it, the politics of imperialism turned both on issues of substance in the policy debate as well as on institutional rivalries. Since particular institutional actors in the government and political-party system championed particular policies on

19. Hirano, pp. 76–85; Coox, "The Kwantung Army Dimension," pp. 393–400.
20. I am indebted to Y. Tak Matsusaka for a very stimulating conceptualization of the problem of "dual diplomacy" presented at his Japan Forum lecture at Harvard University on October 23, 1992. In print see Y. Tak Matsusaka, "Managing Occupied Manchuria, 1931–1934," in Peter Duus, Ramon H. Myers, and Mark R. Peattie, eds., *The Japanese Wartime Empire, 1931–1945* (Princeton: Princeton University Press, 1996), esp. pp. 101–102; and Y. Tak Matsusaka, "Japanese Imperialism and the South Manchurian Railway Company, 1904–1914," Ph.D. dissertation, Harvard University, 1993.

the Manchurian question, the fortunes of the policies and their backers rose and fell together. For this reason, shifts in the prevailing climate of opinion brought about a transformation of the institutional framework of policy.

Between September 1931 and December 1933, a series of political compromises transformed Japanese foreign policy. Before 1931, foreign policy was premised on participation in international arms limitations, resolution of the China problem through diplomatic negotiation, and cooperation with the League of Nations. The autonomous foreign policy that followed, however, abandoned all three principles. The new policy, christened a "Monroe Doctrine for Asia," committed the country to building up military strength sufficient to neutralize the influence of the Soviet Union, the Nationalist government of China, and the Anglo-American nations.[21] This paradigmatic shift reshaped the institutional context of foreign policy, helping to bring the army to power at home and in the empire. Although this shift represented a watershed in Japanese foreign and domestic policies, the change did not happen overnight. Rather, it took place incrementally, decision by decision, over the course of three cabinets.

The first changes occurred under the Wakatsuki cabinet (April 1931–December 1931). When faced with the unauthorized military actions of the Kwantung Army, Wakatsuki decided to overrule the advice of his foreign and finance ministers that the government publicly challenge the legality of army action. Instead, he elected to follow the compromise course suggested by his army minister. Accordingly, the cabinet endorsed the military acts of September 18–22, in exchange for which the army high command promised to restrain further Kwantung Army operations and prevent it from installing any new political authorities in the regions under its control. The advantage of this course, the cabinet agreed, was that the government could then use the Mukden (Fengtian) Incident to wrest a new treaty from the Nationalist government and guarantee Japanese rights and interests in Manchuria.[22] By the end of November, however, it was clear that the "nonexpansion policy" had failed, for throughout October and November, the Kwantung Army continued to expand its operations against cabinet orders—while the cabinet continued to endorse the Manchurian faits accomplis.

Such was the pattern in the cabinets that followed. The veteran politician Inukai Tsuyoshi headed the Seiyūkai cabinet that came to power in

---

21. James Crowley treats this in *Japan's Quest for Autonomy,* p. 195.
22. Ibid., pp. 123–127.

December. Like his predecessors, Inukai practiced a policy of appeasement toward the army—yielding similar results. He quickly authorized the occupation of Jinzhou, a city in the southwestern corner of Manchuria with significant British investments, and then of north Manchuria, bringing the Japanese army into the territory of the Soviet-owned Chinese Eastern Railway. In the meantime, he deployed personal emissaries to negotiate a settlement with the Nationalist government, aiming to secure Jiang Jieshi's endorsement of the new political arrangements in Manchuria while preserving the facade of Chinese suzerainty.[23] By this time, however, the army was committed to an independent state in Manchuria, politically severed from the Nationalist government. Opposed by the army, Inukai's private diplomacy failed, just as his policy of appeasement proved inadequate to prevent the fabrication of an incident in Shanghai and its escalation into a major naval operation.

Admiral Saitō Makoto, former governor of Korea, headed the cabinet that replaced Inukai's in May 1932. That summer, Saitō's foreign minister Uchida Yasuya stepped up confrontation with the League of Nations, culminating in the decision to withdraw from the League in February 1933. Since the Chinese Nationalist government first appealed to the League for intervention in the Sino-Japanese dispute on September 21, 1931, the reception of Japan's case had steadily deteriorated. The League Council was initially sympathetic to Japan; a resolution passed on September 30 urged only that troops be withdrawn as soon as possible. But by February 1932, the League Council had formally interpreted Japanese actions in Manchuria to be in violation of the Kellogg-Briand Pact and the Covenant of the League.[24] This meant, among other things, that new political arrangements imposed unilaterally by Japan were not legitimate in the eyes of international law. The council created a commission of inquiry to determine the origins and specifics of the Manchurian Incident and propose a resolution equitable to both China and Japan.

The Inukai cabinet had tried to diffuse the hostility toward Japan in the League by withholding formal recognition from Manchukuo upon its establishment in March 1932. The Saitō cabinet, however, reversed this policy in the summer of 1932, deciding to grant recognition to Manchukuo and begin preparing for a confrontation with the League. Fielding ques-

---

23. For these negotiations, see Ogata, pp. 139–142.
24. The League controversy is described in Westel W. Willoughby, *The Sino-Japanese Controversy and the League of Nations* (1935; reprint, New York: Greenwood Press, 1968).

tions on a Diet speech in which he discussed Japan's imminent recognition of Manchukuo, Foreign Minister Uchida declared that "the Japanese people are united as one man on this issue . . . determined not to yield a single inch even if the country turned into scorched earth."[25] Such bravado notwithstanding, when the League was discussing the Lytton Commission Report (released in October 1932), Uchida counseled restraint in army plans to occupy the province of Rehe and expand the border of Manchukuo south to the Great Wall. Not until it became clear, by early winter, that the League was going to follow the commission's rejection of Japan's case did the Saitō cabinet give the green light to the occupation of Rehe and prepare for withdrawal from the League.

Each of these cabinet decisions represented a capitulation to the demands of the army. The army's victory in the policy battle also signaled the expansion of its power in the institutions of government, a position which would grow stronger over the 1930s. At a loss was the Foreign Ministry, whose authority in Manchuria was greatly curtailed in the new administrative structure, giving the army a lasting advantage in their age-old turf war. The other clear losers were the political parties, whose influence from the executive wing of government was largely eliminated with the establishment of the bureaucratic "national unity" cabinet of Saitō Makoto. From that moment until the end of the war, political party members were precluded from holding the premiership and kept out of all but the most minor cabinet posts.

The loss in May 1932 of political-party power over the executive branch of government represented a reversal of institutional gains made over the previous four decades. Party access to the cabinet was secured by precedent not law; the parties had no constitutional basis for choosing the prime minister, who was selected by a group of elder statesmen and appointed by the emperor. In forty years of parliamentary life, the parties had succeeded in using limited constitutional authority—particularly the right to veto the budget—as a bridgehead to penetrating the executive wing of government. By the 1920s it was customary for the majority party to assume the premiership and control cabinet and bureaucratic appointments.

That the parties were forced to relinquish this hard-won position in 1932 was due, in good part, to army pressure, adroitly applied. Maneuvering against the parties and the Foreign Ministry, the Army Ministry

25. Kajima heiwa kenkyūjo, ed., Manshū jihen, vol. 8 of Nihon gaikōshi (Kajima heiwa kenkyūjo shuppankai, 1973), pp. 334–335.

used the threat of military terrorism and insubordination to take control of foreign policy. In situation after situation, the high command promised to do its best to control the officer corps, insisting at the same time that unless some concessions were made, this might prove impossible. Indeed, the wave of army conspiracies in 1931 and 1932 put teeth into such threats. In September and October, officers in the Kwantung and Korea Armies maneuvered against their superiors, acting without authorization to occupy Fengtian, cross the border into Manchuria, bomb Jinzhou, and set up new political arrangements. But probably more alarming to the army's opponents was a rash of domestic terrorism. In March 1931 plans for a coup d'etat by a group of officers fell apart at the last minute because of disunity, but their organization—the Cherry Society—drew up a second plan for October of the same year, again halted at the eleventh hour. The March plot called for the use of mock bombs to strike at party headquarters and the premier's residence (where the cabinet met); in the confusion that would follow, the conspirators planned to demand the resignation of the cabinet and install their own government. The October plot envisioned a larger-scale operation, mobilizing twelve companies of troops and sixteen planes, and using real bombs to wipe out the cabinet during a meeting.[26]

Close on the heels of the October Incident, a series of assassinations also stunned the political world. In the spring of 1932, an organization of naval officers and civilian ultranationalists calling themselves the Blood Pledge League compiled an assassination list of political, business, and government leaders, killing former finance minister Inoue Junnosuke and the head of the Mitsui business conglomerate Dan Takuma before the main culprits were arrested. On May 15, the remnants of the Blood Pledge League joined army cadets in another attempted coup. This time, a plan for the assassination of Prime Minister Inukai Tsuyoshi, together with coordinated attacks on the Bank of Japan, the Metropolitan Police Office, party headquarters, and other government buildings was actually carried out. However, the army's failure to rise in sympathy scuttled the group's ambitions for a Shōwa restoration of imperial power and the end of parliamentary government.

Although in all instances the conspirators failed to assume control of the government, military terrorism created an atmosphere of fear and uncertainty concerning the army, weakening the resolve to oppose demands of the high command. The ambiguity of the role played by senior officers certainly added to feelings of apprehension. A number were implicated by

26. For an account of army terrorism, see Yoshihashi, pp. 83–95, 194–206.

the inevitable rumors; whatever the extent of their actual involvement, army leaders showed extraordinary leniency in dealing with the conspirators. The March plotters, for example, were placed under "house arrest" at a luxurious inn for several weeks, and, speaking publicly for the assassins of Inukai Tsuyoshi, the army minister emphasized that "they acted neither for the sake of fame nor gain nor treason. . . . They acted upon the genuine belief that this was for the interest of the Imperial country." When negotiating on the successor to Inukai, army leaders flatly refused to participate in a party cabinet. Civilian statesmen were told that young officers were "fundamentally in agreement with the principles held by [the assassins]. Should the cabinet again be handed over to a political party, second and third incidents would recur."[27]

The success of the army in securing greater control over government was not simply the product of such heavy-handed negotiating tactics, but was due in large part to the activities of political parties themselves. In the fall of 1931 a dissident faction in the Minseitō led by Home Minister Adachi Kenzō maneuvered to replace the Wakatsuki cabinet with a promilitary two-party cabinet. It was Adachi, not the army minister, who brought the cabinet down in December. For its part, the jingoistic Seiyūkai platform did as much to conscribe policy options of the Inukai administration as the army. Indeed, Mori Kaku, cabinet secretary and head of the right-wing faction of the party, led the effort to undermine Inukai's negotiations with Jiang Jieshi. Like Adachi, Mori maneuvered to bring down his own cabinet, hoping to replace it with an ultranationalist Seiyūkai-army coalition government. Elections in February brought a resounding victory for the Seiyūkai and its hard-line platform (Seiyūkai, 304; Minseitō, 147), thus strengthening the right-wing factions in both parties. After Inukai was assassinated, the rightists in both parties dominated the negotiations for a successor cabinet: the Minseitō proposed a new version of Adachi's two-party cabinet plan while the Seiyūkai lobbied for Mori's army-Seiyūkai government.[28] Moving both parties steadily to the right, internal party politics weakened the parties' bargaining position in the spring of 1932, reversing the institutional gains of the previous decades and ending their control over the cabinet. With pro-military factions dominating the parties, the army felt safe in vetoing party participation in the cabinet, for the Diet was likely to support its program regardless.

27. Ogata, pp. 153–155.
28. Awaya, *Shōwa no seitō*, pp. 279–288.

In one sense the rise of army political power after 1931 represented a return to the position and prestige it had enjoyed in the late Meiji period, during the early years of parliamentary politics. At that time, the wishes of army leaders had been in sympathy with the other members of the military oligarchy, and the armaments programs of 1882 and 1896 enjoyed broad political support. The army and navy faced serious resistance to their budgets for the first time in 1907 and 1911, when competing claims for local development and demands for tax reduction forced the services to scuttle plans for new divisions and an expansion of the fleet. Political scandals involving the military in 1913 and 1914 gave the parties opportunities to flex their new political muscles, as the army's Katsura cabinet and then the navy's Yamamoto cabinet fell in disgrace. During the Siberian Intervention (1918–1922), the Hara cabinet insisted on administrative authority, giving the parties control over the army for the first time.[29]

Thrown off guard by the parties' political offensive, the army took some time to develop a counter-strategy appropriate to the emerging mass politics of Taishō. The political defeats suffered by the army in the teens and twenties led to a politicization of the officer corps and the decision to abandon the Meiji proscription against involvement in politics. With ambition and skill schooled by the setbacks of the previous two decades, the Manchurian Incident offered the army the opportunity to outmaneuver the parties in the political game. The army used this opportunity to great effect, engineering a major shift in policy at the same time that it projected itself back into the seat of power. It accomplished this not through a putsch, but rather through incrementally negotiated compromises with the Foreign Ministry and political parties.

The policy shift and institutional transformations this shift engendered linked Japan's domestic and international politics and illustrated how, in concrete ways, aggression abroad brought about the militarization of politics at home. The bubble of enthusiasm for the Manchurian occupation restructured the balance of bureaucratic power in favor of the army, which in turn ensured the perpetuation of the new policy of military expansionism.[30]

---

29. Crowley, *Japan's Quest for Autonomy*, pp. 11–16, 24.

30. This phenomenon has been characterized by political scientists as "path dependence." As Stephen Krasner explains, "Path-dependent patterns are characterized by self-reinforcing positive feedback. Initial choices, often small and random, may determine future historical trajectories. Once a particular path is chosen, it precludes other paths even if these alternatives might, in the long run, have

ARMY PROPAGANDA AND THE CONSTRUCTION OF
A "PUBLIC OPINION"

One of the points in the army's favor, as observers at the time repeatedly pointed out, was that public opinion supported the army's cause. They referred in part to the outpouring of jingoism in the mass media. But this was not all, for drawing on political lessons of the 1920s, the army itself undertook a large-scale propaganda campaign in 1931–1932, aiming to mobilize popular support and mold it into a political force. These efforts made "public opinion" a building block of total empire. Riding the wave of enthusiasm for empire that had been stirred up by the unofficial propagandists in the mass media, the "campaign to spread the idea of national defense" (*kokubō shisō fukyū undō*) became a public relations triumph for the army. Their success was achieved in part by following the lead of the mass media. Over the course of the propaganda campaign the army began to experiment with new technologies of direct mobilization, borrowing marketing strategies employed by the culture industries. In the process, the army forged new links between the military and society.

Of course, army administrators had long been concerned with raising the level of popular support for the military; in 1931 they launched the propaganda campaign in pursuit of this larger goal. Two things were accomplished. First, reaching down into local politics, the army brought new constituencies into its political embrace. Second, in using propaganda to mobilize not just the elite who wielded political influence but the masses who did not, the army expanded the scope of its public and helped redefine the idea of a "public opinion."

Begun prior to the Manchurian Incident, the *kokubō* (national defense) propaganda campaign concentrated initially on raising public consciousness about the perils of disarmament, using the "Manchurian problem" to argue the need for a strong defense. During the previous decade, diplomatic and financial pressures had forced the army to accept a series of cutbacks. Sixty thousand officers and men were demobilized in 1922; two independent garrison units and five military preparatory schools were dissolved in 1923. Most painful of all, the Takata, Toyohashi, Okayama, and Kurume divisions were eliminated in 1925, demobilizing 34,000 officers and men,

---

proven more efficient or adaptive." Stephen D. Krasner, "Sovereignty: An Institutional Perspective," in James A. Caporaso, ed., *The Elusive State: International and Comparative Perspectives* (Newbury Park, Calif.: Sage Publications, 1989), p. 86.

and decommissioning 6,000 mounts.[31] Facing renewed pressures from the financial community for budget retrenchment, looking toward yet another disarmament conference scheduled for 1932, and determined to accept no further cutbacks, army leaders decided that extraordinary measures were required to win their cause. At the forefront of their minds was the negative example of the 1930 London Naval Treaty, which the Hamaguchi cabinet signed against the strong opposition of the navy general staff. The army took two lessons from this incident. Army planners judged that navalists were defeated, first, because the navy itself was divided on the question of arms limitation, and, second, because a campaign to arouse public opinion against the treaty was too little, too late. The army would not make the same mistake.

Although army preoccupation with public attitudes toward the military was long-standing, the strategy of using a propaganda campaign to forge public support was fairly new. Influenced by new ideas about "total war," army planners began to study techniques of propaganda and "spiritual mobilization" in the wake of World War I.[32] At the same time, concern about left-wing organizations led the Education, Home, and Army ministries to attempt to combat "dangerous ideas" through public education. In designing its own "movement to spread the idea of national defense," Army Ministry staff officers drew on the experience of the government's first nationwide propaganda campaign initiated by the Home and Education ministries in 1929.[33]

Initial plans for the *kokubō* campaign laid in June 1930 drew a gloomy picture of public opinion on the question of military preparedness, lamenting the "ongoing spread of anti-military feeling." Army planners placed the blame for this situation on "journalists and writers with influence and social position," and attached paramount importance to "winning the understanding of the intellectual class, especially youth, concerning the issue of disarmament." To combat this situation, the Army Ministry

31. Yoshihashi, p. 102.

32. Minami et al., *Shōwa bunka*, pp. 358–359; Fujiwara Akira and Kunugi Toshihiro, "Kaisetsu," in Fujiwara Akira and Kunugi Toshihiro, eds., *Manshū jihen to kokumin dōin*, vol. 8 of *Shiryō Nihon gendaishi* (Ōtsuki shoten, 1983), pp. 581–589.

33. On the 1929 "kyōka undō" (public enlightenment campaign): Kokuritsu kyōiku kenkyūjo, ed., *Kyōiku seisaku 1*, vol. 1 of *Nihon kindai kyōiku hyakunen-shi* (Kyōiku kenkyū shinkōkai, 1974), pp. 320–323; and Fujiwara and Kunugi, "Kaisetsu," pp. 586–587.

directed the publication of a series of pamphlets on Manchuria, the state of military preparedness of Russia, China, and the Great Powers, and Japan's own state of military ill-preparedness. These were to be distributed to party offices, universities, chambers of commerce, newspapers, and magazines, and special efforts were made to secure their publication in the mass media.[34] In the aftermath of the Manchurian Incident, however, efforts to sway elite opinion through propaganda pamphlets were quickly eclipsed by a more broad-based lecture campaign. Coordinated locally through the country's regimental districts and carried out principally by the army reservist associations, the Army Ministry aimed to rouse public opinion at a grassroots level. The first propaganda effort of its kind, this attempt to mobilize direct political support for the army changed the nature of the relationship between the military and society.

From the establishment of a modern army and the introduction of conscription in 1872, two institutions—the schools and local regiments—mediated this military-society relationship. Despite an educational curriculum and military-training system designed to promote loyalty to the country and reverence for the army as a symbol of national pride, army leaders grew concerned that these institutions were insufficient for the task of creating a nation of patriotic "civilian soldiers." Compulsory education lasted a scant four years (expanded to six in 1907); and since the peacetime army remained small until 1937 (under 300,000), only 12 to 16 percent of conscript-age men (about 100,000) were actually drafted each year.[35]

To fill the gaps, the army established a number of auxiliary institutions after the Russo-Japanese War. In 1910 the military reservist association (*zaigo gunjinkai*) was created, unifying thousands of local veteran, martial, and reserve organizations into a national association. Independent on paper, the reservist association was in fact one of a growing number of semipublic voluntary organizations with administrative ties to the central government and financial support from local authorities. The rural branches of the reservists tended to exert more influence over their communities than urban branches: a higher percentage of those eligible joined, the leadership was better integrated with other local elites, and their structure reflected more closely the social hierarchy of their surrounding commu-

---

34. Rikugunshō shinbunhan, "Kokubō shisō fukyū keikaku ni kansuru ken" (30 June 1930), in Fujiwara and Kunugi, *Manshū jihen to kokumin dōin*, pp. 202–204.

35. Richard J. Smethurst, *A Social Basis for Prewar Japanese Militarism: The Army and the Rural Community* (Berkeley: University of California Press, 1974), p. 6.

nities. The centrality of their position in the community arose in part from the variety of important tasks these reservists performed, mobilizing manpower for local ceremonies, construction projects, and disaster relief, and supplementing the labor of families with men in service. The organizations were open to men between twenty and forty years of age who passed the yearly physical examination required, with a few exceptions, of all twenty-year-old males. By 1918 there were thirteen thousand branches nationwide reaching a membership of 2.3 million men.[36]

Following the pattern of the *zaigo gunjinkai*, the army joined the Home and Education ministries in creating a parallel organization for post-elementary school, preconscript-age boys. In 1915, thousands of existing youth groups were unified into a national youth association, soon matching the dimensions of the reservist association. By 1935 the national youth association boasted 2.7 million members, about 40 percent of all those eligible.[37] In addition, military training facilities were expanded with the establishment in 1926 of four-year youth-training centers for elementary school graduates and the posting of officers to middle schools to supervise military drill for those who continued their education past elementary school.[38]

Although on paper this seemed a formidable network of institutions, even as it was tightening the net the army discovered that mere organization did not guarantee the desired outcome. In fact, youth and reservist groups sometimes provided institutional vehicles for activities anathema to the army. In 1918, youth and reservist associations spearheaded rice riots against landlords and rice merchants in Osaka, Okayama, Kyoto, Hyōgo, Shizuoka, Yamaguchi, and elsewhere. As Michael Lewis points out, "the most common feature of the more than eight thousand riot suspects throughout the nation was membership in a reservist or youth association." Nine hundred and ninety reservists and 868 youth association members were arrested for riot-related crimes.[39] In Aomori, Nagano, and elsewhere, liberal and left-wing youths established competing organizations or simply took over the local youth association, turning it into a base for political activity.[40]

Accompanying these distressing developments, the army witnessed an

36. Ibid., pp. 1–21; statistics: p. 20.
37. Ibid., p. 74.
38. Ibid., pp. 22–43.
39. Lewis, pp. 26–27, 128, 160–165.
40. Awaya, *Shōwa no seitō*, pp. 230–231; Smethurst, pp. 36–37.

alarming rise in opposition to the draft. Despite severe punishments for desertion, over 2,000 soldiers deserted every year during the 1920s.[41] Rejecting army attempts to make the army medical exam into a rite of passage, many young men concocted ways to avoid what they considered "empty patriotic service" (kara hōkō). Although the army extolled "class-A" status as a great honor, youths took secret trips to local shrines to make a chōhei nozoke no gokitō—a prayer for failure in the exam.[42] A Nagano newspaper reported with some amusement a "startlingly high" number of cases of "psychological illness" and "imbecility" among conscript-age men in 1927, "driving to distraction" the authorities in charge of the exam.[43] Some young men went even further, amputating a finger or impairing their sight in order to avoid serving.[44]

Through the propaganda campaign, army leaders hoped to reverse these developments, recapture their network of institutions and create from these a political wing of the army. To this end, in the initial phase of the campaign, the army directed its energies toward enlisting the aid of sympathetic reservist associations, youth groups, and local military units to disseminate national defense ideas. In the week preceding the outbreak of the Manchurian Incident, records of the progress of the campaign in the 16th Division district reported, typically, that reservist associations, local military units, and local government organizations held twenty-eight of thirty-three kokubō events.[45] After September 18, as the campaigning in Manchuria improved the popular image of the military, nationalist elements in the more wayward voluntary organizations were able to reassert themselves, assuring the army success in its efforts to mobilize this constituency. Moreover, the spread of war fever encouraged the army to expand the scope of its efforts, reaching out to new groups to promote its message of strengthening the national defense. Local newspapers and busi-

41. Awaya, "Fasshoka to minshū ishiki," p. 280.

42. Sakawa chōshi hensan iinkai, ed., Sakawa chōshi, vol. 2 (Sakawa, Kōchi: Sakawa machi yakuba, 1981), pp. 671–672; Okayama kenshi hensan iinkai, ed., Kindai 3, vol. 12 of Okayama kenshi (Okayama: San'yō shinbunsha, 1989), p. 319.

43. The article was from the July 24, 1927, issue of Shinano mainichi shinbun, included in the document collection compiled by Nagano-ken, Gunji, keisatsu, shihō, vol. 4 of Nagano kenshi kindai shiryōhen (Nagano: Nagano-ken, 1988), pp. 64–65.

44. Shibata shishi hensan iinkai, ed., Shibata shishi, vol. 2 (Shibata: Shibata shishi hensan iinkai, 1981), p. 586.

45. Kenpei shireikan Toyama Bunzō, "Kokubō shisō fukyū kōenkai jōkyō narabi sono hankyō ni kansuru ken hōkoku" (22 September 1931), in Fujiwara and Kunugi, Manshū jihen to kokumin dōin, pp. 19–25.

nesses began to answer the call, joining the list of sponsors for *kokubō* events. Well-to-do residents of Tokyo's Kameido district formed a club to promote the campaign, sending membership dues to the central office of the reservist associations.[46] In Kyoto, a department store made part of its fourth floor available for a *kokubō* exhibit, budgeting 5,500 yen for the project and distributing some 2,000 advertising posters throughout the city. A city theater owner offered his stage free of charge for the local reservists to hold meetings and lectures.[47] In Gifu prefecture, the local press sponsored a *kokubō* rally on October 5, announcing its intent to send two reporters to Manchuria to "comfort troops" and get a firsthand view of events.[48] This willingness of groups outside the army's network raised the stakes in the propaganda campaign. Now the army aimed not merely to recapture its network, but to expand it.

As greater numbers of civilian organizations joined in the *kokubō* campaign, they began to alter the character of the movement. At first, the army used the lecture format almost exclusively. Behind the podium stood active-duty officers, usually natives of the region and, if possible, veterans of the Manchurian campaigns. Echoing the themes of Army Ministry pamphlets, the lectures concentrated on hammering a few points solidly; speakers told audiences of the need for "firm handling" of the Manchuria problem and explained the "lifeline of rights and interests." The "outrageous and insolent" attitude of the Chinese was pointed out, and the interfering and hypocritical attitude of the League of Nations denounced. Often following the lectures, such local elites as teachers, journalists, principals, businessmen, and landlords would gather on stage, voicing support for the army's sentiments in a roundtable discussion.[49]

Before long campaign organizers began to replace these lecture pro-

46. Kenpei shireikan Toyama Bunzō, "Kokubō shisō fukyū kōenkai no jōkyō narabi ni sono hankyō ni kansuru ken hōkoku," (26 October 1931), in Fujiwara and Kunugi, *Manshū jihen to kokumin dōin*, p. 61.

47. Kenpei shireikan Toyama Bunzō, "Kokubō shisō fukyū kōenkai no jōkyō narabi sono hankyō ni kansuru ken hōkoku" (30 September 1931), in Fujiwara and Kunugi, *Manshū jihen to kokumin dōin*, p. 39; and Kenpei shireikan Toyama Bunzō, "Kokubō shisō fukyū kōenkai no jōkyō narabi ni sono hankyō ni kansuru ken hōkoku" (26 October 1931), in Fujiwara and Kunugi, *Manshū jihen to kokumin dōin*, p. 61.

48. Kenpei shireikan Toyama Bunzō, "Kokubō shisō fukyū kōenkai no jōkyō narabini sono hankyō ni kansuru ken hōkoku" (31 October 1931), in Fujiwara and Kunugi, *Manshū jihen to kokumin dōin*, p. 73.

49. Kenpei shireikan Toyama Bunzō, "Kokubō shisō fukyū kōenkai no jōkyō narabi sono hankyō ni kansuru ken hōkoku" (30 September 1931), in Fujiwara and Kunugi, *Manshū jihen to kokumin dōin*, pp. 38–44.

grams with festivals and pageantry. In Nagano, the local regiment launched its celebration of Manchurian Incident Day on September 18, 1932, with a ceremony, followed by a procession to the local shrine to pray for the "protection of the national polity" and the "eternal good fortunes of the imperial army."[50] In 1934 the Utsunomiya Regiment planned to promote the *kokubō* idea through holiday parades and spectacles, with newsreels screened to the accompaniment of "brand-new records," and, because "the people of Ibaraki prefecture love minstrel chanting, patriotic *naniwabushi* troupes."[51] By 1934 the army had come a long distance from its plans to direct propaganda efforts to the intelligentsia and disseminate the message through pamphlets. Following the example of the mass media, campaign planners learned to employ the artistry of jingoism to reach out to a mass audience.

The public greeted the army campaign with the same enthusiasm it had shown the mass media's unofficial propagandists. In the first month after the beginning of the Manchurian Incident, 1,655,410 people (out of a population of 65,000,000) attended 1,866 events held nationwide.[52] In contrast to earlier army projections of growing anti-war sentiment, reports on the *kokubō* campaign after September 18 jubilantly relayed that "audiences were wildly enthusiastic," and that "the *kokubō* campaign is an unprecedented hit."[53] In Nagoya meetings were held on a daily basis, and in other parts of the country campaign coordinators were inundated with "a continuous stream of requests for lecture sponsors and soldiers to speak."[54] Observing that "public opinion in local areas has become hard-line, demanding an immediate and thoroughgoing resolution of the China prob-

50. Teikoku zaigo gunjinkai Kamitakaigun rengō bunkai, teikoku butokukai Nagano-ken shibu Kamitakaigun shijo, "Senden; ketsugi" (15 November 1931), in Fujiwara and Kunugi, *Manshū jihen to kokumin dōin*, pp. 527–528.

51. Utsunomiya rentaiku shireibu, "Shōwa 9 nendo tainai yoron shidō keikaku" (1934), in Fujiwara and Kunugi, *Manshū jihen to kokumin dōin*, pp. 561–562.

52. Kenpei shireikan Toyama Bunzō, "Kokubō shisō fukyū kōenkai no jōkyō narabini sono hankyō ni kansuru ken hōkoku" (31 October 1931), in Fujiwara and Kunugi, *Manshū jihen to kokumin dōin*, p. 72.

53. Kenpei shireikan Toyama Bunzō, "Kokubō shisō fukyū kōenkai no jōkyō narabi sono hankyō ni kansuru ken hōkoku" (30 September 1931), in Fujiwara and Kunugi, *Manshū jihen to kokumin dōin*, p. 38.

54. Eguchi, "Manshū jihen to minshū dōin," pp. 125–142; Kenpei shireikan Toyama Bunzō, "Kokubō shisō fukyū kōenkai no jōkyō narabi sono hankyō ni kansuru ken hōkoku" (30 September 1931), in Fujiwara and Kunugi, *Manshū jihen to kokumin dōin*, p. 39.

lem," army bureaucrats congratulated themselves that "since the initiation of the *kokubō* movement, the officials and the people have been imbued with a keen appreciation of the need for a strong national defense and the protection of Manchurian rights and interests."[55]

Polls taken at the time support army assessments. After two lectures held at Tokyo University, 854 students were asked, first, if they regarded Manchuria as Japan's lifeline, and, second, whether they felt the Manchurian problem should be resolved with military action. Ninety percent answered yes to both questions.[56] A different poll conducted by a Nagoya city publisher asked 230 business and political leaders by postcard whether Japan "should punish China" or "show restraint." Of the 208 replies, 164 opted to "punish," and only 44 wanted "restraint."[57] Though these polls surveyed only elite opinion, they reveal that a significant proportion of the elite did agree with the army's message. Together the parallel propaganda efforts of the mass media and the army appear to have shaped a public opinion that supported Japanese aggression in China.

After bringing its message to the people and constructing a public opinion on China policy and disarmament, the *kokubō* campaign gave political expression to that opinion, first, through the establishment of political associations and, second, through a petition drive. In the eighteen months following the onset of the Manchurian Incident, local army divisions and reservist associations established "national-defense societies" (*kokubō kenkyūkai*) at neighborhood, city, and prefectural levels. In Takada city, the 2d Division headquarters invited the resident press corps and men of influence to participate in a conference on national defense, out of which grew the Takada National Defense Repletion League (*Kokubō jūjitsu kisei dōmei*). Similarly, the Manchurian-Mongolian Study Group of Motosu county (Gifu prefecture) was created during a roundtable discussion between the heads of the Motosu reservist associations, village and neighborhood leaders, and teachers.[58] Such groups quickly proliferated: four

55. Kenpei shireikan Toyama Bunzō, "Kokubō shisō fukyū kōenkai no jōkyō narabi sono hankyō ni kansuru ken hōkoku" (6 October 1931), in Fujiwara and Kunugi, *Manshū jihen to kokumin dōin*, pp. 45–46.

56. Kenpei shireikan Toyama Bunzō, "Kokubō shisō fukyū kōenkai no jōkyō narabi ni sono hankyō ni kansuru ken hōkoku" (30 September 1931), in Fujiwara and Kunugi, *Manshū jihen to kokumin dōin*, p. 57.

57. Kenpei shireikan Toyama Bunzō, "Kokubō shisō fukyū kōenkai no jōkyō narabi sono hankyō ni kansuru ken hōkoku" (6 October 1931), in Fujiwara and Kunugi, *Manshū jihen to kokumin dōin*, p. 46.

58. Kenpei shireikan Toyama Bunzō, "Kokubō shisō fukyū kōenkai no jōkyō

national-defense societies formed in the city of Nagoya, while in Ishikawa prefecture, eighty different groups emerged by April 1933.[59]

The national-defense societies represented a victory for the army at the local political level. Not only did they create civilian organizations to carry out the army's propaganda campaign, but these organizations were headed by the local elite—government officials, businessmen, wealthy landholders, newspaper executives, educational and religious leaders, and heads of the voluntary associations.[60] Community leaders, in turn, used the institutions at their disposal—newspapers and magazines, shrines and temples, businesses, schools, and reservist, youth, and women's groups—to mobilize support for the army. In Sapporo, for example, the founding ceremony for the Hokkaidō National Defense Assembly on October 9, 1931, boasted 2,000 participants: 500 reservists, 500 public officials, 100 students, 30 housewives, and 870 others. Founding members included the leadership of the 7th Division; the "father of Hokkaidō University," Baron Satō Shōsuke; its current president, Minami Takajirō; the mayor of Sapporo; the chairman of the prefectural assembly; and 30 members of the Sapporo city council. From the prefectural governor down, virtually the entire roster of local elite pledged themselves, in the words of the Assembly's charter oath, "to arouse public sentiment . . . to recognize the crisis in East Asia, understand that Japan cannot be shaken from its administration over Manchuria-Mongolia which it has maintained since the Meiji Restoration [sic], comprehend fully that Manchuria-Mongolia represents the current and future profit and well-being of our race, and rise above differences of political party and faction to unify the country behind the goal of the repletion of our national defense."[61] This was a ringing endorsement of the army agenda at home and in the empire.

Such groups became a powerful political tool for the army, mediating a

narabi sono hankyō ni kansuru ken hōkoku" (30 September 1931), in Fujiwara and Kunugi, *Manshū jihen to kokumin dōin,* p. 41.

59. Eguchi, "Manshū jihen to minshū dōin," pp. 128–135; Nakajima Kinji, "Manshū jihenki no jūgo katsudō to minshū: Ishikawa-ken imonkai setsuritsu o meguru jōkyō," Master's thesis, Kanazawa daigaku, January 1988.

60. Kenpei shireikan Hata Shinji, "Manshū jihen ni kiinshi setsuritsu serare-taru gunji kankei dantai no jōkyō ni kansuru ken hōkoku" (21 November 1932), in Fujiwara and Kunugi, *Manshū jihen to kokumin dōin,* p. 223; "Nagano-ken kokubō kōenkai setsuritsu kankei shiryō" (September 1932–April 1933), in Fujiwara and Kunugi, *Manshū jihen to kokumin dōin,* p. 530.

61. Kenpei shireikan Toyama Bunzō, "Hokkaidō kokubō gikai hakkai shiki kyokō ni kansuru ken hōkoku" (9 October 1931), in Fujiwara and Kunugi, *Manshū jihen to kokumin dōin,* pp. 54, 56.

new relationship between policy makers at the center and a politicized public at the peripheries of power. Looking out from Tokyo, policy makers who made crucial decisions about budget and foreign policy beheld a phalanx of national-defense associations, just as tenant farmers, shopkeepers, and housewives found that those to whom they looked for guidance seemed to be in full support of the army. These proliferating national-defense organizations not only expanded the network of institutions that mediated the relationship between military and society, but also provided one of the building blocks of the national unity in whose name a military-dominated government acted.

While the organization of national-defense associations secured the army's local political flank, a petition campaign sought to influence cabinet ministers, diplomats, members of both houses of the Diet, and other national government representatives. Lectures, meetings of national-defense associations, and other *kokubō* events frequently concluded with the drafting of a resolution. Expressing sentiments that echoed the manifesto of the Hokkaidō National Defense Assembly, multiple copies of the resolutions were sent to the authorities and to the press. The procedure of appealing to the authorities through popular manifestos was a political tradition of long standing. What was different about the Manchurian Incident petition drive was the attempt to manipulate this device to convey a sense of national unity on a critical political question. The leadership of the organization drafted the manifesto; the rank and file endorsed it. When these manifestos were distributed to political leaders and the press, they purported to express the will not just of the elite, but of "the people" of Hokkaidō or Nagano. Though the people did not draft the manifestos, they were included in the definition of the public whose opinion mattered.

A plan drawn up by the 5th Division command (Hiroshima) laid out the army's expectations for the petition drive. First, "regular local officials and people" were to be "prevailed upon to telegraph numerous messages (at the very least one per neighborhood and village) to the big newspapers in Tokyo and Osaka urging them to prepare the public for withdrawal from the League"; second, petition-drive leaders would "have every town and village petition the Diet members of both houses from their electoral district about the resolve of the people." Although it is doubtful that every hamlet in Hiroshima sent off a petition, a public rally celebrating Founding Day in Hiroshima city in February 1933 drafted, as anticipated in the same 5th Division plan, a manifesto and resolution expressing "the zeal of the people" which was dispatched by telegraph to "the prime minister, the army minister, the navy minister, the chief of staff, Ambassador Matsuoka

Yōsuke" and by mail to "all division commanders, regimental commanders, and prefectural governors."[62] In this way the army campaign sought to use the petition drive as a means of giving political expression to a newly constructed public opinion.

The effectiveness of the army's *kokubō* campaign made it a model for a succession of similar campaigns in the years that followed. In the fall of 1933, Army Minister Araki Sadao set his bureaucracy to work spreading the news of an impending "crisis of 1936," when the London and Washington naval treaties were scheduled to expire. The so-called movement to clarify the national entity (*kokutai meichō undō*) in the winter of 1934–1935 and the Home Ministry's election-regulation (*senkyō shukusei*) movement in 1935 used the same techniques to attack liberal academics in the former instance and parliamentary politics in the latter. Like the army's *kokubō* movement, these campaigns represented attempts on the part of political factions within the state to circumvent the institutions of representative parliamentary government and forge direct, independent links with the people. In the process, they changed the meaning of public opinion. Mobilization strategies in the *kokubō* campaign concentrated on using the media and extraparliamentary political practices to address a mass audience. This had the effect of making "the people"—regardless of their age, wealth, status, gender, or franchise—the target of the campaign to arouse public opinion. Now they, too, joined the small community of journalists, politicians, and "men of substance" who had constituted the public opinion in the past. The new equation of the masses with public opinion through direct political appeals contributed to their symbolic political empowerment, even while, ironically, it turned them away from representative democracy.

THE OFFICIAL STORY OF THE MANCHURIAN INCIDENT

The construction of a political consensus on the occupation of Manchuria and the withdrawal from the League was not accomplished without a protracted political struggle. The outcome of this struggle led to a reconfiguration of political institutions and determined the rise and fall of political

62. Daigoshidanchō Ninomiya Nobushige, "Yoron kanki ni kansuru ken hōkoku" (13 February 1933), in Fujiwara and Kunugi, *Manshū jihen to kokumin dōin*, p. 241; and Daigoshidanchō Ninomiya Nobushige, "Yoron kanki ni kansuru ken hōkoku" (14 February 1933), in Fujiwara and Kunugi, *Manshū jihen to kokumin dōin*, p. 243.

fortunes. Victory for one side also involved the acceptance, in and out of government, of the victor's version of events in Northeast China and in the League. This became the official story, designed to persuade audiences at home and abroad of the legitimacy of the military occupation. The official version of the Manchurian Incident publically articulated the government's justification of the new military imperialism being practiced on the continent. It transformed into the moral language of ideology the paradigmatic shift in Japanese foreign policy that was taking place. Because this shift did not occur overnight, the government case which defended the new policy was also worked out over time. What both the army and the Foreign Ministry were saying in the fall of 1931 had changed considerably by the following year. These changes reflected a distillation of the evolving consensus in high political circles on the direction of policy. At the same time, through all the revisions made to accommodate the rapidly shifting circumstances in Manchuria and the League, a master narrative of national victimization emerged, drawing on the reservoir of fears and resentments that had long been attached to Japan's imperial mythology.

Initial army pronouncements on the outbreak of hostilities between the Japanese and Chinese armies at Fengtian and other points along the South Manchurian Railway sought to explain why the Kwantung Army had launched an all-out assault on Chinese Army positions in South Manchuria. Describing Chinese behavior toward Japan with words such as *aggression* (*chōsen*), *derision* (*bubetsu*), *persecution* (*hakugai*), and even *extermination* (*kuchiku*), the army accused the Chinese government of scheming to drive Japan out of Manchuria. Explaining how a railway explosion had escalated into a major military action, an army pamphlet issued on September 25, 1931, spared no effort to convince readers that the army had attacked at every turn in simple self-defense. In order to pursue the Chinese troops that had "attacked Japanese railway guards" and subsequently fled into the barracks of the Chinese garrison at Fengtian, the Japanese did not attack, but attempted to "enter" (*shinnyū*) the barracks. When showered by "hot artillery fire from the Chinese Army," the Japanese were forced to take it a step further, having no choice but to surround and occupy the entire barracks. The hostile acts of Chinese troops and the clash of forces at Fengtian placed Japanese lives in jeopardy, forcing army units stationed outside Fengtian to counter-attack and remove the Chinese Army from the Kwantung Leased Territory and the railway zone. Thus, "self-defense" required the army to expand greatly the theater of operations, carrying out rapid "mopping-up operations" in the Changchun area at the northern terminus of the South Manchurian Railway.[63]

After the initial ejection of the Chinese military from Fengtian and Changchun over the night of September 18 and the following morning, the Kwantung Army began to extend operations outside its legal zone of activity in the railway zone, driving Zhang Xueliang and allied warlord armies out of Northeast China and bringing the entire region under Japanese military occupation. These operations were carried out in the face of Chinese nonresistance. Under the advice of Jiang Jieshi, head of the Guomindang central government to which Zhang Xueliang declared allegiance in 1928, Zhang's army responded to Japanese aggression with voluntary disarmament, while Guomindang diplomats appealed to the League of Nations for diplomatic intervention in the Sino-Japanese dispute. As its war aims expanded, the Japanese Army revised the official story, constructing a new justification for continued military action against an enemy that refused to fight back.[64]

The army anchored its new case against China on a simple assertion: "all bandits are soldiers and therefore all soldiers are bandits." Proof was

---

63. Rikugunshō, *Manshū jihen gaiyō* (Rikugunshō, 1931), pp. 2–3. This pamphlet was one of a series of some 123 propaganda pamphlets published between September 1931 and March 1937 through which the Army Ministry publicized the official story of the Manchurian Incident. Planned as part of the army's campaign to spread the idea of national defense, the army pamphlets were distributed to organs of the mass media, and to the offices of voluntary associations, political organizations, business associations, and government institutions. For an Army Ministry planning document on the use of propaganda pamphlets in the *kokubō* campaign, see note 34 in this chapter. For a discussion of the pamphlets, see Eguchi Keiichi, "Manshū jihenki no Rikugunshō panfuretto," *Hōkei ronshū*, no. 113 (Aichi daigaku, February 1987), pp. 165–197.

64. Army Ministry pamphlets that justified the occupation of Chinese territory outside the railway zone and the Kwantung Leased Territory included Rikugunshō, *Manshū fuan no jissō* [The Truth about Unrest in Manchuria] (Rikugunshō, 1931); Rikugunshō, *Mantetsu fuzokuchigai shutsudō butai hikiage no fukanō naru yuen ni tsuite* [Why It Is Impossible to Withdraw Troops Back within the Railway Zone] (Rikugunshō, 1931); Rikugunshō, *Manshū jihen ni okeru Donkō kahan no sentō ni tsuite* [About the Manchurian Incident Battles along the Nen Riverbank] (Rikugunshō, 1931); Rikugunshō, *Manshū jihen ni okeru Kōkōkei fukin no sentō ni tsuite* [About the Manchurian Incident Battles in the Angangji Vicinity] (Rikugunshō, 1931); Rikugunshō, *Chō Gakuryō Kinshū seiken no taiNichi kōsen junbi ni tsuite* [Zhang Xueliang's Jinzhou Government Prepares for War against Japan] (Rikugunshō, 1931); Rikugunshō, *Ryōsei chihō heihi tōbatsu yori Shinagun kannai tettai made* [From the Anti-Bandit Expeditions in the Laioxi Region to the Withdrawal of the Chinese Army within the Great Wall] (Rikugunshō, 1932); Rikugunshō, *Harupin fukin no sentō ni tsuite* [About the Battles in the Harbin Vicinity] (Rikugunshō, 1932).

furnished in the first instance by arguing that 1) Zhang Xueliang was engaged in "machinations" (*sakudō*) which "clearly aimed at disturbing the peace and casting every region of Manchuria into a state of unrest"; and 2) in order to carry this out he was "dispatching soldiers in civilian clothes throughout the region and instigating mounted bandits (*bazoku*) to cause disturbances, as well as planning the arson and destruction of important buildings."[65] The army implied, in effect, that all outlaws were acting as hired mercenaries of the Chinese Army and that crimes committed in any part of Manchuria were part of the machinations of Zhang Xueliang.

After establishing that all bandits were soldiers, the army demonstrated that the reverse was also true. Pamphlets explained that as Chinese forces retreated, "although some retained their unity ... most scattered to the four winds. Having scattered, Chinese soldiers will, as they always have in the past, quickly turn to banditry."[66] Moreover, as "soldier-bandits" (*heizoku* or *heihi*, as distinguished from "mounted bandits," *bazoku*, and "criminal bandits," *hizoku*), Chinese soldiers engaged in "looting and violence" and other "atrocities" against "Japanese subjects and Japanese rights and interests all over Manchuria," thus "disturbing the peace and menacing the railway zone."[67] In this way, the army transformed Zhang and his allies into disorganized gangs of thugs, at the same time insinuating that any type of armed resistance to the Japanese occupation was a form of banditry. Such sophistry resolved the difficulties of justifying continued action against an enemy that had, in fact, surrendered.

To justify military measures against the new threat, the army began to speak of "preserving the peace" (*chian o kakushin*), using the term *self-defense* (*jiei sensō*) less and less often over the course of 1932. The revised goal of military action was to "wipe out" (*sōtō*), "pacify" (*chinbu*), or "suppress" (*tōbatsu*) banditry.[68] The gradual substitution of peace preservation for self-defense signaled a reinterpretation of the Kwantung Army's military mandate. Peace preservation was a woolly phrase associated with domestic traditions of political suppression, as in the Peace Preservation Law of 1925, which forbade political opposition to the system of private property and the *kokutai* (national polity). Used in the Manchurian context, the new terminology transformed the Manchurian Incident from a battle

65. Rikugunshō, *Manshū fuan no jissō*, pp. 1, 9.
66. Rikugunshō, *Mantetsu fuzokuchi*, p. 3.
67. Ibid., pp. 2–3; Rikugunshō, *Chō Gakuryō*, p. 92.
68. Rikugunshō, *Mantetsu fuzokuchi*, p. 20.

between two national armies to a matter of internal police work. The underlying message was unmistakable: the whole of Manchuria was Japanese territory.

After completing the military occupation of Manchuria and dispatching troops to Shanghai to the south in order to suppress the anti-Japanese boycott that emerged as a protest to the Manchurian Incident, the Kwantung Army turned its attention in January 1933 to Rehe province and the border area between north China and Manchukuo. To justify yet another escalation of force—moving to occupy militarily points outside of Manchukuo and south of China's Great Wall—army propagandists revised their story once again. Articulated in pamphlets published over the first six months of 1933, a new Chinese threat to the army came in the form of a Guomindang-backed plot by Zhang Xueliang to invade Manchuria.[69] The language of self-defense was back, now referring to the protection of Manchukuo from its enemies across the border.

The army blamed China for the Japanese invasion across the Manchukuo-China border by telling what was by now a familiar story to the people at home. Army propagandists started with an account of Chinese preparations for an invasion of Manchukuo, explaining that "remaining anti-Japanese forces . . . have taken refuge in Rehe province" where they have joined with "massing anti-Japanese forces . . . supported by the Chinese Nationalist government" and led by the army's arch villain Zhang Xueliang.[70] Estimating Zhang's forces at 74,000 troops, the army claimed China was mounting a campaign to seize Manchuria from Japan. To forestall this invasion, the army stationed itself along the northern side of the Great Wall, which marked the new national boundary. As the army explained, there the Chinese provoked Japan into crossing the Great Wall into the south.[71]

69. Army pamphlets justifying the invasion of China south of the Great Wall included Rikugunshō, *Nekka ni tsuite* [About Rehe] (Rikugunshō, 1933); Rikugunshō, *Shōwa 7 nen 8 gatsu ikō ni okeru Manshū no sōhi to chian no jōtai* [Anti-Bandit Operations since August 1932 and the Condition of Public Order in Manchuria] (Rikugunshō, 1933); Rikugunshō, *Nekka tōbatsu keika gaiyō: furoku Beikoku tsūshin'in no mitaru Nekka sakusen* [An Overview of the Progress of the Rehe Expedition and Supplement on American Reporters' View of the Rehe Operations] (Rikugunshō, 1933); Rikugunshō, *Nekka shukuseigo no Hokushi jōsei to teisen kōshō* [Conditions in North China after the Purge of Rehe and Negotiations for a Ceasefire] (Rikugunshō, 1933); Rikugunshō, *Shōwa 8 nen ni okeru Kantōgun no kōdō ni tsuite* [Kwantung Army Activities in 1933] (Rikugunshō, 1934).

70. Rikugunshō, *Shōwa 7 nen*, p. 18.

71. Ibid., pp. 12–19; Rikugunshō, *Shōwa 8 nen*, pp. 4–6.

Once again, the army's argument portrayed itself reacting to the latest incarnation of the Chinese menace. First appearing in the form of an anti-Japanese movement, the menace reemerged as peace-destroying bandits, and finally appeared again in a Guomindang plot to seize Manchuria. Inverting the roles of victim and aggressor, the army's story transformed a Japanese military conspiracy into a righteous war of self-defense.

While they pointed the finger at the Chinese aggressors, army propagandists took note of the equally serious threat posed by Western expansion in Asia.[72] In army pamphlets chronicling the events leading up to Japan's departure from the League in March 1933, Japan was portrayed as isolated and surrounded at Geneva well before February 1933, when the League in fact condemned Japanese actions. "The various countries have attempted to intervene in the Sino-Japanese Incident," wrote the author of a July 1932 pamphlet, explaining that "the atmosphere was already very bad in the first League Council meeting"—a meeting during which the council had actually voted to leave Japan alone.[73] Not only did they back-date the timing of unified League opposition to Japan, but army pamphlets inflated its significance, expressing what was no more than a war of words in the language of physical force. Using terms like *coerce (iatsu)*, *pressure*

---

72. Army pamphlets publicizing the Western threat included Rikugunshō, *Beikoku Karibian seisaku to Manmō mondai* [America's Caribbean Policy and the Manchurian-Mongolian Problem] (Rikugunshō, 1931); Rikugunshō, *Kokusai renmei ni okeru Manshū jihen keika no gaiyō* [An Overview of the Progress of the Manchurian Incident at the League of Nations] (Rikugunshō, 1931); Rikugunshō, *Daisanji kokusai renmei rijikai ni okeru Manshū jihen* [The Manchurian Incident at the Third Meeting of the Council of the League of Nations] (Rikugunshō, 1931); Rikugunshō, *Nisshi funsō o meguru renmei dōkō o mite* [Looking at League Trends Concerning the Sino-Japanese Conflict] (Rikugunshō, 1932); Rikugunshō, *Hakka ni sonaeyo* [Guard against the White Peril] (Rikugunshō, 1932); Rikugunshō, *Waga Manmō hatten no rekishi to rekkoku kanshō no kaiko* [The History of Japanese Development of Manchuria-Mongolia and a Review of Great Power Intervention] (Rikugunshō, 1932); Rikugunshō, *Manshūkoku no shōnin ni tsuite* [About the Recognition of Manchukuo] (Rikugunshō, 1932); Rikugunshō, *Renmei sōkai ni chokumen shite* [Facing the League Assembly] (Rikugunshō, 1932); Rikugunshō, *Saikin ni okeru Nisshi funsō to kokusai renmei* [The Current Situation of the Sino-Japanese Conflict and the League of Nations] (Rikugunshō, 1933); Rikugunshō, *Renmei dattai to kokumin no kakugo* [Withdrawal from the League and the Resolution of the Japanese People] (Rikugunshō, 1933); Rikugunshō, *Renmei dattai no keii* [The Circumstances of the Withdrawal from the League] (Rikugunshō, 1933); Rikugunshō, *Shina o chūshin to suru renmei narabini Ōbei kakkoku no katsudō ni tsuite* [Activities of America, Europe, and the League toward China] (Rikugunshō, 1933); Rikugunshō, *Yakushin Nihon to rekkyō no jūatsu* [Japan's Advance and Great Power Pressure] (Rikugunshō, 1934).

73. Rikugunshō, *Waga Manmō*, p. 45.

(*appaku*), and *restrain* (*seisuru*), pamphlets described the diplomatic process as an attempt by the West to force Japan to "submit" (*kussuru*).[74] Such strong-arm tactics, it was explained, were merely the latest in a long history of Great Power oppression. A pamphlet on *The History of Japanese Development of Manchuria-Mongolia and a Review of Great Power Intervention* alerted readers to "take a lesson from the long history of Western intervention and pressure on our continental policy going back to the Sino-Japanese War in order to understand why the Great Powers are currently cooperating with China's policy of playing one power off against another." Looking back, army propagandists felt "it was not an overstatement to call all of history since the Meiji period the history of Great Power intervention and oppression."[75]

This history, the army reminded the Japanese, began with the Triple Intervention of 1895, when Japan was deprived of "its foothold on the Asian continent." Subsequent "Great Power aggression on China" led the way to the Russo-Japanese War. After the war, Japan "went through torture" (*kuniku*) to disarm Western loan and railroad-building schemes aimed at "driving Japan from Manchuria." After these trials, Japan enjoyed a brief moment of progress during World War I, followed by the catastrophic "rights loss conference" of 1922 which ushered in an "era of forced retreat from Manchuria" in the 1920s.[76] Thus the army's chronicle of the previous four decades—the period of Japan's stunning rise as an Asian imperial power, during which it acquired two colonies, a sphere of influence in Manchuria, the Pacific Islands mandate, and various other imperial interests—stressed failure, loss, and imperial decline.

The army reserved a special place for the threat to national security posed by the Soviet Union.[77] Explaining the Russian peril, one army pam-

---

74. Rikugunshō, *Manshū jihen boppatsu man'ichinen* (Rikugunshō, 1932), pp. 3–4; Rikugunshō, *Kokusai renmei*, pp. 74–75; Rikugunshō, *Manshūkoku*, pp. 4, 10, 12, 17.

75. Rikugunshō, *Waga Manmō*, pp. 2–3.

76. Ibid., pp. 2–3, 9–11, 17–23, 35, 38–39, 44.

77. Pamphlets dealing with the Russian peril included Rikugunshō, *Hakka ni sonaeyo* [Guard against the White Peril]; Rikugunshō, *Sorenpō daiichiji gonen keikaku no seika to dainiji gonen keikaku no tenbō* [The Outcome of the Soviet Union's First Five-Year Plan and Prospects for the Second Five-Year Plan] (Rikugunshō, 1932); Rikugunshō, *Shina ni okeru kyōsantō no katsudō* [Communist Party Activity in China] (Rikugunshō, 1932); Rikugunshō, *Waga Manmō hatten no rekishi to rekkoku kanshō no kaiko* [The History of Japanese Development of Manchuria-Mongolia and a Review of Great Power Intervention]; Rikugunshō, *Manmō mondai no saininshiki to kokumin no kakugo* [A New Understanding of

phlet declared, "If you want to understand the national character of the Russian people you have only to look at their history. In a word the history of the Russian people is the history of aggression." The latest manifestation of the Russian predilection for territorial expansion was "red aggression" (*akka shinryaku*): "The aggressive character of the Russian people is no different under the Soviet Union from the tsar. For Russians aggression is their temperament and their national policy. . . . Since the establishment of the Soviet Union, without a single day of rest, the Russian people have . . . spread the evil of Bolshevism everywhere . . . and the poison has even seeped into the Japanese Empire." The five-year plans, warned the army, were integral to the Soviet plan to Bolshevize Asia and aimed at "strengthening national defense and preparing for war."[78] Therefore Japan "must be on the alert for military aggression" and other machinations to "imperil Japan through economic disruption or inciting Chinese and Koreans to spread evil ideas."[79]

The language of hostility and confrontation that the army used to describe its relationships with Europe and the United States was part of a strategy to demonize the West. As one pamphlet title summarized the message, *Guard against the White Peril.* "If we look we can see that the entire history of diplomacy in East Asia is in fact the history of aggression on Asia by the white races. They talk about justice, humanity, and peace . . . but toward undeveloped areas they act only to menace [*ikaku*], deceive [*giman*], and aggress [*shinryaku*]. The yellow races must be prepared for the rise of the White Peril in the East, for to end the deadlock in white civilization, the white races must aggress upon and victimize Asia."[80] In such tracts, the army used Japanese sensitivity to Western racism to fan a sense of isolation from the imperialist community, at the same time providing their own racial justification for a new military imperialism in Asia.

In consciously inflammatory terms, the army advocated a bold new vision of empire, one which, as army pamphleteers hastened to explain,

---

the Manchuria-Mongolia Problem and the Resolution of the Japanese People] (Rikugunshō, 1932); Rikugunshō, *Manshū ni okeru kyōsantō* [The Communist Party in Manchuria] (Rikugunshō, 1933); Rikugunshō, *Shina henkyō ni taisuru Sorenpō no sakudō* [The Schemes of the Soviet Union on the China Frontier] (Rikugunshō, 1933); Rikugunshō, *Sorenpō buryokusen junbi no shinten* [The Progress of Soviet Preparations for War] (Rikugunshō, 1933).

78. "Shii no jōsei to kokubō," in Rikugunshō, *Manmō mondai*, pp. 8–12.

79. Rikugunshō, *Hakka ni sonaeyo*, p. 8.

80. Ibid., pp. 3–4.

required a comprehensive revision of Japan's foreign-policy approach. This meant not only providing more forceful leadership of Asia, but also standing up to the West. "As we have seen," lectured army spokesmen,

> the permanent resolution of the Manchurian-Mongolian problem is not possible by the mere resolution of our problems with China. Up until now our hesitation to restrain China's high-handedness was nothing more than deference to the oppression of foreign countries. As history clearly shows, if we do not stop adjusting our policies to accommodate the Great Powers, even the application of real force against China would simply be a waste of our national strength. Therefore we need to resolve to overcome intervention by third countries in the future, for if we do not pursue an autonomous foreign policy it is clear that we cannot expect a positive outcome of the China problem.[81]

Calling this approach a "Monroe Doctrine for Asia," army representatives explained that the new policy signified the purge of "lackey diplomacy" and "bankrupt foreign-policy conservatism," and represented an "epoch-making" leap forward toward an "autonomous foreign policy" (*jishu dokushu gaikō*).[82]

In essence, autonomous foreign policy was a game of brinksmanship. If you stood your ground, you won the day. But this meant that the Japanese "had to be prepared for the worst-case scenario."[83] Capturing the Manichaean proportions of the army's vision of an imperialist high noon, an army pamphlet published in early 1934 depicted a great showdown between Japan and the West in Asia: "The Manchurian Incident . . . was for Imperial Japan a holy war in self-defense. The time of heaven had arrived and Japan acted decisively. . . . Now Japan stands at the center of a world which has entered the Pacific Age. . . . The Manchurian Incident changed world history. Japan, looked upon in the past as a mere watchdog of the Far East, has now become one of the powerful countries of the world. The age of white race omnipotence is passing and Japan is leading the world into an era of international morality."[84] Saturating its propaganda with war words and confrontational images, the army tried to stir up feelings of hostility and paranoia toward the West, using fear tactics to promote the cause of military imperialism in Manchukuo.

---

81. Rikugunshō, *Waga Manmō*, pp. 48–49.
82. Rikugunshō, *Manshūkoku*, p. 5.
83. Rikugunshō, *Waga Manmō*, p. 45; Rikugunshō, *Manshūkoku*, p. 17.
84. From Rikugunshō, *Nichiro sengo nijūkūnen kōkoku wa taiheiyō jidai no sekai jikushin ni tatsu* (1934). Quoted in Eguchi, "Manshū jihenki no Rikugunshō panfuretto," p. 189.

This message resonated with the new xenophobia in the mass media, placing the official story of the Manchurian Incident within a master narrative of national victimization and expansion in self-defense. By 1931 the image of Japan surrounded by a hostile crowd of Western bullies was a familiar one to most Japanese. It expressed the sense of powerlessness and isolation that had shaped perceptions of Japan's place in the world since the humiliating Triple Intervention of 1895. Just as familiar and equally powerful was the picture of Japan, provoked beyond endurance, punching its way out of this hostile crowd. Since the 1870s, when Japanese began to advocate intervention in Korea as a means of protecting Japan from the incursions of the Western powers, imperial ideology sanctioned expansionism as the necessary corollary to self-defense. Though outside the country few people were persuaded that Japan was the victim of Chinese aggression in the Manchurian Incident, to Japanese it made sense in the context of this ideology of imperialism. In other words, the official story was effective because it explained the Manchurian Incident through the conventions of imperial mythology.

JAPAN'S CASE AT THE LEAGUE OF NATIONS

While the army portrayed Japan as a victim of white imperialism and Chinese aggression, reports emerging from the Foreign Ministry on the fate of Japan's case in the League were also fostering "a sense of ill usage." When Chinese diplomats brought Zhang Xueliang's case to the League, they challenged the Japanese army's self-defense argument and accused Japan of an illegal invasion of Chinese territory. To defend their nation against the Chinese charges and to quell doubts within Japan about the adverse impact of the Manchurian occupation on relations with the West, Japanese diplomats sought to depict Japan as the victim of Chinese mendacity and Western ignorance.

The Foreign Ministry gave first priority to an indirect strategy of defense, countering China's string of charges with a campaign of vilification directed at the Chinese government. Foreign Ministry representatives asserted repeatedly that officials of the Chinese government had become international outlaws "by their campaigns for the unilateral denunciation of treaties, by their anti-foreign agitation, and by their systematic violation of undertakings solemnly entered into." By such illegal means, the Foreign Ministry asserted, "the Chinese central authorities and the rulers of Manchuria, particularly Marshal Chang Hsueh-liang [Zhang Xueliang], have attempted and are still attempting to destroy all the work of the Japanese in Manchuria."[85] It was, as one official summed it up, "warfare of an in-sidious character."[86]

Later, after the release of the Lytton Commission Report in the fall of 1932, the Foreign Ministry introduced a new theme in the strategy of national character assassination. Pointing out that China had "for more than ten years been in a state of civil war, in a condition of complete chaos and incredible anarchy" brought about by "wars between the Chinese generals," Japanese diplomats announced, "the Japanese Government do not and cannot consider that China is an 'organized people' within the meaning of the Covenant of the League of Nations." By asserting that China was not an organized state, Japanese diplomats implied it was not a legitimate member of the community of nations and hence could not be entitled to any of the rights or protections of international law. "Had such difficulties arisen in another country which had a properly organized and efficient administration," the Foreign Ministry ruefully concluded, "our action would have been different. There would have been no need for us to go to the point we have reached now.... We could have observed literally the provisions of the Covenant." But because of China's internal chaos, "countries with interests in China have often been compelled to employ methods which would not have been permitted if the same difficulties had occurred elsewhere in a really organized country.... We are obliged to take the protection of the lives and rights of our nationals into our own hands."[87]

While laboring to discredit China, the Foreign Ministry tried to present Japan as an upstanding international citizen. Responding to charges of an unjustified military invasion of Chinese territory in the fall of 1931, diplomats insisted that Japan was only protecting rights derived "from lawfully concluded treaties and agreements and many acquired interests." Since these "rights and interests" were "absolutely essential to Japan's existence," diplomats declared, "the Japanese nation was unanimous in demanding" that they "be safeguarded." In the hands of the Foreign Ministry, the Sino-Japanese controversy at the League was turned into a contest of character. On one side stood Japan: law-abiding, sincere, and determined—a model member of international society. On the other

85. Willoughby, pp. 214–216.
86. Japanese Delegation to the League of Nations, *The Manchurian Question: Japan's Case in the Sino-Japanese Dispute as Presented before the League of Nations* (Geneva: League of Nations, 1933), p. 78.
87. Willoughby, pp. 243–245.

stood China, a disorganized band of lawless treaty-breakers. As Matsuoka Yōsuke expressed it to the League in 1932, who was the more reliable? "I earnestly beg you to deal with us on our terms and give us your confidence. Our history during the past sixty years is, I think, a guarantee of our good faith; is that history of no worth beside China's history, the history of creating disturbances and bringing about catastrophes in the Far East?"[88]

Having opted from the outset to turn the discussions in the League into a popularity contest between Japan and China, the Foreign Ministry found itself in a bind when the first round of discussions in the fall of 1931 failed to give Japan a clear victory. Still committed, at that stage, to maintaining Japan's good standing in the League and hoping to bring the Kwantung Army under control, Shidehara Kijūrō's Foreign Ministry played a very cautious game that fall. Shidehara put on a generally impassive face in response to the three League resolutions of the fall of 1931, though there was a considerable difference in the terms of the first two. The September 30 resolution, which accepted Japanese assurances and merely urged both parties to withdraw forces as soon as practicable, favored Japan; it passed unanimously. The October 24 resolution, in contrast, presented Japan with a two-week deadline to withdraw the Kwantung Army from the newly occupied areas. It failed only when Japan exercised its veto power in the face of otherwise unanimous support. Despite the shift in League posture represented by the failed October resolution, the Foreign Ministry took pains to avoid publicly emphasizing the differences. To the extent that Japanese diplomats offered public comment on the significance of the resolutions for Japan or China, they signaled approval of the first by repeated declarations of the government's intent to comply with its provisions, and showed disapproval of the second by maintaining a dignified silence on the subject.[89]

The third resolution of December 10 temporarily shelved the League discussions by providing for the establishment of a Commission of Inquiry to establish the facts of the controversy and recommend measures for its solution. Since the report of such a commission would have great moral authority, unless the Foreign Ministry could guarantee favorable content, the resolution posed a threat to a positive diplomatic outcome for Japan. Moreover, although Japanese diplomats repeatedly denied the right of third

88. Ibid., pp. 215–216, 489.
89. Ibid., p. 302; Tonedachi Masao, ed., *Manshū Shanhai jihen zenki* (Asahi shinbunsha, 1932), p. 163.

parties to intervene in the Sino-Japanese controversy, by endorsing the commission, Japan in effect sanctioned the right of a third party to judge the matter. For these reasons, the Foreign Ministry had strenuously objected when a commission had been suggested earlier.

In December, however, Japanese representatives publicly took credit for proposing it themselves. The Foreign Ministry presented the commission as a great opportunity for explaining, and therefore exonerating, Japan's position. Unveiling the proposal, the Japanese delegate to the League declared his hope that it would give the world a "clear view of realities" and "impartial information on the situation" which "the Japanese Government considers the essential condition of a fundamental solution."[90] Hopes were publicly entertained that the commission would become a tool for "educating the League" on the "conditions in China which are at the root of the disturbances of peace of the Far East," but would not "be empowered to intervene in the negotiations . . . between the two parties, or to supervise the movements of the military forces of either." This sanguine view of the scope of the commission's investigations raised hopes in Japan for a report that would bear out its own case against China and abstain from any review of Japan's actions.[91] This public nod of approval, and the efforts of the Foreign Ministry to portray a resolution of dubious benefit in terms of a public relations victory, testified to the strength of the Foreign Ministry's desire to minimize diplomatic friction between Japan and the West in the fall of 1931.

By the time the Lytton Commission released its report and the League reopened discussions of the Sino-Japanese controversy in November 1932, the foreign minister's portfolio had changed hands several times and the Saitō "national unity" cabinet had hardened Japan's diplomatic tone. Although the Lytton Commission offered its share of criticism of China, their findings were devastating for Japan. The report found that China had a weak, but viable central government, rejecting Japan's disorganized state thesis; that Japan's actions on September 18 were not justified by legitimate requirements of self-defense; that Manchuria was an integral part of China; and that the Manchukuo regime was a product of Japanese sponsorship rather than an autonomous independence movement. The report recommended, moreover, that the solution to the controversy did not lie in the recognition of the Manchukuo regime but rather in the creation of

90. Willoughby, pp. 172, 302.
91. Kajima heiwa kenkyūjo, p. 263; Willoughby, p. 172.

a multination advisory conference to create a new administration and to effect the demilitarization of the region.[92]

Alternating between shock, disbelief, and indignation, the Foreign Ministry saw only one way to interpret the verdict of the Lytton Commission Report: the world had "taken sides with China against Japan."[93] Commenting on the report, Japanese delegate Matsuoka Yōsuke conceded that "for Westerners, to whom the conditions of China" were a myth "hard to unravel," it was difficult "to detect and know some of the undercurrents connected with . . . the Orient."[94] But this was no excuse for calling Japan a liar. "The Commission, declining to accept the solemn declarations of the Japanese Government and attaching too little value to the detailed documents presented by them have . . . apparently listened to the opinion of unidentified persons and given credence to letters and communications of doubtful or unknown origin."[95]

Shortly before the release of the Lytton Report, the Foreign Ministry began preparing people at home for a confrontation in the League. Foreign Minister Uchida made his famous "scorched-earth diplomacy" (*shōdo gaikō*) declaration,[96] and speeches of Matsuoka Yōsuke, Japanese delegate to the League of Nations, took on a tone of defiant isolationism. As Matsuoka declared to the League,

> I owe it to candour to state—although it may shock some of you—that the irresponsible and misguided voices which were raised in the autumn of last year and the spring of this year in Geneva scared some of our people so much that they made up their minds to confront even the severest sanction under the Covenant—that is to say, economic boycott. They were ready to face it if need be, and I have to tell you, Gentlemen—and this does not imply any threat on our part . . . that even today our nation is prepared to undergo it. And why? Because they believe that it is a question of now or never. They bow not before threats, they stoop not down even under sanctions. They will calmly face them because, rightly or wrongly they believe that—now or never! And they do believe that they are right.[97]

From their podiums in Tokyo and the stage at Geneva, Japanese diplomats spoke self-righteously of sacrifice in the face of international censure, os-

---

92. Willoughby, pp. 380–413; Japanese Delegation to the League of Nations, pp. 11–76.

93. Japanese Delegation to the League of Nations, p. 165.

94. Ibid., pp. 88, 105.

95. Ibid., p. 45.

96. Kajima heiwa kenkyūjo, pp. 334–335.

97. Japanese Delegation to the League of Nations, p. 160.

tracism, boycotts, sanctions, and even self-destruction—all for the sake of Manchukuo.

Responding to the League's rejection of the Japanese case, Matsuoka sought to portray Japan's defiance of the League as the martyred act of a latter-day Jesus.

> Suppose public opinion were so absolutely against Japan as some of the people try to make out, are you sure that the so-called world opinion will persist forever and never change? Humanity crucified Jesus of Nazareth two thousand years ago. And today? Can any of you assure me that the so-called world opinion can make no mistake? We Japanese feel that we are now put on trial. Some of the people in Europe and America may wish even to crucify Japan in the twentieth century. Gentlemen, Japan stands ready to be crucified! But we do believe, and firmly believe, that in a very few years, world opinion will be changed and that we also shall be understood by the world as Jesus of Nazareth was.[98]

Matsuoka's narrative of Japan's martyrdom in the League reinforced images of national victimization promoted by the army's tales of white perils and Chinese menaces. Promoting the view that Japan had been backed into aggression, the official story created the impression that Japan was not responsible for its military and diplomatic actions of 1931–1933 because it had no choice in the matter. Thus, making an association that carried through the subsequent attacks on China, the Soviet Union, the United States, and Britain, a sense of victimization was used to justify military aggression.

The official story was designed to provide cover and legitimation for the Manchurian Incident, but the narrative of victimization and isolation disseminated by the state held much broader implications. Indeed, the official story heralded Japan's policy shift to a new military imperialism in Asia, for it spelled out the necessity of employing new strategies for dealing with both the West and Asia. Depictions of Western imperialists in league against Japan rejected the possibility of cooperative diplomacy. At the same time, the unyielding call to arms to defend Japanese colonial interests against the threat of incipient Asian nationalism endorsed a more comprehensive use of force in the empire. All this the government proclaimed to the world opinion of foreign nations and the public opinion of Japanese subjects. In the latter case, government efforts to give ideological legitimacy to the new foreign policy were strongly aided by the coverage of current events in the mass media as discussed in Chapter Three. Un-

98. Ibid., p. 166.

official propagandists ably seconded the more self-conscious, directed operations undertaken by government propagandists; their narratives complemented one another.

Together, government propaganda and imperial jingoism produced two modifications to the evolving mythology of empire. First, they forged an unshakable commitment to Manchuria as the heart—the lifeline—of the empire. Second, they greatly strengthened the view that Japan stood alone and isolated in a hostile world. The hardening language of international isolation and military confrontation spoken by government officials did more than just publicly proclaim the shift in foreign policy or revise imperial mythology. Official storytellers also buttressed the new domestic politics of imperialism. Most conspicuously, the rhetoric of international embattlement provided a rallying point for political consensus at home about the army's direction of government. In the process, the propaganda message reinforced the redefinition of the idea of "the public" that was taking place in the context of the army's "campaign to promote the idea of national defense." The official story wove both images of Chinese aggression and Japanese martyrdom into a constructed narrative of national unity in which "the people" stood together against their enemies in the battlefield and their detractors in the community of nations. Symbolically empowering the people in the empire, government propaganda abetted the object of the army's campaign to mobilize a new, more broadly construed public opinion for its own political purposes.

EMPIRE IN THE LOCALITIES

Japan's official storytellers were neither the first nor the last to observe that imperialism and nationalism go hand-in-hand. From the nineteenth century, empire building, particularly imperial warfare, stimulated the growth of national sentiment. State expansion outside the national boundaries and the effort to establish domination as a nation over ethnic and racial "others" required mobilization of support within a national context, even as it created opportunities for constructing the imagined community of nation.[99] The nation thus became the cultural vessel for all of these projects.

But it is easy to lose sight, in this larger picture, of the ways in which imperialism also stimulated the growth of plural identities within the na-

---

99. The phrase comes from Benedict Anderson, *Imagined Communities: Reflections on the Origin and Spread of Nationalism*, rev. ed. (London: Verso, 1991).

kill it before it
multiplies

tional fabric. Looking instead from a grassroots perspective, the social history of the Manchurian Incident emerged in the war support movements that took hold in neighborhoods throughout the country. In this context, popular support for the occupation of Manchuria was mobilized through local institutions that drew on loyalties to region, class, gender, and other subnational communities of interest. Organizational strategies appealed to hierarchies of power and authority far removed from the national government in Tokyo; they expressed social and political agendas bearing little relation to the national interest in Manchuria. Although war support campaigns organized in the fall of 1931 were trumpeted as a demonstration of national determination and commitment, in many instances, the "spontaneous outpouring of support" for the nation that official storytellers laid claim to was, in fact, an expression of parochial concerns.

In 1931 the national press took the lead in organizing the *imon*, or war relief, movement, mobilizing people to send letters and gifts to the troops as well as to help support their families back at home. On September 21, just three days after the onset of fighting, the Osaka *Asahi* began to run articles urging readers to donate money for the support of Japanese troops. In mid October, both the *Asahi* and *Mainichi* newspapers unfurled large-scale fundraising drives; within two months the *Asahi* raised 250,000 and the *Mainichi* 95,000 yen—enough to buy twice that number of gift packets to send to the front.[100]

The national dailies fostered such enthusiasm for their campaign through two devices. First, they published daily columns of donations, listing the name of the individual or organization and the donation amount. Presidents of leading corporations were particularly eager to see their names on the list, for it testified to both their patriotism and their public-spiritedness. Second, to encourage the spirit of sacrifice among citizens of lesser means, the newspapers ran inspirational stories (*bidan*) about impoverished women donating the family's supper money or schoolgirls selling flowers to scrape together a few yen. Such devices fostered a competition among contributors—for the largest donation or the most noble sacrifice—while using the prospect of seeing their deeds celebrated in print to entice readers to participate.

By 1931, readers were long familiar with press-sponsored charity drives for victims of natural and man-made disasters. Like the collections taken up for the Saitama flood victims of 1890 or for soldiers' families in the earlier imperial wars, the campaigns during the Manchurian Incident were

100. Eguchi, *Nihon teikokushugi shiron*, p. 182.

part marketing ploy to increase reader involvement in the newspaper, and part strategy to raise the prestige and stature of the newspaper through public service. As Eleanor Westney points out, by involving readers in one region with the trials of their countrymen elsewhere, such campaigns reinforced a growing sense of national identity.[101] During the Manchurian Incident, the wide use of phrases like "national unity" (*kyōkoku itchi*) and "compatriots in Manchuria" (*zaiMan dōhō*) in reports on the *imon* campaign bolstered the idea of national community. Nevertheless, as the movement spread and formed local organizational bases throughout the country, support for troops defending the empire was articulated increasingly in terms of local pride and loyalty, giving a distinctly local cast to the imagined community of nation.

Following the examples of the *Asahi* and *Mainichi*, local papers throughout the country started their own *imon* campaigns. In Ishikawa, the prefecture's largest paper, the *Hokkoku shinpō*, began to collect donations in mid November. By the end of February, the newspaper had collected 10,000 yen. At the same time in Aichi prefecture, the *Aichi, Shin Aichi, Nagoya,* and *Nagoya mainichi* newspapers joined with local government offices and the chamber of commerce to organize a fundraising movement. By the end of April, they raised 80,725 yen.[102]

Mirroring the parade of national heroes like the "three human bombs" celebrated in the mass media, the prefectural press memorialized local heroes of the Manchurian campaigns. In Yamanashi, the *Yamanashi nichinichi* and *Yamanashi shinpō* sensationalized the prefecture's first battlefield death. Drawn by the papers' articles on the heroic demise of Private Morishita, 15,000 turned out for his Kōfu city funeral on February 28. The press advertised the stage dramatization of Morishita's story and published children's essays and poetry on this model soldier. The two papers also ran stories about Morishita's grieving mother, reporting her exhortations to young men to "destroy the hateful Chinese soldiers."[103]

The mobilization of the local regiment often inspired the organization of a local *imon* movement. The units stationed in Manchuria when the fighting broke out were from northeast Japan—Miyagi, Niigata, and Fukushima. Thus, it was not surprising that the earliest local efforts to or-

---

101. Westney, pp. 187–188.

102. Nakajima Kinji, pp. 25–26, Graph 2; Eguchi, "Manshū jihen to minshū dōin," pp. 152–167, Table 13.

103. Kosuge Nobuko, "Manshū jihen to minshū ishiki: Yamanashi-kenka ni okeru gunkoku netsu to haigai netsu" (paper presented to the Awaya Kentarō Seminar, Rikkyō University, Tokyo, June 1989, photocopy).

ganize war relief came from these regions. In Miyagi, home of the first twenty-nine casualties, articles on the fatalities in the *Kahoku shinpō* were quickly followed by reports of *imon* packets flowing into the regimental headquarters from youth groups, reservist organizations, schools, women's groups, and factories. By early October, local government offices were overseeing a burgeoning *imon* campaign.[104]

This local identification became even clearer in the *kokubō kenkin*, or national defense fundraising drive, which sprung up in the wake of the *imon* movement. In early November, seeing a photo of a front-line unit in which half the soldiers lacked metal helmets, concerned citizens of Takasaki city (Gumma prefecture) began to take up collections to buy those soldiers headgear. Around the same time, a Tokyo youth group, with the cooperation of the *Asahi* and *Mainichi*, started a nationwide appeal for funds to buy an airplane for the Kwantung Army. The Army Ministry decided to encourage military donations by inscribing the contributor's name in bold characters along the side of airplanes built with donated funds. This tactic proved an enormous hit, and between November and April, local governments, business and professional organizations, and student and youth groups throughout the country formed fundraising drives to buy a plane with their own name on it.[105]

Of all the groups collecting money, city and prefectural-based organizations demonstrated the greatest fundraising ability. Of the seventy-six aircraft donated to the army by May 1933, thirty-nine were bestowed by prefectures, two by cities, and thirteen by Japanese residents in Manchuria, Korea, or Taiwan.[106] With the names of those localities emblazoned on their sides, these fifty-four planes—representing close to half of the 10.5 million yen raised by September 1933—left quite visible traces of the local construction of support for empire.[107]

104. Fujii Tadatoshi, *Kokubō fujinkai: hinomaru to kappogi* (Iwanami shoten, 1985), pp. 2–9. Headlines and some text of articles on the Manchurian Incident published in the *Kahoku shinpō* between September 19, 1931, and December 31, 1931, are reprinted in "Sono koro minshū wa: *Kahoku shinpō* kiji ni miru hyakunichikan," *Kikan gendaishi*, no. 1 (November 1972), pp. 172–203; henceforth abbreviated as "Sono koro minshū wa." Coverage of the *imon* campaign in September and early October issues of *Kahoku shinpō*: "Sono koro minshū wa," pp. 172–179.

105. Fujii, pp. 2–9; Eguchi, *Jūgonen sensō no kaimaku*, pp. 114–115.

106. Fujii, p. 18.

107. Tokyo *Nichinichi* (17 September 1933), in "Shinbun shiryō kōsei 'gunkoku bidan' no kōzō, Tōkyō *Nichinichi shinbun* 1932–1935," *Kikan gendaishi*, vol. 2 (May 1973), p. 284. Headlines and some text from articles published in the Tokyo *Nichinichi shinbun* from 1932 to 1935 on home-front support for the Manchurian

The success of the fundraising campaigns was an expression both of local pride and of deference to local authority. As the movements spread, the organizational structure of the *imon* and *kenkin* campaigns reproduced the hierarchies of economic and political power that structured local society. From mid November, organizations such as the Takada City (Niigata prefecture) Association for the Protection of Manchurian-Mongolian Rights and Interests, and Yamagata prefecture's Council for the Support of the Imperial Army in Manchuria began to emerge, assuming control over the war-support movements.[108] Frequently merging with the political lobby groups established in the course of the Army Ministry propaganda campaign, their composition mirrored the pattern established in the national-defense societies. Thus, they brought together heads of the reservist associations, army regiments, local presses, chambers of commerce, youth groups, and religious associations, as well as government officials and school authorities. Despite their ties to central government via the Education Ministry (schools), the Home Ministry (local government), and the Army Ministry (regiments and reservists), the war-support associations remained defined by their regional bases.[109] They were not prefectural chapters of national organizations, answering to the call of the central government; the chain of authority ended with mayors and governors. Hence, the effectiveness of fundraising tactics relied on deference to local, rather than national, power and authority.

In Yamagata, for example, after the local regiment was mobilized in November 1931, the Council for the Support of the Imperial Army in Manchuria formed and drew up plans to send gifts and a goodwill mission to express support for their soldiers, as well as to produce pamphlets, books, and photo albums commemorating the prefecture's contributions to the Manchurian Incident. To underwrite these activities, the council called for a contribution of ten sen per household to be collected on a neighborhood by neighborhood basis. It also proposed a one-sen donation from school-

---

Incident are reprinted in "Shinbun shiryō kōsei 'gunkoku bidan' no kōzō, Tōkyō *Nichinichi shinbun* 1932–1935," *Kikan gendaishi*, vol. 2 (May 1973), pp. 260–307. Henceforth abbreviated as "Shinbun shiryō kōsei."

108. Niigata-ken, *Kindai* 3, vol. 8 of *Niigata kenshi tsūshihen* (Niigata: Niigata-ken, 1988), pp. 408–409; Yamagata-ken, ed., *Kingendai* 2, vol. 5 of *Yamagata kenshi* (Yamagata: Yamagata-ken, 1986), pp. 693–694.

109. The cooperation of government and civilian leadership in the war support movements and the links with central government were characteristic of the Russo-Japanese War, as well. During that war, budgetary limitations led central government officials to reach out to localities for donations. They pressured the local elite to donate funds through community organizations. See Iguchi, pp. 112–115.

children, and members of youth and women's groups. The latter, campaign planners calculated, would bring in donations from 120,000 school children, 31,000 youth-group members, 29,000 technical-school students, 25,000 youth-center trainees, 60,000 reservists, and 35,000 Patriotic Women's Association members.[110]

The tactic of targeting neighborhoods, schools, and voluntary organizations was calculated to compel contributions through peer pressure as well as deference to authority. Fixed sums were set for each neighborhood or youth-association branch; since the group was collectively responsible to meet the target, a great deal of pressure was brought to bear on individuals to pay their share.[111] Because the leadership of the voluntary organizations was composed of the wealthy, well educated, and high-status members of the community, this pressure was expressed in the currency of interpersonal debt and obligation.[112] Exhortations to donate from one's landlord, the principal of the school where local children studied, or the general store owner who ran up tabs for customers were difficult appeals to turn down. These fundraising tactics differed from the newspaper campaign strategy, which appealed for collections through advertisements and rewarded contributors with publicity. Targeted group contributions effectively turned the fundraising campaigns into an informal system of taxation.

There were cases in which people were simply unable to pay. In Miyagi prefecture, devastated by a crop failure, a meeting of mayors petitioned the prefectural government to end the campaign in their areas. In the end, most of the actual contributions came from wealthy households who were pressured to make up the difference by officials overseeing the campaign.[113] In Yamanashi, a silk-producing region hard hit by the collapse of the American market, prefectural campaign organizers also found people uncooperative. By November 1932, after nine months, they managed to raise only 1,500 yen, well short of the 70,000 required to buy an airplane. Campaign organizers drew up a new set of targets, pressing Kōfu city to take on a larger share of the burden and asking those who paid taxes of over 10 yen to make up two-thirds of the city's target. To raise interest, the prefectural government published a collection of *Inspirational Tales of Patriotic Donations*, filled with eulogies to local heroes. Campaign organizers

110. Yamagata-ken, pp. 693–694.
111. For a discussion of the collection tactics, see Nakajima Kinji.
112. On local leadership of voluntary associations, see Smethurst, pp. 89–140.
113. Awaya, "Fasshoka to minshū ishiki," p. 266.

even resorted to strong-arm tactics, sending police along to beat up recalcitrants. In the end, these strategies succeeded; the following April the army christened the *Yamanashi Patriot*.[114]

In such campaigns the coercive power of the state was articulated in distinctly local terms: Yamanashi citizens were pressured to sacrifice so that Yamanashi did its part "for the nation." In Yamanashi and elsewhere, the organizations that ran the war-support movement, particularly the *kokubō kenkin* campaign, were almost entirely regional. For this reason, mobilization of public support for the Manchurian Incident both drew on and helped reinforce local identities. Nevertheless, the formation of such imperial localism did not preclude the parallel growth in imperial nationalism. Indeed, one of the most interesting dimensions of the mobilization process in the early thirties was the way these two interacted. At a discursive level, the two fields overlapped; the language of mobilization interwove appeals to region and nation. Yet at an organizational level, there was clear separation; here regional institutions nurtured a local culture that maintained a measure of autonomy from national control. Thus the dynamic interaction between empire, nation, and the localities was a complex one, evading simple categorization as mutually reinforcing on one hand, or oppositional on the other.

LABOR, WOMEN, AND EMPIRE

These dynamics of popular mobilization applied to social collectivities as well, in particular the groups of factory workers, youths, and women who actively participated in the war-support campaigns. Throughout 1932 and 1933, the mass media applauded the collective contributions of patriotic citizens. In April, the Tokyo *Nichinichi* triumphantly announced that 360,000 female higher school students throughout the country had raised 31,460 yen. They used the funds to buy an ambulance, a "suitable contribution for women."[115] In June 1932, NHK broadcast live from Tokyo's Yoyogi Parade Grounds the grand christening ceremony of the *Middle School Student Patriot* (a light bomber), the *School Girl Patriot* (a scout plane), the *Elementary Student Patriot,* and the *Preschooler Patriot*.[116] The Tokyo *Nichinichi* praised the 14,000 tobacco merchants' donation of 10,000 yen; it also applauded the Kyūshū barbers' union that sent its members

---

114. Fujii, pp. 20–23.

115. Tokyo *Nichinichi* (14 April 1932), in "Shinbun shiryō kōsei," p. 277.

116. Ikei, "1930 nendai," pp. 149–152; Tokyo *Nichinichi* (5 May 1932), in "Shinbun shiryō kōsei," p. 278.

out "to schools and youth centers, giving discount cuts and selling soap," and raised the 75,000 yen needed to buy a *Kyūshū Barbers* fighter plane.[117] Like regionally organized activities, such participation was mobilized through institutions that defined a corporate identity—schools, youth groups, unions, factories, and women's organizations. Many of the institutions themselves predated the Manchurian Incident, but were transformed as they became vehicles of mass mobilization. In the process, members reshaped their social identities and redefined the limits of their public roles.

Two groups particularly affected by this process were workers and women. Both had been organizing themselves in social movements since before the turn of the century. They had played prominent roles in the politics of identity that took shape in the teens and twenties, joining the list of marginalized people that banded into collectivities to demand a greater share of wealth and power from Japan's political economy. The drawing power of their movements placed workers and women at the vanguard of the social and cultural experimentation that took place during these years.

In the context of the Manchurian Incident war fever, these icons of Taishō democracy seemed to reverse course, turning their movements to support militarism and empire. Like the conversion of the mass media, the volte-face of the labor movement and its affiliated left-wing parties is usually explained as the consequence of government repression. While a step-up in political surveillance, censorship, and arrests certainly placed new limits on the strategies of the social movement, the swell of imperial jingoism that followed the Manchurian Incident also opened up new possibilities for mobilizing organizational support through appeals to patriotism and defense of the empire. Viewed in this light, the support of labor and women for militarism is less a reversal than a continuation of efforts to secure social and political power by whatever means offered them.

In the wake of the Manchurian Incident, the battle lines laid down over the course of the twenties quickly transformed into the competing war-support drives carried out by capital and labor. After over a decade of intense labor strife, both sides welcomed the opportunity to win public sympathy by demonstrations of patriotism. Beginning in World War I, labor organizations had taken root in Japan's industrial centers. Though

117. Tokyo *Nichinichi* (9 February 1933), in "Shinbun shiryō kōsei," p. 281; and Tokyo *Nichinichi* (21 September 1933), in "Shinbun shiryō kōsei," p. 284.

only a small percentage of workers were organized, the visibility and militancy of unions compelled the attention of industrialists and government officials, winning concessions from both. In 1930 and 1931, the depression sparked a new rash of disputes, as owners and managers responded to the crisis with pay cuts, dismissals, and speedups. Both sides were desperate, and their mutual accusations began to echo the rhetoric of right-wing extremism and fascism. Thus, labor attacked the selfishness and greed of capital, while capital predicted that labor activism threatened Japan with social catastrophe.[118]

Defensive and embattled, businessmen tried to diffuse a perceived widespread anti-capitalist sentiment by giving public and enthusiastic support for the imperial campaigns in 1931 and 1932. Business organizations throughout the country took up donations for the troops. In Yamanashi and Aichi prefectures, chambers of commerce led the local *imon* and *kenkin* drives.[119] The chambers of commerce in Kobe, Tokyo, Osaka, and Nagoya drew up a plan to raise donations of 400 yen from each of their members: the money raised was hand-delivered by a goodwill mission to Manchuria in November 1931.[120] In Osaka, the city's business leaders donated most of the funds for an aerial defense fundraising campaign that began in March 1932, 300,000 yen from Sumitomo, 50,000 from Mitsui, 50,000 from Mitsubishi, 30,000 from Ōsaka shōkō, and 20,000 each from Kōnoike, Yamaguchi, Meiji seimei, Nomura Tokushichi, and Wada Chūzaemon.[121]

The money donated by businesses represented substantial outlays for these organizations. Some businessmen made dramatic individual contributions, such as the Tokyo stockbroker Obuse Shinzaburō, who bought two *Obuse Patriots* for the army.[122] Other firms, in particular the *zaibatsu* conglomerates like Mitsui and Mitsubishi which had branches throughout the country and were active in a variety of business organizations, made multiple contributions; 50,000 yen here and 50,000 yen there must have added up. The business community tried to buy public sympathy through their conspicuous enthusiasm for the occupation of Manchuria. Demon-

---

118. For the labor situation of 1930–1932, see Gordon, *Labor and Imperial Democracy,* pp. 240–241.

119. Eguchi, "Manshū jihen to minshū dōin," pp. 152–167; Kosuge.

120. Nihon shōkōkaigisho, "Manshūgun imon ni kansuru kiroku" (1932), Tōkyō shōkō kaigisho microreel no. 138: 2810–2837.

121. Fujii, pp. 30–31.

122. Tokyo *Nichinichi* (6 February 1932), in "Shinbun shiryō kōsei," p. 275.

strations of wartime charity and corporate beneficence sent a message to the public that, labor leaders' accusations to the contrary, capitalists were patriotic and supported the national unity on the Manchurian question.

The prominent public support of capital for the Manchurian Incident was a challenge to workers, who were determined not to let capital steal the show in the press or monopolize the legitimating mantle of patriotism. Workers carried out their own collection drives, demonstrating the strength of their organizations by getting their names in the newspapers. Workers earned encomiums from the *Asahi* when they ranked first on the list of large contributions to the newspaper's campaign, accounting for almost a quarter (22.8 percent) of donations.[123] Thirty thousand miners and refinery operatives from fourteen Mitsui coal mines (including Mitsui kōzan, Matsushima tankō, and Kamaishi kōzan) began a collection drive under the slogan "Show the Power of Labor." Motivated, the Tokyo *Nichinichi* reported, by "indignation at the indifference of the bourgeoisie toward the Manchurian Incident," the group raised 70,000 yen to purchase an attack plane for the army.[124] In this way, workers used fundraising campaigns to distinguish themselves from capital and project an image of worker solidarity in the service of patriotism. In other instances, they draped demands for concessions in the flag. When the management of the Tokyo subway decided to dismiss drafted employees, workers struck, singing military marches to underscore the point that it was unpatriotic for management to fire workers who were serving their country.[125]

The tactic of using patriotism as a rallying cry for labor solidarity had its costs for some groups in the labor movement. For a labor movement split, by the late twenties, into right- and left-wing factions, the nationalist appeals strengthened the hand of the conservatives. In December 1932, Kamino Shin'ichi, the right-wing Japanist labor leader and head of the Ishikawajima Shipyard Jikyō kumiai, brought four Tokyo and Yokohama labor federations together to form an airplane fundraising association. After successfully raising 100,000 yen, Kamino went south to sign on unions in the Kansai and Kyūshū regions. Applauding Kamino's success, the Tokyo *Nichinichi* reported, "though at first workers made no donations, since August of 1932 their contributions have grown to a point where they

123. Awaya, "Fasshoka to minshū ishiki," p. 276.
124. Tokyo *Nichinichi* (5 May 1932), in "Shinbun shiryō kōsei," p. 278.
125. Kanda Fuhito, ed., *Shōwashi nenpyō: Taishō 12 nen 9 gatsu 1 nichi— Heisei gannen 12 gatsu 31 nichi: nenpyō de tsuzuru Shōwa no ayumi* (Shōgakkan, 1990), p. 19.

reached 164,900 yen for March alone—24.8 percent of the total. . . . Labor unions all over the country are uniting under the slogan 'Protect the Fatherland.' "[126] Extolling worker patriotism, such reports gave public legitimacy to the labor movement and advertised the strength of its organization.

Yet, although this may have been a public relations victory for labor in general, it represented an organizational triumph for the right wing within the specific factional context of the movement. Writing in 1933 on the status of the right-wing labor movement, Kamino regarded the fundraising drive as a tactical victory for his side. He argued, first, that such activities represented an ideological counteroffensive to the socialist- and Communist-inspired labor movement, replacing class with national consciousness. Second, Kamino pointed out that the "Patriotic Labor Festival" which emerged from the fundraising drive created an alternative to and undermined support for the left-wing workers' May Day. The numbers bore him out, for participants in the 1933 May Day festivities totaled 28,000, down from 41,000 the previous year.[127]

According to Home Ministry reports, an estimated 80,000 organized workers (20 percent of all organized workers) and 20,000 unorganized workers participated in the *kenkin* campaign, excluding workers at army and navy arsenals.[128] The active support of so many workers for the military campaigns in China doubtless played a part in the rightward turn of the proletarian parties. Because of their affiliations with the union movement, social democrats were split into right and left wings mirroring the pattern in organized labor. Prior to the Manchurian Incident both the Social Democratic party (Shakai minshutō) and the National Labor-Farmer Masses party (Zenkoku rōnō taishutō) held strong anti-war, anti-imperialist platforms.[129] But like the union movement, in the wake of the Manchurian Incident proletarian parties perceived an organizational advantage to embracing patriotism and defense of the empire in Northeast China. Within days of the occupation of Fengtian, the general

126. Tokyo *Nichinichi* (19 April 1933), in "Shinbun shiryō kōsei," pp. 282–283. On Kamino's Japanist labor movement, see Andrew Gordon, *The Evolution of Labor Relations in Japan: Heavy Industry, 1853–1955* (Cambridge: Council on East Asian Studies, Harvard University, 1988), pp. 222–232.

127. Kamino Shin'ichi, *Nihonshugi rōdō undō no shinzui* (1933). Quoted in Awaya, "Fasshoka to minshū ishiki," p. 277. Statistics from Awaya, "Fasshoka to minshū ishiki," pp. 276–277.

128. Awaya, "Fasshoka to minshū ishiki," pp. 276–277.

129. On anti-imperialist activism of the proletarian parties in the 1920s, see Eguchi, *Nihon teikokushugi shiron*, pp. 42–43.

secretary of the more conservative Social Democratic party, Akamatsu Katsumaro, announced "unconditional support for the Army Ministry and general staff," signaling the abandonment of party opposition to imperialism.[130]

Both proletarian parties sent representatives to look at the situation in Manchuria; these missions returned with positive reports on army action. A November 22 Diet speech by Matsutani Yojirō, one of the Labor-Farmer Masses party's two Diet representatives, declared that the protection of rights and interests was vital to the survival of labor because without Manchurian resources "national industry would be destroyed."[131] *Kenpeitai* (military police) surveillance reports observed that the party was "thrown into increasing disarray,"[132] as Matsutani's speech splintered it into an antiwar, a national-socialist, and an oscillating main faction.[133] Likewise, the *kenpeitai* reported the tremendous impact of the Manchurian Incident on the Social Democratic party: "It is a turning point for the party, and the argument to abandon socialism and adopt national socialism has suddenly swept the party leadership."[134]

In contrast to the socialist parties, the Manchurian Incident inspired the underground Communist party to new heights of anti-military political activism." In 1931, between September 18 and October 31, the JCP and its affiliated organizations conducted 262 anti-war actions, mostly leaflet distributions. For a short time, the JCP made a vigorous effort to organize within the army, distributing a monthly magazine entitled *The Soldier's Friend*. Army Ministry statistics recorded that anti-military actions rose yearly from 1,055 in 1929 to a peak of 2,437 in 1932. This proved to be the swan song of the JCP as an organized movement, however. In October 1932, the government carried out mass arrests of some 12,622 suspected Communists, the largest crackdown since 12,000 people were rounded up on March 15, 1928. The new wave of political repression broke the back of the movement, with recorded anti-war actions dropping off to 1,694 in 1933 and 597 in 1934.[135]

---

130. Kenpei shireikan Toyama Bunzō, "Manshū jiken ni taisuru hankyō naisa no ken hōkoku" (23 September 1931), in Fujiwara and Kunugi, *Manshū jihen to kokumin dōin*, p. 31.

131. Rikugunshō, "Manshū jihen to shakai undō" (February 1932), in Fujiwara and Kunugi, *Manshū jihen to kokumin dōin*, p. 178.

132. Ibid., p. 179.

133. Hirokawa Tadahide, "Hanfashizumu undōron," in Eguchi Keiichi, ed., *Nihon fashizumu no keisei*, vol. 1 of *Taikei Nihon gendaishi* (Nihon hyōronsha, 1978), pp. 217–218.

134. Rikugunshō, "Manshū jihen to shakai undō" (February 1932), in Fujiwara and Kunugi, *Manshū jihen to kokumin dōin*, p. 180.

135. Ibid., p. 176; Rikugunshō, "Kinji ni okeru hangun undō no keikō ni tsuite"

Even before the arrests decimated their ranks, workers had begun to reject the anti-imperialist appeals of the JCP in favor of the Japanist message of labor leaders like Kamino Shin'ichi. As an Army Ministry report noted in February, months before the arrests, "the zealous propaganda activities of the far left are being overwhelmed by the feverish patriotism of the people. They have no impact whatsoever. Their vague internationalism and anti-war sentiments arouse absolutely no sympathy among the people because the groups they are addressing—the so-called propertyless classes such as laborers and tenants—are the most devoted patriots of all."[136] The "people's patriotism" was due in no small part to the success of the Army Ministry's own zealous propaganda campaign. But it also reflected the success of the right-wing labor movement's strategies of mobilization, not to mention the basic appeal to workers of the imperialist message. This support of workers for the Manchurian Incident, more than government repression, accounted for the increasing marginality of the Communist party and the hasty abandonment of the non-Communist left's anti-war stance. Despite the draconian provisions of the Peace Preservation Law, the left could still oppose empire and war on the eve of the Manchurian Incident, but backed down on their own almost immediately afterward.

Like the participation of labor in war-support movements, the mobilization of women for the Manchurian cause in 1931–1933 transformed the institutions that mediated women's public activities. The dramatic surge of women's activism in this period built on the social and cultural gains of the previous two decades. In the context of the war fever, women, like workers, used their newfound power to endorse the militarization of the state and go-fast imperialism in China. Support for the Manchurian Incident won them, as it had workers, public legitimacy; it also gave women the opportunity to expand dramatically their institutional strength.

The growth of the women's movement in wartime was not a new phenomenon. Whether in 1895, 1905, or 1931, imperial warfare encouraged the rapid expansion of women's organizations and offered women opportunities for new forms of public participation. These efforts must be un-

---

(June 1935), in Fujiwara and Kunugi, *Manshū jihen to kokumin dōin*, p. 192; George M. Beckmann and Genji Ōkubo, *The Japanese Communist Party, 1922–1945* (Stanford: Stanford University Press, 1969), p. 237; George Oakley Totten, *The Social Democratic Movement in Prewar Japan* (New Haven: Yale University Press, 1966), p. 64.

136. Rikugunshō, "Manshū jihen to shakai undō" (February 1932), in Fujiwara and Kunugi, *Manshū jihen to kokumin dōin*, p. 174.

derstood within the context of the legislation of 1889 and 1890, which set the perimeters of women's activism by prohibiting their political partici-pation. Until partially revised in 1922, these laws forbid women to even observe meetings where political subjects were discussed.[137] In the early years, government officials interpreted this legislation broadly and frowned upon most forms of public activism for women. But during the Sino-Japanese War, elite women pushed the limits of such strictures on their activities. In the name of patriotism, they formed groups like the Fukuoka Women's Association and turned women's Buddhist organiza-tions such as the Nagano Shinsei Women's Church to war-support activ-ities.[138] Such organizations convinced officials that there was a legitimate public role for women during wartime, and the government cautiously endorsed the formation of the Aikoku fujinkai (Patriotic Women's Asso-ciation) in 1901. With the backing of the Home and Army ministries, the Aikoku fujinkai set up prefectural branches throughout the country. These branches were made up of upper-class women, the wives of prefectural governors and top-ranking military officers, as well as members of the imperial family and the nobility. Seeing a green light on social activism in the name of public service, over the next few years women formed char-itable organizations in many provincial cities. During the Russo-Japanese War, women's war-support associations mushroomed throughout the country.[139]

Pioneers in the women's movement used official endorsement of these organizations to argue their case for women's political rights. Writing of the Aikoku fujinkai, *Sekai fujin* (International Woman) founder Fukuda Hideko pointed out that "the tens of thousands who formed this organi-zation . . . are the very same women whom the Japanese constitution treats as incompetents [*munōryokusha*]." She argued that because support for the war was a political expression, it was inconsistent for "the government authorities and society in general to lavish praise on the meritorious deeds" of the Patriotic Women's Association, while prohibiting their political par-ticipation.[140] Thus, the call for their public services gave women the op-portunity to make claims for greater social and political authority.

Between 1905 and 1931, the range of women's public participation

---

137. Until the end of World War II, women were denied the right to vote and were prohibited from joining or forming political parties.

138. Kokuritsu kyōiku kenkyūjo, ed., *Shakai kyōiku 1*, vol. 7 of *Nihon kindai kyōiku hyakunenshi* (Kyōiku kenkyū shinkōkai, 1974), pp. 632–633.

139. Ibid., pp. 634, 647–648.

140. Ibid., p. 635.

expanded in a number of directions. First, through a series of public-education campaigns, the Home and Education ministries began to actively promote the formation of women's organizations at the village and hamlet level. As a result, the neighborhood fujinkai (women's association) and kanojokai (young women's association) took their place among the growing list of quasi-governmental voluntary associations. According to a Home Ministry survey taken in 1920, such organizations numbered 5,570 nationwide, with a total membership of 872,407.[141] Government efforts to bring these and such groups as the Aikoku fujinkai together under a single organizational umbrella culminated in the formation of the Dai Nippon rengo fujinkai in 1930. Covering the founding ceremonies, the Tokyo *Asahi* reported that 25,000 representatives from over 6,000 organizations were in attendance, and estimated that the membership of participating women's groups reached 2 million nationwide.[142]

In addition to the growth of women's organizations under government sponsorship, women's participation in socialist organizations and a movement for women's suffrage created a second zone of public activity. Although their numbers were small, women were active in the fledgling socialist Heiminsha (1903–1905) and the Japan Socialist party (1906–1907) before government suppression brought a temporary halt to the movement. When it revived after World War I, socialist women formed the Sekirankai in 1921 and championed women's rights in the proletarian culture movement of the late 1920s. Middle-class intellectual women founded the Bluestocking Society (Seitōsha) in 1911, as well as its successor organizations, the New Women's Society (1919, Shin fujin kyōkai) and the Women's Suffrage League (1925, Fusen kakutoku dōmei). Though ultimately unsuccessful in their fight for suffrage, by bringing their demands into public discourse, these women expanded the boundaries of political possibility.

Finally, the wave of industrialization during World War I opened up new avenues of public activity for women as producers and consumers. Before World War I, in an employment pattern characterized as "life-cycle service," women from tenant-farming families worked in factories before they were married, and on family farms or in family businesses afterward. In the twenties, wives and daughters of the urban middle class began to

---

141. Ibid., pp. 653–666, 1035.
142. Originally reported in the December 23, 1930, issue of the Tokyo *Asahi;* cited in Kokuritsu kyōiku kenkyūjo, ed., *Shakai kyōiku 2*, vol. 8 of *Nihon kindai kyōiku hyakunenshi* (Kyōiku kenkyū shinkōkai, 1974), pp. 349–350.

break this pattern, working in department stores, office buildings, hospitals, and schools.[143] At the same time, the growth of this urban middle class and a relatively well-paid "aristocracy" of labor encouraged the expansion of a consumer market. In 1919 and 1920, department stores opened up in cities throughout the country and over the following years a string of new products came on the market.[144] As managers of household finances, women were the purchasers of the new electrical appliances, household conveniences, food products, clothes, and cosmetics. Starting with the enormously successful *Shufu no tomo*, a flood of women's magazines emerged, creating a public forum for the construction of a women's culture. Public recognition of women's social authority as consumers was symbolized by the appearance of the "modern girl" as the icon of Taishō consumer culture: the public woman defining the cutting edge of modernity.[145]

Through these developments in government organizations, the suffrage movement, and the marketplace, the expansion of forms of public participation for women in the previous two decades laid the foundation for a burst of activity during the Manchurian Incident. Women dominated the early news reports of war-support activities. In the northeast, the *Kahoku shinpō* reported on September 23 that the students of Jobanki Girl's School were sending the first seventy-two *imon* packets to the soldiers. Others soon followed suit. The paper applauded the plan of a thousand female employees in the Katakura Textile Mill to send *imon* presents to Manchuria, and praised the industry of nurses at a university hospital when they sold enough flowers to buy a "mountain" of *imon* presents. Headlines cheered a group of cafe hostesses who donated the money they would have paid for cosmetics to the soldiers in Manchuria, and wrote admiringly of the girl's high school in which the entire student body took an hour of class time to write *imon* letters to the soldiers.[146] Newspapers encouraging nurses out onto the steets to hawk flowers and applauding the actions of such morally compromised figures as cafe hostesses would have been un-

143. Gail Lee Bernstein, "Introduction," in Gail Lee Bernstein, ed., *Recreating Japanese Women, 1600–1945* (Berkeley: University of California Press, 1991), pp. 9–11; Kokuritsu kyōiku kenkyūjo, *Shakai kyōiku* 1, p. 1014.

144. Minami et al., *Taishō bunka*, pp. 248–255.

145. On women and modernism see Barbara Hamill Satō, "Josei: modanizumu to kenri ishiki," in Minami Hiroshi and Shakaishinri kenkyūjo, eds., *Shōwa bunka, 1925–1945* (Keisō shobō, 1987), pp. 198–231; and Barbara Hamill Satō, "The *Moga* Sensation: Perceptions of the *Modan Garu* in Japanese Intellectual Circles during the 1920s," *Gender and History* 5, no. 3 (Autumn 1993), pp. 363–381.

146. *Kahoku shinpō* (26 September, 28 September, and 1 October 1931), in "Sono koro minshū wa," pp. 174–176.

thinkable during the Sino- and Russo-Japanese wars. Acclaim for the ability of these women to leap, almost instantaneously, into public activism in 1931 drew on the social and cultural gains of the teens and twenties.

One way the mass media encouraged a new public activism for women in the Manchurian Incident was through its treatment of the category "military mother." Before 1931, the image of the military mother promoted in textbooks depicted women's support in terms of encouraging sons to give themselves for their country. From their kitchens, women blessed the patriotic effort and released their sons to die.[147] During the Manchurian Incident, magazine articles praised the military mother who was out in front of the station, serving tea to troops as they left for or returned from the front. Wives of military commanders and other women who traveled to Manchuria with the troops were honored as "mother surrogates." For their "tireless efforts" to tend the soldiers they earned the nicknames "Mother of Liaoyang" or "Mother of Fengtian."[148] Bringing her out of the kitchen in 1931, the mass media reconceived the idea of the military mother even as it reworked the female iconography of Taishō popular culture: women now occupied public space, not just in their capacities as workers and consumers, but as mothers.

The reaction of government officials to women's war-support movements furnished another striking contrast with the earlier imperial wars. Unlike in 1895 or 1905, in the *imon* movement of 1931–1932, officials wholeheartedly welcomed women's visibility. Before, even government officials who approved of women's participation in charitable public works insisted that they do so "indirectly" and "remain in the background."[149] Now, military leaders Honjō Shigeru and Araki Sadao wrote articles in women's magazines emphasizing women's responsibility for the home front during the national crisis.[150] The Army Ministry's Manchurian Incident *bidan* collection, published in December 1931, opened the volume with a series of photographs; most were of soldiers in Manchuria—raising the flag, gesturing "banzai," and mourning the dead. The single picture taken in Japan showed two women (wives of Kwantung Army officers)

147. Nakauchi, pp. 59–74.
148. Hashimoto Eiko, "Heitai baasan namida no shuki," *Kingu* (December 1932), p. 200; "Yōryō no jibō (Tamon chūshō fujin) kaeru," *Fujin kurabu* (February 1933), p. 12.
149. Kokuritsu kyōiku kenkyūjo, *Shakai kyōiku* 1, p. 634.
150. Honjō Shigeru, "Hijōji no fujin no kakugo," *Fujin kurabu* (February 1933), p. 67; Araki Sadao, "Hijōji! Nihon fujin no shimei," *Fujin kurabu* (April 1933), pp. 110–113.

standing at the head of a rally, flanked to their left by rows of young women and to their right by young men.[151] Female faces dominated the picture, and they were certainly not in the background. Government officials welcomed women's activism in 1931 because they saw it as an extension of the initiatives of the Home and Education ministries during the 1920s to bring women into the network of government voluntary organizations. In the years between the Russo-Japanese War and the Manchurian Incident, government had reached out to bring women into the public grasp of the state. In 1931, women were returning that embrace.

Women's activism in mobilizing themselves to cooperate in the war effort was apparent in the leading role played by women's groups in organizing local *imon* movements. In Niigata, the prefectural branch of the Aikoku fujinkai became the command center for the region's *imon* activities. Directing the efforts of local women's committees and village and town government offices, they presented 3,050 *imon* packets to the local unit in Manchuria in October 1931. In March and April they screened movies for families of troops, and in May they joined the young women's association in carrying out a "public-service week" for visiting the wounded and families of the dead with condolence money and confections. In March 1933, the Niigata edition of their organizational magazine *Aikoku fujin* proudly announced that their accomplishments included the collection of 21,015 yen, two mailings of *imon* packets to the local unit (a total of 27,433 packets), 17 welcome and send-off rallies, 127 funerals, and 2,391 home visits to bereaved families.[152] Like women's activities elsewhere, the ability of the Niigata Aikoku fujinkai to mount such an effective *imon* campaign built upon the institutional foundations that had developed over the previous decades.

Not only were women's organizations more assertive, leading instead of merely participating in the war-support movement, but the social composition of women involved broadened beyond the narrow elite base of pre-1931 organizations. Working women were among the most active participants. Thirty thousand female operatives at affiliated Katakura textile mills raised 200,000 yen for air defense. Their funds purchased an antiaircraft gun, a military jeep, a searchlight, and an aerial receiver. Six thou-

151. Rikugunshō shinbunhannai "tsuwamono" hensan, ed., *Manshū jihen no unda bidan kawa,* no. 2 (Teikoku zaigo gunjinkai honbunai "tsuwamono" hakkōjo, 1931).

152. Niigata-ken, p. 409.

sand women workers from the Nisshin bōseki factories in Kameido, Senjū, Nagoya, Okazaki, Hamamatsu, Takaoka, Kawagoe, Aoshima, and elsewhere began a company campaign and invited management to join. Together they collected 60,000 yen.[153] *Imon* campaigns at textile factories and among department store shopgirls raised extremely large sums, putting working women at the top of the lists of contributors.[154] Even more dramatic, a group of 500 geisha in Osaka caused a media sensation by including photographs of themselves in 15,000 *imon* packets sent to the front. Later, the same group raised 10,652 yen for an air-defense fundraising drive and marched in force to opening ceremonies of the Kansai National Defense Women's Organization. These activities evoked comment because they were unusual, but as the spokeswoman for the group declared, "even women in our occupation want to do something for our country."[155] The prominent participation of working women in the war-support movements articulated a demand for legitimacy and inclusion. Asserting that their class and occupational identity were assets rather than liabilities to public activity, women like the Osaka geisha insisted that they be part of a collective definition of Japanese women.

The most dramatic expression of the more broad-based public definition of women was the emergence of the National Defense Women's Association (Kokubō fujinkai). Established in connection with an air-defense fundraising drive in Osaka in 1932, the organization soon grew to phenomenal proportions. A membership of 1,000 in January 1933 expanded to 150,000 by the end of the year. Spreading first to the other metropolitan centers of Tokyo, Kobe, and Kyoto, it quickly took root in provincial cities throughout the country. With over 1 million members by the end of 1935, the Kokubō fujinkai overtook its principal competitor, the older Aikoku fujinkai. By 1938, with nearly 8 million members, it had outstripped even the reservist associations. The organization boasted branches in every city, town, and village in the nation, and it still continued to grow. The Kokubō fujinkai expanded so rapidly because it was an inclusive organization. Unlike its elitist competitor, the group actively recruited working, lower-middle class, and even women of disrepute like geisha and cafe girls. Cov-

153. Tokyo *Nichinichi* (24 March 1933, 19 April 1933), in "Shinbun shiryō kōsei," p. 282.

154. Eguchi, *Nihon teikokushugi shiron*, p. 160; Awaya, "Fasshoka to minshū ishiki," p. 276.

155. Fujii, pp. 31, 54–57.

ering over the class differences in women's dress, the white apron uniform of the organization equalized members and was a symbol of its anti-elitist character.[156]

Because the organization was affiliated with the army, and because it espoused the conservative philosophy of "good wife–wise mother," suffragettes like the labor activist Ichikawa Fusae were initially opposed to it. But Ichikawa later changed her mind and joined the leadership of the Kokubō fujinkai. As she explained, "to be released from her home for half a day to listen to a speech—this is women's liberation for the ordinary farm woman who has no time she can call her own."[157] As Ichikawa and other activists adapted to the opportunities that presented themselves, they discovered that mobilizing for empire and war might offer women an alternative path to the political liberation denied by the failure of women's suffrage in the 1920s.

Building on the foundation of the Taishō labor and women's movements, both labor and women's groups used the Manchurian Incident to further their own causes. Expressing claims for social legitimacy through gestures of patriotism, labor and women's organizations both reshaped and reinforced their collective identities. In the process, their participation in fundraising drives, their attendance at rallies, parades, and ceremonies, and their letters and gifts for the troops created the popular upsurge of support for the occupation of Manchuria that gave policy makers the impression of national unity on the issue.

VICARIOUS IMPERIALISM

As Japanese told themselves in books, magazines, newspapers, and speeches, the fundraising campaigns were a phenomenal success. Indeed, the sums collected were impressive. In the first year, the *imon* campaign raised 5,348,444 yen in "soldier's relief money" (*juppeikin*), 3,500,978 donations of *imon* packets, and 20,250,840 donations of *imon* goods such as sake, postcards, daily necessities, loincloths, and charms.[158] All this was collected in the midst of a depression which had brought the number of officially designated paupers (*saimin*) in Tokyo from 59,706 in 1929 to 124,035 in 1931, and which drove unemployment in the city up 29 percent between

---

156. Ibid., pp. 58–64, 90–95; Smethurst, pp. 43–49.
157. Awaya, "Fasshoka to minshū ishiki," p. 275.
158. *Imon* donations from Rikugunshō, *Manshū jihen boppatsu man'ichinen*, p. 22.

November 1930 and October 1931.[159] Even more impressive, at a time when many Japanese earned just 1 yen for a day's work, the *kokubō kenkin* drive yielded 10,500,000 yen over a two-year period. By September 1933, the Army Ministry had used these donations to purchase 100 airplanes (at a cost of between 70,000 and 80,000 yen each); numerous bombers (200,000 yen), tanks (80,000 yen), and machine guns (1,600 yen); and many metal helmets (13.50 yen), winter coats (19 yen), winter boots (8 yen), and winter hats (5 yen).[160]

Although the Army Ministry was glad to encourage these fundraising drives, it was more for ideological than financial reasons. The 20 million yen donated to the Army Ministry by September 1934 represented only a tiny fraction (.008 percent) of the combined military budget of 2.5 billion yen for the years 1932, 1933, and 1934.[161] The symbolic dimension of these campaigns becomes even more marked when one examines which projects inspired the greatest generosity. Although some efforts were made to help bereaved families, in the end few of the goods and funds collected for wartime charity found their way into the hands of the poverty-stricken families of soldiers most in need of succor. Rather, donations were squandered on the families of local heroes, on fancy funerals, parades, and statues, and on books celebrating the glories of the battlefield. In this sense the allocation of the wartime charity represented a public endorsement of the messages purveyed by the mass media and official storytellers. What roused campaign participants to action were the dramas of battlefield valor and heroic sacrifice. Choices about where to give proclaimed the public's desire to participate vicariously in the great military adventure—to share in the glory of the Manchurian Incident. This made campaign participants active agents in the process of imperial myth making. The spectacles and pageantry of the war-support campaigns told their own story of the Manchurian Incident in the language of glory and martyrdom.

Before the Manchurian Incident, practices of wartime charity that evolved during the Sino- and Russo-Japanese wars concentrated on providing aid for the families of soldiers at the front. Although the central government made some nominal provision of financial aid, it in fact fell

---

159. Unemployment figures for Tokyo were 84,264 and 118,027: Eguchi, *Jūgonen sensō no kaimaku*, p. 39. Statistics for *saimin*: Eguchi Keiichi, *Futatsu no taisen*, vol. 14 of *Taikei Nihon no rekishi* (Shōgakkan, 1989), p. 177.

160. Tokyo *Nichinichi* (17 September 1933), in "Shinbun shiryō kōsei," p. 284; Fujii, p. 18; Nakajima Kinji, p. 28.

161. Awaya, *Shōwa no seitō*, p. 305.

upon the local community to take care of these families by helping out with farm labor, money, and medical attention. In Miyagi and other northeastern prefectures whose local regiments saw the first action in 1931, the initial relief efforts were in keeping with the established practice. For the first week of military action, the pages of Miyagi's *Kahoku shinpō* were filled with such stories as "Condolence Visits to Families Bereft by Victims of the Clash Between China and Japan" and "Ways to Console Families of the Dead and Injured." Articles focused special attention on hard-luck cases like the tenant family whose eldest son was killed in action, leaving his bedridden parents and six brothers and sisters in desperate straits. The headline read, "Hero's Mother Laments, 'What shall we do?' "[162] As they were intended to, such articles inspired sympathy and support. The day after the "Hero's Mother" article was published, neighbors rushed to the aid of the bereaved family.[163]

Yet by the end of September, this type of article had all but disappeared, as the focus shifted from the tragic circumstances of potential beneficiaries to the pathos and magnanimity of the benefactors. In the ensuing months the families earned occasional flurries of attention, but for the most part the stories of their personal tragedies had become insignificant sideshows compared to the articles trumpeting the latest sacrificial gesture of a fevered patriot. Miyagi was not alone in exhibiting this trend. A collection of articles on the Manchurian Incident taken from the pages of the Tokyo *Nichinichi* between 1932 and 1935 gives some idea of the relative attention granted the families. Two hundred and ninety articles featured contributors and the amount of their donation, while only thirty-five stories dealt with soldiers' families.[164]

What meager charity there was for soldiers' families was allocated disproportionately: a flood of support for relations of popular casualties, and a small trickle for those of the ordinary dead. The fortunes of the families of the "three human bullets" rose rapidly, making them rich practically overnight. On February 27 the Tokyo *Nichinichi* ran an article entitled "A Flood of Popular Admiration—*Imon* Donations for the Bereaved Families of the Three Human Bullets Top 10,000 Yen." The next day the newspaper announced that it was collecting additional donations for a funeral. On the paper's invitation, the mothers of the unfortunate boys traveled to Kansai to receive donations of 10,000 yen each, handed over personally by the

162. *Kahoku shinpō* (22 September 1931), in "Sono koro minshū wa," p. 173.
163. *Kahoku shinpō* (23 September 1931), in "Sono koro minshū wa," p. 174.
164. Tokyo *Nichinichi* (1932–1935), in "Shinbun shiryō kōsei," pp. 260–307.

Mainichi.[165] In April, a statue was erected to the fallen heroes at a cost of 20,000 yen, and the contributions continued to flow in.[166]

In contrast, provision for the family of a soldier who did not have such media exposure amounted, if it was requested, to a single payment of a maximum of 30 yen from the central government, with a possible additional payment from the prefectural organizations. In Ishikawa, for example, the *imon* association allocated donations in the following manner: 20,000 yen for packages to send to soldiers at the front (5 yen/soldier); 40,000 yen for bereaved families (4 yen/month for 10 months); 10,000 yen for funeral expenses (10 yen/funeral); and 10,000 yen for gifts to convalescing soldiers (20 yen/soldier).[167] Thus, contrary to the munificence of the donations to the three human bombs' relations, the bereaved families of Ishikawa's ordinary war dead could count on a paltry 80 yen from their central and prefectural governments, including funeral expenses.

In early 1932, the Home Ministry grew so concerned with the apparent lack of support for bereaved families that a special committee was convened, attended by both vice-ministers and all department heads, to come up with solutions to what they regarded as a serious problem. The meeting resulted in promises to try to secure more financial support from the central government for families; in the meantime, a mission was sent to local areas to pressure community organizations. Businesses were asked to keep jobs open for returning soldiers, and local government was pressed to provide additional funds for support. The Red Cross, the Patriotic Women's Association, reservists, youth associations, and other voluntary organizations were also urged to carry out more satisfactory charity work for the bereaved.[168]

The lack of attention to soldiers' families showed that the enthusiasm of the participants in the war-support campaigns was not inspired by sympathies for the domestic casualties of imperial warfare. What they were moved by was battlefield glory. While their families starved, soldiers at the front were inundated with *imon*. Comfort packets poured into Kwantung Army headquarters. These usually included a supportive letter nestled amidst a pair of underwear, some toilet paper, a magazine, a tooth-

165. Tokyo *Nichinichi* (10 March 1932, 12 March 1932), in "Shinbun shiryō kōsei," p. 264.

166. Tokyo *Nichinichi* (3 April 1932), in "Shinbun shiryō kōsei," p. 267; Tokyo *Nichinichi* (1 March 1932–29 November 1933), in "Shinbun shiryō kōsei," pp. 264–267.

167. Nakajima Kinji, pp. 42–43.

168. Tokyo *Nichinichi* (27 February 1932), in "Shinbun shiryō kōsei," p. 294.

brush, a charm, and a pickled plum. By mid January the Army Ministry reported donations of *imon* packets had reached 1,533,495, many more than the number of troops on the ground. Observers reported that soldiers were using the cloth wrappers to pad their insufficient winter outergear, that there were ten to twenty charms per soldier, and that on average each man had twenty-six toothbrushes.[169] Overflowing with this beneficence, soldiers grew so concerned with reports of the desperate conditions in their home villages that they began their own *imon* campaign to send money back home.[170] They had good reason to be worried; according to a Miyagi prefecture survey on conditions of families with men at the front, 45 percent of the 1,319 families affected were in distress. Of this 45 percent, only 219 families had requested help, and only 121 families were actually receiving aid.[171]

The dead also received a disproportionate share of attention during the Manchurian Incident. In Miyagi prefecture, when news of the first casualties broke, the local press closely tracked the voyage of soldiers' remains on the long road home. Separate articles reported ceremonies attending stops in Dalian, Kobe, and elsewhere en route, culminating in a solemn reception at Sendai station.[172] It was typical for the war dead of the Manchurian Incident to be honored by multiple ceremonials. Aichi prefecture's first casualty, for example, was mourned no less than six times. A welcome committee made a special trip to Kobe to see his remains off the ship, and another crowd awaited the bones at Nagoya station. A group of mourners met his train as it arrived in his home town, after it made intermediate stops for additional ceremonials. All this occurred before the funeral had even started.[173]

Many local areas spent precious funds on publications honoring the war dead, such as Shiga prefecture's 558-page *Record of Loyal Service*. This tome included a preface by the governor, as well as photographs and short biographies of each of the Shiga soldiers killed in action (one page for each private, three to ten for each officer). Biographies were gilded with such flowery eulogies as "heroic on the battlefield; filial at home," "pride of the Yamato race," "model soldier: fierce yet gentle," "incarnation of the spirit

169. Eguchi, *Jūgonen sensō no kaimaku*, pp. 114–115.

170. *Kahoku shinpō* (31 December 1931), in "Sono koro minshū wa," p. 203.

171. *Kahoku shinpō* (24 October 1931), in "Sono koro minshū wa," p. 179.

172. *Kahoku shinpō* (11 October–24 October 1931), in "Sono koro minshū wa," pp. 178–179.

173. Eguchi, "Manshū jihen to minshū dōin," p. 151.

of sacrifice," or, more simply, "a good youth."[174] Such books, like the funerals, attempted to compensate families for their losses in the currency of national honor. Allocating donated funds to spiritual rather than material compensation may not have been the best use of the money from the individual family's point of view, but from the perspective of the community it was a worthwhile expenditure. Devoting those sums to imperial pageantry, everyone was able to share in the sense of loss, to experience vicariously the sacrifice, and to participate in the martyrdom.

The home-front campaigns made their own contribution to the narrative of Japanese martyrdom and expansion in self-defense. In engagements that yielded comparatively few Japanese fatalities, war stories and public funerals nourished a perception of untold death. While representations of the Manchurian battlefield encouraged an obsession with martyrdom, the treatment of the home-front heroes of the *imon* movement also nurtured a sense of victimization. When the majority of the donations were coming from the rich, the gaze of the mass media fixed on the sacrifice and pathos of the nation's most vulnerable citizens. At the same time, the preoccupation of the National Defense Women's Association and other war-support organizations with aerial defense of the home islands bolstered the self-defense argument. As people poured energies into preparing their aerial self-defense against an enemy that had no air force, they embraced a siege mentality, reinforcing the idea that Japan was engaged in a defensive operation against Zhang Xueliang's troops. In this way the participants in the war-support campaigns joined the efforts of propagandists in the army and the mass media to represent the history of the Manchurian Incident in the familiar categories of imperial mythology. Incorporating the Manchurian Incident into the master narrative of Japanese imperialism, they reinvigorated imperial ideology.

This reinvigorated imperial ideology represented one of the cultural effects of the new military imperialism. Through its influence on women's organizations, the labor movement, the political parties, and the army, the Manchurian Incident produced important political and social effects as well. Whether initiated by politicians, military officers, or women organizers,

174. Shiga-ken shutsudō gunjin ikazoku kōen rinji iinkai, *Manshū Shanhai jihen chūseiroku* (Kyoto: Shiga-ken shutsudō gunjin ikazoku kōen rinji iinkai, 1932).

the efforts to mobilize a community of support for the occupation of Northeast China led to the formation of new linkages between empire, state, and society. These new connections built on a tradition of imperial involvement that went back to the Meiji period. The transformation of this tradition revealed, in concrete ways, how a shift in imperial policy implied domestic changes and vice versa. In the dialectical relationship between empire and metropolis, existing domestic formations of mass society and mass politics conditioned the emergence of a popular imperialism; at the same time, the process of mobilizing for empire stimulated the expansion of these mass institutions.

Why the constellation of internal and external forces produced such an imperial transformation during 1931–1932 remains an important question to answer. The political forces behind the shift from the go-slow imperialism of the twenties to the go-fast imperialism of the thirties can be accounted for by the success of the army's political strategy and the lack of an effective opposition either inside or outside the government bureaucracy. The difference between the tepid social and cultural response to army action in Manchuria in 1928 and the war hysteria of 1931 can be attributed, in large part, to the constraints and imperatives of economic depression. Yet, the answer does not end here, for the war fever and the new military imperialism constituted but one dimension of the paradigmatic shift in Japanese imperialism; empire building did not stop with military occupation of the Northeast. As a Manchurian lifeline defined in terms of economic security began to metamorphose into an economic panacea, Manchukuo became an entirely different kind of imperial project—radical and utopian. It is this project, the Manchurian experiment in colonial development, to which we now turn.

PART III

THE MANCHURIAN EXPERIMENT IN COLONIAL DEVELOPMENT, 1932–1941

5 Uneasy Partnership

Soldiers and Capitalists in the Colonial Economy

Before 1932 Japan's geographical scope of activity in Northeast China had been confined to the Kwantung Leased Territory and the railway zone in South Manchuria. The instrument of penetration, the enormous public-private colonial railway concern everyone knew as Mantetsu, had operated mainly in the carrying trade in soybeans. In the early years of Manchukuo's existence, however, the structures of economic imperialism were radically transformed, altering economic policy in Manchuria and Japan as well as the relationship between the two economies. First, under a new regime of imperial management known as the controlled economy, the army-dominated Manchukuo government undertook an experiment in planned economic development and state capitalism. Second, economic expansion in Manchukuo became a critical tool in Japanese domestic economic policy, helping to reflate a stagnant economy. Large-scale industrial and infrastructural development that was financed by a rush of public and private funds soaked up idle capital, while the accompanying leap in exports to Manchuria helped put Japan's factories back to work. Finally, the integration of the two economies, called the "Japan-Manchuria bloc economy," committed both empire and metropolis to a strategy of mutual dependence from which neither could easily withdraw. In Manchuria, in Japan, and in the relationship between the two, these three phenomena defined the new face of economic imperialism.

Developing Manchukuo was an expensive proposition. Estimates of Japanese investment in Manchukuo between 1932 and 1941 run to 5.9 billion yen, a figure that represented a sizable fraction of domestic investment.[1]

---

1. For a breakdown of investments in Manchukuo, see Tables 1 and 2. Domestic public and private investments in fixed capital rose from 1.2 billion yen in 1930 to 8.6 billion yen in 1940: Andō Yoshio, p. 7, Table b.

Although development became part of European colonial discourse in the interwar period, investment in a colonial economy on this scale was unusual in comparative terms. Like the expanding institutions of the Japanese-run South Manchurian Railway (Mantetsu), European agricultural and medical research centers for the study of economic conditions in their colonies proliferated during this period. European colonial administrators like Albert Saurrat, Louis Franck, and Frederick Guggisberg produced technocratic visions of planned economic development that rivaled Japanese schemes for Manchukuo. But because of the European concern that colonies not become a financial drain on metropolitan treasuries, few plans for colonial development gained financial support until after World War II.[2]

Although Japan did fund economic development in the 1930s, the expense of the project evoked political conflict over Manchukuo, as different groups disagreed on what the scale and the nature of the investments should be. The resolution of these disputes occurred within the framework of a growing cooperation between government and business over economic foreign policy. Sharing a common agenda on international questions of economic security and economic expansion, as well as domestic issues of economic and social stabilization, business executives and government officials increasingly worked together to make economic policy. Identifying a similar trend in interwar America, historians of U.S. foreign policy use the term *corporatism* to describe this convergence of public and private interests, the interpenetration of public and private elites, and the joint formation of policy through such organizational vehicles as trade associations and government bureaucracies.[3] But as Japan's case demonstrates, the fact that the exigencies of the international economy threw public and private interests

2. Raymond F. Betts, "*Uncertain Dimensions*: *Western Overseas Empires in the Twentieth Century* (Minneapolis: University of Minnesota Press, 1985), pp. 76–113; Crawford Young, *The African Colonial State in Comparative Perspective* (New Haven: Yale University Press, 1994), pp. 133–138, 165–180, 208–217.

3. Corporatism has become a major subfield in American diplomatic history. For an overview of this approach, see Michael J. Hogan, "Corporatism," in Michael J. Hogan and Thomas G. Paterson, eds., *Explaining the History of American Foreign Relations* (Cambridge: Cambridge University Press, 1991), pp. 226–236; and the exchange between John Lewis Gaddis, "The Corporatist Synthesis: A Skeptical View," and Michael J. Hogan, "Corporatism: A Positive Appraisal," in *Diplomatic History* 10, no. 4 (Fall 1986), pp. 357–372. For a representative study in the corporatist mold, see Michael J. Hogan, *Informal Entente: The Private Structure of Cooperation in Anglo-American Economic Diplomacy, 1918–1928* (Columbia: University of Missouri Press, 1977).

together did not mean that a smooth cooperation or harmony of interests was the necessary result. The prospect of developing Manchuria brought the big business community and the Kwantung Army together into an uneasy partnership. But between the two parties there emerged a fundamental disagreement over the direction of economic policy, a Japanese corporatism that was riven with internal contradictions.

In certain respects, the business community had the upper hand in this dispute. With their capital and expertise, bankers and industrialists held the power to decide the fate of Manchurian development. Yet the historical record on the role of business is spotty and leaves one with two conflicting impressions. Broadly stated, these suggest, on the one hand, that capitalists boycotted Manchuria because they thought the Kwantung Army's development program was ill-conceived and unprofitable, and on the other, that economic expansion into Manchuria was attended by an export of capital on an unprecedented scale.[4] If business, particularly big business, was not putting up the money, where was it coming from?

The answer to this riddle lies in the peculiar nature of the partnership formed between segments of the business community and the army-run Manchukuo government, for the two did indeed cut a deal on Manchuria.

---

4. Work on economic imperialism in Northeast China falls into two categories. The first consists of policy studies of Manchukuo done mainly by members of the Manshūshi kenkyūkai (Manchurian History Study Group). Although they have done relatively little on the role of the business community, this group has produced excellent studies of the Manchurian economy. See for example, these essays by Hara Akira: " 'DaiTōa kyōeiken' no keizaiteki jittai," *Tochi seido shigaku,* no. 71 (April 1976), pp. 1–28; "1930 nendai," pp. 1–114; " 'Manshū' ni okeru keizai tōsei seisaku no tenkai: Mantetsu kaiso to Mangyō setsuritsu o megutte," in Andō Yoshio, ed., *Nihon keizai seisaku shiron* (Tōkyō daigaku shuppankai, 1976), pp. 209–296; "Senji tōsei keizai no kaishi," in *Kindai 7,* vol. 20 of *Iwanami kōza Nihon rekishi* (Iwanami shoten, 1976), pp. 217–268. See also these Kobayashi Hideo works: "Manshū kin'yū kōzō no saihensei katei: 1930 nendai zenhanki o chūshin ni," in Manshūshi kenkyūkai, ed., *Nihon teikokushugika no Manshū* (Ochanomizu shobō, 1972), pp. 115–212; "1930 nendai 'Manshū kōgyōka' seisaku no tenkai katei: 'Manshū sangyō kaihatsu gokanen keikaku' jisshi katei o chūshin ni," *Tochi seido shigaku,* no. 44 (June 1969), pp. 19–43; "1930 nendai shokuminchi 'kōgyōka' no shotokuchō," *Tochi seido shigaku,* no. 71 (April 1976), p. 29–45; "DaiTōa kyōeiken." More general studies of the wartime economy that give attention to Manchuria tend to look at the problem in terms of the domestic economy. See for example Sakamoto Masako, "Sensō to zaibatsu," in Nakamura Masanori, ed., *Sensō to kokka dokusen shihonshugi,* vol. 4 of *Taikei Nihon gendaishi* (Nihon hyōronsha, 1979), pp. 47–92; Ishii Kanji, "Kokusai kankei," in Ōishi Kaichirō, ed., *Sekai daikyōkōki,* vol. 2 of *Nihon teikokushugishi* (Tōkyō daigaku shuppankai, 1987), pp. 39–76; and Kaneko Fumio, "Shihon yushutsu to shokuminchi," pp. 331–366.

Although they disagreed frequently on the future of Manchukuo and held contradictory goals for economic development, neither wanted open warfare. Since the army could not dismiss the business community without risking censure from the ministries of Finance and Commerce, and the business community could not operate in Manchuria without some dealings with the army, each was stuck with the other. The partnership that grew between the two provided the financial foundation upon which Manchukuo was built. More of a nonaggression pact than a real working alliance, army-business cooperation barely extended beyond public assurances of mutual goodwill. That theirs was, from beginning to end, an uneasy partnership meant that the Manchukuo economy rested on shaky ground; the absence of unity in purpose and action was largely responsible for an emerging crisis in the Manchurian economy and augured ill for efforts to resolve them.

Although many of the particulars of policy divided them, soldiers and capitalists were united by their faith in the potential of economic development in Manchuria. Both saw in the new empire the salvation for economic crisis. Facing obstacles in the domestic and global market, Japan's economy was "deadlocked," in the idiom of the day. Colonial development in Manchukuo became the economic panacea for an uncertain age, the lifeline for a nation set adrift in the stormy waters of the global economy. That the uneasy partnership between soldiers and capitalists endured over the course of Manchukuo's lifetime was testament to the binding power of their shared dreams for the new empire.

THE BUSINESS INITIATIVE OF 1932–1933

In Japan, business leaders began to express excitement about the economic potential of Manchukuo in early 1932. With the establishment of the puppet state in March, businessmen moved quickly to set up organizations to coordinate, lobby for, and generally advance their interests in Manchukuo. Within weeks of Manchukuo's announcement, Tokyo businesses pressured the city assembly to appoint a committee to "look at the prospects for the city's commerce and industry in the Manchurian economy." The results were published in 1933 in a four-hundred-page guide to the Manchurian export market, including a digest of Japanese businesses in Manchuria and exporters in Tokyo.[5] Over the summer, the city's chamber of commerce

---

5. Tōkyō shiyakusho, *Manmō keizai chōsasho* (Tōkyō shiyakusho, 1933), p. 1.

sponsored the formation of a Tokyo Manchuria-Mongolia Export Union.[6] The China Problem Research Committee of the Osaka Chamber of Commerce sent a mission to Manchuria; their findings were published in "A True Picture of the Manchurian Economy."[7] The influential Japan Chamber of Commerce sent a team of business leaders to meet with Kwantung Army officials and tour Manchuria in February 1932.[8] From May to December that year, banking and industrial leaders from Tokyo and Osaka met to formulate a business community position and make recommendations on industrial, tariff, finance, and other policy for Manchuria.[9]

This flurry of activity sent a clear signal that within the domestic business community there was considerable enthusiasm for the economic prospects of a Japanese-occupied Manchuria. The business initiative to develop these opportunities shaped in fundamental ways the imperial corporatism in the Manchurian economy. Two key features of this imperial corporatism emerged in the early years of Manchukuo's existence. First, though the attempt to form a corporate voice for capital interests in the new empire achieved some success in an institutional sense, it was constantly being undermined by the diversity of the Japanese business community. Depending on their position within the larger scope of imperial interests, entrepreneurs differed in their assessment of Manchukuo—weighing the value of the new market against opportunity costs for their other overseas interests. The corporate voice of capital, in other words, was never unified. Second, and compounding this, the Kwantung Army sent mixed signals to capitalists, running hot and cold on the prospect of a joint venture in

6. Tōkyō shōkō kaigisho, "Tōkyō Manmō yushutsu kumiai setsuritsu ni kanshi enjokata irai no ken shingi kiroku" (August–October 1932), Tōkyō shōkō kaigisho microreel no. 139:286–319; Toda Shin'ichirō, *Manmō e no yushutsu annai* (Tōji shoin, 1933), pp. 210–224.

7. Ōsaka shōkō kaigisho taiShi mondai chōsa iinkai, ed., *Genchi chōsa: Manmō keizai no jissō* (Osaka: Ōsaka shōkō kaigisho, 1932).

8. Nihon shōkō kaigisho, *Nihon shōkō kaigisho shusai Manmō keizai shisatsu-dan hōkoku narabini ikenshō* (Nihon shōkō kaigisho, 1932). This trip followed an earlier war-support mission, sponsored by four key business organizations: Nihon keizai renmeikai, Nihon kōgyō kurabu, Nikka jitsugyō kyōkai, and Tōkyō shōkō kaigisho. During the earlier visit war-relief funds (*imonkin*) collected from the business community totaling 268,393 yen were presented to the Kwantung Army, and the war-support mission was rewarded with a personal invitation from Army Commander Honjō Shigeru to return. Nihon shōkō kaigisho, "Manshūgun imon ni kansuru kiroku," Tōkyō shōkō kaigisho microreel no. 138:2850–2876.

9. "Nichiman sangyō teikei ni kansuru iinkai" (1933), Tōkyō shōkō kaigisho microreel no. 107:329–655.

Manchuria. Interpolating distrust and ambivalence into the corporatist alliance, the Kwantung Army deepened the divisions already introduced by capitalists.

The divisions within the business camp were apparent in reactions to the early phases of the Manchurian occupation. A number of key sectors of the business community were affected, but not all the same way. In their calculations of advantages and disadvantages to the extension of military control in China, businessmen were divided along two major lines. The first set Japanese commercial and transportation capital in Manchuria apart from domestic businesses; the second divided metropolitan businesses with ties to the China market into those whose primary concern was the China market outside of Manchuria (textile producers) and those with diversified interests throughout China (the large financial-industrial conglomerates known as *zaibatsu*). In the first case, because they felt more immediately threatened by the Chinese rights recovery movement, Japanese-owned businesses in Manchuria welcomed military intervention to protect their interests. Represented by the Manchurian chambers of commerce and Mantetsu, Manchurian-based businesses were well organized, united, and outspoken in their support for army. But while Japanese rights and interests in Manchuria constituted the single, central issue for empire-based capital, the situation was different for metropolitan businesses. At home, businessmen were less informed, less involved, and less unified on what course of action to pursue in Manchuria. Partially this was because many businessmen had no experience in Manchuria or elsewhere in China. But even among those with long-standing ties to the China market, possible advantages of military intervention in Manchuria were balanced against a multitude of other factors.

For *zaibatsu*, the balance sheet on military action was particularly complex. *Zaibatsu* capital was heavily involved in the Manchurian economy and held the lion's share of Mantetsu's privately owned stock. But *zaibatsu* were also committed to the China market south of the Great Wall, as well as dominating Japan's overseas trade inside and outside the Japanese Empire. In addition to their trading divisions, *zaibatsu* like Mitsui and Mitsubishi maintained a host of investments at home and in the empire and were diversified with mining, banking, manufacturing, and other operations.[10] Hence, in deciding to publicly endorse the military takeover, they

10. For *zaibatsu* financing of Mantetsu in the 1920s, see Iwamizu Akira, "Taigai tōshi," in Ono Kazuichirō, ed., *Senkanki no teikokushugi* (Sekai shisōsha, 1985),

would have assessed the impact of the Manchurian Incident on their Mantetsu stock within a much broader context of economic interests.

Even beyond the complexities of the economic balance sheet, *zaibatsu* had other factors to take into consideration before making a public stand on the Manchurian Incident. Probably more important than hard economic interests in determining this public stand was the crisis in public faith that confronted the *zaibatsu* in the early 1930s. In addition to antipathies toward big business over income disparities and the widespread perception that Mitsui and Mitsubishi had respectively "bought" the Seiyūkai and Minseitō political parties,[11] the *zaibatsu* were rocked by a series of public scandals in 1931 and 1932 which earned them a reputation as traitors to the national interest. The "dollar-buying incident" of fall 1931 was the most notorious of these. After insisting for years that Japan maintain a convertable currency, the *zaibatsu* bankers engaged in a fever of highly lucrative speculation against the yen in September and October of 1931, undermining the frantic efforts of the government to shore up the value of the yen in order to keep Japan on the gold standard.[12] Moreover, the news that Mitsui bussan sold barbed wire to the Chinese 19th Route Army (the troops that fought against Japan in Shanghai in 1932) and salt to Zhang Xueliang (the enemy in Manchuria) evoked widespread condemnation of *zaibatsu* willingness to sell out the nation for financial gain.[13] Public hostility took its most extreme form in the assassination of Mitsui executive Dan Takuma in March 1932 and the appearance with alarming regularity of *zaibatsu* leaders on the hit lists of right-wing terrorist groups. All this brought considerable public pressure on *zaibatsu* to demonstrate their patriotic support for Manchukuo. Thus, in the early days of the oc-

---

pp. 105–109; and Sakurai Tōru, "Minami Manshū tetsudō no keiei to zaibatsu," in Fujii Mitsuo et al., eds., *Nihon takokuseki kigyō no shiteki tenkai*, vol. 1 (Ōtsuki shoten, 1979), pp. 23–50.

11. For commentary on the party "sell out" to the *zaibatsu*, see Ōyama Ikuo, "Taishu tōsō no shinron ni tatsu 'Daisan seiri,' " *Chūō kōron* (July 1931), pp. 143–144; Iwafuji Yukio, "Tetsudō dōmyaku-demo no ken'i," *Chūō kōron* (July 1931), p. 295; and Sasa Hirō, "Wagakuni kin'yū katō seiji," in "Gendai taishū tokuon" section of *Chūō kōron* (July 1931), pp. 3–6. I am grateful to Hyung Gu Lynn for calling my attention to these articles as well as to the information cited in note 13 in this chapter.

12. William Miles Fletcher, *The Japanese Business Community and National Trade Policy, 1920–1942* (Chapel Hill: University of North Carolina Press, 1989), pp. 65–71.

13. Miyake Seiki and Saitō Eizaburō, eds., *Nihon zaikai jinbutsu retsuden*, vol. 2 (Seichō shuppan, 1963), p. 414.

cupation, when the Minseitō cabinet opposed expanding the occupation, the *zaibatsu*-dominated Japan Industrial Club petitioned the government to end its nonexpansion policy.[14] This support for the army continued, as Mitsui, Mitsubishi, Sumitomo, and others set examples of corporate beneficence in the Manchurian Incident fundraising drives.[15]

The domestic business interests with the most to lose from military action in Manchuria, however, were the manufacturing, trading, and shipping companies involved in the textile industry. Since the 1890s, textile manufacturing concentrated in the Kansai region around Osaka and Kobe had led Japan's industrialization. Growing sales in Asian markets quickly made textiles a key export, second only to raw silk. The only sector of industry not dominated by *zaibatsu* capital, textile manufacturers organized early into what became the nation's most durable and powerful industrial cartel—the Japan Spinners' Association, founded in 1882.[16] From the unequal Sino-Japanese commercial treaty of 1896, acquired through China's military defeat, to the Manchurian Incident of 1931, the growth of the textile industry was dependent on the China market. As exports took an increasing share of production (from 8 percent in 1900 to 42 percent in 1930), China provided the key to export expansion. In 1900, 30 percent of textile exports went to China, rising to 78 percent in 1910, then tapering off to 47 percent in 1920, and 42 percent in 1930.[17] Until World War I, these exports were primarily cotton yarn, but with the emergence of a native Chinese cotton-spinning industry and the expansion of Japanese-owned textile mills in China, the composition of Japanese exports to China changed from yarn to cloth and piece goods.

Most of these exports were directed not to the Northeast, but to China proper, that is, south of the Great Wall. It was here, in Shanghai and Qingdao, that the overseas investments of Japanese textile producers were overwhelmingly concentrated. Throughout the twenties, Manchuria absorbed less than a tenth of textile exports to China proper.[18] In contrast to the heavily guarded South Manchurian Railway in the warlord-controlled

14. Eguchi, *Nihon teikokushugi shiron*, p. 75.

15. For business participation in the fundraising campaigns, see Chapter 4.

16. Fletcher, *The Japanese Business Community*, pp. 15–17.

17. These figures include the Kwantung Leased Territory: Peter Duus, "Zaikabō: Japanese Cotton Mills in China, 1895–1937," in Peter Duus, Ramon H. Myers, and Mark R. Peattie, eds., *The Japanese Informal Empire in China, 1895–1937* (Princeton: Princeton University Press, 1989), pp. 72–73.

18. Ibid.

Northeast, textile interests in China proper were a vulnerable target for nationalist protest. Major boycotts against Japanese goods were carried out in 1915, 1919, 1923, 1925, 1927, and 1928, and Japanese-owned mills in Shanghai were struck 119 times between 1918 and 1929.[19] For this reason, the news of military action against Chinese Nationalists in the Northeast inspired a dual response within the Kansai business community.

Initially, Kansai capitalists were inclined to join the *zaibatsu* with a public show of support for the military. In a public climate of resentment toward capital, businessmen throughout the country tried to diffuse some of the hostility by making generous donations to war-support campaigns and ensuring that their names headed the lists of contributors published in the newspapers. In this spirit, on September 28 twelve Osaka business organizations (including the Osaka Chamber of Commerce, the League of China Cotton Spinners, and the Osaka Economic Association) formed the China Business Federation to publicize their support for military action. Resolving to "arouse general commercial and industrial opinion to support the settlement of the Manchurian-Mongolian problem and the thorough-going chastisement of China," the federation sent envoys to Tokyo and petitioned the cabinet and diplomatic leaders to abandon the nonexpansion policy.[20] Very quickly, however, this enthusiastic response began to evaporate in the face of a new anti-Japanese boycott movement and a wave of strikes protesting the military occupation of Manchuria. The Guomindang-led movement devasted the textile industry; in one month Japanese exports to China proper dropped 76 percent, and many factories in Qingdao and Shanghai were forced to close in early October.[21] Fearing that a continuation of the forward policy might lead to all-out war with China, frus-

19. Ibid., p. 87.

20. Since the army was concerned that the Kansai business community might be a strong source of opposition to its Manchurian policy, the military police monitored its activities during the fall and winter of 1931–1932. These surveillance reports have been published in Fujiwara and Kunugi, *Manshū jihen to kokumin dōin*, pp. 136–173. Covering the China Business Federation is Kenpei shireikan Toyama Bunzō, "Manshū jihen ni taisuru Ōsaka zaikai hōmen no hankyō ni kansuru ken hōkoku" (30 September 1931, 1 October 1931, 2 October 1931, and 6 October 1931), in Fujiwara and Kunugi, *Manshū jihen to kokumin dōin*, pp. 136–145. See also Eguchi, *Nihon teikokushugi shiron*, p. 75.

21. Kenpei shireikan Toyama Bunzō, "Manshū jihen ni taisuru Ōsaka zaikai hōmen no hankyō ni kansuru ken hōkoku" (7 October 1931), and Kenpei shireikan Toyama Bunzō, "Manshū jihen no Ōsaka jitsugyōka ni ataetaru eikyō ni kansuru ken hōkoku" (9 October 1931), in Fujiwara and Kunugi, *Manshū jihen to kokumin dōin*, pp. 145, 151.

tration bubbled over into sharp criticism of the army in a closed meeting among the big textile interests on October 6.[22] By mid-month, textile industry sentiment seemed to be turning against the army, with businessmen grumbling that "the military makes too much of the protection of Manchurian-Mongolian rights and interests and neglects the importance of the China trade."[23]

The initial reaction of the business community to the Manchurian Incident was complex and diverse. Watching the steamroller of public enthusiasm for the occupation bear down on opponents to the war, capitalists took care to remove themselves from its path. But there was more at stake here than public relations. The ambivalence of the Kansai textile producers to the military occupation of Manchuria emerged from their structural relationship to imperial markets. Their position in the geometry of empire set them apart from *zaibatsu*, Japanese commercial interests in Dalian and Fengtian, and the host of other business enterprises who lent their voices to the business initiative in Manchukuo. What was striking about the business community opinion on Manchuria at this stage was not merely its lack of unity, but the absence of an unambiguous "no" vote even among those with the most to lose.

The first attempt to create an organization to advocate business concerns in the puppet state of Manchukuo imported both the disharmony of interests and the tempered enthusiasm expressed in the textile industry's go-stop message to the Kwantung Army. In spite of these difficulties, business leaders in Tokyo worked energetically to build a national-level organization that could transcend divisions of scale, geography, and sector within the business community. The product of a conference held in August 1933, the Japan-Manchuria Business Council was received enthusiastically by merchants and industrialists throughout Japan—including the heads of the Osaka textile industry. Fifty-three different chambers of commerce within the country joined, representing not just the six leading industrial cities of Tokyo, Yokohama, Osaka, Kobe, Nagoya, and Kyoto, but small and mid-sized cities such as Kagoshima, Niigata, Matsumoto, and Aomori. The inclusion of businessmen from smaller and more marginal cities reflected the desire of the Tokyo capitalists who were the driving force behind

22. Kenpei shireikan Toyama Bunzō, "Manshū jihen ni kanshi zai Ōsaka bōseki gyōsha nado kaigō ni kansuru ken hōkoku" (9 October 1931), in Fujiwara and Kunugi, *Manshū jihen to kokumin dōin*, pp. 147–149.
23. Kenpei shireikan Toyama Bunzō, "Manshū jihen ni taisuru zai Ōsaka jitsugyō no jōsei sonota ni kansuru ken hōkoku" (10 October 1931), in Fujiwara and Kunugi, *Manshū jihen to kokumin dōin*, p. 155.

the council to make broad claims for their organization. Negotiating with the Kwantung Army over the direction of economic policy in Manchukuo, council leaders could purport to represent the entire national community of business interests. At the same time, the eagerness of businessmen from cities at the periphery of the domestic economy to participate, despite their lack of experience with the Manchurian market, spoke to the drawing power of Manchukuo.[24]

The Japan-Manchuria Business Council was similarly noteworthy for the variety of interests it represented. In Tokyo, for example, when the organization first called for members in November 1933, bankers, manufacturers, and merchants all joined in large numbers. There seemed to be a role for all to play in Manchurian development and profits enough to spread around. Among the Tokyo firms that signed up immediately were insurance companies, ship builders, flour millers, cement manufacturers, department stores, airplane makers, movie producers, and candy companies. The sectoral diversity and range of size in the enterprises, like their geographical spread, reflected both the organizational strategies of the council's leaders and the basic appeal of their message. Council organizers included everyone because they were keen to disassociate the council from the narrow concerns of the *zaibatsu;* candy manufacturers and the like answered their call because they were persuaded by the message of opportunity in the Manchurian market.[25]

Beneath its mantle of inclusiveness, the Japan-Manchuria Business Council in many ways remained a Tokyo-based, *zaibatsu*-dominated organization. The companies that bought their own memberships (as opposed to participating through their local chamber of commerce) were concentrated in Tokyo. Of the Tokyo membership, *zaibatsu* paid the lion's share of the subscriptions. Mitsui's firms alone—Mitsui Bank, Mitsui Trading, and the holding company, Mitsui Limited—accounted for 70 of the 273 Tokyo corporate subscriptions in February 1934. Between them, Mitsui subsidiaries Ōji Paper, Tokyo Muslin, and Tōyō Rayon purchased another 25.[26] Moreover, the council president, Gō Seinosuke, and vice-president, Yūki Toyotarō, were associated with the *zaibatsu* firms Mitsui and Yasuda, respectively.

24. Nihon shōkō kaigisho, "Nichiman jitsugyō kondankai shussekisha meibo" (July 1933), Tōkyō shōkō kaigisho microreel no. 139:1752–1757.
25. Nichiman jitsugyō kyōkai, *Tōkyō kaiin tokkūsū* (1934), Tōkyō shōkō kaigisho microreel no. 140:2454–2471.
26. Ibid.

Nevertheless, council leaders gave more than lip-service to their mission of inclusiveness. That they took seriously their claim to represent a national community of business interests in Manchuria was demonstrated by the serious efforts undertaken to communicate with membership outside Tokyo. Although the council's central office was based in Tokyo, special care was taken to establish liaison with member chambers of commerce throughout the country. Indeed, one of the council executives spent most of 1934 shuttling throughout Japan, deliberating, explaining results of surveys, and getting input from the provinces.[27] The council tried to redress the problem of Tokyo dominance by setting up an Osaka branch in 1936;[28] and while *zaibatsu* leaders occupied the presidency and vice-presidency of the council, heads of the chambers of commerce in Osaka, Tokyo, Nagoya, Kyoto, Kobe, Yokohama, Hakata, Hiroshima, Moji, and Niigata held positions on the directorship of the organization.[29] Thus, despite divisions in its ranks, the business community forged an institutional unity to represent the corporate voice of capital in Manchukuo.

The involvement of the domestic business community on this scale in the Manchurian economy represented a new departure. Responding to a constituency with little or no experience in Manchuria, a key function of the council became furnishing basic information about the Manchurian economy and explaining how to expand business operations in unfamiliar terrain. In this sense the council mediated the first contact many businessmen had with Manchuria. A large-scale conference held in Dalian in August 1933—at which the Japan-Manchuria Business Council was founded—provided the first chance for many Japanese businessmen to visit Manchuria. Delegates heard lectures by and held discussions with government officials, Mantetsu representatives, and the Japanese business community in Manchuria. Most availed themselves of the opportunity to travel through the country and appraise the situation for themselves. A highlight of the conference was a seven-option tour package taking participants on different routes through Manchukuo. In two weeks of travel, most made stops at Xinjing (the new capital), Fengtian, and Jilin. From there, some routes took side trips into Korea and north China, while others

27. Nichiman jitsugyō kyōkai, *Shōwa 9 nendo Nichiman jitsugyō kyōkai jigyō hōkokusho* (Nichiman jitsugyō kyōkai, 1935), pp. 91–93, 98–99.

28. Ibid., pp. 57–59; Nichiman jitsugyō kyōkai, *Nichiman jitsugyō kyōkai daiyonkai kaiin sōkai hōkokusho* (Nichiman jitsugyō kyōkai, 1937), p. 16.

29. Nichiman jitsugyō kyōkai, *Setsuritsu shuisho, kaisoku oyobi yakuin meibo* (1934), Tōkyō shōkō kaigisho microreel no. 140:2432–2437.

went into north Manchuria or to the mining centers of Anshan and Fu-shun.[30]

The conference was well attended by the nation's business leaders. The 119 businessmen and 12 local officials who took part included officials of fifty-three different chambers of commerce and the mayors of Japan's major cities.[31] By introducing a new aspect of Manchuria to a group that had thought little on the subject before then, the conference made a great impact on the men who controlled the domestic economy. As the mayor of Osaka commented, "Before when I thought of Manchuria, it was the military administration established right after the Russo-Japanese War back in 1906. Now when I see the different dimensions of the new Manchukuo, the only word I can think of to describe my reaction is amazement."[32] In the course of the conference, the mayor of Osaka and other influential Japanese began to see Manchukuo the way the council promoted it: as a land of opportunity. Through seminars and lectures, pamphlets and surveys, the council spread the message to businessmen throughout Japan. The result was the culmination of the business initiative in the early years of Manchukuo and arguably the most profound impact the council was to have—the popularization of the image of economic opportunity in the new empire.

MIXED SIGNALS FROM THE ARMY

While the Japan-Manchuria Business Council had been forming, the Kwantung Army and Manchukuo government had been putting together a policy for economic penetration of the four provinces of Northeast China that were now under military occupation. In the initial phases of policy formation, the Kwantung Army sent mixed signals to the private sector about their role in Manchuria's new economic regime. On one hand, the Kwantung Army made sporadic efforts to court the goodwill of businessmen, inviting the Japan Chamber of Commerce to send delegates to a conference on economic policy in January 1932, and making army representatives

30. Nihon shōkō kaigisho, *Nichiman jitsugyō kondankai yōkō* (1933), Tōkyō shōkō kaigisho microreel no. 139:1714–1744.

31. Ibid.

32. The mayor's remark was published in an Osaka *Mainichi* article on August 28, 1933, and reprinted in the five-hundred-page report on the conference and the founding of the Japan-Manchuria Business Council: Manshū daihakurankai kyō-sankai, *Nichiman jitsugyō kyōkai kiyō* (1933), Tōkyō shōko kaigisho microreel no. 139:1785–2324, article on frame 2263.

available to meet with businessmen and discuss their concerns.[33] On such occasions spokesmen professed the Kwantung Army's desire to cooperate with private industry, and businessmen frequently came away feeling sanguine about working with the army. As one member of a Japan Chamber of Commerce economic mission reported to the press on his return from Manchuria in late March 1932, "We talked with all the key military authorities there as well as important people in and out of government. The military authorities really welcome the investment of domestic capital, and I did not see evidence of the army oppressing capitalists. We at home will take the opportunity to give as much financial support as possible to the construction of the new Manchuria."[34]

Yet this warm show of welcome was shaded by information appearing in the press about Kwantung Army hostility to capital. In a meeting with business leader Yamamoto Jōtarō in December 1931, Army Minister Araki Sadao reportedly declared the army's intention to "exclude monopoly profits of capitalists" from Manchuria and require that earnings be "reinvested in Manchurian development." Even while Kwantung Army Commander Honjō was toasting the fortunes of his corporate guests, he was being quoted as saying, "We want to use Manchuria as the means to renovate [*kaizō*] Japan. Even if this is impossible, at the very least we intend absolutely to exclude finance capital and the influence of political parties from Manchuria." Shared by the right wing and national socialists in Japan, these opinions were summarized in what became known as the Kwantung Army's unofficial slogan for Manchurian development: *zaibatsu wa Manshū ni hairu bekarazu—zaibatsu* must not come into Manchuria.[35]

To many businessmen, proof of Kwantung Army antagonism to their interests came with the announcement of the Manchukuo government's Economic Construction Program in March 1933. Tokyo and Osaka business circles held the opinion, which had been clearly communicated to the army, that state planning and economic controls should be used only for the purpose of discouraging the growth of industries that would compete

---

33. Fletcher, *The Japanese Business Community*, p. 78.
34. The interview was originally published in the Tokyo *Asahi* on April 2, 1932. This remark was quoted in Suzuki Tōzaburō, "Manmō shinkokka to Nihon no kin'yū shihon," *Kaizō* (May 1932), p. 66.
35. Suzuki Takashi, "Manshū keizai kaihatsu to Manshū jūkōgyō no seiritsu," *Tokushima daigaku gakugei kiyō (shakai kagaku)* 13, supplement (1963), p. 99. For typical media treatments see Suzuki Takeo, "Nichiman burokku keizairon no saikentō," *Kaizō* (January 1933), pp. 53–67; Suzuki Tōzaburō, "Manmō shinkokka to Nihon no kin'yū shihon," *Kaizō* (May 1932), pp. 64–71.

with existing domestic production. And as they stressed most vociferously, the controlled economy should not be employed to restrict the freedom of action of capital in the development of Manchuria, interfere in the management of industry, or limit the rate and use of profits.[36] The Economic Construction Program ignored this advice, however, serving notice to big business that "national control" would be "exerted on important economic activities" to protect "the interests of the (Japanese) people as a whole" and to prevent economic development being "monopolized" by an "exclusive class of people."[37]

Calling it the Japan-Manchuria controlled economy or the Japan-Manchuria bloc economy, the Manchukuo government program set up a complicated regulatory procedure to oversee economic development. One group of industries "important from the standpoint of national defense or in the nature of public utility" was subject to state management through special companies. A second group, requiring development "by degrees under necessary control according to domestic demands," was obliged to receive government permits for operation. A third group, everything "not included in the above two categories," was ostensibly open to free enterprise. But in practice, these too required a government license, albeit more easily obtainable than the permits for group two industries.[38]

The announcement of this program signaled the failure of the Japan-Manchuria Business Council's efforts to create a framework for imperial corporatism in Manchukuo. The Kwantung Army had unambiguously rejected their advice and unilaterally cut them out of the decision-making process in Manchukuo. Capitalists responded to the Kwantung Army's action with disgust. As the words of an Osaka industrialist demonstrate, businessmen condemned the Economic Construction Program for its shortsighted hostility to capital:

> If the policy of complete economic control is applied to Manchukuo industrialization, it will act as a check on the flow of urgently needed capital

36. Business views were expressed in the various discussions on economic policy held in Manchuria and Japan throughout 1932 and 1933. For a summary of the positions of Tokyo *zaibatsu* and Osaka industrialists, see "Nichiman tōsei keizai seisakuron no yōshi" (1933), Tōkyō shōkō kaigisho microreel no. 107:608–617. See also Nihon shōkō kaigisho, *Manmō keizai shisatsudan;* and Mantetsu keizai chōsakai, ed., *TaiMan keizai seisaku ni kansuru kakushu iken* (Mantetsu, 1932).

37. The Economic Construction Program was first published in March 1933 as *Manshū keizai kensetsu yōkō*. Reprinted in South Manchurian Railway Company, *Fifth Report on Progress in Manchuria to 1936* (Dalian: South Manchurian Railway Company, 1936), p. 98.

38. Ibid.

from Japan. Such an arbitrary order cannot possibly have any appeal for capital in a capitalist system. Moreover, widely publicizing the fact that certain parties in Manchuria want to exclude capitalists has created an even greater impediment to capital investment. . . . There is no other way for Manchukuo to get the capital it needs except from Japanese capitalists. Capital in the current meaning of the term will not invest on the basis of patriotism.[39]

In a sense, the hot-and-cold attitude of the army toward the involvement of capitalists in Manchurian development merely reinforced the feeling among many businessmen that the army could not be trusted to run the empire. Although the Japan-Manchuria Business Council and other business organizations had made serious efforts to work with the Kwantung Army in the creation of the new economic regime in Manchukuo, they took it in stride when the army rejected the business initiative.

Certainly private enterprise had little intention of backing away from Manchukuo, even though information emanating from Manchukuo and the anti-capital thrust of the Economic Construction Program may have dampened business ardor for participating in state-controlled industrial development. The decision not to abandon Manchukuo to the army was conditioned by the crisis atmosphere in the international and domestic economy. Japanese business had been buffeted by a series of shocks in the late twenties and early thirties: the banking crisis and collapse of stock values, the change on to and then off of the gold standard and the wild fluctuations in exchange rates, the slump in international trade and the rise of protectionism, and the on again, off again anti-Japanese boycott in China. In the midst of crisis and uncertainty, businessmen looked eagerly to the security of a Japanese-dominated Manchurian market. Yet unlike the Manchukuo government, businesses put profits at the top of their agenda. This did not mean that they opposed government policy outright, but rather that they tried to turn the situation to their own advantage. Thus, business organizations adopted a wait-and-see attitude toward the more radical elements of economic construction, such as state ventures in resource development, and moved forward boldly in areas that had proven profitable in the past, like consumer exports.

For this reason, the Japan-Manchuria Business Council chose to give enthusiastic endorsement to the official rhetoric of economic construction in its public statements. The organization's prospectus framed its emergence in the context of "the rapid changes in every aspect of the situation

---

39. Mantetsu keizai chōsakai, pp. 15–16.

following the founding of Manchukuo," and referred grandly to "establishing peace in the East":

> Awakening to the intimate and inseparable relationship . . . referred to under the terms Japan-Manchuria economic partnership and Japan-Manchuria industrial control, we are establishing the Japan-Manchuria Business Council . . . to foster close cooperation and goodwill. Aiming to cooperate in the economic construction of Manchukuo and the Japan-Manchuria economic partnership through the promotion of an unreserved and harmonious partnership between industrialists of both countries, the council aims to lay a path toward the coprosperity and coexistence of both nations.[40]

Rhetorically paying obeisance to the state program of economic control and economic unification, the council signaled the intention of the business community to lend public support to Manchukuo government policy.

Through the Japan-Manchuria Business Council and other organizations, Japanese business leaders actively promoted the new economic imperialism in the development of Manchukuo. In this critical early phase when contracts were signed and irrevocable decisions made, even though executives had fundamental reservations about the Manchukuo government's plan, they judged the best advantage lay in a show of cooperation rather than public antagonism. Thus began what amounted to a hollow partnership between big business and the Manchukuo state. On the surface was bowing and bonhomie, but behind the smiles lay a cynical contempt for each other's goals and a ruthless disregard for the effects of their own actions on their partner's well-being.

"CONFLICTING VISIONS" OF ECONOMIC DEVELOPMENT

Even as spokesmen for private enterprise and the Japanese representatives of the Manchukuo state joined together to promote an economic union between Japan and Manchuria, conflicting visions of this partnership emerged in the public debate over Manchurian development. As this debate spilled out into the organs of the mass media—the daily press, general interest magazines, leading economic journals, and pamphlets published by business organizations and the Manchukuo government—a tangle of slogans and theories jostled one another. Such buzzwords as the "Japan-Manchuria controlled economy," "Japan-Manchuria bloc," "Japan-Manchuria partnership," "inseparable relationship," "economic construction,"

40. Nichiman jitsugyō kyōkai, *Setsuritsu shuisho,* Tōkyō shōkō kaigisho microreel 140:2426.

"economic development," "coexistence and coprosperity," "autarky," and "self-sufficiency" showed the variety of policies that collided under these rubrics were so multifaceted, self-contradictory, and confusing that one observer lightheartedly characterized the problem in terms of excess-knowledge: "This rampant production is leaving people lost in confusion, not because of inadequate knowledge [*ninshiki busoku*], but because of excess-knowledge [*ninshiki kajō*] of Manchurian economic conditions. Isn't it time to subject the uncontrolled and excess production of Japan-Manchuria controlled economy theories itself to some control and consolidation?"[41] These conflicting visions of the new economic imperialism emerging in the early thirties were at least united by a growing conviction that Manchukuo was big enough for everyone. Conflicting interests need not fight over pieces of the pie because the pie itself was inexhaustible. And although both sides viewed Manchukuo in utopian terms, the precise meaning of utopia was in the eye of the beholder.

The Manchurian paradise depicted by Manchukuo government planners was intended to become the model of state capitalism, with industrialization proceeding in steps according to a well-ordered plan. Influenced by the example of Soviet economic planning in the five-year plans, architects of the Manchukuo government's "Outline of Economic Construction in Manchuria" claimed to be practicing "kingly way economics" (*ōdōshugi keizai*), a name invented to disassociate Manchukuo from Marxist ideology.[42] Promising to build "the only economic structure of its kind in the world," army planners envisioned that a radical program of state control over "important economic activities" would permit "coordinated development" between "every branch of the economy." In the "Outline of Economic Construction," army planners used terms like *rationalize, coordinate,* and *control* to announce the fundamental reform of capitalism under state auspices.[43]

---

41. Suzuki Takeo, "Nichiman burokku keizairon no saikentō," *Kaizō* (January 1933), pp. 53–54. The Japanese phrasing of these slogans was *Nichiman tōsei keizai* (Japan-Manchuria controlled economy), *Nichiman burokku* (Japan-Manchuria bloc), *Nichiman teikei* (Japan-Manchuria partnership), *fukabun kankei* (inseparable relationship), *keizai kensetsu* (economic construction), *keizai kaihatsu* (economic development), *kyōzon kyōei* (coexistence and coprosperity), *autaruki* (autarky), and *jikyū jisoku* (self-sufficiency).

42. For a discussion of the "kingly way" (*ōdō*), see Chapter 6, under "The Revolutionary State of Manchukuo."

43. Tanaka Kuichi, "Manshūkoku no keizai jūkanen keikaku: sono keizai ken-

As a strategy for economic expansion, however, these ideas were anything but fresh. State and quasi-state enterprises such as the Oriental Development Company, the Banks of Taiwan and Korea, and Mantetsu had provided the instruments of economic management since Japan set up colonial administrations in Korea, Taiwan, and the Kwantung Leased Territory. In China, too, the state carefully monitored private activities. In 1906, for example, when competition for the Chang (Yangtze) River trade proved ruinous, the government stepped in and ordered four shipping companies to merge into the government-supervised Nisshin kisen kaisha.[44] Public policy firms had always dominated Japan's colonial economies, regulating the terms of private involvement and guiding business operations. State enterprises already coordinated and controlled important economic activities; they had executed long-term plans for railway building and the expansion of rice cultivation. But there were two key differences between these earlier efforts and the Economic Construction Program. First, army planners in Manchukuo wanted to use state capitalism for heavy industrialization—an idea that was both radical and untried. Second, they gilded the program with extravagant predictions that the Manchukuo experiment would usher in a new domestic era of statist harmony. Once capitalism was reformed in Manchuria, the lessons could be applied to the domestic economy as well.

The private sector had its own visions of Manchukuo's future. But rather than looking to a utopia of reformed capitalism, the business community dreamt of relief from economic depression. Articles in economic journals such as *Tōyō keizai shinpō* spoke glowingly of the curative power of the "Manchuria prosperity."[45] They noted that trade was expanding and had given the economy a healthy inflationary boost. The investment world had also "turned its attention to Manchuria." Because of the unshackling of Japanese rights and interests under the new regime, the rise in demand for Japanese goods due to the Economic Construction Program, and the establishment of the Japan-Manchuria bloc economy, "hopes were running

setsu yōkō," *Chūō kōron* (April 1933), pp. 64–70; text of the "Outline of Economic Construction" in South Manchurian Railway Company, p. 98.

44. William D. Wray, *Mitsubishi and the N.Y.K., 1870–1914: Business Strategy in the Japanese Shipping Industry* (Cambridge: Council on East Asian Studies, Harvard University, 1984), pp. 384–394.

45. "Junchō ni kōjō suru Manshū zaikai," *Tōyō keizai shinpō* (9 August 1934), p. 19.

very high" for the new Manchuria.[46] Economist Takahashi Kamekichi explained the popular perception that Manchuria had provided the solution to Japan's economic deadlock in terms of the complementary needs of metropolis and empire:

> In the current era of global overproduction of commodities, much labor and productive capacity lies idle in Japan as well. By simply mobilizing this excess capacity, we can easily supply all the goods urgently required as a result of the Manchurian problem. In the past Japan would have had to pay for the construction of Manchukuo with gold, but now she can pay in goods. . . . Killing two birds with one stone, as it were, the economic construction of Manchukuo is simultaneously furnishing the expenditure for necessary programs of "industrial relief" and "unemployment relief." . . . The League of Nations predicted that the independence of Manchuria would destroy the Japanese economy but far from it, it has been the saving and strengthening of Japanese capitalism.[47]

The mood of self-congratulation and confidence reflected in Takahashi's commentary was characteristic of the business press on the Japan-Manchuria partnership. In 1934, when Takahashi's article was written, businessmen had good reason to feel optimistic. After a precipitous drop in the two years following the onset of global depression, Japanese trade had made a remarkable turnaround in 1932 and 1933. Stimulated by a sharp fall in the value of the yen when Japan went off the gold standard in December 1931, the nation's exports surged worldwide. Together with the rise in military spending, this trade boom helped reflate the domestic economy. By 1933 the signs of recovery were already apparent. While price levels in the United States hit an all-time low and industrial production continued to fall throughout the economies of Europe, in Japan prices had recovered 20 percent and industrial production had risen beyond 1920s' levels. It was a heady moment: the military battles had been won, economic development was changing the face of Manchuria, and while the rest of the world was still mired in depression, the Japanese economy had turned itself around.[48]

In their language and their sense of heady optimism, the tangle of theories on Manchurian development shared a common framework. But

46. "Manshū kankei kaisha no tōshi kachi," *Tōyō keizai shinpō* (9 September 1933), p. 23.

47. Takahashi Kamekichi, "Manshūkoku shisatsu hōkokuki," *Chūō kōron* (October 1934), p. 252.

48. Ōishi Kaichirō, "Sekai daikyōkō to Nihon shihonshugi: mondai no shozai," in Ōishi Kaichirō, ed., *Sekai daikyōkōki*, vol. 2 of *Nihon teikokushugishi* (Tōkyō daigaku shuppankai, 1987), p. 16, and Ishii, pp. 57–64.

under the same grand slogans emerged concrete visions of the Japan-Manchuria partnership that fundamentally contradicted one another. The bloc economy envisioned in the Manchukuo government's Economic Construction Program meant creating an autarkic trading sphere which would provide for self-sufficiency in wartime. As was often pointed out, this argument was based on observations of wartime mobilization during World War I: "From the perspective of the wartime economy, the purpose of the Japan-Manchuria economic bloc is to guarantee resources. . . . Because of the shortage of goods during and immediately after the war in Europe, all countries made it a priority to guarantee the supply of resources. Certain parties advocate Manchurian development on this basis."[49] The army-run Manchukuo government wanted the Northeast as a particular kind of resource base; that is, a source of materials necessary for military industries. Hence, its interest in resource development extended little beyond the progress of mining coal, iron, magnesite, and other materials necessary to heavy industry and light-metals production. Agricultural products—even the famed soybeans—were low on the army's priority list. Moreover, the army's Economic Construction Program proposed not only securing strategic resources in Manchuria, but actually refining and manufacturing them on site. Thus, its picture of the new Manchuria featured a showcase of special companies linking industrialization with national defense and efficiently managing the development and conservation of strategic resources. Manchukuo government and Army Ministry publications vaunted such "industrial successes" as the Manchuria Arsenal Corporation, Showa Steel Works, Manchuria Chemical Industry Company, Manchuria Petroleum Company, and Dowa Automobile Manufacturing Company.[50]

What domestic businessmen envisioned gaining from the Japan-Manchuria partnership was something altogether different. As one Osaka businessman phrased it in 1933,

> Manchuria has recently become an incredible boom area as a consumer market for Japanese goods; this year's exports have approached 300,000 yen, more than ten times what they were only a few years ago, and far surpassing exports to China. . . . Because Osaka products make up between 60 and 70 percent of these exports, we have great hopes for the future of

49. Takahashi Kamekichi, "Manshū keizai no genjō to zentō," *Kaizō* (October 1934), p. 35.

50. Rikugunshō, *Manshū jihen boppatsu man'yonen: Manshūkoku gaikan* (Rikugunshō, 1935), pp. 9–15; Tanaka Kuichi, "Manshūkoku no keizai jūkanen keikaku: sono keizai kensetsu yōkō," *Chūō kōron* (April 1933), pp. 64–70; South Manchuria Railway Company, pp. 79–111.

Manchukuo and want to strive to develop Manchukuo and raise domestic purchasing power. Japan's foreign trade is beginning to face great obstacles, the foremost due to economic pressure from England. Now more than ever Manchuria is an absolutely vital lifeline for domestic commerce and industry—the single free place where we may increase our trade.[51]

Amidst all the talk of bold new solutions to the historic crisis and of following the world trend toward the segmentation of the globe into trading blocs, business hopes for Manchuria harked back to the fabled China market. And yet, this familiar myth had been revised in the course of the past few years. Now it signified not only a market of prodigious size, but one that could be guaranteed. This new ideal market could not be threatened by tariffs or by any of the other forms of trade protectionism that were beginning to cut into Japan's export boom in the British Empire. In contrast to the army's concern for wartime exigencies, businessmen imagined the Japan-Manchuria bloc economy as a peacetime trading sphere. While the army's point of reference was economic mobilization during World War I, businessmen had in their minds the experience of worldwide depression. With the global economy suffering from an excess of production, the argument went, the key was not to guarantee resources (as in the army view) but to guarantee markets.[52] It was in this sense that the Osaka businessman underscored the value of Manchuria as a commercial "lifeline."

Unlike the army, the domestic business community was strongly opposed to the industrialization of Manchuria. In the words of the influential Japan Industrial Club, "As much as possible Manchuria should be made into a supplier of materials. It is a mistake to encourage new industrial production that will compete with Japanese domestic industry. . . . Manchurian tariffs should be kept as low as possible to encourage the import of Japanese products. Industrial goods should be produced within Japan and exported to Manchuria."[53] In other words, businessmen were not looking for fundamental change in the structure of the colonial economic relationship between Japan and Manchuria, which was based on imports to Japan of primary products and the export of consumer goods. Opposed to the growth of a competing manufacturing industry in Manchuria, they defined development quite differently from the army. In the business community's terms, development signified expansion of the agricultural sector,

51. Manshū daihakurankai kyōsankai, Tōkyō shōkō kaigisho microreel no. 139:2248.
52. Takahashi Kamekichi, "Manshū keizai no genjō to zentō," *Kaizō* (October 1934), p. 35.
53. Mantetsu keizai chōsakai, p. 14.

which would mean more money in the hands of Chinese peasants and a larger market for Japanese goods.

As much as businessmen might welcome the idea of a secure market, many of them had mixed feelings about the message a Japan-Manchuria bloc might convey to the rest of the world. In the words of one Osaka industrialist, "this term can be so easily misunderstood. . . . I think the slogan 'Japan-Manchuria partnership and cooperation' [*Nichiman teikei kyōchō*] conveys a much more appropriate image."[54] The concern here was not to give any encouragement to the rise of global protectionism, for business leaders were well aware of their dependence on European and American markets. In this sense, the business view of a Japan-Manchuria partnership was premised on the continuation of a trade relationship with the West, in contrast to the Manchukuo government vision which was premised on the rupture of that relationship.

The conflicting visions of economic development appearing in the early imaginings of Manchukuo reproduced the tensions in the corporatist partnership that took form over the same period. Neither party was blind to the contradictions in the soldier-capitalist alliance; indeed, both sides commented on their fundamental conflict of interest. Knowing this full well, the army and the business community drew together nevertheless, united in their perception of the boundless possibilities of development. Images of Manchukuo as a land of opportunity promoted by the Japan-Manchuria Business Council reinforced the utopian ideals disseminated in the army's plan for a controlled economy; faith in Manchukuo brought them together. Along with the ambivalence, mistrust, and dissent, this faith suffused the corporatist partnership in Manchukuo.

IMPERIAL CORPORATISM AND THE YEN BLOC

The contradictions in the two economic blueprints meant that despite a veneer of cooperation, public and private sectors pursued development plans at cross-purposes. However, despite these fissures in the government-business partnership, the two sides did manage to jointly create a new economic empire in Manchuria. While army bureaucrats laid the plans and oversaw construction, private financiers supplied capital, and private industry purveyed the goods and material necessary to keep the new regime of colonial state capitalism afloat. Although businessmen disagreed fun-

---

54. Manshū daihakurankai kyōsankai, Tōkyō shōkō kaigisho microreel no. 139:2257.

damentally with the course the army was pursuing in Manchukuo, they were willing to lend economic support which, if withheld, would have brought empire building to a grinding halt. They did so not because they feared the stick of government coercion, but because the carrot of benefits was sufficiently enticing.

The formation of the trading sphere known as the yen bloc comprised one key project of the joint venture. For the army, the formation of the Japan-Manchuria bloc economy was a first stab at an autarkic production sphere. For the business community, it represented an attempt to develop a protected export market. Over the course of the 1930s, as both sides pursued their independent agendas, the yen bloc gradually took concrete institutional form. In 1933 and 1934, tax and currency initiatives created a new framework for trade between Japan, its colonies, and Manchukuo. In 1935 and 1936, these initiatives were expanded to include north China. After 1937, with the onset of the China Incident, the extension of Japanese military control brought more and more of China into the embrace of the yen bloc. Finally, with the advance south into the European colonies of Southeast Asia, the dominion of the yen spread into the so-called Co-prosperity Sphere. From its origins in Manchukuo to its embrace of greater East Asia, the yen bloc charted a rocky course. At every stage implementation was impeded first, by problems created by the conflict of public and private interests, and second, by the essential inability of an imperial trade bloc to overcome Japan's economic dependence on Western markets for imports, exports, and capital. Still, to the last the myth of the Manchurian market remained powerful. Over and again unpleasant realities were brushed aside by the optimism and hope that Japanese projected onto Manchukuo.

In the first stage of this process, the business community made energetic efforts to lobby government and promote its agenda for the yen bloc. When business organizations began to exert themselves in pursuit of economic opportunity in Manchuria, their primary goal was to open up an export market for Japanese consumer goods. When the Japan Chamber of Commerce took up the problem of Manchukuo in 1933, the need to decrease universally tariffs on Japanese goods entering Manchuria was high on its agenda.[55] At the founding conference of the Japan-Manchuria Business Council in Dalian later the same year, businessmen took the opportunity to lobby hard on this point.

55. Tōkyō shōkō kaigisho, "Manshūkoku kanzei kaisei ni kansuru iken" (January 1933), Tōkyō shōkō kaigisho microreel no. 139:1211–1227.

The Japan-Manchuria Business Council took up the interests of exporters, pouring its energies in 1934 into "developing long-term policy toward railway freight charges, currency reform, and the tariff problem." The council sponsored a large Manchuria-export conference, attended by members of government and trade associations throughout the country, including Kōchi, Aichi, and Tottori prefectures, as well as Tokyo, Yokohama, and other big cities. The conference sent letters to the Army Ministry, Foreign Ministry, Colonial Ministry, Manchurian Tax Bureau and other government authorities urging reduction of Manchurian import tariffs. The council also organized a series of discussions and lectures on issues concerning exporters and published pamphlets on the Manchurian trade.[56] An offshoot of the Japan-Manchuria Business Council was formed to promote exports from the ports along the Sea of Japan coast and northern Japan. Members joined from the prefectures of Fukui, Ishikawa, Toyama, Akita, Niigata, and Hokkaidō, which were not well served by the ports of Osaka, Yokohama, and Kobe.[57] Numerous local organizations also sprang up to promote exports on this new route across the Japan Sea into Manchuria via Korea. Several of these joined together with Toyama city to hold a large "Japan-Manchuria Industrial Fair" from April through June of 1936. This event aimed to "foster harmonious relations between Japan and Manchuria, raise the level of our production culture, and contribute to the rise of trade."[58] Since such activities consumed the energies of organizations promoting business interests in Manchuria, it seemed clear that what businessmen wanted from Manchuria was a consumer market.

Although export promotion was at the top of private industry's Manchurian agenda, it ranked close to the bottom on the army's list of priorities. Against the ambitions of domestic producers, the army weighed the need to keep the costs of economic development down and to protect Manchukuo government finances (between 1932 and 1936 tariffs accounted for 30–40 percent of government revenue). It had no qualms in sacrificing domestic producers to this end. Hence, tariffs were slashed or eliminated for construction goods (such as wood or cement) and heavy industrial products (steel or machinery), but only modestly reduced for consumer goods.[59] Moreover, the Manchukuo government did little to address what

56. Nichiman jitsugyō kyōkai, *Shōwa 9 nendo*, pp. 59–91.
57. Nichiman jitsugyō kyōkai, *TaiMan shōkō toshite mitaru ura Nihon no shokōwan* (Nichiman jitsugyō kyōkai, 1934).
58. *Toyama-shi shusai Nichiman sangyō daihakurankai* (Toyama: Toyama-shi, 1938), p. 157.
59. Kaneko, "Shihon yushutsu," pp. 350–351.

had become a chronic depression in the Manchurian agricultural sector, a situation which stymied dreams of a burgeoning market among Manchuria's peasantry and urban labor force. In fact, problems caused by the world depression and collapse in soybean market values (Manchuria's principal export commodity) were compounded by Japanese policies. Military operations disrupted production, economic restructuring brought financial dislocation, and limitations on Chinese immigration from the south caused rural labor shortages. Economic policies favored industrial over agricultural development and transferred wealth from the rural Chinese population to the Manchukuo state. By squeezing the peasantry to finance economic development, the Manchukuo government further restricted the already modest purchasing power of the Chinese labor force.[60] Any remaining hopes that the Manchukuo government might aid the exporter's cause were put to rest with the series of laws passed from 1938 on that increasingly restricted the Manchurian import trade in order to mitigate a foreign-exchange crisis.[61]

Still, the expansion of the Manchurian economy under the Economic Construction Program and subsequent development plans did expand Japanese exports to the Northeast, and the booming Manchurian market was hailed as proof of the success of the Japan-Manchuria bloc. The value of Japanese exports tripled by mid-decade, leaping from 136 million yen in 1931 to 507 million yen in 1936. This market, moreover, was increasingly important to Japan; as a percentage of total exports, the Manchukuo trade rose from 17 percent in 1935 to 39 percent in 1940.[62] Despite these encouraging statistics, however, Manchuria never became the vital lifeline for Japanese consumer goods. Instead, Manchukuo government policies stimulated demand for producer goods such as steel and machinery, which were supplied from Japan and which spurred the growth of Japanese heavy industry. For example, Japan's consumer exports to Manchuria rose from approximately 167 million yen in 1932, to 277 million yen in 1936, and

60. Jones, pp. 172–174; Takahashi Kamekichi, "Manshūkoku shisatsu hōkokuki," *Chūō kōron* (October 1934), pp. 255–258; Ōkura Kinmochi, "Manshū keizai no tokushusei o saguru," *Ekonomisuto* (11 July 1935), pp. 13–18.

61. Hara Akira, "DaiTōa kyōeiken," p. 16.

62. Rise in Japanese exports: *Manshū keizai zuhyō* (1934), p. 16; *Manshū keizai zuhyō* (1937), p. 9; and Louise Young, "Mobilizing for Empire: Japan and Manchukuo, 1931–1945," Ph.D. dissertation, Columbia University, 1993, p. 264, Table 5.5. Manchukuo trade as percentage of total exports: Manshū teikoku seifu, ed., *Manshū kenkoku jūnenshi*, vol. 91 of *Meiji hyakunenshi sōsho* (Hara shobō, 1969), p. 625.

again to 660 million yen in 1939. Compared to this, export values of heavy industrial and construction goods increased much more rapidly, from 37 million yen in 1932, to 145 million yen in 1936, reaching 539 million yen in 1939. The more than fifteen-fold expansion of heavy industrial goods dwarfed the four-fold increase in consumer products.[63]

This pattern of growth caused a dramatic shift in the composition of Japanese exports to Northeast China after the establishment of Manchukuo. In 1928 cotton textiles had occupied first place with 34 percent of exports, followed by wheat flour at 6 percent and machinery at 3 percent. However, by 1936 cotton textiles' share had fallen to 15 percent, while machinery and rolling stock took over first place with 16 percent of the total.[64] At the same time, Manchuria's consistently favorable balance of trade with Japan began to reverse itself in the wake of Japanese occupation, as soybean output fell steadily from 5.2 to 3.5 million tons between 1931 and 1940.[65] Consequently, a Manchurian trade surplus of 136 million yen at the close of 1931 was replaced, in 1933, with a 139 million yen deficit. Ever increasing imports from Japan exacerbated this yawning trade deficit, which rose to over 1 billion yen by 1940.[66] These developments transformed the classic colonial pattern of trade that had existed between Japan and Manchuria prior to 1931. From a single-crop export economy and a market for Japanese consumer goods, Manchuria became Japan's first external market for heavy industrial products and lost its own export strength.

Although at the time aggregate trade figures were taken as striking evidence of the formation of the Japan-Manchuria bloc, the rise of Japan's Manchurian trade in fact did little to affect the overall balance of Japan's foreign trade. Both army dreams of building a self-sufficient production sphere and businessmen's visions of creating a protected export market ran aground on the realities of Japan's place in the global economy. The quest

63. Figures for 1932: "Nichiman bōeiki no bunseki," *Ekonomisuto* (11 October 1935), pp. 14–17; figures for 1936 and 1939: Ōkurasho, *Gaikoku bōeki geppyō* (December 1936, December 1939). See also Louise Young, "Mobilizing for Empire," p. 270, Table 5.6.

64. Kaneko, "Shihon yushutsu," p. 353.

65. Iizuka Yasushi and Kazama Hideto, "Nōgyō shigen no shūdatsu," in Asada Kyōji and Kobayashi Hideo, eds., *Nihon teikokushugi no Manshū shihai: jūgonen sensō o chūshin ni* (Jichōsha, 1986), pp. 434, 492.

66. Figures for 1931 and 1933: *Manshū keizai zuhyō* (1934), pp. 13, 16; figure for 1940: Hara Akira, "DaiTōa kyōeiken," p. 19. See also Louise Young, "Mobilizing for Empire," p. 264, Table 5.5.

for economic security on these terms proved quixotic, for the Japanese economy was too deeply integrated into Western-controlled markets to make reorientation to an imperial trade bloc feasible.

In the first place, the army's efforts to promote autarky in the yen bloc failed to mitigate Japan's dependence on Western imports. Far from dissolving these ties, the heavy industrialization of Manchukuo actually stimulated growth in imports of producer goods from countries outside the yen bloc. As the decade wore on, and particularly after 1937, Japan's dependence on the United States and other non-yen-bloc countries for steel, machinery, and petroleum rose dramatically.[67] As Hara Akira has pointed out, the key flaw in the yen bloc was the impossibility of using qualitatively and quantitatively inferior Manchurian products to replace imports from the West.[68]

At the same time, the expansion of Japan-Manchuria trade failed to fulfill businessmen's hopes for a guaranteed consumer export market. Though Manchuria's importance as an export market for heavy industry was decisive, it never absorbed more than a fraction of consumer exports. Since the early thirties, textiles had overtaken raw silk as Japan's principal export. When textile markets in Asia replaced the American raw silk market as Japan's chief source of foreign revenue, the colonial markets of the Dutch East Indies, French Indochina, and British India became Japan's real export lifeline. Although Japanese traders might feel more secure in the knowledge that Japanese officials, rather than hostile colonial governments, were setting tariff rates, in fact, the size of the "guaranteed Manchurian market" did not reach a fraction of British India's, even after the latter imposed severe import restrictions on Japanese goods. Moreover, as a result of their occupation of Northeast China, Japanese traders lost the much larger China market south of the Great Wall. Boycotts against Japanese goods effectively eliminated sales to China, a 304 million yen export market in 1928 cut almost in half by 1936. Thus early gains in Manchuria were almost entirely offset by losses in the rest of China.[69]

Contradictions between the rhetoric and reality of the yen bloc soon

67. For example, imports of iron and steel from the United States rose from 78 million yen in 1936 to 228 million yen in 1939. Imports of machinery from the United States rose from 38 million yen to 149 million yen over the same period: Matsui Kiyoshi, *Kindai Nihon bōekishi*, vol. 3 (Yūhikaku, 1963), pp. 114–115. See also Ishii, p. 62, and Louise Young, "Mobilizing for Empire," pp. 274–275, Tables 5.8 and 5.9.
68. Hara Akira, "Senji tōsei keizai no kaishi," pp. 225–234.
69. Ishii, pp. 61–64, and Kaneko, "Shihon yushutsu," pp. 352–353, 355.

manifested themselves in the development of a chronic shortage of capital to finance Manchurian trade. As early as 1935, business analysts began to point out this deficiency in the Japan-Manchuria bloc economy. Failure to address problems in the agricultural sector had led to a catastrophic fall in soybean exports. The agricultural depression showed no signs of abating, and Japan's import policy only aggravated the problem. To protect its own depressed agricultural sector, Japanese tariffs were raised against Manchurian soybeans, barley, and sorghum.[70] Without the foreign exchange from soybean exports, the financing of rising imports of steel, machinery, and other goods for Manchukuo's economic construction was dependent on the continued inflow of Japanese capital. But by 1935, a recovered domestic economy was competing to invest those funds at home.

After 1936, with the inception of the Five-Year Plan in Manchukuo and the acceleration of the domestic military buildup, the dilemmas of trade finance grew even more serious. The problem lay in the triangular relationship between Japanese, yen-bloc (Manchukuo, occupied China, and the Japanese colonies), and non-yen-bloc trade. Heavy industrialization in Japan caused a sharp rise in imports of machinery and metals from the United States and Europe, leading to a chronic negative balance of Japan's trade outside the yen bloc. Non-yen-bloc exports simply could not earn enough dollars and pounds to buy the materials needed to keep military production going. As capital reserves in Japan dried up and foreign loans proved unavailable, this led to an increasingly urgent balance of payments crisis.

The government tried to address the foreign exchange shortage by limiting imports of nonmilitary goods from outside the yen bloc on one hand and redirecting exports from inside to outside the yen bloc on the other. But when Japanese imports of cotton, wool, and other nonmilitary producer goods were restricted, the ensuing shortages led to a fall in textile and other light-industry production. Since these products represented the core of Japanese exports outside the yen bloc, the restrictions on cotton and wool imports simply exacerbated the foreign exchange crisis. By the close of the decade, not only had shortages driven prices up, but they also brought domestic production to intermittent stoppages. Moreover, yen-bloc trade restrictions were thwarted by galloping inflation rates in Man-

70. "Nichiman bōeki no bunseki," *Ekonomisuto* (11 October 1935), pp. 14–17; Ōkura Kinmochi, "Manshū keizai no tokushūsei o saguru," *Ekonomisuto* (11 July 1935), p. 12; "Shinsetsu kaisha no genkyō ni miru Manshū keizai kōsaku no shinten jōkyō (I)," *Ekonomisuto* (21 November 1935), p. 35.

chukuo and north China which drew Japanese goods toward the highest prices.[71] Producers evaded government restrictions to sell their goods on what became a thriving consumer black market in Manchuria. Ironically, when the dream of the Manchurian market finally materialized, it contributed to the undoing of the home economy.

By 1940 the government clearly had lost its grip on the reins of the East Asian trade sphere. This did not mean, however, that the yen bloc was an unmitigated disaster. Far from it; many fortunes were made from the booming Manchurian trade. Evaluation of success or failure depended on where one was placed in the economic nexus. One company's big break became another's misfortune. Windfall profits on the black market were financed out of the losses of domestic producers whose supplies had dried up. These profits on the yen bloc, moreover, had proved highly volatile. The early years had seen the greatest return for the greatest number. But even toward the end, when the problems of trade finance made it clear to all involved that the yen bloc was unsustainable, the business of money-making in Manchuria continued.

In both the successes and failures of the yen bloc were inscribed the tensions within Japan's imperial corporatism. Though the dream of the Manchurian market inspired the union of soldiers and capitalists, imperial corporatism could never rise above their incompatible interests in the field of foreign trade. The reasons for the uneven record of the yen bloc were rooted in the process of mobilization for economic imperialism. The inclusiveness of the visions for Manchukuo, calculated to draw in a broad spectrum of support, imported into the imperial venue the full range of conflict afflicting Japan's political economy at the time. The diversity of interests that joined together to develop Manchukuo created one of the paradoxes of the imperial project, for diversity imparted to Manchukuo both the strength of dynamism and the weakness of instability.

THE JOINT VENTURE IN STATE CAPITALISM

While Japanese exporters traveled the course from giddy optimism at the beginning of the 1930s to grim despair at the decade's close, investors who supplied the capital for Manchurian development followed a different path to the same conclusion. Unlike prospects for the export market, business leaders were initially skeptical about the army's plans to industrialize Manchukuo. Yet despite these sentiments, when they could be insulated from

71. Hara Akira, "Senji tōsei keizai no kaishi," pp. 225–234.

the risks and guaranteed a profit, capitalists were willing to underwrite the army's development project. Indeed, investment in state capitalism in Manchuria grew at an astounding rate. Between 1932 and 1941, 5.86 billion yen was transferred to Manchuria, an unprecedented export of Japanese capital.[72] These investments gave meaning to the rhetoric of an inseparable relationship, over time committing Japan to a strategy from which it could not easily withdraw. They also demonstrated the extent of private-sector support for the army experiment that business leaders allegedly condemned.

During the first half of the thirties, the economic construction period of Manchurian development, Japanese investment had two salient characteristics. First, it was overwhelmingly concentrated in state-controlled ventures (see Table 1). Of the approximately 1.2 billion yen invested between 1932 and 1936, over 77 percent (891 million yen) was channeled through the semipublic Mantetsu and the Manchukuo government itself. Second, the importance of loans was striking. About two-thirds (779 million yen) of total investment was financed either through purchases of government securities and company bonds, or direct loans (see Table 2). The remaining third of the capital was invested through stock purchases.

In this decisive early phase, Japanese investors chose to finance Manchurian development through bonds rather than stocks and through government enterprises rather than private ventures. These choices were driven by a desire to minimize liability for what they saw as a dicey experiment. While stocks might be more profitable, if the venture failed, the loss fell completely on the investor. Bonds, on the other hand, cushioned the investor from such adversities. The rate of return was fixed and repayment set within a short period of time. Bonds were a conservative, risk-minimizing investment. By purchasing bonds for government enterprises, the investor distanced himself from risk still further. Although corporate bonds might lose their value if the company went bankrupt, government bonds were guaranteed.

Although private enterprise deplored the army's brand of state capitalism, it was investment choices of capitalists that ensured survival of the army's program. Because they backed state enterprises, state enterprises flourished. Because they neglected private investment, no network of private industries emerged to counterbalance state power. And because they chose to invest their money with minimal direct involvement, army planners had the field to themselves. Thus, private-sector choices as well as

72. Hikita, pp. 866, 889.

Table 1. Investment in Public and Private Enterprises
in Manchukuo (in Millions of Yen)

	Public	Private	Both Types
1932–1941	4,441	1,421	5,862
1932–1936	891	265	1,156
1932	86	12	97
1933	131	30	161
1934	186	66	252
1935	321	61	382
1936	168	96	264
1937–1941	3,550	1,156	4,706
1937	324	129	453
1938	376	150	526
1939	785	291	1,076
1940	1,029	197	1,226
1941	1,036	389	1,425

SOURCES: Kaneko Fumio, "Shihon yushutsu to shokuminchi," in Ōishi Kaichirō, ed., *Sekai daikyōkōki*, vol. 2 of *Nihon teikokushugishi* (Tōkyō daigaku shuppankai, 1987), p. 337; Hayashi Takehisa, Yamazaki Hiroaki, and Shibagaki Kazuo, *Nihon shihonshugi*, vol. 6 of *Kōza teikokushugi no kenkyū: ryōtaisenkan ni okeru sono saihensei* (Aoki shoten, 1973), pp. 872–877; and Hikita Yasuyuki, "Zaisei, kin'yū kōzō," in Asada Kyōji and Kobayashi Hideo, eds., *Nihon teikokushugi no Manshū shihai: jūgonen sensō o chūshin ni* (Jichōsha, 1986), pp. 866, 889, 890.

NOTE: Public enterprises include the Manchukuo government, Mantetsu, Manchurian Heavy Industries, and the Manchurian Industrial Bank. Mantetsu-affiliated "special companies" are classified here under private enterprises.

government policy worked to create an economic order that excluded private industry.

These private-sector decisions were largely dictated by the *zaibatsu*, about which there are two key points to be made. The first concerns a distinction often drawn in discussions of the involvement of *zaibatsu* in Manchuria (and the wartime economy more generally) between new *zaibatsu* like Nissan, who tied their fortunes to the military-industrial complex in the empire, and old *zaibatsu* such as Mitsui and Mitsubishi, who allegedly shunned it.[73] In fact, as indicated in Table 3, the biggest single

73. "Old *zaibatsu*" refers to the financial-industrial conglomerates like Mitsui, Mitsubishi, Sumitomo, and Yasuda, which emerged in the late nineteenth century under the patronage of the Meiji government. In contrast, "new *zaibatsu*" such as Nissan and Nitchitsu grew to prominence during the World War I boom. Whereas old *zaibatsu* were associated with mining, trading, and banking, the new *zaibatsu*

Table 2. Capital Investment in Manchukuo through Stocks,
Loans, and Bonds (in Millions of Yen)

	Stocks	Loans and Bonds	All Types
1932–1941	2,035	3,783	5,818
1932–1936			
Mantetsu	212	480	692
Private corporations	197	103	300
Manchukuo government	0	180	180
Total (1932–1936)	409	763	1,172
1937–1941			
Mantetsu	366	1,102	1,468
Manchurian Heavy Industries	774	395	1,169
Manchurian Industrial Bank	0	125	125
Private corporations	486	663	1,149
Manchukuo government	0	735	735
Total (1937–1941)	1,626	3,020	4,646

SOURCES: Kaneko Fumio, "Shihon yushutsu to shokuminchi," in Ōishi Kaichirō, ed., *Sekai daikyōkōki*, vol. 2 of *Nihon teikokushugishi* (Tōkyō daigaku shuppankai, 1987), p. 337; Hayashi Takehisa, Yamazaki Hiroaki, and Shibagaki Kazuo, *Nihon shihonshugi*, vol. 6 of *Kōza teikokushugi no kenkyū: ryōtaisenkan ni okeru sono saihensei* (Aoki shoten, 1973), pp. 872–877; and Hikita Yasuyuki, "Zaisei, kin'yū kōzō," in Asada Kyōji and Kobayashi Hideo, eds., *Nihon teikokushugi no Manshū shihai: jūgonen sensō o chūshin ni* (Jichōsha, 1986), pp. 866, 889, 890.

source of direct investment was the old, not the new *zaibatsu*. In Manchukuo's first five years old *zaibatsu* invested an estimated 187.1 million yen, compared with 11.4 million yen for new *zaibatsu*. Even in the second half of the decade, when Nissan moved its operations to Manchukuo, direct investments of the old zaibatsu still exceeded the new zaibatsu by 33.4 million yen.[74] The second point about the *zaibatsu* and Manchukuo relates

---

were involved with heavy and chemical industries. For a classic statement of the "old *zaibatsu* rejects Manchukuo; new *zaibatsu* embraces Manchukuo" thesis, see Jones, pp. 142–148. For a more recent restatement stressing that the "army rejects old *zaibatsu*, embraces new *zaibatsu*," see Johnson, *MITI and the Japanese Miracle*, pp. 130–131.

74. I have used Hara Akira's figures as the basis of Table 3, but he cautions that because of gaps and inaccuracies in the statistics of this period, readers should interpret these figures somewhat loosely: Hara Akira, "1930 nendai," p. 57.

Table 3. Direct Investment in Manchukuo by New
and Old *Zaibatsu* (in Millions of Yen)

	Old Zaibatsu	*New* Zaibatsu
1932–1941	387.0	177.9
1932–1936	187.1	11.4
1932	6.5	0
1933	9.2	1.3
1934	63.8	7.5
1935	49.4	0.1
1936	58.2	2.5
1937–1941	199.9	166.5
1937	43.5	61.4
1938	37.4	30.5
1939	107.1	66.9
1940	5.7	2.7
1941	6.2	5.0

SOURCE: Hara Akira, "1930 nendai no Manshū keizai tōsei seisaku," in Manshūshi kenkyūkai, ed., *Nihon teikokushugika no Manshū* (Ochanomizu shobō, 1972), p. 55.

NOTE: Of the *zaibatsu* listed in Hara's table, Mitsui, Mitsubishi, Sumitomo, Ōkura, and Asano are categorized here as old *zaibatsu;* Nomura, Suzuki [*sic*], Nissan, Nitchitsu, and Nezu are classified as new *zaibatsu.*

to the fact, frequently observed, that direct *zaibatsu* investments occupied a relatively small share of overall capital flows to the new empire. According to Hara Akira's figures, between 1932 and 1941 *zaibatsu* directly invested some 565 million yen, under 10 percent of the 5.86 billion yen transferred to Manchuria from Japan over the same period. These sums, however, reflect only a fraction of the capital the *zaibatsu* actually furnished to Manchuria. In the early thirties, *zaibatsu* banks formed syndicates to buy up Mantetsu and Manchukuo bonds. The Mantetsu bond syndicate, for example, was made up of ten banks, including the three semipublic banks (Japan Industrial Bank, Yokohama Specie Bank, and Bank of Korea) as well as Daiichi, Mitsui, Mitsubishi, Yasuda, and Sumitomo Banks. After 1937 the syndicate system expanded to accommodate the increased capital demands of the first Five-Year Industrial Development Plan. Between 1937 and 1941, banking syndicates invested a total of 2,707 million yen in Manchurian development. This figure included 1,031 million yen furnished to Mantetsu, 630 million yen to Manchukuo government securities, and 395 million yen to Manchurian Heavy Industries.[75]

The willingness of these banks, with their notoriously conservative investment policies, to invest in what they saw as unprofitable, high-risk Manchurian development companies was premised increasingly throughout the decade on government guarantees on profits and principal.[76] In their quid pro quo with the army, the *zaibatsu* agreed, in effect, to stay out of policy decisions in exchange for government assumption of all the risk for their investments. In the early thirties, because of the depressed condition of the domestic economy and the low demand for investment, a temporary structural excess of capital put the army in a better bargaining position vis-à-vis capital suppliers. Under these conditions, bonds of the reputable Mantetsu became a profitable and safe location for bankers to channel surplus capital.[77] But by 1936, with economic recovery under way, the situation had reversed; it was now a suppliers' market. Yet instead of using their new bargaining power to impose conditions on the way the money was being used, bankers insisted on more and greater guarantees on the return of their investments. By the late thirties it was typical for the government to fully guarantee and back by real security both the principal and the interest on Manchurian bonds. In fact, several laws were passed in 1938 to legalize the new collateral system for corporate debentures.[78]

Even when *zaibatsu* did invest money directly by establishing new ventures in Manchukuo, the terms of their investments conformed to the same pattern of letting the Manchukuo government make key decisions and shoulder most of the risk. Of course when businessmen made direct investments they were risking their own capital, but they agreed to permit government intervention in management decisions in exchange for guarantees on their investment. The case of the new *zaibatsu* Nissan was a classic example. In 1937 Nissan founder Aikawa Yoshisuke moved his firm to Manchuria, reorganizing it as Manchurian Heavy Industries, or Man-

75. Hikita, pp. 888–892, figures from p. 890.
76. Particularly after the bank panic of 1927, most of the nation's finance capital was concentrated in *zaibatsu* banks. Very conservative, these banks invested in activities of firms within their organization, and in the buying and selling of currency, government securities, or call-back loans outside the organization. Traditionally they were not in the business of making the sort of long-term loans or investments required by Manchurian development companies.
77. Kaneko, "Shihon yushutsu," p. 341.
78. Hikita, p. 890.

gyō. Like Mantetsu, Mangyō became a "public-policy corporation" (ko-kusaku kaisha). As such it was both half-owned by the Manchukuo government and subject to its control. In exchange for carrying out the army's Five-Year Plan, Aikawa Yoshisuke secured a host of guarantees for his investment. These included: 1) a three-way division of profits, two parts to privately held shares, one part to Manchukuo government shares; 2) in case of dissolution, division of remaining equity on the same basis; 3) principal and 6 percent minimum dividends guaranteed by the Manchukuo government for ten years after Mangyō's founding; 4) special tax privileges; 5) no ceiling on dividends or restrictions on their use; and 6) protections against fluctuations in the market value of the company's shares on the stock market.[79]

Although Aikawa clearly had a say in running the Mangyō operations, the real authority remained in the hands of the Manchukuo government. In signing away control over his company in exchange for investment guarantees, Aikawa got what he bargained for. Although profits were low, subsidies from the Manchukuo treasury made up the difference, enabling him to pay 10 percent on privately owned shares and 5 percent on government shares by 1940. But the price tag on this financial security was high. Feuds between Nissan managers and Manchukuo government planners obstructed operations from the beginning and eventually led Aikawa to resign the presidency in disgust in 1942.[80]

The quid pro quo between businessmen and the army worked well enough during the first phase of Manchurian development. As the thirties wore on, however, the results of army management began to tell not only on the Manchukuo economy, but on Japan's as well. In the early days, the rush of capital to Manchukuo had financed a boom in Japanese exports to the region and helped pull the domestic economy out of depression.[81] But

79. In contrast to other zaibatsu, Aikawa's willingness to move his operations to Manchuria arose partly because of the attractiveness of the deal offered him by the army and partly because of the crisis facing him at home. A tax hike imposed in 1937 was extremely disadvantageous to Nissan, and, combined with a capital crisis growing out of his rapid expansion in the early 1930s, Aikawa was facing bankruptcy in 1936 and 1937: Hara Akira, " 'Manshū' ni okeru keizai tōsei seisaku," pp. 237–248.

80. Jones, pp. 150–151.

81. The causes of the economic reflation of the early 1930s are a matter of debate among economic historians. The standard interpretation accounts for economic recovery through a combination of "military inflation" (Finance Minister Takahashi's deficit spending for military production) and "social dumping" (the export boom based on low domestic wages and the fall in the yen value). Against this Takafusa Nakamura has advanced the argument that recovery was spurred not

by the mid thirties, danger signs began to appear in the Manchurian controlled economy. In 1935, economists reported that progress in Manchukuo development had come to an impasse. The Manchukuo government's Economic Construction Program was about to run aground due to a lack of capital, and the small amount of direct private investment was in "deep trouble." Most worrisome was the failing health of Mantetsu, still the anchor of Manchurian development. Under army direction, Mantetsu resources had been diverted into such unprofitable military-related activities as the construction of strategic railroads and the development of special companies like the Dowa Automobile Manufacturing Company and the Manchurian Chemical Industry Company. Bankers complained that Mantetsu's recent activities had badly overextended it, turning a healthy company into one whose prospects were "unpromising."[82]

Meanwhile, the flow of funds into Northeast China was starting to affect the domestic economy adversely, and Finance Minister Takahashi issued a public warning against the "continuation of unrestrained financing of Manchukuo."[83] A competition for funds by Manchukuo bonds, domestic government bonds to cover Finance Minister Takahashi's deficit-spending program, and the new demand for capital by a recovered domestic industry had led, by 1935, to a shortage of capital. Becoming increasingly acute as the decade wore on, by the late thirties the capital shortage led to an inflationary spiral as the government began to print money to make up the shortfall.[84]

Though historians have endorsed the view of business analysts at the

---

by military demand but by government spending on rural investment to combat the agricultural depression. Others, such as Hashimoto Jurō, Sanwa Ryōichi, and Ishii Kanji have called attention to the stimulation to heavy industry caused by exports to Manchukuo: Ōishi, p. 16; Ishii, pp. 39–76; and Hashimoto Jurō, "Keizai seisaku," in Ōishi Kaichirō, ed., *Sekai daikyōkōki,* vol. 2 of *Nihon teikokushugishi* (Tōkyō daigaku shuppankai, 1987), pp. 77–118. Nakamura's argument is in Takafusa Nakamura, "Depression, Recovery, and War, 1920–1945," in Peter Duus, ed., *The Twentieth Century,* vol. 6 of *The Cambridge History of Japan* (Cambridge: Cambridge University Press, 1988), pp. 451–493.

82. For representative contemporary comment, see "Mantetsu no kokkateki shimei to sono jitai," *Ekonomisuto* (11 September 1935), pp. 24–25; Ōkura Kinmochi, "Manshū keizai no tokushūsei o saguru," *Ekonomisuto* (11 July 1935), p. 12; "Shinsetsu kaisha no genkyō ni miru Manshū keizai kōsaku no shinten jōkyō (I)," *Ekonomisuto* (21 November 1935), p. 35. For a historical analysis, see Kaneko, "Shihon yushutsu," pp. 337–339.

83. Kojima Seiichi, "Manshū kaihatsu seisaku to Nihon infure keiki no zento," *Ekonomisuto* (1 April 1935), pp. 51–53.

84. Hara Akira, "Senji tōsei keizai," pp. 220, 231.

time that inexperience and the misplaced priorities of army planners created the problems in the controlled economy, private capital played an
equal role in setting the direction of Manchurian development. Private
industry underwrote the army-run experiment in state capitalism with
financial investment on a staggering scale unprecedented in the history of
the empire. This investment gave the army the capital resources essential
to set in motion and sustain state capitalism in Manchukuo. The decision
to channel funds into low-risk, state-controlled ventures instead of private
enterprise strengthened the position of the state in the Manchurian economy. Thus, the formation of state capitalism in Manchukuo was dramatic
testimony not to the power and vision of the army, but to the impact of
the imperial corporatism of the 1930s. Private industry supplied the capital,
the army made policy, and Japanese taxpayers assumed the risk.

In the joint venture over Manchurian development, the dreams of business executives and army planners proved equally elusive. Neither the vital
lifeline for Japanese consumer goods nor the regime of state capitalism
lived up to expectations. It was already clear by the mid 1930s that plans
for the Japan-Manchuria partnership were failing; both the trade bloc and
the production bloc were in serious difficulties. Yet instead of stepping back
and cutting their losses, Japanese plunged further into what became an
economic quagmire. Despite the often lucid and penetrating analyses of
the impasse in Manchurian development in 1935, the opening of north
China to Japanese economic penetration at the end of the year and the
announcement of a five-year development plan in 1936 inspired a new
surge of optimism. Articles in the business press heaped praise on the Five-
Year Plan and applauded Aikawa Yoshisuke's decision to move Nissan to
Manchuria in 1937. Transferring hopes to a Japan-Manchuria-China bloc,
economists optimistically predicted that what had failed in Manchuria
would work in China. It would be much easier, economists blithely asserted, to develop that consumer market in densely populated north
China.[85]

The brief flash of criticism of the Japan-Manchuria bloc that appeared
and then quickly disappeared in the mid thirties testified to the growing
power of the Manchurian ideal. The dream of economic panacea had taken

85. "Tairiku seisaku no hatten to waga zaikai," *Ekonomisuto* (11 May 1936), pp.
9–22; Naitō Kumaki, "Hokushi keizai shinshutsu ni kansuru shiken," *Tōyō keizai
shinpō* (27 November 1937), pp. 30–36; "Tōkaku sōsai Yasukawa Yūnosukeshi ni
Hokushi keizai kōsaku o kiku," *Tōyō keizai shinpō* (13 November 1937), pp. 29–35;
"Manshū sangyō gokanen keikaku no zenbō," *Ekonomisuto* (11 May 1937), pp. 31–
33; "Chōmanshi tōshi no zentō," *Ekonomisuto* (21 December 1936), pp. 25–28.

firm root, not to be dislodged by warning signs or nagging doubts. Indeed, obstacles and setbacks only served to steel the belief in the grail of economic security. Taking that fatal step forward into north China, Japan committed itself to military action to protect an expanded perimeter of economic security and precipitated the renewal of war with China.

Although I have drawn attention here to the unrealistic dimensions of the planning and implementation of economic policy in Manchukuo, this should not gainsay the very real accomplishments of this policy. For all its flaws, Manchurian development was highly profitable for the corporate interests involved; under army direction, the Manchurian economy was transformed in the space of a few years. In this sense the "Manchurian success story" was not just empty rhetoric. This was another paradox of total empire: the same excess of optimism that produced the spectacular failures of Manchukuo gave rise to its equally dramatic successes.

A MANCHURIAN BLUEPRINT FOR EAST ASIA

In July 1937 the outbreak of what was called the China Incident kindled Japan's second war fever of the decade. As in the Manchurian Incident five years earlier, the mass media played a major role in mobilizing popular support for militarism on the continent. Triumphant headlines reported success after military success, as the Japanese Army drove south from Beijing and spread out over north China and Inner Mongolia, moving into Shanghai, the Chang River Valley, and Nanjing in the fall of 1937.[86]

The same combination of victory euphoria and anxiety over domestic and international economic crises infused the public mood of 1937–1939. Just as they had five years before, people turned eagerly to the economic promise opened up on the continent. Books, newspapers, magazines, and radio programs buzzed with excitement over the possibilities of the China market in Japanese hands and applauded the Konoe cabinet's dramatic unfurling of the "New Order in East Asia" (*Tōa shinchitsujo*) in November 1938. A day scarcely passed without the invention of a new name to describe the transformation of the empire. The "Japan-Manchuria bloc" became a relic of an earlier era, replaced by "management of the continent" (*tairiku keiei*), "East Asian league" (*Tōa renmei*), "East Asian cooperative community" (*Tōa kyōdōtai*), "Japan-Manchuria-China bloc economy"

---

86. Ikei Masaru, "Nitchū sensō to masu media no taiō," in Inoue Kiyoshi and Etō Shinkichi, eds., *Nitchū sensō to Nitchū kankei: Rokōkyō jiken gojusshūnen Nitchū gakujutsu ronkai kiroku* (Hara shobō, 1988), pp. 211–223.

(*Nichimanshi burokku keizai*), the "East Asian coordinated economy" (*Tōa sōgōtai*), and the "new economic structure" (*shinkeizai taisei*).

The new thicket of slogans which grew up around the China Incident promoted the belief that Japan's economic security was linked with continental expansion over the whole of China. Under its multiple labels, the New Order in East Asia was essentially a reformulation of the Manchurian solution on a grander scale. The vision of the New Order invoked the two key elements of the Manchurian program: the trade bloc and the controlled economy. Extending the purview of the bloc to include China, the New Order continued the pursuit of a guaranteed market for exports and raw materials. Like before, this aimed to mitigate Japan's economic vulnerability to the vagaries of the global marketplace and political interventions by Western countries in the markets under their control. The New Order also appropriated strategies for state management of the economy that had been developed for Manchukuo, making Japanese-controlled puppet states throughout China the agents of planned and regulated economic development of industries important to Japan.

Both these formulas emerged out of the particular history of Japan in Manchuria. The plan to develop the Northeast, where Japanese had at their service the extensive operations of Mantetsu, was now expanded to an area of vastly greater size, vastly more dense population, and where investments were limited to the treaty port operations of Japanese shipping lines, trading houses, and textile mills. With little or no thought to its applicability to the whole of China, Japanese simply expanded formulas devised for Manchukuo to encompass first north China, then Inner Mongolia, then central and south China. Etched in people's minds as a remedy for economic ills, the experiment which had produced such mixed results in Manchuria nevertheless became the blueprint for the New Order in East Asia. This virtually seamless transition from Manchuria to China highlights an often overlooked dimension of Japan's thrust into China in the 1930s. We tend to think of the "China quagmire" in military terms: the relentless logic of military expansionism bogged Japan down in an unwinnable war. But the logic of economic expansionism was equally powerful. In this sense, a "pathology of security" that prescribed the perpetual enlargement of the perimeter of defense paralleled a "pathology of development" that drew Japan incrementally southward into the same territories.

In the early stages of the economic advance into China, high-brow journals and the business press became forums of a public debate over the direction of the new economic order. In many ways, the debate of 1938–1939 echoed discussions of Manchuria in 1933–1934. It took place in the same organs of the mass media; it maintained the same basic division between a radical statist vision promoted by government and a conventional capitalist vision championed by businessmen; and it was infused by the same collective faith in the new frontier of economic opportunity. But there were striking differences as well. The venue, of course, was China and not Manchuria, and with this shift came an amplification of ambition and confidence. The other important difference related to a shift in the composition of the spokesmen for the government side to the debate. A new group of actors entered the picture, joining radical elements in the army who advocated state capitalism in the empire. While the Japanese government cast about for a solution to the China Incident that would satisfy the competing demands of the Army, Navy, Commerce, Foreign, and Finance ministries, the initiative fell into the hands of the intellectual luminaries staffing the Konoe brain trust, that is, the Shōwa kenkyūkai, formed in November 1936 to advise Konoe Fumimaro (senior politician and three-time prime minister) on national policy.

The key players in the Shōwa kenkyūkai formed a group of radical intellectuals that included Ryū Shintarō, Rōyama Masamichi, Kada Tetsuji, Takahashi Kamekichi, Ozaki Hotsumi, and others. The story of the mobilization of the radical intelligentsia by the state belongs more properly in the following chapter, but I will anticipate somewhat the argument laid out there. Marxist-informed intellectuals who had flirted with left-wing politics joined Konoe's brain trust in the hopes that they could help steer the state toward the restructuring of capitalism. When the army passed the torch of imperial radicalism into their hands, these intellectuals articulated a new vision of cooperative imperialism that they hoped would complete the experiment in state-reformed capitalism begun by the army in Manchuria.

The Shōwa kenkyūkai intellectuals christened their vision the "East Asian Cooperative Community" (*Tōa kyōdōtai*). The new continental policy, they confidently predicted, would "dramatically expand the original scope" of Manchurian development.[87] What they meant by this was not merely the assimilation of China into the bloc, but fulfilling the "true spirit of nation building in Manchukuo" (*Manshū kenkoku ideorogii no risō*). In the estimation of the Shōwa kenkyūkai, the army's original plan for Manchukuo was betrayed by the demands of Japanese capitalism. Un-

---

87. Ozaki Hotsumi, "Tōa shinchitsujo no genzai oyobi shōrai: Tōa kyōdōtairon o chūshin ni" (1939), in Ozaki Hotsumi, *Ozaki Hotsumi chosakushū*, vol. 2 (Keisō shobō, 1977), p. 357.

daunted by the recognition that "this danger still existed," the Shōwa kenkyūkai took strength from the conviction that they had discovered the formula to reform the practices of both imperialism and capitalism from within.[88]

In the imagery of the Shōwa kenkyūkai intellectuals, Japan's continental aspirations began to assume fantastic proportions. In books, magazines, and policy proposals, pictures of a rosy imperial future were drawn out in prose laden with promises of an "escape route" (shutsuro) from the trials besetting Japan's China policy. The Tōa kyōdōtai offered a means to "overcome" (chōkoku) China's warped anti-foreign nationalism. It was a "panacea" (bannōkō) that constituted the single comprehensive solution to the dilemmas of Japanese imperialism. As Rōyama Masamichi expansively predicted, by building the community, Japan could "shake free [dakkyaku] of the current global crisis" and "liberate and overcome the spatial and regional limitations of the Japanese economy."[89] Such transcendental language surpassed by far the already extravagant claims made for the controlled economy by the army in 1933. In its expanded form, the Manchurian model became the solution not just to Japan's problems in China, but to the entire globe.

For the Shōwa kenkyūkai intellectuals, the first task of continental policy was to come to grips with Chinese nationalism. Rōyama Masamichi, Ozaki Hotsumi, Kada Tetsuji, and others poured their energy into impressing the public with the seriousness of the Nationalist movement and the need to look beyond a military strategy for overcoming it. As Ozaki explained:

> Most Japanese are not at war with China because they hate the Chinese masses. They fight the Nationalist government to make it rethink the errors of its policies. But to the Chinese, this is a nationalist struggle for which they willingly gamble national survival. We can use military power to divide China into enemy and allied regions, but this will not solve the

88. Ibid., pp. 357–359.
89. Overcoming Chinese nationalism: Moritani Katsumi, "Tōa shinchitsujo e no rironteki tankyū," Kaizō (June 1939), pp. 44–45; and Rōyama Masamichi, "Tōa kyōdōtai no riron," Kaizō (November 1938), p. 15. Rōyama's predictions: Rōyama Masamichi, "Tōa kyōdōtai to teikokushugi," Chūō kōron (September 1939), p. 10; and Rōyama Masamichi, "Kokumin kyōdōtai no keisei," Kaizō (May 1939), p. 5. See also three essays by Ozaki Hotsumi in Ozaki: " 'Tōa kyōdōtai' no rinen to sono seiritsu no kyakkanteki kiso" (1939), pp. 309–318; "Tōa seikyoku ni okeru ichijiteki teitai to aratanaru hatten no yosō" (1939), pp. 340–349; and "Tōa shinchitsujo no genzai oyobi shōrai: Tōa kyōdōtairon o chūshin ni" (1939), pp. 350–359.

problem of nationalism. Even if we were to suppose that the war would finish in a manner to our liking and that Japan should achieve a decisive victory, we would still be faced with the vexing problem of Chinese nationalism. The current direction of the Nationalist movement in China stands directly athwart Japan's path. . . . We are starting to get a sense of how difficult it will be to remove this from our path militarily.[90]

In the late thirties, it was no easy task to write persuasively against the prosecution of the war without appearing to be unpatriotic or running afoul of the censors. Nevertheless, this was the message Ozaki was trying to get across: the Chinese Nationalist movement doomed a military resolution to Sino-Japanese conflict.

The solution offered by Ozaki and his colleagues was to win "the voluntary cooperation of the Chinese," a task that depended on Japan's giving up "traditional imperialistic demands" and ending its "unilateral approach to economic organization in East Asian countries."[91] In this connection, the renovationist intellectuals distinguished their ideas from what they identified as the "economic-bloc approach," which, as practiced by England, France, and the United States, was just another version of imperialism. Those in Japan who advocated imperialistic economic blocism were on the wrong track. It was not simply morality which argued against economic blocism, but "practical considerations for securing native sources of development capital and avoiding the threat of political unrest." Most important of all, it was dubious that "the Japanese economy could withstand the demands of both prosecuting a war and developing the continent."[92] Instead of endorsing the immoral and unrealistic program of traditional imperialism, the Shōwa kenkyūkai put forth its own impractical solution: join forces with the Chinese Nationalist movement. Ozaki thought this could be done through land reform, thus converging with the anti-feudal component of the Nationalist movement. Kada advanced the idea of cultivating Chinese capital for joint-development projects. Although the various proposals for accommodating Chinese nationalism shared an uncompromising "rejection of imperialism," none proposed retreat from the continent.[93]

90. Ozaki Hotsumi, " 'Tōa kyōdōtai' no rinen to sono seiritsu no kyakkanteki kiso," in Ozaki, pp. 312–313.

91. Ibid., pp. 311, 314.

92. Ibid., p. 311; Rōyama Masamichi, "Tōa kyōdōtai to teikokushugi," *Chūō kōron* (September 1939), pp. 10–14.

93. In addition to the articles cited earlier, see also discussion of *Tōa kyōdōtai* in Shōwa dōjinkai, ed., *Shōwa kenkyūkai* (Keizai ōraisha, 1968), pp. 139–252; and Takahashi Hisashi, " 'Tōa kyōdōtairon': Rōyama Masamichi, Ozaki Hotsumi, Kada

The belief that the blueprint for the *Tōa kyōdōtai* could somehow alter the nature of Japan's military and economic expansion in China, much less coopt the Nationalist movement, seems particularly quixotic. Vague appeals to cooperativism stood no chance in the face of the bloodlust of the army in their campaigns of annihilation against the Nationalist Army and the avarice of war profiteers in Japanese-occupied China. Indeed, the striking gap between the rhetoric of cooperativism and the realities of the occupation makes it tempting to dismiss the vision of the Shōwa kenkyūkai as cynical propaganda. This would be a mistake, however. The radical intellectuals were sincere, if deluded. Overawed by their rapid ascension into the citadels of power and seduced by their own rhetorical excess, these men invested their words and ideas with a power that in the real world they did not possess.

If the quest for cooperative imperialism seemed deluded, plans to link the creation of the *Tōa kyōdōtai* to domestic reform were no less fantastic. The intention to "use Manchukuo as the means to renovate Japan" was anticipated in army declarations in the early 1930s; the Shōwa kenkyūkai now called for the overhaul of Japanese capitalism to lay the groundwork for this cooperative imperialism. Although there were variations in the Shōwa kenkyūkai reform package, Ryū Shintarō's *The Reorganization of the Japanese Economy* undoubtedly became the most famous statement of the new approach. Ryū's book (which went through forty-four printings between its first publication in December 1939 and the following fall) laid down the battle plans for a frontal assault on the free enterprise system— beginning with an attack on profits and ending with the nationalization of industry. Since the pursuit of profit and sectoral interests impeded rational allocation of resources for the optimum national economic performance, profits were to be limited and economic managers shielded from intervention by the owners of capital. Following the "separation of management from capital," a hierarchical structure of industrial cartels and economic management committees would be created to allow economic planning and national supervision of industry. But unlike the old-style profit-maximizing industrial collusion, the new cartels would work to lower prices and increase productivity through the socialization of production. Reorganized into this new structure, industry would abandon the profit motive in favor of a "new economic ethic" of "cooperativism." Ideally the voluntary cooperation of capital with national policy would obviate the necessity for

---

Tetsuji no baai," in Miwa Kimitada, ed., *Nihon no 1930 nendai: kuni no uchi to soto kara* (Sōryūsha, 1980), pp. 50–79.

some imposition of benevolent authoritarianism, but the new structure gave the state the power to compel cooperation if necessary.[94]

In the Shōwa kenkyūkai program for domestic reform, the idea of jointly renovating Manchukuo and Japan germinated by army planners in the early 1930s had grown into a scheme of prodigious proportions, linking the reform of imperialism to the reform of capitalism. The army's notion of linked renovation had tended to imagine that what could be quietly accomplished in Manchukuo could later be used as a means of unloosing the stranglehold of private capital over the economy at home. Men like Ryū felt, in contrast, that the success of their program in the empire was premised on the achievement of the transformations they sought at home. Cooperativism with China would follow from cooperativism in Japan. Thus they reversed the order of business, putting the reform of domestic capitalism ahead of the new order in the empire. That both goals were doomed in the political-economic environment in which they operated is something that appears clear from hindsight. From the vantage point of the late 1930s, however, the mercurial pace of change in Manchuria did not warrant such pessimism. Rather, the atmosphere of radicalism and chaos seemed an auspicious time for the revolutions dreamed by the Shōwa kenkyūkai.

The radical vision of economic restructuring promoted by Shōwa kenkyūkai intellectuals and their allies in the bureaucracy and the military was opposed by key sectors of the business community. Initially, business leaders concentrated their efforts on quiet noncooperation with domestic reform initiatives to counter what they regarded as a Communist conspiracy. Later, they mounted the counteroffensive that brought about the purge of "reds" from the government and the downfall of the Shōwa kenkyūkai in late 1941.[95] The failure to predict the ferocity and power of this counteroffensive provided clear evidence of Shōwa kenkyūkai members' tenuous grip on the realities of their situation.

Shōwa kenkyūkai members were lured into a false sense of confidence because at first, the public reaction of businessmen to economic reform seemed favorable. Indeed, public statements of business organizations and the business press in 1938 and 1939 echoed the slogans coined by "red" planners. In what was standard procedure, the published deliberations of

94. Ozaki Hotsumi, "Tōa shinchitsujo no genzai oyobi shōrai: Tōa kyōdōtairon o chūshin ni," in Ozaki, p. 353; Fletcher, *The Search for a New Order*, pp. 121–133, 147–150; Shōwa dōjinkai, pp. 139–252; Takahashi Hisashi, pp. 49–80.
95. Johnson, *MITI and the Japanese Miracle*, pp. 143–152.

a Japan-Manchuria-China economic policy conference attended by business leaders opened by endorsing the New Order in East Asia and the new economic structure.[96] In part this show of support for the New Order was a public relations move. As they did during the Manchurian Incident, businessmen rallied round the flag in the early years of the China Incident in an effort to dispel the reputation of capitalists as unpatriotic. Chilled by the assassination of Finance Minister Takahashi Korekiyo in 1936 for his open opposition to maintaining current levels of defense spending, as well as by the spectacle of business leaders being vilified as traitors for opposing passage of the economic mobilization plan in 1937, many businessmen chose to keep their criticisms to themselves. On the other hand, the business community's initial enthusiasm for the New Order was not entirely forced. This was because, unlike the Shōwa kenkyūkai, businessmen drew a line between the New Order at home and the New Order in the empire. While they were adamantly opposed to such elements of the reform agenda as the control of profits and nationalization of industry in Japan, businessmen were by no means hostile to the imperial dimension of the New Order. The crisis precipitated by the China Incident inspired a reappraisal of the economic significance of the continent that was quite genuine. In 1938 and 1939 a new confidence in Manchurian development expressed itself in a flood of articles in *Ekonomisuto* and *Tōyō keizai shinpō*, calling attention to new continental opportunities. Headlines reported the emergence of a "new appreciation" (*saininshiki*) of the bloc economy, the "leap forward in the understanding of Manchuria" (*taiMan ninshiki no hiyaku*), and the "reconsideration [*saikentō*] of investment in Manchurian industry."[97] Economists applauded the recent "acceleration in the development of the East Asian bloc" and explained that its "necessity" was much more clear than had been the case "at the time of the Manchurian Incident."[98]

Unlike the Shōwa kenkyūkai's vision, which sought to break with the past in the creation of an anti-imperialist empire, the business press's reappraisal of Manchurian development placed the new empire-building initiatives squarely within the framework of Japan's imperial tradition. Business analysts defined that tradition in economic terms, pointing to a

96. *Nichimanshi keizai kondankai hōkokusho* (Nichiman chūō kyōkai, 1939), unpaginated preface and opening remarks.
97. "Manshūkoku keizai kaihatsu no shinkō jōtai," *Ekonomisuto*, (21 July 1939), p. 20; Kikuchi Kazue, "Senji keizai to Manshū sangyō no saikentō," *Tōyō keizai shinpō* (8 April 1939), p. 38.
98. "Reimeiki no Tōa burokku," *Ekonomisuto* (1 April 1938), pp. 34–35.

historical link between "continental policy and Japanese capitalism."[99] As one writer explained, "since the 1870s Japan has relied on continental policy for both the survival and the development of Japanese capitalism. As we can see in our present policy of looking to the East Asia bloc to guarantee an export market and resources for our country, in the past as well as in the present continental policy has provided the foundation of Japanese capitalism."[100] In other words, the outbreak of war with China did not signify any change in Japanese policy.

The continuity theme was underscored in arguments that suggested that in both past and present, war was the inevitable by-product of economic growth. One analysis of the East Asian bloc noted that the Sino- and Russo-Japanese wars of 1894–1895 and 1904–1905 were "a predestined enterprise for the development of Japanese capitalism."[101] And while those conflicts had aimed to secure markets in China and Korea for Japanese textile producers, the current hostilities emerged out of Japan's "desire to trade with all of China and to develop resources in north China."[102] Reiterating constantly that it was "unnecessary to reiterate that the survival of Japanese capitalism required the expansion of continental policy in the current China Incident,"[103] business analysts proclaimed their support for the use of force to expand the empire into central and south China. With such arguments, businessmen convinced themselves that the creation of a Japan-Manchuria-China bloc was a sound economic proposition and that the second Sino-Japanese War was necessary to ensure their economic survival.

Like Shōwa kenkyūkai members, business analysts broadened the meaning of development when they applied it to the "New Asian Order." It continued to mean creating the guaranteed export market for Japanese goods, but now these goods included products of both heavy and light industry. In addition, "development" now signified the construction of a secure source of coal, iron, cotton, and other resources needed by Japanese industries. As industrialists dreamed of Japanese capital unlocking the "unopened treasurehouse" of north China, Inner Mongolia, and central and south China, images of two, three, or many Manchukuos leapt forth from

99. "ShinTōa kensetsu no keizaiteki kiso," *Tōyō keizai shinpō* (4 February 1939), p. 60.

100. "Reimeiki no tōa burokku," *Ekonomisuto* (1 April 1938), p. 35.

101. "Tōa burokku no kihon mondai," *Ekonomisuto* (11 February 1938), p. 11.

102. "ShinTōa kensetsu no keizaiteki kiso," *Tōyō keizai shinpō* (4 February 1939), p. 60.

103. "Tōa burokku no kihon mondai," *Ekonomisuto* (11 February 1938), p. 11.

the China continent.[104] In their new appreciation for resources, businessmen endorsed what they had earlier so vigorously opposed: the army's vision of development.

In contrast to earlier prescriptions for the Manchurian economy, in the late 1930s businessmen insisted that the best formula for continental development was the strategy perfected in Japanese colonial enterprises— "Japanese capital and know-how combined with China's resources." As Fujiwara Gin, president of Ōji Paper Industries, declared, "we have developed Taiwan and we have developed Korea and we have developed Hokkaidō. In the same way we will shock the world by transforming the continent within the space of ten or twenty years . . . with Japanese capital, Japanese efforts, and Japanese technology."[105] For Fujiwara and other business executives, this marked a much more enthusiastic embrace of colonial investment than they had shown in the early years of Manchukuo. Indeed, the new language used to describe continental development in 1938 and 1939 reflected a shift in the frame of reference. Before, "Manchurian development" was based on images of a mythical China market and the experience of trade expansion in the informal treaty-port empire of China proper. Now, what business leaders referred to was the whole colonial empire: building a Taiwanese sugar industry, increasing Korean rice production, developing the coal mines of Hokkaidō, and the creation of roads, railways, and harbors everywhere.

For businessmen, the New Order was a business proposition. In this sense, it was clearly the bottom line that led businessmen to revise their estimation of Manchuria from a mere outlet for consumer goods to a profitable field for investment. Jubilant reports of a boom in Manchurian securities in the spring and summer of 1939 harkened back to the Manchurian prosperity of 1934. Trying to account for the "sudden popularity of Manchurian stocks," the *Ekonomisuto* suggested that it was a combination of the "poor performance of the domestic market" and the fact that "even timid capital" was "finally beginning to understand Manchuria." Citing a remarkable turnaround of the two anchors of the Manchurian economy, Mantetsu and Manchurian Heavy Industries (Mangyō), the same article warmly recommended both corporate stocks.[106] A *Tōyō keizai shinpō* ed-

104. Ibid., pp. 11–19; "Manshūkoku keizai kaihatsu no shinkō jōtai," *Ekonomisuto* (21 July 1939), pp. 20–31; "Reimeiki no Tōa burokku," *Ekonomisuto* (1 April 1938), pp. 29–82; "Tairiku keiei no genjō dashin," *Ekonomisuto* (21 December 1938), pp. 9–17.

105. *Nichimanshi keizai kondankai hōkokusho*, p. 15.

106. Kawamura Ikeru, "Tairiku mondai," *Ekonomisuto* (11 July 1939), p. 10.

itorial on "the remarkable rise of Manchurian stocks" expressed the same opinion, further explaining that "Japanese capitalists have come to appreciate certain features of the controlled economy in Manchuria" such as "lower taxes" which made Manchurian companies "a much more profitable investment than domestic corporations."[107] As media coverage of Manchurian development showed, the new interest in the continent was spurred by an old interest in profits.

In certain respects, the collective vision of continental development appeared to be more uniform than it had been in the early thirties. Businessmen, like the Shōwa kenkyūkai, saw continental expansion as a "solution to the present crisis."[108] Both groups felt that economic modernization and the growth of Japanese capitalism made economic integration in East Asia a historic "inevitability" (*hitsuzensei*) and often spoke of the bloc as Japan's "destiny" (*shukumei*). Spokesmen for both the business community and government planning agencies now admitted the importance of maintaining economic relationships with Europe and the United States. Since development of the bloc required borrowing from Western capital markets and importing Western products, this in turn required Japan to continue exporting to these countries. They both seemed to concur that national-level economic planning was called for and that bloc development required a unified industrial policy. Representatives on both sides called for multilevel economic integration, recognizing that finance, industry, and trade were interdependent facets of bloc development.

Despite agreement on these points, however, the consensus on continental development was just as contradictory and conflict-riddled in the late thirties as it had been in the early thirties. What the Shōwa kenkyūkai considered the inevitable decline of capitalism and its replacement with a new economic paradigm meant precisely the opposite to businessmen. While the Shōwa kenkyūkai linked transformation in the imperial relationship with the overturning of capitalism at home, businessmen tied the survival of domestic capitalism to old-style continental expansionism. Moreover, competing demands for capital and resources to supply north China, Manchukuo, and home industry left everyone short and no one

107. Kikuchi Kazue, "Senji keizai to Manshū sangyō no saikentō," *Tōyō keizai shinpō* (8 April 1939), pp. 38–39.

108. The choice of words in the business press such as "*yukizumari no dakai*" (solution to the current deadlock) or "*fukyō no kirinuki*" (escape from depression) reflected their interest in the bloc as a policy of relief from the business cycle. See "Manshūkoku keizai kaihatsu no shinkō jōtai," *Ekonomisuto* (21 July 1939), pp. 20–21; and "Reimeiki no Tōa burokku," *Ekonomisuto* (1 April 1938), p. 35.

satisfied. Agreement was reached not by compromising and setting priorities, but by making a longer wish-list. Like the Japan-Manchuria bloc five years earlier, the East Asian wish-list took on the appearance of a bloated omnibus bill. By the time all the interested parties had added their requirement to the list, bloc development was so loaded down that it lost all coherence.

Predictably, the bloc-development omnibus steered an erratic course and by 1940 was widely criticized for stalling the economy. Business organizations complained sharply of shortages and the inadequacies of the trade bloc.[109] The example of economic cooperativism in the collaborationist regimes of Prince Teh in Inner Mongolia and Wang Kemin in north China failed to inspire a change of heart within the Chinese resistance movement. As the war with China dragged on, Ozaki and others saw their slogans being used simply to justify more and more slaughter. But once again, Japanese set aside their doubts, smoothed over their irritations, and muted their criticisms when the prospect of including Southeast Asia in the bloc arose before them. In a virtual recapitulation of the bloc criticisms of the mid thirties, the cautionary voice was sounded briefly at the close of the decade only to be drowned out by the enthusiastic fanfare attending the establishment of the Greater East Asia Co-prosperity Sphere.[110]

The application of the Manchurian blueprint to China and then to Southeast Asia demonstrated the staying power of the imperial corporatism of state and private enterprise. Though the partnership forged by the army and *zaibatsu* leadership in the early thirties seemed insecure and unstable, it yielded stunning results in Manchukuo with the creation of the command economy and the yen bloc. Like the original blueprint for Manchukuo, plans for the New Order were the product of contradictory visions for the colonial economy. The New Order embraced both the radicalism of the Shōwa kenkyūkai and the opportunism of the business com-

109. For example, see complaints voiced in the East Asia Business Council meetings of May 1940, in Tōa keizai kondankai, *Nichiman keizai kondankai hōkokusho* (Tōa keizai kondankai, 1940).

110. Gōko Kiyoshi, "DaiTōa keizai kensetsu no kihon shisetsu," *Ekonomisuto* 20, no. 5 (1942), pp. 11–13; Ōshima Kenzō, "DaiTōa kyōeiken no tsūka shintaisei," *Ekonomisuto* 20, no. 3 (1942), pp. 11–12; "Nihon shihaika no senryaku shigen," *Ekonomisuto* 20, no. 5 (1942), pp. 19–28; "DaiTōa senka no Nihon sangyō (1)," *Ekonomisuto* 20, no. 2 (1942), pp. 18–29; "DaiTōa senka no Nihon sangyō (2)," *Ekonomisuto* 20, no. 3 (1942), pp. 18–35. Beginning in January 1941, the *Ekonomisuto* stopped identifying issues by month and day. Therefore all citations to *Ekonomisuto* after this date refer to volume and number only, with the year in parentheses.

munity. Though the two groups were at odds with one another, they jointly endorsed the concept of the New Order as well as the use of force to bring China into the grasp of Japan's state-managed economic imperium. Both groups placed great faith in the power of the colonial state to accomplish the herculean tasks set before it. This being said, it was undoubtedly easier to take such a leap of faith than to try to halt the process of economic development. Once set in motion in the early thirties, colonial state capitalism was propelled by its own momentum incrementally and inexorably forward. It was this pathology of development, as much as the quest for military security on the continent, that led Japan even deeper into war with China.

THE BUSINESS INITIATIVE OF 1940–1941

As the mounting optimism of the early thirties gave way to deepening gloom at the end of the decade, business organizations made a considerable effort to forestall disaster by opening a new set of negotiations with the government on the problems of Manchurian development. In essence, the business initiative of 1940–1941 undertook to renegotiate the terms of imperial corporatism. The key demand was for more policy input; private capital was no longer willing to allow the government to run the Manchurian economy single-handedly. An organization called the East Asia Business Council (*Tōa keizai kondankai*), composed of four leading business organizations, the Japan Economic Federation, the Federated Chambers of Commerce, the Japan-China Business Council, and the Japan-Manchuria Business Council, set up a series of conferences on the Manchurian economy in the early 1940s. Bringing together representatives from all sectors of economic activity, the East Asia Business Council, like the Japan-Manchuria Business Council before it, tried to present a corporate voice for business on economic policy in the empire. This time, however, there was a sense of urgency not evident in earlier appeals to the government. Surprisingly late, businessmen began to understand what they had not seen in 1933 or even 1937—that they were not in fact insulated from damage if the Manchukuo experiment collapsed. As long as it seemed that they could generate profits without personal risk, entrepreneurs were happy to let the government keep the reins. When it finally dawned on them that the losses would have to be shared, business leaders suddenly decided that they should be made real partners in the decision making for Manchukuo.

At a conference held in May 1940, members of the home and Manchukuo governments were invited to take part in a government-business brainstorming session on Manchurian economic problems. Businessmen were outspoken in identifying the global nature of the problems plaguing the Manchurian experiment. They reserved their sharpest criticism, however, for those areas where the government's development plan had become a drain on the domestic economy. Spokesmen for the financial community were unequivocal that the loans to Manchukuo—"800 million yen or nearly one-third of the national debt between 1937 and 1939"—were wreaking havoc on domestic finances. The excessive financing of Manchuria was making it impossible for bankers to fulfill their mission to support national policy by "securing the domestic capital supply." There must, they insisted, "be limits placed on further loans to Manchukuo."[111]

Manufacturers echoed these complaints, insisting that supplying the bottomless demands of Manchurian industry for producer goods was killing the home islands. As Mitsubishi Heavy Industries president Shiba Kōshirō illustrated the problem, borrowing the favored metaphor of Manchukuo officialdom, Should the parent starve itself to feed a child?

> Because of shortages of locally produced materials, Manchurian production depends on Japan for production materials. Since Japan is also short of materials, it is extremely difficult for us to respond to this demand. Of course, as we all know, since Manchukuo is the child and Japan the parent, when the child is in trouble it is the parent's responsibility to come to its aid. Nevertheless, even if we—the parent—would willingly reduce our meals from three times to once a day to help Manchuria, the problem for the home islands has gone beyond this. . . . In some cases our shortages are more severe than those in Manchuria.[112]

Discussions on trade were similarly dominated by businesses' concern with the rush of goods out of, and consequent shortages within, Japan.[113] While they found much about which to disagree, financiers, manufacturers, and merchants were united in their urgent sense that Manchurian development was in trouble. This newfound concern with the government's management of Manchukuo was not animated by the poor performance of Manchurian industry, but rather the conviction that Manchuria was proving to be the undoing of the domestic economy.

Business leaders at the conference took special pains to distance themselves from what had happened in Manchuria, claiming disingenuously

---

111. Tōa keizai kondankai, pp. 235–236, 242–244.
112. Ibid., pp. 144, 146–147.
113. Ibid., p. 184.

that there was no profit motive for their involvement in the Manchurian economy. In the early thirties, the Kwantung Army had been warned to abate its anti-*zaibatsu* rhetoric because capital would not invest in Manchuria on the basis of patriotism; now, businessmen claimed that patriotism was the only thing that had brought them to Manchuria. As president of Mitsubishi Heavy Industries Shiba Kōshirō exclaimed self-righteously, "Japanese industrialists have paid enormously to move operations into Manchuria. And we have had to deal with the friction that has resulted with domestic producers.... However, since the government made this their policy, as industrialists we made huge sacrifices to support this policy and advance into Manchuria."[114] As Shiba tried to present the matter, Manchukuo was entirely a government project. The contributions of private industry were made solely at the behest of government; businessmen, therefore, bore no responsibility for the current mess in the Manchurian economy.

Apparently finding nothing to fault in their own handling of Manchurian issues, businessmen were indiscriminate in their condemnation of government mismanagement. They repeatedly pointed out basic failures in the operation of the command economy in Manchuria. After listening to a government planner trumpet the achievement of production goals, one industrialist observed acidly, "Although production is allegedly bountiful, the private sector is unable to secure supplies of anything. We cannot produce for lack of coal. These facts clearly indicate the failure of economic controls.... It is not true that there are no goods in Manchuria. There are considerable goods, but it is precisely because of the controlled economy that these things disappear from the market or vanish into the hinterland. Controlling the economy is extremely difficult ... but misguided government policy makes the situation much worse."[115] Thus businessmen at the conference took a hard line with government officials in a way that departed from precedent. Favorable official reports were no longer allowed to go publicly unchallenged. Government performance was subject to open scrutiny, and shortcomings were criticized without ceremony.

A large part of the problem, as businessmen pointed out at this late date, was that government planners lacked the necessary expertise and experience to carry out their policies.

> We are in danger of falling into the evil of so-called bureaucratic control—management based on no real experience, but simply churning out laws

114. Ibid., p. 144.
115. Ibid., pp. 146–147.

and abusing administrative authority. Even if intentions are good there is a real danger that the results will run against the goal (of economic partnership). . . . The most pressing demand in Manchuria is for science, technology, and experience. The government needs to mobilize this precious resource for national defense, production, and livelihood. . . . It is imperative to mobilize enough knowledge and experience to prevent falling into the evil of so-called bureaucratic self-righteousness.[116]

Thus, after years of silence, businessmen finally came forward to tell the government that without business's input, Manchurian development would founder.

If businessmen were agreed on the nature of the economic crisis, they were equally united on the need for bold solutions. Although the government's policy of economic control had come under considerable criticism, the solutions proposed by business leaders involved more, rather than less, control. In such key areas as finance, where the slightest movement produced a ripple effect in Japan, businessmen cried out for an extension of the command economy. Most of the proposals put forward involved the establishment of some version of a government-business agency for coordinating economic policy within the yen bloc. Tsushima Juichi, a vice-president of the Bank of Japan, suggested such an organization be set up to control inflation:

> It is absolutely vital that a comprehensive and unified policy be developed for price control. The most appropriate method to accomplish this would be to establish a Japan-Manchuria permanent control agency which would aim at comprehensive price controls between the two countries. Above all, regulating the flow of goods must be the basis of achieving price control. Thus, our most urgent task is to examine the relationship between supply and demand of goods in both countries and establish a long-term plan for the joint mobilization of resources in Japan and Manchuria.[117]

Others, including director of the Tokyo Chamber of Commerce Kuwabara Yoshine, thought such a committee should include China as well.[118] Whether it was a two- or three-country agency, the proposal outlined a kind of permanent executive economic-planning committee that would deal with problems globally rather than on an ad hoc basis. Since agencies like the Cabinet Planning Board that aimed to do precisely this on a national level already existed, businessmen were really suggesting that they bring some measure of domestic control over what had been a largely

116. Ibid., pp. 57–59.
117. Ibid., p. 238.
118. Ibid., p. 185.

autonomous state management of the Manchurian economy. Manchukuo bureaucrats needed to be stripped of some of their power to give the home islands a chance to deal with their own economic woes.

As conceived by businessmen, not only would such a committee bring Manchuria under metropolitan control, but it would also give the private sector a real voice in economic governance. As Kuwabara saw it,

> Since last year the government authorities from Japan, Manchuria, and China have held various conferences to promote economic partnership between the three countries . . . and we have high hopes for the outcome. . . . However, when key economic policies are being decided upon, it is important that such meetings consist not only of government officials, but also include as much as possible specialists from the private sector. These specialists have ideas which need to be heard if you want to construct a realistic policy that has any chance of actually being carried out.[119]

According to Kuwabara, this constructive exchange of opinions would be carried out within the familiar category of a "public-private council" (*kanmin kyōgikai*) granted comprehensive policy-making authority. Kuwabara and others were suggesting, in effect, a modification of the terms of imperial corporatism: now state and capital jointly would manage the yen bloc.

In addition to selling private-sector expertise and other advantages, promoters of the new partnership idea informed the government of what the costs of noncooperation might be. In what amounted to a thinly veiled threat, the director of the Japan-Manchuria Business Council pointed out that "controlling prices and the movement of goods is something which, unlike most other laws, requires the full understanding and cooperation of the people. In other words, it is not something that can succeed merely by the exercise of authority from above, but requires cooperation from below. You cannot simply impose punishments on violators, but must gain the full understanding of such people. As long as the government fails to secure such understanding, it is quite clear that the policy will fail."[120] The Manchukuo government was being told, in so many words, that unless they were consulted in the making of such laws, businessmen could not be expected to obey them.

The Manchukuo government's response to these proposals at the conference was chilly. Businessmen were told that the government "would look into the possibility" and that a "joint government policy to control

119. Ibid., p. 186.
120. Ibid., p. 187.

resources was already being carried out."[121] This lack of enthusiasm was perhaps not surprising. Left alone for all these years, institutions of industrial policy making in Manchukuo were shaped to exclude business input; the institutional culture was nurtured on the prerogatives of autonomy. There was no reason to expect in 1941 that Manchukuo government officials would suddenly feel constrained to consult avowedly hostile domestic business leaders. It was even less likely that they would reassemble the machinery of government in order to accommodate a group of people clearly bent on disrupting the current policy.

For business leaders rejection had its advantages. Entrepreneurs could view themselves as victims of government policy. After Japan's defeat, they emerged from the Manchukuo fiasco with the moral high ground, able to argue that the controlled economy was not their idea and that, to the end, the Kwantung Army would not let them near it. Although such an impression has survived until the present day, in fact, soldiers and capitalists together determined the shape of the Manchurian economy. Ultimately the choice not to intervene earlier in the management of their Manchurian investments belonged to businessmen alone, and its impact was probably equal in weight to the whole string of Kwantung Army initiatives.

Both parties were well aware of the tensions in the army-business relationship. Even so, neither side tried very hard to improve the alliance when it still could have helped to solve both Manchurian and domestic economic problems. Neither the Kwantung Army's overweening notions of what it could achieve in Manchukuo, nor private enterprise's miscalculation of the scale of the Manchurian disaster underwent any significant modification until the end of the decade, when the situation had slipped from their control. Both misperceptions were based on a kind of blinkered optimism about Manchurian development. Five-year plans were fashioned of wishful thinking; money was loaned on best-case scenarios. There was something very make-believe about the ever elusive "development of Manchuria."

The vision of economic panacea may have been an illusion, but the rail lines, the factories, and the hydro-electric plants built in its name left very real traces of the power of an idea. Today, of course, Japan no longer possesses these monuments to Manchurian development—testimony, no less vivid, to the illusion of power. Herein lies one of the interesting contra-

121. Ibid., pp. 190–191.

dictions of Manchukuo. The dreams of Manchukuo fed the pride and reck-
lessness of the Japanese, leading them to overextend themselves in the
empire and making the project unsustainable. At the same time, these
dreams provided Japanese with the ambition, the confidence, the creativity,
and the energy to carry out the Manchurian experiment in colonial development.

The contradictory fortifying and destabilizing impulses of imperial
dreams were an intrinsic part of Japan's total empire in Manchuria. In the
colonial economy, as in the military project in the Northeast, optimism set
the tone of the dreams. Because such imperial projects were multidimensional, the mobilization of support among their divergent interests required an inclusive vision that promised something for everyone. Since
strategies of mobilization increasingly had to accommodate competing interests and conflicting agendas, imperial promoters became, in effect, a
Pollyanna chorus, redoubling their efforts to stress the positive, the promising, and the propitious.

The multidimensional nature of imperial projects like economic development had other consequences as well. Pursued by different people for
different reasons and drawing in diverse social groups with increasing intensity, imperial projects developed a bloated and dangerously incoherent
quality. As the imperial relationship deepened and the web of connections
between empire and metropolis grew, internal contradictions proliferated
and pulled the empire in different directions. Military men in Manchuria
subverted metropolitan government authorities. Within the home government, the Army Ministry conspired against the Navy Ministry, and together both ministries conspired against the Foreign Ministry. Whether it
was periphery against metropole, bureaucracy against bureaucracy, or civilian against military, imperial-policy formation involved intense competition and conflict. In this sense, strategies of mobilization that sought
greater inclusion by bringing a variety of institutionally organized private
and public interest groups into the imperial project considerably complicated the decision-making process. The collective formulation of policy
required negotiations both within and between state and society. Such was
the outcome of empire pursued by a complex, bureaucratic state and a
complex, stratified society.

Though divisions within the corporatist alliance of imperial interests
were not unique to Japan, the economic project in Manchukuo took Japanese imperialism down paths untrodden by its imperialist cohort. Like
other nineteenth- and twentieth-century imperialists, Japan looked to its
colonies for markets to provide a field for its expanding industrial capital-

ism. This project involved the development and shaping of the colonial economy in order to integrate it into the metropolitan economy. The construction of ports and railways to foster commercial exchange was a common feature of colonial policy in this era. What was unique about the Manchukuo experiment was the scale of the endeavor—both the size of the investment and the magnitude of the ambition. Manchurian development was not just a question of adding infrastructure—a few roads, a new port, more railway lines—though this was clearly part of it. Neither was it merely a question of improving the existing colonial relationship by raising the production of soybeans and opening up new markets for Japanese consumer exports. The truly radical and novel facet of Manchurian development lay in the plans for heavy industrialization and the hope to make Manchukuo the advance guard of Japanese industrial capitalism. By turning Manchukuo into a testing ground for industrial management and planning techniques, Japan departed from existing colonial practices.

Manchurian development displayed other elements of colonial radicalism, as the following pages will show. Joining the efforts of army officers and businessmen, Japanese intellectuals took the visions of empire in Northeast China into realms yet uncharted in the heat of the war fever. There they added a new dimension to the cultural edifice of Manchukuo, an empire of hope in which Manchurian development seemed to promise all things to all people. In the crucible of fascism, war, and revolution, Japanese imagined a brave new empire that would at once shield the nation from economic storm and provide an arena in which to test formulas for planned political and social change.

6 Brave New Empire
Utopian Vision and the Intelligentsia

"Brave New" = the poor, deluded guys

Under the auspices of Manchurian development, Japanese professionals and intellectuals set about building an imperial state that was both modern and radical. Over the course of the 1930s, the funds pouring into Manchukuo financed elaborate construction plans that criss-crossed the landscape with new rail lines and changed the face of Manchuria's urban centers. With state-of-the-art technology and the talents of a bright young breed of civic planners, architects, and engineers, the Manchukuo government railway and urban construction programs were designed to build cities fitted with all the modern conveniences and equipped for rapid population growth. As hundreds and thousands of Japanese arrived every year to help build these cities of the future, they recast their colonial communities in the image of a modernist utopia.

At the same time, Japanese scholars and China experts <u>flocked</u> to Manchuria to take up research and planning posts in the rapidly expanding colonial state. Heavily influenced by left-wing ideas and often sympathetic to Chinese nationalist aspirations, Japan's China hands saw in Manchukuo the solution to the dilemmas of Sino-Japanese relations. For them, Manchurian development and the establishment of the state of Manchukuo promised the birth of a new kind of empire that would accommodate Japanese economic imperialism and Chinese nationalism. From their positions in the think tanks of the South Manchurian Railway (Mantetsu) and the puppet state, these intellectuals dreamed revolutionary dreams of creating a new, just society out of the chaos of twentieth-century China.

The extravagance of Japanese plans for the construction of a utopia in Manchuria matched the optimism of the blueprints for the yen bloc and the command economy. As Richard Stites notes in his study of utopianism in the Russian revolution, social dreaming takes many forms: imagining a society of equals or a society of plenty; reveries of cosmopolitan urbanity or the rustic, simple life; visions of mechanization or a return to nature.[1] In all its forms, utopian vision constructed an alternative to the status quo. For architects of the yen bloc and the controlled economy, the status quo that needed changing was capitalism; hence they imagined renovating its structures of finance, industry, and commerce. The social dreams of the technocrats, artists, and Sinologists conjured up alternatives to a different catalog of grievances with the status quo, including outmoded cityscapes, the inconveniences of daily life, and the misery and exploitation of the laboring class. Frustrated in their attempts to put social dreams into practice at home, they took them to the empire, projecting onto Manchukuo utopian fantasies of modernism and revolution. Their utopian vision of development turned Northeast China into a brave new empire where the infrastructures of urban modernity would liberate Japanese colonizers at the same time that political and social revolution would liberate the Chinese colonized.

"Stereotypes of imperialism" in this period tend to imagine colonies in Schumpeter's terms: the province of atavistic, retrograde autocrats and bullies. In fact, Japan's colonial architects included the progressive intelligentsia who stood at the vanguard of the most forward-looking social and cultural movements of the day. As idealistic reformers and sometimes revolutionaries, the scholars, journalists, artists, engineers, and architects who comprised the progressive intelligentsia were concerned with social justice and welfare. Such lofty concerns dovetailed conveniently with interests somewhat closer to home. With the mass resignations of left-wing scholars from Kyoto University in 1933 in response to the firing of law professor Takigawa for alleged Communist sympathies, the escalation of ideological repression in Japan began to threaten the livelihood of the progressive intelligentsia. Just as they were being harassed and driven from jobs and cultural organizations at home, in Manchuria the funds flowing into colonial development were opening up a plethora of job prospects for the educated elite. In this sense Manchukuo was, first, an empire of opportunity; as they joined the colonial enterprise, the progressive intelligentsia made it the object of their utopian vision.

Utopian social dreaming was not unique to Japanese imperialism. Indeed, particularly after World War I, the vocabularies of progressive reformism, Wilsonian self-determination, and revolutionary socialism en-

---

1. Richard Stites, *Revolutionary Dreams: Utopian Vision and Experimental Life in the Russian Revolution* (Oxford: Oxford University Press, 1989).

tered colonial discourses around the world. The intellectual climate of the interwar period encouraged the participation of Britain's T. E. Lawrence in the Arab nationalist movement and sanctioned the involvement of American personalities as divergent as Agnes Smedley and Joseph Stilwell in the revolutionary nationalist effort in China.[2] The modernist imagining of the colonial city in Manchukuo was likewise a common feature of colonial urban planning in the European empires. In colonies as disparate as French Morocco, British India, and Italian Libya, Europeans embarked on ambitious urban plans in the teens and twenties to make municipal showcases of the colonial cities of Casablanca, New Delhi, and Tripoli.[3] As in Japan, the reformist and modernist articulations of the colonial project in Europe and the United States represented a twentieth-century incarnation of that long-time staple of colonialist discourse—the civilizing mission. Although in retrospect, such ideas appear to be self-serving, even cynical, rationalizations of an endeavor that everybody knew rested on violence and exploitation, at the time they inspired people to participate in an enterprise whose unsavory aspects were mitigated by a commitment to progress and other lofty goals.

In this sense the civilizing mission was directed not at the Chinese subjects of the new empire, but rather toward the Japanese population. Designed to mobilize support for Manchukuo, plans for urban development, and social and political reform ennobled the imperial project for the Japanese who took part in its creation.

CITIES OF THE FUTURE

In the fourteen years between the start of the Manchurian Incident in 1931 and the end of the war in 1945, Mantetsu added approximately 5,300 kilometers of new track to their railway network, excluding construction

2. On Lawrence, see Jeffrey Meyers, *The Wounded Spirit: A Study of the Seven Pillars of Wisdom* (London: Martin Brian and O'Keefe, 1973). On Smedley, see Janice R. MacKinnon and Stephen R. MacKinnon, *Agnes Smedley: The Life and Times of an American Radical* (Berkeley: University of California Press, 1988). On Stilwell, see Barbara W. Tuchman, *Stilwell and the American Experience in China 1911–1945* (New York: Macmillan, 1971).

3. On colonial urbanism, see Nezar AlSayyad, ed., *Forms of Dominance: On the Architecture and Urbanism of the Colonial Enterprise* (Aldershot, England: Avebury, 1992); Gwendolyn Wright, *The Politics of Design in French Colonial Urbanism* (Chicago: University of Chicago Press, 1991); Anthony D. King, *Urbanism, Colonialism, and the World-Economy: Cultural and Spatial Foundations of the World Urban System* (New York: Routledge, 1990); and the chapter on colonial cities in Betts.

of double tracks. The construction boom began immediately; two-thirds (3,510 kilometers) of the new lines went up in Manchukuo's first five years. To supplement the rail lines, Mantetsu built an additional 5,030 kilometers of new roadbed between 1932 and 1938.[4] The thirty-two new rail lines branched out in three directions. The first series of new lines in the east linked Sipingjie, Jilin, Harbin, and Suihua—railway hubs in central Manchuria—with Ji'an, Tumen, Dongning, and Hulin—railway towns on the Manchurian-Korean border. These tied the Manchurian rail network more closely to the Korean transportation network, both improving strategic access and developing new trade routes through Korea. In addition, the line running north from Tumen to Jiamusi brought a new region of northeastern Manchuria under Japanese economic domination and spurred the development of the timber industry. A second series of new lines went north, opening the former Russian sphere of influence to Japanese military and commercial penetration. These included lines connecting Harbin with Jilin and Lafa in north-central Manchuria and Xinjing to Baicheng and Halunashan in the remote northwest, and a network that extended the northern spurs from Harbin and Qiqihar through Bei'an and Nenjiang, all the way north to a meeting point at the Manchurian-Siberian border town of Heihe. Finally, a third set of new lines, running through Xilitun and Rehe to Gubeikou, extended Japanese enterprise into Rehe province and created a new trade route into China.

While Mantetsu built these lines, the Manchukuo government undertook a series of urban construction plans, creating the urban infrastructure for Manchurian development. The first and most ambitious of these projects aimed to turn the trading town of Changchun into a magnificent capital city for the new regime. In the renamed Xinjing ("new capital"), Japanese erected 105 new public buildings (17 for the Manchukuo government and 88 for other corporations), 3,001 special residences, 5,550 ordinary buildings, 1,067 rental office units, and 421 other houses—all by the end of the first phase of construction in 1937.[5]

While the building boom went on in the new Manchukuo capital, similar efforts were under way to rebuild the entrepôts of Fengtian and Harbin. In 1934 and 1935, as railway expansion brought additional cities into the Japanese economic perimeter, committees went to work drawing blueprints

4. Manshikai, vol. 1, pp. 384–387.
5. Manshū jijō annaijo, ed., *Manshūkoku kakuken jijō* (Xinjing: Manshū jijō annaijo, 1939), pp. 2–3.

for new towns in Mudanjiang, Jiamusi, Qiqihar, Tao'an, Bei'an, Heihe, Yanji, Tumen, Rehe, and Chifeng. Between 1932 and 1938, town plans were established for forty-eight Manchurian cities. While the extent of urban development varied, and few towns matched the extravagance of the plans for the new capital, most of the new Japanese cities were fitted with the basic essentials. These basics included running water and sewer systems, gas and electricity, telephone and telegraph lines, and a road network connecting to the railway station. In addition, the new development created a variety of public amenities including parks, a public square, sports facilities, a hospital, and a Japanese cemetery.[6] Most important from the point of view of the Kwantung Army, the new settlements were all provided with military facilities. These both fortified Japanese investments and made the new towns into bases for anti-insurgency campaigns and border operations against China to the south and the Soviet Union to the north. In this sense, urban construction, like the expanded rail network, was geared to both strategic and economic policy goals.

Together the railway and the town plan became the twin symbols of Manchukuo's modernity. Their power in the imperial context drew on the reservoirs of meaning that had accumulated in the discourse on Japanese modernization. Since the Meiji period, definitions of modernity took Europe and the United States as their referent, measuring Japanese progress against Western technological, political, and economic advances. The discourse on empire was closely bound up in this comparison, for modernization was seen as the way to protect Japan from Western aggression. This meant not only Japanese modernization, but also that of China and Korea. In this way, Meiji conceptions of Korean and Chinese backwardness provided justification for Japanese expansion. From the interventions of Japanese liberals in the Korean reform movement in the 1880s to the establishment of Japanese-style educational and police institutions in the colonies, the reformist impulse provided one of the driving forces behind empire building. Whether in the ideas of Japanese liberals that once reform succeeded on the continent, reform of Japan would be "automatic," or in the hopes of colonial officials to modernize Asia in the image of the Meiji reforms, visions of empire closely tied Japan's progress with that of its Asian neighbors.[7]

---

6. Koshizawa Akira, *Harupin no toshi keikaku, 1898–1945* (Sōwasha, 1989), pp. 202–203; Manshū teikoku seifu, pp. 225–247.

7. On Japanese liberals and the reform of Korea, see Conroy, pp. 124–168; quotation from p. 133. On the domestic model for colonial institutions, see E. Pa-

The railway exemplified Japanese apprehensions of this relationship between modernity in the West, Japan, and the empire. As Carol Gluck has
pointed out, the locomotive emerged in the Meiji period as a popular icon
of civilization and progress. It was first introduced into Japan in the min-
iature form of a "fire-wheeled car" model that American treaty seekers
brought with them in the 1850s to impress Japanese with the technological
might of the West. The Meiji government was convinced, and actively
promoted railway construction as part of its program to encourage economic development. The first line connecting Tokyo's Shinbashi with Yokohama was opened in 1872; by 1905 nearly 5,000 miles of railway line
linked urban and rural communities on all four of the main islands of the
Japanese archipelago. Increasing the mobility of both goods and persons,
the railway stimulated commerce and urbanization. By the end of the Meiji
period it was regarded as the preeminent agent of modernization.[8]

In the early decades of colonial rule this Western import acquired an
imperial facade, as Japan built railways in Taiwan and Korea, and expanded
the South Manchurian network taken over from Russia. Like the image
of the railway in Japan itself, the colonial railroad represented an engine
of civilization and progress. In Manchukuo, the development of the high-
speed "Asia Express" took this one step further. Surpassing records in Japan
and matching the railway technology of the West, the Asia Express became
the symbol of an ultramodern empire where technological feats opened up
new vistas of possibility for Japan.

Inaugurated in 1934, the Asia Express ran from Dalian to Xinjing, making intermediate stops in Dashiqiao, Fengtian, and Sipingjie. The whole
trip took eight and a half hours, with the train traveling at an average
speed of 82.5 kilometers per hour. Its top speed was 110 kilometers an
hour, 15 kilometers faster than its closest rival in Japan, the Tsubame
Express, and equaling express trains in the United States and Europe. Mantetsu engineers accomplished this feat in part through innovations in
steam-locomotive design. New, more powerful engines were encased in an
aerodynamically streamlined shell, turning the complex contours of the
engine car into a flat tube and giving the train a sleek, modern look. At

tricia Tsurumi, "Colonial Education in Korea and Taiwan," in Ramon H. Myers
and Mark R. Peattie, eds., *The Japanese Colonial Empire, 1895–1945* (Princeton:
Princeton University Press, 1984), pp. 275–311.

8. Gluck, *Japan's Modern Myths*, pp. 101, 247, 261; Fujiwara Akira, Imai Seiichi, and Ōe Shinobu, eds., *Kindai Nihonshi no kisō chishiki: shijitsu no seikakuna
rikai no tame ni*, rev. ed. (Yūhikaku, 1979), pp. 196–197.

the time, aerodynamic designs were beginning to be used for automobiles and railway cars, but the intricate structure of the engine car presented more of a challenge. In addition, the Asia Express possessed the unusual feature of a glass-enclosed observation deck. One of two first-class cars, the observation lounge was much photographed, with its salon-style arrangement of elegantly upholstered chairs, tables, and a bookshelf. Mantetsu engineers also traveled to the United States to learn techniques for refrigeration and air conditioning; these were incorporated into designs for the Asia Express, which was equipped with facilities for heating, cooling, drying and adding moisture to the air. This was another aspect in which it outclassed the Tsubame Express, where only the dining car circulated heated and cooled air.

The application of these new technologies to the Asia Express made this a train ahead of its time. Indeed, railway designs employed within Japan did not catch up with many of its innovations until after the end of the war. Mantetsu was proud of its new prize, and subsequent promotional literature turned the train into the company mascot. Pamphlets and posters invariably featured an ultramodern image of the Asia Express. It became a familiar sight in photo collections, guidebooks, and travel literature on Manchukuo. The revised series of primary-school literature textbooks used from 1934 even included an essay "On Board the Asia Express."[9] All this conveyed the message that the new train, like Manchukuo itself, represented something much more advanced than anything produced at home. In contrast to a culturally, politically, and economically backward China, likened to a Japan of the past, Manchukuo represented the Japan of the future.

Like the railway, by 1931 the concept of urban planning had acquired both domestic and colonial associations. Of more recent vintage, urban planning was nevertheless in the process of becoming an equally powerful symbol of modernity. In the 1880s, national leaders expressed enthusiasm for remodeling Tokyo into a capital city appropriate to their image of a modern nation. Although their interest was diverted in the 1890s by more pressing international concerns, problems caused by the strains of rapid population growth in Osaka, Kobe, Nagoya, and elsewhere brought the issue of urban reform to the attention of local governments. During the teens, city councils began to consider urban planning as the solution to problems of housing, traffic, and public health. After World War I, architects, civil engineers, city administrators, developers, and academics formed

9. Harada Katsumasa, *Mantetsu* (Iwanami shoten, 1981), pp. 171–180.

three organizations devoted to the problem of urban reform: the Urban Studies Association (Toshi kenkyūkai), the Architectural Academy (Kenchiku gakkai), and the Kansai Association of Architects (Kansai kenchiku kyōkai, later renamed Nihon kenchiku kyōkai). The vision of the city of the future produced by these specialists was heavily influenced by European and American models. Without an academic program on city planning in Japan itself, many had trained in the West. Widely read in the Western literature, they took inspiration from Baron Haussmann's nineteenth-century remodeling of Paris, Frederick Law Olmsted's park systems, and the city beautiful movement.[10]

By the time interest in the problems of city planning was growing at home, colonial administrators had already acquired hands-on experience in urban development. Under the direction of Gotō Shinpei, the cityscape of Taipei, capital of Japan's first colony, took shape in the late 1890s. In the years that followed, city plans were drawn up and executed for seats of colonial administration in Seoul, Dalian, and elsewhere in the empire. Gotō Shinpei, considered by architectural historians as the "father of modern city planning" in Japan, was also Mantetsu's first president, and as such had a hand in urban development in the Japanese concessions in the railway zone.[11] A physician by training, Gotō was particularly interested in the problems of public health and the need for adequate sewage systems and a clean water supply. After he was posted back to Japan, Gotō applied the interest and experience he acquired in problems of city planning in the empire to urban problems at home. He headed the Urban Studies Association and used his political authority to aid the efforts of a group of eager neophyte urban planners, charging them to redesign Tokyo after the devastation of the 1923 earthquake.

The combined efforts of the three city-reform organizations led to the creation of a city-planning agency within the Home Ministry in 1918, and in 1919, a building code and city-planning ordinance. Yet despite the great hopes fostered by these achievements, elaborate plans worked up by members of the professional organizations for the remodeling of Osaka and Tokyo were doomed to disappointment. In both cases a shortage of financial support, together with the political opposition of various landowning interests, forced planners to abandon the best parts of their envisioned cities. It was this group of frustrated planners that formed the team of

10. Koshizawa Akira, *Manshūkoku no shuto keikaku: Tōkyō no genzai to mirai o tou* (Nihon keizai hyōronsha, 1988), pp. 9–12, 14–20.

11. Ibid., pp. 2, 12–14.

urban developers who transformed the face of Manchukuo's cities. They took their pent-up energy and their unfulfilled dreams to the empire, where, with the political and financial support of the colonial state behind them, they encountered none of the obstacles that had tripped them up in Japan. Manchukuo became a blank canvas on which to paint the ideal cities of the future. The designs for Manchukuo, as Koshizawa Akira observed, "assimilated all the Japanese plans of the past, and comprehensively applied their accumulated knowledge and technology to this one enormous testing ground."[12]

Like the Asia Express, the new Manchurian cities were widely advertised as symbols of the ultramodern character of Manchukuo. This was especially true of Xinjing, the crowning achievement of Manchukuo planners. Like Haussmann's Paris and the city beautiful ideal, Xinjing was laid out with wide, tree-lined boulevards in axial formations radiating from architectural monuments to Japan's colonial presence: a war memorial, the palace of the puppet emperor, the train station, and key government buildings. The geometric symmetry of this street pattern could not pose a more striking contrast than with the twisted maze of narrow roads that meandered through Japan's own cities.

In addition to the giant tree-filled plazas where the boulevards converged, the landscaped cemeteries, and the arbors of trees lining the main streets, city planners built several elegant parks. Together, the percentage of city space devoted to greenery rivaled the greenest of European cities. With botanical gardens, decorative lakes and streams, a zoo, and other amenities, lavish city parks became another monument to the munificence of the colonial state. To Japanese residents and visitors accustomed to a fraction of this green space in their cities back home, the parks were one more feature of an ideal urban landscape.[13]

At a time when sewage disposal was a basic measure of urban progress, the construction of waste pipes and water closets in the new cities placed Manchukuo at the vanguard of public hygiene. Sano Toshikata, the disciple of Gotō Shinpei who oversaw the construction of Xinjing, was particularly concerned, like his mentor, with the problem of public health. He insisted that water closets be built in all-new construction. Sano and his team were proud of their achievement when Xinjing became the first city in Asia in which all residential, commercial, and industrial buildings were equipped with water closets. Books like *The New Face of Manchurian Cities* proudly

12. Ibid., pp. 14–25; quotation from p. 2.
13. Ibid., pp. 120–133, 139–144.

pointed to the "world class" sewage systems in the capital.[14] In contrast to the ultrahygienic state of Manchukuo's construction, few buildings in Japan had water closets at that time. Indeed, it would be thirty years before they were found in most ordinary households.[15]

With their state-of-the-art roads, parks, and water closets, the cities of Manchuria became a showcase of municipal splendor, projecting the power of the colonial state as the agent of modernity. That the colonial state took up this role was largely due to the influence of progressive intellectuals within its bureaucratic ranks. Using their positions in Mantetsu and the Manchukuo government, designers, architects, and engineers gave free rein to their creative vision. Unlike in Japan, no considerations of finance or politics restrained their soaring imaginations. In Manchukuo they could build the fastest train or the greenest city because they held at their disposal the power to seize land at will, to appropriate resources, and to silence dissenting voices; their modernist utopia rested on the foundation of the absolute power of the colonial state. But if absolutism sounded a discordant note in the brave new empire of the progressive intelligentsia, they did not speak of it. In their glorification of colonial development they conveyed instead the dazzling magnificence of their futuristic cityscapes, and the heady exhilaration of turning dreams to reality.

CITIES OF OPPORTUNITY

While they were being remade into cities of the future, these towns were also stimulated by the Manchukuo government's railway and urban construction plans to become Manchurian cities of opportunity for Japanese entrepreneurs. The unfaltering construction boom throughout the country brought a steady influx of fortune seekers who answered Manchuria's call. Between 1930 and 1941, the civilian population of Manchuria rose by 800,000, making this the largest concentration of Japanese overseas. The stream of Japanese into Manchuria soon meant that every stop on the South Manchurian Railway had a Japantown; in many cities the Japanese outnumbered the Chinese. Urban Manchuria was not only being designed and built by Japanese, it was being populated by them as well. Taking up residence in the dreamtowns of urban architects, the Manchurian Japanese set about fulfilling the extravagant ambitions of Kwantung Army planners.

14. Manshū nichinichi shinbun, ed., *Manshū toshi no shinsōbō* (Manshū nichinichi shinbunsha, 1937), p. 5.
15. Koshizawa, *Manshūkoku*, pp. 135–136.

If they did not find the much vaunted "paradise on earth" (*shintenchi*), they encountered something close to it in the free flow of money, the luxury, and the cosmopolitanism of their new life.

After 1931, the rapid entry of new commercial and industrial enterprise transformed the geography of Japanese capital in the Northeast. Before the Manchurian Incident, there were 1,242 Japanese corporations operating in the Kwantung Leased Territory and the railway zone, with a total paid-in capital of 627,820,000 yen (see Table 4). This capital was overwhelmingly concentrated in the port city of Dalian, the political and commercial center of the Kwantung Leased Territory. Of the 1,180 Japanese corporations in Manchuria at the end of 1930, 728 were in Dalian (61.7 percent), as was an even higher proportion of Japanese capital (87.6 percent or 556,280,000 yen). Fengtian, the power base of Zhang Xueliang and the largest of the Japanese concessions in the railway zone, was a distant second runner. Only 14.7 percent (174) of Japanese companies and 4.8 percent (5,590,000 yen) of Japanese capital was based there.[16] As the seat of the Kwantung governor general, the headquarters of Mantetsu, and the center for the majority of Japanese businesses, Dalian towered above the other outposts of Japanese enterprise in Manchuria.

The rush of new companies after 1931 ended Dalian's monopoly on Japanese capital in the Northeast and altered the region's make-up. Between January 1932 and December 1937, 690 new companies were created with a paid-in capital of over 1 billion yen (see Table 5). A comparison of the figures in Tables 5 and 6 (neither of which includes smaller unincorporated enterprises) reveals a number of differences in the composition of larger Japanese capital interests before and after the Manchurian Incident. First, while investment in transportation remained overwhelmingly dominant through both periods, it was 65 percent of the pre-1932 investment, but only 59 percent after 1931. Second, in the earlier period, though the number of commercial enterprises was higher than mining and manufacturing businesses (682 compared with 436), in terms of paid-in capital the two sectors were more or less balanced (96,460 yen for commerce, 110,650 yen for mining and manufacturing). In the later period, in contrast, new manufacturing and mining firms shot dramatically ahead of those in commerce, both in overall numbers (240 compared with 138) and in terms of paid-in capital (277,528 yen for manufacturing, 37,312 yen for commerce).

Many of these new manufacturing firms built their plants in locations

16. Manshikai, vol. 2, p. 716.

Table 4. Japanese Companies in Manchuria, 1931

Type	Number of Companies	Paid-in Capital (yen)
Agriculture	31	9,600,000
Fishing	6	420,000
Mining	23	15,050,000
Manufacturing	413	95,600,000
Commerce	682	96,460,000
Transportation	86	410,690,000
Total	1,241	627,820,000

SOURCE: Manshikai, *Manshū kaihatsu yonjūnenshi,* vol. 2 (Manshū kaihatsu yonjūnenshi kankōkai, 1964), p. 716.
NOTE: Includes Kwantung Leased Territory and the railway zone.

Table 5. New Corporations in Manchukuo and the Kwantung Leased Territory, January 1932–December 1937

Type	Number of Companies	Paid-in Capital (yen)
Service and finance	220	99,305,000
Transportation	40	673,060,000
Commerce	138	37,312,000
Manufacturing	240	277,528,000
Agricultural settlement and development	32	44,303,000
Other	20	2,010,000
Total	690	1,133,518,000

SOURCE: Manshikai, *Manshū kaihatsu yonjūnenshi,* vol. 2 (Manshū kaihatsu yonjūnenshi kankōkai, 1964), p. 722.

other than Dalian. In 1931, only 403 Japanese factories operated outside the Kwantung Leased Territory. Between 1932 and 1940, this number increased to 1,853.[17] This expansion of the Japanese manufacturing base in central and north Manchuria signaled a change in the character of eco-

17. *Manshūkoku kōjo tōkei (B): Kōnei 7 nen* (Xinjing: Manshūkoku keizaibu kōmushi, 1942), pp. 2–3. Note that there are two series of pages in this statistical yearbook. The statistics cited here and later are from the second series, under the heading "Kōjō tōkeihyō."

Table 6. Growth of Japanese Population in Selected Manchukuo Cities

	1931	1933	1935	1937	1939	1941
Dalian	102,768	121,611	143,329	155,224	169,953	192,059
Fengtian	47,567	—	66,674	83,542	110,736	163,591
Harbin	4,151	11,856	27,399	36,347	38,220	53,295
Xinjing	17,464	37,130	51,780	65,222	90,560	128,582
Andong	12,570	14,958	15,251	16,625	18,277	24,917
Fushun	—	—	21,543	25,372	32,015	41,688
Yingkou	—	—	372	5,433	6,270	7,739
Jilin	—	—	6,519	12,493	11,031	21,694
Mudanjiang	—	—	1,345	13,073	16,538	56,400
Anshan	—	—	15,470	22,206	36,809	46,375
Jinzhou	—	—	4,584	8,649	12,334	—
Sipingjie	—	—	6,400	7,169	—	9,215
Qiqihar	—	—	6,898	7,085	—	13,823

SOURCE: *Manshū keizai zuhyō* (Dalian: Dalian shōkō kaigisho, 1934–1940); Tōa ryokō-sha, ed., *Manshi ryokō nenkan: Shōwa 18 nen* (Fengtian: Tōa ryokōsha, 1942), pp. 540–541.

nomic imperialism. Before 1931, the rule of Dalian demonstrated the centrality of the port and the dominance of trading capital. Japan was a strong, if peripheral presence, bleeding Manchuria through the big toe, as it were. After 1931, however, Japanese enterprises began to dominate internal trade and commerce as well as manufacturing. With this geographic and sectoral diversification, Japanese interests succeeded in tapping the main arteries of the Manchurian economy.

As the economic thrust of Japanese imperialism shifted northward, a number of cities emerged as centers of Japan's new economic power. Probably the most dramatic transformation occurred in Changchun, which in 1931 was Mantetsu's final stop and the northernmost Japanese settlement in the railway zone. As the principal connection between Mantetsu and the Russian-owned Chinese Eastern Railway, Changchun thrived on the commercial interactions between the two railways and the companies for which they shipped merchandise. It was an entrepôt for transshipment of soybeans and lumber from the north to the port of Dalian. Chinese capital interests dominated the local economy, which was based on warehousing, general goods stores, the oil-pressing industry, and cottage industries such as ceramics. At that time, Japanese capital investment was minimal; it included only the Changchun Electric Company and the Manchurian Milling and Jilin Match Company plants.

After the Manchurian Incident, Changchun became the new capital of Xinjing, and the city was transformed into the political and administrative center of the Northeast. Thousands of Japanese arrived every year to take up posts in the expanding state apparatus, making Xinjing the fastest growing of all the Japanese communities in the Northeast. The government's urban development stimulated the growth of a construction industry; lumberyards, cement, brick-making and glass factories flourished while developers and contractors flocked to the city to ride the construction boom. Xinjing's importance as a transshipment point only increased as Mantetsu's expanded railway network directed trade from all corners of Manchuria toward the central arterial line running from Harbin to Dalian. The major commercial operations had offices in Xinjing, and many were headquartered there. It also became one of the new manufacturing centers, especially for consumer products aimed at the expatriate Japanese community.[18] Of the Japanese communities outside the Kwantung Leased Territory, only Fengtian had more factories (780) than Xinjing (227) in 1940.[19] The vast majority of Xinjing's factories were engaged in the production of construction materials like bricks and lumber, or such consumer goods as books and newspapers, confections, hand-tailored clothing, and leather products. The burgeoning Japanese community drew in small merchants as well. By the end of 1936 there were already 938 Japanese shops, restaurants, hotels, and other small business establishments in Xinjing.[20]

If the political center of the Japanese presence shifted from Dalian to Xinjing, Fengtian took over as the industrial capital. Although Dalian had more Japanese residents, with a population of 332,000 in 1931, Fengtian was the largest city in the Northeast. Like Xinjing, it was a major com-

18. On the transformation of the Xinjing economy: Manshū keizai jijō annaijo hōkoku, "Kokuto Shinkyō keizai jijō," *Manmō* (May 1933), pp. 125–149; Manshū keizai jijō annaijo hōkoku, "Kokuto Shinkyō keizai jijō," *Manmō* (June 1933), pp. 59–87; Manshū kōhō kyōkai, *Manshū no shinbun to tsūshin* (Xinjing: Manshū kōhō kyōkai, 1940), pp. 64–68; Shinkyō shōkō kaigisho, *Shinkyō shōkō jijō* (Xinjing: Shinkyō shōkō kaigisho, 1942), pp. 2–6; *Manshūkoku kōjo tōkei (A): Kōnei 7 nen* (Xinjing: Manshūkoku keizai kōmushi, 1942), pp. 16–23; and Manshū jijō annaijō, pp. 1–10.

19. In descending order, numbers of Japanese factories in key industrial regions of Manchukuo in 1940 were 780 in Fengtian, 227 in Xinjing, 150 in Mudanjiang, 149 in Andong, 116 in Binjiang, and 113 in Jilin: *Manshūkoku kōjo tōkei (A): Kōnei 7 nen* (1942), pp. 16, 24, 48, 54, 72, 86.

20. Manshū nichinichi shinbun, p. 15.

munications hub, traversed by the Hun River and intersected by several rail lines. Hence, it prospered before 1931 as a distributing center for a section of central Manchuria. Under the stimulation of the Manchukuo government's development of heavy industry, Fengtian and the nearby iron- and coal-mining complexes at Anshan and Fushun became the industrial heartland of the Northeast. Although there were only 72 Japanese factories operating in Fengtian city in 1931, by the end of the decade there were 780 manufacturing plants in Fengtian province.[21] With the exception of a handful of industries in Yingkou, these were all located in the three-city industrial belt.

At Anshan, the new Showa Steel Works, which was built on the foundation of an ironworks created by Mantetsu in 1918, represented one of the centerpieces of Manchurian industrialization. Machine manufacturing plants like Sumitomo Steel Pipe and Manchurian Roll Manufacturing soon established themselves nearby to process the pig iron and steel produced at Showa Steel. Coal-mining operations at Fushun, located thirty-five kilometers east of Fengtian, spun off a cluster of industrial enterprises of its own—electric power, coal liquification, and cement and brick manufacture. At Fengtian itself, the establishment of Manchukuo ushered in what was called a golden age for Japanese industry.

The magnet for the influx of new industries to Fengtian was a special industrial zone, inaugurated in 1934. The construction of the new West Industrial District set off a building boom that rivaled Xinjing, making Fengtian a showpiece of modern industry. Japanese poured money into the construction work in Fengtian. Between 1931 and 1937, 136.6 million yen was spent, a modest 1 million yen in 1931 rising to 47 million yen in 1937.[22] By the end of 1936, the district had forty kilometers of road and six kilometers of rail to connect factories with Mantetsu's Fengtian Station. It had water, gas, and electricity, as well as telephone, telegraph, and postal services. There were 175 new factories in the West Industrial District at the end of 1935, and another 59 went into operation in the following two years. Most of these produced heavy industrial goods. For example, of the 48 new factories in 1937, 14 manufactured iron and steel, 12 made machinery and tools, and 6 produced chemicals.[23]

21. *Manshūkoku kōjo tōkei (A): Kōnei 7 nen* (1942), p. 86.
22. For further details see Geo. White, "Construction Work in Mukden," *Manchuria* (1 April 1938), p. 188.
23. This discussion of the industrialization of Fengtian, Anshan, and Fushun draws on the following sources. Fengtian: "The Flourishing City of Mukden," *Manchuria* (15 December 1936), pp. 390–392; Geo. White, "Construction Work in

Manchurian development offered the best opportunities for Japanese entrepreneurs, but some Chinese also prospered under the economic stimulation of the 1930s. Chinese entrepreneurial associates of Zhang Xueliang were clear losers under the new regime. Their businesses, such as the Fengtian Arsenal and the Fengtian Provincial Bank, were simply appropriated by the Kwantung Army and turned into Manchukuo government enterprises. The army took over most of the modern Chinese production facilities in the Northeast, particularly those infant industries created by Zhang Zuolin in the 1920s in the effort to drive an economic wedge against Japanese imperialism. This left traditional and cottage industries such as bean-oil pressing, flour milling, and pottery, which Chinese capital continued to dominate. Even more important than manufacturing, however, was commerce. Before the Manchurian Incident, Chinese merchants handled the majority of goods brought into and carried out of the city. In 1931, for example, Chinese controlled 62 percent of Fengtian's trade, worth 56 million yen, while the Japanese controlled only 38 percent. These shares reversed after the creation of Manchukuo; by 1935, Japanese merchants handled 60 percent and Chinese only 40 percent of goods moving in and out of the city. But trade shares told only one part of the story. With the increasing importance of Fengtian as a transshipment center, the city's trade volume boomed and figures for Chinese merchants rose accordingly. The volume of goods handled by Chinese merchants was 35 million yen in 1931 and 130 million yen in 1935, almost a four-fold increase.[24] Although many segments of Chinese society in the Northeast—the peasantry and the old regime in particular—lost considerably under Japanese rule, others were able to profit from economic development.

While the expansion of Japanese power and influence produced the most dramatic changes in Xinjing and Fengtian, a number of other cities underwent similar transformations on a smaller scale. In 1941, there were five Manchurian cities with over 50,000 Japanese residents: Dalian

---

Mukden," *Manchuria* (1 April 1938), pp. 188–189; Hōten shōkō kaigisho, *Hōten keizai jijō* (Fengtian: Hōten shōkō kaigisho, 1936), pp. 10–27; Hōten shōkō kaigisho, *Kōgyō toshi Hōten* (Fengtian: Hōten shōkō kaigisho, 1934); and Hōten shōkō kaigisho, *Kigyōchi toshite no Hōten* (Fengtian: Hōten shōkō kaigisho, 1932). Fushun: "Fushun—Manchurian City of Industry," *Manchuria* (1 October 1936), pp. 234–235. Anshan: "The Showa Steel Works at Anshan," *Manchuria* (15 October 1936), p. 255.

24. "The Flourishing City of Mukden," *Manchuria* (15 December 1936), pp. 390–392; Hōten shōkō kaigisho, *Hōten keizai jijō*, pp. 10–27, statistics on pp. 11–12.

(192,059), Fengtian (163,591), Xinjing (128,582), Harbin (53,295), and Mudanjiang (56,400) (see Table 6). Another four—Anshan, Fushun, Andong, and Jilin—were home to communities of between 20,000 and 50,000 Japanese. In these smaller Japanese communities, as in the larger ones, some of the funds flowing into heavily capitalized state-managed corporations trickled out into the hands of small businessmen. In Harbin, for example, 946 new Japanese businesses established themselves between 1932 and 1935, 83 in 1932, 110 in 1933, 192 in 1934, and 346 in 1935. Of these, 163 were cafes and restaurants, 70 were building contractors, and about 200 were in the sex trade and other fly-by-night businesses. The petit-bourgeois character of the new businesses in Harbin was reflected in the changing composition of the Japanese Chamber of Commerce of Harbin. There were twelve ranks of membership a business could select, depending on the size of the firm and the amount of dues it was willing to pay. Between 1932 and 1935, members in the top six ranks increased from 24 to 28, while those in the bottom six ranks rose from 103 to 275. Of the latter 172 new members, 130 were from the last three ranks.[25] The variety of opportunities offered to Japanese entrepreneurs in Manchuria was reflected in a 1939 Japanese Chamber of Commerce directory of business for Andong, a city of 17,192 at the time. Most of the 868 businesses listed were involved in retail and service enterprises that catered to the local Japanese population. This included the ubiquitous hotels, restaurants, and cafes, as well as bicycle, office supply, sports equipment, and furniture stores. Japanese ran pawn shops, employment agencies, bathhouses, and movies theaters. And there was sufficient demand among the Andong population to support ten photography studios.[26]

The throng that answered the call of these cities of opportunity swelled the Japanese population of Manchukuo. By 1940, over a million Japanese lived in the Northeast; almost 80 percent arrived after the Manchurian Incident.[27] Before 1930, the Japanese population rose at an average rate of 9,350 per year. The most rapid influx was immediately after the Russo-Japanese War and again during the World War I boom. In the 1930s, the rate of population growth shot up to an average of 83,132 per year—almost ten times the rate before 1931.

25. Harupin Nihon shōkō kaigisho, *Harupin keizai gaikan* (Harbin: Harupin Nihon shōkō kaigisho, 1937), pp. 111–112.

26. Antō shōkō kaigisho, *Antō shōkō annai* (Andong: Antō shōkō kaigisho, 1939), pp. 47–124.

27. Manshikai, vol. 1, p. 84.

These newcomers came from all over Japan. The business capitals of Osaka and Tokyo sent large contingents, but these were just a fraction of the total number. The greatest percentage came from the southern island of Kyūshū, situated geographically at the closest proximity to the continent.[28] Aside from geography, it is not altogether clear why so many of the Manchurian Japanese came from Kyūshū, though the majority of Japanese residents in the Chinese treaty-port settlements also came from Kyūshū.[29] Perhaps the connections established with the treaty-port settlements since 1895 had produced local institutions facilitating the flow of people to the continent. Certainly the prefectural associations, present in all the areas of Japanese settlement in China and Manchuria, represented one such institution.[30]

As it had been before the Manchurian Incident, the Japanese community in the Northeast was overwhelmingly middle class in character. Though the Japanese population increased by half between 1930 and 1935, the occupational composition remained almost identical. Japanese moved to Manchuria to take up posts in the colonial government (22 percent), to work in a shipping company or for Mantetsu (18 percent), to engage in commerce (25 percent), or to work at one of Manchukuo's manufacturing plants (21 percent).[31] Japanese working in government, transportation, and commerce were virtually exclusively white-collar workers and professionals: bureaucrats, business executives, planners, engineers, managers, office workers and shop clerks. Only in the fields of manufacture and the building trades were there significant numbers of blue-collar Japanese in Manchuria, and even these were an aristocracy of skilled labor.[32] Wage rates were

28. For example, in December 1937 the Japanese population of the Kwantung Leased Territory was 177,784. Of this number 63,065 were born in Kyūshū, 26,197 in Chūgoku, 18,214 in Kantō, 12,008 in Tōhoku, 11,259 in Shikoku, 9,241 in Hokuriku, 8,612 in Tōkai, 6,665 in Tōsan, 1,993 in Hokkaidō, and 3,190 in the empire and Okinawa. Kantōkyoku, *Shōwa 12 nen: dai 32 tōkeisho* (Dalian: Kantōkyoku, 1939), p. 39.

29. Mark R. Peattie, "Japanese Treaty Port Settlements in China, 1895–1937," in Peter Duus, Ramon H. Myers, and Mark R. Peattie, eds., *The Japanese Informal Empire in China, 1895–1937* (Princeton: Princeton University Press, 1989), pp. 170–171.

30. For a directory of prefectural associations throughout China (including the Northeast) and statistics on their membership, see Tōa ryokōsha, ed., *Manshi ryokō nenkan: Shōwa 18 nen* (Fengtian: Tōa ryokōsha, 1942), pp. 483–493. It was standard practice to list names and addresses of prefectural associations in travel guidebooks of the period.

31. Manshikai, vol. 1, p. 85.

32. According to Manchukuo government statistics, of the 27,778 Japanese em-

considerably higher than within Japan itself; for example, in 1934 Japanese carpenters and plasterers in Dalian, Fengtian, and Xinjing made almost twice what they did in Tokyo, Nagoya, or Osaka.[33]

Thus for the new colonial elite pouring into Northeast China from Japan, Manchukuo represented not only the world of the colonial future, but also the world of their future. And from where they stood in the mid 1930s, that future looked bright indeed. The march of progress in the empire promised the reordering of the colonial landscape into the rational lines of urban modernism. For the colonial elite themselves, urban development and the construction boom were filled with seemingly boundless opportunities for profit and advancement, and made possible a cosmopolitan lifestyle and standard of living not available to them at home. For the million Japanese in urban Manchuria, experience made good on some, at least, of the extravagant promises of Manchurian development. The disjunction between dreams and deeds, between rhetoric and reality, so jarring in other dimensions of the imperial project, was less evident here in the cities of opportunity.

THE MANCHURIAN TRAVEL BOOM

The colonial elite were not the only Japanese able to sample the offerings of Manchukuo's new urban showcase. Students, teachers, principals, photographers, painters, and novelists all joined the swelling ranks of continental travelers in the 1930s, drawn by the Manchurian dream. The surging demand for the Manchurian tour among Japan's educated classes accelerated the commercialization of tourism inside and outside Japan that had begun in the twenties. The flourishing travel industry that emerged became one of the cultural cornerstones of Manchukuo. Images of Manchurian development became advertisements for the continental tour: the bustling Dalian wharf, the magnificent new government buildings in Xinjing's central plaza, and Mantetsu's pride, the sleek Asia Express. Disseminating promotional literature on the Manchurian tour, the travel industry assumed the role of unofficial publicity agent for the new empire. Whether people saw Manchuria's highlights for themselves or simply dreamed about them, the packaged tour shaped their understanding of the imperial project.

---

ployees in Manchukuo factories in 1940, 7,461 were engaged in managerial and clerical occupations, 6,760 in technical and engineering occupations, and 13,557 in skilled labor. *Manshūkoku kōjo tōkei (B): Kōnei 7 nen* (1942), pp. 70–73.

33. Hōten shōkō kaigisho, *Kōgyō toshi Hōten*, pp. 16–17.

Japanese tourism had long been a part of the cultural dimension of Japanese imperialism. With their easy access by ship and rail, Korea and South Manchuria attracted the largest number of visitors to the empire. Tourist facilities quickly emerged to accommodate the growing number of travelers. Two years after the founding in 1912 of the central agency for organized tourism in prewar Japan, the Japan tsūrisuto byūrō (JTB), a Dalian branch was opened.[34] The network of continental services under JTB's Dalian branch expanded so rapidly that it assumed budgetary independence from the Japan office in the late 1920s. By 1930, JTB-Dalian managed twelve major service centers (annaijo), five smaller tourist information offices (shutchōjo), and seven outlets (chūzaiin) both in Northeast China and south of the Great Wall.[35]

The Manchurian network grew even faster after 1931. JTB-Dalian opened and expanded facilities one after another, including a new office in the Chinese section of Fengtian in 1932, an outlet in the Manchurian-Korean border city of Tumen in 1933 (upgraded to a service center in 1935), and service centers to the north in Harbin and Manzhouli in 1935. By 1936 JTB-Dalian had seventeen annaijo, seven shutchōjo, and two chūzaiin in Manchuria alone. The number of staff had risen from 48 in 1927 to 321 in 1936, a six-fold increase. The agency had begun offering special promotions for continental tourism, such as the "East Asia Pass" (Tōa yūran-ken), which gave the bearer 20 percent discounts on rail and 30 percent on ship travel in China, Japan, and Manchuria. JTB-Dalian also began publishing travel digests of fare and schedule information for train, ship, and air travel, as well as the magazine Travel Manchuria (Manshū ryokō) in 1934.[36]

JTB's expansion in Manchuria reflected only a small part of a booming market. Hotels, restaurants, and sight-seeing buses catering to Japanese

---

34. The JTB was founded at the initiative of officials in the Imperial Railway Bureau after railway nationalization in 1906. Originally JTB was created to promote European and American tourism in the empire and the home islands, though it later shifted its energies toward Japanese tourists. After JTB's creation, both Mantetsu and the Imperial Railway Bureau (changed to the Ministry of Railroads in 1920) continued to promote passenger traffic on their lines through advertisements and their own tourism offices as well as working with JTB. The Japan tsūrisuto byūrō is the precursor to the present-day Nihon kōtsū kōsha; it acquired the latter name when it was reorganized in 1945. For the establishment of JTB, see Nihon kōtsū kōsha shashi hensanshitsu, ed., Nihon kōtsū kōsha nanajūnenshi (Nihon kōtsū kōsha, 1982), pp. 10–18.

35. Ibid., pp. 70–71.

36. Ibid., pp. 58, 71, and chronology (paginated separately), pp. 22–31.

tourists established operations throughout Manchukuo. The 1941 *Manchuria-China Travel Yearbook* recommended forty-two accommodations in Dalian, twenty-four in Fengtian, twenty-eight in Xinjing, and at least one in 143 other Manchurian cities.[37] The domestic trade association, Japan League of Tourism (Nihon kankō renmei), reorganized itself in 1936 to include Korean- and Manchurian-based enterprises.[38] As of 1937, Manchurian businesses had their own trade association, the Manshū kankō renmei, which actively promoted tourism through exhibits, tourism weeks, service centers, and the publication of pamphlets, leaflets, and postcards.[39] Starting in 1935, local Japanese chambers of commerce throughout Manchuria established leagues of tourism to undertake these sorts of promotions for their own areas. Within five years such organizations existed in Dalian, Lüshun, Anshan, Fengtian, Tieling, Sipingjie, Benxi, Xinjing, Andong, Yingkou, Jilin, Harbin, Qiqihar, Jinzhou, Rehe, and East Manchuria.[40]

This network of facilities offered Japanese travelers accommodations at a variety of attractions. These attractions included not just the booming urban centers but everything from hunting, fishing, and mountain-climbing regions to famous battle sites and archaeological wonders. Japanese could visit horse-racing tracks, golf courses, and hot springs; they had ski resorts for the winter and sunbathing beaches for the summer. Shinto shrines were available for prayers throughout Manchukuo, and memorial stamps could be had at some 230 train stations and tourist attractions.[41] The Manchurian travel boom was helping to redefine the tourist industry in terms of a standard menu of recreational activities. Pilgrimages to important religious sites, rustication at hot-springs resorts, and mountain climbing were all familiar to travelers at home, but activities of more aristocratic and European associations, such as golf, skiing, and horse-racing, also became very popular. With the rise of continental travel, Japanese were beginning to associate tourism with the exoticism, the luxury, and the ultramodernity of Manchuria's travel facilities.

Evidence suggests that these aspects of tourism held greater allure than the sights in Japan, for the pace of growth in Manchuria quickly outstripped JTB's expansion in the home islands. For example, *annaijo* were

37. Japan tsūrisuto byūrō, ed., *Manshi ryokō nenkan: Shōwa 16 nen* (Hakubunkan, 1941), pp. 350–357.
38. Nihon kōtsū kōsha shashi hensanshitsu, chronology, p. 31.
39. Japan tsūrisuto byūrō, pp. 365–366.
40. Ibid., pp. 365–383.
41. Ibid., pp. 33–160, 205–206.

opened in the mid-sized Manchurian cities of Jilin and Qiqihar before
Sendai and Kumamoto, major cities in northeast and southern Japan. Similarly, Anshan, Tumen, and Mudanjiang all had JTB service centers before
Gifu or Toyama.[42] Employee statistics reflect the same trend. JTB's main
office in Japan employed a staff of 160 in 1931, expanding to 1,021 in 1941.
During the same period, the staff of JTB-Dalian rose from 91 to 1,408,
starting behind and ending ahead of the main office.[43] With its modern
luxuries and exotic opulence, the Manchurian tour clearly exerted a strong
pull on the growing number of Japanese travelers.

   Well into the war, JTB poured resources into promoting travel in Manchuria. In 1941, JTB opened four new offices in their domestic network of
Manchuria-Korea travel service centers: Nagoya, Tsuruya, Nagasaki, and
Otaru.[44] The Dalian branch was even forced to hire women and Chinese
because continued expansion had created such an acute shortage of male
Japanese candidates to fill its staffing demands. A new instruction program
for the 200 Chinese employees was introduced in 1942, and a number were
sent back to Japan for additional training.[45]

   The experience in Manchuria taught the Japanese government how useful tourism could be as a vehicle for imperial propaganda. These lessons
were quickly applied as JTB, following in the wake of the Japanese military,
undertook a massive expansion into the newly occupied territories of the
Co-prosperity Sphere. In 1942 the government reorganized JTB into the
Tōa ryokōsha (East Asia Travel Corporation). Capital assets leapt from
5,707 yen in 1941 to 32,541 yen in 1942 and 55,805 yen in 1943, as the
Tōa ryokōsha absorbed most privately owned tourist businesses under a
huge corporate umbrella.[46] At the late date of 1943, the new president
Ōkura Kinmochi unveiled a spectacular plan that included the establishment of branches throughout the Co-prosperity Sphere, the compilation
of a series of guidebooks to all areas of "Greater East Asia," the expansion
of the network of service centers, the promotion of cultural intercourse
among the literati of the Co-prosperity Sphere, a massive hiring drive, and
an across-the-board salary raise for staff.[47] At a time when the fortunes of

---

42. Nihon kōtsū kōsha shashi hensanshitsu, chronology, pp. 25–27.
43. The biggest staff increases for JTB-Dalian were after 1937, when it employed 417 people, rising to 609 in 1938, 1,047 in 1939, and 1,258 in 1940: ibid.,
p. 72.
44. Ibid., chronology, p. 40.
45. Ibid., pp. 67–69.
46. Ibid., p. 194, document no. 15.
47. Ibid., pp. 79–86.

war had shifted against Japan, the extravagance of this plan for expansion of tourist facilities was testimony either to Ōkura's insanity, or to the importance of propaganda and cultural mobilization in the strategic scheme of the government.

Unfortunately, statistics on Japanese travelers in the last years of the war are unavailable, though it is difficult to imagine that there was much more than a faint echo of the Manchurian travel boom in occupied Southeast Asia. However, figures for the continent in the 1930s are plentiful. These show that demand for Manchurian services was heavy and rose throughout the decade. Numbers of passengers arriving at the principal ports of Dalian, Yingkou, and Andong totaled 530,962 in 1930, 696,241 in 1934, and 964,610 in 1939.[48] Of course, these were neither exclusively Japanese nor limited to tourists. Ridership of sightseeing buses, however, was overwhelmingly comprised of Japanese tourists, and sightseeing bus ticket sales rose dramatically year after year. Dalian's tour-bus ridership quadrupled in three years; Xinjing's went from 905 in 1936 to 38,741 in 1939.[49] Hotel statistics reflected the same trend. Guests at Mantetsu-managed hotels rose from 21,865 in 1932 to 42,112 in 1936. By 1939 Mantetsu hotels were accommodating 58,207 guests in a single year.[50] The figures for Japanese hotel patrons shown in Table 7 tell the same story. Between 1934 and 1939 the number of guests at Dalian hotels doubled (to over 100,000), increased ten-fold in Fengtian (to 1,259,250), and went from 20,000 to over 1,000,000 in Harbin.

Although large in number, the Manchurian travelers were composed of a relatively narrow segment of Japanese society. The costs of continental travel made it impossible for most Japanese to consider the journey. Estimates of the cost of a two-week trip to Manchuria and Korea inclusive of transportation, accommodations, and meals ran to 183.43 or 124.97 yen, based on second-class and third-class group rates, respectively.[51] In wage equivalents, this represented many months' salary for most white-collar workers with higher degrees. To a female department store employee with a higher school degree, a third-class trip represented five months of work; a local elementary schoolteacher with a normal school degree would need to save his or her entire salary for three months; and a university graduate

48. Japan tsūrisuto byūrō, p. 283.
49. Ibid., p. 287.
50. Ibid., p. 293.
51. Ibid., pp. 24–25.

Table 7. Japanese Hotel Patrons in Selected
Manchukuo Cities, 1934–1939

	1934	*1937*	*1939*
Southern Route			
Dalian	58,639	71,903	116,125
Anshan	22,000	334,500	53,890
Fengtian	113,576	254,573	1,259,250
Fushun	18,400	28,600	34,900
Yingkou	—	9,557	20,172
Andong	25,439	31,570	65,500
Total (south)	238,054	730,703	1,549,837
Central Route			
Sipingjie	3,390	5,277	10,903
Xinjing	—	163,980	182,520
Jilin	—	46,328	54,216
Total (central)	3,390	215,585	247,639
Northern Route			
Harbin	21,633	15,252	1,083,220
Qiqihar	40,100	61,300	83,600
Manzhouli	835	1,947	—
Total (north)	62,568	78,499	1,166,820
Total (all)	304,012	1,024,787	2,964,296

SOURCE: Japan tsūrisuto byūrō, ed., *Manshi ryokō nenkan: Shōwa 16 nen* (Hakubunkan, 1941), pp. 293–295.

who worked for the Tokyo metropolitan government would have to save for two months to buy the same package tour.[52]

According to the *Manchuria-China Travel Yearbook*, in 1939 prices, an evening meal cost 1.20 yen, or what a month's newspaper subscription came to back home. Without meals, lodging could be found for 2 to 3 yen a night, making it the equivalent of the monthly rent on a 4.5-mat Tokyo apartment. A cheap city-bus trip in Manchuria was worth a bowl of soba

52. Kōdansha, ed., *Ichioku no "shintaisei": Shōwa 13 nen–15 nen*, vol. 5 of *Shōwa nimannichi no zenkiroku* (Kōdansha, 1989), pp. 143, 167, 173.

or a packet of cigarettes back home. One-way third-class tickets between Dalian and Harbin cost 17 yen, about the same as 5 men's shirts. The same one-way, third-class fare on the Ōsaka shōsen kaisha line between Dalian and Kobe ran 19 yen, about the price of a background check on a prospective spouse in Japan.[53]

Clearly continental travel was a major expense, even for middle-class Japanese. One way people managed to afford it was by joining a travel club, like the Nihon ryokō kurabu, and buying the trip on installment through monthly membership fees.[54] Others had their way paid or partially paid, such as in the case of economic missions sent by business organizations, school principal tour groups backed by private and public funds, or trips taken by journalists and artists on commission. The most common subsidies, however, were those given to student tours. Because student groups were granted hefty discounts on railways, boats, and hotels, and because their trips often were partially underwritten by the Ministry of Education, students flocked to Manchuria.[55]

According to statistics gathered in the *Manchuria-China Travel Year-book*, seventy percent (9,854) of the 14,141 Japanese who traveled to Manchuria in 1939 on JTB tours were students. All of these came from elite-track educational institutions such as teacher training schools like the Kumamoto Normal School, technical schools like the Fukuoka Women's Technical College, or business schools like Takamatsu Commercial College.[56] These tours were important milestones in a student's life. Often graduation trips, the event marked a rite of passage and was for many the only travel they would do outside the home islands. The journeys made lasting impressions and could change the course of a life, as it did for Mantetsu researcher Itō Takeo. Recalling how his high school trip first interested him in the study of China, Itō wrote:

> My trip to Manchuria, Korea, and China . . . enormously stirred my interest in the Chinese people and made me feel that they were much more interesting than the Japanese. . . . I began this forty-five day trip . . . as

53. Ibid., pp. 193, 199, 211; Japan tsūrisuto byūrō, pp. 24–25, 253–268, 350–358.
54. Nihon kōtsū kōsha shashi hensanshitsu, pp. 60–61.
55. Ibid., chronology, p. 35; Japan tsūrisuto byūrō, pp. 212–214.
56. Statistics on group tours to Manchukuo were collected for JTB booking centers in Tokyo, Osaka, Moji, and Niigata. In addition to student travelers in 1939, other group tours included 49 groups investigating sites for prospective farm immigration, 43 groups of teachers and educational administrators, 25 business organizations, 5 groups traveling for police training activities, 13 travel clubs, 6 youth groups, and 24 groups on government business: Japan tsūrisuto byūrō, pp. 297–302.

one of over twenty members of the group organized by my high school. The previous year the high school had sent a group to the South Seas area, the newly occupied regions of the island of Saipan and the Truk Islands. Our group was the second such overseas trip. The aim of our voyage was to observe our newly occupied areas, and, by accepting offers of hospitality to stay at Japanese military installations along the way, we traveled extremely cheaply. In our case, this overseas trip cost each person seventy-five yen. Even considering how cheap prices were then, this was still very inexpensive. It also corroborates how well students were treated at that time.[57]

Although Itō's journey was taken in 1917, long before the establishment of Manchukuo, his experience captured the intellectual impact continental travel made on an impressionable young person.

The travel industry mobilized artists, photographers, journalists, and novelists to promote the Manchurian tour. Travel clubs, trade associations, and tourist agencies called on the services of "persons of culture" (*bunkajin*) for their publicity campaigns. The Manchurian Tourism League, for example, invited photographers to submit images and writers to pen a few poetic phrases for a poster contest on the theme "Sacred Manchuria." The same year, 1939, it brought two famous photographers from Japan to help put together a set of travel-promotion photographs, and photographers and journalists from the magazine *Bungei shunjū* for the same purpose. The league also sponsored a "tourism week," which included city clean-up days, a tourism art exhibit, radio dramas, and a transportation ethics drive. The Dalian Tourism Association commissioned postcards of city sights, which were not sold to tourists but sent home to Japan and to other areas of Manchuria to lure travelers to Dalian. The Fengtian Tourist Association commissioned pastel paintings of the city and held several exhibits on local tourism. Trade associations also sponsored endless exhibitions of "sightseeing art," travel photos, and local products in Japan and Manchuria.[58]

Spreading the word on the imperial showcase, Japan's men and women of culture lent to Manchukuo a decided high-brow cachet. In doing so, this host of creative talents followed the tradition of Natsume Sōseki, who wrote *Mankan tokoro dokoro* (Around Manchuria and Korea) in 1909 at the behest of Mantetsu.[59] Over the decade of the 1930s most of Japan's

57. Itō Takeo, *Life along the South Manchurian Railway: The Memoirs of Itō Takeo*, trans. Joshua A. Fogel (New York: M. E. Sharpe, 1988), pp. 29–30.

58. Japan tsūrisuto byūrō, pp. 365–376.

59. Kawabata Yasunari, Shiga Naoya, and Satō Haruo, comps., *Chūgokuhen* 2, vol. 11 of *Sekai kikō bungaku zenshū* (Shūdōsha, 1960), pp. 89–135.

finest writers recorded their impressions of Manchuria, as the continental tour became de rigueur for membership of this elite fraternity. The pages of the magazine *Kaizō*, for example, contained a continuous stream of travel essays, or *kikōbun*, by literary personalities. The January 1934 issue featured an article on Harbin nightlife entitled "A Harbin Fantasy" by well-known liberal journalist Hasegawa Nyozekan and an assessment of the Rehe range by the famous mountaineer and travel writer Fujiki Kuzō. Issues of 1937 included descriptions of Manchukuo's cities by the renowned China hand Murata Shirō and travel sketches by the celebrated artist Yasui Sōtarō. Yamamoto Sanehiko, onetime president of Tokyo *Mainichi* and founder of *Kaizō*, volubly described his own impressions of the continent in the pages of his magazine and in books entitled *Mongolia* and *Crossing the Continent*.[60] Prize-winning novelist Araki Takeshi wrote up his impressions of "A Summer's Travel through North Manchuria" in October 1938, and another member of his literary circle, Nitta Jun, published several travel pieces the same year. Cartoonist Yokoyama Ryūichi, renowned creator of the serial comic "Edokko Kenchan" (Little Ken, Edo boy), and others put together a collection of travel impressions in annotated cartoon form entitled "Only in Manchuria" (Manshū naradewa) in December 1938. In 1939, *Kaizō* offered a travelogue by the literary critic Kobayashi Hideo and artistic renderings by poet Wakayama Kishiko. In addition, outside the pages of *Kaizō*, Hayashi Fumiko, Yada Tsuseko, Dan Kazuo, Yasuda Yojūro, Asami Fukashi, Takami Jun, Fukuda Kiyoto, and Itō Hitoshi all wrote *kikōbun* on Manchuria.[61] This parade of literary luminaries made the Manchurian tour into a badge of cultural distinction. Not unlike a year's study in Europe or the United States in earlier years, a visit to the empire bestowed cultural legitimation on those who aspired to the high arts.

60. *Mongolia* (*Mōko*) was published in 1935 and *Crossing the Continent* (*Tairiku ōdan*) in 1938. See abstracts in Tōyō bunko kindai Chūgoku kenkyū iinkai, ed., *Meiji ikō Nihonjin no Chūgoku ryokōki* (Tōyō bunko, 1980), pp. 97, 105.

61. Other *kikōbun* that achieved some renown included poet and literary critic Haruyama Yukuo's *Manshū fūdoki* [The Manchurian Climate]; *Nekka fūkei* [Pictures of Rehe], by seasoned traveler and associate of many Chinese writers Matsumura Shōfu; *Harupin shishū* [A Harbin Poetry Collection], by poet Murō Saisei; *Manshi kono goro* [Manchuria and China in These Times], by Nagayo Yoshio, a lesser figure in the Literary White Birch Society. For discussion of these works, see Kawamura Minato, *Ikyō no Shōwa bungaku: "Manshū" to kindai Nihon* (Iwanami shoten, 1990), pp. 23–24, 99–138; Tōyō bunko kindai Chūgoku kenkyū iinkai, pp. 87–117; Kawabata, Shiga, and Satō, p. 382; *Shuppan nenkan* (Tōkyōdō, 1937), pp. 350–352, 480.

Both tour guides and travel diaries portrayed a specific face of the empire. The travel industry packaged Manchukuo by whistle-stops, speeding the sightseer past a series of monuments to Japanese achievement. The standard tour stopped first at the new city centers, the pride of the town planners and architects for whom Manchurian development was a dream come true; it then went through the exotic and rather smelly Chinatown, whose chaotic market and picturesque slums stood in marked contrast to the opulence and order that characterized the Japanese sections of town. Both the travel experience and travel literature were structured around this dichotomy of the old and the new, the Chinese and the Japanese. Such contrasts became, in effect, a "before and after" advertisement for Manchurian development which rarely failed to sell the product. In this way the travel industry and the *kikōbun* pouring from the pens of Japan's literary establishment packaged Manchukuo for domestic consumption. Joining the efforts of the urban planners and entrepreneurs who were developing Manchuria's cities, they disseminated an image of Manchukuo as urban utopia—a modernist El Dorado that Japan had fabricated on the vast, open plains of the Manchurian frontier.

REPRESSION, MOBILIZATION, AND JAPAN'S CHINA HANDS

In the meantime, a different group of Japanese were putting together yet another piece of the utopian mosaic: the vision of the colonial state as the agent of political and social revolution in China. The driving force behind the new "revolutionary" imperialism in the Northeast came from the intellectuals who made up Japan's Sinological establishment. Like the artists and designers who dreamed of building a modernist utopia in Manchuria, China specialists were members of a progressive intelligentsia. Based in an academy in which Marxism had become the fashion of the 1920s, these scholars and experts tended to situate themselves on the far left of the spectrum of progressive opinion. They studied and taught Marxism, and they employed Marxist categories in their historical research and their analyses of contemporary events. Many considered themselves scholar-activists; they linked their research to political activities organizing industrial workers, tenant farmers, and the fledgling Japanese Communist Party.

Until the 1930s, left-wing intellectuals were secure, more or less, in their positions at home; but the subsequent escalation of censorship in the academy drastically changed this. Under the pressures of ideological suppression, large numbers of revolutionaries packed their bags for Manchukuo, where they found a haven in the expanding bureaucracy of the puppet government and the research wing of Mantetsu. Deeply conflicted about imperialism, Sinologists nevertheless embraced Manchukuo. They regarded it, much as Manchukuo's city planners did, as a place where dreams of social transformation could take shape. Driven out of Japan by repression and drawn to the empire by Manchukuo's utopian promise, left-wing Sinologists provided the research and planning for Manchurian development and designed the ideology of the new state.

Herein lay one of the most striking contradictions in the political environment of the 1930s: the Japanese government's simultaneous suppression and mobilization of the revolutionary intelligentsia. Circumstances brought left-wing researchers and right-wing officers together in the puppet state and there they remained, strange bedfellows, into the early forties when a wave of arrests purged leftists from Mantetsu and the Manchukuo government, ending this bizarre collaboration. The destructiveness of the rupture, in both personal and institutional terms, demonstrated the hazards of total-empire building: coalitions of competing interests were inherently unstable. Once again, the strategy of inclusive mobilization imparted to Manchukuo both strength and weakness. The Sinologists delivered erudition, experience, and creativity to the development project, even as they brought divisiveness into the very heart of the colonial state.

Though the contradictions became more acute in the 1930s, the ambivalent relationship between Sinology and empire emerged long before the creation of Manchukuo. The network of elite cultural institutions that produced an intellectually hegemonic discourse on Sino-Japanese relations was forged in the crucible of empire. Even so, Sinology produced strong currents of opposition to Japanese expansion on the continent, for China held special meaning for these intellectuals: it was at once a symbol of their cultural roots, a foil for the problems of modernity, and the referent for their concept of Asia. Their attitudes toward China may have been complex, but through the institutions they inhabited Sinologists were deeply implicated in the cultural processes of continental expansion.

At the university level, Sinology developed within the discipline of Asian history. *Tōyōshi*, as it was known, spawned the subfield of Manchurian-Korean history (*Manchōshi*) in the 1910s, soon after Japan had acquired a foothold in Northeast China and annexed Korea.[62] The invented historical

---

62. Hatada Takashi, *Nihonjin no Chōsenkan* (Keisō shobō, 1969), pp. 36–41; Hara Kakuten, *Gendai Ajia kenkyū seiritsu shiron: Mantetsu chōsabu, Tōa kenkyūjo, IPR no kenkyū* (Keisō shobō, 1984), pp. 494–508.

subject *Manchōshi* violated the geographical and cultural boundaries of both China and Korea. In forcibly merging *Manshū* and *Chōsen*, places which shared Japanese domination, scholarship imitated empire. Academic studies, moreover, divided subjects into the historical disciplines, which rarely ventured into the nineteenth century, and colonial studies, which dealt with modern China. Thus scholarship segregated past eras of "high civilization," in which Japan acquired its cultural debt to China, from the present period of "decay and backwardness," during which Japan was justified in colonizing China.[63]

The second pillar of Japanese Sinology was the handful of research institutes that emerged to provide the research and development for empire. One of the best known was the East Asian Common Culture Institute (Tōa dōbun shoin), a training and research agency established in Shanghai which produced a wealth of empirical investigations for the Kwantung Army, the Foreign Ministry, and other organizations. Graduates of this prestigious institute became eminent Sinologists, colonial bureaucrats, and China traders.[64] Japanese business enterprises active in China, including Mitsui, the Bank of Korea, the Bank of Taiwan, and, of course, Mantetsu, often had research divisions. Mantetsu's vast Research Department, established with the company in 1906, was certainly the single most powerful center for China studies, for it did not limit its research to Manchuria, and the scope and quality of its production was extraordinary. One bibliography of Mantetsu publications lists 6,284 volumes on subjects ranging from railroad surveys and studies of racial minorities in Manchuria to research on the resources of China and Southeast Asia.[65]

---

63. For the development of Tōyōshi and colonial studies, see Stefan Tanaka, *Japan's Orient: Rendering Pasts into History* (Berkeley: University of California Press, 1993); Joshua A. Fogel, *Politics and Sinology: The Case of Naitō Konan (1866–1934)* (Cambridge: Council on East Asian Studies, Harvard University, 1984); Andō Hokotarō, *Nihonjin no Chūgokukan* (Keisō shobō, 1971); Asada Kyōji, *Nihon chishikijin no shokuminchi ninshiki* (Azekura shobō, 1985); Asada Kyōji, *Nihon shokuminchi kenkyū shiron* (Miraisha, 1990); and Hara Kakuten.

64. Ishidō Kiyotomo, Noma Kiyoshi, Nonomura Kazuo, and Kobayashi Shōichi, *Jūgonen sensō to Mantetsu chōsabu* (Hara shobō, 1986), p. 32; Hara Kakuten, pp. 10–15; Douglas R. Reynolds, "Training Young China Hands: Tōa Dōbun Shoin and Its Precursors, 1886–1945," in Peter Duus, Ramon H. Myers, and Mark R. Peattie, eds., *The Japanese Informal Empire in China, 1895–1937* (Princeton: Princeton University Press, 1989), pp. 210–271.

65. John Young, *The Research Activities of the South Manchurian Railway Company 1907–1945: A History and Bibliography* (New York: East Asian Institute, Columbia University, 1966). Over the thirty years of its existence, Mantetsu's

The intellectual publishing establishment composed the third link in the Sinology network. Demand among an educated readership for sophisticated analysis of "the China problem" and "the Manchuria problem" supported a surprising volume of publications on these topics. Such major newspapers as the *Asahi* employed erudite scholars for their China desks, and elite monthlies such as *Kaizō* (Reconstruction) and *Chūō kōron* (The Central Review) regularly published pieces by Japan's most eminent Sinologists. In addition, there was a host of specialty magazines. The *Magazine Yearbook* of 1939 listed thirty-two magazines on the empire, most of which focused on China. These included journals associated with Mantetsu, such as *Shintenchi* (New Paradise), *Shin Tōa* (New East Asia), or *Tōa* (East Asia); magazines catering to the increased interest in Manchuria after 1931, such as *Manshū hyōron* (The Manchurian Review) and *Manshū gurafu* (Photo Manchuria); and the "rise of Asia" (*kōa*) magazines that emerged in the late thirties such as *Kaizō*'s sister publication *Tairiku* (The Continent) and *Bungei shunjū*'s *Taiyō* (The East).[66] Thus, Japan's highbrow publishing establishment covered China extensively, providing ample opportunities for China specialists to communicate their views to an educated reading public and reflecting an avid interest in China among educated Japanese.

The China specialists who inhabited this network of universities, research institutes, and publishers made up a small, cohesive group that bound the different institutions together. Most did not stay long at a single job, but moved back and forth among institutions. Ozaki Hotsumi, a luminary of Japanese Sinology who was later arrested and executed as a

---

Research Department underwent numerous reorganizations and was renamed several times. When established in 1906 it was called the Research Department (Chōsabu). In 1908 it was renamed the Research Section (Chōsaka), and although administration of the Research Section was shifted around the organization, this name persisted until 1932. In 1932 the Research Section was reorganized as the Economic Research Association (Keizai chōsakai). This lasted until 1936, during which time the research activities were greatly expanded, with new offices opened in Tianjin, Shanghai, and Harbin. In 1936 there was another large reorganization, and between 1936 and 1938, all Mantetsu's research activities were handled by the Industrial Department (Sangyōbu). In 1938, Mantetsu established the Research Department (Chōsabu), which lasted until 1943, when Mantetsu's main offices were moved to Xinjing and once again the Research Department was reorganized, this time into the Research Bureau (Chōsakyoku). For this history see John Young, pp. 2–15, 26–34.

66. *Zasshi nenkan* (Nihon dokusho shinbunsha, 1939), pp. 315–318; *Zasshi nenkan* (1940), p. 23.

Comintern spy, was a typical example of the migratory career movements of the China hands. After graduating from the preeminent First Higher School and Tokyo Imperial University, Ozaki went to work for the *Asahi shinbun* and was eventually sent as a special correspondent to Shanghai, where he participated in study groups at the Dōbun shoin. He took part in China seminars at the Ōhara Social Problems Research Institute, became a key member in the *Asahi*'s Research Association on East Asian issues (established in 1934), and later became a central figure in the public-policy think tank, the Shōwa kenkyūkai. He served as an adviser to Mantetsu, and wrote regularly for a variety of publications including Mantetsu journals, the opinion monthlies, and Foreign Ministry mouthpieces such as *Contemporary Japan* and *Contemporary Manchuria*. Although Ozaki's career path largely mirrored that of other Sinologists, he was exceptional in two respects. The first, of course, was his affiliation with the Comintern through the Sorge spy ring; the second was the fact that he served the Japanese government directly as an adviser to the Konoe cabinet. Men like Ozaki, though they worked for such government-affiliated institutions as the imperial universities, Konoe's brain trust, the Shōwa kenkyūkai, or Mantetsu, typically did not work in the government itself.[67]

Like Ozaki, virtually all the leading China hands had peripatetic career histories. Tachibana Shiraki was known principally for his editorship of *Manshū hyōron*, but he worked for a score of newspapers before assuming that position. While editing *Manshū hyōron*, Tachibana also consulted for Mantetsu and participated in the Shōwa kenkyūkai. Hosokawa Karoku, the famous Marxist scholar of colonial studies, was a graduate, like Ozaki, of the First Higher School and Tokyo Imperial University. During his career he served at the Ōhara Institute, at Mantetsu, and with the Shōwa kenkyūkai, and also contributed frequently to journals. Suzue Gen'ichi was a left-wing activist who had become a respected Sinologist, like a number of others, by way of his involvement with the Chinese Nationalist movement during the twenties. He worked for a variety of Japanese newspapers and news services in China, wrote for magazines in Japan, and in the thirties became a researcher for the Foreign Ministry Cultural Affairs Division and consultant to Mantetsu.[68]

The group spirit among Japan's Sinologists and the facility with which these men moved among institutions was largely attributable to a shared

67. Chalmers Johnson, *An Instance of Treason: Ozaki Hotsumi and the Sorge Spy Ring*, rev. ed. (Stanford: Stanford University Press, 1990), pp. 21–40.
68. Ibid., pp. 17, 37–39, 115; Itō, 42–43, 69–70, 186–190.

academic background. Many were graduates of Tokyo Imperial University and had joined the same student groups, such as the left-wing Shinjinkai, in the 1920s. It was the contacts established in student days that became the currency with which job opportunities were later negotiated. For example, the core members of the Ōhara Institute staff were Tokyo Imperial University graduates.[69] Ozaki Hotsumi used his influence to recommend his old school friends to both Mantetsu and the Shōwa kenkyūkai.[70] Others at Mantetsu used their influence to similar effect. Kawasaki Misaburō got his friend Shimojō Hideo a job; and Hazama Genzō brought in Hirose Yūichi and Nonomura Kazuo, two friends from his alma mater, Osaka Commercial University.[71] Useful contacts from student days were not limited to scholars and journalists, but applied equally to friendships formed with men destined to become part of the bureaucratic establishment. It was such a connection that brought Ozaki into the Institute for Pacific Relations in 1936 and led to his appointment as an adviser to the Konoe cabinet.[72]

Before the 1930s, the Sinology establishment had tolerated ideological diversity within its ranks to a remarkable degree. Considering that institutions like Tokyo Imperial University were the training grounds for the nation's future leaders in all spheres of society, and more importantly that such institutions were affiliated with or directly under state jurisdiction, the degree of tolerance for radical right- and left-wing critiques of Japanese imperialism is striking. Although under the direction of Yamamoto Miono the Kyoto University School of Colonial Studies was supportive of state expansionism, the Tokyo University school, under the direction of liberal Yanaihara Tadao, produced arguments that imperial expansion was deadlocked and sharply criticized policies of colonial exploitation and monopoly privilege.[73] Both the East Asian Common Culture Institute and Mantetsu were hotbeds of radicalism. Ōkawa Shūmei—along with Kita Ikki, a doyen of right-wing extremism and an advocate of pan-Asianism and a Shōwa Restoration—was a prominent researcher at Mantetsu, as were right-wingers Kasagi Yoshiaki, Inoue Nisshō, and Miyazaki Masayoshi.[74] Many

69. This included the head, Tanaka Iwasaburō, as well as others such as Morito Tatsuo, Ōuchi Hyōei, Kuruma Samezō, and Hosokawa Karoku.

70. Itō, p. 175.

71. Ishidō Kiyotomo, "Mantetsu chōsabu wa nan de atta ka (II)," p. 55.

72. Johnson, *An Instance of Treason*, pp. 111–113.

73. Hara Kakuten, p. 70.

74. Joshua A. Fogel, "Introduction: Itō Takeo and the Research Work of the South Manchurian Railway Company," in Itō, pp. vii–xxxi; and Itō, pp. 43–45.

of Japan's most famous Marxists worked alongside them, men like Sano Manabu, Ōgami Suehiro, Itō Ritsu, Nakanishi Kō, and others.[75]

Underlying this intellectual openness was both the tacit support of the state as well as a tolerance among intellectuals themselves for political diversity in their ranks. It was an intellectual establishment that had grown up in essential ways as a bulwark of empire. Yet this never meant that its members were simply the servants of state imperialism. The relationship between Sinologists and the state was a much more subtle and conflicted one. Intellectuals worked within a system with which they might disagree because they felt their work positively influenced imperial policy. Government bureaucrats tolerated political vipers in their midst because they felt it was the price they had to pay for good research.

The coexistence of rightists, leftists, and liberals characteristic of the Sinological establishment in the early phases of Japanese imperialism underwent a sharp transformation in the 1930s, as tolerance for any form of opposition shrunk. Although the ideological repression of the thirties happened alongside a crackdown on left-wing political organizations, the assault on academic freedom was qualitatively different from the mass arrests of Communists in 1928 and 1932–1933, which were consistent with a long-standing policy of government suppression that periodically turned violent. Repression in the academy reflected a shift in the balance between fear of subversive ideas on the one hand and the value placed on the benefits of intellectual freedom on the other. On an unprecedented scale, conservative bureaucrats and right-wing scholars now purged from the academy intellectuals such as Takigawa Yukitoki and Minobe Tatsukichi, whose teachings had long run counter to official orthodoxy. Thus, in the series of university incidents that punctuated the decade, scientific analysis of Japan's history, polity, and society came increasingly under attack.

Sinology was profoundly affected by this transformation of the academic environment. The expansion of the imperial project in Manchuria brought new pressures on Sinologists to cooperate, just as it opened up new opportunities for them. At the same time, the increasing limitations on freedom of expression forced Sinologists to maintain a show of public support for official government aims on the continent. Depending on political convictions, scholars responded to these changes in a variety of ways. In the last analysis, however, they had two options: mobilization or repression.

Probably the choice was easiest for those right-wing intellectuals such

75. Fogel, "Introduction," pp. xiii–xvi.

as Kyoto University professor Yano Jin'ichi, who had advocated a larger Japanese presence in Manchuria in the twenties. Immediately after the establishment of the puppet state, Yano packed his bags for Manchukuo, where he helped design the doctrine of the kingly way (*ōdō*) as the philosophical underpinning of the new state. He further aided the cause with a flurry of books, articles, and radio appearances publicizing *ōdō*. Inaba Iwakichi, a Manchurian-Korean history specialist who had written the official history of Korea for the governor general of the colony, also became a voluble proponent of the kingly way from his podium at Manchukuo's new state university, Manshū kenkoku daigaku. To mobilize the talents of men like these, the Foreign Ministry established the Japan Manchukuo Cultural Association and commissioned it to undertake research into Manchurian and Mongolian history. Research offices were set up at Tokyo University under the leadership of Manchurian-Korean history expert Ikeuchi Hiroshi, and at Kyoto University under the direction of eminent Sinologist Naitō Konan.[76]

For many left and liberal critics of Japanese expansion, however, to remain true to their beliefs meant the loss of a job or the threat of more serious punishment. Yanaihara Tadao, the liberal head of colonial studies at Tokyo University, was forced along with countless others to sit out the war years under intellectual house arrest. Articles Yanaihara published in *Chūō kōron* in late 1937 opposing military aggression in China incited a wave of protest from right-wing Tokyo Imperial University professors and brought pressure from the Ministry of Education on the university administration to oust him from his teaching position.[77] Under Yanaihara's successors, colonial studies at Tokyo Imperial University veered away from contemporary policy analysis into arcane debates over methodology and the burning question of whether colonial studies could be said to comprise an academic field or not.[78]

Although Yano Jin'ichi and Yanaihara Tadao took divergent paths in response to the suppression of the thirties, both remained faithful to political beliefs that they had held in the twenties. A whole segment of Japanese intellectuals, however, abandoned their former faiths, suddenly lending their support to a policy of imperial aggression in China that was in total violation of the anti-imperialist positions they had previously cham-

76. Fogel, *Politics and Sinology*, pp. 255–259.

77. Asada, *Nihon shokuminchi kenkyū shiron*, pp. 499–505; Hara Kakuten, p. 73.

78. Hara Kakuten, pp. 73–75.

pioned. From their own descriptions of their activities in the 1930s, these *tenkōsha*, or converts, as they were known, divide into two categories: those who truly believed in official goals for Manchukuo, and those who feigned support in order to continue public life.[79]

Sinologist Tachibana Shiraki was an example of a genuine *tenkōsha*. A pioneering Marxist analyst of Chinese society in the twenties, Tachibana had sympathized deeply with the Chinese revolution and nationalist goals. Yet in the journal he started in 1931, Tachibana showed himself to have become an ardent supporter of Manchukuo, believing that in the multi-ethnic state promised by the "harmony of the five races" (*gozoku kyōwa*), the downtrodden Chinese peasantry would find liberation from rapacious landlords and Japanese expansionism would make peace with Chinese nationalism. These ideas meshed well with the Manchukuo government propaganda directed toward the native population, which portrayed the puppet government rescuing the Chinese masses from the depredations of Zhang Xueliang. Tachibana eventually grew disenchanted with state management of Manchukuo, discovering that *gozoku kyōwa* in theory and the harmony of the five races in practice bore little resemblance. Yet, although Tachibana's journal, *Manshū hyōron*, became a forum for his measured criticism of the way state ideals were being put into practice, Tachibana continued to support the idea of Manchukuo until his arrest in the mass roundup of liberals and leftists in 1942 and 1943.[80]

Unlike Tachibana's sincere change of heart, other left-wing Sinologists

---

79. Mobilization of intellectuals by promoting *tenkō* was an outgrowth of a police strategy for reintegrating detained political activists into society. To secure release, the prisoner had to renounce his or her left-wing views and declare support for the state. Beginning with the prison recantations of Communists Sano Manabu and Nabeyama Sadachika in 1933, a *tenkō* wave decimated the left. Many followed suit by undergoing an informal *tenkō*, in other words practicing self-censorship and becoming supportive of state policies in order to keep positions and avoid arrest: Henry Dewitt Smith II, *Japan's First Student Radicals* (Cambridge: Harvard University Press, 1972), pp. 202–204, 221–222, 247–259; Kazuko Tsurumi, *Social Change and the Individual: Japan before and after Defeat in World War II* (Princeton: Princeton University Press, 1966), pp. 29–79; Shunsuke Tsurumi, *An Intellectual History of Wartime Japan, 1931–1945* (London: Routledge and Kegan, 1986), pp. 10–11; and Shisō no kagaku kenkyūkai, ed., *Kyōdō kenkyū, tenkō*, 3 vols. (Heibonsha, 1959–1962).

80. Nakanishi Katsuhiko, "Tachibana Shiraki no shisō keisei: tokō dōki to no kakawari de," *Hōgaku zasshi*, vol. 22, no. 1 (September 1975), pp. 27–48; Johnson, *An Instance of Treason*, p. 17; Yamamoto Hideo, *Tachibana Shiraki* (Chūō kōron-sha, 1977), pp. 196–275.

made "disguised conversions" (*gisō tenkō*). They gave public support to the army's advance into China in the hopes that by working within the system their efforts could somehow stop the military takeover of the government or mitigate the assault on China. Men like Nakanishi Kō and Ozaki Hotsumi underwent such *gisō tenkō* and used their positions as cover for anti-war activities. While conducting research for Mantetsu, Nakanishi secretly worked for the Japanese Communist Party, cooperating with the Chinese Communist movement on the continent.[81] Ozaki became an operative for the Comintern. As Chalmers Johnson argues in his biography, Ozaki felt the best way to help his country was to hasten the end of the war and promote revolution in Asia.[82] Other Marxist scholars followed the example of Ōgami Suehiro. While working for Mantetsu's Research Department, Ōgami tried to use the Kwantung Army as an agent of what he called revolution from above. Calculating that his own hopes for improving the lot of the Chinese peasantry and Kwantung Army desires for increased food production could both be met by the transformation of the semifeudal system of agricultural production, Ōgami attempted to gain army interest in reducing land rents and other measures that would raise the producer's return on agriculture.[83]

Whatever their motivations, and whether their conversions were genuine or not, *tenkōsha* like Tachibana, Ozaki, Nakanishi, and Ōgami provided intellectual support for imperialism in their capacity as researchers and scholars. Collectively they made a great impact on the intellectual underpinnings of empire. This impact was mediated through their participation in the state think tanks like Mantetsu's Research Department, the Shōwa kenkyūkai, and the Cabinet Planning Board's ancillary Tōa kenkyūjo, all of which became the loci of economic planning in the empire during the late thirties.

In the late thirties, these state think tanks had no trouble mobilizing scholars. Earl Kinmonth's research has shown that the job market in Manchuria was a bonanza for university graduates. In striking contrast to the job shortage of the 1920s, student newspapers at Tokyo University, Kyoto

81. Miyanishi Yoshio, "Mantetsu chōsabu to Ozaki Hotsumi, Nakanishi Kō, Himori Torao (I)," no. 18 of "Mantetsu chōsabu kankeisha ni kiku," *Ajia keizai* 28, no. 7 (July 1987), p. 51.

82. Johnson, *An Instance of Treason*, pp. 4–5.

83. Ishidō, Noma, Nonomura, and Kobayashi, pp. 35–36; Miwa Takeshi, "Manshū sangyō kaihatsu einen keikakuan to keizai chōsakai (II)," no. 14 of "Mantetsu chōsabu kankeisha ni kiku," *Ajia keizai* 28, no. 3 (March 1987), pp. 79–81.

University, and Waseda University jubilantly recorded opportunities without limit for the educated job seeker in Manchuria.[84] Particularly as the political crackdown in the universities proceeded, drying up prospects in domestic academic institutions, progressive scholars took advantage of their school connections and flocked to the Manchurian research organizations and state think tanks. After its establishment in 1939, the Cabinet Planning Board's Tōa kenkyūjo quickly lined up 200 full-time researchers; by 1943 it had 1,000 specialists working for it.[85] At its peak, Mantetsu's Research Department had some 2,200 to 2,300 staff members, many of them progressive scholars.[86] As a former researcher at Mantetsu recalled, "When the Enlarged Research Department was founded in 1939, leftists from Japan were entering Mantetsu one after another. A number of these were quite well known: Horie Muraichi, Okazaki Jirō, Itō Kōdō, Yamaguchi Shōgo, Fujiwara Sadamu, Kawasaki Misaburō, Hiradate Toshio, Gushima Kenzaburō, Ishidō Kiyotomo, Ishida Seiichi, Motani Koichirō, Nonomura Kazuo, Andō Jirō, Toki Tsuyoshi, Satō Hiroshi, Ishikawa Masayoshi, Suzuki Shigetoshi, Nishi Masao, Hosokawa Karoku, Ozaki Hotsumi, and Itō Ritsu, among others."[87]

While it might seem strange that the Manchukuo government hired leftists in such large numbers, it did so because of the enormous demand that the controlled economy placed on good research. The state needed social scientists with expertise in China and a good percentage of Japan's trained Sinologists also happened to be left-wing in their political orientation. Moreover, the left-wing cast of the Manchukuo research organizations was enhanced by the double impact of wartime mobilization and wartime repression on the labor market at home. By the late 1930s, wartime mobilization had created a labor shortage for university graduates in Japan. Candidates still seeking work, therefore, were likely to have been those dislodged from their positions by ideological repression in the academy—that is, leftists.

Working for Mantetsu, left-wing, anti-imperialist intellectuals helped draw up the plans for the Economic Construction Program in Manchukuo that started Japan on the road to economic autarky and the absorption of China and Southeast Asia. At the request of the Kwantung Army, Man-

---

84. Earl H. Kinmonth, "The Impact of Military Procurements on the Old Middle Classes in Japan, 1931–1941," *Japan Forum* 4, no. 2 (October 1992), pp. 247–250.

85. Hara Kakuten, p. 103.

86. Ishidō Kiyotomo, "Mantetsu chōsabu wa nan de atta ka (II)," p. 55.

87. Itō, p. 173.

tetsu set up the Keizai chōsakāi (Economic Research Association) in 1932 to provide research and planning support for army policy. Army officers referred to the Keizai chōsakai as a "god-sent child" (*mōshigo*) because of the unexpected cooperation they received from its researchers. Commenting on the changes in Mantetsu after the establishment of Manchukuo, former researcher Noma Kiyoshi recalled the atmosphere at the newly created Keizai chōsakai. Men who disliked the Kwantung Army's attitude and had opposed the occupation, Noma noted, "suddenly began to attack their work with a fanatical gusto." He explained this contradiction in terms of the researchers' sense that they finally had an opportunity to use their knowledge and experience to some purpose—to see their ideas actually being put into practice.[88]

Like other state think tanks, the viability of the Keizai chōsakai was premised on an unspoken quid pro quo between researchers and the Manchukuo government. In return for publicly supporting state goals and carrying out research and planning projects desired by the Kwantung Army, intellectuals were permitted to do their own research as well. Army officers tolerated the Marxist debates which raged in the pages of *Manshū keizai nenpō;* Ōgami was allowed to examine labor relations in Japanese factories; and Amano Motonosuke was able to carry out village studies that aimed to determine the present stage of capitalism in Manchuria.[89] These were published and circulated, in the standard practice for Mantetsu studies, among the community of China scholars in Japan and the empire. Thus Manchukuo provided one of the most stunning examples of the uneven application of political censorship in the 1930s, for while academics in Japanese universities at home were being jailed for seemingly mild critiques of the political system, Sinologists in Manchuria freely expressed unabashedly revolutionary sentiments toward the empire.

The bizarre cooperation between anti-Communist officers and anti-imperialist Marxists was a trademark of the state research organizations of the thirties in both Japan and Manchuria. Although right-wing civilians and bureaucrats managed to conscribe the political limits of expression within the academy, what they accomplished, in effect, was not the elimination of the left, but simply its transfer from the academy to the state itself. As progressive intellectuals ejected from the universities moved into

---

88. Ishidō, Noma, Nonomura, and Kobayashi, pp. 22–23.

89. Itō, p. 112; Ishidō, Noma, Nonomura, and Kobayashi, pp. 31–34; Imai Seiichi, "Mantetsu chōsabu ni kansuru sancho o megutte," *Ajia keizai* 28, no. 11 (November 1987), pp. 95–96.

government think tanks, the tensions between right and left that had formerly expressed themselves through open academic debate now reemerged within policy deliberations in the coded language of *tenkō*. Differences between the various parties were managed by what amounted to a policy of intellectual appeasement: each thought to control the other by cooperation.

In the context of the war, left-wing intellectuals were clear losers in the contest over who was using whom. However much they consoled themselves with the idea that they could use their positions to check army aggression, in the end their work only abetted the military cause. The efforts of Miki Kiyoshi, the philosopher laureate of the New Order and a central figure in the Shōwa kenkyūkai, was a case in point. Miki's "East Asian Cooperative Community" (Tōa kyōdōtai), intended as a formula for promoting peace, in fact provided ideological rationalization for the economic absorption of Manchuria and China. Framing goals to conform with Miki's formula, researchers of the East Asian Economic Bloc Study Group and the China Problem Department drew up policy alternatives for mobilizing Chinese resources to feed the Japanese war machine and expand the front farther south.[90]

Mantetsu's researchers and Sinologists staffing Shōwa kenkyūkai committees tried to provide analyses that took account of the force of Chinese nationalism and advised that military aggression would just make problems worse. The "Investigation of the Resistance Capacity of the Chinese" that was begun in 1938, one of the enormous "integrated" research projects undertaken by Mantetsu at the close of the decade, aimed to convince the army of this point as forcefully as possible. Preparing the ten-volume report absorbed the energies of more than thirty researchers operating out of offices in Shanghai, Dalian, Nanjing, Hankou, Guangzhou, Tokyo, Hong Kong, and elsewhere. Under the general editorship of Japanese Communist Party operative Nakanishi Kō, the report submitted to the Kwantung Army in 1940 argued, among other things, that the Japanese invasion had forced an alliance between the Communists and the Nationalists; that the war was weakening the organizational strength of the Nationalists and boosting that of the Communists; that the real bases of resistance were in an economically self-sufficient countryside; and that the dependence of Japanese-occupied coastal cities on supplies from the rural hinterland made

90. Johnson, *An Instance of Treason*, pp. 119, 122–124; Fletcher, *The Search for a New Order*, p. 123.

prospects for holding these areas bleak.[91] In short, the report asserted that Japan could not win the war with China militarily. But when Nakanishi presented the research team's findings with the recommendation that Japan end the war politically to general staff headquarters in Tokyo, he was greeted with silence and finally one question from a young staff officer: "So, then, what sites would it be best for us to bomb? I'd like to know the key points." Although the army was, at this time, seriously looking at ways to avoid a protracted war (if only through the elusive decisive strike), the defeatist conclusions of the report were soon brushed aside by the victory euphoria of the winter of 1941–1942.[92]

Although some were undoubtedly sincere, the efforts of Sinologists to control militarism from within did more to aid than to impede the army's cause. Even when packaged to convey a discouraging message to military leaders, research projects like the "Investigation of the Resistance Capacity of the Chinese" in fact provided data vital to wartime economic planning. This and other integrated research projects undertaken in the late 1930s— studies of inflation in the Japan-Manchuria-China bloc, reorganization of the wartime economy, availability of strategic resources for Japan in the yen bloc, and the location of industry—all gave army planners the information they needed to push forward with plans for total war and mobilization of China's economic resources.[93]

In hindsight, the thought that intellectuals could blunt the edge of military aggression in China by cooperation seems infeasible, doomed by their subordinate status within an army-dominated colonial state. Yet when compared to the choices available for someone attempting to oppose the military advance on the continent, the idea of working within the system in Manchukuo seems less absurd. Unlike provisions for Italian and German dissidents, the Japanese exclusion law prevented flight to the United States. This left two choices. One could return to Japan, organize, and speak out against the China War until thrown in jail; or, one could sit out the war in silent noncooperation. Given the options, remaining in Manchukuo seemed a reasonable decision to some.

In the sense that they failed to halt the China War, and may even have helped advance it, the decision to stay backfired. But in a host of other ways, the presence of so many revolution-minded intellectuals in the gov-

91. Fogel, "Introduction," pp. xvii–xxi; John Young, pp. 23–24.
92. Fogel, "Introduction," p. xxi; Itō, p. 177.
93. John Young, pp. 12–23.

ernment altered the course of empire building in the Northeast. No less than the impact of idealistic technocrats on Manchukuo's cityscapes, the revolutionary vision of left-wing China hands helped shape the political ideology and the social policies of the puppet state.

THE REVOLUTIONARY STATE OF MANCHUKUO

Out of this odd collaboration between right and left in the Manchukuo government came the plan for the new colonial state and its relationship to Chinese civil society. From the pens of the revolutionary intellectuals who constructed the ideological profile of the new state emerged a picture of a radical new kind of imperialism. Shedding off the venality, despotism, and exploitation that had given empires a bad name, to these scholar-activists, Manchukuo signaled the birth of a remade imperialism. Conceptions of the Manchukuo state accommodated the competing demands of Japanese domination and Chinese nationalism, democracy, and imperial rule. Visionaries of empire imagined, moreover, that in Manchukuo imperialism would become the agent of social revolution, putting modern economic power in the hands of a feudally exploited peasantry. Thus wishful revolutionaries projected a lifetime of hopes onto their puppet state, believing that they, themselves, held the power to make revolution in China.

Revolutionary appeals had inspired "men of purpose" (*shishi*) to support expansion and fight the good fight in Asia since the early years of empire. Japanese pan-Asianism had a long-standing tradition of "continental adventurers" (*tairiku rōnin*) who intervened in Asian politics on the side of reform and revolution. Such men had backed the progressive party of Kim Ok-kiun in the political struggles between reaction and reform in Korea in the 1880s, had conspired with Sun Zhongshan (Sun Yat-sen) to foment revolution in China in the first decade of the twentieth century, and had plotted with Mongol and Manchu aristocrats to create an independent Manchu state in Northeast China in 1911.[94] While Western imperialists justified their actions by invoking a civilizing mission composed of pseudoscientific racism and the imperatives of Christian evangelism, in Japan a "yellow man's burden" called on right-minded Japanese to participate in what promised to be a historic transformation on the continent, as Japan became the architect of Asian revolution.

94. Jansen, *The Japanese and Sun Yat-sen*, pp. 41–49, 83–130, 137–140.

The idea of revolutionary imperialism that emerged in the 1930s, however, went beyond the heritage of Meiji imperialism. Of course, much of what was said simply recycled the notion of exporting revolution—the familiar image of Japanese interventions helping to bring about the overthrow of reactionary forces in East Asia. But in the context of Manchukuo the language of revolution assumed new meaning specific to its time. Stung by the accusations that Chinese nationalists brought against Japan in the 1920s, Japanese labored the rhetoric of empire to make the idea of pan-Asianism and Sino-Japanese cooperation ring true. Moreover, in Manchukuo they elevated the doctrine of a revolutionary imperialism to the position of orthodoxy for the first time. In the past, pan-Asian revolutionaries had operated on the outskirts of official policy; now "revolution" became the official mission of the colonial state.

No one was more active in proselytizing for the revolutionary new state than Tachibana Shiraki, editor of the influential *Manshū hyōron* and well connected within both the Kwantung Army and Mantetsu. Tachibana had resided in China for much of his journalistic career and was on hand to observe both the military occupation and the creation of the puppet state. As noted earlier, Tachibana was one of the more prominent *tenkōsha;* before he became a propagandist for the puppet government, he had tracked the course of the class struggle in China with great sympathy for the Communist party. Even after his ideological conversion, he remained a conscientious scholar and certainly continued to consider himself a friend of the Chinese people. Although in 1932 he witnessed the imposition—through force—of Japanese military administration over the Manchurian Chinese, his writings told a story of liberation and popular empowerment. In the ideology Tachibana helped create for the puppet state, Manchukuo's legitimacy lay in this revolutionary mission. In hindsight this claim may seem vacuous and self-serving, but at the time Tachibana seemed to believe that what was good for the Kwantung Army was providential for the Chinese masses.

One of the first themes Tachibana helped weave into Manchukuo's revolutionary mantle was a purported foundation in the Chinese liberation movement. According to a story circulated by Kwantung Army officers, Manchurian Chinese had grown tired of the disruption of China's civil wars and the transformation of their land into the "Balkans of the Far East." During the 1920s, therefore, disgruntled Chinese adopted the slogan *hokyō anmin*—"secure the borders; pacify the people"—and began to demand that Manchuria be sealed off from China south of the Great Wall.

The Japanese military officers who agitated for Manchurian autonomy in late 1931 and 1932 claimed to be acting in the name of this indigenous independence movement.

As Tachibana explained the Manchurian liberation movement, the Chinese masses and the Japanese found common cause in their loathing of the warlord regime of Zhang Xueliang. The *hokyō anmin* movement had emerged when the various ethnic groups of Northeast China and their constituent social classes—landlords and allied merchants, tenants and agricultural laborers, the working class and lumpen proletariat—had come to understand "consciously and unconsciously" that in spite of "differing social circumstances" they were bound together by their "common interest" in ridding themselves of Zhang. The fact that the Japanese shared "the same dream for different reasons" meant that by working together Japanese and Chinese could achieve the establishment of an independent state.[95] With this small rhetorical contrivance, Tachibana put the key elements of Manchukuo's founding myth in place: a Sino-Japanese alliance for independence and mass Chinese support for Zhang's ouster.

Tachibana's narrative of liberation sketched out the goals of the *hokyō anmin* movement in terms of sweeping and noble abstractions. As he declared expansively, the movement championed local autonomy against central power, pacifism against militarism, an agrarian against an industrial economy, and agrarian democracy against semifeudal tyranny. In this world where the forces of progress battled the forces of reaction, the *hokyō anmin* movement represented revolutionary opposition to Zhang Xueliang and his "regime born of the queer alliance between the bourgeoisie and semifeudal tyranny," despite what Tachibana admitted was a "social base among the wealthy rural landlord class."[96] It was dramatic language, but the message was simple: big landlords were the heroes leading the Chinese masses to liberation against the opposition of warlords and capitalists. The irony of this scenario was, of course, that it cast as agents of revolution the most reactionary elements of the old regime. The wealthy rural landlords, the warlord clique, and the bourgeoisie they were alleged to oppose were in fact one and the same, for there existed no clear demarcation between landholding, commercial, and manufacturing capital in Manchuria.

In the economy of the predominantly agricultural Northeast, wealthy landlords operated the warehouses and general-goods stores that domi-

95. Yamamoto Hideo, *Tachibana Shiraki*, p. 203.
96. Ibid., p. 205.

nated rural commerce. They also served as local bankers and often had investments in agricultural-processing industries. Before 1931 they tended to be politically allied with warlord armies, both those of Zhang Xueliang as well as strongmen in Jilin and Heilongjiang provinces. Though political patrons of the warlords were often rewarded with land grants and other favors, they were also forced to finance the frequent wars. Such patronage relationships were never very strong; loyalty ebbed and flowed, subject to the shifting sands of warlord alliances. In 1932 some Chinese landlords stood with Zhang and some went over to the Japanese, becoming collaborators in the puppet state. Tachibana, however, cast these opportunists as the protagonists of revolution, a suggestion almost as preposterous as the label "bourgeois" for Zhang Xueliang. The forced logic of his argument reflected a desperation on Tachibana's part to furnish Manchukuo with revolutionary credentials. Tachibana and the other China hands who helped construct the ideology for the new state needed to convince themselves that Japan's military interventions were liberating the Chinese masses, for this would justify all.

Another element in the ideological trappings of the new state was the doctrine of "kingly way," or *ōdō*, which like *hokyō anmin* assumed a revolutionary pretense. The idea of *ōdō* had a long currency in Japanese political tradition but was appealing in this context because of its origins in Chinese philosophy. The Chinese term for "kingly way," *wang dao*, was based on the classical Confucian concept of sage statesmanship, which legitimated imperial rule by positing the ruler as the mediator between heaven and earth—an intermediary between god and the people. Confucian political philosophy juxtaposed the leadership style of *ōdō* with *hadō*—the military way. Whereas the sage-king ruled by virtuous example, his military counterpart ruled through force. In the teens and twenties, Japanese began to play with the idea of *ōdō* as an alternative to European models of political leadership in China. During World War I, members of the Terauchi cabinet had appropriated the Confucian rubric of "kingly way" to describe a new Japanese diplomatic initiative in China. Japan could lead China more effectively, they asserted, by employing the virtues of conciliatory, economic diplomacy than by threatening force, as had the previous cabinet.[97] In the 1920s, Japanese Sinologists like Tachibana as well as Chinese revolutionaries like Sun Zhongsha had revived the idea

97. Terauchi was criticizing the gunboat diplomacy of the Ōkuma cabinet for its presentation of the Twenty-one Demands to China. I am indebted to Arthur Tiedemann for calling this usage of *ōdō* to my attention.

of *ōdō/wang dao* as the basis of a program for political transformation more suited to Chinese conditions than the Marxist formula for proletarian revolution. These various readings of *ōdō* as an Asian political tradition of reform and revolution were brought together in the conceptualization of the Manchukuo polity. Japanese used the doctrine of the "kingly way" to justify the restoration of the deposed Qing emperor Pu Yi onto a Manchurian throne.

Again, the chain of logic bringing Tachibana to the conclusion that the restoration of imperial rule was a revolutionary act had a certain forced quality. The first link was identifying the new head of state as the "sage-king" of Confucian lore. Tachibana argued that overthrowing the despotic warlord government of Zhang Xueliang had cleared the way for the "moralization of politics" through the enlightened rule of Pu Yi, the twentieth-century incarnation of the sage-king. In acting to "protect the livelihood of the people," the loyal Japanese ministers of Pu Yi in the Manchukuo government would oversee the "realization of the Confucian ideal of the society of great unity [*daidō*]."[98] Under the enlightened absolutism of Pu Yi's kingly way—and here was the second link—feudal institutions could be transformed from instruments of oppression to instruments of liberation. According to Tachibana, this social alchemy was quite simple: feudalism became liberating when "the people are emancipated from the shackles of feudal despotism and left free to live according to their traditional principles and self-governing institutions."[99]

The key to Tachibana's *ōdō* system and the final logical step that tied restoration to revolution was the relationship between local self-government (*jichi*) and the kingly way (*ōdō*). In his vision, the good life (the great unity of *daidō*) was truly achieved when the people lived by *jichi* alone. At such time society would become self-sufficient and self-regulating. The virtuous ruler could withdraw from the enterprise of statesmanship, and sage rule would simply wither away. However, when the structures of local society failed to ensure the welfare of the people, statesmanship was needed to strengthen the powers of local self-governing institutions. This explained why, despite *ōdō*'s mandate for a "decentralized self-governing state," Tachibana supported the creation of a centralized, authoritarian, and activist state for the foreseeable future.[100]

To *hokyō anmin* and *ōdō* was added *minzoku kyōwa*—"racial har-

98. Yamamoto Hideo, *Tachibana Shiraki*, p. 206; Nakanishi Katsuhiko, p. 46.
99. Yamamoto Hideo, *Tachibana Shiraki*, pp. 206–207.
100. Ibid., pp. 222–224.

mony"—to complete Manchukuo's triad of revolutionary credentials. This rubric pledged the commitment of the new state to political revolution in addition to "national" (but in reality provincial) liberation. Under the slogan *minzoku kyōwa*, the Manchukuo puppet state was trumpeted as the wellspring of an entirely new political structure that promised to extend power to the Chinese peasantry and bring it into the embrace of the state. The origin of this idea was a group of Japanese Mantetsu employees who called themselves the Manchurian Youth League (Manshū seinen renmeikai) and who lobbied for Manchurian independence in the late 1920s. As the Manchurian Youth League defined the banner of their movement, *minzoku kyōwa* bitterly opposed parliamentary politics, the anti-Japanese movement, and Japanese racial prejudice, in that order.[101] Instead, the *minzoku kyōwa* movement proposed a "multiracial polity in which Chinese, Manchus, Mongols, Koreans, and Japanese" would "cooperate" as "equal citizens in a self-governing unit." This new political structure would permit "Chinese and Japanese to mix harmoniously in a single society" where "human beings loved one another" and which would bring to reality the "ideal of coexistence and coprosperity."[102] In July 1932 *minzoku kyōwa* became the guiding vision of the newly created Chinese mass political organization called the Kyōwakai, or Concordia Association, as well as a cornerstone of the new state.

The Kyōwakai was created as part of the Kwantung Army's strategy to eliminate resistance to the new regime and extend its political control over Chinese society. Initially set up as a propaganda and information-gathering agency, the Kyōwakai was intended to complement the network of peace and preservation committees which organized cities, towns, and villages into neighborhood units responsible collectively for maintaining order within their jurisdictions. Headquartered in Xinjing, the organization had branches and local units throughout the country. The Kwantung Army worked to recruit landlords, merchants, and other members of the local

101. For the formation of the Manchurian Youth League and the ideology of racial harmony, see Matsuzawa Tetsunari, "Manshū jihen to 'minzoku kyōwa' undo," *Kokusai seiji* 43, no. 1 (1970), pp. 77–99, esp. pp. 96–99; and David George Egler, "Japanese Mass Organizations in Manchuria, 1928–1945: The Ideology of Racial Harmony," Ph.D. dissertation, University of Arizona, 1977, pp. 78–146. See also voluminous publications of Yamaguchi Jūji, founding member and primary pamphleteer of the Manchurian Youth League, e.g., Yamaguchi Jūji, *Manshū kenkoku to Minzoku kyōwa shisō no genten* (Osaka: Ōminato shobō, 1976); and Yamaguchi Jūji, *Shiryō Manshū kenkoku e no isho daiichibu: minzoku kyōwa kara Tōa renmei e Ishiwara Kanji totomoni* (Osaka: Ōminato shobō, 1980).

102. Matsuzawa, p. 97.

elite to join the Kyōwakai and collaborate with the new regime; by 1934 the party boasted 300,000 members. At first, the Kyōwakai concentrated on promoting and publicizing the new regime as well as soliciting the views of the local elite on government policy, thus trying to instill enthusiastic support for Manchukuo among the native ruling class.[103]

Japanese publicists heralded the Kyōwakai as a pioneering political form that could overcome the trials besetting Japan in China. In their eyes, the Kyōwakai rejected bourgeois Western-style democracy in favor of a single-party system where "representatives . . . truly express the opinions of the multitude"; where "councils . . . come to a conclusion by unanimity"; where "people say frankly what they think to officials"; where "officials get people to understand what they intend to do"; and where "both the people and the officials cooperate." The institutional structure of the Kyō-wakai was essentially autocratic: it was tightly controlled from the center through appointments of local representatives and a unilateral establishment of the political agenda. The language of "natural leadership," "consensus decision making," and "unity of the officials and the people" in Japanese propaganda pamphlets, however, gave the Kyōwakai a populist gloss.[104]

Whether or not the Chinese elite were taken in by this rhetoric, the stated political goals of the Kyōwakai appealed strongly to progressive Japanese intellectuals. China hands like Tachibana who were sympathetic to Chinese nationalist aspirations had faced a difficult choice when the Chinese nationalist movement began to focus its energies against Japanese imperialism—would they betray Chinese aspirations or their own national loyalties? Rejecting the principle of racial self-determination, the formula of a multiracial state resolved their dilemma, constructing an alternative to the two-sided struggle between Japanese imperialism and Chinese nationalism. As Tachibana insisted, Japanese were "by no means the only race who were the founders or even the essential constituents of the new state"; "of course Chinese were involved as were all other races."[105] This

103. Kazama Hideto, "Nōson gyōsei shihai," in Asada Kyōji and Kobayashi Hideo, eds., *Nihon teikokushugi no Manshū shihai: jūgonen sensō o chūshin ni* (Jichōsha, 1986), pp. 278–279.

104. Tomio Muto, "The Spirit of Hsieh-ho: A New Philosophy," *Manchuria* (20 July 1938), p. 7. This article was part of a special issue of *Manchuria* on the Kyōwakai and Japan's cultural activities in Manchukuo. The issue was entitled "Concordia and Culture in Manchukuo."

105. Yamamoto Hideo, ed., *"Manshū hyōron" kaidai: sōmokuji* (Fuji shuppan, 1982), pp. 14, 32–33.

was a comforting fiction, abetting the delusion that Manchukuo had ended Sino-Japanese conflict in the Northeast. Herein lay one of the central appeals of the Kyōwakai and the doctrine of "racial harmony": it allowed progressive Japanese intellectuals to believe that they could be patriots and friends of the Chinese people at the same time.

To Japanese progressives, the other principal attraction of the Kyōwakai was its promise to put political power in the hands of the Chinese masses whom they stereotyped and romanticized as a homogeneous, downtrodden peasantry, ripe for revolutionary enlightenment. Tachibana called the Kyōwakai "an attempt to create a society controlled by producers instead of capitalists."[106] In the overwhelmingly agricultural economy of Manchukuo, the producer class meant the peasants. As Tachibana envisioned it, the reorganization of Manchurian society along anarco-syndicalist lines would empower the toiling peasant masses; local councils of the Kyōwakai would provide a channel of communication between producer groups, the self-regulating village society (*jichi*), and the central government.[107] The prospect of participating directly in the political education and mobilization of the Chinese masses captivated many China hands. As one Mantetsu researcher recalled, "lots of idealists went into the Kyōwakai from Japan because they wanted to make contact with the Chinese people at the grass roots of society."[108] Deluding themselves that the Kyōwakai was an instrument of peasant empowerment, Japanese progressives seemed to feel that by working for it they had their fingers on the pulse of Chinese revolution.

Although the inherent difficulties of using an army of occupation as the instrument of peasant empowerment might have invited skepticism from the outset, Tachibana and his partners in revolution seemed genuinely shocked when the Kwantung Army reorganized the Kyōwakai in October 1934, to Tachibana's mind eliminating its revolutionary potential.[109] Indeed, transformed from a mass party into a vehicle for indoctrination and espionage, the Kyōwakai subsequently joined the military police (*kenpeitai*) to mobilize support for the puppet regime through counterinsurgency tactics.[110] In the restructured Kyōwakai, even the ideal of

106. Yamamoto Hideo, *Tachibana Shiraki*, p. 247.

107. Ibid., pp. 221–224.

108. Ishidō Kiyotomo, "Mantetsu chōsabu wa nan de atta ka (I)," no. 16 of "Mantetsu chōsabu kankeisha ni kiku," *Ajia keizai* 28, no. 5 (May 1987), p. 78.

109. Yamamoto Hideo, *Tachibana Shiraki*, p. 247.

110. For use of Kyōwakai for counterinsurgency, see Jones, pp. 50–54; Okabe, pp. 127–128; and Kazama, pp. 304–321. See also the study of Japanese counterinsurgency tactics commissioned by the Rand Corporation to aid in American war

racial equality fell by the wayside. A 1939 pamphlet on "Manchuria and Racial Harmony—For New Citizens" devoted an entire chapter to explaining "Japanese as the leading race."[111]

Yet, despite its obvious degeneration, many Japanese continued to hope that the Kyōwakai could be salvaged. Tachibana never completely lost faith and began writing again about the "liberating mission" of the Kyōwakai.[112] Revolution-minded Japanese continued to flock to the organization—to the extent that the Kwantung Army felt it necessary to carry out yearly purges to eliminate "red elements" from its ranks. Progressives who worked for the Kyōwakai told themselves they were "working for the good of the Chinese masses within the limits of what was possible." This might have settled the matter with their own consciences, but the Chinese peasants who were the object of their solicitude did not necessarily appreciate the subtleties of such moral calculations. Their judgments of any Japanese working with an army of occupation were harsh and unequivocal, as the story told by former Mantetsu researcher Ishidō Kiyotomo reveals: One of Ishidō's friends, described as a leftist and an idealist, had joined the Kyōwakai, like many others, "to work with the peasants." After managing to escape the red purges year after year, he was murdered in the end by Chinese villagers following Japan's defeat. As Ishidō remarked, "We need to think more about why it was that our good intentions . . . did not communicate to the Chinese masses."[113]

For Ishidō and his cohort, good intentions continued to define the essence of Manchukuo. Whether the new state was in fact able to achieve the prized political harmony between Japanese imperialists and their Chinese subjects was, in a sense, irrelevant because they measured Manchukuo's value against the nobility of the attempt itself. Japanese inscribed this noble dream with the trio of official slogans they created for Manchukuo: the founding myth of the *hokyō anmin* liberation movement, autonomy and self-government under the enlightened rule of *ōdō*, and a Sino-Japanese partnership in the political revolution of *minzoku kyōwa*. All this was designed, of course, as propaganda. It was a justification of Japan's new role in Northeast China that aimed to persuade fellow impe-

planning in Vietnam: Chong-sik Lee, *Counterinsurgency in Manchuria: The Japanese Experience, 1931–1940* (Santa Monica, Calif.: Rand Corporation, 1967).

111. Manshū teikoku kyōwakai chūō honbu, *Minzoku kyōwa no Manshūkoku shutoshite shin nyūMansha no tameni* (Manshū teikoku kyōwakai chūō honbu, 1939), p. 27.

112. Yamamoto Hideo, *Tachibana Shiraki*, pp. 260–261.

113. Ishidō Kiyotomo, "Mantetsu chōsabu wa nan de atta ka (I)," p. 78.

rialists, the Manchurian Chinese, and the Japanese themselves of Manchukuo's legitimacy. The message did not find much favor in places like the League of Nations, but among Japanese intellectuals it was tremendously appealing. However imperfectly realized, the doctrine of revolution set forth the high-minded ideals of empire in terms that demonstrated the virtues of imperialism. If no one else, they at least persuaded themselves that what mattered was the loftiness of their intentions rather than the shortcomings of their achievement.

THE LEFT AND THE SOCIAL LABORATORY OF EMPIRE

Social dreamers projected their hopes in many directions. Like the idea of a liberating colonial state, the vision of social transformation in Manchuria became a kind of magnet for displaced Japanese revolutionaries. Frustrated by the increasingly repressive atmosphere within Japan, left-wing intellectuals were drawn by opportunities for social activism in the new empire. Though affected by the pressures for ideological conformity issuing from the metropolis, geographical separation buffered Manchukuo and muted their impact. As Mantetsu researcher Hama Masao put it, "Between Japan and Manchuria there was an 'intellectual time-zone change.' "[114] This relative openness enhanced Manchukuo's appeal, making it appear all the more exciting—a place (unlike Japan) that welcomed new ideas, invited experimentation, and offered an open field to the creativity of city designers, artists, photographers, and left-wing academics. Even more attractive to leftists who were politically marginalized at home, Manchukuo offered power. Joining the bureaucracy of the new state, leftist intellectuals had an unprecedented opportunity to lay their hands on the levers of governmental authority: they were finally at the center of the action. Intellectuals took full advantage of their newfound power, moving quickly to put revolutionary ideas into practice. From their positions in Mantetsu and the Manchukuo government, they tried to turn the new empire into a kind of social laboratory, a controlled environment in which to test out theories of social transformation.

Proximity to the absolute power of the colonial state did not corrupt the leftists or lead them astray from the righteous path of revolution. Instead, it nurtured delusions of grandeur. Having witnessed the sputtering shifts and starts in the Chinese revolutionary movement since 1911, and particularly the debilitating clash between the Nationalist and Communist

114. Fogel, "Introduction," p. xvi.

parties in the twenties, Japanese leftists felt the Chinese were in need of assistance. Manchukuo provided a unique opportunity to come to their aid. Intellectuals believed that from their positions in the puppet state they could guide Northeast China to revolution. Undertaking a scientific analysis of the stage of capitalist development, a correct diagnosis of the obstacles to revolution, and a program for guided social change, they aimed to make Manchukuo a model for the Chinese to follow. Thus leftists imagined that by working for the puppet state they were helping teach their Chinese brothers the business of revolution, opening up a path to a just society out of the political morass the Chinese had created.

The ambition to make Manchukuo the cauldron of the Chinese revolution first took root in the context of a debate on the Manchurian economy. The *Manshū keizai ronsō*, as this debate was known, raged in the pages of Tachibana's *Manshū hyōron* (The Manchurian Review) and Mantetsu's *Manshū keizai nenpō* (Manchurian Economic Yearbook) between 1934 and 1936. The principal participants were Ōgami Suehiro, Nakanishi Kō, and Suzuki Kōhei, all men with long histories of involvement with the left-wing movement in Japan who were eventually arrested for similar crimes in Manchuria. These men considered themselves both activists and scholars; in their minds, therefore, the debate over these theoretical points was not mere armchair philosophizing, but the necessary first step to develop a strategy for social revolution.

The *Manshū keizai ronsō* did not emerge out of an intellectual vacuum, but essentially continued—in a different venue—the so-called debate on Chinese society (Chūgoku shakaishi ronsen). This earlier debate had been touched off by the debacle of the Chinese revolution of 1927–1928, when the attempt to unify the country under a united front of Nationalist and Communist parties culminated in Jiang Jieshi's bloody anti-Communist coup and the outbreak of civil war between the two forces. Focusing on China south of the Great Wall, the debate on Chinese society took up the "what went wrong" question and offered various diagnoses of the impediments to making revolution in China's agricultural society.[115] Given their concern with the fate of the Chinese revolution, it was significant that Japanese Sinologists abruptly shifted venue in 1934 and began to address the same question by looking at Manchuria. The inception of the *Manshū*

---

115. Nakajima Hōzō, "'Chūgoku shakaishi ronsen' ni kansuru chōsa," no. 15 of "Mantetsu chōsabu kankeisha ni kiku," *Ajia keizai* 28, no. 4 (April 1987), pp. 67–68; Itō, pp. 102–114.

keizai ronsō signaled their consideration of the Northeast as the new staging ground for the revolution.

Essays on the nature of capitalism in Manchuria by Ōgami, Nakanishi, and Suzuki revolved around the same key issue that had animated the earlier debate on Chinese society: Was the economy more properly characterized as feudal or capitalist? To prove that the underlying social structure was either feudalistic or capitalistic in nature, they argued over the significance of high land rents paid in kind, the stratification of the agricultural laboring class, and the existence of a labor market. They debated whether landlords' power to extract surplus from peasants was purely economic or whether a web of social pressures (extraeconomic coercion) held peasants in serflike bondage to landlords. They interpreted the landlord alternately as a capitalist investing in real estate and as a feudal baron working his lands. They haggled over the degree of integration into a world capitalist market and the significance of integration for the commercialization of the local economy, a point which hinged on the theoretical problem: Could a feudal productive system be integrated into a capitalist market? They regarded the role of foreign imperialism as either retarding capitalist development or promoting it, depending on how they evaluated the alliance between foreign and domestic capital and the strength of the links with the international market.[116]

These matters were important because they illuminated the critical problem of revolutionary strategy: prescriptions for correct social action had to be based on an accurate identification of the stage of capitalist development. For this reason, it was of overriding importance to decide whether Ōgami was right in asserting that despite certain capitalistic features the Manchurian economy remained feudalistic, or whether Nakanishi was more correct in arguing that despite feudal remnants Manchuria was essentially a capitalist economy. In the mechanistic formulas of Japa-

116. For discussion of these debates, see Asada, *Nihon chishikijin*, pp. 47–106, 187–312; Ishida Seiichi, "Kita 'Manshū' nōson ni okeru konō no seishitsu," no. 4 of "Mantetsu chōsabu kankeisha ni kiku," *Ajia keizai* 26, no. 7 (July 1985), pp. 57–75; Nakajima Hōzō, pp. 61–82; Miyanishi, "Mantetsu chōsabu to Ozaki Hotsumi, Nakanishi Kō, Himori Torao (I)," pp. 51–68; Miyanishi Yoshio, "Mantetsu chōsabu to Ozaki Hotsumi, Nakanishi Kō, Himori Torao (II)," no. 19 of "Mantetsu chōsabu kankeisha ni kiku," *Ajia keizai* 28, no. 8 (August 1987), pp. 76–93; Miwa Takeshi, "Keizai chōsakai kara chōsabu made (I)," no. 27 of "Mantetsu chōsabu kankeisha ni kiku," *Ajia keizai* 29, no. 9 (September 1988), pp. 67–91; and Miwa Takeshi, "Keizai chōsakai kara chōsabu made (II)," no. 28 of "Mantetsu chōsabu kankeisha ni kiku," *Ajia keizai* 29, no. 10 (October 1988), pp. 56–79.

nese Marxism, what often seemed torturous hairsplitting did, in fact, have method. Theory was needed to determine whether the program of social action called for a one-stage revolution of the proletariat or a two-stage bourgeois-to-proletarian revolution. It was needed to identify the protagonists of revolution from among the host of candidates: peasants, workers, native capital, the Communist party, the Nationalist party, or a united front. Only through thorough analysis could it be decided whether society was ripe for revolution and whether internal conditions had generated the revolutionary energy to spark social action from within or if external stimulation was required. If nothing else, the debate on the Manchurian economy furnished Japanese intellectuals with a clear answer to this last question: Manchuria needed an external push toward revolution, and Japanese imperialism could provide it. In this way, at least, the *Manshū keizai ronsō* had established the theoretical potential for social revolution in Manchuria.

These arguments went over familiar terrain for Japanese leftists. They had covered it not only in their debate on Chinese society but also in their analyses of the nature of capitalism within Japan itself. The interpretive division over whether the Manchurian economy was essentially feudal or essentially capitalist mirrored the split within Japanese Marxism between the *kōza* (Japan-as-feudal) and *rōnō* (Japan-as-capitalist) camps. Indeed, Marxist analyses of China, Manchuria, and Japan converged so precisely that a substitution of place-names would make them virtually interchangeable. The questions, the terms, the categories, the logic, and the points of debate were all identical. Such congruity suggested that the new interest in the revolutionary potential of Manchuria involved a double displacement: intellectuals were relocating both Chinese and Japanese revolutions to Manchuria. Just as the rupture of the Communist-Nationalist alliance in China stalled the revolution in China, the decimation of the Japanese Communist party in 1933 through mass arrests and a *tenkō* wave killed hopes for Japan. On the heels of this double disappointment, Japanese Sinologists began to take up the question: Could there be revolution in Manchuria? The rapidity of this shift revealed both the confusion and the optimism of Japanese Marxists as they cast about for a stage for Asian revolution. In their search the ground might shift beneath them, but their vision of social justice remained firm.

Having captured their imaginations, the idea of making revolution in Manchuria guided the actions of Japanese Sinologists as they began their work for the puppet state. A remarkable capacity for self-deception helped them ignore the disjunction between what they thought they were doing—liberating the masses—and what they were actually accomplishing—

tightening Japanese control over the masses. Recollections of these researchers present a romantic self-portrait of an intellectual version of the *tairiku rōnin,* the swashbuckling continental adventurer who operated in the exotic underworld of Asian political insurrection. Nakanishi Kō's memoirs, *In the Tempest of the Chinese Revolution,* recount in boastful detail his critical role as a freedom fighter on the continent.[117] In the revolutionary underground, researchers imagined themselves "discovering a new society" and believed they were "developing a closeness to the Chinese peasants, a sense of intimacy with the lives . . . not just of landlords or rich farmers but of the people who actually practiced agriculture."[118]

The contradiction between this romantic self-image and their role as servants of Japanese imperialism emerged with particular force in the context of a series of empirical village studies conducted by Mantetsu after 1935. The team that carried them out was from the agricultural section of Mantetsu's Economic Research Association (later reorganized into the Industrial Department and again into the Research Department), commissioned by the Kwantung Army–run Manchukuo government to undertake the surveys in order to aid in agricultural policy formation.[119] In spite of what intellectuals wanted to believe, the Manchukuo government's mandate to them was clear: find a way to squeeze more productivity out of agriculture.

Japanese village studies of Manchuria were carried out on a large scale, involving the efforts of many of Mantetsu's most talented researchers. Surveys were planned for every year through 1940, but the bulk of the research was done in 1935 and 1936 when some 40 villages were surveyed and 24 volumes of results published.[120] As the area under Japanese occu-

117. Nakanishi Kō, *Chūgoku kakumei no arashi no naka de* (Aoki shoten, 1974). Nakanishi also published his wartime correspondence with his wife under the equally dramatic title, *Writing from the Face of Death: Shi no kabe no naka kara: tsuma e no tegami* (Iwanami shoten, 1971). For an evaluation of Nakanishi's writings by colleagues, see Miyanishi, "Mantetsu chōsabu to Ozaki Hotsumi, Nakanishi Kō, Himori Torao (I)," pp. 56–57.

118. Noma Kiyoshi, " 'Manshū' nōson jittai chōsa ibun (I)," no. 1 of "Mantetsu chōsabu kankeisha ni kiku," *Ajia keizai* 26, no. 4 (April 1985), p. 73; and Noma Kiyoshi, " 'Manshū' nōson jittai chōsa ibun (II)," no. 2 of "Mantetsu chōsabu kankeisha ni kiku," *Ajia keizai* 26, no. 5 (May 1985), p. 83.

119. The Economic Research Association was reorganized during 1936 into the Industrial Department, and again in 1938 into the Research Department. See note 65 of this chapter.

120. The 1935 studies were carried out in sixteen prefectures in north Manchuria but were not published. The 1936 survey of twenty-one prefectures over much of South Manchuria was published in two series: Manshūkoku kokumuin

pation spread southward, village investigators soon followed. Mantetsu also produced an impressive volume of village studies on China in the late 1930s. In addition to the numerous articles brought out in journals like *Mantetsu chōsa geppō*, Mantetsu published 178 separate village studies between 1936 and 1942, many of which ran to multiple volumes. The village studies reached their peak with the ambitious project on agricultural customs of north China launched in 1940 and completed in 1942, the scholarly value of which is highly regarded even today.[121] Together these village studies comprised the intellectual product of a host of scholar-activists, men who envisioned themselves as the intellectual foot soldiers of the revolution.

For the researchers, the starting point of their investigations was the theoretical debate over Manchuria's revolutionary potential set forth in the *Manshū keizai ronsō*. Recalling the "soaring interest in village studies within the ranks of Mantetsu," one former employee explained that researchers were inspired by the desire to prove Ōgami right and "reveal the semifeudal character of Manchurian farm villages."[122] As they collected data for the puppet state, Sinologists imagined they were amassing information vital to the course of the revolution.

With Suzuki Kōhei's treatise *The Structure of Manchurian Agriculture* as their bible, Japanese researchers boldly set out to assay the revolutionary potential of Chinese society—flanked by a mounted security force to protect them from "anti-Japanese elements." Although this force undoubtedly added to the sense of high drama, nothing illustrated more clearly the researchers' relationship to the Japanese colonial state. It was typical for a survey party of six or seven to travel with five to six interpreters and ten to twenty cavalry soldiers—and this was in parts of Manchuria considered safe. Any area regarded as even slightly questionable was placed off limits to research teams.[123] Adventure, in any case, lost its appeal in the face of the real discomforts of life among the masses. As one participant recounted,

---

jitsugyōbu rinji sangyō chōsakyoku, *Keitoku 3 nendo nōson jittai chōsa hōkokusho*, 4 vols. (1936), and Manshūkoku kokumuin jitsugyōbu rinji sangyō chōsakyoku, *Keitoku 3 nendo nōson jittai chōsa ippan chōsa hōkokusho*, 20 vols. (1936): Ishida, p. 59.

121. Noma Kiyoshi and Fukushima Masao, "Chūgoku nōson kankō chōsa (I)," no. 10 of "Mantetsu chōsabu kankeisha ni kiku," *Ajia keizai* 27, no. 4 (April 1986), p. 11; John Young, pp. 429–454; Fogel, "Introduction," pp. xvi–xvii.

122. Noma, "'Manshū' nōson jittai chōsa ibun (I)," pp. 62–67; and Noma, "'Manshū' nōson jittai chōsa ibun (II)," p. 76.

123. Noma, "'Manshū' nōson jittai chōsa ibun (II)," pp. 76, 83.

"we brought our own food and had it prepared according to our recipes. But the Chinese cook always made it too greasy. Probably because of the food, even the more adventurous types had had it after about a week. The atmosphere got pretty tense—it was all we could do to prevent bickering."[124] Dashing self-images notwithstanding, the revolutionary commitment of village researchers was undone within a week by a peevish intolerance for greasy food, squalid accommodations, and their own wearing company.

Rationalizing their relationship with the colonial state, former researchers used such phrases as "moral sense," "integrity," "purely motivated," or "good judgment" to describe their impartial attitude. As Noma Kiyoshi explained, "we did not do the surveys because we thought they were useful for policy—this was not our personal perspective. The term 'scholarly' is perhaps misleading but it captures the kind of pure and unsullied curiosity that was at the heart of our interest in the surveys and which fueled our passion for continuing even though the surveys were extremely wearing to the nerves."[125] Some went further, claiming that surveyists became champions of the peasantry. "We didn't face the peasants as representatives of the ruling class or government authority, but the opposite," maintained Suzuki Tatsuo. "We became advocates for the peasants with the provincial authorities."[126]

However much the surveyists may have wanted to believe that they could separate themselves from the colonial state, the cold truth was that they were collecting data to facilitate the making of Manchukuo agricultural policy, policy aimed to increase both Japanese control over and Japan's share of agricultural production. To peasants watching the survey team descend upon them with armed guards, the relationship must have seemed very clear indeed. In hindsight, former researchers realized that this explained the high degree of noncooperation with the surveys. As they recalled, Chinese peasants sometimes simply refused to answer questions and often employed the more subtle weapons of the weak: feigned forgetfulness, ignorance, or stupidity.[127]

Although when facing the peasants researchers found it convenient to ignore the implications of their relationship with the colonial state, under

124. Ibid., p. 76.
125. Noma, "'Manshū' nōson jittai chōsa ibun (I)," pp. 72–73.
126. Noma, "'Manshū' nōson jittai chōsa ibun (II)," p. 83.
127. Noma, "'Manshū' nōson jittai chōsa ibun (I)," p. 70; Noma, "'Manshū' nōson jittai chōsa ibun (II)," p. 76.

other circumstances they attached too much significance to their positions. For most researchers, Manchukuo was the first occasion in which they enjoyed such proximity to power; often it went to their heads. Nowhere was this more clear than in ambitions to use their influence over the government to promote, in Ōgami Suehiro's words, "revolution from above." The notion that through their limited access to Manchukuo officialdom and modest input in policy deliberations they could manipulate the Kwantung Army into piloting a social revolution in Manchuria was a monumental conceit. Such hubris cost them dearly in the end, when their efforts on behalf of the Chinese peasantry aroused the anti-Communist paranoia of the Kwantung Army and brought the iron fist of the colonial state down upon their own heads.

Believing that the land question held the key to social revolution in an agricultural society, the Mantetsu researchers first targeted the land tenure system in Manchurian villages. Since the villages had long been viewed as a social problem within Japan itself, researchers and policy makers were accustomed to thinking about the agricultural economy in terms of social structure—particularly landholding arrangements within a village. Throughout the twenties, advocates of land reform in Japan had proposed a succession of measures to bolster the position of tenants and encourage the growth of a stable yeoman-farmer class. In the face of landlord opposition, however, meaningful reform had proved impossible within Japan. Nevertheless, in reform proposals for Manchuria, Mantetsu researchers undertook to dislodge the oppressive hold of the landlords in the new empire in an attempt at "revolution from above."

Their first opportunity came in 1936, when the Kwantung Army requested that a Mantetsu committee prepare a draft proposal for a five-year development plan for Manchukuo. The committee, made up of Ōgami, Oshikawa Ichirō, Saitō Masao, Noma Kiyoshi, Yamanaka Jirō, and others, used meetings with Kwantung Army planners to press its case for agricultural reform. Arguing that the shortcomings of the first experiment with economic planning in Manchukuo (the "Outline of Economic Construction" initiated in March 1933) were due entirely to excessive attention to the industrial sector, Mantetsu scholars pressed hard for making "agricultural policy the foundation of industrial policy."[128] Initial suggestions that "the extremely complex land system be modernized to promote Manchurian socioeconomic development" were met with a positive response to

128. The committee's proposals were published as *Manshū einen keikaku shiryō:* Hara Kakuten, pp. 616–617, 621.

"gradualist reforms." Kwantung Army planners agreed that land reform was necessary in principle to "raise agricultural productivity and to create a pool of labor for the development of mining and manufacture and in this way to insure the smooth progress of industrial development."[129] Encouraged by the prospect of seeing a moderate reform package adopted, Ōgami temporarily abandoned ambitions for a comprehensive land reform. His proposals left the existing land-tenure system intact, advocating simply the state appropriation and sale of uncultivated lands in north Manchuria, the institution of agricultural cooperatives, the mechanization of agriculture, and the development of permanent tenancy rights.[130]

Despite these promising beginnings, and with the single exception of agricultural cooperatives, Mantetsu reform proposals were eliminated in the final round of revisions. In the words of the senior officer responsible, "These proposals will make the Manchurians in the government uneasy and stir them up. Moreover, the influence of such reforms on Japan would be very grave."[131] Thus, in the first attempt at revolution, Ōgami's conservative strategy met with failure. As he was told, land reform, no matter how watered down, was still a political taboo in both Manchuria and Japan. Although the argument that land reform in the empire would be intolerable to entrenched landlord interests at home was just an excuse, the danger it presented to "the Manchurians in the government" was very real and very problematic. This hazard existed for the simple reason that what Ōgami called the semifeudal social structure in the countryside still comprised the political-economic core of Manchukuo. Chinese landlords were the collaborators who manned the puppet regime; without them Manchukuo would collapse. The colonial state was not about to oversee a revolution that would ensure its own demise.

Even with these setbacks, would-be revolutionaries did not give up. Under the leadership of Satō Daishirō, another attempt at revolution from above was made through participation in an agricultural cooperative movement in north Manchuria. Starting as early as 1932, the Manchukuo government had experimented with using different forms of agricultural cooperatives as a means of increasing government control over local commerce and raising agricultural productivity. Each of these initiatives

129. Miwa Takeshi, "Manshū sangyō kaihatsu einen keikakuan to keizai chō-sakai (I)," no. 13 of "Mantetsu chōsabu kankeisha ni kiku," *Ajia keizai* 28, no. 1 (January 1987), pp. 64–66.
130. Ibid., p. 67.
131. Ibid.

involved limiting the power of landlord-owned *lian hao* (general-goods stores) in the local economy. A combination of commercial and loan capital, *lian hao* carried out a multitude of functions. These general-goods stores marketed consumer goods and agricultural inputs, purchased and stored agricultural produce, acted as money exchanges, and carried out basic agricultural processing, producing wine, bean cakes, flour, and oil. The strength of *lian hao* stemmed from combining assets through a guildlike organization that linked village stores to district stores and large central stores in the provincial capital. Because of their multifold activities and organizational structure, *lian hao* maintained a stranglehold on the local economy. The agricultural cooperative movement aimed to establish parallel financial and marketing networks that would bypass *lian hao* and link producers directly to the state.[132]

To Japanese revolutionaries, the cooperative movement offered a means to end the feudalistic oppression of the peasantry at the hands of *lian hao* by using state authority to bolster their economic power and independence. As Satō declared, "By organizing the impoverished peasant class we will support the development of true economic power. . . . In time when the organization begins to acquire real strength the organized peasant masses will become the popular foundation for a new kind of government authority which will be able to truly resolve the social problems of the village."[133] What Satō had in mind when he spoke of a final resolution of social problems was inspired by the physiocratic paradise of Japanese agrarian (*nōhonshugi*) romantics. He envisioned the cooperative movement not simply as the vehicle for economic empowerment of the most impoverished and exploited of the peasant class, but as the instrument for eliminating class divisions entirely. The cooperative organization would embrace "all peasants within a hamlet without regard to wealth or poverty, allowing the self-regulating community which had been warped by class divisions to develop and correct itself through the vehicle of the cooperative movement."[134]

Japanese organizers tended to rate the significance of the cooperative

132. Bix, "Japanese Imperialism and the Manchurian Economy," pp. 426–427. For an extended discussion of *lian hao*, see Iizuka and Kazama, "Nōgyō shigen no shūdatsu," pp. 255–326.

133. The original statement was made in the preface to Satō Daishirō's *Suikaken nōson kyōdō kumiai hōshin taikō* (1937). Quoted in Yamamoto Hideo, *Tachibana Shiraki*, p. 270.

134. Yamamoto Hideo, *Tachibana Shiraki*, p. 266.

movement and their own role in it very highly. They believed that their tiny campaign in one small segment of north Manchuria would show the way to an "Asian liberation movement built not by the proletariat but by the peasant masses . . . which would offer an ideological alternative to a Western-inspired democratic or socialist peasant movement." Inflating the significance of their own leadership, they envisioned themselves as the "vanguard who had mastered the peasant consciousness."[135]

The gratifying triumphs of the cooperative movement proved to be short-lived, however. Before their revolutionary organization had time to gather much strength, Satō, Suzuki Kōhei, and about fifty others were arrested by the military police for subversive activities in November 1941, the first in the wave of arrests that decimated the Research Department of Mantetsu in 1942 and 1943. The so-called Mantetsu Incident of 1942–1943 was part of a series of arrests that continued through the end of the war. These arrests included the editors of *Manshū hyōron* in Manchuria and swept through the elite publishing world in Japan, affecting magazines like *Kaizō, Chūō kōron, Nihon hyōron,* and *Tōyō keizai shinpō,* the *Asahi* newspaper, and the Iwanami publishing company. Researchers with the Cabinet Planning Board and the Shōwa kenkyūkai were all arrested, as the Japanese government tried to make a clean sweep of suspect scholars.[136]

Within Manchuria, the Kwantung Army justified the purge of leftists and liberals from Mantetsu by claiming to have discovered a widespread Communist conspiracy among Japanese residents of Manchukuo. Demobilization of the intelligentsia through repression spelled the dying gasp of Manchurian development. As crises mounted, the foundation for cooperation fell away and the anti-Communist paranoia of the army raged out of control. While allied forces pressed in on Japan and the Manchurian economy was grinding to a halt, the Kwantung Army assigned precious resources to a massive internal investigation to substantiate the Communist conspiracy theory. The resulting 850-page *ZaiMan Nikkei kyōsanshugi undō* (The Communist Movement of Japanese in Manchuria) analyzed hundreds of Mantetsu publications and minutely investigated the background and activities of scores of researchers looking for "red" proclivities.[137] Whether the army was in fact trying to create a scapegoat for

135. Ibid., pp. 268–270.
136. Fogel, "Introduction," pp. xxi–xxv; Itō, pp. 186–203; John Young, pp. 26–33.
137. Fogel, "Introduction," p. xxii.

the sinking fortunes of war, or whether the powers behind the purge had simply become consumed with paranoia, remains unclear.[138] Whatever the motivation, researchers in Mantetsu suddenly found themselves betrayed by the colonial state in which they had placed such high hopes. The peculiar alliance between the progressive intellectuals and the Manchukuo government was over.

Whether as architects of Manchukuo's futuristic cityscapes or scientists in the social laboratory of revolution, the new middle classes stood at the vanguard of the effort to build a brave new empire in Northeast China. Although this changed after the outbreak of the Sino-Japanese War in 1937, in the early years of Manchukuo the new empire drew intellectuals and white-collar professionals in such numbers in part because opportunities in Japan for ambitious and privileged graduates of higher secondary schools and colleges had all but dried up. Not only was there a glut of educated youth on the job market, but finding and keeping employment proved increasingly difficult for those of left-wing and liberal dispositions. Even for the lucky ones who had work in Japan, opportunities for rapid advance, for bold and creative action, or for making a name for themselves were few and far between. But just a short distance away, Manchukuo beckoned to idealistic and enterprising young professionals. The empire offered a fertile field for the cultivation of power and influence, of fame and fortune.

The men, and in some cases, women, who answered the call of this land of opportunity brought with them tremendous ambition and drive. In their efforts to remake their own lives, they remade the empire. They invested it with their preoccupation with modernity and their dreams of a utopian future. They pushed it to embrace an idealistic rhetoric of social reform and to justify itself in terms of Chinese nationalist aspirations. They turned it to architectural ostentation and the heady luxury of colonial consumption. They made it into a project of radical change, experimentation, and possibility.

This utopian and feel-good imperialism was an essential part of empire building in the early twentieth century, not only for Japan, but for Europe and the United States as well. Colonial discourses on urban modernism,

138. Ibid., pp. xxi–xxii; Yamaguchi Hiroichi, " 'Mantetsu chōsabu jiken' (1942–45 nen) ni tsuite," no. 29 of "Mantetsu chōsabu kankeisha ni kiku," *Ajia keizai* 29, no. 11 (November 1988), pp. 63–66.

economic development, and social reform represented efforts to mobilize political and social support for the imperial venture. Mobilizing support through hope and optimism, such development projects confirmed and reproduced the sense of colonial mission. In the process, development projects converted people to the idea that imperialism was good, a force of modernization and progress. In Japan, this twentieth-century version of the civilizing mission made imperialists out of liberals and radicals who had no love for the army and every sympathy for the Chinese nationalist movement. And yet, through their belief in the development of Manchukuo, they also supported the military assault against Chinese nationalism.

This last point is an important one, for it reminds us that the power used by progressive intellectuals to put their ideals into practice drew on the institutionalized violence and political autocracy of the colonial state. Even though Japanese progressives imagined themselves to be undermining militarism from within, their participation only strengthened the power of the Kwantung Army's puppet state. For the Chinese subjects of this brave new empire, Japanese utopianism, progressivism, and experimentation were experienced through the iron fist of a despotic alien power. But from the vantage point of the colonizer, it was easy to avoid looking at the underside of empire. Telling themselves that they were working for the good of the Chinese masses, Japanese progressives had trouble seeing that the benefits of colonial progress were largely enjoyed by the Japanese.

PART IV

THE NEW SOCIAL IMPERIALISM
AND THE FARM COLONIZATION
PROGRAM, 1932–1945

7 Reinventing Agrarianism
Rural Crisis and the Wedding of
Agriculture to Empire

The announcement of the Japanese government, in 1936, of a program of mass colonization of Northeast China ushered in a third phase in the creation of Manchukuo. This ambitious plan undertook to send a million farm households, one-fifth of Japan's 1936 farm population, to the new state of Manchukuo over the space of twenty years. Though the colonization plan fell short of its ambitious yearly targets, over 300,000 Japanese resettled in Manchuria before the campaign was interrupted by Japan's surrender in 1945.

As in the Manchurian war fever and economic boom that came before, extragovernmental forces provided an important impetus for Manchurian settlement. Although adoption as a government priority after 1936 did much to ensure its extraordinary achievements, Manchurian colonization was a social movement before it became a state initiative. Indeed, it was the groundswell of popular support that emerged in rural Japan in the early 1930s that persuaded government officials to place the institutional and financial backing of the state behind this enterprise. Hence the first stage—and the first achievement—of the colonization project was the mobilization of the state by a movement advocating Manchurian emigration.

The project was designed, in part, to cure the social ills of the Japanese farm village by exporting the rural poor to the empire. Although the Manchurian solution only emerged in the 1930s, the rural crisis it sought to address was long-standing. Since before the turn of the century, under the banner of the agrarianist *nōhonshugi* movement, advocates of rural reform had labored to overcome the social dislocations that industrialization produced in the Japanese villages. Against the backdrop of protracted rural crisis, the agrarianist movement joined forces with the equally long-standing emigration movement, itself galvanized into activity by the depression. Their fusion produced the Manchurian colonization movement, which seized on mass emigration to the empire as the solution to the dilemmas of agricultural modernization.

In this sense, the rural crisis in Japan stimulated the emergence of a new social imperialism. Since J. A. Schumpeter popularized the term, historians have used *social imperialism* to describe the relationship between industrial capitalism, social conflict, and the new imperialism of the late nineteenth and early twentieth centuries. In essence, the social imperialism thesis looks at empire building as a political strategy of elites to produce social stability and win the support of the masses. Faced with the emergence of a politically organized working class demanding social reform, entrenched political elites promoted the social and economic benefits of colonial expansionism as an alternative to social welfare policies. Thus social imperialism represented a phenomenon of the fledgling welfare state: one of a range of socially interventionist policies developed to deal with the consequences of uneven capitalist development and the social unrest caused by cyclical business downturns.[1]

The difference between this formulation of social imperialism and the Japanese case was social geography. Japanese social imperialism of the 1930s emerged with greatest force not in the urban centers, but in rural peripheries of political and economic power. It was in the agrarian political economy that the impact of uneven economic growth was felt most keenly and in the world of the village elites that social imperialism became the answer to calls for social justice by an agrarian proletariat of tenant farmers. For the countryside, the advent of industrial capitalism meant the incorporation in and increasing vulnerability to a national and global market, a process that pitted landlords against tenants in the struggle to achieve social security against the vagaries of the market. Rejecting the tension-ridden modernity that capitalism had wrought in agrarian society, local elites looked to Manchurian colonization as an avenue for social reform, hoping to open up an alternative path to agrarian modernity in their communities.

Government-sponsored settlement programs like Japan's colonization

1. Joseph A. Schumpeter, "Imperialism and Capitalism," in Joseph A. Schumpeter, *Imperialism and Social Classes*, trans. Heinz Norden, ed. Paul M. Sweezy (1951; reprint, Philadelphia: Orion, 1991), pp. 83–130, esp. pp. 114–115. See also Bernard Semmel, *Imperialism and Social Reform: English Social-Imperial Thought, 1895–1914* (Cambridge: Harvard University Press, 1960); and Wehler, "Bismarck's Imperialism."

of Manchukuo were not a prominent part of twentieth-century empire building, although they had been during the seventeenth and eighteenth centuries. For most colonial powers, including Japan, unassisted migration from the metropolis overwhelmingly flowed into colonial cities, usually trading entrepôts. Though members of the colonizing society did not always have the preponderance of numbers, they possessed the preponderance of power. Colonial cities thus became the creations and the base of the expatriate colonizer. In trying to promote the growth of an expatriate community in the Manchurian countryside in the 1930s, the Japanese government undertook a project unusual both in the context of its own imperial history as well as among its imperial cohort. Two other cases of rural migration stood alongside Japan. First, beginning in the 1880s, tsarist Russia promoted peasant emigration into its newly acquired holdings in Central Asia, particularly Kazakh and Turkestan. Official encouragement dramatically reshaped the demography of the steppe: by 1914 some 40 percent of its inhabitants were immigrants, the great majority of whom lived in rural areas.[2] In the 1930s, Italy, too, promoted mass agricultural settlement in colonial Libya. In a dramatic commemoration of the fascist march on Rome, the state engineered the transport of 20,000 Italian peasants from Italy in 1938, placing them in an armada of nine ships with an escort of eight destroyers.[3]

Both the Italian and the Russian agricultural settlement projects possessed features similar to Japan's. In all three cases emigration came to be seen as a panacea for a discontented—and increasingly politically and socially destabilizing—peasantry; in all three cases large amounts of state aid were granted to facilitate relocation; and all three projects tried to create utopian agrarian communities in colonial settings. To accomplish these goals, all three displaced indigenous communities from their lands in order to create a settlement frontier for agricultural colonists.

In Japan, as in Russia and Italy, agrarian social imperialism forged new links between agriculture and empire. When they tied their fortunes to Manchukuo, Japanese rural reformers expanded the definition of agrarianism to accommodate the empire even as they broadened the meaning of imperialism to include farm colonization. To this end, they imagined, on the one hand, a new imperial agrarianism in which mass agricultural re-

2. D. K. Fieldhouse, *The Colonial Empires: A Comparative Survey from the Eighteenth Century* (New York: Delacorte Press, 1966), pp. 336–337.

3. Betts, pp. 50–51, and Claudio G. Segrè, *Fourth Shore: The Italian Colonization of Libya* (Chicago: University of Chicago Press, 1974), esp. Chapter 5.

settlement in Manchuria would provide the vehicle for rehabilitating the agricultural village in Japan. And on the other hand, they envisioned a new agrarian imperialism in which the creation of model farm communities in Manchuria would provide an enduring social foundation for the imperial project.

EMIGRATION AND EXPANSIONISM

Before the establishment of Manchukuo, almost no one considered Japanese agricultural migration an indispensable pillar of empire in Northeast China. Although various schemes for migration had been discussed since Gotō Shinpei first introduced the idea during his term as president of Mantetsu (the South Manchurian Railway) in 1906, general opinion weighed against it. As one emigration analyst noted in 1932, "In the past there have been both optimistic and pessimistic views of Manchurian migration, but I think the pessimists prevailed."[4] In fact, this greatly understated the case. Early publications on Manchuria showed little interest in farm migration, let alone an energetic debate over its prospects. A bibliography of scholarly books and articles on "The Imperatives and Possibilities for Manchurian Migration" compiled in 1936 by the Japanese Association for the Advancement of Science listed thirty-one titles published before the Manchurian Incident. Few of these dealt with the problem of agricultural migrants, and many did not refer to Japanese migration at all.[5] Moreover, it was not yet clear that the kind of migrants Manchuria needed was agricultural. A "Guide to Manchuria" published in early 1932 by the venerable Nihon shokumin kyōkai (Japanese Colonization Society) gave little space to farmers. After a lengthy introduction to Manchuria's cities, financial and product instruction for aspiring merchants, information on daily and monthly wage rates, and a job-hunting guide, the 406-page manual allotted 6 pages to farm settlements.[6]

All this began to change after the founding of the puppet state. In the words of a contemporary, "After the establishment of Manchukuo the old

4. Nakajima Jinnōsuke, "Manmō imin mondai no tenbō," *Shakai seisaku jihō*, no. 140 (May 1932), p. 86.

5. *Manshū nōgyō imin bunken mokuroku* (Nihon gakujutsu shinkōkai, 1936), pp. 1–20.

6. Nihon shokumin kyōkai, *Manmō annai*, vol. 1 of *Imin kōza* Tōhō shoin, 1932). On the founding of the Colonization Society in 1893, see Akira Iriye, *Pacific Estrangement: Japanese and American Expansion, 1897–1911* (Cambridge: Harvard University Press, 1972), pp. 40–41.

pessimism towards migration was suddenly transformed into optimism."[7] A flood of articles with titles like "A Practical Proposal on Emigrating Farm Labor to Manchuria" and "The Foundation of Manchukuo and Unemployment in Japan" poured out of academic and public policy journals, Manchurian affairs monthlies, and economic, agricultural, and general affairs magazines. The 1936 Japanese Association for the Advancement of Science bibliography, which surveyed journals such as *Teikoku nōkai jihō* (Bulletin of the Imperial Agricultural Association), *Ekonomisuto* (Economist), *Kaizō* (Reconstruction), *Shakai seisaku jihō* (Social Policy), *Gaikō jihō* (Foreign Affairs), and *Manmō* (Manchuria Mongolia), furnished 196 references to works published between January 1932 and June 1935. Interest in the Manchurian migration debate peaked in 1932 when a voluble chorus of Japan's most eminent academics, bureaucrats, and journalists expounded on how Manchurian migration could best be accomplished.[8]

This surge of interest in agricultural colonization in 1932 seemed to have appeared out of thin air, but in fact it emerged out of a long-standing association of emigration with Japanese expansion. This began in the 1870s, when the northern island of Hokkaidō (known previously as Ezo) became the first target of mass-colonization schemes. Before organized Japanese settlement in the late nineteenth century, Hokkaidō was populated virtually exclusively by the ethnically distinct Ainu people. Until that time, they had maintained an existence politically and culturally separate from the Japanese of the other main islands. The establishment of the Hokkaidō Colonization Board (Kaitakushi) in 1869, however, drastically altered the Ainu's situation. The colonization board oversaw the dispossession of Ainu from most of their lands, turning them over to Japanese immigrants in order to promote economic development. The precipitous fall in Ainu population through the disease and poverty that ensued, along with the steady increase in Japanese immigrants, meant that the Ainu fell from a 95 percent majority to a minority of 22 percent between 1873 and 1897. In the appropriation of Ezo from the Ainu, Hokkaidō became the first venue for the use of emigration as a tool of expansion.

The initial wave of Japanese emigration to Hokkaidō shaped the insti-

7. Nakajima Jinnōsuke, "Manmō imin mondai no tenbō," *Shakai seisaku jihō*, no. 140 (May 1932), p. 86.

8. The two titles cited were published in a special issue on "Manchurian Migration" in *Shakai seisaku jihō*, no. 140 (May 1932). One hundred and seven of the articles listed in the bibliography were published in 1932, 44 in 1933, 30 in 1944, and 6 during the first six months of 1935. Nine were undated: *Manshū nōgyō imin bunken mokuroku*, pp. 4–19.

tutions and ideology of what became the emigration movement in two ways. First, like most enterprises of the early Meiji, the early emigration movement bore the strong imprint of the state. Through the agency of the colonization board, the government encouraged emigration with grants, subsidies, and other forms of state aid. The ultimate success of the venture rested, of course, on a vigorous popular response. Nevertheless, the involvement of the state gave the movement a heavy coloration of paternalism which would carry through in later incarnations. Second, since Hokkaidō could be considered Japan's first colony, mass settlement of the island established the precedent of "mixed colonization"—extending control through both administrative rule and settlement. Although Japan never reproduced the success of Hokkaidō settlement in any of its other colonies, the mixed-colony ideal entered the canon of Japanese colonial philosophy.

From its birth in the colonization of Hokkaidō, the emigration movement expanded its purview to target the European settlement societies of the Americas and the Pacific. Beginning with the legalization of emigration in 1884, Japanese were encouraged by government officials and private organizations to move to Hawaii, the west coast of the United States and Canada, South America, Australia, and New Zealand. In contrast to the colonization of Hokkaidō, which was quite successful, the idea of settlement in the more foreign and distant lands across the ocean seemed more popular in the abstract than in reality. The vast majority of its promoters had no intention of moving themselves, but they thought it imperative that others should. Already in the early Meiji period a clamorous assembly of bureaucrats, businessmen, and intellectuals lectured each other and a largely unresponsive populace on the benefits of colonization. Taking part in the *bunmei kaika* (civilization and enlightenment) boom in foreign-cultural imports of the 1870s and 1880s, Fukuzawa Yukichi, Kanda Kōhei, Amano Tamesuke, Taguchi Ukichi, and others promoted Western theories of colonization with their translations of the population theories of Thomas Malthus and their interpretations of the role of colonization in the expansion of the West. The Meiji neologism for colonization—*shokumin*—soon passed into common usage as organizations such as the Shokumin kyōkai (Colonization Society), Nihon rikkō kai (Japanese Striving Association), and Shinano kaigai kyōkai (Shinano Overseas Association) proliferated after the turn of the century. A host of specialty magazines appeared, ranging from the scholarly *Takushoku jijō* (Colonization Affairs) to the Foreign Ministry publication *Kaigai ijū* (Overseas Settlement), and including the numerous promotional magazines published by emigration societies, such as the Shinano Overseas Association's *Umi no soto* (Across the Sea).⁹

With the exhortation and material aid furnished by these institutions, some 227,830 Japanese resettled in North and South America and another 144,295 in Hawaii between the legalization of emigration in 1884 and 1930 (see Table 8). Although these figures nurtured ambitions for a Japanese diaspora that would match the neo-Europes in the Americas and the Pacific, the numbers of Japanese moving overseas never approached those of Europe. In comparative terms, if emigration between 1850 and 1950 is expressed as a percentage of population increase, the emigration rates of such countries as England (75 percent), Italy (47 percent), Germany (24 percent), Denmark (22 percent), and France (6 percent) far exceeded Japan's 1 percent.¹⁰

Although the numbers involved were never large in comparative terms, Japanese emigration was increasing just as the nation burst onto the world stage as the single nonwhite imperialist power. Imperial rivalries took on racial overtones, and the identification of immigrants with empire was at least partially responsible for the United States' annexation of Hawaii in 1897 and subsequent limitations on Japanese immigration in the Americas and the Pacific. These restrictions included the White Australia and White New Zealand policies of 1901 and 1903, the Gentlemen's Agreements with the United States and Canada of 1907 and 1908, initiatives to curb immigration to Peru and Brazil, and what would always be remembered as the crowning insult, the exclusion of Japanese altogether in the U.S. Immigration Act of 1924.

Since Japanese regarded the treatment of their nationals as a reflection of international prestige, diplomats worked hard to attain what amounted to honorary white status for Japanese. From their perspective, possession of an empire entitled them to be spared the racial discrimination visited

---

9. The Shokumin kyōkai was established in 1893 to promote the settlement of Hokkaidō, the Rikkōkai in 1900 to encourage emigration to America, and the Shinano kaigai kyōkai in 1923 to support emigration from Nagano prefecture. Nagano-ken kaitaku jikōkai Manshū kaitakushi kankōkai, *Nagano-ken Manshū kaitakushi*, vol. 1, overview (Nagano: Nagano-ken kaitaku jikōkai Manshū kaitakushi kankōkai, 1984), pp. 35–38, 55–70; *Zasshi nenkan* (1939), pp. 218–220; Peattie, "Japanese Attitudes toward Colonialism," pp. 80–90; Kaneko Fumio, "Nihon ni okeru shokuminchi kenkyū no seiritsu jijō," in Kojima Reiitsu, ed., *Nihon teikokushugi to Higashi Ajia* (Ajia keizai kenkyūjo, 1979), pp. 49–94; Iriye, *Pacific Estrangement*, pp. 17–25, 35–62; Pyle, pp. 87–91; Hara Kakuten, pp. 63–66.

10. Kōdansha, ed., *Encyclopedia of Japan* (New York: Kōdansha, 1983), s.v. "emigration."

Table 8. Japanese Overseas Population in 1930

Asia	
China	
Manchuria	
Kwantung Leased Territory	119,770
South Manchurian Railway Zone	100,268
Manchuria outside Japanese occupation	13,282
Total (Manchuria)	233,320
China proper	53,632
Total (China and Manchuria)	286,952
Korea	500,000
Taiwan	228,000
Philippines	19,695
Other Asian areas	19,409
Total (Asia)	1,054,056
Americas	
Continental United States	103,996
Canada	20,156
Mexico	5,930
Brazil	119,740
Argentina	4,846
Peru	20,650
Other American areas	2,512
Total (Americas)	277,830

(Continued on next page)

upon the colonized peoples of Asia and Africa. The failure of diplomatic efforts on the immigration question fed a sense of resentment and rivalry toward the Western powers; the issue vexed Japanese foreign relations for much of the prewar period. Interpreted as a sign of Japan's exclusion from the imperialist club, emigration became linked, again, with empire.[11]

This second wave of emigration reinforced the cultural patterns the

11. These conclusions are based on my discussion of the racial dimensions of Japanese foreign relations and the Japanese diplomatic initiative at the Paris Peace Conference in 1919: Louise Young, "Power and Color."

Table 8—*Continued*

Pacific	
Hawaii	144,295
Japanese-administered Pacific islands	20,000
Other Pacific areas	3,525
Total (Pacific)	167,820
Europe	
Total (Europe)	3,696
Africa	
Total (Africa)	104
Total Japanese population overseas	1,503,506

SOURCES: Figures for Manchuria from *Kantōchō tōkeisho*, vol. 26 (1931), p. 19; and *Manshū keizai zuhyō* (Dalian: Dalian shōkō kaigisho, 1936), p. 2. Figures for Taiwan, Korea, and the Japanese-administered Pacific islands from W. G. Beasley, *Japanese Imperialism 1894–1945* (Oxford: Clarendon Press, 1987), pp. 151–155. Other figures from *DaiNippon teikoku tōkei nenkan* (1933), p. 67.

colonization of Hokkaidō inscribed in the emigration movement. The paternalism of the movement, so apparent in its initial phase, continued to shape the institutions and ideology of emigration. This was a movement of promoters, not migrants; it was emigration preached from above by a welfare-minded elite, not pushed from below by land-hungry farmers. Moreover, just as the colonization of Hokkaidō was viewed as a means to enrich the nation and expand Japanese territory, emigration to the Americas and the Pacific became tied to ideas of world power and national pride. In the literature on colonization one did not read inspirational tales of rags to riches, though ready material for such stories could be extracted from the experiences of cane workers in Hawaii and houseboys in California who saved and became farmers of independent means. The message of the emigration movement focused, rather, on Japan's population problem and the utility of Japanese overseas communities for amassing national wealth and power. In other words, the movement dealt in the ideological currency of nationalism, not individual opportunity.

Both the success of Hokkaidō's colonization and the unfulfilled dreams of a Japanese diaspora in the Americas and the Pacific shaped aspirations for another wave of emigration when a new frontier of settlement opened up in Japan's expanding colonial empire. In 1909, Foreign Minister Komura Jutarō unveiled before the Imperial Diet a plan for sending a million Japanese emigrants to Manchuria within the space of twenty years.[12] Several years later, the historian Taketoshi Yosaburō exuberantly reported that, whereas before 1895 Japan had colonists but no colonies, "now Korea has room for ten million immigrants and Formosa [Taiwan] two million."[13] This plan proved impossible to implement in Taiwan, where Japanese sugar companies organized local labor into a profitable system for sugar production and had little interest in diverting lands for the use of Japanese settlers. But in Korea and the Kwantung Leased Territory in South Manchuria, rosy estimations of undeveloped lands and the desire to raise production of rice and other goods with which Japanese farmers were familiar led policy makers to adopt colonization plans.

In order to oversee the anticipated flood of immigration into Korea, business leaders Shibusawa Eiichi, Toyokawa Ryōhei, and Nakano Buei worked together with Finance Ministry bureaucrats to create the semi-public Tōyō takushoku kaisha (Oriental Development Company, or Tōtaku) in 1908. Initially capitalized at ten million yen, the company planned to settle 2 million Japanese farmers over a ten-year period to provide a bulwark against Korean resistance. This ambitious plan was never actually put into effect, however. After Tōtaku began to send employees into the field to draw up a more concrete program, it was discovered that the only land suitable for Japanese farmers was already being cultivated by Koreans—who were present in numbers grossly underestimated by the early Japanese statistics.[14] The goal to recruit 30,000 Japanese farm households per year was scaled down to 1,500, and Tōtaku assisted these families by appropriating land for them, subsidizing their moving expenses, and financing their production through long-term, low-interest loans. Although Tōtaku grew rapidly in size and had to be recapitalized at fifty million yen within twelve years, immigration figures remained disappointing. A mere 20,000 Japanese farmers resided in Korea by 1926, and many of these were landlords.[15] In the meantime, the company had become one of the colony's

12. Matsumura Takao, "Manshūkoku seiritsu ikō ni okeru imin rōdō seisaku no keisei to tenkai," in Manshūshi kenkyūkai, ed., *Nihon teikokushugika no Manshū* (Ochanomizu shobō, 1972), p. 216.

13. Peattie, "Japanese Attitudes toward Colonialism," p. 89.

14. Estimates of 10 million were eventually revised to 15 million.

15. Karl Moskowitz, "The Creation of the Oriental Development Company: Japanese Illusions Meet Korean Reality," *Occasional Papers on Korea*, no. 2 (March

biggest landlords itself. By 1931 Tōtaku holdings reached 153,175 *chō* (375,279 acres), on which it collected rents from an estimated 80,000 Korean tenants.[16]

The history of Japanese management of its leaseholds in the Kwantung Peninsula and the South Manchurian Railway Zone prior to the Manchurian Incident was likewise strewn with failed attempts at farm colonization. With aims similar to the Korean project, most of these were small-scale group settlements overseen either by Mantetsu or the governor general of the Kwantung Leased Territory. Despite these efforts, less than 1,000 farmers made the move to Manchuria before 1931, and of these all but a couple hundred returned home.[17] Such failures meant that though almost 1 million of the 1.5 million overseas Japanese in 1930 lived in the empire, only a tiny fraction of these were farmers. The composition of the Japanese expatriate community was in fact that of a temporary colonial elite: government bureaucrats as well as the technicians and managers involved in commerce, railroads, and manufacturing. These statistics did not stop the dreaming, however. Despite the disappointing results of the early experiments with Korean and Manchurian immigration, these movements provided important models upon which the post–1931 colonization plans were founded.

Over the course of the emigration movement that developed in Japan in the late nineteenth and early twentieth centuries, the Meiji notion of colonization acquired a thick encrustation of meaning. Its associations were, foremost, imperial. Japanese regarded the growth of their overseas communities as a form of "peaceful expansionism," to borrow Akira Iriye's term.[18] In their eyes, the treatment of Japanese in European settlement societies was a matter of national prestige and reflected Japan's standing in the world. In the colonial empire, they viewed the growth of a stable population of Japanese colonists as a tool for imperial management. Emigration had become part of the project of empire building.

1974), pp. 73–111; Duus, "Economic Dimensions of Meiji Imperialism," pp. 160–161; Beasley, pp. 151–153.

16. Asada Kyōji, *Nihon teikokushugi to kyūshokuminchi jinushisei: Taiwan, Chōsen, "Manshū" ni okeru Nihonjin daitochi shoyū no shiteki bunseki*, rev. ed. (Ryūkei shosha, 1989), pp. 114–121, 384–385. The tenancy figure of 80,000 in 1931 is estimated from Asada's 1938 figure of 78,667. Since land holdings of Tōtaku fell slightly between 1931 and 1938 (from 153,175 to 145,236 *chō*), one may assume that the number of tenants fell slightly as well.

17. South Manchurian Railway Company, pp. 129–133; Matsumura, pp. 215–226.

18. Iriye, *Pacific Estrangement*, pp. 35–47.

It had also grown into a broad-based social movement, albeit one geared toward promoting emigration from above. Over the decades the movement developed an elaborate institutional apparatus, with an army of promoters and an extensive publishing wing. Although before 1931 the emigration movement advocated farm settlement, it maintained only tenuous ideological and institutional ties to Japanese agrarianism: its mission was to build the empire, not to save Japanese agriculture. This would change after the creation of Manchukuo in 1932, when the emigration and agrarianist movements joined forces in the Manchurian colonization campaign and their two missions became fused.

Believing that Manchukuo opened up a new frontier for farm colonization, emigration promoters quickly gathered their forces to lobby the government on the prospects for Manchurian settlement. At the center of this effort was a group of scholars and bureaucrats associated with the figure of Katō Kanji.[19] The so-called Katō group included Nasu Kō and Hashimoto Den'emon of the Tokyo and Kyoto University Departments of Agriculture, respectively; Ishida Tadayuki and Kodaira Ken'ichi of the Ministry of Agriculture and Forestry; and Yamazaki Yoshio and Sō Teruhiko, both heads of rural youth-training centers. The leader of the group, Katō Kanji, was a right-wing agrarianist educator who had founded schools for rural youth in Yamagata and Ibaraki. A long-time advocate of agrarian imperialism, Katō used his schools to sponsor many of the unsuccessful attempts at farm colonization of Korea and Manchuria in the 1920s.[20] In 1932, when the future of Manchukuo was being widely discussed, Katō and his colleagues seized the opportunity to press for their long-cherished dreams of continental settlement.

In the context of the Taishō agrarianist movement, Katō's advocacy of colonial settlement was unusual—one of the few links between the agrarianist and emigration movements. Though his interest in both would later serve as a bridge between the two movements, in 1932 proponents of Manchurian settlement still argued their case in the paternalist and expansionist language of emigration. Since agricultural land in Manchukuo, like the Korean colony before it, was already under cultivation by a large popu-

19. This Katō Kanji should not be confused with the admiral of the same name who led the naval fleet faction opposition to the London naval treaty of 1930.

20. Asada Kyōji, "Takumushō no Manshū nogyō imin keikaku (shiken iminki)," *Keizai gakubu kenkyū kiyō*, no. 32 (Komazawa daigaku, March 1974), pp. 89–91; Yamada Gōichi, "Manshū ni okeru hanMan kōNichi undō to nōgyō imin (I)," *Rekishi hyōron*, no. 142 (June 1962), pp. 56–57.

lation of Chinese peasants, resurrecting the old formulas for colonization destined the initial Manchurian plan to the fate of the Korean experiment.

This was the most forceful objection raised by opponents to Manchurian colonization in 1932. As Yanaihara Tadao, the eminent professor of colonial studies at Tokyo University, pointed out, the reasons for the failure of Japanese farm colonization in the empire in the past still held in the present. Getting rid of Zhang Xueliang did not alter the fact that Japanese farmers would face the difficulty of competing in the agricultural marketplace with Chinese who both lived more cheaply and were more experienced in Manchurian cultivation.

> As a rule people migrate from an area of low wages and living standards to an area of high wages and living standards. Migrating in the opposite direction is unnatural, rather like trying to make water flow upstream against the current. In contrast to bureaucrats, military officers, company managers, and engineers who are insulated from the local labor market by virtue of their special status, laborers and farmers migrating to Manchuria are violating this basic economic rule of migration.[21]

Yanaihara and other critics insisted that economic law doomed Japanese farm settlement: there were no "pull" factors to lure Japanese farmers into Manchurian agriculture.

The Katō group answered this objection with the standard appeal of emigration activists: colonization could succeed with "support from government and conviction from the settlers."[22] Echoing arguments promoting the creation of a quasi-government agency to oversee Korean settlement twenty-five years earlier, the Katō group insisted Manchurian colonization could overcome the laws of economic competition if the government took an active role in subsidizing and managing the settlements. The policies proposed by the colonization advocates aimed, first, to lend state aid in making the settlements self-sufficient, thus shielding them from having to compete in the market with Chinese farmers. Second, they suggested that the state train colonists in superior (to Chinese) agricultural techniques and methods, furnish land grants to ensure economies of scale, and finance the purchase of new mechanized farm equipment. To accomplish

---

21. Yanaihara Tadao, "Manmō shokumin keikaku no busshitsuteki oyobi sei-shinteki yōso," *Shakai seisaku jihō,* no. 140 (May 1932), p. 52.

22. Hashimoto Denzaemon, "Manmō to nōgyō imin," *Ekonomisuto* (1 April 1932), p. 66; Nasu Kō, "Manshū nōgyō imin no jikkō hōhō ni tsuite," *Shakai seisaku jihō,* no. 140 (May 1932), pp. 152–154.

these goals, promoters of Manchurian colonization generated a welter of proposals on the proper selection of land and crops, optimum holdings, and means to give financial, technical, and other aid to settlements.[23] Once again, emigrant promoters imagined paternalism could overcome a multitude of obstacles.

For emigration enthusiasts the more serious problem was posed by inappropriate attitudes toward emigration on the part of the Japanese masses. The Manchurian migration debate was filled with the familiar litany of complaints on this score. As Tokyo University professor Kawazu Susumu phrased it, the Japanese evinced a much regretted "attachment to their native place" (*aichakushin*), which explained why in the past "population pressure had not translated into overseas settlement."[24] Even more troubling, those who did go were motivated by the wrong reasons. Thinking only to "strike it rich" (*ikkaku senkin*), earlier Japanese migrants had been little more than *riken'ya*, grafters who had no proper concept of developing resources but came only to make a quick profit and leave. As Mantetsu researcher Okagawa Eizō indignantly exclaimed, "The people moving into agriculture did not place even a single foot in Manchuria but acted as a kind of absentee landlord . . . squeezing out profits like petty capitalists."[25] The condemnation of the desire for upward mobility and personal gain as illegitimate motivations for resettlement emerged straight out of the canon of the emigration movement. Proponents conceived Manchurian settlement not in terms of economic opportunity but as a patriotic enterprise. Moreover, in the presumption that the Japanese masses stood in need of enlightenment on the proper attitude toward emigration they reproduced the didactic tendency that had long defined the movement's culture.

In spite of the enthusiastic support circulating among colonization spe-

23. Kawazu Susumu, "Manshū imin ni tsuite," *Shakai seisaku jihō*, no. 140 (May 1932), p. 33; Hijikata Seibi, "Manshū imin to jinkō mondai," *Shakai seisaku jihō*, no. 140 (May 1932), p. 44; Sawamura Yasushi, "Manmō nōgyō imin seisaku no sho mondai," *Shakai seisaku jihō*, no. 140 (May 1932), p. 130; Nishigori Hideo, "Manmō nōgyō imin no hitsuyō to kanōsei," *Shakai seisaku jihō*, no. 140 (May 1932), p. 145; Nasu Kō, "Manshū nōgyō imin no jikkō hōhō ni tsuite," *Shakai seisaku jihō*, no. 140 (May 1932), p. 156; Sō Mitsuhiko, "Manmō shokumin no gutaiteki hōsaku," *Shakai seisaku jihō*, no. 140 (May 1932), p. 156; Sō Mitsuhiko, "Manmō shokumin no gutaiteki hōsaku," *Shakai seisaku jihō*, no. 140 (May 1932), p. 169.

24. Kawazu Susumu, "Manshū imin ni tsuite," *Shakai seisaku jihō*, no. 140 (May 1932), pp. 29–30, 44.

25. "Manshū keiei wa naze seikō shinakatta ka," *Ekonomisuto* (1 April 1932), p. 26; Kawazu Susumu, "Manshū imin ni tsuite," *Shakai seisaku jihō*, no. 140 (May 1932), p. 31; Okagawa Eizō, *Shakai seisaku jihō*, no. 140 (May 1932), pp. 171–172.

cialists in 1932, consensus among policy makers for state sponsorship did not emerge immediately. Like the complicated politics of imperialism which set in motion the creation of Tōtaku in 1908, the expense of inaugurating the Manchurian colonization project required a political consensus of far-flung proportions. Although the Katō group quickly won the support of the Colonial Ministry, the Finance Ministry objected to proposals for mass colonization on economic and financial grounds. But after an initial rejection in March 1932, by June intense lobbying by the Katō group persuaded the guardians of the national purse to grant a modest 100,000-yen research budget. In August, a trial emigration plan based on the ideas of Nasu Kō and Hashimoto Den'emon of the Katō group was approved by both the cabinet and the Diet.[26] After August 1932 the government made yearly budget allocations for trial colonies of a small number of households (between 500 and 1,000) to be resettled in Manchuria under the auspices of the Colonial Ministry. The experiment with Manchurian colonization had begun.

In the Manchurian migration debate and the process of consensus building that took place over the course of 1932, there was little new about the ideas of colonization except the surge of interest in Manchuria as a location. The ease with which the Katō group gained government support followed earlier precedents of state involvement with emigration. Moreover, the government granted minimal support—little more than a sop—to the Katō group and their allies in the Kwantung Army and the Colonial Ministry. In short, there was nothing in the initial phase of the Manchurian migration movement to indicate that the Katō group would succeed where so many had failed in the past. In 1932, this looked like just one more pipe dream in the armchair imperialism of the emigration movement.

THE MANCHURIAN SOLUTION TO THE "PROBLEM OF THE VILLAGES"

Contrary to precedent, the modest trial emigration project of 1932–1935 grew into the prodigious "Millions to Manchuria" (*Manshū e hyakumanto*) program of 1936.[27] The institutional vehicles of the movement proliferated rapidly, and rural Japan was deluged with literature promoting resettlement in Manchuria. Hundreds of thousands answered the call, con-

26. Asada, "Takumushō no Manshū nōgyō imin keikaku," pp. 89–91, 106–107.
27. This slogan literally translates as "a million households to Manchuria," but since ministry projections assumed an average of five members per household, I have used the plural "millions" in my translation.

trary to the expectations of critics like Yanaihara Tadao who could see no appeal for Japanese farmers in the Manchurian frontier. As the Katō group predicted, government support was critical in bringing about this reversal of fortune for the emigration movement, for after 1936 Manchurian colonization became a pillar of government policy in Japan and Manchukuo. In fact, one of the reasons for the relative success of Manchurian colonization resulted from the enormous expansion of the state in the context of this movement. But before looking at the growth of the state, one question needs to be answered: Who mobilized the state to begin with? As impassioned as they were, it took more than the arguments of the Katō group to convince the government to back Manchurian colonization on such an extravagant scale.

The government was finally won over by the rise of a significant constituency of support from among the rural community. This support emerged within the context of a nationwide agrarianist movement aimed at resolving what was called the "problem of the villages." Hard hit by a series of economic shocks in the early thirties, Japan's farm villages became the site of an intensifying social crisis. As embattled local elites searched for a means to deal with the effects of rural depression, they began to listen with new receptivity to the solution proposed by advocates of Manchurian settlement.

The Manchurian solution to the problem of the villages represented a radical departure for an agrarianist movement that had long been part of rural political culture. The roots of agrarianism went back to the 1890s and 1900s, when the term *nōhonshugi* (making "agriculture the root" of Japan's social order) first emerged, together with its institutional vehicles and ideological authority. Described by Carol Gluck as an "ideological offensive against social change," the early agrarian movement sought to protect the rural sector from the socioeconomic transformations brought about by economic development and the integration of Japan into a world economy.[28] To this end, the early *nōhonshugisha* (agrarianists) constructed a vision of the traditional village community that countered mounting class tensions with evocations of a harmony of community interests and wielded exhortations of self-help and self-reliance as shields against the growing commercialization of agriculture. In the imagined agrarianist

28. For early agrarianism, see Gluck, *Japan's Modern Myths,* pp. 178–186; R. P. Dore, *Land Reform in Japan* (New York: Schocken Books, 1985), pp. 56–107; and Thomas R. H. Havens, *Farm and Nation in Modern Japan: Agrarian Nationalism, 1870–1940* (Princeton: Princeton University Press, 1974), pp. 56–111.

countryside, self-government and local autonomy would guide local administration in the face of what was, in fact, an increasingly powerful and intrusive national government. Moreover, agrarianists championed the role of the owner-cultivator as the backbone of their idealized village communities at a time when the concentration of lands had fractured rural society into a complex hierarchy of landowning and tenant classes, leaving the independent owner-cultivator a distinct minority.

In 1930 the idea of *nōhonshugi* reflected a half century of accumulated resentments toward the world of the city and all it represented. From the Meiji on, both the industrial policy of government and private-sector initiatives had tended to support urban and industrial development at the expense of the agricultural sector. Throughout the period farmers complained, with justice, that farm incomes bore a disproportionate share of the national tax burden. With brief exceptions in the late 1870s and during World War I, the relative prices of agricultural commodities and consumer goods affected the rural-urban terms of trade to the disadvantage of the villages. Wage differentials and the dream of social mobility drew agricultural labor to the cities, but workers returned to their home villages if unemployed by a business downturn or because of illness. In this sense, villages were forced to absorb many of the social, as well as capital, costs of industrialization. Such inequities fueled agrarianist hostilities toward big industry, capitalism, and central government, all of which they identified with Japan's increasingly powerful cities. Over the course of a forty-year history, therefore, the agrarianist movement had vetted various strategies for sealing off the villages from the corrosive influence of the city. But none had proven equal to this task, and in the face of the new crisis of the 1930s, these long-accumulated frustrations and resentments helped steer the attention of many agrarianists to the empire as the potential instrument of village salvation. Manchurian settlement now appeared to offer a route to a future of social stability that circumvented the city.

When these agrarianists finally embraced the Manchurian solution, they embraced it wholeheartedly. But endorsing the depopulation of rural Japan was a big step, and it took something cataclysmic to propel rural activists into this position. The devastating depression of the early 1930s catalysed the fusion of the agrarian and emigration movements, providing the groundswell of popular support that turned Manchurian colonization into a mass movement. The sense among agrarianists that, once again, the villages were suffering disproportionately the social costs of a nationwide crisis of capitalism explained why forces behind social imperialism in the 1930s gathered with particular intensity in the countryside.

Well before the shock waves from the Wall Street Crash hit Japan, pressures for agrarian social imperialism were building in the villages. The rural economy, which provided the livelihood for 50 percent of the gainfully employed population, had been under siege since the post–World War I depression. Volatile prices of the two mainstays of agriculture, rice and silk cocoons, had shaved profits on agriculture. Landlords' returns on leased paddy fields fell sharply from 7.92 percent in 1919 to 5.67 percent in 1925, and again to 3.69 percent in 1931. Although the rate of return on manufacturing and agricultural investment had been more or less equal before 1925, by 1931 corporate stocks and bonds were twice as profitable. The shrinking returns on agriculture caused an outbreak of disputes between landlords and tenants over rents. Though the growth of tenancy itself had leveled off around the turn of the century, spurred by the rise in social activism through Japan during the 1920s, the number of tenancy disputes leapt from 256 in 1918 to 1,532 in 1924, and to 2,478 by 1930.[29]

The global reverberations of the Wall Street Crash of 1929 dealt the rural economy, already in a weakened condition, a stunning blow. The villages were a major supplier of the urban labor force and when the factories shut down these workers came home to their families. White-collar workers and capitalists likewise returned to ancestral lands if they became unemployed or were left bankrupt. Rural society was thus forced to absorb much of the social dislocation caused by the depression. On top of this, the precipitous fall in rice and silk prices, as well as widespread crop failures in northern Japan, made the early 1930s years of catastrophe for farmers.[30] In the north, famine victims from Aomori, Iwate, Akita, and Hokkaidō numbered close to half a million; Home Ministry officials recorded the sale of 11,604 Aomori, Akita, Yamagata, Fukushima, and Niigata girls into service, mostly as prostitutes. As painful as the effects of depression were in the cities, because agricultural prices fell further and came back more slowly than those of manufacturing goods, the villages were hit harder and took longer to recover.[31] This sense of relative deprivation heightened

29. In 1902, 33.9 percent of farm households owned their land, 38 percent owned part and leased part, and 28.1 percent leased all their land. The corresponding figures for 1930 were 31.1 percent, 42.3 percent, and 26.5 percent: Andō Yoshio, pp. 15, 107.

30. Kinbara Samon and Takemae Eiji, eds., *Shōwashi: kokumin no naka no haran to gekidō no hanseiki,* rev. ed. (Yūhikaku, 1989), pp. 16–27.

31. Eguchi, *Jūgonen sensō no kaimaku,* pp. 181–183. For a comparison of prices of agricultural and manufactured goods, see Andō Yoshio, p. 116.

the urgency of the appeals for help that bombarded the government in 1931 and 1932.

These urgent appeals came from a variety of directions. Right-wing agrarianists led by Gondō Seikyō, Tachibana Kōsaburō, Nagano Rō, Inamura Ryūichi, Wagō Tsuneo, and others formed the Jichi nōmin kyōkai (Farmers' Self-Government Alliance), which spearheaded a petition drive in early 1932. During this time, 28,887 signatures were collected on an appeal to the government demanding, first, a three-year moratorium on farm-household debt, second, fertilizer subsidies, and third, fifty million yen in aid for Manchurian emigration; a revised list of demands was submitted later with 42,505 signatures. Since a number of the conspirators in the spectacular May 15 coup d'etat attempt were associated with Tachibana's agrarian training center, Aikyō juku, the news of the assassination of the prime minister and attacks on other power centers conferred added significance to the petition movement in the eyes of government officials. In the meantime, petitions continued to pour in from farm organizations all over the country, finally inducing the government to convoke a special "save agriculture" session of the Imperial Diet in 1932.[32]

The proposals that were most closely reflected in the government's policy response came from the Imperial Agricultural Association, Teikoku nōkai. Representing landlord interests, the association's proposals aimed at shoring up their own position through price supports and the suppression of class conflict within the villages. It was hardly surprising that the measures adopted by the government for debt relief, public works, and *jiriki kōsei* (rehabilitation through self-help) had the effect of exacerbating class divisions, as the upper and particularly the middle stratum of landowners took advantage of programs that left poorer tenant farmers out in the cold.[33]

Consequently, tenancy disputes continued to increase throughout the first half of the 1930s, rising from 2,478 incidents in 1930 to a peak of 6,804 incidents in 1936.[34] There was an important distinction between these disputes and those of the previous decade which was related to the

32. Eguchi, *Jūgonen sensō no kaimaku*, pp. 186–191; Fujiwara, Imai, and Ōe, pp. 386–387; Takahashi Yasutaka, "Nihon fashizumu to nōson keizai kōsei undō no tenkai: Shōwaki 'kyūnō' seisaku ni tsuite no kōsatsu," *Tochi seido shigaku*, no. 65 (October 1974), pp. 1–26.

33. Takahashi Yasutaka, "Nihon fashizumu to nōson keizai kōsei undō," pp. 4–8; Dore, pp. 98–106.

34. For statistics on tenancy disputes, see Andō Yoshio, p. 107.

intricate nature of the tenancy system in prewar Japan. Japanese village society was defined by the relationships between landowners and tenants, which were complicated by the diversity in both these categories. Landowners could be absentee or resident, could own land parcels ranging from under a half *chō* (1.23 acres) to over 1,000 *chō* (2,450 acres), could have sidelines in light manufacturing, commerce, or moneylending, and were divided between those who worked their own land, those who leased it, and a combination of the two. The taxonomy of tenancy was equally complex, with divisions between pure tenants and part-tenant/part-owners, as well as between those who engaged in farming full-time and those who were part-time farmers.[35]

The protracted agricultural crisis had intensified conflict between the middle stratum of landowners and the lower stratum of tenants; these tensions were reflected in the new character of the tenancy disputes of the 1930s. Wedged in between a land tax paid in cash and a fixed-tenancy fee paid in kind, and with few assets to cushion them from economic hardship, small-scale landowners were hit hard by the fall in rice prices. Consequently, they responded to the agricultural crisis in one of three ways: evicting tenants in order to expand the area of land they cultivated themselves; selling the land they had hitherto leased; or renting the land out at a higher price. Such practices were facilitated by the influx of unemployed labor from the cities and the intensification of competition for land. Thus the number of disputes over eviction rose sharply in the 1930s while those concerned with rent reduction fell.[36] All this tended to focus attention on the issue of land shortage. As one bureaucrat from the Ministry of Agriculture and Forestry summarized, "The deadlock in the rural economy is decidedly not caused by irrationality in the economic structure of the farm community, the need for more organization, a lack of planning, or even, as some argue, the feudal character of the farmers. The basic problem always comes back to the inability to adjust population to land resources."[37] To observers at the time, it seemed that the problem of the villages boiled down to too many farmers competing for too little land.

Against this backdrop, support gathered for funding the resettlement of this excess population in the reputedly limitless Manchurian frontier. Groups proposing that rural poverty could be solved by Manchurian em-

---

35. For discussion of these social categories, see Dore, pp. 3–53; for statistical representation, see Andō Yoshio, pp. 13–16.

36. Ann Waswo, *Japanese Landlords: The Decline of a Rural Elite* (Berkeley: University of California Press, 1977), pp. 127–134.

37. Sugino Tadao, *Nōson kōsei undō to bunson keikaku*, no. 3 of *Bunson keikaku sōsho* (Nōson kōsei kyōkai, 1938), p. 3.

igration mushroomed in farm villages throughout the country. Already by September 1932 (only six months after the establishment of Manchukuo) more than eighty-four local organizations had drawn up emigration plans.[38] Such organizations were receptive to the Malthusian-inspired predictions of the dire implications of Japan's surplus population and promising estimations of vast tracts of empty lands in Manchuria that were circulated by the Katō group in the first years of the puppet state. Advocates of Manchurian colonization hammered this theme home, arguing that resettlement offered the sole remedy of a diseased society. Claiming that overpopulation "has made Japan putrid, like stagnant water," and that it was solely responsible for "the tragedies of family suicide and unemployment which inundate the pages of the daily press," promoters of Manchurian emigration saw population resettlement as a means to "purify" Japan.[39] In an argument widely circulated but disproved before the end of the decade, the experts insisted that industrial expansion could never absorb Japan's excess labor; "the only possibility remaining was overseas settlement."[40] While they were lamenting Japan's overpopulation problem, colonization advocates hailed readers with various calculations of Manchuria's "absorptive power" (*shūshōryoku*). As every tract on Manchurian migration ritualistically observed, Manchuria was "153 percent larger than Japan" but had only "33 percent of the population." This left room, in the optimistic prediction of House of Peers member Nakajima Kumakichi, for "a trillion (Japanese) immigrants."[41] In sounding the overpopulation theme, emigration activists had found a message that resonated with the concerns of the agrarianist movement. Conceptually, a link was established between the two.

At this point (1932), however, neither farm organizations like Nōkai and Sangyō kumiai, nor the prefectural and national leadership of the Ministry of Agriculture and Forestry expressed much interest in the ideas

38. Manshū kaitakushi kankōkai, *Manshū kaitakushi* (Manshū kaitakushi kankōkai, 1966), p. 33.

39. Hijikata Seibi, "Manshū imin to jinkō mondai," *Shakai seisaku jihō*, no. 140 (May 1932), pp. 37, 45; Nakajima Jinnosuke, "Manmō imin mondai no tenbō," *Shakai seisaku jihō*, no. 140 (May 1932), p. 94.

40. Hijikata Seibi, "Manshū imin to jinkō mondai," *Shakai seisaku jihō*, no. 140 (May 1932), pp. 37, 43–45; Nakajima Jinnosuke, "Manmō imin mondai no tenbō," *Shakai seisaku jihō*, no. 140 (May 1932), p. 94; Yanaihara Tadao, "Manshū shokumin keikaku no busshitsuteki oyobi seishinteki yōso," *Shakai seisaku jihō*, no. 140 (May 1932), p. 50.

41. Nakajima Kumakichi, "Manshū shinkokka to kyokutō keizai burokku," *Shakai seisaku jihō*, no. 140 (May 1932), pp. 5–6.

of the emigration movement or the schemes of a few local organizations. Yet within a few years the conservative reform measures of the rural rehabilitation program were proving a failure, and as a spokesman for the program admitted, they "had only deepened the class divisions in the villages."[42] Casting about for new policies, rural elites began to entertain the more radical solution of exporting the problem. Thus, in 1937, with encouragement from local communities and farm organizations, the Ministry of Agriculture and Forestry adopted a program to help finance group emigration in villages that wished to participate. Embracing the overall goal of exporting nearly one-third of the domestic farm population, the ministry made mass emigration the new cornerstone of its revamped rural rehabilitation policy.

The impact of this new policy was dramatic. From the experimental settlements of 1932 through 1936, to the peak of emigration fever in the late 1930s and into the years of the Pacific War, 321,882 emigrants were mobilized to participate in the Manchurian project. Disproportionately, the Manchurian emigrants came from specific regions of Japan. Nagano and Yamagata prefectures sent by far the greatest numbers, together accounting for 17 percent of the total (see Table 9). With a single exception, the seven top-ranking prefectures were clustered in the same region, forming a line that ran from Gifu in east central Japan to Miyagi in the northeast.[43] If that group is expanded to include prefectures sending 6,000 emigrants or more (the top 18), the pattern becomes even more pronounced.[44]

Although the professed reason for promoting emigration was overpopulation in the countryside, this factor did not appear to have much effect on a community's decision to adopt an emigration plan. According to the Ministry of Agriculture and Forestry's own calculations, the problem of overpopulation was most extreme in Oita, which had 61 percent more people than land to support them properly. But Oita and the second most overpopulated prefecture, Nagasaki, sent very few emigrants—ranking close to the bottom of the prefectural list. Moreover, only three of the thirteen prefectures "more than 41 percent overpopulated" were among the top eleven emigrating prefectures, while five of the twelve least overpopulated (less than 30 percent excess population) were in this group.

42. Sugino, *Nōson kōsei undō*, p. 4.
43. Rankings are determined on a national scale of Japan's forty-seven administrative units (*dōfuken*), which includes one province, or *dō* (Hokkaidō), three metropolitan districts, or *fu* (Tokyo, Osaka, Kyoto), and forty-three prefectures, or *ken*. When designated in the collective, *dōfuken* will be referred to as prefectures.
44. Nagano-ken kaitaku jikōkai Manshū kaitakushi kankōkai, vol. 1, p. 309.

Table 9. Emigration by Prefecture

Rank	Prefecture	Number of Emigrants
1	Nagano	37,859
2	Yamagata	17,177
3	Kumamoto	12,680
4	Fukushima	12,673
5	Niigata	12,651
6	Miyagi	12,419
7	Gifu	12,090
8	Hiroshima	11,172
9	Tokyo	11,111
10	Kōchi	10,482
11	Akita	9,452
12	Shizuoka	9,206
13	Gumma	8,775
14	Aomori	8,365
15	Kagawa	7,885
16	Ishikawa	7,271
17	Yamaguchi	6,508
18	Iwate	6,436
19	Okayama	5,786
20	Kagoshima	5,700
21	Nara	5,243
22	Toyama	5,200
23	Fukui	5,136
24	Yamanashi	5,104
25	Saitama	4,864
26	Ehime	4,525
27	Hyōgo	4,400
28	Saga	4,300
29	Tochigi	4,231
30	Osaka	4,155
31	Mie	4,062
32	Tottori	3,626
33	Ibaraki	3,573
34	Miyazaki	3,382
35	Kyoto	3,370

(Continued on next page)

Table 9—*Continued*

Rank	Prefecture	Number of Emigrants
36	Tokushima	3,325
37	Wakayama	3,149
38	Hokkaidō	3,129
39	Fukuoka	3,114
40	Shimane	3,035
41	Okinawa	2,994
42	Oita	2,571
43	Aichi	2,358
44	Nagasaki	2,150
45	Chiba	2,148
46	Kanagawa	1,588
47	Shiga	1,447

SOURCE: Nagano-ken kaitaku jikōkai Manshū kaitakushi kankōkai, *Nagano-ken Manshū kaitakushi,* vol. 1 (Nagano: Nagano-ken kaitaku jikōkai Manshū kaitakushi kankōkai, 1984), p. 309.

In fact, it was not distress caused by overpopulation, but rather the unevenly felt agricultural crisis that led certain regions to promote Manchurian emigration. The impact of the drop in rice prices affected agriculture as a whole, but the fall in the value of silk and the crop failures of 1933 and 1934 were more localized disasters. The most active prefecture in the emigration movement was Nagano, also the nation's number one silk producer. Seventy percent of Nagano's agricultural revenue came from sericulture.[45] Together the six prefectures of the Tōhoku, the northeast region most affected by the crop failures, sent 66,522 emigrants, or 21 percent of the total. In all six prefectures, adverse weather conditions caused precipitous drops in rice production.[46]

These conditions led both to the disintegration of village finances and to an intensification of social conflict. Household debt and tenancy disputes were good predictors of community participation in the emigration move-

45. Kōdansha, ed., *Hijōji Nihon: Shōwa 7 nen–9 nen,* vol. 3 of *Shōwa nimannichi no zenkiroku* (Kōdansha, 1989), p. 255.

46. As a percentage of the 1929–1933 average, rice production in 1934 fell to 45.73 percent in Iwate, to 53.6 percent in Aomori, to 54.07 percent in Yamagata, to 61.73 percent in Miyagi, to 66.58 percent in Fukushima, and to 74.44 percent in Akita: ibid., p. 308.

ment. In terms of the former, with an average household debt of 666.7 yen, Nagano was again at the top of the national list. Akita (596.1 yen), Fukushima (558.4 yen), Yamagata (526.9 yen), Niigata (517.8 yen), and Miyagi (495.6 yen) were also among the ten prefectures with the highest rates of debt.[47] During the 1930s tenancy disputes were most prevalent in emigration centers of the Tōhoku and Chūbu regions, and in the Tōhoku this represented a 616 percent rise in disputes from the previous decade. Moreover, in contrast to regions such as the Kinki, a high proportion of the Tōhoku disputes (78 percent in 1937) concerned eviction.[48] Landlords in the Tōhoku region thus had a greater incentive for supporting the re-settlement of their tenants overseas.

However, a disproportionate degree of economic hardship did not in itself translate into a strong local emigration movement. Yamanashi was a major silk-producing region, but unlike Nagano sent few emigrants. The rice harvest was much worse in Iwate than Niigata, yet the latter sent about twice as many emigrants. Unusually high household debts plagued rural communities in Shimane and Saga, yet they did not send many either. Clearly, economic hardship provided a necessary but not sufficient condition for the development of an emigration movement. The additional requirement was the existence of local institutions already active in pro-moting emigration. The new agrarian social imperialism mobilized the institutions of the emigration movement.

The prefectures that led the nation in sending colonists to Manchuria all possessed long histories of involvement with colonization. The leading source of emigrants, Nagano, had perhaps the most extensive local tradi-tion. The prefectural Board of Education, Shinano kyōikukai, had assidu-ously promoted emigration since 1888, the date of its first publication on the subject. Numerous local emigration associations formed after the Russo-Japanese War, including Nagano's Shinano Overseas Association (Shinano kaigai kyōkai). The latter steadily extended the scope of its ac-tivities, and in the 1920s sponsored a mass emigration plan to establish a Nagano village in Brazil.[49] In the number two position, Yamagata had a similar history. Between 1910 and 1940, an average of 1,698 Yamagatans emigrated per year, a movement which peaked after World War I. Local organizations had energetically pushed mass emigration to Hokkaidō,

47. Ibid., p. 316.
48. Waswo, pp. 97, 102.
49. Nagano-ken kaitaku jikōkai Manshū kaitakushi kankōkai, vol. 1, pp. 1–70, 101–120.

South America, and the Pacific Islands (Nan'yō).[50] Ranking eighth among prefectures in out-migration, Hiroshima, too, had been promoting emigration for decades before Manchukuo. Hiroshima created the nation's first prefectural Overseas Settlement Council and sent almost twice as many immigrants to the United States as any other prefecture.[51] Miyagi, Niigata, and other key prefectures also had parallel experiences.[52]

After World War I these same prefectures became centers for Katō Kanji's agrarian training institutes, spreading ideas about farm colonization of the empire which were later assimilated in the government's settlement program. With prefectural support, Katō built his original youth-training center in Yamagata in 1915. Graduates from this center formed the core of the experimental Korean and Manchurian farm colonies of the 1920s.[53] Miyagi, Nagano, and Niigata also offered fertile soil for an expanding network of youth-training centers to disseminate Katō's ideas and indoctrinate the young men who would lead the Manchurian farm colonies in the 1930s.[54]

These flourishing local traditions provided a critical foundation for the rapid growth of a Manchurian emigration movement in the early thirties. This trial emigration period before Manchurian colonization became national policy in 1936 was a decisive organizational phase for the prefectures that would spearhead the full-blown emigration movement. Nowhere was this more true than in Nagano. By 1932 local organizations had drafted

50. Yamagata-ken, p. 736.

51. Hiroshima maintained this position among Japanese emigrating to the United States before 1922. Kumamoto, the third largest source of Manchurian emigrants, was second to Hiroshima in terms of emigrants to the United States: Nagano-ken kaitaku jikōkai Manshū kaitakushi kankōkai, vol. 1, pp. 35, 55.

52. Mainichi shirizu shuppan henshu, ed., *Miyagi-ken no Shōwashi: kindai hyakunen no kiroku*, vol. 1 (Mainichi shinbunsha, 1983), pp. 282–284; Niigata-ken, p. 741.

53. Yamagata shishi hensan iinkai, ed., *Kingendaihen* of *Yamagata shishi* (Yamagata: Yamagata-shi, 1980), pp. 277–282.

54. Yunoki Shun'ichi, "Shōwa nōgyō kyōkō to Shōnaigata imin keikaku no tenkai: Yamato-mura bunson imin o chūshin toshite," *Keizaigaku kenkyū*, no. 4 (Komazawa daigaku daigakuin, March 1976), pp. 133–158; Yunoki Shun'ichi, "Shōwa nōgyō kyōkō to Manshū imin: Miyagi-ken Nangō-mura imin no bunseki," *Kenkyū kiyō*, no. 14 (Tōkyō-to senshū gakkō kakushu gakkō kyōkai, March 1978), pp. 131–138; Yunoki Shun'ichi, "Manshū imin undō no tenkai to ronri: Miyagi-ken Nangō-mura imin undō no bunseki," *Shakai keizai shigaku* 48, no. 3 (August 1982), pp. 52–71; Yunoki Shun'ichi, " 'Manshū' nōgyō imin seisaku to 'Shōnaigata' imin: Yamagata-ken Yamato-mura imin keikaku o chūshin ni," *Shakai keizai shigaku* 42, no. 5 (March 1977), pp. 44–69; Nagano-ken kaitaku jikōkai Manshū kaitakushi kankōkai, vol. 1, pp. 150–158.

five separate emigration plans. Among these the Shinano kaigai kyōkai drew up a ten-year scheme to send 400 households each year in order to build a colony they called the Manshū aikoku Shinano-mura (Manchurian Patriotic Nagano Village). Local government officials also matched the enthusiasm of private organizations for Manchurian colonization. Although the regimental command had been assigned the task of recruiting volunteers from Nagano for the government's Trial Emigration Program, by 1934 prefectural bureaucrats had all but taken over the job. Initiating the involvement of the prefectural government, the Shinano Board of Education sent an inspection tour to Manchuria in 1932. The following year the board established a "Manchurian-Mongolian Research Office" and began to add positions to handle the growing emigration-related workload. The prefectural branch of the national farm cooperative, Sangyō kumiai, also demonstrated an early interest in Manchurian emigration by setting up the Manmō ijū kenkyūkai (Manchurian Mongolian Settlement Society) in 1932. All these organizations began to deluge the rural community with exhortations to emigrate. By 1935, the Shinano kaigai kyōkai alone had held 200 lectures and distributed 4,000 books, 15,000 pamphlets, and 350,000 posters promoting Manchurian colonization.[55] Although Nagano stood out from the rest of the country in terms of sheer magnitude of activity, Yamagata, Hiroshima, Niigata, Miyagi, and other prefectures also built up their local emigration machines before 1936.

In this way, local movements first anticipated and then provided the momentum behind the national movement. Support for Manchurian colonization in places like Nagano and Yamagata brought together the hitherto separate social movements supporting agrarianism and emigration. The acute agricultural crisis of the 1930s forced agrarianists to adopt colonization as the solution for the villages. At the same time, the opening of a new colonial frontier in Manchukuo led emigration organizations to concentrate their hopes on farmers as the vehicles for Japan's demographic expansion overseas. Out of the fusion of these two movements emerged a powerful agrarian social imperialism.

In its power and form the social imperialism of the 1930s was a new phenomenon. Although people had been discussing agricultural coloni-

---

55. Nagano-ken kaitaku jikōkai Manshū kaitakushi kankōkai, vol. 1, pp. 70–101, 121–166; Higashichikuma-gun, Matsumoto-shi, Shiojiri-shi kyōdō shiryō hensankai, ed., *Gendai 1*, vol. 3 of *Higashichikuma-gun, Matsumoto-shi, Shiojiri-shishi* (Nagano: Higashichikuma-gun, Matsumoto-shi, Shiojiri-shi kyōdō shiryō hensankai, 1962), pp. 391–392.

zation for decades, and a similar project had been both proposed and partially implemented in Korea, the Manchurian program went further and involved a much larger scale of popular support. It was also significant that the pressures for social imperialism emerged with greatest strength from the countryside. All the forces propelling imperialism in Northeast China in the 1930s contained an element of social imperialism; the Manchurian Incident war fever certainly fed on economic ills, as did ambitions for the yen bloc. Yet it was the villages that produced the most intense and sustained movement for social imperialism. Moreover, agrarian social imperialism sought succor with unmatched literalness. In cases of military occupation and Manchurian development, hopes for the empire represented displacements and distractions from domestic social tensions. In contrast, Manchurian agrarian colonization undertook the direct export of the rural social problem.

IMPERIAL AGRARIANISM IN JAPAN

When they tied their fortunes to the emigration movement, agrarianists revised their prescriptions for social reform to accommodate the empire. This new, imperial agrarianism rendered empire as space: vast empty tracts of fertile farmland providing lebensraum for Japan's overcrowded and socially conflicted villages. In the past, problems such as farmers' debt and the land shortage had proved resistant to agrarianist remedies. These solutions had ultimately foundered on the inability to reconcile competing interests of landlords and tenants. With the addition of the unlimited lands of Manchuria into the formula for rural rehabilitation, however, all these problems suddenly disappeared. In the context of empire, agrarianism became transmuted from an ideological tradition expressing rural interests against city interests, and landlords against tenants, into a nationalist ideology. This shift was the key to the success of the Manchurian settlement movement in building a broad consensus among the policy-making elite at the center and periphery of the Japanese polity.

Because of its evocations of an imagined, harmonious past to which it sought return, as well as its association with the fascist movement, agrarianism is often regarded as a reactionary philosophy. Yet in its imperial variant, agrarianism was concerned more with the future than the past: its prescriptions for social reform had a radical and "modern" flavor. The Millions to Manchuria planners envisioned rehabilitating villages through new technologies of social engineering on a grand scale, unlike anything envisioned before. Employing the language of scientific management, social policy, and industrial rationalization which had begun to circulate in the 1920s, emigration planners hoped to modernize the Japanese farm village from above. Seeking the creation of an alternative modernity to that which capitalism had produced in the villages, they were determined to turn the clock forward, not back.

The emigration plans counted heavily on the marvels of social science. In the 1937 study that set the terms of the new national policy of Manchurian settlement, Ministry of Agriculture and Forestry officials surveyed small landowning households in 1,000 villages throughout the country to determine the minimal plot size required to practice farming without incurring long-term debt. From this survey emerged the magic figure of 1.6 *chō* (4 acres) to designate the amount of land a farm household required to maintain itself free of debt, and hence, out of poverty. Identifying this 1.6 *chō* figure as the "standard optimum holding" (*hyōjun keiei menseki*), the ministry calculated that to stretch existing land resources so that all farm households could have optimum holdings, 31 percent of the nation's farm population would have to go.[56] Confident in the powers of social science, the organizers of the emigration movement proceeded with great certitude to plan the resettlement of one-third of rural Japan based on this simple calculation.

To engineer such a depopulation of rural Japan, ministry officials hoped to persuade local communities throughout the country to send enough of their members to Manchuria so that those left behind would have landholdings sufficient to become independent farmers. Drawing up an elaborate set of guidelines for how a local community should plan and organize its own Manchurian emigration movement, ministry officials tried to sell village elites on the Manchurian solution to their local problems. Sugino Tadao, who authored many of the ministry's promotional pamphlets, described the proffered package of reforms in the language of radical transformation. In various contexts he called it a program for "social renovation" (*shakai kaizō*), "comprehensive reform" (*dāinaru kakushin*), "restructuring of Japanese farm villages" (*nōson no saihensei*), and "agricultural revolution" (*nōgyō kakumei*).[57] Such language distinguished

56. This survey was published by Nōrinshō keizai kōseibu, *Manshū nōgyō imin ni kansuru chihō jijō chōsa gaiyō* (1937), and included in "Manshū nōgyō imin ni kansuru shoshiryō," *Naigai chōsa shiryō* 10, no. 11 (November 1938), pp. 241–262; for standard optimum holding, see pp. 241–242; for excess population, see p. 249.

57. Sugino Tadao, *Bunson keikaku no igi: sono shidō seishin ni tsuite*, no. 2 of *Bunson keikaku sōsho* (Nōson kōsei kyōkai, 1938), pp. 3–4, 13–14; Sugino Tadao,

proposals for Manchurian emigration from past policies, suggesting that the ministry had abandoned the discredited measures of the earlier rural rehabilitation movement in favor of thoroughgoing and truly effective agricultural reform.

Even while holding out the hope of real solutions, advocates of Manchurian colonization hastened to silence alarms that such words of change might sound among the village wealthy. Earlier policies of debt relief, public works, and self-help had failed to give relief to the poorest strata of rural society because they ran afoul of landlords, who refused to curtail their powers and prerogatives. From this experience rural rehabilitators took a key lesson: to be effective, agricultural reform must not threaten entrenched class interests. With this in mind, planners took careful stock of potential obstacles. They anticipated that landlords would object to emigration because, by altering the population-to-land ratio, village colonization was likely to drive down the price of land and tenancy fees. In addition, since many tenants were chronically indebted to landlords, planners worried that the debt problem "could act as a brake" on colonization, especially if suspicions were raised that the emigration planners were encouraging debtors to "escape by cover of night" from their creditors. Moreover, if wealthy landlords did not cooperate with plans for the disposal of vacated lands, the entire project could be placed in jeopardy. Planners wanted to prevent both the further concentration of land in the hands of large landowners as well as an influx of new tenants from outside the village.[58]

The emigration plan aimed to resolve these problems by the unlimited extension of village lands into Manchuria. With the grant of a large tract of land from the Manchukuo government, the mother village would send its poor farmers off to establish a branch village in the empire. Although technically separated by miles of land and water, ties of custom and blood bound the two villages together in an imagined community. These ties would endure and provide infinitely expandable farmlands to which the mother village could send her sons on into the future. With the creation of a greater village community, the dream of reshaping the mother village into a uniform population of middle-class farmers no longer stood at var-

Seishōnen ni uttau, no. 1 of *Bunson keikaku sōsho* (Nōson kōsei kyōkai, 1938), pp. 3–4.

58. Nōrinshō keizai kōseibu, ed., *Shinnōson no kensetsu: tairiku e bunson daiidō* (Asahi shinbunsha, 1939), pp. 27–32; Sugino Tadao, *Bunson keikaku to sono hantairon*, no. 5 of *Bunson keikaku sōsho* (Nōson kōsei kyōkai, 1938), pp. 1–20.

iance with the protection of existing landlord interests. No one need give anything up because the village poor would happily move to Manchuria for the land, the land they left behind could be distributed to those who needed it, and the landholdings of the wealthy would be left intact. A land reform, boasted Sugino Tadao, that must please every landlord, "village colonization" resolved the tenancy problem "to the best advantage of tenants without exacting a major sacrifice from landlords."[59]

Conceived in this way, vexatious problems "like the land question" suddenly seemed "easy to take care of."[60] The Ministry of Agriculture and Forestry issued a list of suggestions to solve the land problem through the "rational distribution of land" freed up by mass emigration. Local village plans interpreted these in various ways. For example, in Fujimi village "most of this land" would be "bought by [the co-op association] Sangyō kumiai," which in turn would "distribute it appropriately among neighborhood farm cooperatives for communal farm plots." Thus the Fujimi Committee placed priority on using this land to refashion their community into a model of "cooperativism."[61] The Yomikaki village plan, in contrast, allocated virtually all the vacated lands to the creation of *chūnō*, or middle-sized farmers. Through the resale of some lands and the transfer of leaseholds on others, village authorities aimed to transform their community into the middle-holder ideal. Projections of the structure of village landholdings showed a community before emigration in which over 50 percent of the households managed under half a *chō* (1.2 acres) of land each. The village envisioned after emigration was one where almost 57 percent of households managed a half to one *chō* (1.2 to 2.45 acres) of land and the remaining 43 percent managed upward of one *chō* (2.45 acres). Thus, households managing under a half *chō* (1.2 acres) of land were completely eliminated, without touching the big landowners.[62]

The emigration plan also resolved the seemingly intractable problem of tenant debt. As the Rehabilitation Division of the Ministry of Agriculture and Forestry recommended for the case of debt clearance, promoting trust between debtors and creditors was the key to the whole problem. If liquidating farmers' assets did not cover the sum of their obligations, officials proposed the familiar course of committees, cooperatives, plans, and ne-

59. Sugino, *Seishōnen ni uttau,* p. 6.

60. Sugino, *Bunson keikaku no igi,* p. 5.

61. Teikoku nōkai, *Fujimi-mura no bunson undō ni tsuite (Nagano-ken Suwa-gun Fujimi-mura chōsa)* (Teikoku nōkai, 1942), p. 23.

62. Nagano-ken keizaibu, *Bunson keikaku jirei: Nishichikuma-gun Yomikaki-mura,* no. 37 of *Keizai kōseisankō shiryō* (Nagano-ken keizaibu, 1939), p. 64.

gotiations be tried to resolve emigrants' indebtedness before they moved to Manchuria. Where none of this availed, emigrants would have no alternative but to repay their debt from Manchuria, an option purportedly made possible by the "good offices of village authorities" and a feeling of "good faith" on both sides.[63] All this good feeling was to spring from the carefully nurtured sense of connection between the village and colony. Allowing debtors to move out of the locality, creditors were giving up effective control over the situation in the illusion that their debtors were still well within reach. What had been, until then, a persistent obstacle to social reform, the debt problem was suddenly resolved by an imagined set of connections with an imperial colony yet to be established.

Although creditors may not always have been persuaded by this logic, to the emigration planners it was unimpeachable. They were convinced that the new tracts of farmland from Manchukuo, when properly administered with social scientific techniques for planning and analysis, would finally resolve the deadlock between the village haves and have-nots. Thus their confidence in the tools of scientific management was matched by a faith in the future of the empire. Indeed, in the scheme of Manchurian colonization planners, empire became a kind of deus ex machina which could magically whisk away long-standing social obstacles to rural reform. The revised formulas of imperial agrarianists promised to end social conflict between rich and poor without requiring landowners to forfeit any of their lands, wealth, or status. The acquisition of unlimited Manchurian land meant that rural poverty could be eliminated without any sacrifice from the wealthy.

Hopes restored by the new possibilities opened up in the empire, rural reformers focused their energies on using Manchurian colonization to create a rural population of *chūnō* (middle-sized farmers). As one of Sugino's tracts explained, "The purpose of the village colonization plan is to turn all of the farmers in the village into *chūnō* through the planned limitation of farm households." Thus Sugino and his colleagues claimed they could forge a nation of uniform, comfortably independent small farmers out of the bewildering array of tenants, part-tenants, landlords, and part-landlords which characterized the real social fabric of the Japanese village.

Colonization plans deployed the agrarian shibboleth that if all farmers were *chūnō*, problems such as poverty and class conflict would disappear. Meticulous new research supported this claim, showing that "solvent farm households" were "generally found among the middle-sized farmer class."

---

63. Nōrinshō keizai kōseibu, *Shinnōson no kensetsu*, pp. 27–28.

Recasting all farm households in this mold would "put an end to rapacious starvation tenancy . . . and overturn serf-like relations between landlord and tenant." It would permit "the creation of fair and just conditions of tenancy and tenacy fees." In short, it would finally resolve the "land question."[64]

Not only would social problems disappear, promised the planners, but a village of *chūnō* could engineer untold improvements in agricultural production. Since "the middle-sized farmer class" was "exceptional in terms of labor productivity," it was optimistically calculated that "even if the agricultural population is reduced by half, a group of solid, middle-sized farmers working together could ensure that far from suffering a reduction in agricultural production, the nation will very likely experience a rise in output."[65]

Finally, the expansion of the *chūnō* class would provide a "material foundation for mutual aid and cooperativism" within the hamlet, a cherished dream of the agrarianists. With land freed up by emigrants, "community farms" could be established, becoming in turn "the mainstay of cooperative activity in the village." At last the "rationalization of agricultural management" would "become possible." With the reduction of the agricultural labor force, farmers would have to increase productivity by "joint management of lands," "increased use of livestock and machinery," and "planned allocation of labor"—all measures long "planned for but never actually put into practice."[66] Thus, in the vision of imperial agrarianism, the middle-class farm household represented the key to an economically healthy, socially harmonious farm village. Through the social construction of the *chūnō* ideal, rural reformers hoped to build a utopian alternative to the flawed modernity that capitalism had wrought.

As the terms used to describe the concept of *chūnō* reflected, planners were never quite sure whether they were talking about actual people or a constructed ideal. The middle-farmer was both representative (*daihyō*) and ideal (*risō*), "someone any ordinary person could identify with" and a "model" (*mohan*).[67] This ambiguity gave local emigration committees wide leeway to define their goals as they saw fit, while giving lip service to the program's established guidelines.

---

64. Sugino, *Seishōnen ni uttau*, pp. 5–6.
65. Ibid.
66. Ibid., p. 7.
67. See e.g. Sugino Tadao, *Bunson keikaku no jissai mondai: jirei o chūshin toshite*, no. 4 of *Bunson keikaku sōsho* (Nōson kōsei kyōkai, 1938), pp. 1–18.

Whether the *chūnō* to which they referred was a real farmer or an ideal image of one, he did possess one defining characteristic: his farm ran a modest surplus. He did this by combining traditional agrarianist values with the techniques of modern farm management. First, the *chūnō* relied exclusively on the traditional family system for his labor needs, upholding the family unit as the foundation of the ideal farm household economy. At the time, driven by economic necessity and desires for upward mobility, fewer and fewer of the younger children of farm households—rich or poor—were staying at home to work on the family farm full time. Rural rehabilitators hoped to reverse this trend, reinforcing the strength of the family system by providing a livelihood for all its members. Second, while he upheld tradition, the ideal farmer also employed modern budgetary and cultivation practices. Model "in-the-black" households managed the lands at their disposal "rationally," minimizing cash outflow by double-entry bookkeeping and a scientific mix of crops.

Most important of all, the model farmer possessed enough land to accomplish this. Any number of methods were employed to determine, within the scope of a particular emigration plan, what should constitute "the appropriate scale standard farm household." As one emigration manual instructed, this should be calculated from estimates of "the scale of land necessary to provide a stable household income but which could be managed within the limits set by labor power of the household." Accordingly, in many localities like the Shōnai district (Yamagata prefecture), emigration committees conducted elaborate surveys to determine their choice of scale. Selecting twenty-two households, the Shōnai District Committee minutely measured labor-power values for each family member and analyzed the household accounts sen by sen. Other local committees took the advice of the manual to "eyeball it," skipping the survey and simply picking a local farmer who "looked right" as a standard.[68]

It was not surprising, therefore, to find that estimations of the standard household plot varied considerably. One of the pioneering surveys carried out in four counties in Ibaraki prefecture by the Rural Rehabilitation Council in 1936 declared that the in-the-black household needed 2 *chō* (4.9 acres) of land.[69] The nationwide survey undertaken by the Ministry of Agriculture and Forestry in 1937 adopted 1.6 *chō* (4 acres) as a national

68. Nōrinshō keizai kōseibu, *Shinnōson no kensetsu*, p. 21; *Shōnai bunkyō keikaku chōsa hōkoku* (Manshū ijū kyōkai, 1938), pp. 2–7.
69. Sugino, *Nōson kōsei undō*, p. 180.

standard.[70] The Shōnai District Committee based its calculations on the introduction of certain changes in farm management. Since its "stable farm household" abjured income from "entertainment, sericulture, lumbering, fishing, or tenancy fees" and supplied its own household demand for food-stuffs, 3.3 *chō* (8 acres) were needed to keep the accounts in the black.[71] Plans published by Yomikaki village and Fujimi village, located close to-gether in Nagano prefecture, differed in their targets by a matter of .74 *chō* (1.8 acres).[72] Since the idea was to bring all farmers up to this standard, a matter of a half a *chō* could mean a significant difference in the aggregate acreage required to upgrade the entire village to *chūnō*.

As these local variations showed, in spite of the herculean research efforts by the Ministry of Agriculture and Forestry, the agricultural as-sociation Nōkai, the agricultural cooperative Sangyō kumiai, and the re-spective local governments, there was no exact ratio of land to farmer that would socially engineer a stable rural middle class. Yet, though these vil-lage studies varied in their calculations of the standard holding, they were united in their fixation on the question of land: everything followed from an adequate plot size. This preoccupation with land was the defining char-acteristic of imperial agrarianism, for when they brought empire into their field of vision, agrarianists revised their prescriptions for social reform. Now instructions for measuring and allocating land occupied a central place, while homilies of frugality, community spirit, and other staples of agrarian philosophy retreated into the background. Because to rural re-formers empire signified land, when they adopted the Manchurian solution to the problem of the villages they transformed their agrarianism from a moral philosophy that idealized farm life into a program for land reform. In this way the tie to Manchuria strengthened progressive tendencies in agrarianism, demonstrating, once again, how the forces of social reform harnessed themselves to the empire in the 1930s.

AGRARIAN IMPERIALISM IN MANCHURIA

Within Japan, rural reformers understood that planning for ideal com-munities had to take into account existing social reality. In contrast, ar-

70. Nōrinshō keizai kōseibu, *Shinnōson no kensetsu*, p. 518.

71. *Shōnai bunkyō keikaku chōsa hōkoku*, pp. 2–7.

72. Yomikaki-mura set a .76-*chō* target and Fujimi-mura a 1.5-*chō* target: Teikoku nōkai, *Fujimi-mura*, p. 20; Nagano-ken keizaibu, *Bunson keikaku jirei*, p. 35.

chitects of the new Manchurian settlements felt completely unfettered by such constraints. Although planners were well acquainted with the complexities of Chinese agricultural society in the region, blueprints for Japanese settlements projected visions of self-contained communities growing up in a pristine socioeconomic wilderness.

The vastly greater scope for action afforded planners in Manchuria by their position within an all-powerful colonial state was reflected in the more elaborate set of prescriptions for creating their version of agrarian utopia. Whereas planners in Japan restricted their gaze to the one sphere where they had some control—land—and ended by diluting the moral flavor of agrarianism, the architects of the Manchurian settlements placed traditional agrarian precepts at the foundations of their vision of agrarian imperialism. Unlike rural reformers in Japan, whose unit of analysis was the individual farm household, planners in Manchuria took up the community as a whole. Yet, in spite of these differences, agrarian imperialism shared a great deal with its metropolitan counterpart. Both sought to use the Manchurian colonization program as a vehicle for creating an alternative modernity in the Japanese farm village, one that would insulate the village from the demonstrated impact of capitalism on the rural economy. Both raised the possibilities of social engineering to new heights and drew on vocabularies of the social bureaucrats of the 1920s. Finally, they shared their shortcomings. Both failed to save the villages from the inroads of capitalism and both proved unable to control human beings in the ways suggested by the mechanical metaphors of social engineering.

In October 1935 the Colonial Ministry published the planning document that became sacred writ for Japanese settlement, the "Proposed Standards for the Management of Collective Farm Immigrants in North Manchuria."[73] This document represented the Manchurian counterpart to the 1937 Japanese government survey that established standards for village rehabilitation plans at home. Echoing the hopes of rural rehabilitators in Japan, the "Proposed Standards" provided instructions for building model rural communities without social conflict, villages of the future that could exist outside capitalism. Guided by the same ideal of the independent middle-holder, Manchurian settlements were structured to prevent absolutely the emergence of the class divisions and the tenancy system that plagued rural society in Japan. Not only would this new classless community avoid importing social problems from home, but it would be stable,

73. Takumushō takumukyoku, "Hokuman ni okeru shūdan nōgyō imin no keiei hyōjun'an," *Naigai chōsa shiryō* 10, no. 11 (November 1938), pp. 8–45.

unchanging, and, above all, enduring. This was not just idealism; stability was essential if the settlements were to fulfill their function as anchors for a permanent Japanese population in the Manchurian countryside.

The "Proposed Standards" used the term *jisakunō* (yeoman farmer) to describe the independent farmer who provided the linchpin of stability in the settlements themselves. Planners felt that a stable population of independent cultivators could be engineered socially, given the correct materials, the appropriate organization, and the right plan. Accordingly, the "Proposed Standards" set out in great detail the ingredients required to metamorphose the outcasts of rural Japan into *jisakunō*. In addition to their twenty *chō* (forty-nine acres) of land, immigrants were promised one cow, one horse, one female pig, and ten female sheep. They were to be issued one plow and other sundry farm tools as well as three storage sheds and one wagon. They shared one well among 5 families, an enclosing wall with the other 29 families of their hamlet, and a flour mill, a rice huller, an oil press, a foundry, various barns, and a truck among the 300 households of the village. From such a precise combination of ingredients, it was alleged, would emerge the mythical figure of the *jisakunō*—the independent cultivator of the settlement planners' dreams. These facile predictions of the efficacies of social engineering in the Japanese settlements assumed that settlers, too, would arrive in a standardized form, like so many products off an assembly line. Identical when they arrived, they would be allocated identical materials and thus grow into a socially identical population of Japanese settlers. Every household of every hamlet of every village of every province throughout Manchukuo, every one of the million would be just like the rest.

If standard issue started colonists out on equal footing, provisions for the cooperative organization of the settlement aimed to keep everyone that way. The "Proposed Standards" called for cooperativism to extend to all aspects of farm management, including joint cultivation, collective management of livestock, cooperative management of such joint-production facilities as oil presses and foundries, and the sharing of profits and losses through cooperative marketing arrangements. All this was to be accomplished through an extensive cooperative bureaucracy that ran the daily operations of the settlement. In this way planners thought to eliminate possibilities for private accumulation, seeking to discourage the profit motive among settlers who had been lured to Manchuria with promises of private holdings and dreams of upward mobility.

With materials and organization in place, all that remained to engineer the ideal community, in the minds of the planners, was the plan itself. The

"Proposed Standards" offered a model settlement plan which promised to make the community self-sustaining within three years. The key to the plan was self-sufficiency and isolation from the market economy, thus bringing to Manchuria the same policy swords used by agrarian ideologues in their attempt to fend off the demons of capitalist modernity. Like the proscriptions against private accumulation, the requirement for self-sufficiency contradicted one of the cases being made for Manchurian colonization back in Japan. In the policy debate of the early 1930s many Japanese, particularly businessmen, were won over by the argument that the growth of a substantial Japanese population would create a consumer market for Japanese goods. Neither this contradiction nor the fact that self-sufficiency had proved unworkable in Japan stopped planners in Manchuria from drawing up a strict program for colonies to supply their own consumption requirements through diversified farming practices. The consumption program was divided into subsistance categories of shelter, clothing, and food. Shelter, according to the "Proposed Standards," was taken care of in the start-up package. Clothing colonists could make for themselves from settlement-produced wool during the winter season. This left food, which could be self-supplied almost completely, assuming settlers sustained themselves on the meal plan set forth in the "Proposed Standards." In this way, visions of minimal market interaction rested on the questionable assumptions that buildings in the settlement would require no improvements in three years, that home fuel and lighting could be locally furnished, that colonists would need no additional accoutrements or furnishings, that colonists would wear only wool, and that they wanted to eat rice mixed with millet, local game, and local vegetables.

On the production side, a program of diversified cropping and mixed-crop and livestock farming would serve the dual purpose of supplying all local demand and minimizing the impact of price fluctuations on whatever marketable surplus there was. Accordingly, the model plan included yearly targets for rice, soybeans, barley, millet, wheat, and maize production, and set the number of sheep, cattle, horses, and pigs which settlers should breed. Since the "Proposed Standards" prescribed self-supply of feed, fertilizer, and seed, management of the farm, like management of the household, was geared to minimize dependence on the market. Planners anticipated the achievement of all this in a three-year time frame, leaving no room for shortages of farm implements, livestock, or other start-up materials. Moreover, the plan provided no margin for the errors sure to be made by settlers who had never seen a sheep before let alone raised one, and who were otherwise unfamiliar with the crops, the tools, the methods, and the size of their new farms.

The "Proposed Standards" defined what became known as the four principles of settlement: owner-cultivatorism, mixed cultivation, self-sufficiency, and cooperativism. Aiming to create an ideal village in Manchuria, the four principles purported to improve upon a Japanese model which had never actually existed. Communities whose social fabric would not alter, the Manchurian settlements were designed to be self-sustaining and self-contained—protected islands within the sea of Chinese humanity.

Despite this grand vision, specific proposals to ensure survival rejected new departures in favor of the well-worn moralism of traditional agrarianism. The treatment of the issue of economic competition in the "Proposed Standards" was a case in point. As all parties to the early 1930s debate over Manchurian migration conceded, under free-market conditions the native Chinese farmers would undersell Japanese settlers because it cost them less to maintain their lower standard of living. In choosing to address this problem through self-sufficiency, the "Proposed Standards" ignored the welter of advice that raising productivity through farm technology was the only way Japanese settlers could compete with Chinese farmers. As Tokyo University professor Nishigori Hideo argued, Japanese settlers were entering an agrarian society where their "lifestyle would never be the same as the Chinese farmers," but where the more numerous Chinese set the terms of the marketplace. The only way Japanese settlers could take control of the situation and turn the market terms to their advantage was by bringing a "superior agricultural technology" to Manchuria. This way, reasoned Professor Nishigori, not only could settlers compete with natives but natives would gradually adopt Japanese farming methods in order to improve their own standards of living. For most migration experts, technology was vital to the settlement project.[74]

Although the "Proposed Standards" made no mention of agricultural technology, and tractors, harvesters, and other mechanical farm equipment were nowhere to be found in the standard issue for new immigrants, within Japan the pamphlets, books, and articles exhorting farmers to resettle on the continent referred to modern continental farming methods and showed illustrations and photographs of smiling Manchurian settlers astride the enormous tractors that were unknown in Japan outside of Hokkaidō. In-

74. Nishigori Hideo, "Manmō nōgyō imin no hitsuyō to sono kanōsei," *Shakai seisaku jihō*, no. 140 (May 1932), p. 145.

deed, these tractors became one of the symbols of the Manchurian farm settlements.[75] Yet for all the expert advice and the high expectations, the first blueprints for continental settlement spurned technology in favor of spirit. In essence, the elaborate prescriptions for cooperative management and self-supply were little more than a paraphrase of habitual exhortations to Japanese farmers to solve the economic problems of rural society through frugality and self-help.

Just as self-sufficiency, self-help, and cooperativism had failed to solve the social and economic problems of the farm village in Japan, they yielded unfortunate results in Manchuria. Research teams tracking the progress of the settlements could see clearly that a variety of problems were emerging, most of which stemmed from shortcomings in technology.[76] Accustomed to intensively cultivating less than a half *chō* (1.23 acres) of land, settlers could not hope, under their own labor power and without adopting new mechanized farming practices, to manage the more than 20 *chō* (49 acres) of land assigned to them in Manchuria. Since they lacked the machines, they used people, who were readily available. But in turning to hired labor and tenants to help them work the land, settlers violated the first principle of owner-cultivatorism. In turn, the huge cash outlays for wages wrecked the perfect budget plans.

Japanese tourbooks heaped praise on one of the first farm colonies established in Manchukuo, Chiburi village. But if travel writers had read the colony's balance sheet between 1938 and 1941, perhaps they would not have been so impressed. The settlement registered an average loss of over 2,000 yen per year, largely due to average yearly wage payments of over 700 yen. To try to offset such cash outlays, most settlements produced large numbers of cash crops such as rice and soybeans, and marketed perhaps 50 percent of their produce. Concentrating on marketable crops, colonists basically abandoned animal husbandry. For example, in colonies established in 1939, the average household possessed six-tenths of a draft animal, one-tenth of a sheep, one-fifth of a pig, and one-tenth of a chicken.

75. See e.g. "Manshū kaitaku tokugo," *Ie no hikari* (October 1939), p. 2; "Hirake iku tairiku," *Ie no hikari* (April 1939).

76. These reports are analyzed in research by Asada Kyōji and Kobayashi Hideo: Asada Kyōji, "Manshū imin no nōgyō keiei jōkyō," *Keizaigaku ronshū* 9, no. 1 (Komazawa daigaku keizai gakkai, June 1977), pp. 77–99; Asada Kyōji, "Manshū nōgyō imin no funōka jinushika jōkyō," *Keizaigaku ronshū* 8, no. 3 (Komazawa daigaku keizai gakkai, December 1976), pp. 39–94; Kobayashi Hideo, "Manshū nōgyō imin no einō jittai," in Manshū iminshi kenkyūkai, ed., *Nihon teikokushugika no Manshū imin* (Ryūkei shosha, 1976), pp. 387–490.

Clearly the second of the "Proposed Standards," the principle of mixed cultivation, was not being met.[77]

Since settlements were marketing such a high percentage of their production, there was not enough to supply their own needs, leading to the betrayal of the third golden rule—self-sufficiency. The Iyasaka settlement, for example, needed to buy 43.8 percent of their fertilizer, seed, and other necessities from outside the colony. The record on household consumption was even worse, with 60 percent supplied by the market. The disappointing household accounts appeared to stem mainly from the fact that, contrary to expectations, settlers were able to supply only 47 percent of their own food consumption.[78]

Cooperativism, the last of the four principles, met the same fate as the other three. In this case, hopes of government planners were frustrated by aspirations of the settlers themselves for individualistic success and private gain. Complaining vociferously about cooperative management, colonists demanded that settlement lands be divided into individual plots for private management. A report on settlements established in 1939 noted that "because of cooperative management," settlers were "not motivated to work hard," and "few even went out to the fields." Since their discontent was having an adverse effect on production, the settlements abandoned cooperative cultivation in stages. A thirty-household collective in the Iyasaka settlement, for example, first broke into mini-cooperatives of three to four families, then privatized completely. As researchers concluded, "Cooperative management was nothing more than a dream."[79]

The failure of the four principles was accompanied by the disturbing specter of colonists leaving the land and the appearance of income disparities within the settlement. To combat such blights on their ideal villages, planners drew up a new "Basic Outline of Manchurian Settlement Policy" in December 1939, and over the following two years issued the triad of laws that put these policy guidelines into effect: the Settlement Law of April 1940, the Settlement Cooperative Law of July 1940, and the Settlement Farm Law of November 1941.[80] Despite the ready availability of high-quality research on the socioeconomic conditions of Manchurian ag-

77. Asada, "Manshū imin no nōgyō keiei jōtai," pp. 88, 85–89; Asada, "Manshū nōgyō imin no funōka jinushika jōkyō," p. 62; Kobayashi, "Manshū nōgyō imin no einō jittai," pp. 432–433.

78. Asada, "Manshū imin no nōgyō keiei jōtai," pp. 82–83.

79. Ibid., p. 92.

80. Text of the "Basic Outline" and the new settlement laws reprinted as "Kaitaku kankei shohōki," in Manshū kaitakushi kankōkai, appendix 1, pp. 773–803.

riculture and the problems encountered by Japanese settlers operating in this context, the new "Basic Outline" predicated its proposals on the imagined autonomy and isolation of the Japanese settlements. It was as if planners had become victims of their own propaganda. Driven by images of "breaking fertile soil," their blueprints swept clear the social landscape and pretended that settlers were actually entering an "empty plain."

One dramatic expression of this was the treatment of the native (*genjūmin*) problem. Settlement plans took little note of the fact that the Manchurian countryside was filled with Chinese (and to a lesser extent, Korean) peasants whose economic activity shaped the market context in which Japanese colonists operated. Yet, although the Japanese colonies were tiny islands in a sea of Chinese humanity, the "Basic Outline" ignored this native community as a social force. Instead, natives appeared in the "Basic Outline" in only two connections. First, provisions for mixed residence among neighboring cooperative hamlets (though not within a single hamlet) and transactions between Japanese and Chinese cooperatives treated natives within the context of the Japanese settlement. Second, the "Basic Outline" provided guidelines for relocating natives when necessary to make way for Japanese settlements. In this way, the "Basic Outline" pretended that all interactions between settler and native took place within the purview of the settlement and suggested that people, like forests, could be cleared at will. Settlement planners had convinced themselves that Manchuria was truly a social wilderness.

This refusal to face up to the fact that, as Yanaihara Tadao had warned during the initial debate over Manchurian settlement, Japanese colonists could not compete in a marketplace dominated by Chinese agriculturists was apparent in the "Basic Outline" correctives for the failure of the four principles. Indeed, the bulk of the "Basic Outline" was devoted to strengthening the four principles and assuring, through legal means if necessary, that colonies of purportedly self-sufficient independent cultivators would stay put on the land. The Settlement Cooperative Law strengthened powers of the cooperative and required that any deviation from prescribed form receive authorization from the colonial government authorities. The Settlement Law spelled out the "duties and obligations" of the settlers to take part in collective cultivation and other joint production in the settlement. Colonists were tied to their farms by stipulations that any change in occupation required approval of the head of the settlement. Limits were placed on capital accumulation through the strict prohibition of market and cash transactions outside of the cooperative. Finally, the Settlement Farm Law gave the farm household legal form, investing authority in the head of household and defining the legal entity of the family in terms of its connection to the land. Thus family and land were bound together in legal eternity, ensuring that the land could not be broken up or alienated from the family, but would pass undivided from one generation to another. Trying to build legal dams to stem the economic current, settlement planners persisted in their belief that the settlers could and should be kept out of its flow.

The inability of the settlement planners to factor the economic agency of the settlers into their plans reflected, at a deeper level, a constitutive unwillingness to accommodate Manchurian colonization to the wishes of the colonists themselves. This "we know best" attitude on the part of planners was consistent with the paternalism of earlier ideas of emigration and the institutional culture of an emigration movement that had been shaped by the desires of promoters, not the aspirations of emigrants. In the context of Manchukuo, such tendencies were invigorated by the new faith in social science and the efficacy of social planning, even as they were empowered by the absolutism of the colonial state. Zeal for paternalistic social engineering inspired the plans for village rehabilitation in Japan as well, but the colonial context encouraged a certain ruthlessness in the treatment of the Japanese settlers that went beyond the condescension toward poor tenant farmers at home. Ultimately, the Manchurian settlers were pawns in an imperial strategy that transcended agrarian imperialism, and when the game began to turn against Japan they would be sacrificed to this greater goal.

While the story of the specific impact of the Manchurian colonization movement on the lives of the settlers awaits telling in Chapter Nine, some conclusions about its influence on Japanese agrarianism may be drawn here. As I have argued, the formation of the Manchurian colonization movement reinvented agrarianism in at least four ways. The first reinvention occurred when the institutionally separate and ideologically distinct movements of emigration and agrarianism were forged into a single movement. Brought together by the rural crisis of the early 1930s, activists in the two movements joined hands to promote Manchurian colonization. In the process, the institutional strength of agrarianism was effectively doubled, giving agrarianists access to the cultural resources, the political connections, and the social base that emigrationists had been developing for fifty years.

This institutional fusion brought about the second aspect of reinvention: the reshaping of agrarianist philosophy to accommodate the tenets of emigrationism. The ideology of the Manchurian colonization movement assimilated the expansionist mandate of the emigration movement into the agrarian banner of rural revitalization. Wedding agriculture to empire, the colonization movement articulated a new agrarian vision that linked imperial agrarianism in Japan with agrarian imperialism in Manchuria. Although before the 1930s agrarianism had formed little part of the imperial vision, the literature of the colonization movement popularized the idea that Japan's agrarian spirit was a key instrument of imperial expansion. While the first groups of settlers were adapting to their new life in Manchuria, propagandists were populating the imaginary landscape of empire with novel images of stalwart yeoman farmers and bucolic Japanese farm villages. At the same time, the new agrarian vision wove the spaces of empire into their formulas for rural rejuvenation. Movement into the vast, fertile Manchurian plains now became an opportunity for village activists to mold residents into the *chūnō* ideal. In the past they had struggled to save the villages without touching land tenure; now land reform was the centerpiece of programs for rural rehabilitation.

Third, the wedding of agriculture and empire reinvented agrarianism in the form of a social imperialist movement. After decades of grappling with the problems of rural poverty and backwardness, agrarianist prescriptions proved unequal to the rural crisis of the early 1930s. Any serious efforts to alleviate the sufferings of the rural poor came up against the entrenched interests of landlords. Against this backdrop, agrarianists turned to the empire for alternatives to failed social welfare policies and in an attempt to bring social harmony back to villages riven by the social turbulence of tenant-landlord conflicts. Trumpeting Manchurian colonization as the solution to the problem of the villages, agrarianists tried to buy off demands from the rural masses for social justice with promises of social benefits in the empire.

Adopting the social imperialist solution allowed agrarianists to imagine modernity in utopian rather than dystopian terms: this was the fourth reinvention. In the past agrarianists had labored to stem the tides of social change, attempting to return villages to a mythical era of self-sufficiency and social harmony, a time before commerce and industry drained the villages of vitality, before the state impoverished agriculture to enrich industry, and before the heartless and corrupt money-culture of the city spread to the villages. In other words, they demonized modernity as the destroyer of the agricultural way of life. The Manchurian solution gave them a reason to embrace the future. Driven by a vision of an alternative modernity, they stopped trying to slow the processes of social transformation and now began to engineer them. Enthusiastically taking up the latest techniques of social management and drawing on the resources of the modern nation-state, agrarianists sought to create a class-free society through the export of village poverty to Manchuria. Relying on the power of their modern colonial army to appropriate an endless supply of colonial land, agrarianists foresaw the reversal of agriculture's decline. They could now imagine a future where, continuously revitalized by the imperial connection, Japan's flourishing farm economy would hold its own against the pressures of industry and commerce. Empire, in short, helped them make peace with modernity.

8 The Migration Machine
*Manchurian Colonization
and State Growth*

The story of the Manchurian colonization movement would have remained a footnote to Manchukuo were it not for its success in mobilizing the national government behind the project. In 1936, the Hirota cabinet adopted Manchurian colonization as one of the pillars of national policy. Throwing the resources and authority of the state into the colonization project, the Japanese government reshaped a local movement with many supporters but few settlers into a national movement that transformed rural society at home and in the empire.

No one expected hundreds of thousands of farmers to spontaneously up and move to Manchuria. Architects of the policy anticipated that much exhortation, bribery, and bullying would be required to convince poor farmers to leave their country for a new home in the empire. To accomplish this, they created what was, in effect, a huge migration machine. A well-organized movement tied to an elaborate bureaucratic apparatus performed the tasks of planning, recruiting, financing, transporting, settling, and supplying the new settlements. The new bureaucratic institutions and the activities they undertook represented a new scale of state intervention in Japanese society.

The success of the government campaign rested on the shoulders of a host of grassroots agents of empire. In scores of villages throughout the country, local activists reached out to embrace government initiatives. In the service of state and empire they labored to promote the Manchurian colonization program in their communities, an endeavor that involved, first, building a consensus among the village wealthy and, second, recruiting volunteers from among the village poor. These grassroots activists mediated the new relationship between state and society, inviting the government into the lives of the rural populace.

Together social activists at the center and periphery of state power encouraged the growth of a socially interventionist state. Like other industrializing societies, from the late nineteenth century on, the Japanese state exhibited strong tendencies to intervene in private affairs, particularly in the economic and political realms. In Japan, as elsewhere, the state involved itself actively in projects of nation building through the creation of democratic political institutions, a conscript army, and universal primary education. In this sense the idea of an interventionist state was a nineteenth-century invention.

The extension of these initiatives into the sphere of social reform came somewhat later. Social policy became part of the language of government in the teens and twenties, when a new breed of social bureaucrats undertook to mediate social conflict between capital and labor through the creation of laws affecting factory workers, public health, and tenancy. In the early years of this experimentation with social policy, the state took on the challenge of the Manchurian colonization project.

The choice of an imperial project as one of the first tasks of social management profoundly influenced the direction of state growth in the 1930s. New state institutions were tailored to serve the demands of Manchurian policy and justified in the language of Japan's colonial mission. At the same time, the village communities that joined the Manchurian colonization campaign understood their new partnership with government in terms of imperial goals. Local organizers of the colonization movement framed their appeals to fellow villagers in a language that heroized social activism in the service of the state even as it ennobled the role of the farmer in the imperial project.

The way that imperialism shaped the growth of government in Japan is particularly striking when considered in a comparative frame of reference, for the 1930s was a decade of rapid government expansion throughout the industrialized world. As in Japan's case, institutional expansion was accompanied by the construction of new ideological justifications for state interventionism. In the name of "revolution from above," the Soviet Union expanded the social power of the state through agricultural collectivization and central economic planning. Under the banner of the New Deal, the United States government grew a thicket of institutional acronyms, bearing witness to the rise of the regulatory state. In Germany, the Nazis deployed racial doctrines to legitimate the creation of new apparatuses for propaganda and censorship, internal policing, and a vast escalation of public expenditure. Although mobilization for empire was related in some fashion to this process in each of these countries, in the main state goals articulated domestic concerns: promoting the revolution, regulating the market, purifying the race. In Japan, however, the empire assumed central importance, setting the country on an alternate path toward the social expansion of the state.

In essence, the processes of state building and empire building became intertwined in Japan. In both cases the result was integration. The social engineering of the migration machine created new connections between state and society; as the government assumed greater control over people's lives, social conditions became an increasing preoccupation of the government. At the same time, the linking of social policy at home to that in Manchukuo facilitated the integration of empire and metropolis, bringing more of Japan into Manchukuo and more of Manchukuo into Japan. The migration machine tells the story of this doubled transformation.

THE BUREAUCRACY OF EMPIRE

Migration normally occurs in the context of what are known as push and pull factors. In the case of Japanese migration to rural Manchuria, protracted agricultural depression and a serious land shortage provided considerable push. When asked, 17 percent of young people polled in the 1937 Ministry of Agriculture and Forestry's 1,000-village survey said they wanted to emigrate.[1] Nevertheless, at no time during the tenure of Manchukuo did this expressed desire in itself translate into commensurate action. Conditions were neither sufficiently bad at home nor sufficiently better in Manchuria to induce Japanese farmers to pack their bags and remove themselves to the empire. Even when the government created a strong incentive for resettlement by granting immunity from military conscription for male settlers—an incentive that grew increasingly attractive as the war escalated—for most Japanese farmers the move to Manchuria was not tenable in the absence of outside assistance. To provide the necessary impetus, to get farmers to go to Manchuria and stay in their new homes, an elaborate structure of both pulls in Manchuria and pushes in Japan had to be constructed. The government institutions created to fulfill this requirement drew on Japan's experience with colonial management, at the same time generating new techniques of state intervention in society.

This process transformed the apparatuses of government. The bureaucratic initiative to resettle millions of Japanese in Manchuria stimulated

---

1. Nōrinshō keizai kōseibu, *Manshū nōgyō imin*, p. 260.

rapid growth of government institutions and the deployment of financial resources into new fields of government activity. Both these developments involved a redefinition of the legitimate province of government action, and gave rise to new expectations for institutional and financial support of policy directives. At the same time, though some of the specific initiatives were new, such a transformation of government itself was not without precedent. In the rapid institution building of the early Meiji, as well as the mobilizations for the Sino- and Russo-Japanese wars, Japanese had expanded their government and redefined its mission.

Even in the absence of the Millions to Manchuria program, some sort of expansion and experimentation would have taken place in the 1930s, as the government struggled to combat the ravages of depression. But the institution building that occurred, and the migration machine it produced, was designed specifically for imperial needs. Two implications followed from this. First, the new bureaucracy served dual masters: policy makers in Manchuria and policy makers in Japan. Because the migration machine linked social policy at home and in the empire, a certain amount of coordination was required between the two spheres, and the machine became a bureaucratic bridge between colonial and metropolitan state apparatuses. Second, because of this connection, the colonial state became a model for metropolitan institution building and helped to influence the heavily bureaucratic and paternalistic character of the migration machine in Japan.

Within the Manchukuo government, an extensive bureaucracy emerged after 1936 to administer the new settlement policy. The Colonization Bureau (Kaitaku sōkyoku), with its four divisions and twelve departments, deployed an army of bureaucrats to issue orders to colonization companies and permits to immigrant groups, oversee land transfers and the resettlement of displaced Chinese peasants, give out licenses and stamp forms, and, of course, write the reports and tabulate the statistics which documented their labors. Though the Colonization Bureau itself was a new institution, the colonial state had long involved itself in real estate transactions and controlling the movement of population across borders. The extensive size of the Colonization Bureau and density of its personnel were likewise consistent with the bureaucrat-intensive character of Japanese colonial management as it had evolved over the previous thirty years. In the past, the efforts of the colonial state concentrated primarily on providing communications, ports, and other infrastructure for the development of Japanese commercial enterprise. Secondarily, in Mantetsu-managed Japanese towns in the railway zone and in the colonial capitals of Seoul and Taipei administered by the governors general, a colonial state provided for the expatriate Japanese community such urban amenities as housing, schools, and hospitals, and in Manchuria, a consumer cooperative. With the creation of the bureaucratic machinery of mass colonization, the concept of a paternalistic and developmental state was applied to a whole new sphere of activity. In the process, the idea of colonial government was refigured to include the new objective of rural population management through interventions in land tenure and cultivation practices, relocations of Chinese, Korean, and Japanese communities, and other forms of social engineering.

Under the Colonization Bureau the labor of managing the new settlements was divided among a number of affiliated institutions. The most important of these was the quasi-public colonial development company, Manshū takushoku kōsha, or Mantaku. Modeled on the original conception of the Oriental Development Company in Korea, Mantaku was created to act as a general intermediary between Japanese immigrants and the society into which they moved. In the first instance, the company served as an agent in the project of land acquisition. This meant finding a suitable location (meeting both the cultivation needs of the settlers as well as the Manchukuo government's paramilitary goals), acquiring title to the land (often over the opposition of existing owners), and funding its purchase. It also meant facilitating, and often forcing, the resettlement of the existing community of Chinese or Korean peasants. As banker as well as purchaser and sales agent, Mantaku acted as a buffer that protected the settlers from having to deal directly with the Manchurian market.

To meet the enormous demands placed upon it, Mantaku was recapitalized several times, with an initial 50 million yen in 1937 expanded to 130 million yen by 1943. Its budget for Japanese immigration in 1943 was about 120 million yen. Headquartered in Xinjing, the company had main branches in Tokyo and Seoul, and twelve additional centers elsewhere. These collectively administered a total of fifty-six offices, fifty-three management stations, and twelve farm stations, giving the company command over a huge bureaucracy and staff.[2]

In 1940, following the expansion of a youth settlement program known as the Patriotic Youth Brigade, a separate agency was created to administer

2. Manshūkoku tsūshinsha, ed., *Manshū kaitaku nenkan* (1944; reprint, Howa shuppan, 1986), pp. 52–55; Kimijima Kazuhiko, "Manshū nōgyō imin kankei kikan no setsuritsu katei to katsudō jōkyō: Manshū takushoku kaisha to Manshū takushoku kōsha o chūshin ni," in Manshū iminshi kenkyūkai, ed., *Nihon teikoku-shugika no Manshū imin* (Ryūkei shosha, 1976), p. 190.

the yearly influx of 10,000 to 20,000 young colonists. A paramilitary organization inaugurated in 1938, the Patriotic Youth Brigade mobilized young men aged fourteen to twenty-one to spend three years in Manchurian training camps and exempted them from the draft if they elected to join other adult settlers in the farm communities. The Seinen giyūtai kunren honbu (Youth Brigade Training Headquarters) was made up of five divisions and eleven departments, employed 222 bureaucrats, and had liaison offices in seven key Manchurian prefectural offices. With a budget that grew from forty million yen in 1940 to almost fifty-two million by 1943, the main activity of this bureaucracy was to oversee the network of ninety-two training camps built between 1938 and 1941. Initial training camps accommodated between 1,500 and 6,000 youths for their first year of training, after which they were sent to smaller camps (housing 300 colonists-in-training) for an additional two years.[3]

In addition to Mantaku and the training centers, the Manchukuo government established a network of colonial research stations known as the Kaitaku kenkyūjo. This network included offices in the capital of Xinjing, the northern railway hub of Harbin, Heihe on the Soviet-Manchukuo border, and Jiamusi in the northeast. Provided a budget of nearly one million yen and a staff of 118 in 1943, the research network surveyed and scrutinized the progress of the settlements. The idea of creating a research wing for the settlement project drew on the illustrious example of Mantetsu, which boasted libraries and museums, statisticians, surveyists, and planners, as well as a host of affiliated research agencies for industrial and agricultural experimentation, the survey of geological and natural resources, and the study of social hygiene and animal disease. Though the more modest research network of the Kaitaku kenkyūjo could not compete with Mantetsu's voluminous output, their findings and policy recommendations were published in the magazine *Tairiku kaitaku* (Continental Settlement) and in individual village studies.[4]

The support apparatus furnished by these and other organizations attempted to create the conditions necessary to lure Japanese settlers to Manchuria. In addition to the land, financing, and ongoing assistance provided by Mantaku, each settlement was provided with farming experts, police and defense directors, physicians, and veterinarians. Immigrants were endowed with "common equipment and facilities" such as "hospitals, bar-

---

3. Manshūkoku tsūshinsha, *Manshū kaitaku nenkan* (1944), pp. 49–51; Manshū kaitakushi kankōkai, pp. 241–250.

4. Manshūkoku tsūshinsha, *Manshū kaitaku nenkan* (1944), pp. 46–47.

racks, baths, wells, defense walls, shops, factories, and schools." Aid granted
in 1936 by the Colonial Ministry alone budgeted 250 yen per household
for transportation and another 650 yen for other expenditures, intended
to support several families for their first year. The village as a whole received a one-time payment of 4,750 yen and another 14,733 yen per year
for three years to defray the expenses for experts and directors. It also was
granted 8,750 yen to build and staff a medical clinic, which was given an
operating budget of 14,733 yen per year for a ten-year period.[5] Above and
beyond subsidies for agricultural production itself, these funds were meant
to provide immigrants an entire prefabricated social infrastructure. On one
hand the settlers would be protected from a social climate in which they
could not survive, and on the other they would be comforted by some of
the familiarities of home. In this way the farm colonists were to remain
tight within the protective embrace of Mantaku, much as their urban counterparts had been insulated from the native Chinese community by the
interventions of Mantetsu. Thus did a new colonial society of agricultural
immigrants and a new state apparatus designed to minister to that society
cling to one another, in the process inaugurating a new phase in the paternalistic tradition of colonial state-society interaction.

Domestically, the Millions to Manchuria policy generated the emergence of an equally dense network of institutions and programs to push
emigration. At the national level, the machinery to propel migration
became the work of two government bureaucracies, the Colonial Ministry and the Ministry of Agriculture and Forestry. The Colonial Ministry
(which after 1942 was amalgamated into the Greater East Asian Ministry)
coordinated policy with the Manchurian bureaucracy and administered
government funding for transportation and settlement. Through its over-
sight of the Nōson kōsei undō (Rural Rehabilitation Movement), the Ministry of Agriculture and Forestry helped recruit candidates for emigration
and dispensed funds to communities involved in the emigration campaign.
Both ministries were awarded large budgets to carry out their tasks; in
1937 alone the Colonial Ministry earmarked nine million yen to promote
the emigration of 6,000 households while Agriculture and Forestry designated five million yen for aid to participating communities.[6]

Together this represented an enormous and unorthodox expenditure
for what was, essentially, social welfare. Of course, as stated earlier, state

---

5. South Manchurian Railway Company, p. 130; Manshū kaitakushi kankōkai,
pp. 182–183.
6. Manshū kaitakushi kankōkai, pp. 203, 807.

intervention in domestic society was not without precedent. Like the colonial state in Manchuria, the developmentalist orientation of metropolitan government was of long-standing tradition. Since the initiation of a "rich country–strong military" policy in the early Meiji period, the Japanese state involved itself in encouraging modern industry through financial subsidies and other forms of government promotion. The government invested in railroads and other infrastructural development. Likewise, since the Meiji government initiated universal primary education and universal male conscription, the project of nation building made the state an increasingly intrusive presence in the lives of the people. Although within Japan itself this presence could not rival the intimacy that emerged between colonial governments and expatriate Japanese communities, over the early decades of the twentieth century, the Home, Army, and Education ministries developed networks of voluntary organizations through which they exercised initiatives of guardianship and surveillance over Japanese society. As Sheldon Garon has noted, the commitment to state activism was inspired, in the case of a growing number of bureaucrats, by German ideas of state welfare which "infused the state with the ethical mission of protecting the weak from the ravages of industrialization in the interests of social order and national greatness."[7] In the teens and twenties, this principle was enshrined in legislation to regulate factory and tenant conditions, to support the price of rice, and to improve public health conditions in urban areas. Still, until the 1930s, state paternalism was not supported by fiscal largesse on the part of the central government. The expense for state initiatives in areas of education, public health, and elsewhere was borne overwhelmingly by local communities. In this sense, the fiscal support for Manchurian colonization departed from previous practice, and this signaled the ordination of a fundamental principle of the welfare state: the central government assumed fiscal responsibility for social policy.

With its generous allocations from the national budget for Manchurian settlement, the Colonial Ministry established a semipublic corporation called the Manchurian Immigration Council (Manshū ijū kyōkai) and a network of Settlement Training Centers. The Manchurian Immigration Council acted essentially as a propaganda organization, drawing on the pioneering techniques developed in the course of the Home Ministry's "enlightenment movement" of the late 1920s to counter the spread of left-wing ideas and the Army Ministry's "campaign to disseminate the idea of

7. Sheldon Garon, *The State and Labor in Modern Japan* (Berkeley: University of California Press, 1987), p. 25; see also Lewis, pp. 246–248.

national defense" during the Manchurian Incident. Targeting specific areas for saturation propaganda, the council established offices in select prefectures each year and concentrated its energies on a key group of villages within those prefectures. Some of the council's personnel worked at the head office editing pamphlets and the monthly magazine *Hirake Manmō* (Opening Manchuria-Mongolia, later changed to *Shin Manmō*), analyzing data and writing reports, and drawing up plans for the years to come. At the same time, an army of council agents descended on the villages. Gearing their activities to two different audiences, recruiters made their rounds with one packet of materials to convince the local leadership and another to enroll prospective emigrants.[8]

Training centers became another pillar of the new bureaucratic apparatus of emigration support. Like the involvement of government in propaganda, the creation of state-run training and indoctrination centers represented the elaboration of a recent innovation in state techniques for mass mobilization. The idea of adult education emerged in the 1920s when the Education Ministry adopted the term *social education* to express a host of new initiatives directed toward continuing government education of the post-primary school population. These initiatives included the creation of public libraries, museums, and sports facilities, as well as the use of existing educational institutions to carry out adult training courses and lectures. At the same time, the Education Ministry deepened its ties with local voluntary organizations, mobilizing national networks of reservists' associations, women's organizations, youth groups, and the like to serve as vehicles for adult education campaigns.[9]

In addition to government experiments with social education in the 1920s, the institutionalization of state training centers for emigrants drew on the experience of the rural training centers. Known as *nōmin dōjo*, these agricultural academies sprang up throughout the country in the teens and twenties (fifty-eight were established between 1911 and 1920). With an average of twenty to thirty students, *nōmin dōjo* such as Katō Kanji's famous Nihon kokumin kōtō gakkō dedicated themselves to rearing community leaders committed to agriculture as a way of life. In the early thirties, the central government began to involve itself with the *nōmin dōjo*. As part of its Rural Rehabilitation Movement, the Ministry of Agriculture and Forestry started to subsidize the *nōmin dōjo* and take a hand in strengthening the agrarianist content of the curriculum. A number of

8. Manshū kaitakushi kankōkai, pp. 187–188.
9. Kokuritsu kyōiku kenkyūjo, *Kyōiku seisaku* 1, pp. 315–319.

these rural academies were mobilized to carry out colonial training in the late 1930s.[10]

Before leaving the country (and in addition to training they would receive in Manchuria) adult recruits were given at least a month of "spiritual training" to prepare them for their new life. A national network of 50 centers was erected between 1937 and 1940, with all prefectures tied into it. The Colonial Ministry agreed to cover half the cost of building new facilities, which were estimated to reach 12,000 yen per center if the facilities had to be constructed from scratch.[11] In addition, an entirely separate system of domestic training centers was created for the Patriotic Youth Brigade. All recruits received two months of training at the national complex at Uchiwara in Ibaraki prefecture, designed to handle 50,000 trainees per year. Moreover, 380 camps scattered throughout the country (excepting Hokkaidō and Kanagawa prefectures) provided an opportunity for graduating middle-school classes to spend a week with their teachers taking a course in *kōa kyōiku* (rise-of-Asia education), after which they were invited to enlist en masse with the Patriotic Youth Brigade.[12]

Since most of the real work of emigrant recruiting took place at the local level, each prefecture set up its own promotional apparatus. Nagano, the prefecture which sent the most emigrants, assigned bureaucrats in departments of Labor, Social Welfare, and Planning to work on surveys, publications, propaganda, recruitment, advising, and so on. The prefecture ran training centers built with the aid of the Colonial Ministry and maintained technical institutes to instruct young men in theories and methods of colonization. The proliferation of emigration support was reflected in the prefectural payroll. Although only twenty-one bureaucrats were engaged full-time on the settlement project in 1935, by 1940 their number had multiplied six-fold. The prefectural budget for emigration showed the same exponential expansion; expenditures of 6,500 yen in 1936 leapt to 74,763 yen in 1940 and to 515,783 yen in 1944.[13] Thus Manchurian settlement stimulated the expansion of the welfare state at the prefectural, as well as national, level.

10. Kokuritsu kyōiku kenkyūjo, *Shakai kyōiku* 2, pp. 493–501.
11. Manshū kaitakushi kankōkai, pp. 200–203.
12. Sakuramoto Tomio, *Manmō kaitaku seishōnen giyūgun* (Aoki shoten, 1987), pp. 57–67, 153–154; Shiratori Michihiro, " 'Manmō kaitaku seishōnen giyūgun' no hen'yō (1938–1941 nen): 'kyōdō butai hensei' dōnyū no igi," *Kyōiku gakubu kiyō*, no. 54 (Hokkaidō daigaku, February 1990), p. 73.
13. Nagano-ken kaitaku jikōkai Manshū kaitakushi kankōkai, vol. 1, pp. 250–255.

The state's newly constructed emigration machine exerted a variety of pressures on the village to induce farmers to leave. Table 10 shows a model budget for the array of activities considered necessary to produce the population exodus. As the yen budgeted for village colonization demonstrated, the program involved a considerable expense by both national and local government. Herein lay one of the striking features of the bureaucratic machine built to push emigration to Manchuria: its reliance on financial incentives. In the past, the Japanese government had tried to resolve the social dislocations of an industrializing society by throwing words at the problem; now they weighted the message with money. This certainly strengthened the impact of social policy. In the process, however, the definition of government was altered. Now the state had a financial stake in its social policy. Like the colonial state apparatus created to pull migrants to Manchuria, the funding of an emigration movement at home led to the expansion of state initiatives into new spheres of social management, at the same time bringing about an increasing intimacy in state-society relations. This continued a process begun earlier. Social welfare institutions in development in the 1920s, like social education, turned to mobilizing for empire. As these new initiatives transformed the bureaucratic apparatuses of government into a tool for social policy, they also reshaped them into an instrument for empire building.

RACIAL EXPANSIONISM

Part of the process of reshaping government involved the construction of a mission that both articulated the purpose and justified the existence of the migration machine. Ideas inspiring the movements of the early thirties were taken up by the new state bureaucracy and reconstructed into a racial mission to expand. Like the ideology of the New Deal in the context of the fledgling American welfare state, Japan's racial mission legitimated the new scale of public involvement in local towns and villages. Although in Japan's case the ideological justification for state growth appealed more overtly to race, American initiatives in public health and public education were driven by eugenic concerns and made the same connections between social reform and racial improvement.[14]

Japan's racial mission was communicated through the staggering vol-

---

14. See Daniel J. Kevles, *In the Name of Eugenics: Genetics and the Uses of Human Heredity* (New York: Knopf, 1985), and Stephen Jay Gould, *The Mismeasure of Man* (New York: Norton, 1981).

Table 10. Village Colonization Model Budget

Category	Amount (yen)	Source
Full-time office in village to promote immigration	600 per year for 3 years	Village funds
Survey	20	Village funds
Publication	30	Village funds
Two-person yearly fact-finding team sent to Manchuria	160 per year for 3 years	Prefectural funds
Five-member immigrant representative team sent to Manchuria	50 for 1 trip	Village funds
Special training for youth leaders at rural training centers (five people per year)	50 per year for 3 years	Village funds
Lectures and movies	50 per year for 3 years	Village funds
Informational materials	100	Village funds
Immigrant bonus money	50 per immigrant; total of 10,000	Village funds
Aid for remaining families	24,000	National government
Family training	150 per year for 3 years	Village funds
Farewell parties	240 over 3 years	Village funds
Purchase of land vacated by emigrants	86,000	National government
Debt settlement	300	Village funds
Misc. expenses for disposal of property	100 per year for 3 years	Village funds
Correspondence and communications	100 per year for 3 years	Village funds

SOURCE: Nōrinshō keizai kōseibu, ed., *Shinnōson no kensetsu: tairiku e bunson daiidō* (Asahi shinbunsha, 1939), pp. 539–541.

ume of propaganda and recruitment literature produced by local commit-tees, prefectural bureaucracies, the Manchurian Emigration Council, and the Ministry of Agriculture and Forestry. The idea of colonization dissem-inated through the diverse channels of the migration machine, like the statecraft of the machine itself, introduced a new vision of empire even as it borrowed from the past. Drawing on an existing colonial discourse, the mission to expand racially became the latest imperative in an already multifaceted colonial mission that embraced Taiwan, Korea, the Pacific Islands, and China.

The obvious source for the appropriation of ideas to legitimate the migration machine was the emigration movement, which had long advocated overseas settlement in the name of empire. In keeping with this tradition, propaganda for Manchurian colonization phrased its appeals in the language of patriotism rather than economic opportunity. Hence, speeches by ministers of colonization urged "soldiers of the hoe" to "Go! Go and colonize the continent! For the development of the Yamato race [*Yamato minzoku*], to build the new order in Asia!"[15] Koiso Kuniaki, head of the ministry in late 1939, titled one tribute to the "pioneers who battled with the soil of North Manchuria," "The Strength of One Hoe." He exhorted farmers to take up this "holy endeavor of the race," while he urged the public to express "gratitude" and support.[16] The grandiose rhetoric made immigration something much more than a mere economic prospect for impoverished and land-hungry farmers; it was the means to seed the empire with the racial spirit of the Yamato people.

For Japan, like other colonial powers, the colonial discourse was in part a discourse on self and other, expressed, increasingly, in the language of race. From the first steps toward empire in the 1870s to the military expansionism of the 1930s and 1940s, the incorporation of racial doctrines into a Japanese discourse on colonialism took place in three phases. The first occurred in the late nineteenth century, when Confucian ideas of proper place in social hierarchies and Shinto beliefs in the divine ancestry of the Japanese people were overlaid by the framework of Western racial science. Imported along with craniometry, Social Darwinism, and the notion of racial types was the European confusion between national, ethnolinguistic, and phenotypical definitions of race. In Japan these ambiguities appeared in the inconsistent and often interchangeable usage of the terms *minzoku* and *jinshū* to designate race. The ideographs for *minzoku* translate literally as "people-kinsmen," and the term evoked the ethnic and national meanings of the word race, whereas *jinshū*—"human type"—implied a biological classification. Both terms were employed to contrast Asian with Western and yellow with white; at the same time they could

15. Hatta Yoshiaki, "Tairiku no yokudo wa maneku," *Ie no hikari* (April 1939), p. 35.

16. Koiso Kuniaki, "Ichi kuwa no chikara," *Ie no hikari* (October 1939), p. 31.

refer to ethnic categories within Asia—Han, Manchu, Mongolian, Ainu, and so on.[17]

Beginning in 1895, the acquisition of a colonial empire stimulated the formation of an academic and official discourse on colonial rule. The debates over the relative merits of racial assimilation or association marked a second stage in the interpenetration of racial and colonial discourses in Japan. These debates over whether it was possible and appropriate to Japanize colonial subjects set in motion a process of defining and articulating the nature of difference between Japanese and other Asians in a colonial context, where social separation and absolute political authority conditioned the perceptions of this difference. It has frequently been observed that in European colonial settings the differences between policies of association and assimilation were more rhetorical than real, both resting on de facto segregation, discrimination, and a sense of an impassable gulf between the races. The same was true for Japan, with an interesting distinction which suggested that the rhetoric mattered after all. Whereas European colonial theory tended to gravitate over time to the associationist position, discouraging the diffusion of Western institutions, Japanese colonial discourse moved in the opposite direction toward assimilation, as Mark Peattie has pointed out.[18]

By the mid 1930s, the enthusiastic embrace of the idea of racial assimilation marked the third phase in the discourse of race and colonialism. Official colonial policy became more overtly racial; it was justified by the blend of mythohistorical, Confucian, and pseudoscientific constructions of race that had evolved over the previous half century. This was apparent in the *kōminka* (imperialization) policy adopted in Taiwan and Korea, which attempted to force racial assimilation through coercive diffusion of Japanese language, Japanese names, and shrine Shinto. The racialization of colonial policy was also evident in planning for administration of the Co-

17. The theoretical literature on race is prodigious, particularly the intellectual history of race and racial pseudoscience. For the study of race thinking outside European and neo-European societies, see Frank Dikötter's pioneering study, *The Discourse of Race in Modern China* (Stanford: Stanford University Press, 1992). For race as a social construction, see Barbara Jeanne Fields, "Slavery, Race and Ideology in the United States of America," *New Left Review*, no. 181 (May–June 1990), pp. 95–118; and for an exploration of the relationship between nationalism and racism, see Etienne Balibar, "Racism and Nationalism," in Etienne Balibar and Immanuel Wallerstein, eds., *Race, Nation, Class: Ambiguous Identities* (New York: Verso, 1991), pp. 37–67.

18. Peattie, "Japanese Attitudes toward Colonialism," p. 97.

prosperity Sphere, as seen in documents such as the 4,000-page "Investigation of Global Policy with Yamato Race as Nucleus" produced by the population and race section of the Ministry of Health and Welfare Research Bureau.[19] Finally, it also could be seen in the newly fashioned mission to colonize Manchukuo, which articulated, for the first time in the history of Japanese colonialism, an official policy of racial expansionism.

The racial expressions that filled the new lexicon of empire were evident in the choice of slogans to represent the emigration project. The literature on colonization frequently referred to Manchuria as a "brother country to which Japan had given birth" (*Nihon ga unda kyōdaikoku*).[20] The idea that Japan and its colonies represented a brotherhood of nations was, of course, a stock image in Confucian-inspired representations of the Japanese empire. Manchurian colonization took this one step further, reinforcing the Confucian family metaphor with the Shinto-inspired idea of the family-state. Enshrined in the Meiji Constitution and disseminated through primary-school textbooks, the concept of a family-state rested on the mythohistorical account of a common racial ancestry. Classical texts traced the origins of the Japanese people back to the divinely descended Emperor Jimmu, founder of the Japanese state at Yamato in B.C. 660 and mythic progenitor of what was called the Yamato race. In these terms, the nation constituted an extended family linked by blood, and the imperial head of state was also the paternal head of this extended national household. When emigration propaganda applied the biological language of kinship to the colonization of Manchukuo, the empire was brought into the racial embrace of the family-state. As one article explained, Manchukuo was not just a colony of Japan, but blood kin. The imperial relationship became an extension of the Japanese family system where "Japan is the stem family and Manchuria is the branch family." Observing the hierarchical relations maintained between stem and branch, Japan acted as parent to the infant nation of Manchukuo, rearing it to become a "splendid nation just like Japan."[21] Thus, in the new language of colonization, colonies became kinsmen and the family-state became the family-empire.

The policy of recruiting second and third sons to set up branch families

19. See Dower's analysis of this document in *War without Mercy*, pp. 262–292.

20. Hatta Yoshiaki, "Tairiku no yokudo wa maneku," *Ie no hikari* (April 1939), p. 35; Koiso Kuniaki, "Ichi kuwa no chikara," *Ie no hikari* (October 1939), p. 31.

21. "Tokugo: tairiku wa maneku Manshū kaitakusha montō," *Ie no hikari* (April 1939), p. 141.

in Manchuria buttressed this idea of colonial kinship. Recruiting literature stressed that "the rich soil of the continent beckoned" especially to second and third sons whose "bleak expressions registered their despair at making a life for themselves on the family farm."[22] In similar fashion, the language of the village colonization program literally signified the creation of a "branch village" (bunson). As one caption urged, "Set up a branch family in Manchuria through village colonization" (bunson imin de Manshū e bunke).[23] In this way the metaphors of reproduction and family were invoked to suggest a new connection of race and blood between empire and metropolis.

In keeping with the idea of racial seeding, emigration promoters strongly sounded the youth theme. Echoing Horace Greeley's famous admonition "Go west, young man," Baron Ōkura Kinmochi of the Manchurian Emigration Council instructed Japanese youth, "Go to the continent young man," for "a new land awaits the village youth."[24] In popular settlement songs the "frontier spirit" overflowed, invariably, "with the blood of youth."[25] The prominence of images of youth in colonialist discourse and the representation of Japanese overseas expansion in the figure of a virile young man can be traced back to the 1870s and 1880s and the Japanese representation of a youthful and progressive Japan guiding aged and decrepit Asian neighbors down the path to Western-style civilization and enlightenment. In the 1930s, the cultural content in the metaphor of nation as youth thinned, and was replaced by biological and physiological meanings. The anthems of the Youth Brigade eulogized the physical vigor and power of the young, qualities needed to plant the race on the continent. Lyricist Hoshikawa Ryōka referred to the "capable fists" and "strength" of youth in his prize-winning tune "We Are the Young Volunteers." The song "Frontier March" popularized phrases like "stalwart sons of the holy land" (shishū no kendanji), and the "Patriotic Youth Brigade Song" proclaimed:

> With our young lives,
> We are Japan's advance guard onto the soil.

22. Hatta Yoshiaki, "Tairiku no yokudo wa maneku," Ie no hikari (April 1939), p. 35.

23. "Tokugo: tairiku wa maneku Manshū kaitakusha montō," Ie no hikari (April 1939), p. 145.

24. Ōkura Kinmochi, "Seinen yo tairiku ni idō seyo," Ie no hikari (January 1938), p. 34.

25. Shimada Keita, "Kaitaku damashii," Ie no hikari (September 1941), pp. 34–35.

Our emotion burns bright;
We come gripping hoes
So we will open the land —
The great land of Manchuria.[26]

There were, of course, practical reasons for advocates of colonization to pay particular attention to recruiting young people. Literature on Manchurian colonization laid great stress on the responsibility of Japan's youth to seed the new empire with the Yamato race and expand the nation's living space onto colonial soil. In the words of a colonization manual, Japanese youth were uniquely capable of founding a new continental generation and a "new continental Japan."[27] Under the caption "The Joy of Becoming a Progenitor," one article asked, "What could be better than creating a new country and of becoming the founding fathers to that country? There is no life more worth living. There is no task more worth doing."[28] Giving a new twist to the Russo-Japanese War image of the Manchurian grave, joyful settlers in the pages of *Ie no hikari* declared their burning desire to "bury our bones in an unknown land . . . and build a paradise for the children and grandchildren yet to be born."[29]

Women also figured prominently in this imagined Manchukuo, appearing for the first time as active agents of Japan's colonial mission. "Continental mothers" and "continental brides" were the target of frequent appeals to the patriotic spirit of Japanese women. *Ie no hikari* was filled with *bidan*, or inspirational tales, about these female pioneers, highlighting the unique contribution that a woman's strength and endurance made to the building of colonial society. One such story, entitled "The New Brides Who Protected the Village," explained how the men in a settlement of recruits from the Tokyo area had, after a bad harvest, given up and decided to disband the settlement. Several young brides, who "had come to the continent burning with hope," then "bravely stood up and argued with their husbands" to put a stop to the defeatism, delivering the following speech:

26. Hoshikawa Ryōka's "Wareware wa wakaki giyūgun" and Tobishi Aiko's "Kaitaku yuki" shared first prize in a song contest held by *Hirake Manmō* for the official anthem of the Youth Brigade. Shimao Atsunari wrote "The Patriotic Youth Brigade Song" ("Seishōnen giyūgun no uta"): Sakuramoto, pp. 53–54, 101.

27. Miura Etsurō, ed., *Manshū ijū tokuhon* (Kaizōsha, 1939), p. 34.

28. Katō Takeo, "Seishōnen giyūgun no seikatsu," *Ie no hikari* (December 1938), pp. 231–232.

29. "Tairiku no hanayome," *Ie no hikari* (July 1938), p. 27.

At our wedding ceremony in Tokyo under the blessing of the governor, did we not pledge our tears to build Tokyo village colony in the Manchurian heaven and to become the cornerstone of peace in the East? . . . At home, too, crops are sometimes a success and sometimes a failure. To declare the soil no good and abandon the settlement after a single crop failure without really knowing the truth—how will this look to those at home who are counting on us? And what about the Manchurians watching we Japanese settlers do this—what will they say? We have pledged our future, and promised to build Tokyo village permanently on this spot. Now more than ever you men need to rouse yourselves to be brave and redouble your efforts for us.[30]

In such stories it was the women who could be counted on to understand and endure hardship, who provided the moral fortitude and the stick-to-itiveness necessary to make the holy mission a success.

Like the focus on youth in the literature of Manchurian colonization, the attention given to women was motivated by practical concerns. For that reason, representations of women constructed gender in physiological terms and emphasized their reproductive characteristics. Depicting them as breeders of a new generation of Manchurian Japanese, drawings and photographs of settler women seemed always to catch them with a baby at the breast. The caption for a drawing entitled "The Joy of the Harvest" explained that it was portraying "immigrant soldiers of the hoe at the close of a day of busy harvesting. The glow of the sunset is reflected in the face of the young father. The Manchurian Japanese baby suckles at the ample breast of his mother. . . . Does this not symbolize the blessings of Japanese youth?"[31] The title of a photograph of a settler and her children, "The Joy of Breeding," referred both to the woman's family and to the herd of sheep grazing in the yard behind her. "Looking out onto a spectacular view, the young mother, the continental dog, and the plump and healthy second generation born in Manchuria play happily together on the second story of the shepherd's house," read the caption.[32]

Although in the early days officials discouraged settlers who had passed the prime of life, in an article published in late 1942, emigrants were exhorted to "take the old folks with them" to help with this second generation. "The birth rate among settlers is high but the incidence of miscar-

30. "Kaitaku bidan: tairiku ni saku Yamato Nadeshiko," *Ie no hikari* (October 1940), pp. 15–17.

31. "Shūtaku no yorokobi," *Ie no hikari* (November 1939).

32. "Manshū kaitaku tokugō," *Ie no hikari* (October 1939), p. 1.

riage, premature birth, and infant mortality is also high. For the most part this appears to be caused by the fact that these are first births and that there is a shortage of experienced people around to help. If the grandparents were available their experience would save not only the family but the whole village from disaster."[33] Thus, the presence of women, children, and grandparents in the imagined imperial landscape reflected the new sense of intimacy with which Japanese now regarded Manchukuo. In this sense the idea of racial expansionism implied the Japanizing of Manchuria both literally and metaphorically. Transplanting entire households to the new empire raised the Japanese percentage of the local population. At the same time, the projection of images of motherhood and connubial life domesticated the empire. The battlefield was transformed into a vegetable garden, the commodity market supplanted by a Japanese farm community. Manchukuo was beginning to look more like home every day.

The racial overlay to the colonizing mission in Manchukuo involved more than a lebensraum-like idea of racial expansionism. It also drew on the racial conceptualization of the relationship between Japanese and other Asians that was the product of the colonial experience in Taiwan and Korea. Applying racial definitions of difference to the so-called land of racial harmony, colonization literature reinforced and invigorated ideas of a natural hierarchy of race and power in Asia. In the representations of the interactions between Japanese and the native Chinese who were called the Manchurians, race was everything. The frequency with which propagandists felt compelled to assert the superiority of the Japanese race was as noteworthy as their ingenuity in varying the iteration of this concept. The position of the Yamato people was expressed variously as the "heart" (*kakushin*), "pivot" (*chūjiku*), and "axis" (*chūsū*) of the five races, the "position of leadership" (*shidōteki chii*), the "guiding role" (*shidōteki yakuwari*), the "leader of the Asian continent" (*Ajia tairiku no meishu*), the "head of the five races" (*gozoku kyōwa no sentō*), the "driving force of racial harmony" (*gozoku kyōwa no suishinryoku*), or all of these at once. Since the early Meiji period, advocates of empire had trumpeted Japan's right to assume the leadership of Asia by virtue of its success in creating a modern civilization. Now, cultural superiority was signified in the language of race.

Race also prescribed the duty of Japanese settlers to "lead and enlighten" (*shidō keihatsu*) the other races of Manchukuo, and to undertake their

---

33. Ikago Kenzō, "Kaitaku no kuwa wa kagayaku: Manshū kenkoku jūshūnen o mukaeru," *Ie no hikari* (September 1942), p. 31.

"moral reform" (*tokka*) and "guidance" (*yūeki*).[34] Detailing the task of racial enlightenment, literature on Manchurian colonization catalogued the racial characteristics that separated Japanese from other Asians. In Japan, as in other colonizing societies, the perception of technological backwardness became a key measure of the racial gap.[35] Books and magazine articles on Manchukuo paid particular attention to the level of material culture among the native Chinese population, contrasting it negatively with Japan. Describing a visit to the home of a wealthy Chinese landlord, one writer "thought it peculiar" that the home was decorated with empty glass bottles because he had heard "glass products were highly prized in Japan about a hundred years ago when Japan was first exposed to Western culture."[36]

The belief that levels of technology reflected racial development led some writers to rearrange the facts in order to maintain the myth of Japanese racial superiority. While the Japanese settlers in Manchuria were frantically trying to learn local cultivation practices from Chinese and Korean farmers, at home settlement propaganda was instructing Japanese farmers of the burning need to go to the new paradise to disseminate superior Japanese farm methods. Noting that Manchurian farm villages were in an appalling state which the Manchukuo government was "working diligently to improve," one pamphlet explained that "because [Chinese] farmers are illiterate, no matter how many times things are explained to them they do not understand." To help them "overcome their failings," the pamphlet counseled, it was necessary "to bring a superior race well-trained in agricultural techniques to guide these backward Chinese farmers in the field."[37]

In addition to the question of technology, colonization literature drew the reader's attention to standards of personal hygiene as a measure of racial difference. One writer, in his "First Look at a New Settlement," devoted a large amount of space to describing his revulsion to the "foul"

34. Miura, pp. 31–35; "Tokugo: tairiku wa maneku Manshū kaitakusha montō," *Ie no hikari* (April 1939), pp. 141–142; Ishihara Jirō, *Manshū imin to seinendan* (Dai Nippon rengō seinendan, 1937), p. 40.

35. For an account of science, technology, and imperial ideologies, see Michael Adas, *Machines as the Measure of Men: Science, Technology, and Ideologies of Western Dominance* (Ithaca: Cornell University Press, 1989).

36. "Manshū imin mura hōmonki (II)," *Ie no hikari* (March 1937), pp. 63–64.

37. Ōkura Kinmochi, *Nōson seinen shokun no funki o unagasu* (Manshū ijū kyōkai, 1936), p. 12.

body odor of a "crowd of Chinese coolies."[38] On their return from a tour of the settlements, a husband and wife team reported enthusiastically of their success in disseminating hygenic practices among the Chinese. Stressing the special role of Japanese women in promoting racial harmony through bathing instruction, Mrs. Koshio observed, "As everybody knows Manchurians are a very dirty race and there are many of them who only take a bath two or three times in their life. But while they are mixing with Japanese women they begin to imitate our bathing customs and learn how to get rid of 'Nanjing vermin' [bed-bugs]."[39] Mr. Koshio followed this story with his own illustration of the "dirty racial habits" of the Chinese, explaining how settlers had "struggled to promote the use of lavatories" through a prize contest. While the soldiers were out bringing law and order to the land with guns and swords, Mrs. Koshio felt this instruction brought about "what I would call true pacification."[40]

Such stories were important because they reinforced the sense, for Japanese, of their proper place in the social hierarchy of Manchukuo. By transplanting a rural underclass to the empire, Manchurian colonization raised disturbing questions of the relationship between the social hierarchy at home and in the empire: in the Manchurian context, the socially inferior at home suddenly became the socially superior. To smooth over the contradictions between domestic underprivilege and colonial overprivilege, propagandists highlighted racial hierarchy and the putative civilization gap between Chinese and Japanese, using a racial construction of difference to obscure the commonalities between poor farmers of both nationalities.

As such reports from the frontier informed readers back home, the Japanization of Manchuria implied not only filling the country with Japanese, but also the cultural Japanization of the native population. Thus, advocates of Manchurian colonization defined racial expansionism in terms both of demographic expansion and of cultural assimilation. In choosing to frame their appeals in the language of race, they helped redefine the ideology of Japanese expansion. This process of redefinition reflected the profundity of the changes engendered by Japan's new social imperialism. As the migration machine integrated social policy at home and in the empire, and brought Japanese into new forms of social contact with colonial subjects, colonization literature began to express a new sense of intimacy

38. "Manshū ijū mura hōmonki (I)," *Ie no hikari* (February 1937), p. 61.

39. "Otoko to onna no tachiba kara Manshū kaitaku mura o miru," *Ie no hikari* (October 1939), p. 139.

40. Ibid., pp. 137, 139.

between Japan and Manchukuo. Imperial propagandists conveyed this sense of intimacy in their depictions of an empire "turning Japanese"—drawing fancied pictures of mass Chinese conversion to a Japanese way of life and painting Japanese settlements in hues of bucolic familiarity. It is worth noting that the way the new social concatenations between Japan and Manchukuo were bringing about this process in reverse—that is, the Manchurianization of Japan—occupied no place in the narrative of racial expansion. In this sense propagandists conveyed a message about the vast assimilating power and impermeability to outside influence of the Japanese nation-state. At a more basic level, the imperative of racial expansionism provided a mission for the proliferating institutional apparatus of the migration machine. The racialized colonial mission legitimated the extension of the colonial project into a new sphere of activity even as it authorized the generation of enormous government budgets, an army of bureaucrats, and mountains of paper.

GRASSROOTS AGENTS OF EMPIRE

From the perspective of Japanese farm communities, the Manchurian colonization program inaugurated a process of mass mobilization. This process enmeshed people in a web of new connections with national and prefectural government organizations, and created new ties between the village community and farm settlements in Manchuria. Along the way, both state and empire began to assume new meaning in people's lives, restructuring village society and popular consciousness.

The forces that reshaped the relationship between community, state, and empire did not emerge solely from the state itself. While government initiatives exerted new kinds of pressures on village communities, at the grassroots level the operation of the bureaucracy of migration relied on the mediation of local elites. Ultimately, the extent to which empire and state were permitted into the village was determined by these elites—the gatekeepers of local autonomy. As I argued in Chapter Seven, involvement in the Manchurian colonization movement was far from uniform; the communities that chose to participate were led to that decision through the influence of community leaders.

Most Japanese adults who emigrated did so through the village colonization program.[41] Under this system an *imindan,* or settlement of be-

---

41. Four hundred twenty-two *imindan* of between 200 and 300 people each were sent to Manchuria. Three hundred nineteen of these were recruited as a town or village unit: Manshū kaitakushi kankōkai, p. 332.

tween 200 and 300 households, was recruited either by subdividing a village and sending a third of its population (*bunson imin*), or by mobilizing volunteers from a number of villages in a particular district (*bunkyō imin*). In effect, this system involved the participating village or district as an entire community. Everybody, from the mayor to the third sons of tenant farmers, was drawn into a collective effort to remake the social, political, and economic structure of the village.[42]

At the village level the mobilization began with the decision to develop countermeasures to alleviate the economic crisis. Sometimes this decision came after pressure from a local emigration movement, sometimes after lobbying from prefectural authorities. In either case, such a decision reflected consensus among the village elite. Next, an office was set up within the town hall with direct connections to the mayor and vice-mayor. This office administered several departments that linked up with local voluntary organizations such as reservists, youth groups, farm co-ops, and so on.

The first task of the emigration office was to conduct a survey of the village to determine how many households ought to go. This was an elaborate project requiring collection of data from each household in the village concerning the size of plot it cultivated, household finances, family size, the number of full-time and part-time cultivators, and the percentage of

42. "Community colonization" programs were closely documented in the host of local studies done by Nōrinshō, Teikoku nōkai, Manshū ijū kyōkai and other organizations in the late 1930s and early 1940s (for specific references see note 43 of this chapter). More recently Takahashi Yasutaka and others have produced a number of article-length studies of local communities participating in the emigration movement. Takahashi Yasutaka, "Nihon fashizumu to Manshū bunson imin no tenkai: Nagano-ken Yomikaki-mura no bunseki o chūshin ni," in Manshū iminshi kenkyūkai, eds., *Nihon teikokushugika no Manshū imin* (Ryūkei shosha, 1976), pp. 309–386; Takahashi Yasutaka, "Nihon fashizumu to 'Manshū' nōgyō imin," *Tochi seido shigaku*, no. 71 (April 1976), pp. 47–67; Yamada Shōji, "Furikaeru Nihon no mirai: kaisetsu, Manshū imin no sekai," in Yamada Shōji, ed., *Manshū imin*, vol. 6 of *Kindai minshū no kiroku* (Shinjinbutsu ōraisha, 1978), pp. 11–52; Kimijima Kazuhiko, "Fashizumuka nōson ni okeru Manshū imin: Hanishina-gun bunkyō imin no jisshi katei," in Ōe Shinobu, ed., *Nihon fashizumu no keisei to nōson* (Azekura shobō, 1978), pp. 297–342; Yunoki, " 'Manshū' nōgyō imin seisaku," pp. 44–68; Yunoki, "Manshū imin undō to ronri," pp. 52–71; Tanaka Tamotsu, "Taiheiyō sensōka no Manshū bunson imin: Kōchi-ken Hata-gun no rei," *"Herumesu": Hitotsubashi daigaku gakusei kenkyūshi*, no. 27 (March 1976), pp. 140–175; Ōtani Tadashi, "Taiheiyō sensō makki ni okeru Manshū imin: daijūsanji daiHyōgo kaitakudan ni miru bunson kaitakudan sōshutsu no jittai," *Kindaishi kenkyū*, vol. 21 (Ōsaka rekishi gakkai, June 1979), pp. 32–58.

land owned or rented. Once this information had been amassed, the standard optimum holding (*hyōjun keiei menseki*) for the village was calculated. The total land holdings of the village were divided by the standard optimum holding, providing the ideal number of village households. According to the emigration plan, any village population in excess of this figure was to be sent to Manchuria. This quota of excess population became the target that the local emigration movement strove to fill.

Recruiting then began in earnest. A rally was held and a fact-finding mission dispatched to gather firsthand information on the prospective site of settlement. On the mission's return, a welcome-back celebration took place, speeches were made, and an exhibit of materials brought back from the continent opened with pomp and circumstance. The prefectural bureaucracy, Manchurian Emigration Council, Colonial Ministry, Ministry of Agriculture and Forestry, and the prefectural leadership of women's groups, youth groups, and farm groups all sent experts to lecture and persuade. Movies were shown and pamphlets distributed. Roundtable discussions were organized by neighborhood to convince people to go. Once recruiting efforts were exhausted, another survey was executed, this time to calculate the subsidies needed to purchase the soon-to-be vacated land, to resolve indebtedness of the emigrants, and to support family members temporarily left behind. "Emigration bonus money" was distributed to recruits, and they departed the village, after yet another ceremony, to begin "spiritual training" at the Prefectural Training Center.

The colonists departed from their villages in waves—every six months over a period of three years. Even after the last groups had gone, the village continued support activities, sending relief packages (*imon bukuro*) and encouragement packages (*shōrei bukuro*), making visits, and sometimes sending new recruits. Thus for most of the villages involved, the frenetic pace of emigration promotion kept residents in a buzz of activity for the entire duration of the war.[43] The intensity of this activity reflected the

43. For an instructional guide see Nagano-ken keizaibu, "Bunson keikaku no tatekata," in Nōrinshō keizai kōseibu, ed., *Shinnōson no kensetsu* (Asahi shinbun-sha, 1939), pp. 533–550. For a description of this process in various participating villages, see the seven local studies in Nōrinshō keizai kōseibu, *Shinnōson no kensetsu*, as well as Teikoku nōkai, *Fujimi-mura*; Nagano-ken keizaibu, *Bunson keikaku jirei*; Sekisetsu chihō nōson keizai chōsajo, *Manshū nōgyō imin boson keizai jittai chōsa: Yamagata-ken Higashitagawa-gun Yamato-mura* (Sekisetsu chihō nōson keizai chōsajo, 1941); Nichiman nōsei kenkyūkai, *Kaitaku seisaku ni kansuru kenkyū: Manshū kaitakumin no sōshutsu jōkyō ni kansuru chōsa oyobi kaitaku seisaku ni kansuru jakkan no kōsatsu* (Nichiman nōsei kenkyūkai, 1940); Teikoku nōkai, *Manshū kaitakumin sōshutsu ni kansuru chōsa*, no. 1 (Teikoku

profound grassroots impact of the migration machine. The Manchurian colonization movement caught entire communities up in a process that brought about the integration of community and state on one hand, and village and empire on the other.

Mobilization of a community of support was critical, because potential emigrants were not clamoring to go to Manchuria. They needed to be convinced, and the Manchurian colonization movement used peer and community pressure to accomplish the task. It must be underscored that in this sense the Community Emigration Program was not a movement of emigrants; it was a recruitment drive. Since the program involved mobilizing support not just of individuals, but of communities, one of the main tasks of the campaign was to organize the organizers. Village elites stood at the center of this process.

The initiative was first seized by people designated in the numerous emigration "how-to" manuals as *chūshin jinbutsu*—"core individuals"— who lobbied local power brokers to place emigration on the political agenda. Typically these *chūshin jinbutsu* were young men from small landowning families who had been active as leaders of local Sangyō kumiai (cooperatives) or were products of one of the agrarianist training centers. Passionate converts to continental emigration as the solution to their villages' woes, these young men often joined local recruits and became leaders in the Manchurian colonies.[44] But before they could lead their flock to the promised land, they had to convert community leaders to the Manchurian solution.

At the local—the county and village—level, this meant convincing the village and county councils, the county school board, the local chapters of the Imperial Agricultural Association (Teikoku nōkai), and the umbrella farming cooperative organization, Sangyō kumiai. These organizations provided the executive structure for the local emigration movement and mobilized the next tier of recruiters—school principals and heads of youth groups, women's groups, reservist associations, neighborhood associations, credit and marketing cooperatives, teachers' organizations, and other voluntary associations. In turn, they mobilized their members to help with the campaign, recruiting ever more recruiters.

---

nōkai, 1942); Takumushō takuhokukyoku, *Nagano-ken Yomikaki-mura bunson jijō chōsasho* (Takumushō takuhokukyoku, 1942); and Teikoku nōkai, *Nagano-ken Suwa-gun Fujimi-mura*, no. 2 of *Manshū kaitakumin sōshutsu chōsa* (Teikoku nōkai, 1942).

44. Nōrinshō keizai kōseibu, *Shinnōson no kensetsu*, pp. 19–20.

The key to the mobilization of rural support for the Manchurian emigration project was the nexus of national, prefectural, and local initiatives. This was made possible by the position of local elites in a prefectural and national network of organizations that tied the village community to the state. The same voluntary associations that constituted the core of the village emigration movement were also active at higher levels. In Nagano prefecture, for example, the Prefectural Council of Mayors and Village Heads, the Shinano School Board, the prefectural councils of Sangyō kumiai, Nōkai, the Aikoku fujinkai (Patriotic Women's Association), and the youth groups all played key roles. Local leaders of these organizations represented the channel through which prefectural government pressure was exerted on the local population.[45]

Standing at the intersection of government and community, local elites played their role, in part, by carrying out initiatives directed from above. Emigration policy was backed by a considerable bureaucratic drive, coming from the multiple state agencies of the Kwantung Army, Manchukuo government, and the national and prefectural bureaucracies in Japan. But this growth in the capacity of state intervention did not imply a totalitarian control over local society. The state was increasingly able to structure the options faced by rural communities, but this still left a considerable range of choice in community hands. In the end it was the village that decided whether or not to participate in Manchurian colonization, and the local landowning elites who made this decision. The mayor and vice-mayor, the village council, school principals, and the heads of the farm guilds and voluntary organizations typically composed the membership of the committee that adopted an emigration plan. They provided leadership and drive, and helped mobilize the local organizations they dominated to carry out the labor-intensive tasks of the local emigration movement. Thus, in both its formative and mature phases, the colonization movement represented a dialectic of local and national initiatives, and of public and private interventions.

The village colonization program for adult farm households dominated the Manchurian colonization movement from 1936 to 1938. After that, momentum shifted to a program known as the Patriotic Youth Brigade. Accounting for more than a third of the Manchurian emigrants, the Patriotic Youth Brigade recruited males between fourteen and twenty-one years of age to stake their future on the continent. In the first two years

45. Nagano-ken kaitaku jikōkai Manshū kaitakushi kankōkai, vol. 1, pp. 273–308.

of the program, 1938 and 1939, the Colonial Ministry set prefecture-wide targets which relied on local regiments, reservist associations, and youth associations to promote the program and recruit candidates. Although this system worked well in 1938, by 1939 numbers of recruits were dropping off sharply and reports of homesickness and dissatisfaction in the Manchurian training camps were causing alarm among the program's promoters. Starting in 1940, the Colonial Ministry changed its method of recruitment. Following the adult emigration program which targeted a local community as a whole, the Youth Brigade began to recruit boys in local units through the school system.[46]

The centerpiece of this strategy was the implementation of what were called *Takushoku kunren* (Colonial Training Courses). The graduating classes of higher primary schools (the equivalent of eighth grade) were encouraged to take part in a week's retreat at one of the prefectural training camps run, typically, by the county board of education.[47] The participants from each school formed into squads of 10 students, which became the basic units in the paramilitary organization maintained during the week's training. Commanding the troops in the program of military, spiritual, and physical training were their teachers, youth association leaders, prefectural bureaucrats, and officers from the local regiment and reservist association.[48] Most prefectures held a number of training courses per year at several different locations. Okayama, for example, held twenty training sessions in 1940 attended by a total of 1,121 students.[49] Nationwide, the *Manchurian Settlement Yearbook* of 1941 recorded 20,000 schoolboys taking part in these courses during the same year.[50]

Teachers remained the key to mobilizing youth support for Manchurian colonization. Much as they had encouraged students to participate in the fundraising campaigns and write letters to soldiers during the Manchurian Incident, primary school teachers were agents of empire in the late 1930s, urging their charges to leave their homes for the new frontier. Thirteen-

46. Shiratori, " 'Manmō kaitaku seishōnen giyūgun' no hen'yō," pp. 50–64.
47. Since 1896 the Japanese educational system mandated eight years of compulsory education. After 1908 these were divided between six years of primary school (*jinjō shōgakkō*) and two years of higher primary school (*kōtō shōgakkō*). In the wartime educational reform of 1941 these became amalgamated into a single school (*kokumin gakkō*), but the division between a lower course of six years (*shōtōka*) and an upper course of two years (*kōtōka*) remained unchanged.
48. Sakuramoto, pp. 154–192.
49. Okayama kenshi hensan iinkai, p. 364.
50. Manshūkoku tsūshinsha, ed., *Manshū kaitaku nenkan* (Xinjing: Manshūkoku tsūshinsha, 1941), p. 445.

and fourteen-year-old students deciding on their future were highly susceptible to the advice of their teachers and sometimes followed this advice even over the objections of their parents. In 1941, for example, 77 percent of Youth Brigade recruits declared their reason for volunteering to be the recommendation of a teacher.[51]

The fact that the schools played such an active role in turning the energies of students toward imperialism and war has led postwar opponents of Japanese militarism to direct harsh criticism toward teachers, textbooks, and schools. In books by Tsurumi Kazuko, Ienaga Saburō, and others, the prewar educational system is depicted as an institution that operated, since the Meiji period, to socialize Japanese for death. In this narrative of the institutionalization of thought control and inexorable progress toward war, teachers become the drill sergeants of militarism, using ultranationalistic textbooks to indoctrinate children with an irrational ideology of the emperor-cult.[52]

Yet the reality was not quite so simple. In fact, like other institutions that helped mobilize popular support for imperialism in the 1930s, schools had provided vehicles for the spread of democratic and liberal ideas in the 1920s. Beginning after the Russo-Japanese War and accelerating during World War I, the currents of student activism, labor organizing, and bourgeois cultural experimentation began to affect the educational community. Influenced by the ideas of John Dewey and other Western advocates of utilitarian, child-centered education, educational administrators like Sawayanagi Masatarō created new elementary schools that promoted individual development and self-reliance. Social activists, such as the women's movement pioneer Hani Motoko, became principals of these alternative primary schools and took their ideals of social justice to the classroom. Left-wing writers like Takakura Teru helped found free universities (*jiyū daigaku*) in Nagano and elsewhere, institutions designed to democratize access to higher education by providing advanced study for people of humble means. Artists like Yamamoto Kanae began to teach art in primary schools, inspiring a wave of interest both in children's art and in art for children.[53]

51. Shiratori, " 'Manmō kaitaku seishōnen giyūgun' no hen'yō," p. 76.
52. Kazuko Tsurumi, pp. 99–137; Saburō Ienaga, *The Pacific War, 1931–1945,* trans. Frank Baldwin (New York: Pantheon Books, 1978), pp. 13–32.
53. Kokuritsu kyōiku kenkyūjo, *Kyōiku seisaku* 1, pp. 304–306, 323–328; Nihon kindaishi kenkyūkai, ed., *Kiro ni tatsu Shōwa Nihon,* vol. 9 of *Gahō Nihon kindai no rekishi* (Sanseidō, 1980), pp. 84–85; Nihon kindaishi kenkyūkai, ed., *Minponshugi no chōryū,* vol. 8 of *Gahō Nihon kindai no rekishi* (Sanseidō, 1980),

As activists and artists became involved in building educational institutions to promote social reform and individual development, teachers, too, were drawn into what was called the new education movement. Teachers began to organize groups to study Tolstoy and socialism, and formed unions to press for educational reform and better working conditions. They published magazines and tried to establish alternative teacher training academies that would bypass the state-run normal schools. There were two socioeconomic developments underpinning the new social activism of teachers in the 1920s. First, the wartime inflation of the late teens eroded the already precarious economic situation of elementary school instructors. The further reduction of their purchasing power led teachers, whose low salary put them in an income category below many factory laborers, to follow the example of workers around them and organize for better conditions. Second, this increase in teacher activism had to do with changes in the social origins of teachers during the teens and twenties. As opportunities for careers in the higher civil service declined in a period of "employment difficulties" (*shūshokunan*), educated middle-class youth turned to less prestigious vocations such as teaching and journalism. Products of the elite education system, this new breed of teachers brought with it the current fashions in social reform that were sweeping Japan's universities.[54]

A combination of factors led to the decline of the new education movement in the early thirties. Its strength was sapped, in part, by the economic depression; funding to support the journals, unions, and private schools simply dried up. At the same time, opposition within the government and local communities became increasingly organized and effective. Yet, although many of the specific initiatives associated with the new education movement faltered as a result, the reformist impulse of the movement did not die out. Indeed, as educational historian Kawai Akira notes, many of the key figures in the reform movement of the 1920s later turned their energies toward wartime mobilization, and after the war became enthusiastic exponents of democratization.[55] While for some this double flip-flop may have been an opportunistic reaction to the trends of the times, for

---

pp. 140–141, 162–163; *Taishō demokurashii*, vol. 10 of *Nihonjin no hyakunen* (Sekai bunkasha, 1972), pp. 40–55, 114–119; Yamazumi Masami, *Nihon kyōiku shōshi* (Iwanami Shoten, 1987), pp. 77–117.

54. Kokuritsu kyōiku kenkyūjo, *Kyōiku seisaku 1*, pp. 308–312; Gluck, *Japan's Modern Myths*, pp. 152–154.

55. Kawai's study was coauthored by Kawai, Yasukawa Junnosuke, Morikawa Terumichi, and Kawaguchi Yukihiro. See Kawai et al., *Nihon gendai kyōikushi* (ShinNihon shuppansha, 1984), pp. 160–161.

others the shift from liberal to fascist to democrat represented a consistent pursuit of social ideals. In Nagano, for example, many of the young teachers who were fired in the early thirties for "red proclivities" later volunteered to lead Youth Brigades to Manchuria.[56] One can speculate that teachers like these who pushed their students to join the Youth Brigade did so not to get children to sacrifice themselves for the war machine, but rather because they hoped to give them an opportunity for a better life. In other words, they probably sent their children to Manchuria because they believed in the cause themselves.

Government administrators of the Youth Brigade policy recognized the importance of teachers and spared no effort to enlist their help. Numerous programs were made available to schoolteachers to raise their consciousness about Manchurian colonization. During summer and winter breaks they could participate in the Manmō kaitaku seishō giyūtai kyōgaku hōshitai (Patriotic Youth Brigade Education Corps), which financed a month's tour of selected training camps in Manchuria.[57] If they missed that opportunity, teachers could join a Manchurian tour sponsored by their county or prefectural board of education. And if they had no inclination to go overseas, they could enroll in one of the many teacher-training courses run by local, prefectural, and national educational administrators, or take part in a "rise-of-Asia" (kōa) study group.[58]

At the same time, administrators initiated changes in curriculum. In January 1940 the content of a new "rise-of-Asia" course in the higher primary schools was the subject of a national meeting in Tokyo. In 1943 the Manchurian Emigration Council established a network of prefectural rise-of-Asia education guidance boards to facilitate national leadership of what became known as the kōa kyōiku, or "rise-of-Asia education" movement. Local boards of education in Nagano and elsewhere moved to introduce kōa kyōiku into the curriculum. As the Higashi Chikuma Board announced, the goal was to promote support for the Patriotic Youth Brigade by teaching students of "the danger faced by Asia because of white aggression" and "the importance of the continental advance of the Japanese race for the construction of Asia."[59] By 1942 this movement had grown to

56. Ibid., p. 161.
57. Shiratori, " 'Manmō kaitaku seishōnen giyūgun' no hen'yō," p. 81.
58. Okayama kenshi hensan iinkai, pp. 363–364; Higashichikuma-gun, Matsumoto-shi, Shiojiri-shi kyōdō shiryō hensankai, pp. 397–400.
59. Okayama kenshi hensan iinkai, pp. 363–364; Higashichikuma-gun, Matsumoto-shi, Shiojiri-shi kyōdō shiryō hensankai, p. 400; Sakuramoto, pp. 172–180; Nagano-ken kaitaku jikōkai Manshū kaitakushi kankōkai, vol. 1, pp. 431–433.

the extent that the textbook publisher Meguro shoten began to track its trends in a monthly journal entitled *Kōa kyōiku* (Rise-of-Asia Education).[60]

The *kōa kyōiku* campaign drew administrators, teachers, and even parents into a community education movement to disseminate the idea of Asian colonization. In this way the recruitment strategy for the Patriotic Youth Brigade involved both the mobilization of the nation's higher primary schools as well as a widening circle of institutions that had potential influence over the target age group of children. Directed only secondarily toward students themselves, the *kōa kyōiku* movement was much more than a program of instruction for potential Youth Brigade settlers. Like the village colonization program, it became a vehicle for the mobilization of rural Japan behind the Manchurian project.

The idea of Manchurian colonization appealed to teachers and other grassroots agents of empire because it seemed to offer an alternative for a rural underclass trapped in poverty and oppression. Projecting progressive impulses onto a settlement frontier, rural reformers were engaged in much the same process as their urban counterparts: transferring dreams of domestic social transformation onto the empire. The magnetic power of Manchukuo as a space for social dreaming reminds us, once again, that for many Japanese who lived through it, the empire building of the 1930s was not defined simply by militarism.

At another level, the story of grassroots activism in the Manchurian colonization movement illustrates the role of local communities in directing the growth of the state over these years. The migration machine was a joint endeavor of government and community. In this sense it represented the product both of the extension of the state into new spheres of social management and the penetration of the state by social activists.

HEROIZING MANCHURIAN COLONIZATION

Cultural representations of the colonization movement glorified the efforts of these grassroots agents of empire. Expressed through the same propaganda and recruitment literature that had ennobled the bureaucratic enterprise of colonization, the story of movement activists served as the social counterpart to the narrative of racial expansionism. While the racial mission represented colonists as part of a transcendental, racial aggregate, this narrative focused on individual participants: village activists, movement

60. Sakuramoto, pp. 150–152.

leaders, and the boys of the Youth Brigade. The journalists, writers, and artists who created the propaganda of colonization appealed to potential recruits to become heroes in the challenging but worthy enterprise of Manchurian settlement. Like the racial mission, the heroic narrative worked at two levels, celebrating the role of local activists in the new public-private partnership on one hand, and fostering a new sense of intimacy between villagers and their empire in Manchukuo on the other.

In the first instance, this process of celebrating local activists involved mythologizing the experiences of Japanese colonists, rendering heroic and meaningful individual sacrifices for the sake of state and empire. The outlines of what became the Manchurian frontier myth began to appear in 1937, just when the Millions to Manchuria policy entered its first year. At this juncture it was important to put to rest the doubts and suspicions raised by several years of bad press on the fortunes of the first experimental settlements. Hence, when Japanese read pamphlets or articles about Manchurian migration, they were treated to a historical account of the project that focused exclusively on these early years of trial, making heroes of the participants and celebrating the passing of the colonization project from a past era of hardship into a present period of bounty.

Previously, emigration promoters had simply tried to minimize the reports of the terrors of unremitting Chinese bandit attacks and other hardships. In 1935 a Colonial Ministry official insisted that the bandits that "people at home were so worried about" were "not as numerous as the sensationalistic press accounts would have us believe." The president of an emigration society also dismissed the significance of a bandit problem, exclaiming, "Why, the true character of these bandits is no different from the household burglars you read about every day in the Japanese papers."[61]

The historical accounts of migration drawn up after 1937 abandoned this line, glorifying instead the dangers of banditry and the corresponding heroism of the settlers. For example, a Mantetsu pamphlet on *Manchuria: The Settler's Paradise* focused, as became the pattern, on the adventures of the first and second settlements in Iyasaka and Chiburi. These settlements suffered more than any subsequent groups from armed attack, poor production, and high desertion rates. As *The Settler's Paradise* described their plight, "With banditry still rampant . . . the settlers had to arm themselves . . . with a hoe in one hand and a gun in the other. . . . The first and second settlements got drawn into a struggle for their lives even as they

61. Yoshizaki Senshū, "Manshū imin no senku dantai no kūshin," *Ie no hikari* (April 1935), p. 124; "Yowatari annai," *Ie no hikari* (February 1935), p. 146.

struggled to open the land. . . . In May 1934 the first and second settle-ments were completely surrounded by a group of several thousand bandits. However, they fought bravely and refused to yield even one step to the enemy. On the contrary they drove the bandit forces to retreat."[62] But the incident took its toll, the authors noted grimly, with twenty-four dead and many others wounded. Forty percent of the colonists withdrew in frustra-tion, making this the low point of Manchurian settlement.

The pamphlet followed this gloomy picture with a stirring speech given by the colonists who decided to stick it out. Comparing the Japanese col-onization of Manchukuo with the mythic founding of Japan by the divine emperor Jimmu, one colonist declared, "We are the apostles who descended to Manchuria from the holy land of Japan. Just as in the ancient age of the gods the children of heaven descended to the home of the gods, now we will build a new home of the gods [*takamagawara*] in a corner of north Manchuria."[63] With these words the story shifted and the fate of the col-onists suddenly changed. Continental brides arrived, children were born, and the colony began to flourish. Explaining the "joy of ending a desperate fight," *The Settler's Paradise* concluded its historical summary with the happy news that "in thirty skirmishes over five years the colonists dem-onstrated their bold fighting spirit and the large and small bandit groups in the area no longer dared to touch them."[64]

Such stories, circulated in the late thirties, made the Iyasaka and Chiburi settlements household names by the early forties. As a Colonial Ministry researcher boasted, in 1934 "no one had heard" of Iyasaka and Chiburi, but in 1942 there was "not a soul who do not know their names." Thus, in the space of a few years, an orthodox history of Manchurian colonization had been etched into public memory.[65] In the course of repetition, certain details of this narrative became writ in stone. Even abridged versions, such as the account in the Japan Tourist Bureau's *Travel Guide to Manchuria*, referred to the five years and thirty engagements before the colonists tri-umphed over the bandits; and no one failed to mention the arrival of the women and the "baby rush" (*akachan rasshu*). The settlers were invariably designated the "desperate trial colonists" (*chimidorona shiken imin*), and

---

62. *Manshū wa imin no rakudo* (Dalian: Mantetsu, 1937), pp. 1–7, quotation from p. 5.

63. Ibid., p. 6.

64. Ibid.

65. "Kaitaku jūnen no kaiko," *Ie no hikari* (December 1942), p. 74.

the account always ended with the "fear of the colonists" ("*kaitakudan osorubeshi" no shinnen*) planted in the minds of the bandits.[66]

As a result of the dissemination of this heroic tale, Iyasaka and Chiburi were usually at the top of the sightseer's agenda. Indeed, both colonies soon built hotels to accommodate the crowds that converged on these twin "meccas of settlement."[67] The deluge of visitors was such that many settlers were reportedly forced to give up farming altogether in order to devote full time to "showing people around." Explaining the popularity of this "immigration showcase," one travel diary related the excitement of "witnessing the scars left by the trials of their early experiences," and realizing how far Japanese colonists had come since then. The Iyasaka and Chiburi colonists were "living testimony to the pain and struggle" of settlement; they demonstrated the perseverance required "to build the flourishing settlements you see today." Chiburi, it was noted, "even has a department store"—the ultimate proof of success.[68]

By flocking to the site of the "bandit" attacks, sightseers reinforced the imperial legend of settler heroics and helped the legend grow. Telling and retelling the story of the settlement to successive groups of visitors, settler tour guides gave shape to the narrative. Adding polish and embroidering details, travel writers left their mark as well. The mythologizing of Manchurian colonization, in other words, was a collective process. Bureaucrats, journalists, and even simple tourists all took part in the construction of a colonial frontier myth designed to dispel fears aroused by the hardships of early settlement.

Out of this epic narrative two figures emerged to become the twin champions of Manchurian colonization: Tomiya Kaneo and Katō Kanji. Both men had been involved in the Manchurian colonization movement in its organizational phase in the early 1930s. Tomiya was an army officer who embraced expansionist causes. He was peripherally associated with right-wing patriotic societies operating in China and imagined himself to belong to the company of *tairiku rōnin*, continental adventurers who conspired to advance Japan's position in China. A passionate Russophobe, in the early thirties Tomiya pushed hard for paramilitary Japanese settlements in north Manchuria as a bulwark against the Soviet Union. Katō,

66. Japan tsūrisuto byūrō, p. 164.
67. Ibid., p. 174; Asahi shinbunsha Tōa mondai chōsakai, ed., *Manshū imin*, vol. 2 of *Asahi Tōa ripōto* (Asahi shinbunsha, 1939), pp. 24–25.
68. Asahi shinbunsha Tōa mondai chōsakai, pp. 24–25.

on the other hand, was a leading *nōhonshugi* ideologue. He headed the group of agrarian reformers and scholars who advocated Manchurian colonization in the early 1930s and was instrumental in persuading the government to establish a small number of farm colonies on a trial basis.[69] Both Tomiya and Katō were represented in colonization propaganda as government "outsiders"—spokesmen for the popular groundswell of interest in the settlement of the Manchurian frontier. Moreover, both men were symbolically important to a narrative that sought to valorize equally the role of movement activists in Manchuria and at home. In this sense Tomiya stood as spiritual forefather of the colonial pioneers, while Katō personified the patriarch of the homeside emigration movement.

Descriptions of the two men stressed their similarities, from the identical shaggy goatees they sported to their kindred spirits and their shared trials. Possessed by the same dream, the two men had "overcome a thousand obstacles" to bring that dream to reality. Like the narratives of the trial immigrants, their stories were told in a manner intended to disarm negative images. Popular biographers celebrated the fact that Tomiya and Katō were "once laughed at as the immigration maniacs [*iminkyō*]," contrasting this derogatory nickname with the more flattering replacement, "the immigration gods."[70] In this way their stories communicated the same message as the retold tale of the pioneer immigrants: success follows great suffering and hardship.

The images of Tomiya conveyed in songs like Shiratori Seigo's "Colonel Tomiya—Father of Colonization," and in the obituaries following his death in battle against China in the fall of 1937 were of a man who embodied the spirit of the continental adventurer. With Tomiya, "one glance at his wild beard and fearless countenance" revealed a "fierce warrior." His reputation was such that "bandit chiefs had only to hear his name to start quaking in their boots." In addition to god and father of immigration, Tomiya was crowned with numerous other popular sobriquets. He was called the "sentimental warrior" because of his reputation as a poet, and "the ballast stone of continental expansion" (*tairiku hatten no suteishi*) from a line in one of his own poems. He was also known as the "fisherman of Sanjiang," referring to his military adventuring in north Manchuria,

69. For more on Katō, see Chapter Seven herein and Havens, *Farm and Nation in Modern Japan*, pp. 275–294.
70. Hata Kennosuke, "Imin no chichi Tōmiya taisa," *Ie no hikari* (June 1938), pp. 60–62.

and (his personal favorite) *"hokushin,"* or "strike north," the slogan embraced by advocates of war with the Soviet Union. As his various nicknames attest, depictions of Tomiya as explorer, warrior, firebrand, and patriot drew on stock images of Japanese continental adventurers to set the standards for manly virtue to which settlement pioneers could aspire.[71]

In the meantime, as the inspiration for the homeside movement, Katō Kanji was carefully styled in the image of the philosopher laureate of imperial agrarianism. One admiring account likened Katō to two of the most celebrated figures of the agrarianist movement, Ninomiya Sontoku and Tanaka Shōzō. The allusion to Ninomiya, the legendary "peasant sage" of the Tokugawa period, greatly flattered Katō, ranking him with the man whose moral system of "repaying virtue" had provided the guiding philosophy of the modern agrarianist movement. The comparison to the village activist and champion of local autonomy, Tanaka Shōzō, credited Katō with the same selfless and single-minded pursuit of justice for which Tanaka had become famous in his battle against Ashio Copper Mine pollution in the 1890s. Inheriting the mantle of these two inspirational leaders, Katō reportedly embodied "the spirit of the soil and the spirits of the departed." Combining Ninomiya's moral wisdom with Tanaka's stern adherence to principle, Katō's teachings were to sustain Japanese settlers through the trials of life in their new home. Such rapturous descriptions made Katō sound like a charismatic quasi-religious leader and sage. Thus Katō, the "idealist" and the "man of spirit," complemented Tomiya, the "man of action," as champions of Manchurian colonization.[72]

In addition to constructing an epic of frontier settlement and grooming Tomiya and Katō to be champions of the grassroots agents of empire, the literature on colonization celebrated mass participation by fabricating popular symbols for the two key programs of village colonization and the Youth Brigade. Significantly, these symbols were drawn not from the settlement experience in Manchuria, but from the mobilization experience at home. Complementing the epic tale of the Iyasaka and Chiburi pioneers that took place in Manchukuo, paeans to the home-front heroes of colo-

71. Kami Shōichirō, *Manmō kaitaku seishōnen giyūgun* (Chūō kōronsha, 1973), pp. 14–15; "Tairiku hatten no suteishi," *Ie no hikari* (June 1938), p. 23; Sakuramoto, p. 107; Hata Kennosuke, "Imin no chichi Tōmiya taisa," *Ie no hikari* (June 1938), pp. 60–63.

72. Katō Takeo, "Manshū kaitaku no chichi Katō Kanjishi o kataru," *Ie no hikari* (November 1941), pp. 38–40; Hata Kennosuke, "Imin no chichi Tōmiya taisa," *Ie no hikari* (June 1938), p. 62.

nization told the same tale of integration of home and empire. Here, the story illustrated how the process of mobilizing for empire helped to bring a conflicted rural community into social harmony.

Literature on the village colonization movement always included examples of the "three models of village colonization," Miyagi prefecture's Nangō village, Yamagata prefecture's Shōnai district, and Nagano prefecture's Ōhinata village.[73] Of the three, the story of Ōhinata became by far the most famous. One of the first villages to participate in the Ministry of Agriculture and Forestry's Village Colonization Program, Ōhinata was carefully developed as a test case and model. To this end, large groups of Ministry of Agriculture and Forestry officials made several visits to the village. Kodaira Ken'ichi, head of the Rural Rehabilitation Division in charge of the program, made a personal appearance. Kodaira's wife recalls that her husband stayed up all night in order to convince villagers to support the scheme, demonstrating the importance the ministry attached to its success with Ōhinata. In particular, ministry officials felt that the appearance of unanimous village support for emigration was critical. Moreover, the village received a generous government grant for its participation, before any official subsidy program was established. And although a number of settlers were recruited from neighboring villages to fill the targets for Ōhinata, this fact was hidden to cultivate a myth of origin that all settlers in the colony came from the same native place. Such efforts aimed to guarantee not only that Ōhinata was a success, but also that it set an appropriate model to follow.[74]

The popularizing of the Ōhinata myth largely took place after 1939, when the initial surge of enthusiasm for village colonization was fading and recruitment began to fall off sharply. Partly due to the encouragement of emigration officials, movie companies, playhouses, record companies, and publishers created a boom in Ōhinata village productions. Tokyo theaters sent troops of actors to visit the village and prepare themselves for their roles. The Ministry of Agriculture and Forestry invited leaders of the local movement to advise a Shinbashi playhouse on how to dramatize their story. In movie, novel, short story, photo essay, and song form, the moving story of Ōhinata's struggles to better the conditions of the community became an advertisement for the village colonization movement. As one actor playing the settlement leader urged the audience from the stage at

73. Miura, pp. 95–96; Nōrinshō keizai kōseibu, *Shinnōson no kensetsu*.
74. Yamada Shōji, pp. 29–30, 36.

the close of the play: "You must follow us in great multitudes and build two, three, many Ōhinata villages!"[75]

The cultural monument to the Ōhinata village colonization movement was Wada Tsutō's classic novel *Ōhinata-mura*, upon which the movies and plays were based. A prominent member of the anti-urban anti-Marxist rural literature movement (*nōmin bungaku undō*), Wada joined with Minister of Agriculture and Forestry Arima Yoriyasu in 1938 to form the first of the so-called national policy literature organizations, the Nōmin bungaku konwakai. Under the auspices of this organization, Wada spent time with the villagers in Ōhinata interviewing and collecting information for a documentary novel, after which he took a paid one-month tour to visit the colony in Manchuria. The product of these efforts was published in mid 1939 by the *Asahi* newspaper and again in 1941 as one volume in the *Asahi*'s "Colonial Literature Series."[76]

Wada's narrative focused almost exclusively on the efforts of the leaders of the village colonization movement in Ōhinata, newly appointed village head Asakawa Takemaro and Sangyō kumiai organizer Horikawa Kiyomi, to mobilize their community. As the story opens, the two men despair at the intractable poverty of their village, the villagers' debt peonage to a rapacious local merchant, and the bleak future of the young people. Hearing how Horikawa's attempts to use the Sangyō kumiai to oppose the financial grip of the merchant had failed in the past, Asakawa was suddenly struck with inspiration: Manchuria was the solution. Before Asakawa can bring his dream to reality, however, he must convince the poor villagers, defuse the plots of the villainous merchant, and secure government aid to finance the project. After great struggles and the suicide of a tubercular villager to release her family and fiancé to make the trip to the new land, the movement finally triumphs. Everyone in the village—anxious parents, reluctant landlords, and even the evil merchant—falls into the group spirit and joins the fanfare as the story closes with a joyous send-off ceremony.

The Ōhinata story took place entirely in Japan. The empire was central to the plot, but it did not comprise a theater of action. This was significant,

75. "Shibai monogatari Ōhinata-mura," *Ie no hikari* (January 1940), pp. 104–109; Yamada Shōji, pp. 36–38.
76. Wada Tsutō, *Ōhinata-mura* (1941), in Shōwa sensō bungaku zenshū henshū iinkai, ed., *Senka Manshū ni agaru*, vol. 1 of *Shōwa sensō bungaku zenshū* (Shūeisha, 1964), pp. 115–171. See also discussion of Wada's work in Shōwa sensō bungaku zenshū henshū iinkai, ed., *Senka Manshū ni agaru*, vol. 1 of *Shōwa sensō bungaku zenshū* (Shūeisha, 1964), p. 494; and Kawamura, pp. 28–33.

for it underscored the message that empire transformed Japan for the better, not just the other way round. Moreover, by making the mother village into the symbol of imperial emigration, the story domesticated the process of colonization, making it less fearsome. No bandits made an appearance, and the hardships were all too familiar.

Like the village colonization movement, the symbol for the Patriotic Youth Brigade emerged from the domestic landscape. Although extensive press coverage of the Youth Brigade's precursor offered excellent candidates for a brigade hallmark, these were bypassed in favor of the gigantic domestic training complex in Ibaraki prefecture, where youths were sent for their initial months of training. Uchiwara Training Center consisted of fields, an enormous parade ground, and about 500 distinctively shaped round barracks. It was these curious "sun-shaped barracks" (*nichirin heisha*) that became the popular symbol for the Youth Brigade.

Like Ōhinata, writers and artists played a large role in popularizing the new imperial symbol. Fukuda Kiyohito, another central figure in the rural literary movement and founder of Tairiku kaitaku bungei konwakai (Continental Colonization Literary Association), in 1939 titled his popular novel on the Youth Brigade *Nichirin heisha*.[77] Tatsumi Seika, the celebrated children's poet, published a collection entitled *Nichirin heisha no asa* (Morning in the Sun-shaped Barracks). Like many of the songs about Uchiwara, Tatsumi's poems described what he imagined to be the excitement of the boys who were answering the call to empire. For the new recruits, the camp purportedly fulfilled a "long-cherished dream, these barracks that imitate the sun." To this fabled retreat with its exotic "Mongolian" flavor boys came to play at empire.

> Through the dew-drenched leaves
> You can see the sun-shaped barracks . . .
> Those sun-shaped barracks
> Looking like conical Mongolian hats,
> Those perfectly round roofs
> Thatched with cedar.
> Inside them young men
> Silently reading, writing,
> Earnestly preparing themselves.
> These boys of tender years
> Gather from throughout the nation,
> Wishing to give to their country,

77. Fukuda Kiyohito, *Nichirin heisha* (Asahi shinbunsha, 1939).

Burning with the bold and valiant
Colonial spirit.[78]

Uchiwara was designed to imitate empire. The huge parade ground and
the camp shrine were both named after the first of the trial settlements,
Iyasaka. Katō Kanji had borrowed the idea of the round barracks from a
design used by the Kwantung Army for maximum protection against
armed attack. Originally the invention of architect and long-time China
resident Koga Hirome, these were not drawn from any indigenous Manchurian model, but out of Japan's imperial tradition.[79] Yet when they gazed
at Uchiwara, Japanese thought they were seeing something that represented the Manchurian folk tradition. In a work entitled *Stalwart Uchiwara*, one observer wrote:

> You could see several roofs like conical Mongolian hats and barracks
> shaped rather like upside-down kettles. They call them *nichirin heisha* but
> basically they are put together on the outside with split pine logs and on
> the inside wood slabs. Perhaps five hundred of these sun-shaped barracks
> are nestled among forty *chō* of pine woods that stretch between an ex-
> panse of hills and fields. When your eye confronts the specter of these
> alien buildings, you feel for an instant that you are nowhere near Tokyo,
> indeed, that you have been transported to a corner of Mongolia in the far
> reaches of Manchuria.[80]

Intrigued by Uchiwara's exotic imperial feel, Japanese chose its distinctive
round barracks as the symbol for the Youth Brigade. It was a symbol well
suited to the aspirations for a new intimacy between empire and metropolis. Planting a piece of Manchuria in Japan, Uchiwara domesticated empire
even as the settlement project was Japanizing Manchuria.

With the construction and popularization of a heroic myth of the Manchurian frontier, the colonization movement assimilated new ideas into the
ideology of Japanese colonialism. The incorporation of the farm community into the imperial project brought new groups into the process of expansion. As Manchukuo became a land of rural opportunity for poor farmers, villages became symbolic, as well as material, beneficiaries of empire.
Before, imperial mythology had reserved the heroes' gallery for soldiers
and opportunities for the colonial elite. Now the stalwart farmer-colonists

78. Sakuramoto, pp. 71–72, 78–79.
79. Ibid., pp. 69–70.
80. The original work by Itō Kinjirō, *Takumashiki Uchiwara*, was published in
1938. Passage quoted in ibid., p. 69.

partook of the heady success and the glorious heroism of empire building in the service of the state, and all of rural Japan could take vicarious pride in their accomplishments. By heroizing Manchurian colonization, movement literature valorized the village embrace of the empire even as it sanctified the social embrace of the state.

THE TYRANNY OF THE MACHINE

From its origins in the nationwide movement to save the villages in the early 1930s, a dialectic of local and national initiatives, and of public and private interventions, gave rise by the end of the decade to the formidable bureaucratic apparatus of the migration machine. But like many complex institutions, once set in motion, the machine assumed a life of its own and its operations were no longer responsive to those forces that had given it birth. In the final years of the war, when the national priority was to mobilize soldiers, not migrants, and the farm villages were suffering from acute labor shortages, the migration machine continued to resettle large numbers of Japanese in Manchurian farm colonies. The relentless pursuit of its mission against utility or logic had turned the migration machine into a tyrannical force within the state and rural society. The ways in which, by 1942, Manchurian colonization was undermining the war effort illustrated how the growth of the state, paradoxically, could also contribute to its disintegration.

As early as 1937, the constellation of forces that promoted the colonization movement began to come apart. In the countryside, though economic recovery came relatively late, by 1936 prices of most agricultural commodities (with the exception of raw silk) had returned to pre-1929 levels, and industrial expansion had reversed the in-migration from urban areas.[81] As war spread from China to the Pacific, the ever-growing demands of military and industrial mobilization gave rise to a severe agricultural labor shortage. Between 1936 and 1941, the expansion of the armed forces alone mobilized over 2 million men, as troop strength grew from 564,000 to 2,391,000. Over the same period the Japanese military death toll reached 230,000. Both these figures, of course, rose precipitously after 1941.[82]

81. Mori Takemaro, "Senjika nōson no kōzō henka," in *Kindai* 7, vol. 20 of *Iwanami kōza Nihon rekishi* (Iwanami shoten, 1976), p. 317.
82. Hara Akira, "Senji tōsei keizai no kaishi," p. 240.

Moreover, over the course of the war, industrial expansion absorbed an estimated 1.5 million new workers from the villages.[83]

This mass mobilization began to strain labor reserves well before the outbreak of the Pacific War. Already by 1938, over half of the men fighting in China were reserve soldiers in their thirties. By 1939 the labor shortage for wartime industry had necessitated the implementation of a labor draft. Between 1936 and 1941 the rural population dropped by over 100,000 households and the percentage of farmers engaged full-time in agriculture fell from 75 percent to 42 percent. For the first time anyone could remember, villages were faced with a labor shortage. The resulting crisis in food production grew so bad that the government began importing "Patriotic Farm Labor Brigades" of urban youths into the countryside.[84]

Consequently, it became increasingly difficult to meet recruiting targets for Manchurian emigrants. As shown in Table 11, the emigration movement surpassed the modest targets of the trial emigration period, but recruited less than half the hoped-for number between 1937 and 1941, and only 16 percent afterward. The drop in interest was reflected in local statistics, too. For example, village emigration planners in Kōchi prefecture's Hata county managed to recruit 47 percent of their targets through 1942 but only 9.5 percent during the final years of the war.[85]

Still, a surprising number of communities continued to push Manchurian emigration. Between 1942 and 1945, 97,740 people moved to Manchuria (see Table 12). Even though from a national perspective the settlement project had become a clear drain on the war effort, emigration planners kept the bureaucratic machinery running full throttle in the belief that their part in Asian coprosperity was equally important to the war industry or the armed forces. As interest fell off among adults, all-out efforts were made to recruit children into the Patriotic Youth Brigade. After 1941, these young men made up over one-third of the number of colonists. Although the Youth Brigade program was initially set up to overcome

83. Mori, pp. 354–355. Mori estimates 1.8 million left the village for industrial employment or emigration to Manchuria.

84. Reserve soldiers in China: Fujiwara Akira, "Nihon fashizumu to tai-Chūgoku shinryaku sensō," in Fujiwara Akira and Nozawa Yutaka, eds., *Nihon fashizumu to Higashi Ajia* (Aoki shoten, 1977), p. 14; the labor draft: Awaya Kentarō, "Kokumin dōin to teikō," in *Kindai* 8, vol. 21 of *Iwanami kōza Nihon rekishi* (Iwanami shoten, 1976), p. 182; agricultural labor shortage: Mori, pp. 323, 354–357. According to Mori, the rural population was 5,597,465 in 1936 and 5,498,826 in 1941.

85. Tanaka Tamotsu, p. 144.

Table 11. Emigration Targets and Percentage of Target Achieved

Year	Adult Emigrants		Youth Brigade	
	Target	%	Target	%
1932–1936	14,500	104	0	0
1937	30,000	67	0	0
1938	30,000	86	30,000	66
1939	55,000	71	30,000	36
1940	101,000	41	12,600	73
1941	154,250	9	12,000	106
Total (1937–1941)	370,250	38	84,600	63
1942	65,000	36	10,200	114
1943	128,000	12	15,000	71
1944	165,000	12	13,500	58
1945	205,000	3	10,000	38
Total (1942–1945)	563,000	11	48,700	70

SOURCES: Figures for 1932–1935 from Matsumura Takao, "Manshūkoku seiritsu ikō ni okeru imin, rōdō seisaku no keisei to tenkai," in Manshūshi kenkyūkai, ed., Nihon teikokushugika no Manshū (Ochanomizu shobō, 1972), pp. 220–221. Figures for 1937–1941 from Manshū teikoku seifu, ed., Manshū kenkoku jūnenshi, vol. 91 of Meiji hyakunenshi sōsho (Hara shobō, 1969), pp. 374–375. Figures for 1942–1945 from Asada Kyōji, "Manshū nōgyō imin seisaku no ritsuan katei," in Manshū iminshi kenkyūkai, ed., Nihon teikokushugika no Manshū imin (Ryūkei shosha, 1976), p. 100; and Sakuramoto Tomio, Manmō kaitaku seishōnen giyūgun (Aoki shoten, 1987), p. 147.

NOTE: In the original planning documents, targets for adult emigrants were set for households whereas those for the Youth Brigade were set for individuals. To make these units compatible I have adjusted the numbers for the adult emigrants by multiplying the targeted number of households by five. Emigration plans were based on an estimated average household size of five persons.

labor shortages among adult settlements, it soon became the means of meeting the ambitious goals of the colonization project.[86]

In addition to the expanding Youth Brigade, programs designed to try to drum up interest in emigration proliferated. In one of the more suc-

86. For an examination of Youth Brigade policy, see Shiratori Michihiro's series of articles: " 'Manmō kaitaku seishōnen giyūgun' no sōsetsu katei," Kyōiku gakubu kiyō, no. 45 (Hokkaidō daigaku, December 1984), pp. 189–222; " 'Manshū' imin seisaku to 'Manmō kaitaku seishōnen giyūgun,' " Kyōiku gakubu kiyō, no. 47 (Hokkaidō daigaku, February 1986), pp. 107–139; and " 'Manmō kaitaku seishōnen giyūgun' no hen'yō," pp. 33–96.

Table 12. Manchurian Emigration, 1932–1945

Year	Adult Emigrants Households	Adult Emigrants Estimated Emigrants	Youth Brigade Emigrants
1932	493	2,569	0
1933	494	2,574	0
1934	298	1,553	0
1935	500	2,605	0
1936	1,109	5,778	0
Total (1932–1936)	2,894	15,079	0
1937	3,857	20,095	319
1938	4,924	25,654	19,830
1939	7,489	39,018	10,818
1940	7,930	41,315	9,156
1941	2,741	14,281	12,753
Total (1937–1941)	26,941	140,363	52,876
1942	4,526	23,580	11,604
1943	2,895	15,083	10,658
1944	3,738	19,475	7,799
1945	1,056	5,502	3,848
Total (1942–1945)	12,215	63,640	33,909
Total (1932–1945)	42,050	219,082	86,785

SOURCES: Figures for 1932–1935 from Matsumura Takao, "Manshūkoku seiritsu ikō ni okeru imin, rōdō seisaku no keisei to tenkai," in Manshūshi kenkyūkai, ed., *Nihon teikokushugika no Manshū* (Ochanomizu shobō, 1972), pp. 220–221. Figures for 1937–1941 from Manshū teikoku seifu, ed., *Manshū kenkoku jūnenshi*, vol. 91 of *Meiji hyakunenshi sōsho* (Hara shobō, 1969), pp. 374–375. Figures for 1942–1945 from Asada Kyōji, "Manshū nōgyō imin seisaku no ritsuan katei," in Manshū iminshi kenkyūkai, ed., *Nihon teikokushugika no Manshū imin* (Ryūkei shosha, 1976), p. 100; and Sakuramoto Tomio, *Manmō kaitaku seishōnen giyūgun* (Aoki shoten, 1987), p. 147.

NOTE: Original statistics on adult emigration were collected on a household basis, whereas those for the Youth Brigade reflect individual emigrants. To make these numbers compatible, I have included estimates of numbers of individual emigrants, based on a calculation of five persons per household.

cessful of these programs, emigration planners turned to cities for recruits in what was known as the *Tairiku kinō kaitakumin* (Return to Agriculture Continental Emigration) program. Return to Agriculture campaigns in Kōbe, Hiroshima, Sendai, and Kashiwazaki targeted people who had lost their livelihood due to the wartime downfall of small-scale domestic consumer industries. Return to Agriculture colonists represented a large proportion of those sent during the last years of the war. In Niigata prefecture, for example, 48 percent of emigrants during this period did not farm by trade, and neither did 1,328 of the 4,477 emigrants from Hiroshima prefecture.[87]

But this was not all. Nagano, Hiroshima, and Yamagata prefectures energetically promoted the recruitment of "continental brides" as mates for Youth Brigade settlers who had come of age. Hiroshima's Continental Bride Training Center, one of seven in the nation, boasted 316 graduates for 1942 and 1943.[88] The Manchurian Voluntary Labor Corps sent young men and women over for a short-term period to help the settlers.[89] In 1942 the Greater East Asian Ministry inaugurated the *Tokubetsu shidō gun undō* (special county leadership movement), targeting a select group of about a dozen counties nationwide for saturation recruitment.[90] Throughout the country, *imin kōenkai* (emigrant-support associations) sprang up to arrange marriages for bachelor settlers, mail gifts and newspapers, and send visitors to lend comfort and cheer.[91] In these ways the emigration-movement engineers adapted their project to the wartime contingencies, ensuring that the flow of emigrants out of Japan did not stop.

Emerging out of the traditions of agarianism and emigration, the movement to send Millions to Manchuria had gathered strength in the midst

87. On the "return to agriculture continental emigration program," see Niigata-ken, pp. 748–750; Hiroshima-ken, *Kindai* 2, vol. 6 of *Hiroshima kenshi tsūshi* (Hiroshima: Hiroshima-ken, 1981), pp. 983–985, 993–994; Ōtani, p. 33; Mainichi shirizu shuppan henshu, p. 284; and Nagano-ken kaitaku jikōkai Manshū kaitakushi kankōkai, vol. 1, pp. 593–600.

88. For recruitment of continental brides, see Yamagata-ken, pp. 751–752; Nagano-ken kaitaku jikōkai Manshū kaitakushi kankōkai, vol. 1, pp. 646–650; and Hiroshima-ken, p. 995.

89. Manchurian Voluntary Labor Corps: Nagano-ken kaitaku jikōkai Manshū kaitakushi kankōkai, vol. 1, pp. 560–582; Hiroshima-ken, pp. 992–993.

90. Special county leadership movement: Nagano-ken kaitaku jikōkai Manshū kaitakushi kankōkai, vol. 1, pp. 455–456, 499–506, 550–555; Manshūkoku tsūshinsha, *Manshū kaitaku nenkan* (1944), pp. 69–70; Hiroshima-ken, p. 997; Gifu-ken, *Kindai* 1 of *Gifu kenshi tsūshihen* (Gifu: Gifu-ken, 1967), pp. 640–642; Tanaka Tamotsu, p. 144.

91. On emigrant-support associations, see Hiroshima-ken, p. 994.

of economic crisis. It had grown at national, prefectural, and community levels—all essential to make the movement a success. As the apparatus of emigration grew increasingly elaborate at all three levels, emigration promoters lost sight of the original purposes of the machinery at their command; rather than being a means to an end, emigration became the end itself. This tendency to develop a relative autonomy from the rest of the government was not an isolated characteristic of the emigration movement, but represented one of the enduring features of a socially interventionist state. Once a state apparatus is created to carry out a particular social progam, that bureaucracy becomes difficult to dismantle. It develops a cadre of bureaucrats dedicated to its purpose and networks of constituencies dependent on its perpetuation for their own livelihood. It becomes, in short, a state within a state. In the end, the remarkable achievement of the Manchurian colonization movement—resettling hundreds of thousands of Japanese in Manchuria even amidst the exigencies of war—was due to the relative autonomy of the emigration machine within the Japanese state.

Once taken up by the colonial and metropolitan governments, the colonization project set off a process of intense state building and bureaucratic experimentation in techniques of social management and engineering. Welfare state building also took place in other areas of social policy, carried out by the newly constituted Ministry of Health and Welfare (established 1938). But the colonization program monopolized a large share of bureaucratic energy and resources that in the absence of empire doubtless would have flowed into other activities. The opportunity cost of the billions of yen and millions of bureaucratic hours spent planning and proselytizing is, of course, impossible to measure. Even so, some concrete outcomes of the preoccupation of the early social-policy state with empire can be noted. One of these was the introduction of paternalistic and autocratic colonial-state traditions into the metropolitan welfare-state practices. Another was the tendency to expand the "export-the-problem" approach to poverty and underemployment. By the end of the decade, government officials were promoting Manchurian settlement for small-scale urban merchants and manufacturers displaced by the war economy.

In the longer term, one might speculate that the intimate association between social welfare and empire during the war years affected the position of welfare-state apparatuses within the reconstituted postcolonial state. In a sense, when defeat stripped Japan of its empire, it also stripped the fledgling welfare state of its mission. The triple mandate of national defense, economic development, and social welfare that the government assumed in the early twentieth century in order to justify its expanding interventions in the private sphere was dismantled after 1945. The state continued to assume welfare and defense functions, but these largely disappeared from the official policy statements and government pronouncements through which the state communicated with the public. In the postcolonial era the state legitimized itself not through the articulation of missions to end poverty, or conceptions of state as social safety net, or even the imperatives of defense, but in the language of economic development: high growth and income-doubling plans. This strategy of public relations has shaped popular impressions of the postwar state in which the image of economic management predominates.

Of the three imperial projects that defined empire building in Manchukuo, colonization involved the state most actively as an agent of mobilization. States, of course, have human faces, and one consequence of the mobilization efforts undertaken by the government in the late 1930s was to bring the human agents of the state into the lives of Japanese villagers. Planning sessions, surveying teams, and recruitment drives brought waves of prefectural and national government personnel circulating though the villages. As the history of the Manchurian colonization movement shows, rural activists welcomed their new intimacy with these government officials. Their efforts to mobilize government action in the sphere of social policy and their cooperation with government initiatives at the local level were both important forces behind the migration machine. From the perspective of these local agents of empire, the new social activism of the state represented the flip side of their own increasing social activism. In other words, the rise of the socially interventionist state also told the story of a society increasingly able to penetrate and mobilize government. The ideological constructions of the Manchurian colonization movement sanctified both developments, creating a racial mission that justified state expansion and a heroic tradition of colonization that ennobled social activism.

9 Victims of Empire

[handwritten marginalia: KoC victims, yes; active? (no) / ~real / J. colonizers = victims]

The people to whom all this frenetic activity was ostensibly directed <u>had little say</u> about what was happening to them. Very few emigrants sat on the committees that drew up emigration plans or plotted campaign strategy. They did not help make the decision about when to leave or where their new home was going to be. They were given little choice in what they could bring with them and what was to happen to possessions left behind. These were marginal and powerless people who had been enticed, pressured, and in some cases, coerced into migrating to Manchuria. The hundreds of postwar accounts of the Manchurian emigrants convey an image of suffering and victimization, often tidily captured in titles like *Tomb of Grass: A Record of the Abandoned People of the Manchurian Settlements*.[1] But their role in the empire is neither as clear nor as simple as such books might suggest. Indeed, the story of the emigrants reveals the complex ways that ordinary people both exploited and were exploited by their empire.

IMPERIAL PRIVILEGES

[handwritten marginalia: colonizers always do...]

By design, Manchurian immigrants came from the lowest stratum of village society. As the planners of emigration envisioned, the village colonization plan was based on the "principle of rehabilitating poor farmers in Manchuria and middle-class farmers at home."[2] The designation "poor farmer" (*binō*) basically signified a household managing less than 5 *tan*,

1. Fujita Shigeru, *Kusa no hi: Manmō kaitakudan suterareta tami no kiroku* (Kanazawa: Noto insatsu shuppanbu, 1989).
2. Takahashi Yasutaka, "Nihon fashizumu to nōson keizai kōsei undō no tenkai," p. 21.

or 1.25 acres of land; this included one-third of farm households nation-wide. In a typical situation in Nagano's Ōhinata village, one tenant house-hold worked .25 acre of vegetables, .25 acre of rice, and .50 acre of mulberry. A son worked locally as a day laborer and the rest of the family reared silkworms. Because in Japan it was "all they could do to put food on the table," this family elected to emigrate.[3]

The overwhelming majority of Manchurian settlers were such people. Surveys of landholdings among 337 emigrant households in six villages revealed that over half were tenants who owned no land. An additional 31 percent of emigrating households owned under five *tan* of land, putting them in the category of poor farmer. This meant that most emigrants had not been able to survive on cultivation alone and needed to supplement their income through day labor and other side occupations, thus forming part of the rural underclass. For example, the occupational breakdown of the 214 emigrating households from Yomikaki village illustrates clearly the marginal character of this population. Under half (90) were full-time farmers, and of these only 28 were self-cultivating landowners. Thirty-two were part-time farmers with side employment in household charcoal making or day labor, 44 were full-time day laborers, and the remaining 48 were engaged in such miscellaneous occupations as tool making, vending, carpentry, and so on.[4]

Youth Brigade settlers were recruited from the same socioeconomic group as the adult colonists. The chief difference between the two and the greater vulnerability of the former was due, of course, to age. In photo-graphs, Youth Brigade recruits appear startlingly young, dwarfed by the rifles they carried in training exercises and far from ready to be separated from their families and communities.[5] The target age was sixteen to nine-teen, but as time went on the average age decreased and even fourteen-year-olds were encouraged to join (see Table 13).

Whatever their hopes for Manchukuo, upon settling in their new home the immigrants found that their social position underwent a rapid eleva-tion. As the "leading race" in colonial society they acquired a host of formal and informal privileges that transformed them from a rural underclass to

3. Yamada Shōji, pp. 12, 15.
4. Teikoku nōkai, *Manshū kaitakumin sōshutsu ni kansuru chōsa*, pp. 22, 48, 78; Nichiman nōsei kenkyūkai, *Kaitaku seisaku ni kansuru kenkyū*, pp. 14–15; Takahashi Yasutaka, "Nihon fashizumu to nōson keizai kōsei undō no tenkai," pp. 20–21; Takumushō takuhokukyoku, pp. 34–37.
5. Zenkoku takuyū kyōgikai, ed., *Shashinshū Manmō kaitaku seishōnen gi-yūgun* (Ie no hikari kyōkai, 1975).

Table 13. Number of Youth Brigade Recruits by Age,
1940–1942

Age	1940	1941	1942
14	50	58	80
15	1,747	3,140	3,782
16	3,825	6,890	7,133
17	636	897	644
18	509	697	387
19	379	558	271
20	70	170	69
21	2	5	4
Total (age 14–21)	7,218	12,415	12,370

SOURCE: Manshūkoku tsūshinsha, ed., *Manshū kaitaku nenkan* (1944; reprint, Howa shuppan, 1986), p. 192.

a colonial elite. The first of these privileges came in the shape of an enormous land grant—10 hectares (24.7 acres) of vegetable and paddy fields and 10 hectares of grazing lands per household. Altogether, an estimated 10 million hectares of land was required to supply all the projected Japanese settlements.[6] In order to keep costs of land acquisition down and to minimize friction between Japanese settlers and the resident farm population, colonial authorities adopted the policy of buying lands not presently under cultivation. Ideally, undeveloped swamp and forest lands would be drained and cleared for Japanese settlers. If Japanese settlement did require relocation of existing residents, this was supposed to be carried out with the welfare of the dislocated population in mind.[7]

To fulfill their mission colonial authorities began gobbling up lands at a furious pace. By April 1941 Japanese held deeds to 20 million hectares (out of a Manchukuo territory estimated at 140 million hectares), double the projected land required for Japanese colonization. Despite stated goals to the contrary, 3.5 million hectares, or 18 percent of Japanese-held lands, had been previously under cultivation. Thus Japanese land acquisitions took a substantial bite out of the 15 million hectares of Manchurian lands

6. Asada, "Manshū imin no nōgyō keiei jōkyō," p. 77.
7. Manshūkoku kaitaku sōkyoku, *Manmō kaitaku seisaku kihon yōkō* (Kaitaku sōkyoku, 1939), p. 11; Kimijima, "Manshū nōgyō imin kankei kikan," pp. 196–197.

under cultivation at the time, dislocating Chinese and Korean peasants from more than a quarter of this area.[8]

This enormous land transfer was accomplished through price manipulations, coerced sales, and forced evictions. Japanese officials grossly undervalued the land they bought. In Sanjiang they paid 15 yen for cultivated lands worth between 50 and 100 yen, and 2 to 4 yen for undeveloped lands whose market value ranged between 5 and 25 yen.[9] Chinese sellers frequently complained that Japanese kept prices artificially low by systematically misclassifying cultivated fields as uncultivated.[10] In addition, having yielded up the deed to the land, former owners often had to wait indefinitely for remuneration. In 1941 only 10.8 million of the 20 million hectares in Japanese possession had been paid for.[11] The Kwantung Army frequently sent soldiers along to hover in the background when land sales were being arranged. If Chinese proved unresponsive to this veiled threat, people were roughed up, and in extreme cases additional troops were brought in to occupy the village until the sale was agreed to.[12] Residents were often relocated without regard to season, interrupting the harvest or moving them too late to get the year's crop planted. Although they were given new lands in exchange for those they were forced to give up, for the most part these were inferior, uncultivated, and undeveloped lands.[13]

Evidence suggests that Japanese colonists were aware that their new land had belonged to other people before they left Japan. In Ōhinata village in Nagano, colonists who had been sent ahead to inspect the site of colonization reported that the current residents were "worried that they had

---

8. Only 200,000 hectares of the land taken away from Chinese and Korean farmers were used by Japanese settlements, most of the remaining land simply was allowed to lay fallow: Asada, *Nihon teikokushugi to kyūshokuminchi jinushisei*, pp. 205–207; Asada Kyōji, "Nihon teikokushugi to 'Manshū' imin," in *Manshū imin to hisabetsu buraku: dōwa seisaku no gisei to natta Kutami kaitakudan* (Ōsaka jinken rekishi shiryōkan, 1989), pp. 39–40.

9. Asada, *Nihon teikokushugi to kyūshokuminchi jinushisei*, pp. 207–208.

10. Manshūkoku saikō kensatsuchō, "Manshūkoku kaitakuchi hanzai gaiyō" (1941), in Yamada Shōji, ed., *Manshū imin*, vol. 6 of *Kindai minshū no kiroku* (Shinjinbutsu ōraisha, 1978), p. 450.

11. Kimijima, "Manshū nōgyō imin kankei kikan," pp. 199–200.

12. Kami, pp. 128–133; Ronald Suleski, "Northeast China under Japanese Control: The Role of the Manchurian Youth Corps 1934–1945," *Modern China* 7, no. 3 (July 1981), pp. 355–361.

13. Manshūkoku saikō kensatsuchō, pp. 453, 456; Suleski, p. 359; Yoda Yoshiie, "Dainiji taisenka, Nihon no Manshū imin no jittai: imindan kankei no hanzai o chūshin ni," *Shakai kagaku tōkyū* 18, no. 1 (Waseda daigaku shakai kagaku kenkyūjo, 1972), pp. 47–56.

no place to go if Japanese colonists came and bought their land." Yet, as one emigrant put it, rather than causing them to hesitate, this information "encouraged them because if someone else had cultivated the land, well, then so could they."[14]

Not only did imperial privilege allow Japanese settlers to take prime lands away from Chinese farmers, but it also facilitated exploitation of the labor power of many of the same people they had just displaced. Policy makers had imagined that with twenty hectares (twenty *chō* or forty-nine acres) of land, one cow, one horse, and two hired hands for the initial settling-in period, a husband and wife team could live a model farm life as self-sufficient owner-cultivators. The one deviation from the ideal — the requirement for two hired hands — would disappear after a system of labor exchange was created amongst the colonists themselves.

From the beginning, this blueprint proved impossible to follow. Japanese immigrants, accustomed to labor- and land-intensive minute-scale agriculture, had trouble adapting to the scale of the lands they now managed. Despite some attempts and much talk about disseminating large-scale farming techniques practiced in Hokkaidō and raising productivity through mechanization, settlers principally relied on conventional Manchurian farming techniques which they learned from the local population. Such methods were labor-intensive, and because of recruitment shortfalls, the high percentage of colonists involved in village administration, and the heavy labor demands for various construction activities, Japanese settlements were chronically short of labor.[15]

Settlers responded by hiring large numbers of Chinese and Korean farm hands and leasing out substantial portions of their lands, thus exploiting the colonial population in precisely the way they had been exploited at home. In settlement studies investigators found that, on the average, colonists tenanted out between one-third to just under one-half of their lands. When lands managed collectively were included, the percentage of tenanted land rose considerably to between 70 and 90 percent of settlement holdings. These same studies found that on the lands settlers worked themselves, unless the plot was under 5 hectares (5 *chō* or 12.25 acres), at the very most settlers could provide only a third of the labor required to cultivate their holdings.[16]

---

14. Yamada Shōji, p. 13.
15. Kobayashi, "Manshū nōgyō imin no einō jittai," pp. 428–430; Asada, "Manshū nōgyō imin no funōka jinushika jōkyō," pp. 64–65.
16. Kobayashi, "Manshū nōgyō imin no einō jittai," pp. 393–396, 428–430,

Another privilege acquired by Japanese colonists in their move to the empire was a monopoly on the instruments of violence in the new society. While the Kwantung Army was engaged in an ongoing campaign to disarm the local population, Japanese settlers were allowed to possess weapons and were given wide latitude in using force against native peoples. Indeed, a major part of the settlers' training program was taken up in military exercises. Moreover, through training-center indoctrination as well as mass-media images of Manchukuo disseminated in Japan, settlers had been conditioned to look upon Chinese farmers as potential bandits and insurgents. Furthermore, as an anti-insurgency measure, immigrants had been deliberately placed in so-called bandit-infested areas, centers of the anti-Japanese movement in the northeast region of Manchukuo such as Bei'an, Binjiang, Jilin, and Longjiang.[17] Thus settlements were armed and maintained constant military alert against potential anti-Japanese attacks.[18]

For these reasons, Japanese settlers routinely treated the Chinese in their neighborhoods with brutal hostility. Police authorities recorded numerous incidents in which fears of Chinese had erupted into violence. In one case, two colonists saw a fifty-year-old man walking near their settlement engaged in what they believed to be suspicious activity. They began to chase him but when he did not respond to their orders to stop, they shot and killed him.[19] In another case, three Youth Brigade boys tried to warn off a group of Chinese who were attempting to cross their lands.

457–459; Asada, "Manshū nōgyō imin no funōka jinushika jōkyō," pp. 49–53, 72–76.

17. According to statistics in the 1944 *Manchurian Colonization Yearbook,* the ten Manchukuo provinces most densely populated with Japanese agricultural immigrants were Bei'an (10,250 households), Sanjiang (9,951 households), Binjiang (7,964 households), Dongan (7,510 households), Jilin (7,093 households), Longjiang (5,759 households), Mudanjiang (3,649 households), East Xingan (1,879 households), Jinzhou (1,791 households), and Heihe (1,722 households): Manshūkoku tsūshinsha, *Manshū kaitaku nenkan* (1944), p. 28.

18. The frequency of such attacks had declined sharply after a peak in 1934. Nevertheless, police authorities recorded twelve armed attacks on Japanese settlements in 1940, nine in Bei'an province, two in Dongan, and one in Longjiang: Manshūkoku saikō kensatsuchō, pp. 446–447. For an account of anti-Japanese resistance see Tanaka Tsunejirō, "Nihon teikokushugi no Manshū shinryaku to hanMan kōNichi tōsō: Chūgoku kakumei no tenkai to kanren shite," in Manshū iminshi kenkyūkai, ed., *Nihon teikokushugika no Manshū imin* (Ryūkei shosha, 1976), pp. 607–694; and Tanaka Tsunejirō, "HanMan kōNichi undō," in Asada Kyōji and Kobayashi Hideo, eds., *Nihon teikokushugi no Manshū shihai: jūgonen sensō o chūshin ni* (Jichōsha, 1986), pp. 327–420.

19. Yoda, p. 58.

When they were ignored, the youths attacked the Chinese with their hoes, killing one of them.[20]

Chinese and Koreans protested vigorously against their treatment at the hands of Japanese settlers, and these protests were often met with more violence. The friction surrounding these issues grew to such proportions that the colonial police authorities drew up a report in 1941 documenting a long list of illegal land acquisitions and incidents of forced labor as well as violent assaults on persons and property by Youth Brigade boys. Such incidents clearly worried police authorities, who viewed them as a spur to the growth of communism and anti-Japanese resistance.[21] They also revealed the extent to which Japanese settlers enjoyed their imperial privileges at the expense of the other peoples of the oft-evoked land of racial harmony.

IMPERIAL SACRIFICES

The "outbreak" of the Pacific War profoundly affected Japanese immigrants. Already taxed to its limits, the demands on Japan's human and resource base set off by the opening of a new front made the enormous financial, material, and human requirements of the settlement program almost impossible to meet. But rather than abandon the policy, government authorities drove the immigration machine all the harder. They drew up fantastic immigration targets, projected huge production increases, and planned to overcome the labor shortages by a breakneck mechanization of the settlements.[22] All this came at a time when the armed services were calling up new troops at a rate of over one million per year, when all resources were being diverted into armaments production, and when transport facilities were being monopolized by the military.[23] If one could even find them, getting men, tractors, or fertilizers to the settlements posed a logistical

20. Suleski, p. 360.

21. The report, "Manshūkoku kaitakuchi hanzai gaiyō," was compiled by Manshūkoku saikō kensatsuchō. For fears of communism and anti-Japanese movement, see Manshūkoku saikō kensatsuchō, p. 438.

22. Asada Kyōji, "Manshū nōgyō imin seisaku no ritsuan katei," in Manshū iminshi kenkyūkai, ed., *Nihon teikokushugika no Manshū imin* (Ryūkei shosha, 1976), pp. 84–98; and Kobayashi, "Manshū nōgyō imin no einō jittai," pp. 471–483.

23. Troop strength increased from 1.7 million (1940) to 2.4 million (1941), 2.8 million (1942), 3.4 million (1943), 5 million (October 1944), and 7 million (August 1945): Hara Akira, "Senji tōsei keizai no kaishi," pp. 217–268, p. 240 for troop strength.

nightmare. In the face of these obstacles the relentless pursuit of the settlement policy caused enormous suffering among the immigrants themselves. Cynically exploited by their government in a last-ditch effort to shore up a crumbling empire, the settlers were then callously abandoned when defeat became inevitable.

As the war progressed, the strategic thrust of settlement policy, always a priority, grew even more prominent. From the initiation of large-scale immigration in 1937, the first line of settlement had been along the Manchurian-Soviet border as "a military reserve for Imperial Army operations" against the Soviet Union. Policy outlines drawn up late in the war (December 1942 and August 1943) accelerated the pace of settlement in anti-Soviet positions. All of the Youth Brigade settlers (*giyūtai kaitakumin*), participants in the Youth Brigade who elected to reenlist as permanent settlers after completing their three years of training, were destined for the front line. Because Youth Brigade settlers outnumbered regular settlers four to one in the last three years of the war, the overwhelming majority were placed directly in the path of the Soviet Army. By the end of 1943, 50 percent of settlers had been established in the anti-Soviet colonial front line and an additional 40 percent placed in centers of the Chinese resistance.[24]

The original strategic purpose of this settlement pattern was to provide back-up support for the Kwantung Army. But as the fortunes of war turned against Japan, the settlers, unbeknownst to themselves, became the first line of defense—a "human pillbox" (*ningen tōchika*). In 1941, at the peak of its power, the Kwantung Army concentrated the greatest troop strength and the best fighting units of the Japanese military along the Soviet-Manchukuoan border. With the decision to strike south at American and British positions in the Pacific instead of north at the Soviet Union, however, the Kwantung Army began to shrink. After a few fleeting moments of victory, the progress of the Pacific War went from bad to worse, and in the spring of 1943 unit after unit was transferred south from Manchuria. By the second half of 1944, the once mighty Kwantung Army had been reduced to little more than a hollow shell.[25]

The evisceration of the Kwantung Army left the settler communities completely vulnerable. But instead of evacuating them or taking any mea-

24. Between 1943 and 1945, Youth Brigade settlers numbered 30,890 households and regular immigrants 7,889 households: Asada, "Manshū nōgyō imin seisaku no ritsuan katei," pp. 89, 92–103.
25. Shimada, pp. 156, 176–182.

sures to ensure their protection, government authorities did the opposite. Settlements were systematically depleted of able-bodied men by an increasingly exhaustive draft, violating the promise of draft exemption for colonists. For both the boys of the Youth Brigade who had not yet done their military service, and young men in their twenties and thirties who had put in their two years but were still obliged to serve in the reserves, this exemption had been a key reason for emigrating. After 1943, however, reserve soldiers were called up from the settlements and Youth Brigade boys drafted as soon as they reached the age of twenty. In 1944 underage boys in the training camps began to be transferred to military units to protect supply lines and military stores. In mid 1945 the Kwantung Army undertook a "bottom-scraping" (*nekosogi*) mobilization to fortify itself for a final showdown against an anticipated Soviet invasion. In late July and early August the few remaining males were removed from settlements in Dongan province and other Manchukuoan-Soviet border regions. Even after the Soviet Union began its attack on August 8, the army continued to pull men from settlements in central Manchuria.[26]

Since they were filled with young men just coming of draft age, the Youth Brigade settlements were hardest hit by the Kwantung Army's military mobilization. In twenty-nine settlements of Youth Brigade graduates from Nagano prefecture, 1,828 young men were drafted, leaving 1,118 people in the settlements, an average of 40 people per settlement, most of whom were young brides and small children.[27] By the summer of 1945 the adult settlements were hardly better off, with none except the elderly, women, and children remaining. For example, 3,016 of 21,403 adult settlers from Nagano prefecture were drafted between 1943 and 1945.[28] Taken as a whole, 40,277, or one-fifth of the population of both types of settlements, were drafted in the final years of the war (see Table 14).

In the midst of the army's all-out mobilization, immigration authorities continued to bring new settlers over from Japan until the bitter end. During 1945, 3,848 Youth Brigade boys began their training and 1,056 farm families were settled in the Manchurian paradise. One of the last groups from Nagano arrived in May 1945, amidst criticisms from relatives that "all they were going to accomplish was to be taken prisoner by the Soviet

26. Nagano-ken kaitaku jikōkai Manshū kaitakushi kankōkai, vol. 1, pp. 662–670, 682.

27. Ibid., vol. 2, individual settlements, pp. 611–875.

28. Ibid., pp. 113–486.

Table 14. Conscription of Manchurian Settlers

		Conscription	
	Population	*Number*	*%*
Adult settlements	213,666	40,277	19
Youth Brigade training camps	22,518	873	4
Voluntary farm labor corps	4,976	144	3
Total	241,160	41,294	17

SOURCE: Manshū kaitakushi kankōkai, *Manshū kaitakushi* (Manshū kaitakushi kankō-kai, 1966), pp. 433–434.

NOTE: Adult settlements include graduates of the Youth Brigade settled in Manchuria.

Union."[29] More than anything else, the Kwantung Army's attitude of callous irresponsibility toward the settlers ensured that, for many, this prediction was to come true. Beginning in February 1945, the Soviet Union began to bring troops into Siberia from the west in preparation for an invasion of Manchuria, and in April they told Japan they would not renew the neutrality treaty. After the capitulation of Germany in May, the Kwantung Army knew that the invasion was simply a matter of time. Setting up a defense sphere that ran along the rail lines from the city of Tonghua in the east near the Korean border, through the capital of Xinjing in south central Manchuria, and south to the port city of Dalian at the tip of the Kwantung Peninsula, the Kwantung Army prepared to abandon the remaining three-quarters of Manchuria. All units were to be pulled back within the defense sphere and any Japanese civilians outside, including most of the settlers, were to be left to fend for themselves.[30]

In a meeting on July 25, Kwantung Army commanders informed a flabbergasted group of Manchukuo government officials of these plans. When civilian government authorities brought up the question of settlers outside the defense perimeter, the commanders dismissed their concern, stating, "Their only alternative is suicide." At the insistence of government officials a plan for evacuation was drawn up and the army command reluctantly agreed not to draft all the leaders of the immigrant settlements.[31]

29. Ibid., p. 266.
30. Shimada, pp. 183–188.
31. Nagano-ken kaitaku jikōkai Manshū kaitakushi kankōkai, vol. 1, pp. 682–683.

On August 9 the Soviet Union began a three-pronged attack on Manchuria, moving in from the Vladivostock area to east Manchuria and north Korea, across the Amur River into north Manchuria, and from the west toward Hailar. The following day the Kwantung Army staff in charge of civilians ordered the evacuation of *military families only* to safe locations, a move whose callousness was criticized even within army ranks. Anticipating the imminent fall of Xinjing, on August 12 the army and Manchukuo government withdrew from Xinjing to Tonghua, leaving a city full of Japanese civilians behind.[32]

Evacuation orders were issued to settlers by the nearest government outpost on August 9, although no provisions were made to help with the evacuation. Settlers were simply advised to load up their possessions and a week's worth of food onto whatever transport was available and make their way south to one of several main cities. What followed was a period of living hell for the settlers. Some decided to dig in and try to join the fight against the Red Army. Others, in terror of attack by Russians or Chinese, chose mass suicide. Those who moved quickly and were lucky were able to travel south by train before the service stopped on August 13. The rest were forced to make their way on horse and foot, often traveling through swamp and forest to avoid Russian and Chinese attack. Between mid August and mid September the fleeing immigrant communities were assaulted by groups of Chinese—remnants of the former Japanese-trained Manchukuo Army, units from the Chinese resistance, and workers and farmers seeking revenge for loss of land, forced labor, and other depredations they had been made to endure by Japanese. These assaults stripped many settlers of their provisions, increasing the enormous number of deaths due to starvation and disease.[33]

This flight south took a terrible toll on the settlers. Their suffering is documented most dramatically in estimates of the 11,520 settlers who died violently in the aftermath of Japan's defeat. Table 15 shows the number of settler deaths connected with Chinese and Russian assaults on seventy-five settlements. What is striking and tragic about these figures is that such a large number of people should have died by their own hand. Some settlers committed mass suicide in fear of impending attacks; others, having survived one battle, despaired of enduring the long journey home. It was certainly true that the violent rage of Japan's enemies only marked the

32. Shimada, pp. 188–191.
33. Manshū kaitakushi kankōkai, pp. 415–422.

Table 15. Violent Deaths during Evacuation, August–September 1945

	Source of Attack			
Cause of Death	Chinese	Russians	Combination	Total Deaths
Suicide	3,420	759	216	4,395
Killed in action	1,141	1,620	0	2,761
Combination of suicide and battle	476	1,418	0	1,894
Other	—	—	—	612
All causes	5,037	3,797	216	9,662

SOURCE: Manshū kaitakushi kankōkai, *Manshū kaitakushi* (Manshū kaitakushi kankō-kai, 1966), pp. 430–432.

beginning of the settlers' trials. A huge number of them—an estimated 67,000—succumbed to starvation and disease.[34]

Only six groups of Japanese farm immigrants managed to make their way south and back to Japan in the final transportation out in August and September. The majority of those left behind were repatriated between May and October of 1946 under an American-supervised evacuation plan. In the meantime they either tried to survive as refugees in the cities or returned to the countryside to hire themselves out to Chinese farmers or the Chinese Communist Army. Of the estimated 180,000 settlers left alive in November 1946, 110,000, or 61 percent, were already repatriated. Another 34,000 were believed to be held in Soviet POW camps. This still left an estimated 36,000 missing in Manchuria, not all of whom were able to make it out before the intensification of the Chinese civil war suspended repatriation efforts in August 1948. Those left behind had to wait until these efforts resumed in March 1953 before they had another opportunity to return home. At that point, evacuation officials were unsure as to how many of the settlers still missing in August 1948 were actually alive and wanted to repatriate. Nagano prefecture found that as many as 10 percent of the original settler population was trapped in Manchuria by the Chinese civil war.[35]

Final tallies taken after the second and last phase of repatriation carried

34. Ibid., pp. 436–437.
35. Ibid., pp. 423–425, 433–436, 829; Nagano-ken kaitaku jikōkai Manshū kaitakushi kankōkai, vol. 1, pp. 716–717.

out between March and October 1953 revealed the high cost in lives paid by the Manchurian settlers. Based on Foreign Ministry surveys published in 1956, statistics show that of the 223,000 settlers resident in Manchuria at the end of the war only 140,000 (63 percent) ever returned to Japan. More than a third of the settlers—78,500 people—died in the wake of defeat, most due to starvation or illness. That such staggering losses could have been avoided if the settlers had been evacuated earlier or aided in their flight to the urban centers in South Manchuria is clear from a comparison of death rates among settlers and other Japanese expatriates. Although settlers made up no more than 14 percent of the Manchurian Japanese population in 1945, they accounted for 45 percent of the civilian deaths at the end of the war.[36]

It was these last hellish months that the settlers who lived to tell the tale would remember and record in the memoirs of their experiences in Manchuria. They cast themselves in the victims' role—victims of the Chinese, victims of the Russians, and victims of the Kwantung Army. And indeed they were victims of empire. But although settlers may have paid the highest price in the end, they did buy and savor, if only for a short time, their piece of the empire. In this sense they were not so different from most other Japanese, who both benefited and suffered from their imperial "paradise" in Manchuria.

36. Manshū kaitakushi kankōkai, pp. 436–437.

PART V

CONCLUSION

this says only, "I can't ⟶
figure this out;" it isn't
a paradox

10 The Paradox of Total Empire

—what's paradoxical?

Over the course of the 1930s, the Japanese built in Northeast China what I have called a total empire. This book has isolated three imperial projects in Manchukuo—military, economic, and settlement. I have separated them in time, identifying each with a particular phase of empire building, and in space, associating them with different social spheres. But though they did constitute three distinct imperial projects, in the end, they were all Manchukuo. Herein lay the paradox at the heart of total empire. It was at once discrete and interconnected, plural and singular, methodical and random, overdetermined and contingent. This contradictory logic shaped the history of Japan and Manchukuo, and explained how Japanese ended up with a total empire when no one started off that way.

THE METROPOLITAN IMPRINT OF MANCHUKUO

Like most of the modern world, Japan developed in the crucible of empire. During the late nineteenth and early twentieth centuries, the world's territory was carved into a handful of colonial empires. The new imperialism of these years structured global intercourse; with very few exceptions, societies became part of the world system either as practitioners of imperialism or as its objects—as colonizers or colonized. We take for granted the transforming force of imperialism on colonial societies and would find it odd, for example, to write a history of modern Algeria without reference to the impact of French occupation. But the reverse happens all the time. My point of departure in this study is the conviction that Japan, acknowledged as an aggressor, was also dramatically and irrevocably transformed by the process of empire building. And the meaning of Manchukuo for its Japanese colonizers inscribed the patterns of total empire on Japan itself.

Manchukuo reshaped the landscape of Japanese history in the 1930s. Yet it is difficult, if not impossible, to isolate a specific Manchurian imprint within the broader context of global crisis, expansion into China and Southeast Asia, and the process of mobilizing for an escalating, multifront war. Indeed, the Japanese engaged Manchukuo within this larger context: the depression conditioned their reactions to the Manchurian Incident, and they formulated their plans for colonial development with the rest of China very much in mind. In other words, while the process of mobilizing for empire in Manchukuo profoundly influenced domestic society, its impact was connected to and determined by other dimensions of the economic and military crisis. To speak of the metropolitan imprint of Manchukuo is not to slight these other factors but to see how this imperial project affected the direction of historical change in the 1930s. Manchukuo did not cause the technological advances in the mass media or the expansion of state bureaucratic apparatuses, which occurred over the period, but it did influence their development.

I have isolated six sites of transformation, locations in the domestic landscape where the process of mobilization left on Japan a metropolitan imprint of Manchukuo. On each site was erected a building block of empire, one of the many structures that produced and reproduced dominance in Manchukuo. Although my narrative has separated these six sites analytically, none of them singly caused Manchukuo. Rather, it was in their relationship to one another that they defined the topography of a total empire.

The first of these sites was the mass media. The influence of Manchukuo on the Japanese culture industries was perhaps most pronounced during the war fever of the early thirties. Then, imperial jingoism stimulated the growth of a national market for the big dailies, the growth of new media like radio, and the expansion of a host of other cultural manufactures. The rise in demand for media products on the theme of war provided opportunities for experimentation with new media technologies, and encouraged the spread of mass culture from an urban base into rural society.

Although the mass-culture industries did not react with the same intensity either to Manchurian development or Manchurian colonization, the media nevertheless acted as a vehicle through which support was mobilized for both of these endeavors. Publications of the business press, current events magazines, travel literature, and the like tracked the course of Manchurian development for elite audiences. Enthusiastic accounts of the performance of the controlled economy in economic journals popularized the image of a Manchurian success story among the business community.

6 "sits" = nothing

Glossy spreads on new Manchurian cities in highbrow magazines advertised the empire as a land of opportunity for middle-class Japanese. Like the transformations in commercial culture during the war fever, media activism in the economic project led to innovation and expansion. Such changes were evident in the proliferation of pamphlets and brochures on all manner of subjects relating to Manchukuo, in the emergence of new genres of travel and expatriate literature, and in still photography and other visual forms.

Moreover, the Manchurian colonization movement also employed the mass media to mobilize support. Only part of the paper mountains that accumulated on this subject were attributable to commercial publishers, however. Government propagandists quickly copied techniques of communication pioneered by the commercial media, purveying their message through films and records, in novels and magazines, and in pamphlets featuring large print and extensive illustrations. In its promotion of the Millions to Manchuria policy, the challenge of mass recruitment led the government to experiment with new vehicles of propaganda in popular culture.

The second site of transformation was Japan's polity, where imperial interest groups emerged to promote military expansion on the Asian mainland and a confrontational diplomatic posture toward Japan's imperialist rivals. In the shifting political alliances surrounding the new military imperialism, the army emerged as institutionally ascendant and increasingly able to set the terms of China policy. At the same time, home-front support organizations among union members and urban women took new forms, using appeals to imperial patriotism to forge group solidarity and to press for improved social conditions for themselves.

Both these developments revealed the tale of empire in an age of mass society and mass politics, a story that was played out in the projects of economic development and agricultural settlement as well. The political history of business organizations, key institutions in the mobilization of capital for Manchukuo, showed an increasing interpenetration of business and political elites that was manifested in the integration of business organizations into local and national politics. The record of academic institutions told a similar story of organizational proliferation and of the expansion of networks connecting the swelling ranks of the intelligentsia to elite collectivities in government and in the professions. In both these cases, as well as in the rural voluntary organizations involved in the Manchurian colonization movement, the process of mobilizing for empire stimulated organizational development and the articulation of group identities and group interests. Of course, Manchukuo was only one of many catalysts stimulating development of women's groups, the business community, and other interest groups in Japanese society in these years. But it was important, and at certain junctures in their organizational history, decisive. Since mass society was built on the foundations of these smaller social collectivities, in stimulating their growth, total empire opened up new institutional pathways for a mass politics and a mass society.

The third site for metropolitan empire building was in the expanding alliances between hostile public and private interests, driven together by a common desire to bring stability to the socioeconomic crisis of Japanese capitalism. It was here that emerged the uneasy partnership between big business and the army-dominated colonial government over Manchukuo. As with the massification of media and politics, Japanese involvement in Manchuria was only one of many forces that molded the new relationship between *zaibatsu* and military. Yet it was a significant one, for Manchukuo became a testing ground for industrial policy initiatives that required the cooperation of both parties to the relationship. The immense capital requirements of the scheme for Manchurian industrialization drove the anti-capitalist planners of the Manchukuo government into the arms of *zaibatsu* capitalists. Capitalists returned the embrace, motivated by opportunities for guaranteed returns on the stockpile of idle capital they had been amassing since the late 1920s. Conflicting agendas for Manchurian development meant that this alliance rested on shaky foundations. Nevertheless, the partnership endured, providing the framework for the industrial finance of Manchukuo.

Such marriages of convenience were a common feature of all phases of Manchukuo's history. They explained, for instance, the capitulation of liberal and left-wing intellectuals to the army's push for military occupation, and the support lent by Minseitō and social-democratic politicians to the shift to go-fast imperialism and military rearmament. They characterized the alliances between state bureaucrats who held agendas of agrarian social reform and conservative agrarianists who regarded the state with loathing. Landlords, tenants, and yeoman farmers, whom socioeconomic crisis had pitted against one another, joined hands in the Manchurian colonization movement to remake agrarian capitalism. Yet like the uneasy partnership between big business and the army, the cohesion of the agrarian social imperialists was undermined by the divergent agendas for mass migration. Some saw it as the salvation of the landlords at home; some wanted to create an agrarian utopia for poor tenant farmers in Manchuria; and some wanted armed settlers to provide the first line of defense against Chinese insurgents in the empire. In all three phases of empire building in Manchukuo, formulas were found to accommodate such divergent agendas, but the fissures within the alliances at times imperiled the success of each imperial project.

Invariably, such formulas appealed to the faith that most Japanese came to share in the potential of Manchukuo. These utopian dreams constituted a fourth site where Manchukuo left its mark on the Japanese metropolis. Plans for the new empire provided a testing ground for ideas of reform and revolution, a place to project the last, best, hope of a generation. Assimilated into imperial ideology, this spirit of idealism manifested itself in a mission to bring the latest in Japanese progress and civilization to Northeast China. This emerged perhaps most clearly in the brave new empire of Japan's progressive intellectuals, where economic development promised modernist utopia for Manchuria's cities and social justice for its countryside. Of all the imperial projects in Manchukuo, Japanese projected onto this idealistic vision of economic development their utopian dreams for Japan itself. Although not all dimensions of empire building in Manchuria so closely mirrored progressive aspirations for domestic reform, each phase of empire was justified by the idea of "doing good" in the empire. The military campaigns against the army of Zhang Xueliang were carried out in the name of defending Japanese lives and property as well as protecting an exploited and downtrodden Chinese citizenry against the depredations of the warlord regime. Agents of rural colonization appealed to a racial mission to Japanize backward Asians and bring stability to that troubled land.

The construction of a colonial mission through tales of military heroism, shared sacrifice, and the march of Japanese progress in Manchukuo was directed primarily toward mobilizing the Japanese population. Such stories were designed not to convince colonial subjects of the benefits of Japanese overrule, but rather to ennoble imperialism for its practitioners. In this sense it should be hardly surprising that the only figures given any agency in Japanese imperial narratives were the Japanese themselves. Japan's colonial others, when they appeared, were a faceless mass in the background—a force of nature that blended into the alien landscape of Northeast China. In the Manchukuo of their imaginations, Japanese built an empire in which Chinese initially figured as a cowardly and feckless enemy. Once vanquished this enemy retreated from sight, occasionally appearing in coolie barracks but not seen in the new industrial parks, on the new roads and railway tracks, or in the new municipalities created by economic development. Somewhere off in the remote hinterland the numberless toiling Chinese masses suffered silently, stoically, awaiting Japanese leadership to give them voice and show them the way to a better life. With the arrival of the Japanese settlers, even the countryside was emptied of Chinese: the Manchurian colonists were shown breaking new soil, planting Japanese blood in a vast, open plain, and occasionally instructing crude and ignorant natives in the ways of civilization. Such stories, in which Japanese figured as heroic helpers and imperial do-gooders, were designed to appeal to the better instincts of the Japanese. Representing Manchukuo as an idealistic enterprise, they helped people feel right about imperialism. These comforting fictions invariably cast Chinese in a passive role: being bested, being managed, being led, being taught—being done to rather than doing. The inability of Japanese storytellers to give agency to Chinese revealed the limits of the imperial conscience. Japanese liked the idea of doing good in the empire, but only to the extent that they retained total control. In this sense narratives of mission in Manchukuo made compelling appeals to progressive ideals, even while they compromised those ideals by sanctioning the absolutism of Japanese authority.

The fifth site of home-front empire building was within initiatives to expand state interventions in economy and society. Elite proponents of state aid saw such measures as a cure for the socioeconomic crisis of the early 1930s as well as a means to diffuse opposition movements by giving social activists a greater stake in the system. It was within this context that the movement for agrarian social imperialism in Manchuria took shape. Economic depression and social crisis in the farm villages impelled the rural reform movement and the emigration movement to unite under the banner of Manchurian colonization. Bringing together the institutional strength of these two long-standing movements, the Manchurian colonization campaign enabled joint efforts to mobilize the state behind the settlement project. With state support, advocates of Manchurian settlement hoped to resolve the problems in the agrarian economy through the export of surplus Japanese agricultural labor to Manchukuo.

This agrarian example, however, was only one of many ways in which empire became an economic panacea and a tool to smooth over social conflict over resources at home. During the Manchurian Incident, the effects of depression helped to persuade business and labor organizations of the efficacy of supporting the army's drive to hold onto the Manchurian lifeline. In the face of a widely perceived industrial "deadlock," the business press celebrated state-led Manchurian development as the key to economic recovery in Japan. For the ranks of underemployed middle-class professionals, the surging job opportunities in the colonial state gave proof to the rhetoric of a land of opportunity. In these ways the imperial project represented a social imperialism that projected onto Manchuria hopes for government solutions to a market economy in crisis. Colonial-state management of Manchukuo provided a method of increasing the pie of social advantage so that no one need fight over shrinking resources at home.

The sixth dimension of the metropolitan infrastructure of Manchukuo was the governmental institutions that emerged to bolster and facilitate empire building, built upon the site of the proliferating bureaucracy of the modern state. The most striking example of imperial state making was probably the bureaucratic machinery of migration erected in Japan and Manchukuo to engineer the resettlement of Japanese farmers to the Manchurian countryside. But military and economic empire building also stimulated the growth of new state apparatuses and the innovation of new forms of state interventions in polity, economy, and society.

In the Manchurian Incident, the decision to respond to the challenge posed by Chinese nationalism with military action implied an expansion of military apparatuses in the colonial state, a process mirrored throughout the colonial empire and deepened as the armed forces brought new territories under occupation. The new military imperialism was accompanied at home by a series of interventions in the polity, including an increase in censorship activities, political surveillance, incarceration of left-wing activists, and other forms of political repression and thought control. At the same time, the machinery of state propaganda, in Philip Taylor's phrase, the Siamese twin of censorship,[1] expanded with the highly successful Army Ministry campaign "to spread the idea of national defense."

While the Manchurian Incident led to increased government involvement in the political sphere, economic expansion in Manchuria took state-building efforts in another direction. Under the banner of Manchurian development, the colonial state created a battery of new laws that regulated economic activity and greatly expanded the economic planning and research capacity of the state. The widely trumpeted success of the Manchurian experiment in state control over the economy encouraged the exten-

1. The phrase comes from Philip M. Taylor: "Censorship and propaganda are Siamese twins, inseparable and inextricable." See Taylor, *The Projection of Britain: British Overseas Publicity and Propaganda, 1919–1939* (Cambridge: Cambridge University Press, 1981), p. 4.

sion of industrial policy initiatives in Japan, as the home government instituted new techniques of economic management in order to protect and promote industrial capitalism. In these three ways—increased political activism, the rise of state capitalism, and the development of a social-policy state—empire building in Manchukuo helped stimulate and configure the reinvention of government that took place in the 1930s.

Such were the six sites where empire building left its mark on the metropolis, where Japanese erected the institutions necessary to support the imperial project in Manchuria. It was in part because of their centrality in the terrain of Japanese modernity that Manchukuo achieved its peculiar force. Institutions like the mass media, the bureaucratic state, and social interest groups were pivotal in a modern society, conditioning the meaning and experience of everyday life. Moreover, such institutions represented sites where economy, politics, and culture intersected and hence became nodal points of history. Yet none of these sites—not the strategic alliances between public and private interests, or the social interventions of the state, or the impulse for utopian dreaming—could alone have produced Manchukuo. Rather, it was out of their interconnections that the ecology of a total empire emerged.

In the metropolitan sites where empire struck back, as it were, the developments that I discuss might well have taken place with or without Manchukuo. The culture industries would have become more commercial, interest-group alliances between state and society would have proliferated, and utopian reform movements to deal with the crisis of industrial capitalism would have arisen. Such phenomena were everywhere typical of industrial societies in the 1930s. But the point is that Manchukuo directed the particular course that these developments took in Japan. To take one example, the fact that radio revolutionized politics and culture throughout the world in the 1930s suggests that even in the absence of a war fever wireless broadcast would have become a mass media in Japan. The Japanese government was likely to recognize its political potential; Roosevelt certainly did when he began his fireside chats, as did Hitler when he incorporated radio into his mass rallies. It made a difference, however, whether radio was employed to win support for Roosevelt's New Deal, Hitler's Nazi movement, or Japan's empire in Manchukuo. The explosive growth of radio during the military campaigns of the early 1930s, the early radio linkups with the Asian continent, and the increasingly intimate association with the army were all specific products of the Manchurian Incident war fever; as such they left traces of Manchukuo on this, as on many other fragments of Japan's modernity.

" MANY VIETNAMS, TOTAL EMPIRE "

MANY MANCHUKUOS, TOTAL EMPIRE

Because its metropolitan support system was multisited and widely dispersed, the imperial project that Japanese knew as Manchukuo was complex, eclectic, and dynamic. Yet although Manchukuo meant many things to many people, in the end it was one empire. Paradoxically, this unity in diversity represented both the strength and the weakness of Manchukuo, and the tension between its centripetal and centrifugal forces was an integral part of the story of total empire in Manchukuo.

One element of this tension was the plural nature of the decision-making process. Although the accumulating weight of investments pre-structured decisions in favor of the perpetuation of empire, it did not proscribe dissent. Indeed, people expressed resistance throughout the course of empire building in Manchukuo. In the fall of 1931, politicians of the Minseitō party as well as journalists writing for *Chūō kōron, Kaizō,* and *Nihon keizai shinpō* spoke out strongly against the military operations in Manchuria. Throughout the decade, the business press alternatively lambasted and applauded the performance of the Japan-Manchuria bloc economy. In the late 1930s, villagers in many areas of the country registered their opposition to the colonization program by refusing to participate. It was true that landlord opinion carried more weight than that of tenant farmers in a community's decision to reject the program. But as testified by the intensity of the recruiting efforts, tenants were not automatically obedient to the will of their social betters. With rare exceptions, differences between opponents and supporters of the imperial project were resolved through the mechanisms of negotiation and compromise, not by repression. In the end, the energy generated by a plurality of opposing views and the struggles of diverse interest groups over the direction of imperial policy gave momentum to Manchukuo.

This process was consistent with the developing institutions of parliamentary politics and constitutional monarchy that defined the Japanese polity. As a system of representative government, it was flawed on many accounts, as historians have taken care to point out.[2] But for all its shortcomings, the system did, in a limited sense, represent organized interests within Japan's stratified society: regional interests, class interests, professional interests, sectoral interests, and so on. Of course, not all members

---

2. A dated but forcefully expressed analysis of the flaws in the prewar democratic system is found in Robert A. Scalapino, *Democracy and the Party Movement in Prewar Japan: The Failure of the First Attempt* (Berkeley: University of California Press, 1953).

of society were represented organizationally. This, in addition to the enormous disparities of power and influence between organizations, meant that representation was partial and imperfect. Yet with all their limitations, it was these organizations—the Women's National Defense Association, the regional air-defense fundraising organizations, labor unions, chambers of commerce, emigration societies, and landlord groups—that became the social building blocks of empire, the vehicles for the mobilization of mass support for Manchukuo.

Mediating the diverse agendas of these groups was Japan's complex bureaucratic state, which ultimately prevented competing interests from tearing Manchukuo apart. Although the architects of constitutional government designed the system to insulate the administration from political influence, by the inception of Manchukuo, organized private interests had penetrated the bureaucratic citadel and politicized the state. This occurred not only through the creation of political patronage within the prefectural civil services, but through the increasing association of private-sector constituencies with national government ministries: big banks with the Finance Ministry, landlords with Agriculture and Forestry, industrialists with Commerce and Industry. It also happened through the expansion of bureaucratic ties with voluntary associations. Bureaucratic connections with youth groups, reservist associations, and farm co-ops gave the Home, Army, and Education ministries a popular base, while at the same time granting the networks of voluntary organizations access to government aid and limited input to policy.

The proliferation of such linkages between state and society created multiple vectors of influence. Competing demands of the national defense lobbying organizations (to build more planes for the army in China), of the agrarian societies (to finance emigration), and of the chambers of commerce (to expand the China market for Japanese exports) pulled the government in a variety of directions. Reconciling the increasingly divisive conflicts over Manchukuo tested the abilities of the state to manage the plurality of interests that it had come to represent. When the contradictions between competing visions of Manchukuo began to strain the seams of total empire, the state, too, was divided against itself. In this sense, the tension between centripetal and centrifugal forces in the empire was intrinsic to the evolving nature of the state itself.

Such tensions were nothing new to the Japanese state in the 1930s; and neither were they peculiarly Japanese. But by the late 1920s, in Japan as well as in other industrial societies, the process of proliferating linkages between social interest groups and state bureaucracies was sufficiently advanced that a crisis on the scale of the Great Depression was enough to cause paralysis, disintegration, or even violent destruction. In the United States, Great Britain, France, Germany, Italy, and elsewhere—the state was under seige. One can argue that in all these places it took mobilization for total war in the late 1930s and early 1940s to temporarily stabilize the state, as social interest groups set aside their differences to cooperate with the common war effort. In the case of Japan's total empire, too, it was the idea that diverse interests were part of a common enterprise that kept the many Manchukuos precariously intact. And what was true of Manchukuo and Japan probably applied to other total empires as well; in British India and French Algeria the process of empire building doubtless brought about both the integration and the disintegration of the metropolitan state. Of course, the relationship between total empire and the state would have varied considerably depending on time frame and a host of other factors. But whether this process took place over centuries, decades, or years, in each case it was out of the complexity of the modern state that emerged the possibility for total empire.

Much of the dynamism, the pluralism, and the contradictory complexities of total empire rested on "the gossamer foundation of dreams." Most Japanese encountered Manchukuo within their shared universe of symbolic meaning, a place where the evanescent and mutable qualities of popular culture permitted a sense of both unity in principle and diversity in interpretation. In the realm of the imagination, the shared term *Manchukuo* atomized into thousands of variations, each conditioned by individual experience. To a woman who experienced Manchukuo primarily in terms of the military mobilization of the early thirties, the new empire was refracted through her first involvement in public activism and a sense of participation in a national community that rallied together at a time of crisis. To a scholar who joined the staff of Mantetsu, Manchukuo signified both a wonderful job opportunity and a chance to take part in a historic colonial experiment. To a yeoman farmer who led a group of fellow villagers to a new home in China, Manchukuo represented a chance to help end the cycle of poverty and indebtedness that made wretched the lives of tenant farmers, as well as to fulfill personal ambitions for political and social leadership which could not be satisfied at home. Such dreams were at once personal and public. Thus, images of Manchukuo ennobled personal ambitions by association with ideals that transcended those ambitions. What Japanese shared—and what gave to total empire its essential unity— were these transcendental ideals; they made Manchukuo more than just the sum of its disparate parts.

Yet the recurrent disjunctures between dream and reality sorely tested the binding power of these ideals. Nowhere was this more true than in Northeast China itself, where real Japanese soldiers killed real Chinese people and real Japanese farmers tilled real Chinese soil. What happened when the Mantetsu intellectual learned of the genocidal tactics being used in the war against China, or the farm settler realized that the real Manchurian paradise was to be found in the new urban centers? Though such epiphanies were possible, the remarkable compartmentalization of the imperial projects minimized the opportunities for Japanese to draw these sorts of connections. Although they may have caught a brief glimpse of Manchukuo's municipal magnificence en route to their new homes, settlers had few opportunities to return to the urban centers. Although urban Japanese certainly knew of the ongoing anti-bandit campaigns and the harsh treatment meted out to the anti-Japanese resistance, they were rarely forced to witness the brutality of occupation firsthand. Because participants in the military, economic, and settlement projects moved in different social worlds, they were insulated from each other's experiences. In the end, this is what saved many empire builders from disillusionment. Segregation of the imperial projects both in their social realities and in their cultural constructions fostered a sense of dissociation among the three groups, placing each out of the other's reach. The colonial elite saw little connection between their frenetic construction work and the army's campaigns of murderous destruction. The settlers perceived no link between the conspicuous consumption of the urbanites and their own days of endless toil.

As fractured as the experiences of Manchukuo were for its motley crew of builders, however, in the end this was a single empire. The settlement project was an extension of the army's anti-insurgency campaigns; the road and railway construction programs of economic development made possible the establishment of Japanese communities in the Manchurian countryside. Development, too, was geared to military concerns; investment funds were channeled overwhelmingly into defense-related industries, while urban and railroad construction was tailored to strategic designs. Colonial planners concentrated Japanese settlements around the new industrial zones in order to protect Japanese investments from Chinese attack. The Kwantung Army's mandate grew in response to the proliferating investments and the extension of Japanese settlement into rural Manchuria. Much as they were perceived, subjectively, in isolation from one another, the three imperial projects were in fact interactive and reciprocal. It was these connections that bound the different Manchukuos in a total empire.

"quagmire myth"

INCREMENTAL IMPERIALISM

The character of Japan's continental expansion in the 1930s has been captured by one historian in the title *The China Quagmire*.[3] As the phrase
implies, imperialism in China in the 1930s entangled Japan in a morass
from which there was no easy escape. It was not a sudden and concerted
leap that landed the nation in the middle of the bog, but a large number
of small steps taken by a host of independent agents of empire. Each step
made by one person or group limited the choices of another, gradually
cutting off exit routes from the imperial quagmire. The dynamic of incremental imperialism made Manchukuo the first of a succession of territorial
appropriations and the starting point for the series of wars that took place
over these years.

Although in Manchuria's case incremental imperialism ended in total
empire, there was nothing inexorable about this; the process of incremental
imperialism did not necessarily lead to total empire. Yet the two were
clearly connected, and in their connections lay another of the paradoxes
of total empire. The cumulative weight of incremental imperialism created
the leviathan of total empire. Yet each increment was incidental, meaning
that at every juncture the possibility existed for different decisions and,
hence, for retreat from total empire. In other words, the process of incremental imperialism did not constitute a chain of inevitability, but rather a
chain of contingent decisions, one following upon the other and linked in
their cumulative potential to produce total empire. In this sense, the frac-
tures in the timeline of total empire mirrored the fragmentation in the
sites of its production. No more than the single institution of the mass
media could a single decision of Kwantung Army officers in itself bring
about total empire. It was only out of the concatenation of these temporal
and spatial fragments that Manchukuo finally emerged.

The process of incremental imperialism began with the Manchurian
Incident. The initiatives of Kwantung Army officers to engineer the clash
of Chinese and Japanese forces in September 1931 provided cabinet members with a limited set of options. The reaction of the mass media and the
political parties further narrowed those choices. The continued escalation
of military action by the Kwantung Army subverted the Foreign Ministry's negotiating position at the League of Nations. Pinned between League
pressures to cease the military action and army resistance to foreign pres-

3. James William Morley, ed., *The China Quagmire: Japan's Expansion on the
Asian Continent* (New York: Columbia University Press, 1983).

sure, diplomats stalled, gambling on a favorable finding by the Lytton Commission. When this failed to materialize, the cabinet was forced to choose between staying in Manchukuo or staying in the League. Japan withdrew from the League, plunging deeper into the China quagmire.

In a different venue, another series of steps moved Japan from the first plans for a bloc economy toward the runaway inflation of the 1940s. Year after year public and private sources poured increasing amounts of yen into Manchuria: 161 million in 1933, 382 million in 1935, 453 million in 1937, 1,076 million in 1939, 1,425 million in 1941. Paralleling the widening flow of capital were steady rises in Japanese exports to Manchukuo. Thousands of new Japanese-owned businesses opened every year as the Japanese population in Manchuria rose by over three-quarters of a million between 1930 and 1940. Whether measured in terms of the thirty-two new rail lines or the forty-eight new urban centers, or in increasing capital, commodity, and population flows, by the end of the decade the Japanese commitment to Manchukuo had escalated to a scale and complexity that left policy makers with few options for retreat.[4]

The same was true of popular engagement in the colonization project. What began as a hopeful experiment to eliminate rural poverty turned, by the 1940s, into a frantic and increasingly coercive search for warm bodies to shore up the crumbling foundations of the Manchurian settlements. Since the bureaucratic lines of commitment to the continuation of the settlement project were so numerous, even when the diversion of resources to other areas of the war effort created labor and other shortages that imperiled the survival of the settlements, withdrawal was never seriously contemplated.

By the advent of the Pacific War, Manchukuo was clearly destroying itself from within: the production and reproduction of the structures of domination were in fact causing the empire to unravel at its seams. Yet this tendency to disintegrate was still counterbalanced by the collective force of bureaucratic and private interests seeking to perpetuate Manchukuo. Thus, even at the end—on the very eve of its destruction—the unifying forces of total empire preserved the fragile coherence of Manchukuo.

The progress of incremental imperialism entangled Japan in an imperial morass. Because their commitment to Manchuria proscribed retreat, Japanese chose to go forward. In the process, they accumulated a total bill for empire that cost the nation dearly. The occupation of Manchuria set in

4. For details, see Chapters Five and Six herein; statistics on investment: Table 1; statistics on population: Table 6.

motion a perpetual expansion of the perimeter of defense, fueled by a preoccupation with securing Japan's ever-expanding territorial commitments. The price of military occupation proved to be an endlessly expanding war front, as war in Northeast China spread in all directions. In Japanese lives alone the escalating wars for empire took a heavy toll. The engagement with the Soviet Union at Nomonhan cost 18,000 lives;[5] almost 390,000 Japanese soldiers died in the war against China; and another 1,352,350 were lost in the campaigns against the United States and the British Empire.[6] In gradual increments the exhilarating successes of the small war in Manchuria in 1931 moved Japan closer to the hellfires of Hiroshima and Nagasaki in 1945.

In the interim, the Japan-Manchuria bloc became a sinkhole for financial, industrial, and human resources. By the 1940s the continued flow of capital, goods, and services into Manchuria was crippling a domestic economy already stressed by the demands of war. Equally critical, the shift toward an exclusive trade and production sphere in China helped follow diplomatic isolation with economic isolation. First tariffs shut Japan out, then export controls cut Japan off from European and American markets both domestic and colonial. Eventually this economic isolation threatened the nation's very survival.

At the same time, the colonization project was exacting its own price on Japanese both collectively and individually. The program accelerated just as the combined impact of industrial and military mobilization strained labor reserves. But the machinery of mobilization for Manchurian settlement ground on regardless. By diverting scarce labor power from industry and agriculture, the empire of settlement ultimately undermined the war effort. The heaviest price, of course, was paid by the colonists themselves, almost 80,000 of whom died in the retreat from Manchuria in 1945.

When all this began in 1931, no one knew that the total bill for empire would run so high. With the clarity of hindsight, it is possible to appreciate the terrible price the Japanese paid for their empire in Manchukuo. But at the time, there was no master accountant watching over the bills and charges. There was no master strategist who coordinated the disparate agendas for empire and who could foresee that Manchukuo was moving

5. Alvin D. Coox, "The Pacific War," in Peter Duus, ed., *The Twentieth Century,* vol. 6 of *The Cambridge History of Japan* (New York: Cambridge University Press, 1988), p. 322.

6. Dower, *War without Mercy,* p. 297.

Japan deeper into the China quagmire. Rather, the decisions for incremental imperialism were narrowly focused; they were made piecemeal and without coordination. The process was thus plural rather than totalitarian. Only in their cumulative force did these thousands of independent initiatives provide the momentum for a total empire. And if the decisions were multitudinous, then the responsibility was also widely dispersed. There was, in short, plenty of blame to go around for the brutality, hubris, and tragedy of total empire.

MODERNITY AND THE TURN TO TOTAL EMPIRE

For the countries that created them, total empires like Manchukuo were revolutionary and transformative, mass mobilizing and mass consuming, complex and contradictory. Manchukuo was a total empire because its impact on the Japanese metropolis was as profound as Japan's impact on Northeast China. To build Manchukuo Japanese created a network of support at home, reconfiguring the institutions of mass politics, mass society, and mass culture. This process was quintessentially modern. That is to say, the kinds of transformations wrought by imperialism—in both Northeast China as well as Japan—were made possible by the advent of industrial capitalism and the nation-state. Japan's total empire in Manchukuo was the product of a modern state and a modern society whose relationship was mediated by a commercialized mass culture and conditioned by an expanding industrial capitalism. This meant, for instance, that the mass media, the interventionist state, organized interest groups, and an ideology of progress and reform all became instruments of the imperial project. Japanese turned the ideas and institutions of modernity to the purposes of empire; in Manchukuo the culture of Japanese modernity became the culture of imperialism.

It is important to remember that Manchuria did not become this ultimate of modern empires until the 1930s. Before that it was an important part of the Japanese empire, but not its vital center, not the vanguard of imperial strategy, not the hope for Japan's salvation. It became all these things after 1931, when the Manchurian Incident ushered in a new phase of go-fast imperialism for Japan and changed the face of empire throughout the territories under Japanese occupation in the 1930s and 1940s. Three characteristics set this new imperialism apart from earlier phases. First, it was distinguished by its overwhelmingly military character. In the 1930s, a series of military faits accomplis propelled forward an empire that was constructed in the context of ongoing warfare. Second, it articulated a new emphasis on development. This signified colonial industrialization and accelerated integration into the Japanese economy, on one hand, and the creation of social and political institutions that mobilized support among colonial subjects for Japanese rule, on the other. Third, it represented a new social imperialism. The congeries of metropolitan organizations that drove the imperial projects forward sought to export to Manchuria and elsewhere in the wartime empire the social tensions, political divisions, and economic problems that were tearing Japan apart.

The new militarism, the new developmentalism, and the new level of metropolitan involvement all changed the character of Japanese imperialism in the 1930s. The question remains: Why the transformation? Or, focusing simply on the Manchurian case, why did the occupation of Manchuria succeed in 1931 and not 1928, when the Kwantung Army first attempted it? Why did forces mass behind the creation of an autarkic production sphere? Why did agrarian social imperialism succeed in Manchuria in the 1930s, when it failed in Korea in the 1910s? In short, why was 1931 a turning point for empire? I want to suggest two answers to these questions. The first traces the causes of the turn to total empire back to the late nineteenth century, when the empire took shape as a bulwark of Japanese modernity. Dependent for their survival on the perpetuation of the empire, the institutions that propelled modernization also set in motion a long-term logic of expansionism. By the 1930s, this logic of empire dictated the need for some sort of Manchukuo. But it took the immediate historical factors of the economic depression and the rise of the Chinese nationalist movement to determine that Northeast China would provide the site and 1931 the time for the turn to total empire. This historicity provides the second answer to my questions, suggesting that the turning points in the long-term logic of empire were contingent on the short-term catalysts of expansion.

From a long-term perspective, the propulsion behind the new military imperialism of the 1930s emerged from Japan's modern military apparatuses which, by 1931, were deeply invested in the perpetuation and expansion of the empire. Since the strategic mission of Japan's newly created armed services identified a Chinese-dominated Korea as a threat to the security of the home islands, military planning defined national security in terms of an expanding defense perimeter on the Asian continent and in the Pacific. Not only did the army's own sense of mission rest on the expansion of Japan's territory, but the status and reputation of the new military institutions within Japanese society were increasingly tied to the successes of military imperialism. The Sino- and Russo-Japanese wars

i.e., blame it all on militarism

marked periods of enormous institutional growth of the armed services, with generous budget increases, new divisions, and the establishment of the reservist organizations. Moreover, the double victory greatly enhanced the prestige of the military, which was seen as the agent of Japan's ascension to world power.

As military institutions grew more complex and powerful, bureaucratic rivalries provided a source of momentum for empire building. Competition between the army and navy was a prime example. The dual strategic mandate and a military division of labor, where the army focused on the continent and the navy on the Pacific, provided a strong incentive for imperial adventurism in order to justify institutional and budgetary expansion. At the same time, military garrisons in the Kwantung Leased Territory and Korea provided power bases for factional rivals within the army to maneuver against one another. The increasing autonomy of the Kwantung Army encouraged acts of subimperialism that were an integral part of continental expansion long before the Manchurian Incident. The expansionist thrust of such interservice and intraservice rivalries was compounded by army rivalries with other forces, including the Foreign Ministry over China and the political parties over the cabinet. In each case the army asserted political dominance through a hard-line, expansionist approach to the Asian continent, combating its bureaucratic rivals in the theater of empire. The army's practice of using imperial interventions as an institutional power play made bureaucratic rivalries a critical contributor to the dynamic of expansionism and the go-fast imperialism of the 1930s.

The new developmentalist thrust of total empire in the 1930s was also impelled by the logic of Japanese imperialism. From the outset, colonial governments in Taiwan, Korea, the Kwantung Leased Territory, and the Pacific Islands (Nan'yō) focused efforts on restructuring colonial economies to serve the needs of Japan's expanding industrial capitalism, particularly the emerging commercial shipping and trading industries. Through the Oriental Development Company, Mantetsu, and other quasi-public development and railway companies, Japanese investment funds were channeled into infrastructural development of ports and communication networks to expand Japanese commercial control. Colonial state-led development of monocultural economies of sugar in Taiwan, rice in Korea, and soybeans in Manchuria stimulated the growth not only of commerce between Japan and the colonies, but also of Japan's trade in colonial products with Europe and United States. In this way, Japan, from the start, used colonial development as a tool for metropolitan economic development. As

the vanguard of Japanese capitalism shifted from commerce to heavy industry, it was natural for Manchukuo economic planners to turn to the
empire to foster the development of Japanese heavy industrialization.

The other face of development was the cultural reconstruction of the
colonial subject, tying economic to social modernization. Since the first
Japanese interventions in Korea in the 1870s, the mandate for empire was
expressed in the language of exporting Japanese civilization and enlightenment. Educational, police, and other institutions of the colonial state
consciously modeled themselves on metropolitan institutions which were
regarded as engines of modernization. Japanese ambitions to direct the
course of political and social transformation in Taiwan, Korea, and China
emerged from the conviction that Japanese were special because Japan was
the only East Asian nation to have successfully engineered its own modern
revolution. Therefore, Japanese believed that they possessed unique qual-
ifications and the special mandate to sponsor Japanese-style modernization
among their East Asian neighbors. The arrogance, in the 1930s, of Japanese
plans to mobilize the energies of anti-colonial nationalism in service of
their vision of a Japanese-ruled Greater East Asia was merely a more elaborate expression of an overweening faith in the assimilating ability of their
institutions.

Like the new militarism and the new developmentalism of total empire,
the lineages of the new social imperialism went back to the late nineteenth
century, when Japanese began to see empire building as a social nostrum.
Starting with the debates over whether or not to invade Korea during the
turbulent years of the early 1870s, imperial adventures were promoted as
a means to distract the attention of political troublemakers. Government
officials and private citizens were equally quick to grasp the significance of
the surge of patriotism and national unity during the Sino-Japanese and
Russo-Japanese wars, as appeals to empire acquired the rhetorical power
to define a national identity that transcended social divisions. Increasingly,
different groups sought to harness that power to their respective political
causes. Casting themselves as the watchdogs of the empire, opposition
politicians tried to stir up hostility toward whatever government was in
power by attacking its foreign policy. Politicizing in succession the "Korea
problem," the "China problem," and the "Manchuria problem," political
parties brought empire into the mainstream of political discourse. In the
Hibiya Riot of 1905 and other crowd actions in the 1910s, the disenfran-
chised urban poor expressed calls for social justice in the name of the
empire. By 1931, Japanese had thus established a long track record in the
ways of social imperialism.

Moreover, a high degree of social integration with the empire presaged the proliferating entanglements of the 1930s. This was most developed among the middle classes. Japan's academic institutions, for example, developed an extensive imperial network. This network encompassed the research facilities of Mantetsu, the Shanghai Common Culture Institute, and the colonial universities, as well as those attached to the colonial banks, development companies, and overseas subsidiaries of the large trading companies. Colonial service offered a flourishing job market for Japan's educated youth, and elite secondary schools and universities provided feeders for colonial employment. These same schools sent their students on summer trips to the continent, where they saw firsthand the opportunities for participation in the imperial venture and made connections that would further their job prospects. Though the civilian presence in the empire would grow rapidly after 1931, close to a million civilians were already living in Taiwan, Korea, and Manchuria by that time. Through the academic institutions and business organizations to which they belonged, and the civil service and private enterprises for which they worked, this colonial elite was connected to sister and parent institutions in Japan. Moving back and forth between the colonies and the home islands, these Japanese provided a powerful social force for the perpetuation and expansion of empire. The institutional links they established made possible the rapid flow of entrepreneurial and professional Japanese into Manchuria in the 1930s.

Well before the creation of Manchukuo, Japanese projects of modernity and empire had become inextricably linked. Whether in Japan's military, economic, or social entanglements with the empire, the forces driving modern growth also drove imperialism. Such entanglements placed Japan in a large company of modern colonizers. Great Britain and France also developed their modern military institutions in the context of imperial warfare in the nineteenth century. For both those societies, colonial garrisons in Asia and Africa became important agents of subimperialism, helping to precipitate the colonial scramble of the late nineteenth century. As in Japan, European military institutions became politicized, and used empire to jockey for position within an increasingly complicated bureaucratic politics. European empire building also embraced developmentalism, as both ideology and strategy. The language of development did not emerge for European colonial projects until after World War I, but it was anticipated in the colonial state-building efforts that followed the wave of annexations in the late nineteenth century. As in Japan, the desire to make colonialism profitable entailed reconstruction of colonial economies and their integration into a world economy. Like Japanese, Europeans believed that the colonial state could be a social engineer, making modern peoples out of traditional peoples through the spread of Christianity, the work ethic, and the European family structure. Finally, European imperialisms were also socially driven. Whether it was Bismarck's political machinations in Germany in the 1880s, the tactics of Joseph Chamberlain and his Birmingham caucus of supporters to overturn the doctrine of British free trade, or the growing strength of the Colonial party in French politics in the 1890s, certain mass political institutions found empire a useful rallying cry. Colonial civil services also provided employment for the British upper class, channeled through the elite public schools. Such convergences in the experiences of colonizing societies testify to the importance of the relationship between empire and modernity: in all colonizing societies, the forces of modernity propelled imperial expansion.

This point is of considerable significance for the interpretation of Japanese history, since it runs against the idea that the excesses of the wartime empire were the product of an incomplete modernization: social relations distorted by feudal remnants, a warping dualism between modern and traditional sectors of the economy, a democracy that failed to take root and reverted to absolutism, and an intellectual development stultified by thought control. The evidence on Manchukuo suggests, to the contrary, that it was not the leftovers from the old Tokugawa regime but institutions developed after the Meiji Restoration—modern industry, mass culture, political pluralism, and new social organizations—that were the real forces behind the new imperialism. Thus the maturation of modern institutions, and not their stunting, led to the burst of expansionism of the 1930s.

Because modernity in Japan set forth a certain logic of expansionism, the turn to total empire was "imminent" even before 1931. Yet though it was, in this sense, overdetermined by modernity, Manchukuo was also a specific product of its historical moment. In the final analysis, two historical events catalyzed the formation of total empire in Northeast China: the economic depression and the rise of organized Chinese nationalism. The short-term impact of the Guomindang rights recovery movement stirred the Kwantung Army into action to try to seal off Manchuria from Guomindang influence. Though a Manchurian crisis in 1928 had met little response at home in Japan, in 1931 the social crisis and pervasive sense of economic insecurity generated by the depression suddenly made the idea of an imperial lifeline attractive. The ideas of a Japanese-sponsored independence movement, a client state, and a program of social reform pioneered in Manchukuo were all formulas for Sino-Japanese cooperation within a Japanese-controlled Manchuria that responded specifically to the anti-colonial challenge of Chinese nationalism. The bloc economy and the push for economic autarky represented reactions to global depression. The need for countermeasures to armed Chinese resistance to Japanese rule in Manchuria provided a key incentive behind the colonization program. At the same time, the effect of the depression on the agrarian economy at home stimulated support for mass emigration.

All this gave Manchukuo its historicity, for without the congeries of short-term forces unleashed by the depression and the anti-Japanese movement, Manchukuo would have been a different kind of empire. It needed the combination of long-term and short-term causes to direct the shift to a new imperial paradigm. Rather than a single taproot of total empire, Manchukuo was underlaid by a tangled network of separate causes, interrelated and overlapping. In its multiple dimensions and its multiple causes, Manchukuo remained a product of modern times. The logic and momentum of modernization propelled Japan toward empire in Northeast China. At a moment of crisis, Japanese created Manchukuo to answer the dilemmas brought on by modern growth.

I'm going to throw up...

Bibliography

Adas, Michael. *Machines as the Measure of Men: Science, Technology, and Ideologies of Western Dominance*. Ithaca: Cornell University Press, 1989.

AlSayyad, Nezar, ed. *Forms of Dominance: On the Architecture and Urbanism of the Colonial Enterprise*. Aldershot, England: Avebury, 1992.

Anderson, Benedict. *Imagined Communities: Reflections on the Origin and Spread of Nationalism*. Rev. ed. London: Verso, 1991.

Andō Hikotarō, ed. *Mantetsu: Nihon teikokushugi to Chūgoku*. Ochanomizu shobō, 1965.

————. *Nihonjin no Chūgokukan*. Keisō shobō, 1971.

Andō Yoshio, ed. *Kindai Nihon keizaishi yōran*. 2d ed. Tōkyō daigaku shuppankai, 1979.

Antō shōkō kaigisho. *Antō shōkō annai*. Andong: Antō shōkō kaigisho, 1939.

Asada Kyōji. "Manshū imin no nōgyo keiei jōkyō," *Keizaigaku ronshū* 9, no. 1 (Komazawa daigaku keizai gakkai, June 1977), pp. 77–99.

————. "Manshū nōgyō imin no funōka jinushika jōkyō," *Keizaigaku ronshū* 8, no. 3 (Komazawa daigaku keizai gakkai, December 1976), pp. 39–94.

————. "Manshū nōgyō imin seisaku no ritsuan katei." In Manshū iminshi kenkyūkai, ed., *Nihon teikokushugika no Manshū imin*. Ryūkei shosha, 1976.

————. *Nihon chishikijin no shokuminchi ninshiki*. Azekura shobō, 1985.

————. *Nihon shokuminchi kenkyū shiron*. Miraisha, 1990.

————. *Nihon teikokushugi to kyūshokuminchi jinushisei: Taiwan, Chōsen, "Manshū" ni okeru Nihonjin daitochi shoyū no shiteki bunseki*. Rev. ed. Ryūkei shosha, 1989.

————. "Nihon teikokushugi to 'Manshū' imin." In *Manshū imin to hisabetsu buraku: dōwa seisaku no gisei to natta Kutami kaitakudan*. Ōsaka jinken rekishi shiryōkan, 1989.

————. "Takumushō no Manshū nōgyō imin keikaku (shiken iminki)," *Keizai gakubu kenkyū kiyō*, no. 32 (Komazawa daigaku, March 1974), pp. 87–155.

Asada Kyōji and Kobayashi Hideo, eds. *Nihon teikokushugi no Manshū shihai: jūgonen sensōki o chūshin ni*. Jichōsha, 1986.

Asahi nenkan. Asahi shinbunsha, 1931–1936.

437

Asahi shinbunsha Tōa mondai chōsakai, ed. *Manshū imin*, vol. 2 of *Asahi Tōa ripōto*. Asahi shinbunsha, 1939.

Awaya Kentarō. "Fasshoka to minshū ishiki." In Eguchi Keiichi, ed., *Nihon fashizumu no keisei*, vol. 1 of *Taikei Nihon gendaishi*. Nihon hyōronsha, 1978.

———. "Kokumin dōin to teikō." In *Kindai 8*, vol. 21 of *Iwanami kōza Nihon rekishi*. Iwanami shoten, 1976.

———. *Shōwa no seitō: hōkai to sengo no saishuppatsu*, vol. 6 of *Shōwa no rekishi*. Shōgakkan, 1988.

Balibar, Etienne. "Racism and Nationalism." In Etienne Balibar and Immanuel Wallerstein, eds., *Race, Nation, Class: Ambiguous Identities*. New York: Verso, 1991.

Barnhart, Michael A. *Japan Prepares for Total War: The Search for Economic Security, 1919–1941*. Ithaca: Cornell University Press, 1987.

Beasley, W. G. *Japanese Imperialism 1894–1945*. Oxford: Clarendon Press, 1987.

Beckmann, George M., and Genji Ōkubo. *The Japanese Communist Party, 1922–1945*. Stanford: Stanford University Press, 1969.

Berger, Gordon M. "Politics and Mobilization in Japan, 1931–45." In Peter Duus, ed., *The Twentieth Century*, vol. 6 of *The Cambridge History of Japan*. Cambridge: Cambridge University Press, 1988.

Bernstein, Gail Lee. "Introduction." In Gail Lee Bernstein, ed., *Recreating Japanese Women, 1600–1945*. Berkeley: University of California Press, 1991.

Betts, Raymond F. *Uncertain Dimensions: Western Overseas Empires in the Twentieth Century*. Minneapolis: University of Minnesota Press, 1985.

Bix, Herbert P. "Japanese Imperialism and Manchuria, 1890–1931." Ph.D. dissertation, Harvard University, 1972.

———. "Japanese Imperialism and the Manchurian Economy, 1900–1931," *China Quarterly* 51 (July–September 1972), pp. 425–443.

Boyle, John Hunter. *China and Japan at War, 1937–1945: The Politics of Collaboration*. Stanford: Stanford University Press, 1972.

Bungei shunjū. 1931–1944.

Butow, Robert J. C. *Tojo and the Coming of the War*. Stanford: Stanford University Press, 1961.

Chamoto Shigemasa. *Sensō to jaanarizumu*. San'ichi shobō, 1984.

Chao, Kang. *The Economic Development of Manchuria: The Rise of a Frontier Economy*. Michigan Papers in Chinese Studies, no. 43. Ann Arbor: Center for Chinese Studies, 1982.

Chen, Ching-chih. "Police and Community Control Systems in the Empire." In Ramon H. Myers and Mark R. Peattie, eds., *The Japanese Colonial Empire, 1895–1945*. Princeton: Princeton University Press, 1984.

Chi, Madeleine. *China Diplomacy, 1914–1918*. Cambridge: East Asian Research Center, Harvard University, 1970.

Chou, Wan-yao. "The Kōminka Movement in Taiwan and Korea: Comparisons and Interpretations." In Peter Duus, Ramon H. Myers, and Mark R. Peattie, eds., *The Japanese Wartime Empire, 1931–1945*. Princeton: Princeton University Press, 1996.

Chūō kōron. 1931–1944.

Conroy, Hilary. *The Japanese Seizure of Korea, 1868–1910: A Study of Realism and Idealism in International Relations*. Philadelphia: University of Pennsylvania Press, 1960.

Coox, Alvin D. "The Kwantung Army Dimension." In Peter Duus, Ramon H. Myers, and Mark R. Peattie, eds., *The Japanese Informal Empire in China, 1895–1937.* Princeton: Princeton University Press, 1989.

———. *Nomonhan: Japan against Russia, 1939.* 2 vols. Stanford: Stanford University Press, 1985.

———. "The Pacific War." In Peter Duus, ed., *The Twentieth Century,* vol. 6 of *The Cambridge History of Japan.* New York: Cambridge University Press, 1988.

Crowley, James B. "From Closed Door to Empire: The Formation of the Meiji Military Establishment." In Bernard S. Silberman and H. D. Harootunian, eds., *Modern Japanese Leadership: Transition and Change.* Tucson: University of Arizona Press, 1966.

———. *Japan's Quest for Autonomy: National Security and Foreign Policy, 1930–1938.* Princeton: Princeton University Press, 1966.

Dikötter, Frank. *The Discourse of Race in Modern China.* Stanford: Stanford University Press, 1992.

Dirks, Nicholas B., ed. *Colonialism and Culture.* Ann Arbor: University of Michigan Press, 1992.

Dore, R. P. *Land Reform in Japan.* New York: Schocken Books, 1985.

Dore, R. P., and Tsutomu Ōuchi. "Rural Origins of Japanese Fascism." In James William Morley, ed., *Dilemmas of Growth in Prewar Japan.* Princeton: Princeton University Press, 1971.

Dower, John W. *Empire and Aftermath: Yoshida Shigeru and the Japanese Experience, 1878–1954.* Cambridge: Council on East Asian Studies, Harvard University, 1979.

———. *War without Mercy: Race and Power in the Pacific War.* New York: Pantheon Books, 1986.

Duus, Peter. *The Abacus and the Sword: The Japanese Penetration of Korea, 1895–1910.* Berkeley: University of California Press, 1995.

———. "Economic Dimensions of Meiji Imperialism: The Case of Korea, 1895–1910." In Ramon H. Myers and Mark R. Peattie, eds., *The Japanese Colonial Empire, 1895–1945.* Princeton: Princeton University Press, 1984.

———. *Party Rivalry and Political Change in Taisho Japan.* Cambridge: Harvard University Press, 1968.

———. "Zaikabō: Japanese Cotton Mills in China, 1895–1937." In Peter Duus, Ramon H. Myers, and Mark R. Peattie, eds., *The Japanese Informal Empire in China, 1895–1937.* Princeton: Princeton University Press, 1989.

Eckert, Carter J. "Total War, Industrialization, and Social Change in Late Colonial Korea." In Peter Duus, Ramon H. Myers, and Mark R. Peattie, eds., *The Japanese Wartime Empire, 1931–1945.* Princeton: Princeton University Press, 1996.

Egler, David George. "Japanese Mass Organizations in Manchuria, 1928–1945: The Ideology of Racial Harmony." Ph.D. dissertation, University of Arizona, 1977.

Eguchi Keiichi. *Futatsu no taisen,* vol. 14 of *Taikei Nihon no rekishi.* Shōgakkan, 1989.

———. *Jūgonen sensō no kaimaku,* vol. 4 of *Shōwa no rekishi.* Shōgakkan, 1988.

———. "Manshū jihen to daishinbun," *Shisō,* no. 583 (January 1973), pp. 98–113.

———. "Manshū jihen to minshū dōin: Nagoya-shi o chūshin toshite." In Furuya Tetsuo, ed., *Nitchū sensōshi kenkyū.* Yoshikawa kōbunkan, 1984.

———. "Manshū jihenki no Rikugunshō panfuretto," *Hōkei ronshū,* no. 113 (Aichi daigaku, February 1987), pp. 165–197.

————. *Nihon teikokushugi shiron: Manshū jihen zengo.* Aoki shoten, 1975.

Eiga to engei. 1931–1938.

Ekonomisuto. 1931–1944.

Elsbree, Willard H. *Japan's Role in Southeast Asian Nationalist Movements, 1940 to 1945.* Cambridge: Harvard University Press, 1953.

Fairbank, John K. *Trade and Diplomacy on the China Coast: The Opening of the Treaty Ports, 1842–1954.* 2 vols. Cambridge: Harvard University Press, 1953.

Fieldhouse, D. K. *The Colonial Empires: A Comparative Survey from the Eighteenth Century.* New York: Delacorte Press, 1966.

Fields, Barbara Jeanne. "Slavery, Race and Ideology in the United States of America," *New Left Review,* no. 181 (May–June 1990), pp. 95–118.

Fletcher, William Miles. *The Japanese Business Community and National Trade Policy, 1920–1942.* Chapel Hill: University of North Carolina Press, 1989.

————. *The Search for a New Order: Intellectuals and Fascism in Prewar Japan.* Chapel Hill: University of North Carolina Press, 1982.

Fogel, Joshua A. "Introduction: Itō Takeo and the Research Work of the South Manchurian Railway Company." In Itō Takeo, *Life along the South Manchurian Railway: The Memoirs of Itō Takeo,* trans. Joshua A. Fogel. New York: M. E. Sharpe, 1988.

————. *Politics and Sinology: The Case of Naitō Konan (1866–1934).* Cambridge: Council on East Asian Studies, Harvard University, 1984.

Fujii Tadatoshi. *Kokubō fujinkai: hinomaru to kappogi.* Iwanami shoten, 1985.

Fujin kurabu. 1931–1941.

Fujita Shigeru. *Kusa no hi: Manmō kaitakudan suterareta tami no kiroku.* Kanazawa: Noto insatsu shuppanbu, 1989.

Fujiwara Akira. "Nihon fashizumu to taiChūgoku shinryaku sensō." In Fujiwara Akira and Nozawa Yutaka, eds., *Nihon fashizumu to Higashi Ajia: gendaishi shinpojumu.* Aoki shoten, 1977.

————. *Nihon gunjishi.* 2 vols. Nihon hyōronsha, 1987.

Fujiwara Akira and Imai Seiichi, eds. *Manshū jihen,* vol. 1 of *Jūgonen sensōshi.* Aoki shoten, 1988.

Fujiwara Akira, Imai Seiichi, and Ōe shinobu, eds. *Kindai Nihonshi no kisō chishiki: shijitsu no seikakuna rikai no tame ni.* Rev. ed. Yūhikaku, 1979.

Fujiwara Akira and Kunugi Toshihiro. "Kaisetsu." In Fujiwara Akira and Kunugi Toshihiro, eds., *Manshū jihen to kokumin dōin,* vol. 8 of *Shiryō Nihon gendaishi.* Ōtsuki shoten, 1983.

————, eds. *Manshū jihen to kokumin dōin,* vol. 8 of *Shiryō Nihon gendaishi.* Ōtsuki shoten, 1983.

Fukuda Kiyohito. *Nichirin heisha.* Asahi shinbunsha, 1939.

Gaddis, John Lewis. "The Corporatist Synthesis: A Skeptical View," *Diplomatic History* 10, no. 4 (Fall 1986), pp. 357–362.

Gaimushō, ed. *Nihon gaikō nenpyō narabini shūyō bunsho.* Hara shobō, 1976.

Garon, Sheldon. *The State and Labor in Modern Japan.* Berkeley: University of California Press, 1987.

Gifu-ken. *Kindai* 1 of *Gifu kenshi tsūshihen.* Gifu: Gifu-ken, 1967.

Gluck, Carol. "The Idea of Showa," *Daedalus* 119, no. 3 (Summer 1990), pp. 1–13.

————. *Japan's Modern Myths: Ideology in the Late Meiji Period*. Princeton: Princeton University Press, 1985.

Gordon, Andrew. *The Evolution of Labor Relations in Japan: Heavy Industry, 1853–1955*. Cambridge: Council on East Asian Studies, Harvard University, 1988.

————. *Labor and Imperial Democracy in Prewar Japan*. Berkeley: University of California Press, 1991.

Gotō, Ken'ichi. "Cooperation, Submission, and Resistance of Indigenous Elites of Southeast Asia in the Wartime Empire." In Peter Duus, Ramon H. Myers, and Mark R. Peattie, eds., *The Japanese Wartime Empire, 1931–1945*. Princeton: Princeton University Press, 1996.

Gould, Stephen Jay. *The Mismeasure of Man*. New York: Norton, 1981.

Hamano Kenzaburō. *Aa Manshū*. Akimoto shobō, 1970.

Hanzai kagaku. 1931–1933.

Hara Akira. "'DaiTōa kyōeiken' no keizaiteki jittai," *Tochi seido shigaku*, no. 71 (April 1976), pp. 1–28.

————. "'Manshū' ni okeru keizai tōsei seisaku no tenkai: Mantetsu kaiso to Mangyō setsuritsu o megutte." In Andō Yoshio, ed., *Nihon keizai seisaku shiron*. Tōkyō daigaku shuppankai, 1976.

————. "1930 nendai no Manshū keizai tōsei seisaku." In Manshūshi kenkyūkai, ed., *Nihon teikokushugika no Manshū*. Ochanomizu shobō, 1972.

————. "Senji tōsei keizai no kaishi." In *Kindai 7*, vol. 20 of *Iwanami kōza Nihon rekishi*. Iwanami shoten, 1976.

Hara Kakuten. *Gendai Ajia kenkyū seiritsu shiron: Mantetsu chōsabu, Tōa kenkyūjo, IPR no kenkyū*. Keisō shobō, 1984.

Harada Katsumasa. *Mantetsu*. Iwanami shoten, 1981.

Harupin Nihon shōkō kaigisho. *Harupin keizai gaikan*. Harbin: Harupin Nihon shōkō kaigisho, 1937.

Hashimoto Jurō. "Keizai seisaku." In Ōishi Kaichirō, ed., *Sekai daikyōkōki*, vol. 2 of *Nihon teikokushugishi*. Tōkyō daigaku shuppankai, 1987.

Hatada Takashi. *Nihonjin no Chōsenkan*. Keisō shobō, 1969.

Hatano Sumio. "Japanese Foreign Policy, 1931–1945: Historiography." In Sadao Asada, ed., *Japan and the World, 1853–1952: A Bibliographic Guide to Japanese Scholarship in Foreign Relations*. New York: Columbia University Press, 1989.

Havens, Thomas R. H. *Farm and Nation in Modern Japan: Agrarian Nationalism, 1870–1940*. Princeton: Princeton University Press, 1974.

————. *Valley of Darkness: The Japanese People and World War Two*. New York: Norton, 1978.

Hayashi Takehisa, Yamazaki Hiroaki, and Shibagaki Kazuo. *Nihon shihonshugi*, vol. 6 of *Kōza teikokushugi no kenkyū: ryōtaisenkan ni okeru sono saihensei*. Aoki shoten, 1973.

Heinrichs, Waldo H., Jr. "1931–1937." In Ernest R. May and James C. Thomson, Jr., eds., *American-East Asian Relations: A Survey*. Cambridge: Harvard University Press, 1972.

Higashichikuma-gun, Matsumoto-shi, Shiojiri-shi kyōdō shiryō hensankai, ed. *Gendai 1*, vol. 3 of *Higashichikuma-gun, Matsumoto-shi, Shiojiri-shishi*. Nagano: Higashichikuma-gun, Matsumoto-shi, Shiojiri-shi kyōdō shiryō hensankai, 1962.

Hikita Yasuyuki. "Zaisei, kin'yū kōzō." In Asada Kyōji and Kobayashi Hideo, eds., *Nihon teikokushugi no Manshū shihai: jūgonen sensō o chūshin ni.* Jichōsha, 1986.

Hirano, Ken'ichiro. "The Japanese in Manchuria, 1906–1931: A Study of the Historical Background of Manchukuo." Ph.D. dissertation, Harvard University, 1983.

Hirokawa Tadahide. "Hanfashizumu undōron." In Eguchi Keiichi, ed., *Nihon fashizumu no keisei,* vol. 1 of *Taikei Nihon gendaishi.* Nihon hyōronsha, 1978.

Hiroshima-ken. *Kindai 2,* vol. 6 of *Hiroshima kenshi tsūshi.* Hiroshima: Hiroshima-ken, 1981.

Hobsbawm, Eric. *The Age of Empire: 1875–1914.* New York: Vintage Books, 1989.

Hogan, Michael J. "Corporatism." In Michael J. Hogan and Thomas G. Paterson, eds., *Explaining the History of American Foreign Relations.* Cambridge: Cambridge University Press, 1991.

——. "Corporatism: A Positive Appraisal," *Diplomatic History* 10, no. 4 (Fall 1986), pp. 363–372.

——. *Informal Entente: The Private Structure of Cooperation in Anglo-American Economic Diplomacy, 1918–1928.* Columbia: University of Missouri Press, 1977.

Hōten shōkō kaigisho. *Hōten keizai jijō.* Fengtian: Hōten shōkō kaigisho, 1936.

——. *Kigyōchi toshite no Hōten.* Fengtian: Hōten shōkō kaigisho, 1932.

——. *Kōgyō toshi Hōten.* Fengtian: Hōten shōkō kaigisho, 1934.

Ie no hikari. 1931–1945.

Ienaga, Saburō. *The Pacific War, 1931–1945.* Trans. Frank Baldwin. New York: Pantheon Books, 1978.

Iguchi Kazuki. "Nisshin, Nichiro sensōron." In Rekishigaku kenkyūkai and Nihonshi kenkyūkai, eds., *Kindai 2,* vol. 8 of *Kōza Nihon rekishi.* Tōkyō daigaku shuppankai, 1985.

Iizuka Yasushi and Kazama Hideto. "Nōgyō shigen no shūdatsu." In Asada Kyōji and Kobayashi Hideo, eds., *Nihon teikokushugi no Manshū shihai: jūgonen sensō o chūshin ni.* Jichōsha, 1986.

Ikei Masaru. "1930 nendai no masu media: Manshū jihen e no taiō o chūshin toshite." In Miwa Kimitada, ed., *Saikō Taiheiyō sensō zen'ya: Nihon no 1930 nendairon toshite.* Sōseiki, 1981.

——. "Nitchū sensō to masu media no taiō." In Inoue Kiyoshi and Etō Shinkichi, eds., *Nitchū sensō to Nitchū kankei: Rokōkyō jiken gojusshūnen Nitchū gakujutsu ronkai kiroku.* Hara shobō, 1988.

Imai Seiichi. "Mantetsu chōsabu ni kansuru sancho o megutte," *Ajia keizai* 28, no. 11 (November 1987), pp. 93–100.

Inoue Kiyoshi. "'Manshū' shinryaku." In *Kindai 7,* vol. 20 of *Iwanami kōza Nihon rekishi.* Iwanami shoten, 1976.

——. *Nihon teikokushugi no keisei.* Iwanami shoten, 1968.

Inoue Mitsusada et al., eds. *Kindai 2,* vol. 5 of *Nihon rekishi taikei.* Yamakawa shuppansha, 1989.

Iriye, Akira. "The Failure of Economic Expansionism: 1918–1931." In Bernard S. Silberman and H. D. Harootunian, eds., *Japan in Crisis: Essays on Taisho Democracy.* Princeton: Princeton University Press, 1974.

——. *Pacific Estrangement: Japanese and American Expansion, 1897–1911.* Cambridge: Harvard University Press, 1972.

Ishida Seiichi. "Kita 'Manshū' nōson ni okeru konō no seishitsu," no. 4 of "Mantetsu chōsabu kankeisha ni kiku," *Ajia keizai* 26, no. 7 (July 1985), pp. 57–75.

Ishidō Kiyotomo. "Mantetsu chōsabu wa nan de atta ka (I)," no. 16 of "Mantetsu chōsabu kankeisha ni kiku," *Ajia keizai* 28, no. 5 (May 1987), pp. 67–88.

———. "Mantetsu chōsabu wa nan de atta ka (II)," no. 17 of "Mantetsu chōsabu kankeisha ni kiku," *Ajia keizai* 28, no. 6 (June 1987), pp. 47–60.

Ishidō Kiyomoto, Noma Kiyoshi, Nonomura Kazuo, and Kobayashi Shōichi. *Jūgonen sensō to Mantetsu chōsabu.* Hara shobō, 1986.

Ishihara Jirō. *Manshū imin to seinendan.* Dai Nippon rengō seinendan, 1937.

Ishii Kanji. "Kokusai kankei." In Ōishi Kaichirō, ed., *Sekai daikyōkōki*, vol. 2 of *Nihon teikokushugishi.* Tōkyō daigaku shuppankai, 1987.

Itō Takeo. *Life along the South Manchurian Railway: The Memoirs of Itō Takeo.* Trans. Joshua A. Fogel. New York: M. E. Sharpe, 1988.

Iwamizu Akira. "Taigai tōshi." In Ono Kazuichirō, ed., *Senkanki no teikokushugi.* Sekai shisōsha, 1985.

Iwanami shoten henshūbu. *Kindai Nihon sōgō nenpyō.* Iwanami shoten, 1968.

Jansen, Marius B. *China in the Tokugawa World.* Cambridge: Harvard University Press, 1992.

———. *Japan and China: From War to Peace, 1894–1972.* Chicago: Rand McNally, 1975.

———. *The Japanese and Sun Yat-sen.* Cambridge: Harvard University Press, 1967.

Japan tsūrisuto byūrō, ed. *Manshi ryokō nenkan: Shōwa 16 nen.* Hakubunkan, 1941.

Japanese Delegation to the League of Nations. *The Manchurian Question: Japan's Case in the Sino-Japanese Dispute as Presented before the League of Nations.* Geneva: League of Nations, 1933.

Johnson, Chalmers. *An Instance of Treason: Ozaki Hotsumi and the Sorge Spy Ring.* Rev. ed. Stanford: Stanford University Press, 1990.

———. *MITI and the Japanese Miracle: The Growth of Industrial Policy, 1925–1975.* Stanford: Stanford University Press, 1982.

Jones, F. C. *Manchuria since 1931.* New York: Oxford University Press, 1949.

"Kaitaku kankei shohōki." In Manshū kaitakushi kankōkai, *Manshū kaitakushi.* Manshū kaitakushi kankōkai, 1966.

Kaizō. 1931–1944.

Kajima heiwa kenkyūjo, ed. *Manshū jihen*, vol. 8 of *Nihon gaikōshi.* Kajima heiwa kenkyūjo shuppankai, 1973.

Kami Shōichirō. *Manmō kaitaku seishōnen giyūgun.* Chūō kōronsha, 1973.

Kanda Fuhito, ed. *Shōwashi nenpyō: Taishō 12 nen 9 gatsu 1 nichi—Heisei gannen 12 gatsu 31 nichi: nenpyō de tsuzuru Shōwa no ayumi.* Shōgakkan, 1990.

Kaneko Fumio. "Nihon ni okeru shokuminchi kenkyū no seiritsu jijō." In Kojima Reiitsu, ed., *Nihon teikokushugi to Higashi Ajia. Ajia keizai kenkyūjo, 1979.*

———. "Shihon yushutsu to shokuminchi." In Ōishi Kaichirō, ed., *Sekai daikyōkōki*, vol. 2 of *Nihon teikokushugishi.* Tōkyō daigaku shuppankai, 1987.

Kantōkyoku. *Shōwa 12 nen: dai 32 tōkeisho.* Dalian: Kantōkyoku, 1939.

Kaplan, Amy, and Donald E. Pease, eds. *Cultures of United States Imperialism.* Durham, N.C.: Duke University Press, 1993.

Kasza, Gregory J. *The State and Mass Media in Japan, 1918–1945.* Berkeley: University of California Press, 1988.

Kawabata Yasunari, Shiga Naoya, and Satō Haruo, comps. *Chūgokuhen* (2 vols.), vols. 10 and 11 of *Sekai kikō bungaku zenshū*. Shūdōsha, 1960.

Kawai Akira, Yasukawa Junnosuke, Morikawa Terumichi, and Kawaguchi Yukihiro. *Nihon gendai kyōikushi*. ShinNihon shuppansha, 1984.

Kawamura Minato. *Ikyō no Shōwa bungaku: "Manshū" to kindai Nihon*. Iwanami shoten, 1990.

Kazama Hideto. "Nōson gyōsei shihai." In Asada Kyōji and Kobayashi Hideo, eds., *Nihon teikokushugi no Manshū shihai: jūgonen sensō o chūshin ni*. Jichōsha, 1986.

Keene, Donald. "The Sino-Japanese War of 1894–95 and Japanese Culture." In Donald Keene, *Landscapes and Portraits: Appreciations of Japanese Culture*. Tokyo: Kōdansha International, 1971.

Kevles, Daniel J. *In the Name of Eugenics: Genetics and the Uses of Human Heredity*. New York: Knopf, 1985.

Kigyō tōkei sōran. Tōyō keizai shinpōsha, 1943.

Kimijima Kazuhiko. "Fashizumuka nōson ni okeru Manshū imin: Hanishina-gun bunkyō imin no jisshi katei." In Ōe Shinobu, ed., *Nihon fashizumu no keisei to nōson*. Azekura shobō, 1978.

———. "Manshū nōgyō imin kankei kikan no setsuritsu katei to katsudō jōkyō: Manshū takushoku kaisha to Manshū takushoku kōsha o chūshin ni." In Manshū iminshi kenkyūkai, ed., *Nihon teikokushugika no Manshū imin*. Ryūkei shosha, 1976.

Kinbara Samon and Takemae Eiji, eds. *Shōwashi: kokumin no naka no haran to gekidō no hanseiki*. Rev. ed. Yūhikaku, 1989.

King, Anthony D. *Urbanism, Colonialism, and the World-Economy: Cultural and Spatial Foundations of the World Urban System*. New York: Routledge, 1990.

Kingu. 1931–1940.

Kinmonth, Earl H. "The Impact of Military Procurements on the Old Middle Classes in Japan, 1931–1941," *Japan Forum* 4, no. 2 (October 1992), pp. 247–250.

Kinney, Ann Rasmussen. *Japanese Investment in Manchurian Manufacturing, Mining, Transportation, and Communications, 1931–1945*. New York: Garland, 1982.

Kobayashi Hideo. *"DaiTōa kyōeiken" no keisei to hōkai*. Ochanomizu shobō, 1975.

———. "Manshū kin'yū kōzō no saihensei katei: 1930 nendai zenhanki o chūshin ni." In Manshūshi kenkyūkai, ed., *Nihon teikokushugika no Manshū*. Ochanomizu shobō, 1972.

———. "Manshū nōgyō imin no einō jittai." In Manshū iminshi kenkyūkai, ed., *Nihon teikokushugika no Manshū imin*. Ryūkei shosha, 1976.

———. "1930 nendai 'Manshū kōgyōka' seisaku no tenkai katei: 'Manshū sangyō kaihatsu gokanen keikaku' jisshi katei o chūshin ni," *Tochi seido shigaku*, no. 44 (July 1969), pp. 19–43.

———. "1930 nendai shokuminchi 'kōgyōka' no shotokuchō," *Tochi seido shigaku*, no. 71 (April 1976), pp. 29–45.

Kōdan kurabu. 1931–1933.

Kōdansha, ed. *Encyclopedia of Japan*. New York: Kōdansha, 1983.

———. *Hijōji Nihon: Shōwa 7 nen–9 nen*, vol. 3 of *Shōwa nimannichi no zenkiroku*. Kōdansha, 1989.

———. *Ichioku no "shintaisei": Shōwa 13 nen–15 nen*, vol. 5 of *Shōwa nimannichi no zenkiroku*. Kōdansha, 1989.

———. *Nitchū sensō e no michi: Shōwa 10 nen–12 nen,* vol. 4 of *Shōwa nimannichi no zenkiroku.* Kōdansha, 1989.

———. *Shōwa e no kitai: Shōwa gannen–3 nen,* vol. 1 of *Shōwa nimannichi no zenkiroku.* Kōdansha, 1989.

———. *Tairiku ni agaru senka: Shōwa 4 nen–6 nen,* vol. 2 of *Shōwa nimannichi no zenkiroku.* Kōdansha, 1989.

Kokuritsu kyōiku kenkyūjo, ed. *Kyōiku seisaku 1,* vol. 1 of *Nihon kindai kyōiku hyakunenshi.* Kyōiku kenkyū shinkōkai, 1974.

———. *Shakai kyōiku 1,* vol. 7 of *Nihon kindai kyōiku hyakunenshi.* Kyōiku kenkyū shinkōkai, 1974.

———. *Shakai kyōiku 2,* vol. 8 of *Nihon kindai kyōiku hyakunenshi.* Kyōiku kenkyū shinkōkai, 1974.

Koshizawa Akira. *Harupin no toshi keikaku, 1898–1945.* Sōwasha, 1989.

———. *Manshūkoku no shuto keikaku: Tōkyō no genzai to mirai o tou.* Nihon keizai hyōronsha, 1988.

Kosuge Nobuko. "Manshū jihen to minshū ishiki: Yamanashi-kenka ni okeru gonkoku netsu to haigai netsu." Paper presented to the Awaya Kentarō Seminar, Rikkyō University, Tokyo, June 1989, photocopy.

Krasner, Stephen D. "Sovereignty: An Institutional Perspective." In James A. Caporaso, ed., *The Elusive State: International and Comparative Perspectives.* Newbury Park, Calif.: Sage Publications, 1989.

Lebra, Joyce C. *Japanese-Trained Armies in Southeast Asia: Independence and Volunteer Forces in World War II.* New York: Columbia University Press, 1977.

Lee, Chong-sik. *Counterinsurgency in Manchuria: The Japanese Experience, 1931–1940.* Santa Monica, Calif.: Rand Corporation, 1967.

Lewis, Michael. *Rioters and Citizens: Mass Protest in Imperial Japan.* Berkeley: University of California Press, 1990.

Li, Lincoln. *The Japanese Army in North China, 1937–1941: Problems of Political and Economic Control.* New York: Oxford University Press, 1976.

Lowe, Peter. *Great Britain and Japan, 1911–1915: A Study of British Far Eastern Policy.* London: Macmillan, 1969.

McCormack, Gavan. *Chang Tso-lin in Northeast China, 1911–1928: China, Japan, and the Manchurian Idea.* Stanford: Stanford University Press, 1977.

McCoy, Alfred W., ed. *Southeast Asia under Japanese Occupation.* New Haven: Yale University Southeast Asia Studies, 1980.

MacKenzie, John M. *Propaganda and Empire: The Manipulation of British Public Opinion, 1880–1960.* Manchester: Manchester University Press, 1984.

MacKinnon, Janice R., and Stephen R. MacKinnon. *Agnes Smedley: The Life and Times of an American Radical.* Berkeley: University of California Press, 1988.

Mainichi shinbunsha. *Nisshin Nichiro sensō,* vol. 1 of *Ichiokunin no Shōwashi: Nihon no senshi.* Mainichi shinbunsha, 1979.

Mainichi shirizu shuppan henshu, ed. *Miyagi-ken no Shōwashi: kindai hyakunen no kiroku,* vol. 1. Mainichi shinbunsha, 1983.

Manchuria. 1936–1940.

Manmō. 1932–1942.

Manshikai. *Manshū kaihatsu yonjūnenshi.* 3 vols. Manshū kaihatsu yonjūnenshi kankōkai, 1964–1965.

Manshū daihakurankai kyōsankai. *Nichiman jitsugyō kyōkai kiyō.* 1933. Tōkyō shōkō kaigisho microreel no. 139:1785–2324.

Manshū iminshi kenkyūkai, ed. *Nihon teikokushugika no Manshū imin.* Ryūkei shosha, 1976.

Manshū jijō annaijo, ed. *Manshūkoku kakuken jijō.* Xinjing: Manshū jijō annaijo, 1939.

Manshū kaitakushi kankōkai. *Manshū kaitakushi.* Manshū kaitakushi kankōkai, 1966.

Manshū keizai zuhyō. Dalian: Dalian shōkō kaigisho, 1934–1940.

Manshū kōhō kyōkai. *Manshū no shinbun to tsūshin.* Xinjing: Manshū kōhō kyōkai, 1940.

Manshū nichinichi shinbun, ed. *Manshū toshi no shinsōbō.* Manshū nichinichi shinbunsha, 1937.

Manshū nōgyō imin bunken mokuroku. Nihon gakujutsu shinkōkai, 1936.

"Manshū nōgyō imin ni kansuru shoshiryō," *Naigai chōsa shiryō* 10, no. 11 (November 1938), pp. 1–277.

Manshū teikoku kyōwakai chūō honbu. *Minzoku kyōwa no Manshūkoku shutoshite shin nyūMansha no tameni.* Manshū teikoku kyōwakai chūō honbu, 1939.

Manshū teikoku seifu, ed. *Manshū kenkoku jūnenshi,* vol. 91 of *Meiji hyakunenshi sōsho.* Hara shobō, 1969.

Manshū wa imin no rakudo. Dalian: Mantetsu, 1937.

Manshūkoku kaitaku sōkyoku. *Manmō kaitaku seisaku kihon yōkō.* Kaitaku sōkyoku, 1939.

Manshūkoku kōjo tōkei (A): Kōnei 7 nen. Xinjing: Manshūkoku keizaibu kōmushi, 1942.

Manshūkoku kōjo tōkei (B): Kōnei 7 nen. Xinjing: Manshūkoku keizaibu kōmushi, 1942.

Manshūkoku saikō kensatsuchō. "Manshūkoku kaitakuchi hanzai gaiyō." 1941. In Yamada Shōji, ed., *Manshū imin,* vol. 6 of *Kindai minshū no kiroku.* Shinjinbutsu Ōraisha, 1978.

Manshūkoku tsūshinsha, ed. *Manshū kaitaku nenkan.* Xinjing: Manshūkoku tsūshinsha, 1941.

———. *Manshū kaitaku nenkan.* 1944. Reprint, Howa shuppan, 1986.

Manshūshi kenkyūkai, ed. *Nihon teikokushugika no Manshū.* Ochanomizu shobō, 1972.

Mantakukai, ed. *Dokyumento Manshū kaitaku monogatari.* Azusa shoten, 1986.

Mantetsu, ed. *Manshū nenkan: Shōwa 8 nen.* Dalian: Manshū bunka kyōkai, 1933.

Mantetsu keizai chōsakai, ed. *TaiMan keizai seisaku ni kansuru kakushu iken.* Mantetsu, 1932.

Matsui Kiyoshi. *Kindai Nihon bōekishi,* vol. 3. Yūhikaku, 1963.

Matsumura Takao. "Manshūkoku seiritsu ikō ni okeru imin, rōdō seisaku no keisei to tenkai." In Manshūshi kenkyūkai, ed., *Nihon teikokushugika no Manshū.* Ochanomizu shobō, 1972.

Matsusaka, Y. Tak. "Japanese Imperialism and the South Manchurian Railway Company, 1904–1914." Ph.D. dissertation, Harvard University, 1993.

———. "Managing Occupied Manchuria, 1931–1934." In Peter Duus, Ramon H. Myers, and Mark R. Peattie, eds., *The Japanese Wartime Empire, 1931–1945.* Princeton: Princeton University Press, 1996.

Matsuzawa Tetsunari. "Manshū jihen to 'minzoku kyōwa' undō," *Kokusai seiji* 43, no. 1 (1970), pp. 77–99.

Mayo, Marlene J. "Attitudes toward Asia and the Beginnings of Japanese Empire." In Grant K. Goodman, comp., *Imperial Japan and Asia: A Reassessment*. New York: East Asian Institute, Columbia University, 1967.

————, comp. *The Emergence of Imperial Japan: Self-defense or Calculated Aggression?* Lexington, Mass.: D. C. Heath, 1970.

Meyers, Jeffrey. *The Wounded Spirit: A Study of the Seven Pillars of Wisdom*. London: Martin Brian and O'Keefe, 1973.

Minami Hiroshi and Shakai shinri kenkyūjo. *Shōwa bunka, 1925–1945*. Keisō shobō, 1987.

————. *Taishō bunka, 1905–1927*. Keisō shobō, 1987.

Mitchell, Richard H. *Censorship in Imperial Japan*. Princeton: Princeton University Press, 1983.

Miura Etsurō, ed. *Manshū ijū tokuhon*. Kaizōsha, 1939.

Miwa Takeshi. "Keizai chōsakai kara chōsabu made (I)," no. 27 of "Mantetsu chōsabu kankeisha ni kiku," *Ajia keizai* 29, no. 9 (September 1988), pp. 67–91.

————. "Keizai chōsakai kara chōsabu made (II)," no. 28 of "Mantetsu chōsabu kankeisha ni kiku," *Ajia keizai* 29, no. 10 (October 1988), pp. 56–79.

————. "Manshū sangyō kaihatsu einen keikakuan to keizai chōsakai (I)," no. 13 of "Mantetsu chōsabu kankeisha ni kiku," *Ajia keizai* 28, no. 1 (January 1987), pp. 56–76.

————. "Manshū sangyō kaihatsu einen keikakuan to keizai chōsakai (II)," no. 14 of "Mantetsu chōsabu kankeisha ni kiku," *Ajia keizai* 28, no. 3 (March 1987), pp. 75–91.

Miyake Seiki and Saitō Eizaburō, eds. *Nihon zaikai jinbutsu retsuden*, vol. 2. Seichō shuppan, 1963.

Miyanishi Yoshio. "Mantetsu chōsabu to Ozaki Hotsumi, Nakanishi Kō, Himori Torao (I)," no. 18 of "Mantetsu chōsabu kankeisha ni kiku," *Ajia keizai* 28, no. 7 (July 1987), pp. 51–68.

————. "Mantetsu chōsabu to Ozaki Hotsumi, Nakanishi Kō, Himori Torao (II)," no. 19 of "Mantetsu chōsabu kankeisha ni kiku," *Ajia keizai* 28, no. 8 (August 1987), pp. 76–93.

Mommsen, Wolfgang J. *Theories of Imperialism*. Trans. P. S. Falla. Chicago: University of Chicago Press, 1980.

Mori Takemaro. "Senjika nōson no kōzō henka." In *Kindai 7*, vol. 20 of *Iwanami kōza Nihon rekishi*. Iwanami shoten, 1976.

Morley, James William, ed. *The China Quagmire: Japan's Expansion on the Asian Continent*. New York: Columbia University Press, 1983.

————. *Japan Erupts: The London Naval Conference and the Manchurian Incident, 1928–1932*. New York: Columbia University Press, 1984.

Morton, Louis. "1937–1941." In Ernest R. May and James C. Thomson, Jr., eds., *American-East Asian Relations: A Survey*. Cambridge: Harvard University Press, 1972.

Morton, William Fitch. *Tanaka Giichi and Japan's China Policy*. Folkestone, Kent: Dawson, 1980.

Moskowitz, Karl. "The Creation of the Oriental Development Company: Japanese

Illusions Meet Korean Reality," *Occasional Papers on Korea*, no. 2 (March 1974), pp. 73–111.

Myers, Ramon H. *The Japanese Economic Development of Manchuria, 1932 to 1945.* New York: Garland, 1982.

———. "Japanese Imperialism in Manchuria: The South Manchurian Railway Company, 1906–1933." In Peter Duus, Ramon H. Myers, and Mark R. Peattie, eds., *The Japanese Informal Empire in China, 1895–1937.* Princeton: Princeton University Press, 1989.

Nagano-ken. *Gunji, keisatsu, shihō,* vol. 4 of *Nagano kenshi kindai shiryōhen.* Nagano: Nagano-ken, 1988.

Nagano-ken kaitaku jikōkai Manshū kaitakushi kankōkai. *Nagano-ken Manshū kaitakushi.* 3 vols. Nagano: Nagano-ken kaitaku jikōkai Manshū kaitakushi kankōkai, 1984.

Nagano-ken keizaibu. *Bunson keikaku jirei: Nishichikuma-gun Yomikaki-mura,* no. 37 of *Keizai kōsei sankō shiryō.* Nagano-ken keizaibu, 1939.

———. "Bunson keikaku no tatekata." In Nōrinshō keizai kōseibu, ed., *Shinnōson no kensetsu.* Asahi shinbunsha, 1939.

Nakagane Katsuji. "Manchukuo and Economic Development." In Peter Duus, Ramon H. Myers, and Mark R. Peattie, eds., *The Japanese Informal Empire in China, 1895–1937.* Princeton: Princeton University Press, 1989.

Nakajima Hōzō. " 'Chūgoku shakaishi ronsen' ni kansuru chōsa," no. 15 of "Mantetsu chōsabu kankeisha ni kiku," *Ajia keizai* 28, no. 4 (April 1987), pp. 61–82.

Nakajima Kinji. "Manshū jihenki no jūgo katsudō to minshū: Ishikawa-ken imonkai setsuritsu o meguru jōkyō." Master's thesis, Kanazawa daigaku, January 1988.

Nakamura Seishi. "Hyakusha rankingu no hensen." *Chūō kōron keiei mondai,* special issue (Fall 1977).

Nakamura, Takafusa. "Depression, Recovery, and War, 1920–1945." In Peter Duus, ed., *The Twentieth Century,* vol. 6 of *The Cambridge History of Japan.* Cambridge: Cambridge University Press, 1988.

Nakanishi Katsuhiko. "Tachibana Shiraki no shisō keisei: tokō dōki to no kakawari de," *Hōgaku zasshi* 22, no. 1 (September 1975), pp. 27–48.

Nakanishi Kō. *Chūgoku kakumei no arashi no naka de.* Aoki shoten, 1974.

———. *Shi no kabe no naka kara: tsuma e no tegami.* Iwanami shoten, 1971.

Nakauchi Toshio. *Gunkoku bidan to kyōkasho.* Iwanami shoten, 1988.

Nichiman jitsugyō kyōkai. *Nichiman jitsugyō kyōkai daiyonkai kaiin sōkai hōkokusho.* Nichiman jitsugyō kyōkai, 1937.

———. *Setsuritsu shuisho, kaisoku oyobi yakuin meibo.* 1934. Tōkyō shōkō kaigisho microreel no. 140:2425–2437.

———. *Shōwa 9 nendo Nichiman jitsugyō kyōkai jigyō hōkokusho.* Nichiman jitsugyō kyōkai, 1935.

———. *TaiMan shōkō toshite mitaru ura Nihon no shokōwan.* Nichiman jitsugyō kyōkai, 1934.

———. *Tōkyō kaiin tokkūsū.* 1934. Tōkyō shōkō kaigisho microreel no. 140:2454–2471.

Nichiman nōsei kenkyūkai. *Kaitaku seisaku ni kansuru kenkyū: Manshū kaitakumin no sōshutsu jōkyō ni kansuru chōsa oyobi kaitaku seisaku ni kansuru jakkan no kōsatsu.* Nichiman nōsei kenkyūkai, 1940.

"Nichiman sangyō teikei ni kansuru iinkai." 1933. Tōkyō shōkō kaigisho microreel no. 107:329–655.

"Nichiman tōsei keizai seisakuron no yōshi." 1933. Tōkyō shōkō kaigisho microreel no. 107:608–617.

Nichimanshi keizai kondankai hōkokusho. Nichiman chūō kyōkai, 1939.

Nihon hōsō kyōkai. *Nihon hōsōshi,* vol. 1. Nihon hōsō kyōkai, 1961.

———. *Rajio nenkan: Shōwa 8 nen.* Nihon hōsō shuppan kyōkai, 1933.

Nihon kindaishi kenkyūkai, ed. *Kiro ni tatsu Shōwa Nihon,* vol. 9 of *Gahō Nihon kindai no rekishi.* Sanseidō, 1980.

———. *Minponshugi no chōryū,* vol. 8 of *Gahō Nihon kindai no rekishi.* Sanseidō, 1980.

Nihon kōtsū kōsha shashi hensanshitsu, ed. *Nihon kōtsū kōsha nanajūnenshi.* Nihon kōtsū kōsha, 1982.

Nihon shōkō kaigisho. "Manshūgun imon ni kansuru kiroku." 1931–1932. Tōkyō shōkō kaigisho microreel no. 138:2810–2878.

———. "Nichiman jitsugyō kondankai shussekisha meibo." July 1933. Tōkyō shōkō kaigisho microreel no. 139:1752–1757.

———. *Nichiman jitsugyō kondankai yōkō.* 1933. Tōkyō shōkō kaigisho microreel no. 139:1714–1744.

———. *Nihon shōkō kaigisho shusai Manmō keizai shisatsudan hōkoku narabini ikenshō.* Nihon shōkō kaigisho, 1932.

Nihon shokumin kyōkai. *Manmō annai,* vol. 1 of *Imin kōza.* Tōhō shoin, 1932.

Niigata-ken. *Kindai 3,* vol. 8, *Niigata kenshi tsūshihen.* Niigata: Niigata-ken, 1988.

Nish, Ian H. *Alliance in Decline: A Study in Anglo-Japanese Relations 1908–23.* London: Athlone Press, 1972.

———. *The Anglo-Japanese Alliance: The Diplomacy of Two Island Empires 1894–1907.* London: Athlone Press, 1966.

Noma Kiyoshi. "'Manshū' nōson jittai chōsa ibun (I)," no. 1 of "Mantetsu chōsabu kankeisha ni kiku," *Ajia keizai* 26, no. 4 (April 1985), pp. 59–76.

———. "'Manshū' nōson jittai chōsa ibun (II)," no. 2 of "Mantetsu chōsabu kankeisha ni kiku," *Ajia keizai* 26, no. 5 (May 1985), pp. 70–84.

Noma Kiyoshi and Fukushima Masao. "Chūgoku nōson kankō chōsa (I)," no. 10 of "Mantetsu chōsabu kankeisha ni kiku," *Ajia keizai* 27, no. 4 (April 1986), pp. 63–86.

Nōrinshō keizai kōseibu. *Manshū nōgyō imin ni kansuru chihō jijō chōsa gaiyō.* 1937. In "Manshū nōgyō imin ni kansuru shoshiryō," *Naigai chōsa shiryō* 10, no. 11 (November 1938), pp. 241–262.

———. ed. *Shinnōson no kensetsu: tairiku e bunson daiidō.* Asahi shinbunsha, 1939.

Ōe Shinobu et al., eds. *Bōchō suru teikoku no jinryū,* vol. 5 of *Iwanami kōza kindai Nihon to shokuminchi.* Iwanami shoten, 1993.

———. *Bunka no naka no shokuminchi,* vol. 7 of *Iwanami kōza kindai Nihon to shokuminchi.* Iwanami shoten, 1993.

Ogata, Sadako N. *Defiance in Manchuria: The Making of Japanese Foreign Policy, 1931–1932.* 1964. Reprint, Westport, Conn.: Greenwood Press, 1984.

Ōishi Kaichirō. "Sekai daikyōkō to Nihon shihonshugi: mondai no shozai." In Ōishi Kaichirō, ed., *Sekai daikyōkōki,* vol. 2 of *Nihon teikokushugishi.* Tōkyō daigaku shuppankai, 1987.

Okabe Makio. *Manshūkoku.* Sanseidō, 1978.

Okayama kenshi hensan iinkai, ed. *Kindai 3*, vol. 12 of *Okayama kenshi.* Okayama: San'yō shinbunsha, 1989.

Ōkura Kinmochi. *Nōson seinen shokun no funki o unagasu.* Manshū ijū kyōkai, 1936.

Ōkurasho. *Gaikoku bōeki geppyō.* 1936–1941.

Ōsaka shōkō kaigisho taiShi mondai chōsa iinkai, ed. *Genchi chōsa: Manmō keizai no jissō.* Osaka: Ōsaka shōkō kaigisho, 1932.

Ōtani Tadashi. "Taiheiyō sensō makki ni okeru Manshū imin: daijūsanji daiHyōgo kaitakudan ni miru bunson kaitakudan sōshutsu no jittai," *Kindaishi kenkyū,* vol. 21 (Ōsaka rekishi gakkai, June 1979), pp. 32–58.

Owen, Roger, and Bob Sutcliffe, eds. *Studies in the Theory of Imperialism.* London: Longman, 1972.

Ozaki Hotsumi. *Ozaki Hotsumi chosakushū,* vol. 2. Keisō shobō, 1977.

Peattie, Mark R. "Forecasting a Pacific War 1912–1933: The Idea of a Conditional Japanese Victory." In James W. White, Michio Umegaki, and Thomas R. H. Havens, eds., *The Ambivalence of Nationalism: Modern Japan between East and West.* Lanham, Md.: University Press of America, 1990.

———. "Introduction." In Ramon H. Myers and Mark R. Peattie, eds., *The Japanese Colonial Empire, 1895–1945.* Princeton: Princeton University Press, 1984.

———. *Ishiwara Kanji and Japan's Confrontation with the West.* Princeton: Princeton University Press, 1975.

———. "Japanese Attitudes toward Colonialism, 1895–1945." In Ramon H. Myers and Mark R. Peattie, eds., *The Japanese Colonial Empire, 1895–1945.* Princeton: Princeton University Press, 1984.

———. "The Japanese Colonial Empire, 1895–1945." In Peter Duus, ed., *The Twentieth Century,* vol. 6 of *The Cambridge History of Japan.* New York: Cambridge University Press, 1988.

———. "Japanese Treaty Port Settlements in China, 1895–1937." In Peter Duus, Ramon H. Myers, and Mark R. Peattie, eds., *The Japanese Informal Empire in China, 1895–1937.* Princeton: Princeton University Press, 1989.

Pratt, Edward Earl. "Wanpaoshan, 1931: Japanese Imperialism, Chinese Nationalism and the Korean Problem in Northeast China on the Eve of the Manchurian Incident." Master's thesis, University of Virginia, May 1983.

Pyle, Kenneth B. *The New Generation in Meiji Japan: Problems of Cultural Identity, 1885–1895.* Stanford: Stanford University Press, 1969.

Rabson, Steve. "Yosano Akiko on War: To Give One's Life or Not—A Question of Which War," *Journal of the Association of Teachers of Japanese* 25, no. 1 (April 1991), pp. 45–74.

Rekishigaku kenkyūkai, ed. *Manshū jihen,* vol. 1 of *Taiheiyō sensōshi.* Aoki shoten, 1971.

Rekōdo. 1931–1934.

Reynolds, Douglas R. "Training Young China Hands: Tōa Dōbun Shoin and Its Precursors, 1886–1945." In Peter Duus, Ramon H. Myers, and Mark R. Peattie, eds., *The Japanese Informal Empire in China, 1895–1937.* Princeton: Princeton University Press, 1989.

Reynolds, E. Bruce. "Anomaly or Model? Independent Thailand's Role in Japan's Asian Strategy, 1941–1943." In Peter Duus, Ramon H. Myers, and Mark R. Peattie, eds.,

The Japanese Wartime Empire, 1931–1945. Princeton: Princeton University Press, 1996.

Rikugunshō. *Beikoku Karibian seisaku to Manmō mondai.* Rikugunshō, 1931.

———. *Chō Gakuryō Kinshū seiken no taiNichi kōsen junbi ni tsuite.* Rikugunshō, 1931.

———. *Daisanji kokusai renmei rijikai ni okeru Manshū jihen.* Rikugunshō, 1931.

———. *Hakka ni sonaeyo.* Rikugunshō, 1932.

———. *Harupin fukin no sentō ni tsuite.* Rikugunshō, 1932.

———. *Kokusai renmei ni okeru Manshū jihen keika no gaiyō.* Rikugunshō, 1931.

———. *Manmō mondai no saininshiki to kokumin no kakugo.* Rikugunshō, 1932.

———. *Manshū fuan no jissō.* Rikugunshō, 1931.

———. *Manshū jihen boppatsu man'ichinen.* Rikugunshō, 1932.

———. *Manshū jihen boppatsu man'yonen: Manshūkoku gaikan.* Rikugunshō, 1935.

———. *Manshū jihen gaiyō.* Rikugunshō, 1931.

———. *Manshū jihen ni okeru Donkō kahan no sentō ni tsuite.* Rikugunshō, 1931.

———. *Manshū jihen ni okeru Kōkōkei fukin no sentō ni tsuite.* Rikugunshō, 1931.

———. *Manshū ni okeru kyōsantō.* Rikugunshō, 1933.

———. *Manshūkoku no shōnin ni tsuite.* Rikugunshō, 1932.

———. *Mantetsu fuzokuchigai shutsudō butai hikiage no fukanō naru yuen ni tsuite.* Rikugunshō, 1931.

———. *Nekka ni tsuite.* Rikugunshō, 1933.

———. *Nekka shukuseigo no Hokushi jōsei to teisen kōshō.* Rikugunshō, 1933.

———. *Nekka tōbatsu keika gaiyō: furoku Beikoku tsūshin'in no mitaru Nekka sakusen.* Rikugunshō, 1933.

———. *Nisshi funsō o meguru renmei dōkō o mite.* Rikugunshō, 1932.

———. *Renmei dattai no keii.* Rikugunshō, 1933.

———. *Renmei dattai to kokumin no kakugo.* Rikugunshō, 1933.

———. *Renmei sōkai ni chokumen shite.* Rikugunsho, 1932.

———. *Ryōsei chihō heihi tōbatsu yori Shinagun kannai tettai made.* Rikugunshō, 1932.

———. *Saikin ni okeru Nisshi funsō to kokusai renmei.* Rikugunshō, 1933.

———. *Shina henkyō ni taisuru Sorenpō no sakudō.* Rikugunshō, 1933.

———. *Shina ni okeru kyōsantō no katsudō.* Rikugunshō, 1932.

———. *Shina o chūshin to suru renmei narabini Ōbei kakkoku no katsudō ni tsuite.* Rikugunshō, 1933.

———. *Shōwa 7 nen 8 gatsu ikō ni okeru Manshū no sōhi to chian no jōtai.* Rikugunshō, 1933.

———. *Shōwa 8 nen ni okeru Kantōgun no kōdō ni tsuite.* Rikugunshō, 1934.

———. *Sorenpō buryokusen junbi no shinten.* Rikugunshō, 1933.

———. *Sorenpō daiichiji gonen keikaku no seika to dainiji gonen keikaku no tenbō.* Rikugunshō, 1932.

———. *Waga Manmō hatten no rekishi to rekkoku kanshō no kaiko.* Rikugunshō, 1932.

———. *Yakushin Nihon to rekkyō no jūatsu.* Rikugunshō, 1934.

Rikugunshō shinbunhannai "tsuwamono" hensan, ed. *Manshū jihen no unda bidan kawa,* no. 2. Teikoku zaigo gunjinkai honbunai "tsuwamono" hakkōjo, 1931.

Said, Edward W. *Culture and Imperialism*. New York: Knopf, 1993.

———. *Orientalism*. New York: Vintage, 1978.

Sakamoto Masako. "Sensō to zaibatsu." In Nakamura Masanori, ed., *Sensō to kokka dokusen shihonshugi*, vol. 4 of *Taikei Nihon gendaishi*. Nihon hyōronsha, 1979.

Sakawa chōshi hensan iinkai, ed. *Sakawa chōshi*, vol. 2. Sakawa, Kōchi: Sakawa machi yakuba, 1981.

Sakurai Tōru. "Minami Manshū tetsudō no keiei to zaibatsu." In Fujii Mitsuo et al., eds., *Nihon takokuseki kigyō no shiteki tenkai*, vol. 1. Ōtsuki shoten, 1979.

Sakuramoto Tomio. *Manmō kaitaku seishōnen giyūgun*. Aoki shoten, 1987.

Satō, Barbara Hamill. "Josei: modanizumu to kenri ishiki." In Minami Hiroshi and Shakai shinri kenkyūjo, eds., *Shōwa bunka, 1925–1945*. Keisō shobō, 1987.

———. "The *Moga* Sensation: Perceptions of the *Modan Garu* in Japanese Intellectual Circles during the 1920s," *Gender and History* 5, no. 3 (Autumn 1993), pp. 363–381.

Scalapino, Robert A. *Democracy and the Party Movement in Prewar Japan: The Failure of the First Attempt*. Berkeley: University of California Press, 1953.

Schneider, William H. *An Empire for the Masses: The French Popular Image of Africa, 1870–1900*. Westport, Conn.: Greenwood Press, 1982.

Schumpeter, Joseph A. "Imperialism and Capitalism." In Joseph A. Schumpeter, *Imperialism and Social Classes*, trans. Heinz Norden, ed. Paul M. Sweezy. 1951. Reprint, Philadelphia: Orion, 1991.

Segre, Claudio G. *Fourth Shore: The Italian Colonization of Libya*. Chicago: University of Chicago Press, 1974.

Sekisetsu chihō nōson keizai chōsajo. *Manshū nōgyō imin boson keizai jittai chōsa: Yamagata-ken Higashitagawa-gun Yamato-mura*. Sekisetsu chihō nōson keizai chōsajo, 1941.

Semmel, Bernard. *Imperialism and Social Reform: English Social-Imperial Thought, 1895–1914*. Cambridge: Harvard University Press, 1960.

Shakai seisaku jihō, no. 140, May 1932.

Shibata shishi hensan iinkai, ed. *Shibata shishi*, vol. 2. Shibata: Shibata shishi hensan iinkai, 1981.

Shiga-ken shutsudō gunjin ikazoku kōen rinji iinkai. *Manshū Shanhai jihen chūsei-roku*. Kyoto: Shiga-ken shutsudō gunjin ikazoku kōen rinji iinkai, 1932.

Shillony, Ben-Ami. *Politics and Culture in Wartime Japan*. Oxford: Clarendon Press, 1981.

Shimada Toshihiko. *Kantōgun: zaiMan rikugun no dokusō*. Chūō kōronsha, 1965.

"Shinbun shiryō kōsei 'gunkoku bidan' no kōzō, Tōkyō *Nichinichi shinbun* 1932–1935," *Kikan gendaishi*, vol. 2 (May 1973), pp. 260–307.

Shinkyō shōkō kaigisho. *Shinkyō shōkō jijō*. Xinjing: Shinkyō shōkō kaigisho, 1942.

Shiratori Michihiro. "'Manmō kaitaku seishōnen giyūgun' no hen'yō (1938–1941 nen): 'kyōdō butai hensei' dōnyū no igi," *Kyōiku gakubu kiyō*, no. 54 (Hokkaidō daigaku, February 1990), pp. 33–96.

———. "'Manmō kaitaku seishōnen giyūgun' no sōsetsu katei," *Kyōiku gakubu kiyō*, no. 45 (Hokkaidō daigaku, December 1984), pp. 189–222.

———. "'Manshū' imin seisaku to 'Manmō kaitaku seishōnen giyūgun,'" *Kyōiku gakubu kiyō*, no. 47 (Hokkaidō daigaku, February 1986), pp. 107–139.

Shisō no kagaku kenkyūkai, ed. *Kyōdō kenkyū, tenkō*. 3 vols. Heibonsha, 1959–1962.

Shōnai bunkyō keikaku chōsa hōkoku. Manshū ijū kyōkai, 1938.

Shōnen kurabu. 1931–1945.

Shōwa dōjinkai, ed. *Shōwa kenkyūkai.* Keizai ōraisha, 1968.

Shōwa sensō bungaku zenshū henshū iinkai, ed. *Senka Manshū ni agaru,* vol. 1 of *Shōwa sensō bungaku zenshū.* Shūeisha, 1964.

Shuppan nenkan. Tōkyōdō, 1931–1940.

Silverstein, Josef, ed. *Southeast Asia in World War II: Four Essays.* New Haven: Yale University Southeast Asia Studies, 1966.

Slotkin, Richard. *The Fatal Environment: The Myth of the Frontier in the Age of Industrialization, 1800–1890.* New York: Atheneum, 1985.

———. *Gunfighter Nation: The Myth of the Frontier in Twentieth-Century America.* New York: Harper Perennial, 1992.

Smethurst, Richard J. *A Social Basis for Prewar Japanese Militarism: The Army and the Rural Community.* Berkeley: University of California Press, 1974.

Smith, Henry Dewitt, II. *Japan's First Student Radicals.* Cambridge: Harvard University Press, 1972.

Sōgō shuppan nenkan. Tosho kenkyūkai, 1932.

"Sono koro minshū wa: *Kahoku shinpō* kiji ni miru hyakunichikan," *Kikan gendaishi,* no. 1 (November 1972), pp. 172–203.

South Manchurian Railway Company. *Fifth Report on Progress in Manchuria to 1936.* Dalian: South Manchurian Railway Company, 1936.

Stites, Richard. *Revolutionary Dreams: Utopian Vision and Experimental Life in the Russian Revolution.* Oxford: Oxford University Press, 1989.

Sugino Tadao. *Bunson keikau no igi: sono shidō seishin ni tsuite,* no. 2 of *Bunson keikaku sōsho.* Nōson kōsei kyōkai, 1938.

———. *Bunson keikaku no jissai mondai: jirei o chūshin toshite,* no. 4 of *Bunson keikaku sōsho.* Nōson kōsei kyōkai, 1938.

———. *Bunson keikaku to sono hantairon,* no. 5 of *Bunson keikaku sōsho.* Nōson kōsei kyōkai, 1938.

———. *Nōson kōsei undō to bunson keikaku,* no. 3 of *Bunson keikaku sōsho.* Nōson kōsei kyōkai, 1938.

———. *Seishōnen ni uttau,* no. 1 of *Bunson keikaku sōsho.* Nōson kōsei kyōkai, 1938.

Suleski, Ronald. "Northeast China under Japanese Control: The Role of the Manchurian Youth Corps 1934–1945," *Modern China* 7, no. 3 (July 1981), pp. 355–377.

Sun, Kungtu C. *The Economic Development of Manchuria in the First Half of the Twentieth Century.* Cambridge: Council on East Asian Studies, Harvard University, 1973.

Suzuki Takashi. "Manshū keizai kaihatsu to Manshū jūkōgyō no seiritsu." *Tokushima daigaku gakugei kiyō (shakai kagaku)* 13, supplement (1963), pp. 97–114.

Taishō demokurashii, vol. 10 of *Nihonjin no hyakunen.* Sekai bunkasha, 1972.

Takahashi Hikohiro. *Minshū no gawa no sensō sekinin.* Aoki shoten, 1989.

Takahashi Hisashi. "'Tōa kyōdōtairon': Rōyama Masamichi, Ozaki Hotsumi, Kada Tetsuji no baai." In Miwa Kimitada, ed., *Nihon no 1930 nendai: kuni no uchi to soto kara.* Sōryūsha, 1980.

Takahashi Yasutaka. "Nihon fashizumu to Manshū bunson imin no tenkai: Nagano-ken Yomikaki-mura no bunseki o chūshin ni." In Manshū iminshi kenkyūkai, eds. *Nihon teikokushugika no Manshū imin.* Ryūkei shosha, 1976.

————. "Nihon fashizumu to 'Manshū' nōgyō imin," *Tochi seido shigaku*, no. 71 (April 1976), pp. 47–67.

————. "Nihon fashizumu to nōson keizai kōsei undō no tenkai: Shōwaki 'kyūnō' seisaku ni tsuite no kōsatsu," *Tochi seido shigaku*, no. 65 (October 1974), pp. 1–26.

Takumushō takuhokukyoku. *Nagano-ken Yomikaki-mura bunson jijō chōsasho*. Takumushō takuhokukyoku, 1942.

Takumushō takumukyoku. "Hokuman ni okeru shūdan nōgyō imin no keiei hyōjun'an," *Naigai chōsa shiryō* 10, no. 11 (November 1938), pp. 8–45.

Tanaka, Stefan. *Japan's Orient: Rendering Pasts into History*. Berkeley: University of California Press, 1993.

Tanaka Tamotsu. "Taiheiyō sensōka no Manshū bunson imin: Kōchi-ken Hata-gun no rei," *"Herumesu": Hitotsubashi daigaku gakusei kenkyūshi*, no. 27 (March 1976), pp. 140–175.

Tanaka Tsunejirō. "HanMan kōNichi undō." In Asada Kyōji and Kobayashi Hideo, eds., *Nihon teikokushugi no Manshū shihai: jūgonen sensō o chūshin ni*. Jichōsha, 1986.

————. "Nihon teikokushugi no Manshū shinryaku to hanMan kōNichi tōsō: Chūgoku kakumei no tenkai to kanren shite." In Manshū iminshi kenkyūkai, ed., *Nihon teikokushugika no Manshū imin*. Ryūkei shosha, 1976.

Taylor, Philip M. *The Projection of Britain: Britain Overseas Publicity and Propaganda, 1919–1939*. Cambridge: Cambridge University Press, 1981.

Teikoku nōkai. *Fujimi-mura no bunson undō ni tsuite (Nagano-ken Suwa-gun Fujimi mura chōsa)*. Teikoku nōkai, 1942.

————. *Manshū kaitakumin sōshutsu ni kansuru chōsa*, no. 1. Teikoku nōkai, 1942.

————. *Nagano-ken Suwa-gun Fujimi-mura*, no. 2 of *Manshū kaitakumin sōshutsu chōsa*. Teikoku nōkai, 1942.

Tōa keizai kondankai. *Nichiman keizai kondankai hōkokusho*. Tōa keizai kondankai, 1940.

Tōa ryokōsha, ed. *Manshi ryokō nenkan: Shōwa 18 nen*. Fengtian: Tōa ryokōsha, 1942.

Toby, Ronald P. *State and Diplomacy in Early Modern Japan: Asia in the Development of the Tokugawa Bakufu*. Stanford: Stanford University Press, 1984.

Toda Shin'ichirō. *Manmō e no yushutsu annai*. Tōji shoin, 1933.

Tōkyō shiyakusho. *Manmō keizai chōsasho*. Tōkyō shiyakusho, 1933.

Tōkyō shōkō kaigisho. "Manshūkoku kanzei kaisei ni kansuru iken." January 1933. Tōkyō shōkō kaigisho microreel no. 139:1211–1227.

————. "Tōkyō Manmō yushutsu kumiai setsuritsu ni kanshi enjokata irai no ken shingi kiroku." August–October 1932. Tōkyō shōkō kaigisho microreel no. 139:286–319.

Tonedachi Masao, ed. *Manshū Shanhai jihen zenki*. Asahi shinbunsha, 1932.

Totten, George Oakley. *The Social Democratic Movement in Prewar Japan*. New Haven: Yale University Press, 1966.

Toyama-shi shusai Nichiman sangyō daihakurankai. Toyama: Toyama-shi, 1938.

Tōyō bunko kindai Chūgoku kenkyū iinkai, ed. *Meiji ikō Nihonjin no Chūgoku ryokōki*. Tōyō bunko, 1980.

Tōyō keizai shinpō. 1931–1944.

Tsurumi, E. Patricia. "Colonial Education in Korea and Taiwan." In Ramon H. Myers and Mark R. Peattie, eds., *The Japanese Colonial Empire, 1895–1945*. Princeton: Princeton University Press, 1984.

Tsurumi, Kazuko. *Social Change and the Individual: Japan before and after Defeat in World War II*. Princeton: Princeton University Press, 1966.

Tsurumi, Shunsuke. *An Intellectual History of Wartime Japan, 1931–1945*. London: Routledge and Kegan, 1986.

Tuchman, Barbara W. *Stilwell and the American Experience in China 1911–1945*. New York: Macmillan, 1971.

Wada Tsutō. *Ōhinata-mura*. 1941. In Shōwa sensō bungaku zenshū henshū iinkai, ed., *Senka Manshū ni agaru*, vol. 1 of *Shōwa sensō bungaku zenshū*. Shūeisha, 1964.

Waswo, Ann. *Japanese Landlords: The Decline of a Rural Elite*. Berkeley: University of California Press, 1977.

Wehler, Hans-Ulrich. *Bismarck und der Imperialismus*. Cologne: Kiepenheuer and Witsch, 1969.

———. "Bismarck's Imperialism 1862–1890," *Past and Present*, no. 48 (August 1970), pp. 119–155.

Westney, D. Eleanor. *Imitation and Innovation: The Transfer of Western Organizational Patterns to Meiji Japan*. Cambridge: Harvard University Press, 1987.

Willoughby, Westel W. *The Sino-Japanese Controversy and the League of Nations*. 1935. Reprint, New York: Greenwood Press, 1968.

Wray, William D. "Japan's Big-Three Service Enterprises in China, 1896–1936." In Peter Duus, Ramon H. Myers, and Mark R. Peattie, eds., *The Japanese Informal Empire in China, 1895–1937*. Princeton: Princeton University Press, 1989.

———. *Mitsubishi and the N.Y.K., 1870–1914: Business Strategy in the Japanese Shipping Industry*. Cambridge: Council on East Asian Studies, Harvard University, 1984.

Wright, Gwendolyn. *The Politics of Design in French Colonial Urbanism*. Chicago: University of Chicago Press, 1991.

Yamada Gōichi. "Manshū ni okeru hanMan kōNichi undō to nōgyō imin (I)," *Rekishi hyōron*, no. 142 (June 1962), pp. 46–64.

Yamada Shōji. "Furikaeru Nihon no mirai: kaisetsu, Manshū imin no sekai." In Yamada Shōji, ed., *Manshū imin*, vol. 6 of *Kindai minshū no kiroku*. Shinjinbutsu ōraisha, 1978.

Yamagata shishi hensan iinkai, ed. *Kingendaihen* of *Yamagata shishi*. Yamagata: Yamagata-shi, 1980.

Yamagata-ken, ed. *Kingendai 2*, vol. 5 of *Yamagata kenshi*. Yamagata: Yamagata-ken, 1986.

Yamaguchi Hiroichi. " 'Mantetsu chōsabu jiken' (1942–45 nen) ni tsuite," no. 29 of "Mantetsu chōsabu kankeisha ni kiku," *Ajia keizai* 29, no. 11 (November 1988), pp. 62–88.

Yamaguchi Jūji. *Manshū kenkoku to Minzoku kyōwa shisō no genten*. Osaka: Ōminato shobō, 1976.

———. *Shiryō Manshū kenkoku e no isho daiichibu: minzoku kyōwa kara Tōa renmei e Ishiwara Kanji totomoni*. Osaka: Ōminato shobō, 1980.

Yamamoto Hideo. *Tachibana Shiraki*. Chūō kōronsha, 1977.

———, ed. *"Manshū hyōron" kaidai: sōmokuji*. Fuji shuppan, 1982.

Yamamoto Taketoshi. *Kindai Nihon no shinbun dokushasō.* Hōsei daigaku shuppan-kyoku, 1981.

Yamazumi Masami. *Nihon kyōiku shōshi.* Iwanami shoten, 1987.

Yoda Yoshiie. "Dainiji taisenka, Nihon no Manshū imin no jittai: imindan kankei no hanzai o chūshin ni," *Shakai kagaku tōkyū* 18, no. 1 (Waseda daigaku shakai kagaku kenkyūjo, 1972), pp. 41–78.

Yoshihashi, Takehiko. *Conspiracy at Mukden: The Rise of the Japanese Military.* New Haven: Yale University Press, 1963.

Yoshimi Yoshiaki. *Kusa no ne no fashizumu: Nihon minshū no sensō taiken,* vol. 7 of *Atarashii sekaishi.* Tōkyō daigaku shuppankai, 1987.

Young, Crawford. *The African Colonial State in Comparative Perspective.* New Haven: Yale University Press, 1994.

Young, John. *The Research Activities of the South Manchurian Railway Company 1907–1945: A History and Bibliography.* New York: East Asian Institute, Columbia University, 1966.

Young, Louise. "Mobilizing for Empire: Japan and Manchukuo, 1931–1945." Ph.D. dissertation, Columbia University, 1993.

———. "Power and Color: Japanese Imperialism in a White World Order." Master's thesis, Columbia University, May 1987.

Yunoki Shun'ichi. "Manshū imin undō no tenkai to ronri: Miyagi-ken Nangō-mura imin undō no bunseki," *Shakai keizai shigaku* 48, no. 3 (August 1982), pp. 52–71.

———. " 'Manshū' nōgyō imin seisaku to 'Shōnaigata' imin: Yamagata-ken Yamato-mura imin keikaku o chūshin ni," *Shakai keizai shigaku* 42, no. 5 (March 1977), pp. 44–69.

———. "Shōwa nōgyō kyōkō to Manshū imin: Miyagi-ken Nangō-mura imin no bunseki," *Kenkyū kiyō,* no. 14 (Tōkyō-to senshu gakkō kakushu gakkō kyōkai, March 1978), pp. 131–138.

———. "Shōwa nōgyō kyōkō to Shōnaigata imin keikaku no tenkai: Yamato-mura bunson imin o chūshin toshite," *Keizaigaku kenkyū,* no. 4 (Komazawa daigaku daigakuin, March 1976), pp. 133–158.

Zasshi nenkan. Nihon dokusho shinbunsha, 1939–1940.

Zenkoku takuyū kyōgikai, ed. *Shashinshū Manmō kaitaku seishōnen giyūgun.* Ie no hikari kyōkai, 1975.

Index

academic freedom, 274
academic institutions. *See* education, higher
Across the Sea (*Umi no soto*), 313
activism, 382; media, 78–79; political, 422; state, 359; teachers', 381; women's, 167–68, 171–72, 425. *See also* social activism
activists, 16, 80, 352–53, 379–80, 382, 386; intellectuals as, 292, 296; local, 383, 387; rural, 398
Adachi Kenzō, 128
Admiral Nogi, 71
Africa, 9, 314; colonial garrisons in, 434; Japanese population in, 315 (table)
agents of empire, 15–17, 373–82, 387, 427
aggression. *See* military aggression
agrarian imperialism, 310, 318, 341–51
agrarianism, 307–51, 387, 396
agrarian reform. *See* agricultural reform
agrarian societies, 424
agrarian training institutes, 332
agricultural cooperatives, 299–301, 337, 374, 424
agricultural development, 208
agricultural economy, 28, 284, 420; Manchukuo's, 289; Manchuria's, 32, 204, 208, 298
agricultural policy, 295, 297–98
agricultural reform, 298, 336, 386, 418
agricultural settlement programs. *See*
farm colonization; settlement programs
agriculture, 28, 43, 211, 277, 307–51, 360, 392–93, 403; commercialization of, 322; productivity, 295, 299, 403; products, 203. *See also* farmers
Ah—Major Kuramoto and the Blood-stained Flag, 75
"Ah, Our Manchuria!" (Aa waga Man-shū), 72
"Ah! The Imperial Flag Is in Danger," 108
Ah! The Thirty-eight Heroes of Nan-ling, 74
Aichi (prefecture), 60, 65–66, 157, 163, 178, 207; emigrants, 330 (table)
Aichi (newspaper), 157
Aikawa Yoshisuke, 217–18, 220
Aikoku fujin, 172
Aikoku fujinkai (Patriotic Women's Association), 160, 168–69, 172–73, 177, 377
Aikyō juku, 325
Ainu, 311, 365
airplanes, 424; fundraising campaigns for, 158, 161–62, 164, 175. *See also* *specific names*
Akamatsu Katsumaro, 166
Akira Iriye, 317
Akita, 66, 207, 324; debt, 331; emigrants, 329 (table)
Algeria, 13, 415, 425

457

Compositor:	Impressions Book and Journal Services, Inc.
Text:	10/13 Aldus
Display:	Aldus
Printer and binder:	Braun-Brumfield, Inc.

STUDIES OF THE
EAST ASIAN INSTITUTE

Anvil of Victory: The Communist Revolution in Manchuria, by Steven I. Levine. New York: Columbia University Press, 1987.

Japan's Modern Myths: Ideology in the Late Meiji Period, by Carol Gluck. Princeton: Princeton University Press, 1985.

Japan Erupts: The London Naval Conference and the Manchurian Incident, edited by James W. Morley. New York: Columbia University Press, 1984.

Japan and the Asian Development Bank, by Dennis Yasutomo. New York: Praeger, 1983.

The Fateful Choice: Japan's Advance into Southeast Asia, edited by James W. Morley. New York: Columbia University Press, 1980.

Tanaka Giichi and Japan's China Policy, by William F. Morton. Folkestone, England: Dawson, 1980; New York: St. Martin's Press, 1980.

Japanese International Negotiating Style, by Michael Blaker. New York: Columbia University Press, 1977.

Japan's Foreign Policy, 1868–1941: A Research Guide, edited by James W. Morley. New York: Columbia University Press, 1974.

The Japanese Oligarchy and the Russo-Japanese War, by Shumpei Okamoto. New York: Columbia University Press, 1970.

The Japanese Imperial Institution in the Tokugawa Period, by Herschel Webb. New York: Columbia University Press, 1968.

- one-sided history posing as unbiay-
tided
→ to read this book, substitute
Vietnam r US
- it's an apologia
- she's a chip off the old Gluck...

- no better example of the hermetically-
sealed nature of E. Asian country
studies